Mac® OS X Panther For Dummies®

Cheat Sheet

Top Six Things You Should Never Do

6. Pay list price for any hardware or software. What lists for $499 at Pierre's Chrome and Glass Computer Boutique might only cost $275 at Bubba's Mail-Order Warehouse and Chili Emporium.

5. Pay attention to anyone who says that Windows is just like the Mac. Yeah, right. And Yugo is the Eastern-European cousin of BMW.

4. Bump, drop, shake, wobble, dribble, drop kick, or play catch with a hard drive (or PowerBook or iBook, which contain hard drives) while it's running. Don't forget that your desktop Mac has a hard drive inside it, too.

3. Shut off your Mac by pulling the plug or flipping the power switch. Always use the Shut Down command from the Apple menu.

2. Get up from your Mac without saving your work. Just before your butt leaves the chair, your fingers should be pressing ⌘+S. Make it a habit.

1. Keep only one copy of your important documents. Make at least two back-up copies and keep one of them in a safe place. Period.

Do I Need an Antivirus Program?

"Do I need an antivirus program?" You do if you're at risk. How do you know if you're at risk? You're at risk if you

- Download files from the Internet
- Receive e-mail with attachments (and open the attachments)
- Are on a network and share files with others
- Use disks — floppy, Zip, Jaz, Orb, CD-R, or other — that have ever been inserted in anyone else's Mac

These are the ways that viruses spread, so if any or all of the preceding apply to you, you'd be well served to run an antivirus program, such as Virex or Norton AntiVirus for Macintosh. That said, I feel obliged to add that we Mac users are exposed to significantly fewer viral threats than our Windows-using counterparts.

For Dummies: Bestselling Book Series for Beginners

Mac® OS X Panther For Dummies®

Cheat Sheet

Five Awesome Web Sites for Mac OS X Lovers

http://kbase.info.apple.com: The Apple Knowledge Base is a treasure trove of tech notes, software update information, and documentation.

www.MacInTouch.com: The preeminent Mac news and information site, with tips, hints, troubleshooting information, and more. Many users consider MacInTouch (along with MacSurfer and MacFixit) a must to read every day.

www.versiontracker.com: VersionTracker is the place to go to find freeware, shareware, and software updates for Mac OS X. If VersionTracker doesn't have it, it probably doesn't exist.

www.macminute.com: This site is where those in the know go for up-to-the-minute Mac news.

www.apple.com/macosx: Check this official Apple Mac OS X Web site often for updates, news, and info on your favorite operating system.

Keyboard Shortcuts

Make these shortcuts second nature. All of these shortcuts work in the Finder, and many of them work in other application programs as well. See those perforations over there? That's so you can tear this cheat sheet out and memorize these shortcuts. Ready? RIP!

Command	Keyboard Shortcut
Close All Windows	⌘+Option+W
Close Window	⌘+W
Copy	⌘+C
Cut	⌘+X
Duplicate	⌘+D
Eject Disk	⌘+E
Find	⌘+F
Get Info	⌘+I
Make Alias	⌘+L
New Folder	⌘+Shift+N
Open	⌘+O
Paste	⌘+V
Print	⌘+P
Select All	⌘+A
Undo	⌘+Z

For Dummies: Bestselling Book Series for Beginners

Mac OS® X Panther™ FOR DUMMIES®

by Bob LeVitus

WILEY

Wiley Publishing, Inc.

Mac OS® X Panther™ For Dummies®

Published by
Wiley Publishing, Inc.
111 River Street
Hoboken, NJ 07030-5774

www.wiley.com

About the Author

Bob LeVitus, often referred to as "Dr. Mac," has written more than 40 popular computer books, including *Dr. Mac: The OS X Files* and *Mac OS 9 For Dummies* for Wiley, Inc.; *Stupid Mac Tricks* and *Dr. Macintosh,* both for Addison-Wesley; and *The Little iTunes Book, 3rd Edition* and *The Little iDVD Book, 2nd Edition* for Peachpit Press. His books have sold more than a million copies worldwide.

Bob has penned the popular Dr. Mac column for the *Houston Chronicle* for more than six years and has been published in dozens of computer magazines over the past 15 years. His achievements have been documented in major media around the world. (Yes, that was him juggling a keyboard in *USA Today* a few years back!)

Bob is known for his expertise, trademark humorous style, and ability to translate techie jargon into usable and fun advice for regular folks.

Bob is also a prolific public speaker, presenting more than 100 Macworld Expo training sessions in the U.S. and abroad, keynote addresses in three countries, and Macintosh training seminars in many U.S. cities. (He also won the Macworld Expo MacJeopardy World Championship three times before retiring his crown.)

Bob is considered one of the world's leading authorities on Mac OS. From 1989 to 1997, he was a contributing editor/columnist for *MacUser* magazine, writing the Help Folder, Beating the System, Personal Best, and Game Room columns at various times.

Prior to giving his life over to computers, he spent years at Kresser/Craig/ D.I.K., a Los Angeles advertising agency and marketing consultancy and its subsidiary, L & J Research. He holds a B.S. in Marketing from California State University.

Bob LeVitus lives in the Texas hill country with his wife, children, and a small pack of semi-domesticated animals.

Dedication

This book is dedicated to my wife, Lisa, who taught me almost everything I know about almost everything except computers.

Author's Acknowledgments

Special thanks to everyone at Apple who helped me turn this book around in record time: Keri Walker, Nathalie Welch, Bill Evans, Ken Bereskin, Greg (Joz) Joswiak, and all the rest. I couldn't have done it without you.

Thanks also to super-agent Carole "Still-Swifty-After-All-These-Years" McClendon, for more deal-making far beyond the call of duty. You've been my agent since I started in the business 17 years ago, and I want you to know that you're a treasure.

Big-time thanks to the gang at Wiley: Bob "Is the damn thing done yet?" Woerner, Andrea "The New Whipcracker" Boucher, Andy "Boss Man" Cummings, Barry "Still no humorous nickname" Pruett, technical editor Ilene Hoffman, who did a rocking job, and all the others.

Extra special thanks to Dennis R. Cohen, for technical support as well as for updating several of the chapters for me. It's been an honor and a privilege to work with the only guy I know who's been using OS X longer than me. You rock, dude!

Thanks to my family and friends for putting up with me during my all-too-lengthy absences during this book's gestation.

Special thanks to Saccone's Pizza, Lucky Dog Chicago-style hot dogs, John Muller Texas BBQ, Taco Cabana, Bass Ale, Sam Adams, and ShortStop for providing sustenance as I worked.

And finally, thanks to you, gentle reader, for buying this book.

Publisher's Acknowledgments

We're proud of this book; please send us your comments through our online registration form located at www.dummies.com/register/.

Some of the people who helped bring this book to market include the following:

Acquisitions, Editorial, and Media Development

Project Editor: Andrea C. Boucher
  (Previous Edition: Linda Morris)

Acquisitions Editor: Bob Woerner

Technical Editor: Ilene Hoffman

Editorial Manager: Carol Sheehan

Media Development Manager:
  Laura VanWinkle

Media Development Supervisor:
  Richard Graves

Editorial Assistant: Amanda Foxworth

Cartoons: Rich Tennant
  (www.the5thwave.com)

Production

Project Coordinator: Courtney MacIntyre

Layout and Graphics: Joyce Haughey,
  Heather Ryan, Shae Lynn Wilson

Proofreaders: John Tyler Connoley,
  Andy Hollandbeck, Carl William Pierce,
  Dwight Ramsey, Brian H. Walls,
  TECHBOOKS Production Services

Indexer: TECHBOOKS Production Services

Publishing and Editorial for Technology Dummies

  Richard Swadley, Vice President and Executive Group Publisher

  Andy Cummings, Vice President and Publisher

  Mary C. Corder, Editorial Director

Publishing for Consumer Dummies

  Diane Graves Steele, Vice President and Publisher

  Joyce Pepple, Acquisitions Director

Composition Services

  Gerry Fahey, Vice President of Production Services

  Debbie Stailey, Director of Composition Services

Contents at a Glance

Table of Contents

Part II: Rounding Out Your Basic Training 93

Introduction

•••

You made the right choice twice: Mac OS X and this book.

Take a deep breath and get ready to have a rollicking good time. That's right. This is a computer book, but this is going to be fun. What a concept! Whether you're brand spanking new to the Mac or a grizzled old Mac vet, I guarantee that discovering the ins and outs of Mac OS X Panther will be fun and easy. Wiley, Inc. (the publisher of this book) couldn't say it on the cover if it weren't true!

About This Book

This book's roots lie with my international bestseller *Macintosh System 7.5 For Dummies,* an award-winning book so good that it was offered by now-deceased Mac cloner Power Computing in lieu of a system software manual. *Mac OS X Panther For Dummies* is the fifth or sixth sequel, and it has been completely updated. So it combines all the old, familiar features of the previous books (*Mac OS 8 For Dummies, Mac OS 8.5 For Dummies,* and *Mac OS 9 For Dummies,* and two previous editions of *Mac OS X For Dummies*) but with expanded and updated information about the latest, greatest offering from Apple.

Why write a *For Dummies* book about Panther? Well, Panther is a big, complicated personal computer operating system. So I made *Mac OS X Panther For Dummies* a not-so-big, not-very-complicated book that shows you what Panther is all about without boring you to tears, confusing you, or poking you with sharp objects.

I think you'll be so darned comfortable that I wanted to call this book *Panther without Discomfort,* but the publishers wouldn't let me. Apparently we *For Dummies* authors have to follow some rules, and using "Dummies" and "Mac OS X Panther" in this book's title are apparently among them.

And speaking of dummies, remember that it's just a word. I don't think that you're dumb. Quite the opposite! I also considered calling this book *Mac OS X Panther For People Smart Enough to Know They Need Help,* but you can just imagine what Wiley thought of that.

Anyway, the book is chock-full of information and advice, explaining everything that you need to know about Mac OS X in language you can understand, with time-saving tips, tricks, techniques, and step-by-step instructions, all served up in generous quantities.

Conventions Used in This Book

To get the most out of this book, you need to know how I do things and why. Here are a few conventions used in this book to make your life easier:

- ✔ When I want you to open an item in a menu, I write something like "Choose File⇨Open," which means, "Pull down the File menu and choose the Open command."

- ✔ Stuff you're supposed to type appears in bold type, **like this.**

- ✔ **Sometimes an entire a sentence is in bold,** as you'll see when I present a numbered list of steps. **In those cases, I** debold **what you're supposed to type,** like this.

- ✔ Web addresses, programming code (not much in this book), and things that appear onscreen are shown in a special monofont typeface, `like this.`

- ✔ When I refer to the menu, I'm referring to the menu in the upper-left corner of the Finder menu bar that looks like a blue or graphite Apple (called the *Apple menu*). For example, I may say, "From the menu, choose File⇨Open." I do *not* use the symbol to refer to the key on your Mac keyboard that may or may not have both the ⌘ and symbols on it. I refer to that key (called the *Command key*) with the equally funky ⌘ symbol and write something like, "Press the ⌘ key." So, when you see , think Apple menu.

- ✔ For keyboard shortcuts, I write something like ⌘+*A*, which means to hold down the ⌘ key (the one with the little pretzel and/or symbol on it) and then press the letter A on the keyboard. If you see something like ⌘+*Shift*+*A*, that means to hold down the ⌘ and Shift keys while pressing the A key. Again, for absolute clarity, I will never refer to the ⌘ key with the symbol. I reserve that symbol for the menu *(Apple menu)*. For the Command key, I use only the ⌘ symbol.

What You're Not to Read

The first few chapters of this book are where I describe the basic everyday things that you need to understand in order to operate your Mac effectively.

Even though OS X Panther is way different from previous Mac operating systems, this first part is so basic that if you've been using a Mac for long, you may think you know it all. But hey! — not-so-old-timers need a solid foundation. So here's my advice: Skip through stuff that you know to get to the better stuff faster.

Other stuff that you can skip over if you're so inclined are sidebars and any section marked with a Technical Stuff icon, which I talk about in a moment.

Foolish Assumptions

Although I know what happens when you make assumptions, I've made a few anyway. First, I assume that you, gentle reader, know nothing about using Mac OS X. What I do assume is that you know what a Mac is, that you want to use OS X, that you want to understand OS X without digesting an incomprehensible technical manual, and that you made the right choice by selecting this particular book.

And so, I'll do my best to explain each new concept in full and loving detail. Maybe that's foolish, but . . . oh well.

Oh, and I also assume that you can read.

How This Book Is Organized

Mac OS X Panther For Dummies is divided into six logical parts, numbered (surprisingly enough) 1 through 6. By no fault of mine, they're numbered using those stuffy old Roman numerals, so you'll see I–VI where you (in my humble opinion) ought to see Arabic numbers 1–6. Another rule, I think.

Anyway, it's better if you read the parts in order, but if you already know a lot — or think you know a lot — feel free to skip around and read the parts that interest you most.

Part 1: Desktop Madness: Navigating Mac OS X

This first part is very, very basic training. From the mouse to the Desktop, from menus, windows, and icons to the snazzy new Dock, it's all here. A lot of what you need to know to navigate the depths of Mac OS X safely and sanely will be found in this section. And although old-timers may just want to skim through it, you newcomers should probably read every word. Twice.

Part II: Rounding Out Your Basic Training

In this part, I build on the basics of Part I and really get you revving with your Mac. Here I cover additional topics that every Mac user needs to know, coupled with some hands-on, step-by-step instruction. I start with a look at each and every OS X Finder menu; then I move on to talk about the all-important Finder in depth. Next up is a chapter about how to open and save files (a skill you're sure to find handy), and finally I take a look at removable media (which means *ejectable disks* — CDs, DVDs, and even oldies but goodies such as Zip drives) and how to manage it.

Part III: Doing Stuff with Your Mac

This part is chock-full of ways to do cool stuff with your Mac. In this section, you'll discover the Internet first — how to get it working on your Mac, and what to do with it after you do. Next, I show you the ins and outs of printing under OS X. You also read about all the OS X-related applications that come with Panther, plus how to make your Panther look and feel just the way you like it. That's all followed by the lowdown on the Classic Environment, and possibly the most useful chapter in the whole book, Chapter 15, which details each and every gosh-darned System Preference, filled with useful observations and recommendations.

Part IV: U 2 Can B a Guru

Here I get into the nitty-gritty underbelly of Mac OS X, where I cover somewhat more advanced topics, such as file sharing, backing up your files, and the all-important troubleshooting chapter, Chapter 18.

Part V: The Part of Tens

Last, but not least, it's The Part of Tens, which is mostly a Letterman rip-off, although it does include heaping helpings of tips, optional software, great Mac Web sites, and hardware ideas.

Part VI: Appendix

Last, but certainly not least, I cover installing Mac OS X Panther in the Appendix. The whole process has become quite easy with this version of the system software, but if you have to install Panther yourself, it would behoove you to read this helpful Appendix first.

Icons Used in This Book

You'll see little round pictures (icons) off to the left side of the text throughout this book. Consider these icons as miniature road signs, telling you a little something extra about the topic at hand. Here's what the different icons look like and what they all mean.

Look for Tip icons to find the juiciest morsels: shortcuts, tips, and undocumented secrets about Panther. Try them all; impress your friends!

When you see this icon, it means that this particular morsel is something that I think you should memorize (or at least write on your shirt cuff).

Put on your propeller beanie hat and pocket protector; these parts include the truly nerdy stuff. It's certainly not required reading, but it must be interesting or informative or I wouldn't have wasted your time with it.

Read these notes very, very, very carefully. Did I say *very*? Warning icons flag important information. The author and publisher won't be responsible if your Mac explodes or spews flaming parts because you ignored a Warning icon. Just kidding. Macs don't explode or spew (with the exception of a few choice PowerBook 5300s, which won't run Panther anyway). But I got your attention, didn't I? It's a good idea to read Warning notes carefully.

These icons represent my ranting or raving about something that just bugs me. Imagine foam coming from my mouth. Rants are required to be irreverent, irrelevant, or both. I also try to keep them short, more for your sake than mine.

Well, now, what could this icon possibly be about? Named by famous editorial consultant Mr. Obvious, this icon highlights all things new and different in Mac OS X Panther.

Where to Go from Here

Go to a comfortable spot (preferably not far from a Mac) and read the book.

I didn't write this book for myself. I wrote it for you and would love to hear how it worked for you. So please drop me a line or register your comments through the Wiley Online Registration Form located at www.dummies.com.

Did this book work for you? What did you like? What didn't you like? What questions were unanswered? Did you want to know more about something? Did you want to find out less about something? Tell me! I have received more than 100 suggestions about previous editions, most of which are incorporated here. So keep up the good work!

You can send snail mail care of Wiley, Inc. (the mailroom there will see that I receive it), or send e-mail to me directly at `pantherfordummies@ doctormacdirect.com`. I appreciate your feedback, and I will *try* to respond to all e-mail within a few days.

So what are you waiting for? Go — enjoy the book!

Part I
Desktop Madness: Navigating Mac OS X

The 5th Wave   By Rich Tennant

"I don't know what program you been usin', Frank, but it ain't the right one. Look—your menu bar should read, File, Edit, Reap, Gather..."

In this part . . .

Mac OS X Panther sports tons of new goodies and features. I'll get to the hot new goodies soon enough, but you have to crawl before you can walk.

In this part, you discover the most basic of basics, such as how to turn on your Mac. Next, I acquaint you with the Mac OS X Desktop: windows, icons, the Dock, the Finder — the whole shmear.

So get comfortable, roll up your sleeves, fire up your Mac if you like, and settle down with Part I, a delightful little section I like to think of as "The Hassle-Free Way to Get Started with Mac OS X Panther."

Chapter 1

Mac OS X Panther 101 (Prerequisites: None)

***

In This Chapter

▶ Defining Mac OS X Panther

▶ Finding help if you're a beginner

▶ Turning on your Mac

▶ Shutting down your Mac without getting chewed out by it

▶ Knowing what you should see when you turn on your Mac

▶ Taking a refresher course on using a mouse

***

Congratulate yourself on choosing Mac OS X, which stands for Macintosh Operating System X — that's the Roman numeral *ten*, not the letter *X* (pronounced *ten,* not *ex*). You made a smart move because you scored more than just an operating system upgrade. Mac OS X version 10.3 Panther includes dozens of new or improved features to make using your Mac easier as well as dozens more that help you do more work in less time. Now you can use these new features to be more productive, have fewer headaches, reduce your cholesterol level, and fall in love with your Mac all over again.

In this chapter, I start at the very beginning and talk about Mac OS X in mostly abstract terms. You can turn your Mac on if you like, but most of this chapter has no hands-on material. What you will find, however, is a bunch of important stuff that you need to know in order to proceed. If you're a total beginner to the Mac experience, you should probably read every word in this chapter. Even if you're past the beginner stage, you may want to skim these sections anyway to refresh your memory.

Those of you who are upgrading from an earlier version of Mac OS to Mac OS X should read the Appendix right about now for installation information.

Gnawing to the Core of OS X

Along with the code in its read-only memory (ROM), the operating system (that is, the *OS* in *Mac OS X*) is what makes a Mac a Mac. Without it, your Mac is a pile of silicon and circuits — no smarter than a toaster.

"So what does an operating system do?" you ask. Good question. The short answer is that an *operating system* controls the basic and most important operations of your computer. In the case of Mac OS X and your Mac, the operating system

- Manages memory.
- Controls how windows, icons, and menus work.
- Keeps track of files.
- Manages networking.
- Does housekeeping. (No kidding!)

Other forms of software, such as word processors and Web browsers, rely on the operating system to create and maintain the environment in which that software works its magic. When you create a memo, for example, the word processor provides the tools for you to type and format the information. In the background, the operating system is the muscle for the word processor, performing crucial functions like the following:

- Providing the mechanism for drawing and moving the window in which you write the memo
- Keeping track of a file when you save it
- Helping the word processor create drop-down menus and dialogs for you to interact with
- Communicating with other programs
- And much, much more (stuff that only geeks could care about)

So now that you have a little background in operating systems, take a gander at the next section before you do anything else with your Mac.

Don't let that UNIX stuff scare you. It's there if you want it, but if you don't want it or don't care, you'll rarely even know it's there. All you'll know is that your Mac just runs and runs and runs without crashing and crashing and crashing.

The Mac advantage

Most of the world's PCs use Windows. You're among the lucky few to have a computer with an operating system that's intuitive, easy to use, and, dare I say, fun. If you don't believe me, try using Windows for a day or two. Go ahead. You probably won't suffer any permanent damage. In fact, you'll really begin to appreciate how good you have it. Feel free to hug your Mac. Or give it a peck on the CD-ROM drive slot — just try not to get your tongue caught.

As someone once told me, "Claiming that the Macintosh is inferior to Windows because most people use Windows is like saying that all other restaurants serve food that's inferior to McDonald's."

We may be a minority, but we have the best, most stable, most modern all-purpose operating system in the world. Here's why: UNIX — on which Mac OS X is based — is widely regarded as the best industrial-strength operating system. For now, just know that being based on UNIX means that a Mac running OS X will crash less often than an older Mac or a Windows machine, which means less downtime. But perhaps the biggest advantage OS X has is that when an application crashes, it doesn't crash your entire computer, and you don't have to restart to continue working.

A Safety Net for the Absolute Beginner (Or Any User)

In this section, I deal with the stuff that the manual that came with your Mac doesn't cover — or doesn't cover in nearly enough detail. If you're a first-time Macintosh user, please, *please* read this section of the book carefully — it could save your life. Okay, okay, perhaps I'm being overly dramatic. What I mean to say is that reading this section could save your *Mac*. Even if you're an experienced Mac user, you may want to read this section anyway. Chances are that you need a few reminders.

Turning the dang thing on

Okay. This is the big moment — turning on your Mac! Gaze at it longingly first and say something cheesy, such as "You're the most awesome computer I've ever known." If that doesn't turn your Mac on (it probably won't), keep reading.

If you actually thought that flattery would turn on your Mac, you should probably read *Self-Psychotherapy For Dummies* before you continue with this book. (And if you think that book exists, maybe you should check out *Gullibility For Dummies.*)

If you don't know how to turn your Mac on, don't feel bad — just look in the manual that came with your Mac. Apple, in its infinite wisdom, has manufactured Macs with power switches and buttons on every conceivable surface: on the front, side, and back of the computer itself, and even on the keyboard or monitor. Some Macs (including most older PowerBooks) even hide the power button behind a little plastic door. Because of the vast number of different configurations, I can't tell you where the switch is without devoting a whole chapter just to that topic. (Can you say booooo-ring?)

What you should see on startup

When you finally do turn on your Macintosh, you set in motion a sophisticated and complex series of events that culminates in the loading of Mac OS X and the appearance of the Mac OS X Desktop. After a small bit of whirring, buzzing, and flashing (meaning that the operating system is loading), OS X first tests all your hardware — slots, ports, disks, random access memory (RAM) — and so on. If everything passes, you hear a pleasing musical chord and see the tasteful gray Apple logo in the middle of your screen and a small spinning pinwheel cursor somewhere on the screen. Both are shown in Figure 1-1.

✔ **Everything is fine and dandy:** Next, you see the soothing blue Mac OS logo, the words *Mac OS X,* and a status indicator with messages that tell you that the Mac is going through its normal startup motions. Makes you feel kind of warm and fuzzy, doesn't it? If all this fanfare shows up on your screen, Mac OS X is loading properly. In the unlikely event that you don't see the gray Apple logo, the soothing messages, and the familiar Desktop, see Chapter 18 where I show you how to troubleshoot your system.

Then, you may or may not see the Mac OS X login screen, where you enter your name and password. If you do (you'll only see it if your Mac is set up for multiple users; don't worry, I tell you all about this in Chapter 16), press the Enter or Return key and away you go.

If you don't want to have to type your name and password every time you start or restart your Mac (or even if you do), check out Chapter 16 for the scoop on how to turn the login screen on or off.

Either way, the Desktop soon materializes before your eyes. If you haven't customized, configured, or tinkered with your Desktop, it should look something like Figure 1-2. Now is a good time to take a moment for positive thoughts about the person who convinced you that you wanted a Mac. That person was right!

Figure 1-1:
No more smiley Mac or multi-colored beach ball cursor at startup. These are their Panther replacements.

 ✔ **Sad Mac:** If any of your hardware fails when it's tested, you could see a black or gray screen that may or may not display the dreaded sad Mac icon (shown in the left margin) and/or hear a far less pleasing musical chord (in the key of F-minor, I believe), known by Mac aficionados as the *Chimes of Doom.*

Figure 1-2:
The Mac OS X Desktop after a brand, spanking new installation of OS X.

Some older Macs played the sound of a horrible car wreck instead of the chimes, complete with crying tires and busting glass. It was exceptionally unnerving, which may be why Apple doesn't use it anymore.

The fact that something went wrong is no reflection on your prowess as a Macintosh user. Something inside your Mac is broken, and it probably needs to go in for repairs (usually to an Apple dealer). If any of that's already happened to you, check out Chapter 18 to try to get your Mac well again.

If your computer is under warranty, dial 1-800-SOS-APPL, and a customer service person can tell you what to do. Before you do anything, though, skip ahead to Chapter 18. It's entirely possible that one of the suggestions there can get you back on track without you having to spend even a moment on hold.

✔ **Prohibitory sign (formerly known as the flashing question mark disk):** Although it's unlikely that you'll ever see the sad Mac, most users eventually encounter the prohibitory sign shown in the left margin (which replaced the flashing question-mark-on-a-disk icon and flashing folder icon back in OS X 10.2 Jaguar). This icon means that your Mac can't find a startup disk, hard drive, network server, or CD-ROM containing a valid Macintosh operating system. See Chapter 18 to try to ease your Mac's ills.

How do you know which version of the Mac OS your computer has? Simple. Just choose About This Mac from the menu (that's the menu with the symbol in the upper-left corner of the Finder menu bar). The About This Mac window pops up in the middle of your screen, as shown in Figure 1-3. The version that you're running appears just below *Mac OS X* in the center of the window. Click the More Info button to launch Apple System Profiler, which has much more information, including processor speed, bus speed, number of processors, caches, installed memory, networking, storage devices, and much more. Discover more about this program in Chapter 13.

Shutting down properly

Turning off the power without shutting your Mac down properly is one of the worst things you can do to your poor Mac. Shutting down your Mac improperly can really screw up your hard drive, scramble the contents of your most important files, or both.

If a thunderstorm is rumbling nearby or if you're unfortunate enough to have rolling blackouts where you live, you may *really* want to shut your Mac down. (See the next section where I briefly discuss lightning and your Mac.)

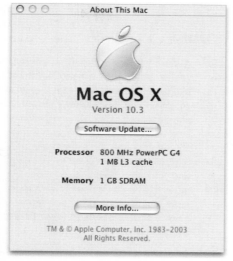

Figure 1-3:
See which
version of
Mac OS X
you're
running.

To turn off your Mac, always use the Shut Down command on the menu (which I discuss in Chapter 6), or you can press the Power key once and then click the Shut Down button. On Apple Pro keyboards, which don't have a Power key, press Ctrl+Eject instead and then click the Shut Down button that appears (or press the Return key, which does the same thing).

TECHNICAL STUFF

The legend of the boot

Boot this. *Boot* that. "I *booted* my Mac and. . . ." or "Did it *boot*?" and so on. Talking about computers for long without hearing the *boot* word is nearly impossible.

But why *boot*? Why not *shoe* or *shirt* or even *shazam*?

Back in the very olden days — maybe the 1960s or a little earlier — starting up a computer required you to toggle little manual switches on the front panel, which began an internal process that loaded the operating system. The process became known as *bootstrapping* because if you toggled the right switches, the

computer would "pull itself up by its bootstraps." This phrase didn't take long to transmogrify into *booting* and finally to *boot*.

Over the years, *booting* has come to mean turning on almost any computer or even a peripheral device, such as a printer. Some people also use it to refer to launching an application: "I booted Excel."

So the next time one of your gearhead friends says the *b*-word, ask whether he knows where the term comes from. Then dazzle him with the depth and breadth of your (not quite useful) knowledge!

Eternally yours . . . *now*

Mac OS X is designed so that you never have to shut it down. You can configure it to sleep after a specified period of inactivity. (See Chapter 15 for more info on the Energy Saver features of OS X.) If you do so, your Mac will consume very little electricity when it's sleeping and will be ready to use just a few seconds after you awaken it (by pressing any key or clicking the mouse). On the other hand, if you're not going to be using it for a few days, you may want to shut it down anyway.

Note: If you leave your Mac on constantly and you're gone when a lightning storm or rolling blackout hits, your Mac may get wasted. So be sure that you have adequate protection if you decide to leave your Mac on and unattended for long periods. See the section "A few things you should definitely NOT do with your Mac" elsewhere in this chapter for more info on lightning and your Mac. If I plan to be away from mine for more than a day, I usually shut it down, just in case. But because OS X is designed to run 24/7, I don't shut it down at night unless it's dark and stormy.

Of course, most of us have broken this rule several times without anything horrible happening. Don't be lulled into a false sense of security, however. Break the rules one time too many or under the wrong circumstances, and your most important file *will* be toast. The only times when you should turn off your Mac without shutting down properly is if your screen is frozen or if you crash and you've already tried everything else. (See Chapter 18 for what those "everything elses" are.) This doesn't happen often — and less often under OS X than ever before — but when it does, turning your Mac off and then back on may be the only solution. Sometimes even that doesn't work, and you may have to unplug the computer from the power outlet to get it to reboot.

A few things you should definitely NOT do with your Mac

In this section, I deal with the bad stuff that can happen to your computer if you do the wrong things with it. If something bad has already happened to you — I know . . . I'm beginning to sound like a broken record — see Chapter 18.

- ✔ **Don't unplug your Mac when it's turned on.** Very bad things can happen, such as having your operating system break. See the preceding section where I discuss shutting your system down properly.

- ✔ **Don't use your Mac when lightning is near.** Here's a simple life equation for you: Mac + lightning = dead Mac. 'Nuff said. Oh, and don't place much faith in inexpensive surge protectors. A good jolt of lightning will fry the surge protector right along with your computer as well as possibly frying your modem, printer, and anything else plugged into it. Some surge protectors can withstand most lightning strikes, but these warriors aren't the cheapies that you buy at your local computer emporium. Unplugging your Mac from the wall during electrical storms is safer and less expensive. (Don't forget to unplug your external modem, network hubs, printers, or other hardware that plugs into the wall as well — lightning can fry them, too.)

- **Don't jostle, bump, shake, kick, throw, dribble, or punt your Mac, especially while it's running.** Your Mac contains a hard drive that spins at 5,400+ revolutions per minute (rpm). A jolt to a hard drive while it's reading or writing a file can cause the head to crash into the disk, which can render many or all the files on it unrecoverable. Ouch!

- **Don't forget to back up your data!** I beg you: Please read Chapter 17 now before something horrible happens to your valuable data! If the stuff on your hard drive means anything to you, you must back it up. Not maybe. You must. Even if your most important file is your last saved game of Tony Hawk Pro Skater 2, you still need to realize how important it is to back up your files.

  In Chapter 17, I discuss how to back up your files, and I *strongly* recommend that you read Chapter 17 sooner rather than later — preferably before you do any significant work on your Mac. Dr. Macintosh sez: "There are only two kinds of Mac users: those who have never lost data and those who will." Which kind will you be?

- **Don't kiss your monitor while wearing stuff on your lips.** For obvious reasons! Use a soft cloth and/or the Klear Screen polish and wipes Apple recommends if you need to clean your display.

Point-and-click boot camp

Are you new to the Mac? Just learning how to move the mouse around? Now is a good time to go over some fundamental stuff that you need to know for just about everything you'll be doing on the Mac. Spend a few minutes reading this section, and soon you'll be clicking, double-clicking, pressing, and pointing all over the place. If you think you've got the whole mousing thing pretty much figured out, feel free to skip this section. I'll catch you on the other side.

Still with me? Good. Now for some basic terminology.

- **Point:** Before you can click or press anything, you have to *point* to it. Place your hand on your mouse and move it so that the cursor arrow is over the object that you want — like on top of an icon or a button. Then click the mouse to select the object or double-click it to run it (if it's an application or an icon that starts up an application). You point and then you click — *point-and-click,* in computer lingo.

✔ **Click:** (Also called *single-click.*) Use your index finger to push the mouse button all the way down and then let go so that it produces a satisfying clicking sound. (If you have one of the new optical Apple Pro mice, you push down the whole thing to click.) Use a single-click to highlight an icon, press a button, or activate a check box or window.

✔ **Double-click:** *Click twice* in rapid succession. With a little practice, you can perfect this technique in no time. Use a double-click to open a folder or to launch a file or application.

✔ **Control-click:** Hold down the Control key while single-clicking. Control-clicking is the same as right-clicking on a Windows system and displays a menu (called a *contextual menu*) where you Control-clicked. In fact, if you are blessed with a two- (or more) button mouse (I personally use the four-button Kensington Turbo Mouse Pro Wireless and recommend it highly), you can right-click and avoid having to hold down the Control key.

✔ **Drag:** *Dragging* something usually accompanies clicking it first. With the mouse button held down, move the mouse on your desk or mouse pad so that the cursor — and whatever you select — moves across the screen. The combination of pressing the mouse and dragging it is usually referred to as *click-and-drag.*

✔ **Press:** A *press* is half a click. Instead of letting go of the mouse button to finish the click, keep holding it down. In most cases, your next step is to drag the mouse somewhere — down a menu to choose a command or across the screen to move an object, for example.

✔ **Choosing an item from a menu:** To get to Mac OS menu commands, you must first open a menu and then pick the option that you want. Point at the name of the menu that you want with your mouse cursor, press your mouse button down, and then drag your mouse downward until you select the command that you want. When the command is highlighted, finish selecting by letting go of the mouse button.

If you're a long-time Mac user, you probably hold down the mouse button the whole time between clicking the name of the menu and selecting the command that you want. You can still do it that way, but you can also click once on the menu name to open it, release the mouse button, and then drag down to the item that you want to select *and then click again.* In other words, OS X menus stay open for a few seconds after you click them, even if you're not holding down the mouse button. Go ahead and give it a try . . . I'll wait.

A pop quiz on mousing

For those of you who need to hone your mousing skills, here's a little quiz:

1. How do you select an icon?

A. Stare at it intently for five seconds.

B. Point to it with your finger, slap the side of your monitor, and say "That one, stupid!"

C. Move the mouse pointer on top of the icon and click once.

2. When do you need to double-click?

A. Whenever you find yourself saying, "There's no place like home."

B. When you're using both hands to control the mouse.

C. When you want to open a file or folder.

3. How do you select multiple items or blocks of text?

A. Get several people to stare intently at the items that you want to select.

B. Attach multiple mice to your Mac.

C. Slide the mouse on your desk, moving the onscreen pointer to the location where you want to begin selecting. Press and hold down the mouse button. Drag the pointer across the items or text that you want to select. Then let go of the mouse button.

4. How do you move a selected item?

A. Call U-Haul.

B. Pick up and tilt your monitor until the item slides to the proper location.

C. Point to the item and hold (press) down the mouse button. With the mouse button still held down, drag the pointer to the new location and let go of the mouse button.

If you haven't figured it out by now, the correct answer to each of these questions is C. If any other answer sounded remotely plausible, sit down with your Mac and just play with it for a while. If you have kids at your disposal, watch them play with your Mac. They'll show you how to use it in no time.

Chapter 2

Meet the Desktop

. . . .

. . . .

*T*his chapter is where I get down to the nitty-gritty about the nifty new Mac OS X Desktop — the place where you start doing stuff with your Mac.

Those of you who've been using a Mac for a while may find some of the information in this chapter repetitive; some features that I describe haven't changed from earlier versions of Mac OS, but in Mac OS X, much more is new than the X in its name. Although you still use the Desktop for many of the same tasks you used it for in OS 9 (and OS 8, and System 7, and so on), it looks very different, with lots of new tools and features and terminology that you need to know before you can call yourself truly Mac OS X savvy.

Besides, if you decide to skip this chapter — just because you think you have all the new stuff figured out — I assure you that you'll miss out on sarcasm, clever wordplay, shortcuts, awesome techniques, a bad pun or two, and some good advice on making the Desktop an easier place to be. If that's not enough to convince you, I also provide a bunch of stuff that Apple didn't bother to tell you (as if you read every word in Mac OS X Help, which is the only user manual Apple provides anyway!).

Tantalized? Let's rock.

Clearing Off the Desktop

Just about everything that you do on your Mac begins and ends with the Desktop. This is where you manage files, store documents, launch programs, adjust the way your Mac works, and much more. If you ever expect to master your Mac, the first step is to master the Desktop.

Some folks use the terms *Desktop* and *Finder* interchangeably to refer to the total Macintosh environment that you see — icons, windows, menus, and all that other cool stuff. Just to make things confusing, the background that you see on your screen — the backdrop behind your hard drive icon and open windows — is also called the Desktop. In this book, I refer to the *Finder* as the Finder, which I discuss in Chapters 7 and 8. When I say *Desktop,* I'm talking about the background behind your windows and Dock, where your hard drive icon appears.

Got it? The Desktop is convenient and fast. Put stuff there.

Check out the default Mac Desktop for OS X in Figure 2-1.

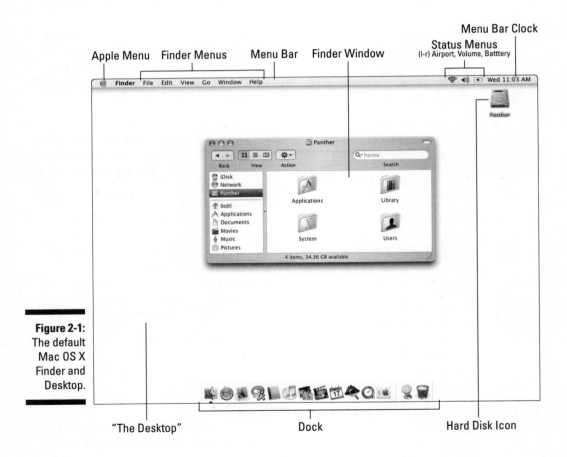

Figure 2-1:
The default
Mac OS X
Finder and
Desktop.

Touring the Desktop

The Desktop is the center of your Mac OS experience, so before I go any further, I need to quickly describe its most prominent features:

- **Desktop:** The *Desktop* is the area behind the windows and the Dock, where your hard drive icon (ordinarily) lives. The Desktop isn't a window, yet it acts like one. Like a folder window or drive window, the Desktop can contain icons. But unlike most windows, which require a bit of navigation to get to, the Desktop is a great place for things that you use a lot, such as folders, applications, or particular documents. The next section discusses the default icons that you see on the Desktop when you first load up OS X.

- **Dock:** The *Dock* is the Finder's main navigation shortcut tool. It makes getting to frequently used icons easy, even when you have a screen full of windows. Like the Desktop, the Dock is a great place for things you use a lot, such as folders, applications, or particular documents. Besides putting your frequently used icons at your fingertips, it's almost infinitely customizable, too; read more about it in Chapter 3.

  If you used an earlier version of Mac OS, think of the Dock as the OS X version of the Apple menu in Mac OS versions of the past. Yes, the OS X Finder *does* have an Apple menu, but it doesn't work at all like the Apple menu in earlier versions of Mac OS. See Chapter 6 for more info on the Apple menu.

- **Icons:** *Icons* are the little pictures that you see in your windows and even on your Desktop. Most icons are containers that hold things that you work with on your Mac, such as programs and documents, which are also represented by — you guessed it — icons. In Chapter 4, I cover icons in detail, and the next section discusses the icons that you see on the OS X Desktop when you first boot up your Mac.

- **Windows:** Opening most icons (by double-clicking them) makes a window appear. Windows in the Finder show you the contents of hard drive and folder icons, and windows in applications usually show you the contents of your documents. For the full scoop on Panther windows, which are very different from Mac windows in previous OS releases, check out Chapter 5.

- **Menus:** *Menus* let you choose to do things, such as create new folders; duplicate files; cut, copy, or paste text; and so on. Find out all about them in Chapter 6.

- **Aliases:** Use *aliases* of things that you use often so that you can keep the originals tucked away in one of your perfectly organized folders. Check out aliases in Chapter 4.

  If all these new terms such as *alias, Dock,* and so on seem strange to you, don't worry — I explain all of them in detail in the rest of the chapters in Part I.

Sniffing out the default Desktop icons

Icons on the Desktop behave the same as icons in a window. You move them and copy them just like you would an icon in a window. The only difference is that Desktop items aren't in a window: They're on the Desktop, which makes them more convenient to use.

Actually, if you look at your Home directory (click the Home button on any Finder window toolbar or use the shortcut ⌘+Shift+H to open a window displaying Home), you see a folder named *Desktop* that contains the same icons that you place on the Desktop (but not the hard drive icons). The reason for this folder is that each user has an individual Desktop. But I'm getting ahead of myself. You find out much more about Home, users, and all that jazz in upcoming chapters.

To move an item to the Desktop, simply click its icon in any window and then, without releasing the mouse button, drag it out of the window and onto the Desktop; then release the mouse button.

✔ **Hard drive icons:** The first icon that you should become familiar with is the icon for your hard drive (refer to Figure 2-1). You can usually find it on the upper-right side of your Finder window when you first start the Mac. Look for the name Macintosh HD, iMac HD, or something like that unless you've already renamed it. (I renamed my hard drive "Panther" when I started working on this book.)

There are two ways to rename your hard drive:

1. Single click the icon's name. When the name highlights, as shown in the middle icon in Figure 2-2, type its new name.

   If you click directly on the icon instead of its name, the icon will be selected but the name will not become highlighted for editing, as shown in the icon on the right in Figure 2-2.

2. Single click the icon itself and then press Return or Enter, and type in a new name.

✔ **Disk icons:** Disk icons appear on the Desktop by default. When you insert a CD or DVD, its icon appears on the Desktop just below your hard drive icon (space permitting).

If you don't see a disk icon on your Desktop, skip ahead to Chapter 6, where I discuss Finder Preferences. That's where you can choose whether to see disks on your Desktop.

Picture this: A picture on your Desktop

I'd be remiss if I didn't mention that you can change the background picture of your Desktop.

Figure 2-2:
An unse-
lected icon
(left); an
icon with its
name
selected
(middle); an
icon that is
selected
(right).

In Figure 2-3, you can see my Desktop with a background picture I made to celebrate the release of Panther. (If you want a reminder of what the default Desktop background looks like, refer to Figure 2-1.)

Figure 2-3:
My
beautified
Desktop.

Here's how you can change your Desktop picture if you care to:

1. **From the Desktop, choose ⟹System Preferences or click the System Preferences icon in the Dock.**

   The System Preferences window appears.

2. **Click the Desktop & Screen Saver icon.**

   The Desktop & Screen Saver Preferences pane appears.

3. **Drag any picture in any folder on your hard disk (it's my Pictures folder in Figure 2-4) to the Desktop & Screen Saver Preferences pane's picture well.**

Another way to change the desktop picture is to select Choose Folder from the list of folders on the left of the window; then select a new picture using the standard Open File dialog box to use as your Desktop picture.

If you don't know how to choose a picture that way, look in Chapter 8. And for more info on using System Preferences, check out Chapter 15.

Figure 2-4:
The picture
well is the
little rec-
tangle to
the left of
the words
Solid White.
The name of
the current
picture
(Solid White
in this case)
appears to
the right of
the well.

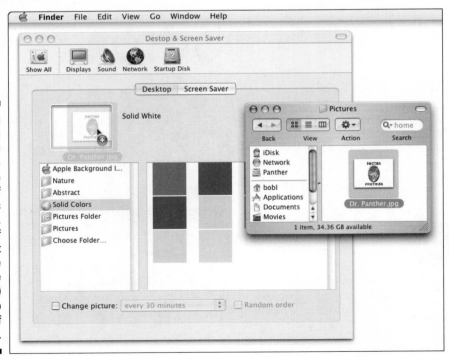

Chapter 3

"What's Up, Dock?"

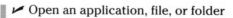

*I*n this chapter, I take a look at the Dock, which is the section of the Desktop that gives you quick access to frequently used applications. The Dock is also a quick way to pull a file or application that's already open to the front so that you can work with it. Read on to discover how to use the Dock and how to customize it so that it works and looks just the way you want.

Running Down the Dock

Take a minute to look at the row of pictures at the bottom of the your Mac OS X Finder screen. That row, ladies and gentlemen, is the *Dock* (shown in Figure 3-1), and those individual pictures are *icons* (which I discuss in Chapter 4). When you click a Dock icon, you either

✔ Open an application, file, or folder

✔ Bring an open application, file, or folder to the front of all others

When you press (click but don't let go) most Dock icons, a menu appears.

By default, the Dock contains a number of commonly used Mac OS X applications, and you can also store your own applications, files, or folders there. I show you how to do that in the "Adding icons to the Dock" section later in this chapter.

Most items that you find on the Dock when you first use Mac OS X are probably familiar to you already. If they aren't, they certainly will be in time. In the following sections, I give you a brief description of each, moving from left to right; I also point you to the parts of this book where I cover the item in more detail.

Figure 3-1:
The Dock
and all of its
default
icons.

Finder

 The Finder application (which I discuss at length in Chapter 7) is always open. Click the Finder icon (shown in the left margin) to open a Finder window if none are open already or to switch to the Finder when another application is active. You can open as many Finder windows as you want by choosing File⇨New Finder Window or by using the keyboard shortcut ⌘+N. (Hold down the ⌘ key and then press the N key.)

Safari

 Click this icon to launch Apple's state-of-the-art OS X Web browser application. I describe Safari in glorious detail in Chapter 11.

Mail

 Click this icon to launch Apple's OS X e-mail application, appropriately named *Mail,* with which you can send and receive e-mail. See Chapter 13 for more on Mail .

iChat

 Click this icon to launch Apple's OS X instant messaging application, *iChat,* with which you can send and receive instant messages (IMs). I cover iChat in loving detail in Chapter 11.

Address Book

 Click this icon to launch Apple OS X's eponymously named address book application, Address Book, where you store information about people (contacts). Go to Chapter 13 for information about Address Book.

iTunes

 iTunes is a major part of Apple's digital hub. With iTunes, you can listen to MP3 files that you download from the Internet, audio CDs, and Internet radio stations, and you can also build your own library of MP3 files from CDs that you already own. I describe iTunes in impressive detail in Chapter 13.

iPhoto

 Use iPhoto, another major part of Apple's digital hub, to download photos from your digital camera, organize them, print them, make slide shows and Web pages from them, and much more. I talk more about iPhoto in Chapter 13.

iMovie

 iMovie is yet another major part of Apple's digital hub. Use iMovie to make high-quality movies complete with transitions and titles. I talk more about iMovie in Chapter 13.

 If you like this sort of digital stuff, check out *The Digital Hub Bible*, written by Dennis Cohen (with a little help from yours truly), published by Wiley Publishing, Inc. This epic tome dedicates hundreds of pages to each of the digital hub applications, making it a great all-in-one reference for the Apple i-apps (iDVD, iMovie, iPhoto, and iDVD). Even if I do say so my iSelf.

iCal

 iCal is Apple's calendar program, discussed in great detail in Chapter 13.

QuickTime Player

 QuickTime, Apple's multimedia application, is yet another part of its digital hub. It provides you with a format for playing movies, audio programs, and streaming audio and video. Read more about QuickTime in Chapter 13.

System Preferences

 Click the System Preferences icon on the Dock to open the System Preferences application. System Preferences, as I describe in Chapter 15, gives you access to all sorts of settings that you use to configure your Mac just the way you like it. Clicking its Dock icon is the same as choosing System Preferences from the Apple menu; both open the System Preferences program.

Apple — Mac OS X

The Apple — Mac OS X icon launches your Web browser (Safari) and takes you to the Mac OS X section of Apple's Web site.

Trash

The Trash icon is unique among Dock items: It's not a file or application that you open. Instead, you drag things to this icon to get rid of them.

Don't want it? Trash it

The *Trash* is a special container where you put the icons that you no longer want on your hard drive or removable media storage device (such as Zip). Got four copies of TextEdit on your hard drive? Drag three of them to the Trash. Tired of tripping over old letters that you don't want to keep? Drag them to the Trash, too. To put something in the Trash, just drag its icon on top of the Trash icon and watch it disappear.

Like other icons, you know that you've connected with the Trash while dragging when the icon is highlighted. And like other Dock icons, the Trash icon's name appears when you move the cursor over the icon.

Taking out the trash

You know how the garbage in the can in your garage sits there until the sanitation engineers come by and pick it up each Thursday? The Mac OS X Trash works the same. When you put something in the Trash, it sits there until you choose the Finder⇨Empty Trash command or use the keyboard shortcut ⌘+Shift+Delete.

While items sit in the Trash waiting for you to empty it, the Trash basket shows you that it has files waiting for you there . . . just like in real life, your unemptied Trash is full of crumpled papers.

You can also empty the Trash from the Dock by pressing the mouse button and holding it down on the Trash icon for a second or two. The Empty Trash menu pops up like magic. Move your mouse over it to select it and then release the mouse button. Control-clicking will pop up the menu immediately.

Think twice before you invoke the Empty Trash command. After you empty the Trash, the files that it contained are (usually) gone forever. My advice: Before you get too bold, read Chapter 17 and back up your hard drive several times. After you get proficient at backups, even though the files are technically gone forever from your hard drive, you can get them back if you like (at least in theory).

Digging stuff out of the Trash (yech!)

As with all icons, you can open the Trash to see what's in there — just click its icon in the Dock. If you decide that you don't want to get rid of an item that's already in the Trash, just drag it back out, either onto the Finder or back into the folder where it belongs.

iDVD

One last thing: If your Mac has a *SuperDrive* — Apple's DVD-RW burner — you may see an icon for iDVD in your Dock. *iDVD* is another digital hub application, used to create beautiful DVDs that can be played on OS X's own DVD Player or any standalone DVD player.

Workin' the Dock

The Dock is a convenient way to get at oft-used icons. By default, the Dock comes pre-stocked with icons that Apple thinks you'll need most frequently, but you can customize it to contain any icons that you choose. In this section, I tell you all about the Dock — how to use it, how to customize it, how to resize it, and more.

Using Dock icons

Dock icons work just like other icons except that instead of double-clicking them, you only single-click them. (I further discuss icons in Chapter 4.) Note that when you single-click a Dock icon, it doesn't become highlighted. Instead, any chosen Dock icon moves up and out of its place on the Dock for a moment, letting you know that you've activated it. Check out Figure 3-2 to see an animated Dock icon — it's still on the Dock, but it's raised higher than the inactive ones.

Figure 3-2:
A raised
Dock icon:
selected
and
opening.

Many Dock icons also do a little bouncy dance when that program isn't active (its menu bar isn't showing and it's not the front-most program) to inform you that it desires your attention. If you notice that the icon for an open application is dancing, give it a click to find out what the program wants or needs.

When an application on the Dock is open, an up-arrow (which looks like a small black pyramid) appears below its Dock icon, as shown in Figure 3-2.

To discover the name of a Dock icon, just move your cursor over any item on the Dock, and the item's name appears above it (as shown in Figure 3-3). This feature is quite handy because you can't view Dock items as a list in the same the way that you can with icons that are stored in windows. And, as you can read in the section "Resizing the Dock" later in this chapter, you can resize the Dock to make the icons smaller (which does make them more difficult to see). Hovering your mouse cursor to discover the name of a teeny icon makes this feature even more useful.

Figure 3-3:
Move your
cursor over
a Dock icon
to display its
name.

Adding icons to the Dock

You can customize your Dock with favorite applications, a document you update daily, or maybe a folder containing your favorite recipes — whatever you need quick access to. The following sections tell you what kind of stuff to put on the Dock and how to add an icon to the Dock.

Knowing what to put on the Dock

Put things on the Dock that you need quick access to and that you use often, or add items that aren't quickly available from menus or the toolbar. If you like using the Dock better than the Go menu or the Finder window toolbar, for example, add your Documents folder to the Dock.

I suggest adding these items to your Dock:

- ✔ **A word processing application:** Most people use word processing software more than any other application.

- ✔ **A project folder:** Suppose that you follow my advice and store all the files that you create in the Documents folder or subfolders thereof. One of those subfolders contains all the documents for your thesis, or the biggest project you have at work, or your massive recipe collection . . . whatever. Add that folder to the Dock and then you can access it much quicker than if you have to open your Documents folder first.

  When you *press* (click but don't let go) on a folder icon, a handy hierarchical menu of its contents appears. Give it a try — it's great.

- ✔ **A special utility or application:** StuffIt Expander is an essential part of my work because I receive a lot of stuffed and zipped files. You may prefer to have handy a *File Transfer Protocol* (FTP) application (used to download files from the Internet), a graphics application such as Photoshop, or your favorite game.

- ✔ **Your favorite URLs:** Save links to sites that you visit every day — ones that you use in your job, your favorite Mac news sites, or your personalized page from an Internet service provider (ISP). Sure, you can make one of these pages your browser's start page, but the Dock lets you add one or more additional URLs.

  Here's how to quickly add a URL to the Dock. Open Safari and go to the page with a URL that you want to save on the Dock. Click and drag the small icon that you find at the left of the URL in the Address bar (denoted with a large number 1 in Figure 3-4) to the right side of the Dock (denoted with a large number 2 in Figure 3-4) and then release the mouse button. The icons in the Dock will slide over and make room for your URL. From now on, when you click the URL icon that you move to your Dock, Safari opens to that page.

  UNIFORM RESOURCE LOCATOR

  You can add several URL icons to the Dock, but bear in mind that the Dock and its icons shrink to accommodate added icons, thus making them harder to see. Perhaps the best idea — if you want easy access to several URLs — is to create a folder full of URLs and put that folder on the Dock. Then you can just press and hold your mouse on the folder (or Control-click the folder) to pop up a menu with all your URLs.

Even though you can make the Dock smaller, you're still limited to one row of icons. The smaller that you make the Dock, the larger the crowd of icons that you can amass. You have to determine for yourself what's best for you: having lots of icons available on the Dock (even though they may be difficult to see because they're so tiny) or having less clutter but fewer icons on your Dock.

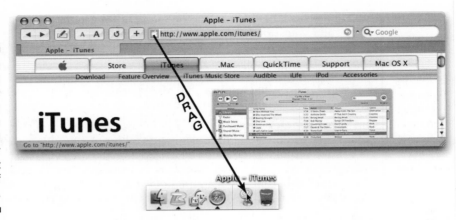

Apple – iTunes

Figure 3-4:
To save a
URL to your
Dock, drag
its little icon
from the
Address bar
to the right
side of
the Dock.

Putting an icon on the Dock

Adding an application, file, or folder to the Dock is as easy as 1, 2, 3. First, open a Finder window that contains an application, file, or folder icon that you use frequently. Now, follow these steps to add it to the Dock:

1. **Click the item that you want to add to the Dock**

   As shown in Figure 3-5, I chose the StuffIt Expander application (it's highlighted). I use StuffIt Expander constantly to decompress archives of files received in e-mail or downloaded from newsgroups on the Internet. (Find the StuffIt Expander application, if you're interested, in the Utilities folder inside your Applications folder.)

2. **Drag the icon out of the Finder window and onto the Dock.**

3. **An icon for this item now appears on the Dock.**

You can add several items at the same time to the Dock by selecting them all and dragging the group to the Dock. However, you can delete only one icon at a time from the Dock.

Removing an icon from the Dock

To remove an item from the Dock, just drag its icon onto the Desktop. It disappears with a cool *poof* animation, as shown in Figure 3-6.

By moving an icon out of the Dock, you aren't moving or copying the item itself — you're just removing its icon from the Dock. Think of it like a library catalog card: Just because you remove the card from the card catalog doesn't mean that the book is gone from the library.

① **②** **③**

Figure 3-5:
Drag an
icon onto
the Dock to
add it.

When you open an application with an icon that doesn't ordinarily appear on the Dock, its icon magically appears on the Dock until you quit that application. And when you quit, its icon magically disappears from the Dock. In other words, you see a temporary Dock icon for every program that's currently open; these temporary icons disappear when you quit the program. If you want to keep an icon in the Dock permanently, you have two ways to tell it to stay around after you quit the program. You can Control-click (or click-and-hold) and then choose Keep in Dock from the menu that pops up, or you can drag the icon (for an application that's currently open) off and then back onto the Dock without letting go.

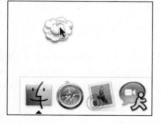

Figure 3-6:
To remove
an icon, drag
it off the
Dock and
POOF — it's
gone.

Setting Dock preferences

You can change a few things about the Dock to make it look and behave just the way you want it to. To do so, just choose Dock⇨Dock Preferences from the menu (or the *Apple menu,* meaning the menu beneath that symbol in the upper-left corner of the Finder menu bar). In the Dock dialog that opens (see Figure 3-7), you can adjust your Dock with the following preferences:

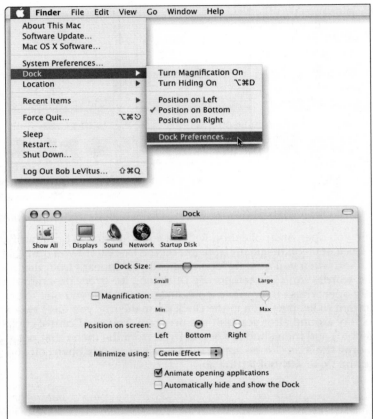

Figure 3-7:
The Dock
menu and
Dock
Preferences
window.

✔ **Dock Size:** Note the slider bar here. Move this slider to the right (larger) or left (smaller) to adjust the size of the Dock on your Finder. As you move the slider, watch the Dock change size. Now *there's* a fun way to spend a Saturday afternoon!

As you add items to the Dock, each icon — and the Dock itself — shrinks to accommodate the new ones.

✔ **Magnification:** This slider controls how big icons grow when you pass the arrow cursor over them. Or you can deselect this check box to turn off magnification entirely.

✔ **Position on Screen:** Choose from these three radio buttons to attach the Dock to the left side, the right side, or the bottom of your screen (the default). Personally, I prefer it on the right side of the screen.

✔ **Minimize Using:** Select from this handy drop-down list to choose the visual effect (animation) that you see when you click a window's Minimize button. The Genie Effect is the default, but the Scale Effect seems a bit faster to me.

✔ **Animate Opening Applications:** Mac OS X animates (bounces) Dock icons when you click them to open an item. If you don't like the animation, deselect this check box, and the bouncing will cease evermore.

✔ **Automatically Hide and Show the Dock:** Don't like the Dock? Maybe you want to free up the screen real estate at the bottom of your monitor? Then select the Automatically Hide and Show the Dock check box; after that, the Dock displays itself only when you move the cursor (mouse) to the bottom of the screen where the dock would ordinarily appear. It's like magic! (Okay, it's like Windows, but I hate to admit it.)

If the Dock isn't visible, deselect (that is, uncheck) this Automatically Hide and Show the Dock check box to bring it back. The option remains turned off unless you change it or choose Dock⇨Turn Hiding Off from the menu (or press ⌘+Option+D).

Resizing the Dock

If the default size of the Dock bugs you, you can make the Dock smaller and save yourself a lot of screen real estate. This space comes in especially handy when you add your own stuff to the Dock.

To shrink or enlarge the Dock (and its icons) without opening the Dock Preferences window, drag its sizer handle. To make the sizer appear (as shown in the left margin), move your cursor over the thin white line that you find on the right side of the Dock. Drag the sizer down to make the Dock smaller, holding onto the mouse button until you find the size you like. The more you drag this control down, the smaller the Dock gets. To enlarge the Dock again, just drag the sizer back up. Poof! Big Dock! You can enlarge the Dock until it fills your screen from side to side.

Chapter 4

I Think Icon! I Think Icon!

*I*f you're going to use a Macintosh, you're going to use icons. Period. They are a fundamental part of what makes a Mac a Mac. I discuss icons a little bit in Chapters 2 and 3, but in this chapter, I get down to the real nitty-gritty and explain them in great detail.

Trust me: By the time you finish this chapter, you'll be so familiar with all the different types of icons that Mac OS X has to offer that you'll probably dream of them tonight.

Introducing . . . Icons!

Icons are those funny little pictographs in your windows. Icons represent things that you work with on your Mac, such as programs, documents, and folders.

Icons come in several shapes and sizes. After you've been around the Macintosh for a while, you get a sixth sense about what an icon contains just by looking at it. The three main types of icons are applications, documents, and folders. Well, there are actually four types — aliases are an icon type in their own right. Don't worry: I show you all four icon types in this section.

Don't confuse icons with buttons; they're sort of alike but different. When you click a button, something else (such as a file, an application, or a folder) opens. *Buttons* are simply pointers. *Icons* actually represent things on your hard drive, such as folders and applications. You can't move buttons around, but you can move icons. And although you double-click icons to open them, you single-click buttons. The toolbar items in the Finder (which I discuss in Chapter 6) are good examples of buttons. And although calling items in the Dock *buttons* is a stretch, they act like buttons because you single-click them to open them.

Application icons

Application icons are linked to *programs* — the software that you use to accomplish tasks on your Mac. Your word processor is an application. So are America Online (AOL) and Adobe Photoshop. Myth III: The Wolf Age and Quake III: Arena are also applications (and great games to boot).

Application icons come in a variety of shapes. For example, application (that is, program) icons are often square-ish. Sometimes, though, they're diamond-shaped, rectangular, or just oddly shaped. In Figure 4-1, you can see application icons of various shapes.

Figure 4-1:
Application
icons come
in many
different
shapes.

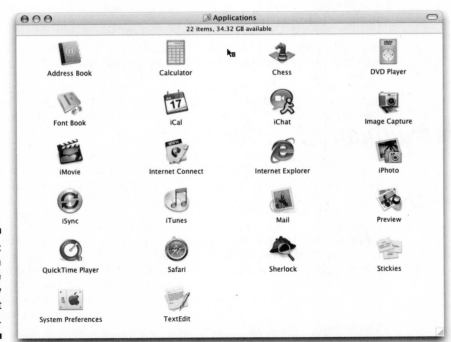

Document icons

Document icons are files that are created by applications. A letter to your mom, which you create in AppleWorks (formerly known as ClarisWorks), is a document. So are my latest column and my Quicken data files. Document icons are almost always reminiscent of a piece of paper, as shown in Figure 4-2.

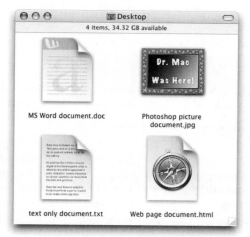

Figure 4-2: Typical document icons.

Folder icons

Folder icons are the Mac's organizational containers. You put icons, usually application or document icons, into folders. You can also put folders inside other folders. Folders look like . . . well, folders . . . and can contain just about any other icon. You use folders to organize your files and applications on your hard drive. You can have as many folders as you want, so don't be afraid to create new ones. The thought behind the whole folders thing is pretty obvious — if your hard drive is a filing cabinet, folders are its drawers and folders (duh!). Figure 4-3 shows some typical folder icons.

Aliases

Aliases are wonderful — no, *fabulous* — organizational tools that Apple introduced in the days of Mac OS 7. (Although Mac OS 7 was originally called *System* 7, Apple didn't begin the Mac OS designation until version 7.6.) I like aliases so much, in fact, that I think they deserve their very own section. Read on for more info on this ultra-useful tool.

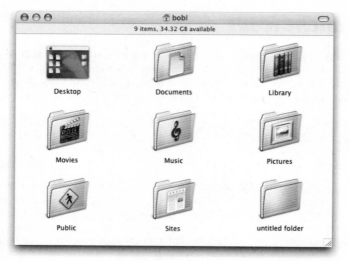

Figure 4-3:
Some run-
of-the-mill
folder icons.

Aliases: The Greatest Invention Since Sliced Bread

An *alias* is a tiny file that automatically opens the file that it represents. Although an alias is technically an icon, it's actually an icon that opens another icon automatically. You can put aliases in convenient places, such as on the Desktop, to help you easily open programs and files that you access often.

Microsoft stole the alias feature from Apple (if you've used Windows, you may know aliases as *shortcuts*). But what else is new?

An alias is different from a duplicated file. For example, Microsoft Word X uses 12.7 megabytes (MB) of disk space. If I *duplicate* it, I have two files, each using 12+MB of disk space. *Creating* an alias of Microsoft Word, on the other hand, uses a mere 52 kilobytes (KB).

So why do I think that aliases are so great? Well, aside from the fact that aliases open any file or folder anywhere on any available disk, here are a few more good reasons:

✔ **Convenience:** Aliases enable you to make items appear to be in more than one place, which on many occasions is exactly what you want to do. For example, keeping an alias of your word processor on your Desktop and another on the Dock is convenient. You may even want a third alias of it in your Documents folder for quick access. Aliases enable you to open your word processor quickly and easily without navigating into the depths of your Applications folder each time that you need it.

✔ **Flexibility:** You can create aliases and store them simultaneously to represent the same document in several different folders. This is a great help when you need to file a document that can logically be stored in any one of several files. For example: If you write a memo to Fred Smith about the Smythe Marketing Campaign to be executed in the fourth quarter, which folder does the document go in? Smith? Smythe? Marketing? Memos? 4th Quarter? All the above?

With aliases, it doesn't matter. You can put the actual file in any folder and then create aliases of the file, placing them in any other applicable folder. Now you can search for a specific document in several places because whichever pertinent folder you open, you can find the memo.

✔ **Integrity:** Some programs need to remain in the same folder as their supporting files and folders. Many Classic programs, for example, won't function properly unless they're in the same folder as their dictionaries, thesauruses, data files (for games), templates, and so on. Thus, you can't put those programs on the Desktop without impairing their functionality.

Creating aliases

When you create an alias, its icon looks the same as the icon that it represents, but the suffix *alias* is tacked onto its name and a tiny arrow called a *badge* appears in the lower-left corner of its icon. Figure 4-4 shows both an alias and its *parent* icon (that is, the icon that will open if you open the alias).

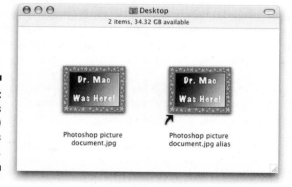

Figure 4-4:
An alias icon (right) and its parent.

To create an alias for an icon, do one of the following:

✔ **Click the parent icon and choose File➪Make Alias.**

✔ **Click the parent icon and press ⌘+L.**

✓ Click any file or folder, press and hold down the ⌘ and Option keys, and then drag the file or folder while continuing to hold down the ⌘ and Option keys.

Presto! An alias appears where you release the mouse button. Better still, aliases created this way don't have that pesky alias suffix tacked onto them.

✓ Click an icon while holding down the Control key and then choose the Make Alias command from the contextual menu that appears.

The alias appears in the same folder as its parent. (I explore contextual menus — which are very cool — in Chapter 6.)

Deleting aliases

This is a short section because deleting an alias is such an easy chore. To delete an alias, simply drag it onto the Trash icon on the Dock. That's it! You can also Control-click it and choose Move to Trash from the contextual menu that appears or select the icon and use the keyboard shortcut ⌘+Delete.

Deleting an alias does *not* delete the parent item. (If you want to delete the parent item, you have to go hunt it down and kill it yourself.)

Hunting down an alias's parent

Suppose that you create an alias of a file, and later you want to delete both the alias and its parent file — but you can't find the parent file! What do you do? Well, you can use the Finder's Find function (try saying that three times real fast) to find it; so here are three fast ways to find the parent icon of an alias:

✓ Select the alias icon and use the keyboard shortcut ⌘+R.

✓ Select the alias icon and choose File➪Show Original.

✓ Ctrl+click the alias icon and choose Show Original from the contextual menu.

Playing with Icons

After checking out the different types of icons, it's time to see what you can do with and to them. In the upcoming sections, I show you how to open, rename, get rid of (again), and select icons. In a matter of moments, you'll be an icon pro!

The temporary alias theory

The Desktop is an excellent place to keep the things that you need most often — whether you use aliases of documents or save the actual files on the Desktop until you figure out where you want to store them. For example, when I first create a file, I save it in its proper folder inside the Documents folder somewhere. If it's a document that I plan to work on for more than a day or two, such as a magazine article, I make an alias of the document (or folder) and plop it on the Desktop. After I finish the article and submit it to an editor, I trash the alias, leaving the original file stashed away in its proper folder.

Of course, you can place that same folder in the Dock as well, so you can use the press-and-hold trick to open its subfolders. But nothing says that you can't have an item appear several places at once for maximum convenience.

Incidentally, you can use a similar technique without the aliases. Just save all your new documents on the Desktop (yourhomefolder/Desktop). Later, as you finish working with each document, you can file it away in its proper folder.

Open sez me! Opening icons

You can open any icon in four ways. (Okay, there are five ways, but one of them belongs to aliases, which I discuss earlier in the section "Introducing . . . Icons!") Anyway, here are the ways:

- ✔ **Click the icon once to select it and then choose File⇨Open.**
- ✔ **Double-click the icon by clicking it twice in rapid succession.**

  If it doesn't open, you double-clicked too slowly. You can test your mouse's sensitivity to double-click speed, as well as adjust it in the Keyboard & Mouse System Preference pane.

- ✔ **Select the icon and then press either ⌘+O or ⌘+↓.**
- ✔ **Click the icon while holding down the Control key and then use the contextual menu's Open command.**

Of course, you can also open any document icon from within an application — skip ahead to Chapter 8 for more on that.

Getting rid of icons

To get rid of an icon — any icon — merely drag it to the Trash on your Dock. (See Chapter 3 for more info on the Dock and the Trash.)

Trashing an alias gets rid of only the alias, not the parent file. But trashing a document, folder, or application icon puts it in the Trash where it will be deleted permanently the next time you Empty the Trash.

Playing the icon name game: Renaming icons

Icon, icon-a, bo-bicon, banana fanna fo-ficon. Betcha can change the name of any old icon! Well, that's not entirely true. . . .

If an icon is locked (see the upcoming section "Info-mation"), busy (an application that's currently open), or you don't have the administrator's permission to rename that icon (see Chapter 16 for details about permissions), you won't be able to rename it. Similarly, you can't rename certain reserved icons, such as the Library, System, and Desktop folders.

To rename an icon, you can either click the icon's name directly (don't click the icon itself because that selects the icon) or click the icon and then press Return (or Enter) on your keyboard once.

Either way, the icon's name is selected and surrounded with a box, and you can now type in a new name (as shown in Figure 4-5). In addition to selecting the name, the cursor changes from a pointer to a text-editing I-beam. An *I-beam cursor* (shown in the left margin) is the Mac's way of telling you that you can type now. At this point, if you click the I-beam cursor anywhere in the name box, you can edit the icon's original name. If you don't click the I-beam cursor in the name box but just begin typing, the icon's original name is replaced by what you type.

If you've never changed an icon's name, give it a try. And don't forget: If you click the icon itself, the icon is selected, and you won't be able to change its name. If you do accidentally select the icon, just press Return (or Enter) one time to edit the name of the icon.

Figure 4-5:
Change an icon's name by typing over the old one when it's high-lighted.

Navigating icons like a supergeek

In addition to the old point-and-click method of navigating icons, you can also move among icons by using the keyboard. In an active window, make sure that no icons are selected and then type the first letter of a file's name. In all views, the first icon that starts with that letter is selected. To move to the next icon alphabetically, press the Tab key. To move to the icon in reverse alphabetical order, press Shift+Tab.

If more than one icon begins with the same letter, type in more than one letter to further restrict the possible results. Suppose that you have three folders in the same window that all begin with *A: Applications, Abstracts,* and *Aunt Mary's Stuff.* To isolate the Applications folder, type **app**.

If no window is active, typing a letter selects the first icon on the Desktop that starts with that letter. Press the Tab key or press Shift+Tab to work your way through the icon names alphabetically forward or backward, respectively. Finally, pressing ⌘+O or ⌘+↓ opens the selected item.

Selecting multiple icons

Sometimes you want to move or copy several items into a single folder. The process is pretty much the same as it is when you copy one file or folder (that is, you just drag the icon to where you want it and drop it there). But you first need to select all the items that you want before you can drag them, en masse, to their destination. You'll find the following method a lot more convenient than selecting and copying files one at a time.

1. **To select more than one icon in a folder, do one of the following:**

   - Click once within the folder window (don't click any one icon) and drag your mouse while continuing to hold down the mouse button. You see an outline of a box around the icons while you drag, and icons within or touching the box become highlighted. (See Figure 4-6.)

   - Click one icon and then hold down the Shift key while you click others. As long as you hold down the Shift key, each new icon that you click is added to the selection. To deselect an icon, click it a second time while still holding down the Shift key.

   - Click one icon and then hold down the Command (⌘) key while you click others. The difference between using the Shift and the ⌘ keys is that using the ⌘ key doesn't select everything between it and the first item selected when your window is in a List or Column view. In an Icon view, it really doesn't make much difference.

Click here

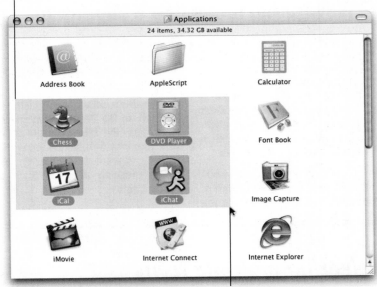

Figure 4-6:
Select more
than one
icon with
your mouse.

Drag to here

To deselect an icon selected in any of these three ways, click it while holding down the ⌘ key.

2. **When you select all the icons that you want, click one of them (don't click anywhere else or you deselect the icons that you just selected) and drag (or Option+drag) them to the location where you want to move (or copy) them.**

Be careful with multiple selections, especially when you drag icons to the Trash. You can easily and accidentally select more than one icon, so watch out that you don't accidentally put an icon in the Trash by not paying close attention.

If you put something in the Trash by accident, you can almost always return it to whence it came. Just invoke the magical Undo command. Choose Edit⇨ Undo or use the keyboard shortcut ⌘+Z. The accidentally trashed file will return to its original location. Usually.

Unfortunately, Undo doesn't work every time — and it only remembers the very last action that you performed when it *does* work — so don't rely on it too much.

Info-mation

Every icon has an Info window that gives you — big surprise! — information about that icon and enables you to choose which other users (if any) that you want to have the privilege of using this icon. (I discuss sharing files and privileges in detail in Chapter 16.) The Info window is also where you lock an icon so that it can't be renamed or dragged to the Trash.

To see an icon's Info window, click the icon and choose File⇨Get Info (or press ⌘+I) The Info window for that icon appears, as in Figure 4-7, which shows the Info window for the QuickTime Player icon.

Figure 4-7:
A typical
Info win-
dow for an
application
(QuickTime
Player, in
this case).

Documents, folders, and disks each have slightly different Info windows. In this section, I give you highlights on the type of information and options that you can find.

The gray triangles reveal what information for an icon is available in this particular Info window. Figure 4-7 shows the options for the QuickTime Player with the General section expanded. The sections that you see for most icons include the following:

- ✔ **General:** For information of the general kind, such as

    - **Kind:** What kind of file this is — an application, document, disk, folder, and so on

    - **Size:** How much disk space this file uses

    - **Where:** The path to the folder that contains this file

- **Created:** The date and time that this file was created

- **Modified:** The date and time that this file was last modified (that is, saved)

- **Version:** Copyright information and the file's version number

✔ **Name & Extension:** Tells the full name, including the (possibly hidden) extension.

✔ **Preview:** When you select a document icon, the menu offers a Preview option that you use to see a glimpse of what's in that document. You can also see this preview when you select a document icon in Column view — it magically appears in the rightmost column. If you select a QuickTime movie or sound, you can even play it right there in the preview pane without launching a separate application. Neat.

✔ **Languages:** Manages the language that the application uses for menus and dialogs. Note that this option only appears if you're using an Info window to look at certain application programs.

✔ **Ownership & Permissions:** Governs which users have access to this icon. (See Chapter 16 for more about privileges.)

✔ **Comments:** Provides a field in which you type your own comments about this icon.

✔ **Open in the Classic Environment check box:** This option is only available for some applications, known as *Carbon apps,* that are developed to run on both OS 9 and OS X. Selecting this check box lets you run the application in the Classic environment. (Don't worry if you don't know what this means — Classic is discussed in full and loving detail, but not until Chapter 6.)

✔ **The Locked check box:** Enabling this shows you whether you can change an icon's name or drag it to the Trash. When an application is *locked* (this check box will be marked), you can't change its name or drag it to the Trash. (I discuss the Trash in Chapter 3.)

Disks can't be locked by merely marking a check box; documents, folders, and applications can.

Folders can be locked by merely selecting the Locked check box in the Info window. In previous versions of Mac OS, you had to open the Sharing panel of the Info window (formerly known as Get Info), but Mac OS X conveniently allows you to lock a folder by selecting the Locked check box in the General area of the Info window. Yea!

✔ **The Stationery check box:** Document icons sport these. Stationery is a special type of document file that acts as a template. When you open any document for which you've marked this check box, the document opens with all the information in it but it's named Untitled — you have to use Save As to save and rename the file.

The Stationery document remains unchanged even after you open it so that you can use it again and again to open a document with some of its content already in place.

Why would you want to run an app in Classic?

I had a great USB printer (Epson Stylus Photo 750) that wasn't supported in OS X, although it worked fine in Classic. I could do most of my printing from Word and Photoshop in Classic, but every so often, I needed to print a file created by some OS X-only program. I couldn't print from OS X, but I could save the file as a PDF (something almost every OS X program can do because PDF support is built into OS X's Quartz imaging architecture). Then, I used the Open in the Classic Environment feature to tell my copy of Acrobat 5 to open as a Classic application instead of a Mac OS X application, thus allowing me to print the formerly unprintable document from Classic.

Chapter 5

Looking through Finder Windows

● ●

● ●

*W*indows are and have always been an integral part of Macintosh computing. Windows in the Finder (sometimes called "on the Desktop") show you the contents of hard drive and folder icons; windows in applications usually show you either the contents of your documents or display information about the active document (or whatever you've selected in the active document.)

Windows are part of what makes your Mac a Mac, which is why knowing how they work and how to use them is so essential.

This chapter focuses on Finder windows. But after you get the hang of Finder windows, you pretty much know how all the display windows that you'll ever see on your Mac work. You'll also have a pretty good idea how document windows work. So relax and don't worry. At the end of this brief chapter, you'll know all you need to work with windows in any application that uses them.

Anatomy of a Window

Like icons, windows are a ubiquitous part of using a Mac. The Finder appears in a window. When you open a folder, it's a window that you see. When you write a letter, the document that you're working on appears in a window, when you browse the Internet, Web pages appear in a window, and so on.

For the most part, windows are windows. As you use different programs, you'll probably notice that some of them (Adobe Photoshop or Microsoft Word, for example) take liberties with windows by adding features such as pop-up menus, or textual information such as zoom percentage or file size in the scroll bar area of a document window.

Don't let it bug you; that extra fluff is just window dressing (pun intended). Maintaining the window metaphor, many information windows display different kinds of information in different *panes*.

Windows in programs running in the Classic environment look different — like Mac OS 9 windows. (I cover the Classic environment in Chapter 14.)

And so, without further ado, the following list gives you a look at the main features of a typical Finder window (as shown in Figure 5-1). I discuss these features in greater detail in later sections of this chapter.

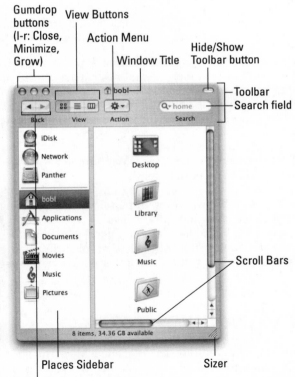

Figure 5-1: A typical Finder window in Mac OS X 10.3 (Panther).

If your windows don't look exactly like the one shown in Figure 5-1, don't be concerned. This chapter and the next two show you how to make your Finder windows look and feel just how you like 'em. Hang in there.

- ✔ **Window Title:** Shows the name of the window.
- ✔ **Scroll bars:** Used for moving around a window pane.
- ✔ **Sidebar:** Where frequently used items live.
- ✔ **Toolbar:** Buttons for frequently used commands and actions live here.
- ✔ **Forward and Back buttons:** Take you to the next or previous folder.

If you're familiar with Web browsers, the Forward and Back buttons in the Finder work exactly the same way. The first time that you open a window, neither button is active. But as you navigate from folder to folder, they remember your path so that you can quickly traverse the path of folders. Another great thing about them is that you can navigate this way from the keyboard by using the shortcuts ⌘+[for Back and ⌘+] for Forward.

If you've enabled the Finder Preference to always open folders in a new window or if you forced a folder to open in a new window (which I'll describe in a bit), the Forward and Back buttons won't work. You need to use the modern, OS X-style window option — the one that uses a single window — or the buttons are useless. These buttons remember only the other folders you've visited in *that* window.

- ✔ **View buttons:** Choose from three exciting views of your window: icon, list, or column.
- ✔ **Action button:** This button is really a popup menu of commands you can apply to the currently selected items in the Finder window.
- ✔ **Close, Minimize, and Expand (gumdrop) buttons:** Shut 'em, shrink 'em, and make 'em grow.
- ✔ **Search field:** Find items in items selected in this window whose names contain the character string you type in this box.
- ✔ **Hide/Show toolbar button:** Causes your computer to melt into a puddle of molten silicon slag. Just kidding! This button actually does what its name implies — hides or shows the toolbar of a window.

Top o' the window to ya!

Take a gander at the top of a window — any window. You see three buttons in the upper-left corner and the name of the window in the top center. These three buttons (called *gumdrop buttons* by some folks because they look like, well, gumdrops) in the upper-left corner of the window — known as Close,

Minimize, and Expand (some people call this button Zoom; I call it by its Mac OS 9 name, Grow) — are colored red, orange, and green (from left to right). Here's what they do:

- **Close (red):** Click this button to *close* the window.

- **Minimize (orange):** Click this button to *minimize* the window. Clicking Minimize appears to close the window, but instead of making it disappear, Minimize adds an icon for the window in the Dock. To view the window again, click the Dock icon for the window that you minimized. If the window happens to be a QuickTime movie, the movie continues to play, albeit at postage stamp size, in its icon in the Dock. (I discuss the Dock in Chapter 3.)

- **Expand (green):** Click this button to make the window larger or smaller, depending on its current size. If you're looking at a standard size window, clicking Zoom *usually* makes it bigger. (I say *usually* because if the window is larger than its contents, clicking this button shrinks the window to the smallest size that can completely enclose the contents without scrolling.) Click Expand again to return the window to its original size.

A scroll new world

Simply click and drag a scroll bar to move it either up or down or side to side. And yes, the scroll bars also look a bit gumdrop-like. As best as I can tell, Steve Jobs (Apple's charismatic CEO) has a thing for gumdrops.

You can scroll in the following four ways:

- **Click a scroll bar and drag.** The content of the window scrolls proportionally to how far you drag the scroll bar.

- **Click in the scroll bar area but not on the scroll bar itself.** The window scrolls either one page up (if you click above the scroll bar) or down (if you click below the scroll bar). If the scroll bar area is white (that is, it doesn't have a blue scroll bar showing), you have no items to scroll to — which means that everything that the window contains is already visible. You can change a setting in your General System Preferences to cause the window to scroll proportionally to where you click. Essentially, this is the same as the OS 9 way, but with a single-click in the place of the click-and-drag.

For what it's worth, the Page Up and Page Down keys function the same as clicking the grayish scroll bar area (the vertical scroll bar only) in the Finder and many applications. But these keys don't work in some programs, so don't get too dependent on them. Also, if you've purchased a mouse, trackball, or other pointing device with a scroll wheel, you can scroll the active window or pane using the scroll wheel.

✔ **Click a scroll arrow at the top or bottom of a scroll area.** The window scrolls a little. Press and hold a scroll arrow, and the window scrolls a lot. Click the up-pointing arrow to scroll toward the beginning and the down-pointing arrow to scroll toward the end.

If you have your General System Preferences set to have the scroll arrows together rather than at top and bottom, they'll be at the bottom and right of the scroll areas, as shown in Figure 5-2. If you don't, you'll see one arrow at each end of the scroll area.

✔ **Use the keyboard.** In the Finder, first click an icon in the window and then use the arrow keys to move up, down, left, or right. Using an arrow key selects the next icon in that direction and automatically scrolls the window, if necessary. In other programs, you may or may not be able to use the keyboard to scroll. The Page Up and Page Down keys work in most programs, but many programs don't use the arrow keys for scrolling their windows. The best advice that I can give you is to try it — either it'll work or it won't.

In the Finder, you can also press the Tab key on the keyboard to select the next icon in the active window alphabetically and press Shift+Tab to select the previous icon alphabetically.

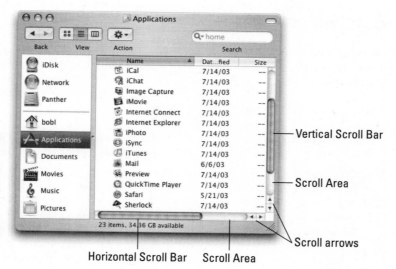

Figure 5-2:
Use scroll bars to navigate a window.

Vertical Scroll Bar

Scroll Area

Scroll arrows

Horizontal Scroll Bar   Scroll Area

(Hyper) Active windows

To work within a window, the window must be *active*. The active window is always the frontmost window, and inactive windows always appear behind the active window. Only one window can be active at a time. To make a window active, click it anywhere — in the middle, on the title bar, or on a scroll bar — it doesn't matter where, with one proviso: You can't click the red, orange, or green gumdrop buttons of an inactive window to activate it.

When you hover your mouse pointer *over* the red, orange, or green gumdrop buttons of an inactive window but don't click your mouse button, the gumdrops light up, thus enabling you to close, minimize, or expand an inactive window without first making it active.

Look at Figure 5-3 for an example of an active window (the Applications window) in front of an inactive window (the Utilities window).

The following is a list of the major visual cues that distinguish active and inactive windows:

✔ The active window's title bar Close, Minimize, and Zoom buttons — the red, orange, and green ones — are, well, red, orange, and green. The inactive windows' buttons are not.

This is a nice visual cue — colored items are active and gray ones are inactive. Better still, If you move your mouse over an inactive window's gumdrop buttons, they light up in their usual colors so you can close, minimize, or expand an inactive window without first making it active. Neat!

Figure 5-3:
An active window in front of an inactive window.

Inactive Window

Active Window

- Other buttons and scroll bars in an active window look different, too — they're bright. In an inactive window, these features are grayed out and more subdued.

- The title bars of inactive document windows are also translucent, thus allowing what is behind them to partially show through. The names on inactive windows are dimmed.

- Active windows have bigger and darker drop shadows than inactive windows.

Dialog Dealie-Boppers

Dialogs are special windows that pop up over the active window. You generally see them when you select a menu item that ends in an ellipsis (...).

Dialogs can contain a number of standard Macintosh features (I call them *dealie-boppers*), such as radio buttons, pop-up menus, text entry boxes, and check boxes. You see these features again and again in dialogs. Take a moment to look at each of these dealie-boppers in Figure 5-4.

- **Radio buttons:** *Radio buttons* are so named because, like the buttons on your car radio (assuming that you have a very old car), only one at a time can be active (when they're active they appear to be pushed in, just like with old radio buttons). Radio buttons always appear in a group of two or more; when you select one, all the others are automatically deselected. Eggheads call this setup *mutually exclusive.* Take a look at Figure 5-4 for an example of radio buttons.

  As shown in Figure 5-4, the first radio button (Rich Text) is selected. If you were to now select the radio button for Plain Text, you deactivate (deselect) Rich Text. Got it? Good. Moving right along. . . .

  Here's a nifty and undocumented shortcut: You can usually select check boxes and radio buttons by clicking their names (instead of the buttons or boxes). Didn't know that, did you?

- **Pop-up menus:** These menus are appropriately named because that's what they do — they pop up when you click them. You can always tell a pop-up menu because it appears in a slightly rounded rectangle and has a double-ended arrow symbol (or, a pair of back-to-back triangles if you like) on the right. For an example, check out Figure 5-4 (the Open and Save pop-up menus both read *Automatic*).

Radio Buttons Text Entry Box   Pop-up Menu

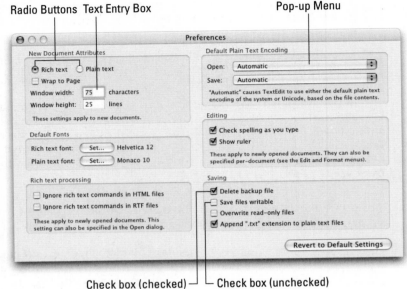

Check box (checked) —— —— Check box (unchecked)

Have you figured out yet what radio buttons and pop-up menus have in common? *Hint:* They both enable you to make a single selection from a group of options.

- **Text entry boxes:** In text entry boxes (sometimes called *fields*), you type in text (including numbers) from the keyboard. When a text entry box (or boxes) appears with a selected radio button, only when that radio button is selected can you make an entry. Take a look at Figure 5-4. The Window Width and Window Height options are both text entry boxes.

- **Check boxes:** The last dealie-bopper that you see frequently is the check box. You use check boxes to choose items that are not mutually exclusive. In a group of check boxes, you can select or deselect each one individually. Check boxes are selected when they contain a check mark, and they are deselected when they're empty. Unlike radio buttons, which force you to choose one and only one item, check boxes are independent. Each one can be either selected or deselected. In Figure 5-4, you can see several check boxes, four of which are selected and five of which are not.

Some applications have what they call *tri-state* checkboxes (and no, we're not talking geography here). These special checkboxes are empty when everything selected doesn't have this feature applied, sport an **x** when everything does, and sport a – when some selected items have the feature and some don't. This type of checkbox is often used for the Custom Install screen of Mac OS X installers.

Working with Windows

In this section, I give you a closer look at windows themselves: how you move them, size them, and use them. And although Mac OS X windows are similar to the windows that you've used in other versions of Mac OS, you'll find some new wrinkles.

If you're relatively new to the Mac, you may want to read this section while sitting at your computer, trying the techniques as you read them. You may find it easier to remember something that you read if actually do it. If you've been using your Mac for a while, you probably figured out how windows work by now.

Resizing windows

If you want to see more (or less) of what's in a window, use the sizer in the extreme lower-right corner of a window. (Refer to Figure 5-1 to see the sizer; it's in the lower-right corner and has little diagonal grippy lines on it.) Just drag the sizer downward and/or to the right to make a window larger. Or drag it upward and/or to the left to make a window smaller. In other words, after you grab the sizer, you can make a window whatever size you like.

Resizing window panes

Display windows, like those in the Finder, frequently consist of multiple panes. In the metal-looking strip between two panes you'll often encounter what looks, at first glance, like a speck of dirt on your monitor. On closer inspection you'll see that it is a tiny knob (look at Figure 5-1, between the Sidebar and the actual contents of the window to the right of it).

When your mouse is over that knob, the cursor changes to a vertical bar (or it could be horizontal if the panes are one above the other), with little arrows pointing out of both sides.

When you see this cursor, you can click and drag anywhere in the strip dividing the Sidebar from the rest of the window to resize the two panes relative to each other (one will get larger and one smaller).

Hunting the seldom-seen Close All command

If you're like me, by the end of the day your Desktop is scattered with open windows — sometimes a dozen or more. Wouldn't you love to be able to close them all at once with a single Close All command? But you don't see a Close All command in any of the menus, do you?

Well, even though Apple (in its infinite wisdom) has hidden this useful command from mere mortals, you can make it come out and play by doing one of the following:

✔ Hold down the Option key and click any window's red gumdrop Close button.

✔ Hold down the Option key and choose File➪Close All. (The Close All command usually reads Close Window but becomes Close All when you hold down the Option key. Release the Option key, and it changes back to Close Window.)

✔ Press ⌘+Option+W.

Moving windows

To move a window, click anywhere in a window's title bar (or anywhere in the metallic part of a display window, except on a knob) and drag the window to wherever you want it. The window moves wherever you move the mouse, stopping dead in its tracks when you release the mouse button.

Shutting yo' windows

Now that I've gone on and on about windows, maybe I should tell you how to close them. You can close an active window in one of three ways (the last two require the window to be active, by the way):

✔ **Click the red Close button in the upper-left corner of the title bar.**

✔ **Choose File➪Close Window from the Finder menu.**

✔ **Press ⌘+W.**

Hold down Option (and occasionally Control, ⌘, or come combination of the three) and pull down menus in both the Finder and in your favorite application programs. It doesn't always reveal anything interesting in the menu, but sometimes it does. Read through Chapter 6 to discover all things menu!

Chapter 6

A Bevy of Delectable Menus

Like icons and windows, menus are a quintessential part of the Macintosh experience. In this chapter, I start with a few menu basics and then move on to the Finder menus. I try to provide an appropriate level of detail based on the menu item's importance; and in many cases, I direct you to another part of the book where that feature is discussed in greater detail.

Menu Basics

Mac menus are often referred to as *pull-down menus*. To check out the Mac OS X menus, click the Finder button in the Dock to activate the Finder and then look at the top of your screen. From left to right you see the Apple menu, the Finder menu, and six other menus that I discuss throughout this chapter, as shown in Figure 6-1. To use an OS X menu, you click its name to make the menu appear and then pull (drag) down to select a menu item. Piece of cake!

Ever since Mac OS 8, menus stay down after you click their names. They stay down until you either select an item or click outside the menu's boundaries.

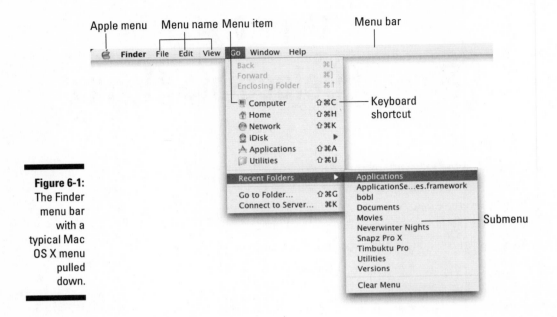

Figure 6-1:
The Finder
menu bar
with a
typical Mac
OS X menu
pulled
down.

Musical menus

Before you start working with OS X menus, you really, really should know this about menus in general: *They can change unexpectedly.* Why? Well, the menus that you see in the menu bar at the top of the screen always reflect the program that's active at the time. When you switch from the Finder to a program — or from one program to another program — the menus change immediately to match whatever you switched to.

For example, when the Finder is active, the menu bar looks like Figure 6-1. But if you launch TextEdit, the menu bar changes to what you see in Figure 6-2.

Figure 6-2 demonstrates a fantastic new Panther feature — TextEdit, which can open documents created by Microsoft Word. The window shown above is a Microsoft Word document; TextEdit was not only able to open the document, but also preserved almost all of its formatting. That's slick.

An easy way to tell which program is active is to look at the left-most menu with a name (the one just to the right of the Apple menu). When you're in the Finder, of course, that menu reads *Finder*. But if you switch to another program (by clicking its icon on the Dock or by clicking any window associated with the program) or launch a new program, that menu changes to the name of the active program.

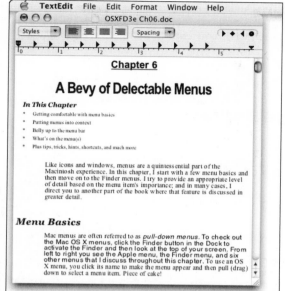

I cover only the menus that are part of OS X here in this chapter. The menus that come with other programs are beyond the purview of this book — this chapter alone would be a set of encyclopedias if I tried to cover them all, and there would always be some new program or version that wasn't covered!

Contextual menus: They're sooo sensitive

Contextual menus list commands that apply to the item that your cursor is over. Contextual menus may be available in windows, on icons, and most places on the Desktop. To use them you hold down the Control key and click — what we Mac users like to call a *Control+click*. (Figure 6-3 shows the contextual menu that appears when you Control+click a document icon.)

Actions appear in contextual menus only if they make sense for the item that you Control+click. For example, if you Control+click inside a window but not on any icon, the contextual menu contains actions that you perform on a window. By contrast, if you Control+click an icon inside a window, you see a contextual menu for that icon. So, you see, a contextual menu for a document differs from the contextual menu for a window.

Don't believe me? Control+click the Desktop (that is, click somewhere that's not in any window and not on any icon). This contextual menu contains only items that apply to the Desktop, and none of the items that pertain to a document. Don't believe me? Compare the Desktop contextual menu shown in Figure 6-4 with the document contextual menu shown in Figure 6-3.

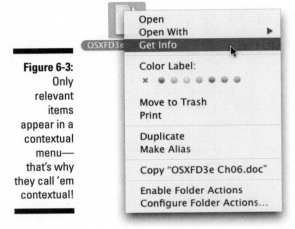

Figure 6-3:
Only relevant items appear in a contextual menu— that's why they call 'em contextual!

Contextual menus are also available in many applications. Open your favorite app and try Control+clicking to find out whether they're there. In most cases, using a contextual menu is a quick way to avoid going to the menu bar to choose a command. In some programs, such as AppleWorks 6, contextual menus are the only way to access certain commands.

Figure 6-4:
This is the Desktop's contextual menu. Notice that it's quite different from a document's contextual menu.

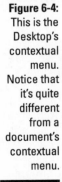
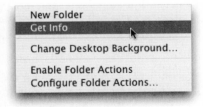

To make the Finder-related contextual menus available to users who didn't have the foresight to purchase this book, Apple added the Actions button to the OS X Finder window toolbar. Now, people who don't know about Control+clicking (or have only one free hand) can access their contextual menus by clicking the Actions button and displaying the contextual menu; you, on the other hand, gentle reader, know how to get at these commands without having to run your mouse all the way up to the toolbar.

I'm a big fan of multi-button mice, and contextual menus are a huge reason for this preference. Just about the first thing I do when I get a new Mac is replace the standard mouse (pretty as it is) with a multi-button mouse. When you have a mouse (or trackball) with at least two buttons, OS X knows that clicking the right button is the same as Control+clicking. Now, I only have to use one hand to access these little beauties.

Get in the habit of Control+clicking items. Before you know it, using contextual menus will become second nature to you.

Disabled options

Menu items that appear in black on a menu are currently available. Menu items not currently available are grayed out, meaning that they're disabled. You can't select a disabled menu item.

In Figure 6-5, the File menu is pulled down while nothing is selected in the Finder; this is why many of the menu items are disabled (in gray). These items are disabled because an item (such as a window or icon) must be selected in order for you to use one of these menu items. For example, the Show Original command is grayed out because it works only if the selected item is an alias.

Submenus

Some menu items have more menus attached to them, and these are called submenus. A *submenu* is just that: a menu under a menu item. You can tell whether a menu item has a submenu if it has a black triangle located to the right of its name.

To use a submenu, click a menu name once to drop down the menu and then slide your cursor down to any item with a black triangle. When the item is highlighted, move your mouse to the right just slightly. The submenu should pop out of the original menu's item. Refer to Figure 6-1 to see the Recent Folders submenu open underneath the Go menu. If you were to release the mouse button while doing exactly what is pictured, a Finder window would pop open, showing you a Finder window displaying your Applications folder.

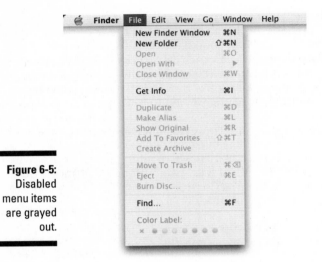

Figure 6-5:
Disabled menu items are grayed out.

The pop-up menus that you see when you click-and-hold or Control+click a Dock icon can also have submenus. In fact, if you were to put your home folder in the Dock, you could access any file in it or its subfolders via the menu and its submenus.

Submenus used to be called *hierarchical* menus, but that's a mouthful. For a while, people liked to call them *pull-right* menus. But these days, just about everyone refers to them as submenus. If you ever hear folks talk about hierarchical menus or pull-rights, they're talking about submenus.

Keyboard shortcut commands

Most menu items, or at least the most common ones, have *keyboard shortcuts* to help you quickly navigate your Mac without having to haggle so much with the mouse. Using these key combinations activates menu items without using the mouse; to use them you press the Command (⌘) key and then press another key (or keys) without releasing the ⌘ key. Memorize the shortcuts that you use often.

Some people refer to the Command key as the Apple key. That's because on most keyboards, that key has both the pretzel-looking Command key symbol (⌘) *and* an Apple logo (⌘) on it. To avoid confusion, I'll stick with Command key. Apple's Help system usually refers to it as the Apple key.

Here are four things that you need to know to properly grasp keyboard shortcuts:

✔ **Keyboard shortcuts are shown in menus.** Refer to Figure 6-5 to see that the keyboard shortcut for the Find command appears on the menu after the word Find: ⌘+F. Any menu item with one of these pretzel-symbol-letter combinations after its name can be executed with that keyboard shortcut. Just press the ⌘ key and the letter shown in the menu — *N* for New Finder Window, *F* for Find, and so on — and the appropriate command executes.

✔ **Capital letters don't mean that you have to press Shift as part of the shortcut.** Although the letters next to the ⌘ symbol in the Finder menus are indeed capital letters, you don't have to press the Shift key to use the keyboard shortcut. For example, if you see ⌘+P, just hold down the ⌘ key and then press *P*. Some programs have keyboard combinations that require the use of ⌘ and the Shift key, but these programs let you know by calling the key combination something like ⇧+⌘+ S or ⇧+⌘+ O. A very few (usually older) programs indicate when you need to use the Shift key by using the word *Shift* rather than the ⇧ symbol.

Of course, there's an exception to every rule, and one of them is Mac Help; you'll get that whole sordid story in a few pages.

✔ **Recognize the funky looking Option key symbol.** You'll see one other symbol sometimes used in keyboard shortcuts: It represents the Option key (sometimes abbreviated in keyboard shortcuts as *Opt* and, on some keyboards, also labeled *Alt*). Check it out next to the Hide Others command, shown in Figure 6-6.

What this freakish symbol means in the Finder menu item (Hide Others in Figure 6-6) is that if you press both the ⌘ and Option keys and *while holding them down* press the H key, all applications other than the Finder will be hidden.

Figure 6-6:
Some keyboard shortcuts, such as Hide Others, use the Option key in combination with the Command key.

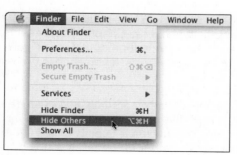

✔ **Okay, there was more than one more symbol.** In some programs, developers may even include a caret (an up-pointing arrowhead, ^) as an abbreviation for the Control key.

✔ **If it makes sense, it's probably a shortcut.** Most keyboard shortcuts have a mnemonic relationship to their names. For example, here are some of the more basic keyboard shortcuts:

Command	Mnemonic Keyboard Shortcut
New Finder Window	⌘+N
New Folder	⌘+Shift+N
Open	⌘+O
Get Info	⌘+I
Select All	⌘+A
Copy	⌘+C
Duplicate	⌘+D

It's elliptical

Another feature of Mac menus is the ellipsis after some menu item names. *Ellipses,* in case your English teacher forgot to mention them, are the three little dots (...) that appear in place of missing text. They basically mean that you can reach more options by clicking the menu item.

Those three little dots aren't separate, though — they comprise one character. If you want to type an ellipsis, you can do so (in most fonts) by holding down the Option key and pressing the foot key, also known as a tick mark or single-quote (').

When you see an ellipsis after a menu item, choosing that item displays a dialog box or sheet (I discuss dialog boxes in Chapter 5 and sheets in Chapter 8), in which you can make further choices. Refer to Figure 6-6 to see that the Preferences command has an ellipsis. If you choose Preferences, the Finder Preferences window opens.

Choosing a menu item with an ellipsis never actually makes anything happen other than to open a dialog box or sheet; from there, you make further choices and then click a button. This button is usually called OK or Cancel, but occasionally, as you'll see in the Finder Preferences dialog box, you use the red Close button/gumdrop in the upper-left corner of the window to dismiss the dialog box.

Underneath the Apple Menu Tree

The Macintosh interface has sported an *Apple* (🍎) *menu* since time immemorial (well, the 1980s anyway). So when the Mac OS X Public Beta appeared without one, Mac users everywhere crawled out of the woodwork to express their outrage. The bruised Apple ultimately relented, and now OS X has an 🍎 menu, just like every version of Mac OS before it. For those of you who used OS 9, the following section discusses the differences between the old 🍎 menu and the new one.

If you never used OS 9, you can skip it.

The sections after "What's in . . . and what's out" describe the Panther 🍎 menu items.

What's in . . . and what's out

The OS X 🍎 menu isn't like any 🍎 menu before it, though. The biggest differences between it and the OS 9 🍎 menu are

- ✔ **The 🍎 in the Apple menu is now blue (the default).** Or gray (if you've selected the Graphite appearance in the General System Preference pane); in either case, it's no longer rainbow striped.

- ✔ **It's not customizable anymore.** You used to be able to add items — applications, folders, documents, aliases, or whatever your heart desired — to your 🍎 menu (desk accessories only before System 7). You can't do that in the OS X 🍎 menu. What you see on the OS X 🍎 menu is what you get. But it's not a big issue because the OS X Dock *is* customizable and does let you add items — applications, folders, documents, aliases, or whatever your heart desires. (I discuss the Dock in Chapter 3.)

If you miss customizing your Apple menu, try Fruit Menu from Unsanity (www.unsanity.com), a fabulous shareware offering that provides all the functionality of the OS 9 🍎 menu and is reasonably priced at $10.

Tiptoeing through the Apple menu items

You won't find any programs available from the new OS X 🍎 menu — no Calculator, no Scrapbook, no programs at all (other than System Preferences and the ones in your Recent Items submenu). Instead, the 🍎 menu provides a set of useful commands, described here, that are always available no matter what program is active.

From top to bottom, the Apple menu's items are

- **About This Mac:** Choose this item to see what version of Mac OS X you're running, what kind of Mac and processor you're using, and how much memory your Mac has. The window that appears also sports a Get Info button that will launch Apple System Profiler where you can find out more than you will probably ever want or need to know about your Mac's hardware and software.

  If you click the version number in this window, it changes to the build number (Apple's internal tracking number for versions). Click the build number in this window, and it changes to the serial number of your Mac. Finally, click the serial number of your Mac in this window, and it changes to the version number again. This interesting effect is shown in Figure 6-7. Any or all of this information may come in handy for troubleshooting, repair, upgrades, or who knows what else. At least now you know where to find it.

- **Software Update:** If you're connected to the Internet, choose this item to have your Mac check with the mothership (Apple) to see whether any updates are available for OS X or its included applications (or even Apple-branded peripheral devices, such as the iPod).

- **Mac OS X Software:** This launches your Web browser and takes you to the Apple Web site.

- **System Preferences:** Choose this item to open the System Preferences window (which I discuss in great detail in Chapter 15).

- **Dock (submenu):** This lets you mess with, well, the Dock! Scour Chapter 3 for more info on the Dock.

- **Location (submenu):** This enables you to quickly switch network configurations. I describe locations and network configurations in Chapter 11.

Figure 6-7: Click on the version, build, or serial number to cycle through these three variations of About This Mac.

- **Recent Items (submenu):** Your Mac keeps track of the applications and documents that you've recently used. Expand this menu item to choose one of them. You can set the maximum number of applications and documents that Recent Items tracks in your General System Preference pane. This feature isn't available in Mac OS X 10.0; it became available in OS X 10.1.

If you're using Mac OS X 10.0, you're missing a lot of other great stuff — new features, bug-fixes, and major speed enhancements. I highly recommend the latest, greatest version, Panther, which happens to be the version this book is about.

- **Force Quit:** When a program misbehaves — freezes or otherwise becomes recalcitrant — this is the command for you. Choosing this brings up the Force Quit Applications dialog box from which you choose the application that you want to quit, as shown in Figure 6-8.

This command is so handy that it has a keyboard shortcut: ⌘+Option+powerbutton. It also has an alternate keyboard shortcut, ⌘+Option+Esc, which is not on the menu but is displayed on the Force Quit Applications window (lower-left of Figure 6-8).

Unlike in earlier versions of Mac OS, you don't need to reboot to continue working after you force a program to quit. If a program ever freaks out on you, Force Quit can almost certainly put it out of its misery and allow you to continue using your Mac.

- **Sleep:** This puts your Mac into its low-powered sleep mode. I talk more about sleep in Chapter 15. (Yawn!)

- **Restart:** Choose this to reboot your Mac, which is essentially the same as shutting down your machine and then turning it back on.

- **Shut Down:** Use this to turn off your Mac safely.

- **Log Out:** Because OS X is a multi-user operating system, you can have multiple users at one Mac. This command enables you to switch users without restarting or shutting down.

Location, location, location

I'm getting a little bit ahead of myself, but because you're probably wondering, a *location* reflects all the settings made in the Network System Preferences pane. They're mostly useful to PowerBook and iBook users, who often have different network configurations (locations) for different places where they may need to use their Mac, such as the office (to connect to an Ethernet network), home (to connect to a Digital Subscriber Line [DSL] or cable connection), and out of town (to connect using an internal modem). Each configuration (office, home, and out of town) is a location, and you can switch from one location to another quickly and painlessly by using this menu item. Got it? If not, you will after you read Chapter 11.

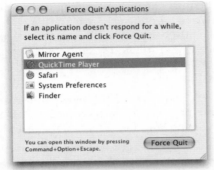

Figure 6-8:
Use Force
Quit
Applications
to exit a
badly
behaved
program.

These last three items have ellipses next to them and will display an Are You Sure dialog box. If you don't want to have to bother with the dialog box, press the Option key before selecting one of them from the menu and the ellipses will disappear and the dialog box won't intrude.

Logging out means that the current user, as identified by username and password, is leaving the scene. The next person to use the Mac (even if it's you) has to enter a username and password to regain entry. All this sharing stuff can be found in Chapter 16.

Your Constant Companion: The Application Menu

The very first menu on the Mac OS X menu bar is the *Application menu* — so named because it includes commands that you use to control the way lots of things work in the current application. But it's really much more than a command center for the application.

When you have an application open, the Application menu name changes to the name of that application, and the commands available change — but just a little bit. (I discuss this unusual phenomenon in the section "Musical menus" earlier in this chapter.) What makes this cool is that you have access to some standard Application menu items even when you're running an application such as AppleWorks or Safari. I have more to say about that as I work my way through the Application menu.

The following list overviews the main items in the Application menu, which is called the Finder menu when the Finder is the active application. It's not too long, but it's packed with useful goodies, such as

✔ **About Finder:** Choose this to find out which version of the Finder is running on your Mac.

TIP

Okay, so this menu item isn't particularly useful, or at least not for very long. But when a different application is running, the About Finder item becomes About *application_name* and usually gives information about the program's version number, the developers (the company and the people), and any other tidbits that those developers decide to throw in. Sometimes these tidbits are useful, sometimes they're interesting, and sometimes they're both.

✔ **Preferences:** Use choices here to control how the Desktop looks and acts. Choosing Preference opens the Finder Preferences window (see Figure 6-9), which has four panes: General, Labels, Sidebar, and Advanced.

Figure 6-9:
Set Finder preferences here.

- In the **General pane,** select the Show These Items on the Desktop check boxes to choose whether hard drives, CDs, DVDs, and other types of disks, and servers appear on the Desktop. OS X selects all three options by default (which mimics earlier versions of Mac OS). But if you don't want disk icons cluttering your beautiful Desktop, you have the option of deselecting (clearing) them. If they're deselected, you can still work with CDs, DVDs, and other types of disks. You just have to open a Finder window and click the one you want from the top portion of the Sidebar.

- You can also choose whether opening a new Finder window displays your Home directory, the Computer window, or some other directory. (Home is the default.)

- The Always open folders in a new window check box makes OS X work the same way as Mac OS 9.

Try it the OS X way — with windows opening "in place" so that you avoid window clutter. Press ⌘ before double-clicking to force a folder to open in a new window. I've learned to love this new way, although I hated it at first. Now, between this feature and the Column view, I find that I rarely need more than two or three windows onscreen, and I get by most of the time with just a single window in Column view.

- Selecting the Open new windows in Column View check box tells the Finder that you want each window to be in Column view when you double-click or (⌘ double-click) to open it. The default behavior is to use whichever view type the folder was last displaying.

- The **Labels pane** lets you rename the colored labels that appear in the File menu. The default names are the same as their color, as shown in Figure 6-9; you can change them to anything you like here.

- The **Sidebar pane** lets you choose which items are displayed in the Sidebar, as shown in Figure 6-9. Check the checkbox to display the item; uncheck the checkbox to not display it.

- Finally, in the **Advanced pane,** the Show Warning before Emptying the Trash check box (on by default) allows you to turn off the nagging dialog box telling you how many items are in the Trash and asking whether you really want to delete them.

- Finally, selecting the Always Show File Extensions check box tells the Finder to display the little three-, four-, or more-character file-name suffixes (like .doc in summary.doc) that make your Mac's file lists look more like those of a Windows user. The Finder hides those from you by default, but if you want to be able to search for files by their extension (Using File⇨Find or ⌘+F), you need to turn this on.

✔ **Empty Trash:** Deletes all items in the Trash from your hard drive — period. I talk about the Trash in Chapter 3 and again in Chapter 4.

Spring-loaded folders have sprung (again)

Spring-loaded folders and windows is a semi-new feature. (This feature *was* in OS 9, then it *wasn't* in OS X 10.0 or 10.1, and made its return, to much fanfare, in Mac OS X version 10.2 Jaguar.) It lets you drag items onto closed folders or disks and have them spring open. It's harder to describe than to do, so try it a few times. Open Finder Preferences, mark the Spring-loaded folders and windows check box, and then follow these steps:

1. Select any icon (except a disk icon).

2. Drag it onto a folder or disk icon (but don't release the mouse button).

3. Press the spacebar (or just wait a few seconds depending on where you've set the Delay slider).

The window of the folder or disk that you dragged onto springs open. If that's the original icon's final destination, release the mouse button now. Or, if you want to drill down deeper in the folder hierarchy, don't release the mouse button and drag the icon onto any folder or disk icon. *Its* window will spring open. And so on.

Spring-loaded folders clean up after themselves, too. When you release the mouse button, regardless of how many windows you've traversed, all windows except the original (if there was one; if you dragged an icon from the Desktop, there wouldn't be) and the destination folder spring shut again, leaving your screen clean and uncluttered. Spring-loaded folders work in all three Finder window views and also with folder or disk icons in the Sidebar. Neat! If you're like me, you'll end up using spring-loaded folders a lot.

I've said it before and I'll say it again: Use this command with a modicum of caution. After a file is trashed and the Trash is emptied, it's gone. (Okay, maybe Norton Utilities can bring it back, but don't bet the farm on it.)

✔ **Secure Empty Trash:** Choosing this option makes the chance of recovery by even the most ardent hacker or expensive disk recovery tool difficult to virtually impossible. Now, the portion of the disk that held the files you're deleting will be overwritten 1, 7, or 35 times (your choice in the submenu) with randomly generated gibberish.

✔ **Services:** One of the really cool features of OS X applications is the accessibility of Services. You can select an e-mail address and create a mail message addressed to that individual, spell-check a document or selection even if the program didn't come with a spell-checker, or calculate exchange rates on currency. Unfortunately, many Carbon-ized applications still don't support Services.

Carbon is an Apple API (Application Program Interface): programming technology that allows software developers to make applications originally created for OS 9 run in OS X with a minimum of modification. Some but not all Carbon applications run under both OS 9 and OS X.

Programs written exclusively for OS X that use Apple's latest generation of development tools are called Cocoa applications. Cocoa apps support OS X features such as Services automatically, unless the developer goes out of his or her way to disable them (see iPhoto for an example).

From your perspective, there's little or no difference between Carbon and Cocoa apps. Some Carbon apps are awesome; some Cocoa programs stink. It's not about the underlying development environment or APIs used.

But I digress yet again. Cocoa and Carbon are far beyond the scope of this book, but at least I snuck in the extremely abridged version.

✓ **Hide Finder (⌘+H):** Use this command when you've got Finder windows open and they're distracting you. Choosing it makes the Finder inactive (another currently running program becomes active) and hides any open Finder windows. To make the Finder visible again, either choose Show All from the Finder menu (or whatever it's called in the active application — the command should still be there) or click the Finder button (shown in the margin here) on the Dock.

The advantage to hiding the Finder — rather than closing or minimizing all your windows to get a clean screen — is that you don't have to open them all again when you're ready to get the windows back. Instead, just choose Show All or click the Finder button in the Dock.

✓ **Hide Others (Option+⌘+ H):** This command hides all windows associated with all running programs except the active program. It appears in most application's Application menus and is good for hiding distractions so you can focus on one thing—the unhidden application.

✓ **Show All:** Use this as the antidote to both hide commands. Choose this, and nothing is hidden anymore.

You used to find these show and hide commands in the Application menu (the menu on the right side of the menu bar that displays the icon of the active application) of older versions of Mac OS. If you're using the Classic environment or a Classic application (which I discuss in Chapter 14), that's where you'll still find them.

File Management and More: Meet the File Menu

The File menu contains many commands that you use to manipulate your files and folders. I discuss file management in Chapter 10, but here I give you the lowdown on the actual Finder File menu itself.

You'll use these commands frequently, so it would behoove you to memorize their keyboard shortcuts.

- **New Finder Window (⌘+N):** Opens a new Finder window. I discuss the Finder window in Chapter 7 and 8 (among other places, such as Chapters 3 and 4).

- **New Folder (⌘+Shift+N):** Creates a new, untitled folder in the active window. If no window is active, it creates a new folder on the Desktop.

In every version of Mac OS since the beginning of time, at least until OS X, the New Folder keyboard shortcut had been ⌘+N — just like the New Document keyboard shortcut in most applications is also ⌘+N. When creating a shortcut for the New Finder Window command in OS X, Apple decided to add the Shift key to the New Folder keyboard shortcut. I admit that this decision kind of makes sense: Opening a new Finder window and opening a new document both create a new window, whereas creating a new folder simply displays a new icon. But if you're a veteran Mac user finally breaking free of OS 9 (or earlier) and entering the world of OS X, you better get used to adding the Shift key to ⌘+N to create a folder or add the New Folder button to your Finder toolbar. (I discuss customizing the Finder toolbar in Chapter 7.)

- **Open (⌘+O):** Opens the selected item, be it icon, window, or folder.

- **Open With:** Lets you open the selected document with an application other than that document's default application. For example, in Figure 6-10, I'm about to open a graphic file. The default application for this document happens to be the wonderful shareware app, GraphicConverter.

If I double-click this document, it would open in GraphicConverter. But that's not what I want. I want it to open it in a graphics viewing program such as Preview because Preview is for displaying graphics, not editing them, and consumes fewer system resources. It opens faster than GraphicConverter, too.

This menu item tells the Finder to do just that.

This command is inactive if the selected icon isn't a document.

Using this menu item from the Contextual menu (Control+click the document icon) or even the Finder toolbar's Action popup button is often easier than it is to reach all the way up to the menu bar to invoke it, as shown in Figure 6-11. With my two-button mouse, described earlier, it's just a right-click and drag 'em in one quick motion.

If you hold down the Option key before you click the File menu, the Open With command changes to Always Open With, as shown in Figure 6-12, which enables you to change the default application for this document permanently.

This Option key trick also works on the contextual menu version of this command!

✔ Close Window (Ô+W): Closes the active window. If no windows are open or if none are selected, the Close Window command is grayed out and can't be chosen.

Most menu commands are intuitive. So how did Apple come up with ⌘+W as a shortcut for Close Window? You think Apple would assign the letter *C*, for *C*lose. However, ⌘+C is the shortcut for Copy.

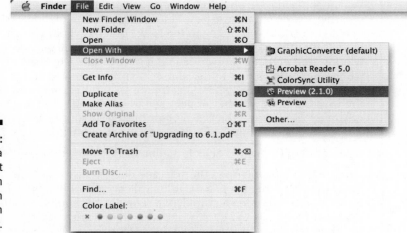

Figure 6-10:
Open a document with an application other than its default.

Figure 6-11:
I prefer the contextual version of this particular menu item.

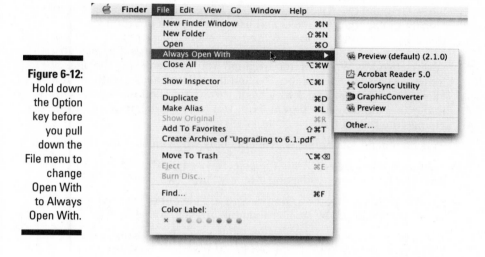

Figure 6-12:
Hold down
the Option
key before
you pull
down the
File menu to
change
Open With
to Always
Open With.

If you press the Option key, the Close Window command changes to
Close All. This very useful command enables you to close all open
Finder windows. But it only shows up if you press the Option key; other-
wise, it remains hidden.

✔ **Get Info (⌘+I):** Opens an Info window for the selected icon. (I tell you all
about the Info window in Chapter 4.)

If you press the Option key, the Get Info command changes to Show
Inspector. The Inspector window is almost identical to a Get Info
window, but it displays information for whatever icon is currently
selected in the Finder. If you click a different icon, the Inspector window
updates to show you information about that item.

A Get Info window, on the other hand, is static. Each one is connected to
one item.

It's good to have choices; sometimes one is more convenient to use for a
particular task than the other, and sometimes you use them both.

✔ **Duplicate (⌘+D):** Makes a copy of the selected icon, adds the word *copy*
to its name, and then places the copy in the same window as the original
icon. You can use the Duplicate command on any icon except a disk icon.

You can't duplicate an entire disk onto itself. But you can copy an entire
disk (call it Disk 1) to any other disk (call it Disk 2). Just hold down
Option and drag Disk 1 onto Disk 2's icon. The contents of Disk 1 will be
copied to Disk 2 and will appear in a folder named Disk 1.

✔ **Make Alias (⌘+L):** Creates an alias for the selected icon in the same
folder as the selected icon (or on the Desktop if the selected icon is on
the Desktop). I cover aliases in detail in Chapter 4.

- ✓ **Show Original (⌘+R):** Switches to the folder that contains the parent icon. Suppose that you make and use an alias, you put it on your Desktop or in your Favorites folder, and everything's peachy. But now you want to delete or move the original file or folder as part of a little spring-cleaning. Where is that original? You've been using the alias so long that you can't remember. To find it, click the alias and then choose File➪Show Original. Quick as a flash, the Finder window switches to the folder that contains the parent icon. You can now delete, copy, move, or change the parent icon.

  This command, of course, is available only when an alias icon is selected.

- ✓ **Add to Sidebar (⌘+T):** Adds the selected item to the Sidebar. You can now reach the item by clicking it in any Finder window's Sidebar.

- ✓ **Create Archive:** Creates a compressed .zip file out of your selection. The compressed file will be smaller than the original, sometimes by quite a bit.

  If you're going to send a file or files as an email enclosure, creating an archive of the file(s) first and sending the archive instead of the original will save you time sending the file and save the recipient time downloading it.

- ✓ **Move to Trash (⌘+Delete):** Moves the selected icon to the Trash.

  The icon (that is, the item that the icon represents) that you move to the Trash is not deleted from your hard drive until you choose the Empty Trash or Secure Empty Trash command from the Finder menu, the Trash pop-up menu, the Finder window's Action popup menu, or the contextual menu.

- ✓ **Eject (⌘+E):** Ejects the selected removable disk (such as a CD, DVD, floppy, or Zip).

- ✓ **Burn Disc:** Burns data to a CD or DVD. If you have a compatible CD-RW or DVD-R drive and you've prepared the media, choosing this command tells the Finder to finish the job and actually burn the data to the CD or DVD. I cover burning CDs and DVDs in Chapter 9.

- ✓ **Find (⌘+F):** Finds a file or folder on your hard drive. Use the File➪Find command when you can't remember where you put it in a file or folder. This command is a Mac OS X feature that really kicks some butt. I discuss finding files in detail in Chapter 12.

The Edit Menu (Which Shoulda Been Called the Clipboard Menu)

In contrast to the File menu, which has commands that mostly deal with file management and are exclusive to the Finder window, the Edit menu's commands and functions are available in almost every Macintosh program ever made.

Because almost every program has an Edit menu and because almost every program uses the same keyboard shortcuts on its Edit menu, it behooves you to know the Edit menu keyboard shortcuts by heart, even if you remember no others.

Personally, I think that the Edit menu should have been called the Clipboard menu because most of its commands deal with the Macintosh Clipboard. Well, I used to think that until Mac OS X version 10.1 came out. With 10.1, Apple included one of the few things that people really like about Windows. You can now use the Copy and Paste commands in the Finder to copy files from one folder to another.

Comprehending the Clipboard

The *Clipboard* is a holding area for the last thing that you cut or copied. That copied item can be text, a picture, a portion of a picture, an object in a drawing program, a column of numbers in a spreadsheet, or just about anything that can be selected. In other words, the Clipboard is the Mac's temporary storage area.

The Clipboard commands in the Edit menu are enabled only when they can actually be used. If the currently selected item can be cut or copied, the Cut and Copy commands in the Edit menu are enabled. If the selected item can't be cut or copied, the commands are unavailable and are dimmed (gray). And when nothing is selected, the Cut, Copy, Paste, and Clear commands are also dimmed.

Copying or cutting to the Clipboard

To cut or copy something to the Clipboard, select the item and then choose Cut or Copy from the Edit menu or use the keyboard shortcuts ⌘+X (cut) or ⌘+C (copy). Choosing Cut *deletes* the selected item and puts it on the Clipboard; choosing Copy *copies* the selected item to the clipboard but does not delete the selected item.

You can cut an icon's name but you can't cut the icon itself; you may only copy an icon.

As a storage area, the Clipboard's contents are temporary. *Very* temporary. When you cut or copy an item, that item remains on the Clipboard only until you cut or copy something else. When you do cut or copy something else, the new item replaces the Clipboard's contents and in turn remains on the Clipboard until you cut or copy something else. And so it goes.

Of course, whatever's on the Clipboard heads straight for oblivion if you crash, lose power, log out, or shut your Mac down, so don't count on it too heavily.

Pasting from the Clipboard

To place the item that's on the Clipboard someplace new, click where you want the item to go and then paste what you've copied or cut (choose Edit⇨Paste or use the keyboard shortcut ⌘+V). Pasting does *not* remove the item from the Clipboard; the item remains there until you cut or copy another item.

Pasting doesn't purge the contents of the Clipboard. In fact, an item stays on the Clipboard until you cut, copy, clear, crash (these used to be called the four Cs of Macintosh computing, but Mac OS X almost never crashes), restart, shut down, or log out. This means that you can paste the same item over and over and over again, which can come in pretty handy at times.

Almost all programs have an Edit menu and use the Macintosh Clipboard, which means that you can usually cut or copy something in a document in one program and paste it into a document from another program. Usually.

Checking out the main Edit menu items

The previous sections give you probably 75 percent of what you need to know about the Edit menu. Still, because I get paid to be thorough and because the Finder's Edit menu has a few commands that aren't Clipboard-related, in this section, I go through the Edit menu's commands one by one.

✔ **Undo/Redo (⌘+Z):** This command undoes the last thing you did. For example, if you change the name of a folder and then choose this command, the name of the folder reverts back to what it was before you changed it. The Undo or Redo command is followed by the name of the action you're about to undo or redo.

The Undo command toggles (that is, switches back and forth) between the new and old states as long as you don't do anything else. For example, if you rename a file from *Do Me* to *Undo Me* and then choose Edit⇨Undo, the file name reverts to *Do Me*. If you pull down the Edit menu now, the Undo command reads Redo instead of Undo. Select Redo, and the name of the file changes back to *Undo Me*. You can continue to Undo and Redo until you click somewhere else.

Don't forget about this command because it can be a lifesaver. Almost every program has an Undo command. Now for the bad news: The Undo command is ephemeral, like the Clipboard: You can only use Undo to reverse your last action. As soon as you do something else — even just clicking a lousy icon — you lose the ability to undo the original action. At least, this is true in the Finder. Some programs, such as Microsoft Word, BBEdit, iMovie, and Adobe Illustrator, allow multiple Undo's.

Here's a cool feature — the Undo command works with certain actions that it never worked with before, such as moving icons. That's way cool because sometimes you drag an icon somewhere and drop it accidentally. Finding it is a hassle. Now you can just undo the move. Kewl beans.

As you find out more about your Mac and OS X, you'll no doubt discover actions that you can't undo. Still, Undo is a great command when available, and I urge you to get in the habit of trying it often.

✔ **Cut (⌘+X):** This command removes the selected item and places it on the Clipboard. You can then paste the item from the Clipboard to another document, text box, or other valid destination. For more info on Cut and the Clipboard, see the earlier section "Copying or cutting to the Clipboard."

✔ **Copy (⌘+C):** This command makes a copy of a selected item and places it on the Clipboard. However, the original is not removed like it is when you cut something. For more info on Copy and the Clipboard, see the earlier section "Copying or cutting to the Clipboard."

✔ **Paste (⌘+V):** This command places the contents of the Clipboard at the place you last clicked. For more info on Paste and the Clipboard, see the earlier section "Pasting from the Clipboard."

✔ **Select All (⌘+A):** This command selects all icons in the active window. Or, if no window is active, using Select All selects every icon on the Desktop. If a window is active, choosing Select All selects every icon in the window, regardless of whether you can see them onscreen.

The Select All command has nothing whatsoever to do with the Clipboard, so why is it on the Edit menu? Is it because selecting is an editing operation and that's why the menu is called Edit? Who knows? The Powers That Be at Apple put it there once upon a time, and there it remains.

✔ **Show Clipboard:** This command summons the Clipboard window, which lists the type of item (such as text, picture, or sound) on the Clipboard and a message letting you know whether the item on the Clipboard can be displayed.

✔ **Special Characters:** This command opens the Character Palette, where you can choose special characters such as mathematical symbols, arrows, ornaments, stars, accented Latin characters, and so on. To insert a character in your document at the insertion point, simply click it and then click the Insert button.

A View from a Window: The View Menu

The View menu controls what the icons and windows look like, how icons and windows are arranged and sorted, and the look of your windows. The View menu affects the icons in the active window; if no window is active, it affects the icons on the Desktop.

The following list gives you a brief description of each of the menu items on the View menu:

✔ **As Icons (⌘+1):** Using Icon view is the traditional Macintosh view — the one most closely associated with the Macintosh experience. In my humble opinion, however, this view is one of the two least useful views because those big horse-y icons take up far too much valuable screen real estate. I discuss Icon view in Chapter 7.

✔ **As List (⌘+2):** In List view, you can copy or move items from different folders with a single motion without opening multiple windows. In either Icon view or Columns view, on the other hand, moving files from two or more different folders requires opening several windows and two separate drags or the use of Copy and Paste introduced in version 10.1.

✔ **As Columns (⌘+3):** This changes the active window to Columns view. Choosing Columns view is a new way (added in Mac OS X) to view your files in a Finder window where the folders on your computer are displayed in a column at the left of the Finder window's Browser pane and the contents of those folders are displayed in columns to the right. See Chapter 7 for more info on Columns view.

✔ **Clean Up:** Choose this to align icons to an invisible grid; you use it to keep your windows and Desktop neat and tidy. (If you like this invisible grid, don't forget that you can turn it on or off for the Desktop and individual windows by using View Options.) Clean Up is available only in Icon view or when no windows are active. If no windows are active, the command instead cleans up your Desktop. (To deactivate all open windows, just click anywhere on the Desktop.)

If you're like me, you've taken great pains to place icons carefully in specific places on your Desktop. Cleaning up your Desktop destroys all your beautiful work and moves all your perfectly arranged icons. And alas, cleaning up your Desktop is not undo-able.

✔ **Arrange:** This rearranges your icons in your choice of six different ways: alphabetical order (by Name); modification date (by Date Modified); creation date (by Date Created); Size; Kind; or Label. Like Clean Up, it's only available for windows viewed as icons, and it's not undo-able.

✔ **Hide/Show Toolbar (⌘+Option+T):** This shows or hides the buttons on the toolbar of the active window. Suppose that you want to see more files and fewer buttons. Because the buttons on this toolbar are also available from the Go menu (see the next section "Going Places"), and the Action button's popup menu is just whatever contextual menu goes with your current selection, you're safe in hiding them. Just choose Hide Toolbar to make the toolbar go away or Show Toolbar to bring it back. (As I detail in Chapter 5, the gray oval button in the upper-right corner of every Finder window does the same thing.) The only thing you lose is the Search field, and you can use Find for that if you want.

What they don't tell you ahead of time, but I will, is that hiding the toolbar also hides the Sidebar. I find this quite annoying because I use the Sidebar a lot, but don't use the toolbar nearly as often (there are keyboard equivalents for all of them).

When the toolbar is hidden, opening a folder opens a *new* Finder window rather than reusing the current one (which is what happens when the toolbar is showing unless you've changed this preference in Finder Preferences) or are using Column view. Go to Chapter 7 for more about the toolbar in Finder windows.

✔ **Customize Toolbar:** This one is way cool — use it to design your own Finder window toolbar. Find out more about this nifty feature in Chapter 7.

✔ **Hide/Show Status Bar:** Shows or hides the status bar for Finder windows, at the bottom of the window. The status bar tells you how many items are in each window and, if any are selected, how many you've selected out of the total, and how much space is available on the hard drive containing this window.

✔ **Show View Options (⌘+J):** Here's where you can soup up the way any (or all) of your windows looks and behaves. You can do this either globally (so that all windows use the same view when opened) or on a window-by-window basis. I discuss Show View Options more in Chapter 7.

Going Places

The Go menu is chock full of shortcuts. The items on this menu take you to places on your Mac — many of the same places that you can go with the Finder window toolbar — and a few other places.

Checking out Go menu items

The following list gives you a brief look at the items on the Go menu.

See the next section for info on some menu items that aren't listed here, such as Computer, Home, iDisk, and Favorites.

✔ **Back (⌘+[ ):** Use this menu option to return to the last Finder window that you had open. It's equivalent to the Back button in the Finder toolbar, in case you have the toolbar hidden.

Think of this command as a breadcrumb trail that moves backward through every folder you open. For example, suppose that you open seven folders to get to the destination folder that you desire — call them folders 1, 2, 3, 4, 5, 6, and 7. Each time that you select the Back command, the previous folder appears — 6, 5, 4, 3, 2, and 1.

✔ **Forward (⌘+]):** This is the opposite of using the Back command, moving you forward through every folder you open. Picking up from the previous example, suppose that you've moved back to folder 1. Each time you select the Forward command, you move forward through those folders — 2, 3, 4, 5, 6, and 7. If you haven't gone back, you can't go forward.

✔ **Enclosing Folder (⌘+up arrow {↑}):** This command tells the Finder window to display the folder where the currently selected item is located.

✔ **Computer (⌘+Shift+C):** This command tells the Finder window to display the Computer level, showing Network and all of your disks.

✔ **Home (⌘+Shift+H):** Use this command to have the Finder window display your Home directory (which is named with your short name).

✔ **Network (⌘+Shift+K):** This command displays whatever is accessible on your network in the Finder window.

✔ **iDisk:** Use this submenu to mount your iDisk (⌘+Shift+I), another user's iDisk, or another user's iDisk Public Folder.

✔ **Applications (⌘+Shift+A):** This command positions the Finder window to your Applications directory, the usual storehouse of all the programs that came with your Mac and the most likely place that programs you install will be placed.

✔ **Utilities (⌘+Shift+U):** This command gets you to the Utilities folder inside the Applications folder in one fell swoop. The Utilities folder is the repository of such useful items as Disk Utility (which lets you erase, format, verify, and repair disks) and Disk Copy (which you use to create and mount disk image files).

✔ **Recent Folders:** Use this submenu to quickly go back to a folder that you recently visited. Every time you open a folder, Mac OS X creates an alias to it and stores it in the Recent Folders folder. You can open any of these aliases from the Recent Folders command in the Go menu.

✔ **Go to Folder (⌘+Shift+G):** This summons the Go to Folder dialog box, as shown in Figure 6-13. Look at your Desktop. Maybe it's cluttered with lots of windows, or maybe it's completely empty. Either way, suppose that you're several clicks away from a folder that you want to open. If you know the path from your hard drive to that folder, you can type the path to the folder that you want in the Go to the Folder text box (separating each folder name with a forward slash [/]) and then click Go to move (relatively) quickly to the folder that you need.

The first character that you type must also be a forward slash, as shown in Figure 6-13, unless you're going to a subdirectory of the current window.

This particular window is clairvoyant, trying to guess which folder you mean by the first letter or two that you type. For example, in Figure 6-13, I typed the letter **A** and paused, and the window guessed that I wanted *Applications;* then I pressed the right-arrow key to accept the guess and typed a **U**, and the window guessed the rest *(tilities)* and filled it in for me. (The final letters I *didn't* type are highlighted in Figure 6-13).

✔ **Connect to Server (⌘+K):** If your Mac is connected to a network or to the Internet, use this command to reach these remote resources.

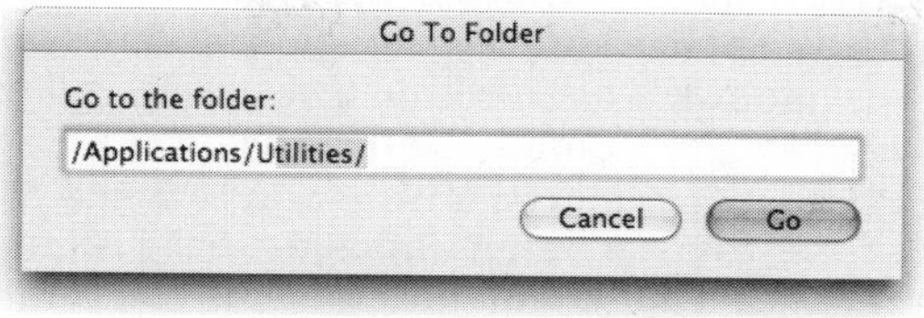

Figure 6-13:
Go to a
folder by
entering its
path.

Go To Folder

Go to the folder:

/Applications/Utilities/

Cancel   Go

Go menu: Keyboard shortcuts at a glance

TIP

Note that the Go menu lists keyboard shortcuts for commands that you also find on the Finder window toolbar and your iDisk. I cover these in detail in Chapter 7 as buttons, and the commands do the same things. But if you want to know the commands and keyboard shortcuts to these commands, here ya go:

Command	Keyboard Shortcut
Computer	⌘+Shift+C
Home	⌘+Shift+H
iDisk	⌘+Shift+I
Network	⌘+Shift+K
Favorites	⌘+Shift+F
Utilities	⌘+Shift+U
Applications	⌘+Shift+A

Window Dressing

Again with the windows! I spend a lot of pages in Chapter 5 giving you the scoop on how to work with windows. The commands on the Window menu provide you with tools that you can use to manage your windows. Here is a brief look at each of the menu items on the Window menu.

✔ **Minimize Window (⌘+M):** Use this command to unclutter your Desktop. It's the same as clicking the orange gumdrop.

REMEMBER

With a Finder window selected (the command will be unavailable — grayed out — if you don't have an active Finder window), using the Minimize Window command makes a file disappear, as it were: The file or folder is still open, but it's not active, and you don't see it on your screen. You do see, however, an icon representing it in the Dock. (Read all about the Dock in Chapter 3.)

✔ **Bring All to Front:** In previous versions of Mac OS, when you clicked a window belonging to an application, *all* that application's windows came to the front. That is, windows moved within layers and as layers. Under OS X, windows interleave. For example, you could have a Finder window, a Word window, a Photoshop window, a Word window, and another Finder window in a front-to-back order. Choosing Bring All to Front enables you to have all the Finder windows move to the front of those belonging to other applications (while keeping their own relative ordering). This essentially allows an emulation of the layering to which Mac (and Windows) users are accustomed.

If you hold down the Option key when you pull down the Window menu, the Minimize Window changes to the Minimize All Windows, and the Bring All to Front command changes to the useful Arrange in Front, which arranges all your Desktop windows neatly starting in the upper-left corner of the Desktop, as shown in Figure 6-14.

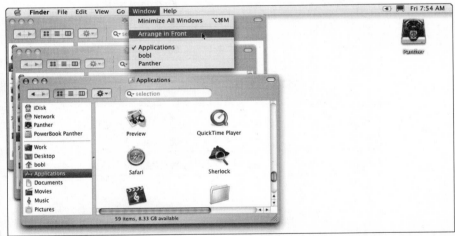

Figure 6-14:
The Arrange in Front command stacks up your windows neatly in the corner.

✔ **Other items:** The remaining items on the Window menu are the names of all currently open Finder windows. Click a window's name to bring it to the front.

The names of windows that you minimize (the ones with icons appearing on the Dock) remain on the Window menu. You can view the window by choosing its name from the Window menu.

Not Just a Beatles Movie: Help and the Help Menu

One of the best features about all Macs since System 7.*x* is the system's excellent built-in help (see Figure 6-15). And Mac OS X doesn't cheat you on that legacy: This system has online help in abundance. When you have a question about how to do something, the Mac Help Center is the first place that you should visit (after this book, of course).

The one exception to the rule that I mention earlier in this chapter — that you don't have to press Shift for capital letters in a keyboard shortcut on a menu — is the keyboard shortcut for Help. This shortcut appears on the Help menu as ⌘+?, and you do have to hold down the Shift key to type the question mark. In fact, if you press ⌘+/ (the Command key and a front slash, which is what you get when you type a lowercase question mark), nothing happens. This is different from earlier versions of Mac OS.

In other words, the shortcut for Help *should be* ⌘+Shift+/ even though the menu says ⌘+?. Got it? If you're wondering why this is, Apple says it's because you're going to be asking questions, and the question mark is a great device for remembering that. Personally, I think it's lame.

To use Mac Help, simply type a word or phrase into the text field at the top right and then press Enter or Return. In a few seconds, your Mac provides you with one or more articles to read, which (theoretically) are related your question. Usually. For example, if you type **menus** and press Return, you get 50 different help articles, as shown in Figure 6-16.

Figure 6-15: Mac Help is nothing if not helpful.

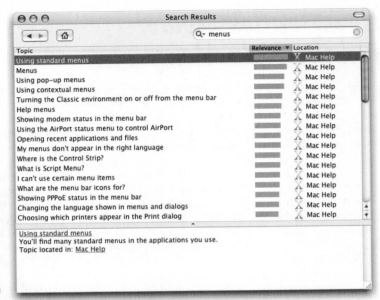

Figure 6-16:
You got
questions?
Mac's got
answers.

Although you don't have to be connected to the Internet to use Mac Help,
you do need an Internet connection to get the most out of it. That's because
OS X installs only certain help articles on your hard drive. If you ask a question that isn't answered by the help articles on your hard drive, Mac Help will
connect to Apple's Web site and download the answer (assuming that you
have an active Internet connection). This can sometimes be inconvenient,
but it's also smart. This way, the help system can be updated at any time by
Apple without requiring any action from you.

Furthermore, after you've asked a question and Mac Help has grabbed the
answer from the Apple Web site, the answer remains on your hard drive forever. If you ask for it again (even in a later date), your computer won't have
to download it from the Apple Web site again.

Part II

Rounding Out Your Basic Training

The 5th Wave   By Rich Tennant

Okay—you were right, I was wrong. F5 opens the garage door, and F6 backs the car out.

In this part . . .

Peruse the chapters in this part to discover how to perform important hands-on tasks. But don't get all worked up: This stuff is easy. In fact, I think of this part as "The Lazy Person's How-To Guide."

First I show you each and every OS X menu, in full and loving detail. Then, it's time to learn more about the all-important Finder, followed by a pair of all-important skills: saving and opening files. You'll also discover how to use removable media with your Mac — a good thing to know!

You're gonna love it!

Chapter 7

New-Fangled Finder

*B*elieve it or not, all the stuff on your Mac can fit in one window — the Finder window. In this window, you can double-click your way to your favorite application, your documents, or out onto the Internet. In fact, the Finder is the place you are when you haven't yet gone any place at all. The Finder window appears on the Desktop when you start up your Mac, and it's always available. And if you close the Finder, you can get it back easily. Even if you're an old hand with Mac OS, I show you how to get the most from the OS X Finder in this chapter.

The Finder is, among other things, a window. A very talented window, but a window just the same. For the lowdown on windows in general, see Chapter 5.

Getting to Know the Finder

A Finder window is a handy friend. And the Finder is indeed a window (or multiple windows) in OS X. Use the Finder to navigate through files, folders, and applications on your hard drive or to connect to other Macs and Internet servers — right from your Desktop.

Hey, I know you!

If you're an experienced Mac user, you know the Finder well. Every version of Mac OS before Max OS X has included the Finder, and its appearance has been pretty much the same since the Mac was introduced in 1984. What's new in Mac OS X is that you can use a single window in the Finder — instead of multiple windows — to view just about everything stored on all your hard drives and removable disks. Instead of opening a new window for each folder, the Finder can display everything in the same window, shifting your view of items as you click or select them with buttons in the window.

Panther changes the appearance of Finder windows just a bit more than previous releases of OS X by adopting the paned (display) window type popularized in iTunes and iPhoto rather than continuing to use the document-type window of all preceding versions.

You still have the option to use multiple windows: When you open an application, for example, it has its own menu bar and windows — just as it always has.

One thing that you won't find is the venerable Chooser. It's gone in OS X, replaced by the Print Center application (which you can read about in Chapter 12) and the Connect to Server menu option (covered in Chapter 6).

If you *really* like multiple Finder windows onscreen the way that many long-time Mac users do, you can tell the Mac to give you what you want so that you don't have to haggle with the above methods of opening a new Finder window. Just hold down the ⌘ key when you double-click any folder, and it'll open in a separate window. Alternatively, you could just set your Finder Preferences (in the Finder menu) to open a new window when you double-click a folder.

Note: If you've hidden the toolbar by clicking a Finder window's Hide/Show Toolbar button, new windows open automatically when you open a folder — you don't have to hold down the ⌘ key at all. It can be disconcerting when the Finder suddenly starts behaving differently. If you want to use the new one-window approach when you've hidden the toolbar or set your Finder Preferences, hold down the Option key when you double-click a folder. It'll open in the same window as if you had never hidden the toolbar and Sidebar.

In Figure 7-1, you can see a typical Finder window, including the following major features:

- ✔ **Toolbar:** From here you can select frequent actions at the click of a button and also search a folder.

- ✔ **Forward and Back buttons:** Click these to go to the last or next folder, respectively, that you viewed in this window. This is sort of like how a Web browser works. However, clicking this Back button takes you back one folder instead of one Web page. Click the Forward button, and you traverse forward in the order that you opened the folders.

Folders are often referred to as *directories* in OS X parlance.

- **View buttons:** The Finder toolbar also sports three view buttons (located to the right of the Forward and Back buttons). Use these buttons to view the contents of your Finder window by icons, list, or columns. Read about these views in the section "Customizing Finder Windows with Views" later in this chapter.

- **Search field:** You can now search for files in a folder (just enter some descriptive text) directly from any window's toolbar. (Its toolbar must be showing, of course.)

- **Icons:** Click these to open your stuff — applications, files, folders, and remote resources, such as Web sites.

- **Status bar:** At the bottom of the window is the *status bar,* which tells you the amount of space available on this hard drive and the number of items in the current folder.

  You can turn the status bar on and off by choosing View⌐Show Status Bar (which toggles to View⌐Hide Status Bar when the status bar is showing).

- **Sidebar:** This handy list, at the left of the window, shows all of your available disks and servers at the top and all of your commonly accessed icons — folders, documents, or applications — at the bottom.

Finding the Finder

If you don't see the Finder window on the Desktop when your Mac finishes the start-up process, you probably closed it the last time that the Mac was on. So how do you find the Finder window again?

- Click the Finder icon in the Dock. (It's the left-most one, with a smiley Mac face on it.)

- Choose File⇨New Finder window (or use the keyboard shortcut ⌘+N), and a Finder window appears. New Finder windows always open up showing your Home directory. In other words, they open up labeled YourShortName, the same as if you chose Go⇨Home or clicked the Home button in the Sidebar.

Note: In Finder Preferences, you can change where your New Finder window opens — to your Home, Computer, Documents folder, or any other folder you choose.

You'll probably open a lot of new windows, so consider memorizing this keyboard shortcut: ⌘+N. This shortcut is good to know because most software programs use the ⌘+N shortcut to create a new document. If your memory is bad, use this mnemonic device: N is for New.

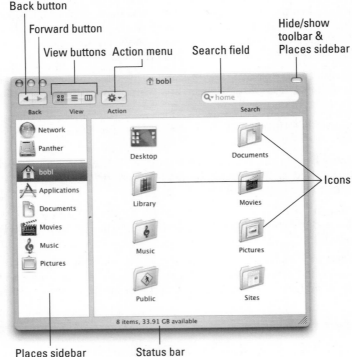

Back button

Forward button

View buttons   Action menu   Search field

Hide/show
toolbar &
Places sidebar

Icons

Figure 7-1:
The
contents of
my Home
folder
displayed in
a Finder
window.

Places sidebar   Status bar

Belly Up to the Toolbar

Right below the title bar, you find the Finder window toolbar (refer to
Figure 7-1). On it are tools and buttons that let you navigate quickly and
act upon selected icons. To activate a toolbar button, click it once.

You say you don't want to see the toolbar at the top of the window? Okay!
Just choose View⇨Hide Toolbar or click the little gray jelly bean-looking
thing in the upper-right corner of every Finder window, and it's gone. If only
life were always so easy!

Alas, hiding the Toolbar also hides the useful (and new in Panther) Sidebar. If
only you could choose to hide them independently . . . .

If you've customized your toolbar, as you discover later in this chapter, it
won't look exactly like this. But, from left to right, here's the lowdown on the
toolbar's default buttons:

✔ **Forward and Back buttons:** Clicking the Forward and Back buttons displays the directories that you've viewed in this window in sequential order. If you've used a Web browser, it's just like that.

The keyboard shortcuts ⌘+[for Back and ⌘+] for Forward are more useful (in my opinion) than using the buttons. For more on this nifty navigation device, see the "Hither and yon: The Forward and Back buttons" section later in this chapter.

✔ **View buttons:** The three view buttons change the way that the window displays its contents. Stay tuned for an entire section on views coming up in just a few pages.

✔ **Action:** Click this button to see a popup menu of all the context-sensitive actions you can perform upon selected icons, as shown in Figure 7-2.

✔ **Search:** The toolbar's Search field is a nifty way to search for files within the current folder and the folders within it, ad infinitum. Just type a word or even just a few letters. After a few seconds, the window will fill with a list of files that match, as shown in Figure 7-3.

Performing a search this way finds files in the current folder or in any of its subfolders. To clear the contents of the Search field, click the little X-in-a-circle on the right side of the Search field. Click the Back button to return to the folder that you were viewing before you searched.

Figure 7-2:
Clicking the Action button displays a menu of actions you can perform on the selected icon or icons in the Finder window.

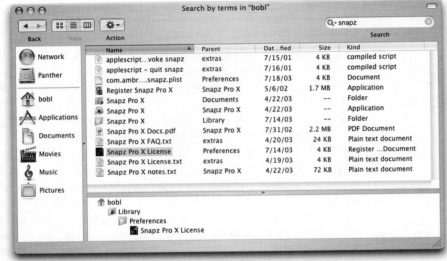

Figure 7-3:
Searching my Home folder for *Snapz* finds these 12 files that contain the word *Snapz*.

For searches using multiple criteria or to search for a word within a document (meaning within the text of the document rather than in its file name), use the more powerful Find command. I take a closer look at it in Chapter 10.

Navigating the Finder: Up, Down, and Backwards

In addition to the Sidebar described previously and some good old-fashioned double-clicking, the Mac OS X Finder window offers a nifty new navigation tool: the aptly named Back button in the toolbar. But first I discuss the current folder pop-up menu, which is essential for understanding where you are in the big scheme of things.

Like a roadmap: The current folder drop-down menu

In the center of the window's title bar is the name of the folder that you're viewing in this window — the highlighted folder. To see a roadmap to this folder from the top level (Computer, a.k.a. PowerBook Panther), ⌘+click and hold on the folder's name (Desktop) in the title bar, as shown in Figure 7-4.

A drop-down menu appears with the current folder (Pictures) at the top.

Figure 7-4:
Traverse
folders
from this
convenient
drop-down
menu.

Select any folder in the menu, and it becomes the highlighted folder in the current window.

Put another way, in Figure 7-4, Desktop is currently the active folder; bobl will become the active folder when I release the mouse.

Use this pop-up menu to move from your current folder all the way to the Computer folder. Now click the Back button. Hey, you're right back where you were before you touched that pop-up menu.

If you like this feature a lot, use the Customize Toolbar command (in the View menu) to add a Path button to your toolbar. It displays the menu of folders previously described without having to hold down the ⌘ key.

To remove an item from the Toolbar, simply hold down the ⌘ key and drag it out of the Toolbar. When you release the mouse button, the item will disappear with a satisfying poof. This technique also works for removing items from the Dock or Sidebar, but you don't have to press the ⌘ key. Just drag them out onto the desktop and poof!

Hither and yon: The Forward and Back buttons

Suppose that you're fiddling around in a Finder window, opening stuff, and maybe even looking for a particular file. You realize that the item you want is in the folder that you just left. D'oh! What to do? Click the Back button — yes, just like with a Web browser. The Back button (shown on the left in the margin) is the left-pointing arrow at the left end of the Finder window toolbar. If you want to move to the last folder you were at, just click the Back button, and there you are! If you use a Web browser (and who doesn't these days?), you're probably a pro at this already.

Here's an example of how the Back button works. Say you're in your Home folder, you click the Favorites button, and then a split-second later you realize that you actually need something in the Home folder. Just a quick click of the Back button and poof! You're back Home.

As for the Forward button, well, it moves you the opposite direction through folders that you've visited in this window.

Play around with them both — you'll find them invaluable. And don't forget even more invaluable keyboard shortcuts — ⌘+[and ⌘+] for Forward and Back, respectively.

Customizing Finder Windows with Views

You have three ways to view a window — Column view, Icon view, and List view. Some people like columns, some like icons, and others love lists. To each her own. Play with the three Finder views to see which one works best for you. For what it's worth, I usually prefer Column view.

The following sections give you a look at each view.

Column view

The Column view is new in Mac OS X; previous versions of Mac OS didn't have anything like it. It's quickly become my favorite way to display windows in the Finder.

 To display a window in the Column view, click the Column view button in the toolbar (as shown in the margin), choose View⇨As Columns from the Finder's menu bar, or use the keyboard shortcut ⌘+3.

You can have as many columns in a Column view window as your screen can handle. Just use the window sizer (a.k.a. the resize control) in the lower-right corner to enlarge your window horizontally so that new columns have room to open. Or click the green Zoom (a.k.a. Maximize) gumdrop to expand the window to its maximum width instantly. (See Chapter 5 for details about the window sizer and Zoom gumdrop . . . er, button.)

 You can use the little grabber handles at the bottom of a column to resize the column widths. When you drag this handle left or right, the column to its left resizes; if you hold down the Option key when you drag, *all* the columns resize at the same time.

See what a Finder window displayed in Column view looks like in Figure 7-5.

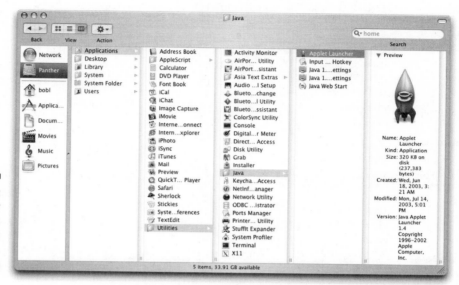

Figure 7-5:
A Finder
window in
Column
view.

Here's how it works: When I click the Panther disk icon in the Sidebar, its contents appear in the column to the right. When I click the Applications folder in this column, its contents appear in the second column. When I click the Utilities folder in the second column, its contents appear in the third column. When I click the Java folder in the third column, its contents appear in the fourth column. Finally, when I click Applet Launcher in the fourth column, a big icon plus some information about this file appears (it's an application, 320K in size, created on June 18, 2003, and so on).

This rightmost column displays information about the highlighted item to its left, but only if that item is not a folder or disk. (If it were, its contents would be in this column, right?) That's the preview column. For most items, the picture is an enlarged view of the file's icon, as shown in Figure 7-5. But if that item is a graphic file (even a PDF) saved in a format that QuickTime can interpret (most graphic file formats), a preview picture appears instead of an icon, as shown in Figure 7-6. If you don't like having the Preview displayed, you can choose View⇨Show View Options and turn off Show Preview Column.

Almost everyone who I've talked to about this view thinks it's a darn handy way to quickly look through a lot of folders at once, especially folders filled with pictures.

Figure 7-6:
The preview
of a graphic
file is a
picture
instead of
an icon.

Icon view

Icon view is a free-form view that allows you to move your icons around within a window to your heart's content. Check out the Finder window in Figure 7-7 to see what Icon view looks like.

 To display a window in the Icon view, click the Icon view button in the toolbar (as shown in the margin), choose View⇨As Icons from the Finder's menu bar, or use the keyboard shortcut ⌘+1.

 To display a window in List view, click the List view button in the toolbar (as shown in the margin), choose View⇨As List from the Finder's menu bar, or use the keyboard shortcut ⌘+2.

List view

Finally, I come to the view that I loved and used most in Mac OS 9 (but have all but forsaken since meeting the Column view): the List view (as shown in Figure 7-8). The main reason why I liked it so much was the little triangles to the left of each folder, known as *disclosure triangles*, which let you open a folder without actually opening a folder. The Library folder is shown in its disclosed state in Figure 7-8.

Icon view: The ol' stick-in-the-mud view

If there's a view that's a dead-ringer for the old Finder interface, it's Icon view. In all fairness, I must say that many perfectly happy Macintosh users love Icon view and refuse to even consider anything else. Fine. But as the number of files on your hard drive increases (as it does for every Mac user), screen real estate becomes more and more valuable. In my humble opinion, the only real advantages that the Icon view has over the Column or List views is the capability to arrange the icons anywhere you like within the window and to put a background picture or color behind your icons. Big deal.

I offer this solution as a compromise. If you still want to see your files and folders in Icon view, make them smaller so that more of them fit in the same space onscreen.

To change the size of a window's icons, choose View⇨Show View Options (or press ⌘+J). In the View Options window that appears, click the This Window Only radio button. Drag the Icon Size slider that you find there to the left. This makes the icons in the active window smaller. Conversely, you could make 'em all bigger by dragging the Icon Size slider to the right. Bigger icons make me crazy, but if you like them that way, your Mac can accommodate you.

If you want to make the icons in *every* window bigger or smaller, click the All Windows radio button in the View Options window and drag the Icon Size slider right or left. This affects all windows displayed in Icon view. (Read more on the View Options window coming up in a page or two. . . .)

Note: If you like Icon view, consider purchasing a larger monitor — I hear that monitors now come in a 23-inch size.

Figure 7-7: Icon view is pretty and very Mac-like but wastes valuable screen real estate.

Figure 7-8:
A window
in List view.

A little triangle-shaped arrow appears next to the name of the selected column in a List view window. (In Figure 7-9, you can see the arrow in the Name column.) If this little arrow points up, the items in the corresponding column sort in descending order; when you click the header (Name) once, the arrow now points down, and the items show up in the opposite (ascending) order, as shown in Figure 7-10. This behavior is true for all columns in List view windows.

To change the order in which columns appear in a window, press and hold on a column's name and then drag it to the left or right until it's where you want it. Release the mouse button, and the column moves. The exception to this (isn't there *always* an exception?) is that the Name column always appears first.

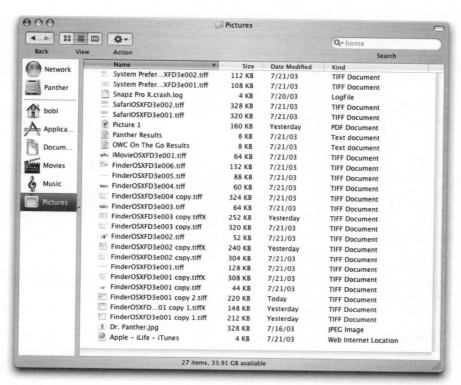

Name	Size	Date Modified	Kind
System Prefer...XFD3e002.tiff	112 KB	7/21/03	TIFF Document
System Prefer...XFD3e001.tiff	108 KB	7/21/03	TIFF Document
Snapz Pro X.crash.log	4 KB	7/20/03	LogFile
SafariOSXFD3e002.tiff	328 KB	7/21/03	TIFF Document
SafariOSXFD3e001.tiff	320 KB	7/21/03	TIFF Document
Picture 1	160 KB	Yesterday	PDF Document
Panther Results	8 KB	7/21/03	Text document
OWC On The Go Results	8 KB	7/21/03	Text document
iMovieOSXFD3e001.tiff	64 KB	7/21/03	TIFF Document
FinderOSXFD3e006.tiff	132 KB	7/21/03	TIFF Document
FinderOSXFD3e005.tiff	88 KB	7/21/03	TIFF Document
FinderOSXFD3e004.tiff	60 KB	7/21/03	TIFF Document
FinderOSXFD3e004 copy.tiff	324 KB	7/21/03	TIFF Document
FinderOSXFD3e003.tiff	64 KB	7/21/03	TIFF Document
FinderOSXFD3e003 copy.tiffX	252 KB	Yesterday	TIFF Document
FinderOSXFD3e003 copy.tiff	320 KB	7/21/03	TIFF Document
FinderOSXFD3e002.tiff	52 KB	7/21/03	TIFF Document
FinderOSXFD3e002 copy.tiffX	240 KB	Yesterday	TIFF Document
FinderOSXFD3e002 copy.tiff	304 KB	7/21/03	TIFF Document
FinderOSXFD3e001.tiff	128 KB	7/21/03	TIFF Document
FinderOSXFD3e001 copy.tiffX	308 KB	7/21/03	TIFF Document
FinderOSXFD3e001 copy.tiff	44 KB	7/21/03	TIFF Document
FinderOSXFD3e001 copy 2.tiff	220 KB	Today	TIFF Document
FinderOSXFD...01 copy 1.tiffX	148 KB	Yesterday	TIFF Document
FinderOSXFD3e001 copy 1.tiff	212 KB	Yesterday	TIFF Document
Dr. Panther.jpg	328 KB	7/16/03	JPEG Image
Apple – iLife – iTunes	4 KB	7/21/03	Web Internet Location

27 items, 33.91 GB available

Figure 7-9:
Sort items in descending order in List view . . .

Showing those View Options

To customize the way Finder windows look, use the View Options window. When you choose View⇨Show View Options from the Finder menu bar (or use the keyboard shortcut ⌘+J), you see the View Options window, as shown in Figure 7-11.

Sharp-eyed readers may notice that the View Options window shown in Figure 7-11 reads Panther in its title bar. That's because the View Options window always bears the name of the active window (the one that will be affected if you mark the This Window Only radio button instead of the All Windows radio button).

Start by selecting the All Windows radio button at the top of the View Options window. Now, whatever choices you set in this window affect *all* Finder windows for which you haven't specified explicit options (by using the This Window Only radio button, which I'll get to in a moment).

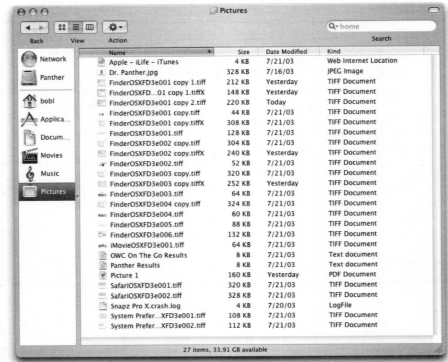

Figure 7-10:
. . . but click the Name header, and items are now in ascending order.

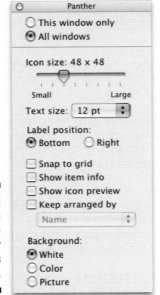

Figure 7-11:
Set the appearance of Finder windows here.

Easy copying and moving in List view

Here's a slick advantage for viewing folders and files in List view with the disclosure triangles. Because you can easily see folders and files with just one window open, you can copy or move items from separate folders with a single dragging motion. You're spared from having to open multiple windows, as you must do in the Icon view or Column view. In those views, moving files from two or more different folders requires opening several windows and two separate file-dragging motions. Of course, you can drag to any folder in the Sidebar, so you can still copy in just one window with Icon or Column view — if you put the destination folder in the Sidebar first.

It's easier to do than to explain, but here goes. In Figure 7-8, you can move any or all three files in the Documents folder into the Desktop, Detritus Library, Movies, Music, Pictures, Public, or Sites folders without opening another window (though you'll have to scroll for the last few). Further, if you've clicked the disclosure triangle for say, Pictures, you can even move the files into a subfolder of Pictures or move files from the Documents and Pictures folder to another folder with one drag.

First decide whether you want to modify the All Windows Icon, List, or Column view by displaying the window in that view. If you choose Icon view, your options apply to all windows in Icon view; if you choose List view, your choices apply to all windows in List view. Because there are no This Window Only choices for Column view, your choices in View Options for Column view always apply to all Column view windows.

The choice that you make determines what options you see in the View Options window. The following sections describe your choices.

Icon View All Windows options

So you just can't kick that icon habit, eh? Okay . . . here's how to make global settings so that all your windows look the same. (If this concept excites you, you really need to get out of the house more!)

In the window, select the All Windows radio button. Now you're really living on the edge — oooh. Now you can set how big you want your icons, how to arrange them in windows, and whether you want to insert a picture as a background for your folder windows (yup, *all* folders) or make the background color something other than white.

The following list describes the View Options that you see after you choose Icon view:

  ✔ **Icon Size:** Use the Icon Size slider to make icons larger or smaller. To save valuable screen real estate space, I recommend that you keep your icons small. The largest icon size is nothing short of huge. *Hint:* Have a Finder window open in which icons are visible as you move the slider so that you can monitor icon size as they shrink or grow, depending on how far you move the slider.

✓ **Text Size:** What it says . . . the size of the icon's name. Just choose the point size that you want from the popup menu here.

✓ **Label Position:** Select either the Bottom or the Right radio button here to set where the icon's name appears — below it or to its right.

✓ **Icon arrangement:** Okay, it doesn't label this group of check boxes, but icon arrangement is what they do. Set here whether those icons should be penned up or free range with these check boxes:

  • **Snap to Grid:** Creates nice, straight lines of icons.

  • **Show Item Info:** Adds a line of text below the icon's name with info about the file (or folder).

  • **Show Icon Preview:** Got me. Nobody I know has figured this one out yet. It doesn't seem to do anything. If you know what it does, please let me know.

  • **Keep Arranged By:** Lets you specify the sort order for your icons from the pop-up menu below. Your choices are Name, Date Modified, Date Created, Size, and Kind.

✓ **Background:** From this list of radio buttons, you can pick a color or picture for your windows or opt for none at all (white, the default). Look at Figure 7-12 to see what a folder looks like with a picture in its background. I'm not sure that windows should have pictures in their backgrounds, but if you like them, this is how it's done.

Whatever you choose — insert a picture, choose a color, or neither — appears in each of your windows if you've chosen the All Windows radio button in the View Options window.

List view All Windows options

Suppose that you prefer List view (instead of Icon view) and want to set global options for viewing your items this way. With your Finder window in List view, choose View➪Show View Options from the Finder menu bar and then select the All Windows radio button from the View Options window that appears. In Figure 7-13, you see a cluster of check boxes beneath the Show Columns heading. Select as many of these check boxes as you like to adjust your List view. When you view a window in List view, those columns will appear.

Most of the options here tell Mac OS X which fields to display or hide. The choices depend on what information you want displayed, such as

✓ Date modified

✓ Date created

✔ Size

✔ Kind

✔ Version

✔ Comments

✔ Labels

(Okay, Labels aren't really new if you're accustomed to OS 9 or earlier, but this is the first version of OS X that has had them.)

Select the ones that you want to see and then decide whether you like the view that you selected. You can always change your selections later if you find that you aren't using a particular field.

Here are two more options that may prove useful. Near the bottom of this window are these two check boxes:

✔ **Use Relative Dates:** Select this check box, and Mac OS X intelligently substitutes relative word equivalents — such as *yesterday* or *today* — for numerical dates.

When you set your clock back a day and look at files that you updated that day before setting your clock back, the relative date reads *tomorrow*. Curious but true.

Figure 7-12:
All windows now have a faux fur Apple logo as their background.

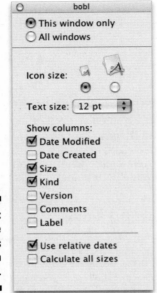

Figure 7-13:
Choose which fields to display in List view.

✔ **Calculate All Sizes:** Selecting this check box instructs Mac OS X to do just that — calculate all sizes. Select this view to see how much stuff is in each folder when you look at it in List view. The items (including folders) in the active window are sorted in descending order from biggest to smallest when you sort by size.

If you don't select the Calculate All Sizes check box, items other than folders are sorted by size, with all folders — regardless of their size — appearing at the bottom of the list (or top, if the sort order is ascending).

Near the top of the View Options dialog box, you find the Icon Size radio buttons. Select from these two radio buttons to choose between small and large icons in your List views. For my money, I think the smallest ones make windows appear noticeably faster and they definitely allow more items to be shown; your mileage may vary.

One more thing. Spring-loaded folders were resurrected in OS X version 10.2 Jaguar. They work in all the views and with icons in the toolbar.

If you were among the millions who requested that Apple bring them back, I'm happy to report that Apple did and that OS X's spring-loaded folders are better than ever. I'll show you why they're so cool in Chapter 10.

TIP

Being really finicky and choosing your views window by window

Perhaps choosing a global look for your Finder windows is just too big of a commitment for you, or you have a setup that you like but need a special view for a particular window. Here's how to adjust your window view settings individually.

1. **Open the window that you want to set up.**

2. **Choose View⇨Show View Options from the menu bar.**

3. **Select the This Window Only radio button in the View Options window.**

4. **Choose View⇨As List or View⇨As Icons to get the view that you want to set.**

The options are conveniently the same as the global options that I describe earlier, so have at it and make this special window look just the way you like it.

Getting Some Action in Your Folders

Apple has this really cool technology called AppleScript. It's been around since System 7 was released and hasn't ever really gotten the respect it deserves. AppleScript lets you program repetitive tasks so that you don't have to go through all the steps yourself every time you want to perform the task.

Almost a decade later (Mac OS 8.5), Apple introduced Folder Actions, a way to attach these AppleScripts to a folder so that whenever the folder was opened, closed, moved, had an item placed in it, or had an item removed, an appropriate script would run.

Having an AppleScript run when items are added to a closed folder sounds like a great tool for drop box-style folders to me — how about you? For example, you could have Mail launch and send a notification to your project leader or project team whenever a new file was added to the folder.

The first thing you need to do is create or obtain AppleScripts to perform the tasks you want performed. Programming AppleScript is beyond the purview of this book (in fact, a book teaching you all about programming AppleScript would be at least the size of this book alone), but you can find some ready-to-go scripts for Folder Actions in your hard disk's Library/Scripts/Folder Action Scripts folder and even more at Apple's Web site in the AppleScript pages (www.apple.com/applescript).

After you've enabled Folder Actions, you can Control+click the folder's icon again and choose a new item from the contextual menu, Attach a Folder Action. This opens a Choose a File dialog box (really an Open dialog box, which I tell you about in Chapter 8) where you can select your Folder Action script. The dialog conveniently defaults to the Folder Action Scripts folder mentioned previously. Select the script, click Choose, and you're set to go.

If you want to know more about writing Folder Action scripts, check out `www.apple.com/applescript/folder_actions`.

Chapter 8

Mastering the Save Sheet and the Open Dialog

Mark my words, this could well be the most important chapter in this book. If you don't understand the Open dialog and Save sheets, you'll never quite get the hang of your Mac. (Actually, there are two Save sheets: Save and Save As sheet, which you see when you choose File⇨Save or File⇨Save As, respectively, in most programs. Similarly, the Open dialog could be a sheet and a variation of it is used to Choose a Folder.) Yet, mastering these essential techniques is perhaps the biggest problem that many Mac users have. Ask any long-time Mac user whether he's ever heard, "Well, I saved the file and now I don't know where it went." It happens all the time with new users.

This chapter is the cure-all for your Save, Save As, and Open woes. Hang with me and pay attention; everything will soon become crystal clear. And keep saying to yourself, "The Save sheets and the Open dialog are just another view of the Finder," as I explain in this chapter.

You work with Open dialogs and Save sheets within applications. You only see them after you launch your favorite application or work within an open or newly created document. For more on launching applications, read through Chapter 4 on icons; for more on creating and opening documents, see the documentation for the program that you're using.

Saving Your Document Before It's Too Late

You can create as many documents as you want, but all is lost if you don't save them to a storage device like your hard drive or some other disk. When you *save* a file, you're committing a copy to a disk — either one mounted on your Desktop, one available over a network, or on a removable disk such as a Zip, floppy, CD-R, CD-RW, DVD-R, or DVD-RW.

In this section, I show you how to save your masterpieces. Prevent unnecessary pain in your life by developing good saving habits. If you take my advice, you'll save your work:

- Every few minutes
- Before you switch to another program
- Before you print a document
- Before you stand up

If you don't heed this advice and the program that you're using crashes while switching programs, printing, or sitting idle (which, not coincidentally, are the three most likely times for a crash), you lose everything that you did since your last save.

The keyboard shortcut for Save in almost every program I know is ⌘+S. Memorize it. See it in your dreams. Train your finger muscles to do it unconsciously. Use it (the keyboard shortcut) or lose it (your unsaved work).

Checking out the Save sheet

When you choose to save a file for the first time (by choosing File⇨Save or pressing ⌘+S), a Save sheet appears in front of the window that you're saving, as shown in Figure 8-1 — we'll call this a Basic sheet. You can choose any folder or volume listed in a Finder window's sidebar by clicking on a Basic sheet's Where popup menu and taking your pick or you can expand the sheet, as shown in Figure 8-2, and navigate folders the same way that you navigate folders in the Finder — by opening them to see their contents.

The Save sheet in Panther offers both Column or List views. In Column view, you click an item on the left to see its contents on the right, just as you do in a Finder window. In List view there are no disclosure triangles (as you see in Finder windows), so you double-click folders to open them and see their contents.

Figure 8-1:
Basic Save
sheets
can look
like this.

In an Expanded sheet, the popup menu shows a path from the currently selected folder similar to what you see when you command-click on a Finder window's title.

Hiding your stuff under the right rock

If you've used previous versions of Mac OS, the rules about where to store things were a lot looser. Storing everything within your Documents folder wasn't at all important. But Mac OS X arranges its system files, applications, and other stuff a bit differently than older versions did.

I *strongly* advise you to store all your document files and the folders that contain them in the Documents folder within your Home folder or your Home folder's Movies folder, Music folder, or Pictures folder if that's where the application (such as iMovie) recommends. Files that you place outside the Documents folder are very likely to get lost while you navigate through a maze of aliases and folders that belong and make sense to certain programs or parts of the system software — and not to you as a user. An

exception to this rule is to place files you need to share with other users in the Shared folder, inside the Users folder in which your Home folder resides.

If other people besides you use your Mac (and they had changed privilege settings to give you access to their directories — see Chapter 16), you could even save a file in another user's folder by accident, in which case you'd probably *never* find it again.

So, trust me when I say that the Documents folder in your Home folder is the right place to start, not only because it's easy to remember but also because it's only a menu command (Go⇨Home) or keyboard shortcut (⌘-H) away, wherever you're working on your Mac.

Working even more like the Finder than ever before, you can also use the Forward and Back buttons as well as the sidebar in an expanded Save dialog box to conveniently navigate your disk.

Before you can navigate the columns in a Save sheet, you need to click the downward-pointing disclosure triangle (to the right of the Where menu, just above the Save button in Figure 8-1) to expand the sheet. Otherwise, you're stuck with the small, slightly less functional version of the Save sheet that you see in Figure 8-1. Click the disclosure triangle and the sheet expands, as shown in Figure 8-2.

Choose between Column and List view in Save sheets by clicking the List or Column view buttons on the left of the popup menu, which look like their counterparts in Finder windows.

Like the List or Column view in a Finder window, you can enlarge the Save sheet to see more. Just drag the lower-right corner of the sheet down or to the right. Then, when you click items in the current right column of the Save sheet (note that you must have the columns showing to have any columns to deal with here), their contents appear in a new, third column.

After you've saved a file for the first time, choosing File➪Save or pressing ⌘+S doesn't bring up a Save sheet anymore. It just saves the file again without any further intervention on your part. Get in the habit of pressing ⌘+S often. It can't hurt and just may save your bacon someday.

In Figures 8-1 and 8-2 you see, respectively, the Save sheet for the TextEdit program, default and expanded, when you haven't chosen Plain Text as the format. In programs other than TextEdit or when you have a Plain Text document in TextEdit, the Save sheet may contain additional options, fewer options, or different options, and therefore may look slightly different. Don't worry. The Save sheet always *works* the same, no matter what options there are.

Figure 8-2:
Expanded
Save sheets
can look like
this or this
(Column
view on left,
List view
on right).

In Mac OS X, you can move the window and attached Save sheet (just as you can any window) by dragging the window's title bar. Just click the title bar and then hold down the mouse button while you drag the window wherever you desire. The Save sheet moves right along with the window. And, unlike the Save dialog in earlier versions of Mac OS, a Save sheet isn't "modal," which means it doesn't prevent you from using other programs or windows when it's onscreen.

Wherefore art thou, Where pop-up menu?

Take some time and get to know the Where pop-up menu. It's a great navigation aid, but a bit confusing for new users. With it, you can quickly move to a location on your hard drive and open or save a file stored there. Consider the Where pop-up menu a shortcut menu to all the items in a Finder window's sidebar.

The Where pop-up menu in OS X Panther in the Basic view looks a lot like the popup menu that appeared at the top of the Open/Save dialogs in earlier versions of Mac OS. But instead of tracing the folder path (as it did in versions of yore, and as it still does in the Expanded view), the Where pop-up menu lists one or more places where you may save your files (Documents, Home,) as well as other folders where you have opened or saved files recently. Both popup menus are shown in Figure 8-3.

After you've chosen a folder from the Where menu you can still navigate to other folders using the sidebar or the List or Column browser.

With all of these ways to navigate to your target folder — the mouse, the Where menu, the sidebar, the browsers, and the arrow keys — you should always be able to get to your target folder (for saving the document) with just a few clicks or keystrokes.

In this section, I run down the parts of the Where pop-up menu. In the process, I show you why it's best to store your files in certain places on your Mac. Finally, I'll show you how to use the Where menu to quickly reach your favorite folders.

The Where menu is contextual and displays different folders based on which view you're in — Basic or Expanded. If you haven't expanded the Save sheet, the Where popup menu displays your currently active directory at the top (Documents in Figure 8-3), followed by your available computers and volumes (Panther PowerBook, iDisk, Network, and Panther in Figure 8-3), followed by folders in your sidebar in Finder windows (Documents, Desktop, bobl, Applications, Movies, Music, and Pictures in Figure 8-3), followed by folders or disks you've used recently (Desktop Pictures and Vintage Typewriter folder in Figure 8-3).

Figure 8-3:
Use the
Where
pop-up
menu to
navigate to
other fol-
ders quickly.
Notice how
its contents
change
depending
upon
whether
you're
using the
Expanded
view (left) or
Basic view
(right).

When you expand the Save sheet, the popup is no longer labeled "Where." And it now displays the hierarchy from the current folder to the Computer level, just like ⌘+clicking on a window's name in the Finder.

Saving to the active folder

In an expanded Save sheet, the name at the top in the Where pop-up menu is the name of the active item (be it a folder, a drive, or the Desktop). In Figure 8-4, the active folder is Folder 2.

A file saved into Folder 2 appears in the column where you see Folder 3 in Figure 8-4.

Think of the active item in a Save sheet as akin to the active window on the Desktop. That's where your file is saved by default if you click the Save button without changing the destination folder at all. This concept is important. In other words, if the Documents folder is the active item (as it is in both Figures 8-1 and 8-2), your document is saved in the Documents folder when you click the Save button. If Folder 2 is the active item (as it is in Figure 8-4), your document is saved in Folder 2 when you click the Save button. And so on.

Figure 8-4:
Saving a file
in Folder 2.

The best places to save

Here's a quick rundown of the folders that appear by default in your sidebar and Where menu (in unexpanded Save sheets):

- ✔ **Documents:** Located within your Home folder, the Documents folder is the best place to store your files (in my humble opinion). You can organize stuff inside your Documents folder by creating sub-folders with meaningful names. For example, in my Documents folder, you'd find sub-folders named Fonts that start with the letter V, Agrapha Icon Sets, NonCom, and so on.

- ✔ **Desktop:** A good place to save files you're going to be using in the short term.

  The Desktop is not a great place for long-term storage of files and folders. If the Desktop becomes overcrowded, you'll have trouble finding files. And, an overcrowded desktop isn't a pretty sight on-screen.

- ✔ **Home:** All users have their own Home folder that contains all their stuff — their documents, their preferences, their applications — everything that belongs to them. You can save documents to your Home folder, which is named for you (that is, bobl in all of this chapter's figures). To save files here, choose Home from the Where menu, or click the Home folder (bobl) in the sidebar, and then click the Save button.

  I don't, however, recommend saving most of your stuff to your Home folder. It quickly gets overcrowded and unmanageable. I find it easier to organize and find files in the Documents folder, away from the Library, Pictures, Music, and other folders that live in Home already.

✔ **Applications:** This is where OS X likes to find your application programs. Do not save documents here! The only reason that it appears in the sidebar and Where popup menu is that you use it a lot in the Finder to select the application you want to launch.

✔ **Movies, Music, and Pictures:** The Movies, Music, and Pictures folders appear in the sidebar by default and are good locations for saving iMovies, songs, and photos or scans, respectively.

Here's a handy shortcut for naming files in the Save sheet. Click on a grayed-out file name in the file list and it becomes the name of the file you're saving, as shown in Figure 8-5.

Be careful using this shortcut — unless you change the name that appears in the Save As field before you click the Save button, you could overwrite the existing file (the one whose name you just clicked), which is probably not what you want to do.

In Figure 8-5, I'd just change the "1" to "4" (or anything other than "2" or "3," which, as you can see, would overwrite existing files).

Even with the proviso above, this can be a handy shortcut as long as you remember to alter the name of the file you're saving so as not to accidentally overwrite an existing file.

Getting active with the Save As field

When a Save sheet appears for the first time, the Save As field is active and displays the name of the document. The document name (often "Untitled") is selected, so when you begin typing, the name will disappear and be replaced by the name you type.

Figure 8-5: Before (left) and after (right) clicking a grayed-out file's name in a Save sheet.

If you press the Tab key while the Save As field is active, it becomes inactive, and the sidebar becomes active. Press the Tab key again and the file list box (the one with the list view or columns in it) becomes active. That's because the file list box, the sidebar, and the Save As field are mutually exclusive. Only one can be active at any time. You select a place, navigate the folder hierarchy, or you name a file.

Look at Figure 8-6. In the top left picture, the Save As field is active; in the top right picture; the sidebar is active; in the bottom picture, the file list box is active.

You can always tell which item is active by the thin blue or gray border around it.

When you want to switch to a different folder to save a file, click the folder in the sidebar (if you're using Column view) or click anywhere in the file list box (Column or List view) to make the file list active.

Figure 8-6:
Check the borders to see active and inactive fields.

Either the Save As field, the sidebar, or the file list box is active at any given time; no two can ever be active at the same time.

The following lists are some things to help you get a hold on this whole active/inactive silliness:

- ✔ Look for the thin border that shows you which part of the Save sheet is active. It's around the Save As field in Figure 8-6 (top left); around the sidebar (top right); and around the file list box (bottom).

- ✔ If you type while the file list box is active, the list scrolls and selects the folder that most closely matches the letter(s) that you type. It's a little strange because you won't see what you type: You'll be typing blind, so to speak. Go ahead and give it a try. For example, typing the letters **no** in the file list box of Figure 8-6 selects the NonCom folder.

- ✔ If you type while the sidebar is active, nothing happens. You can, however, use the up- and down-arrow keys to move around in the sidebar.

- ✔ When the file list is active, the letters that you type don't appear in the Save As field. If you want to type a file name, you have to activate (by clicking in it or using the Tab key) the Save As field again to type in it.

- ✔ Regardless of which box or field is active at the time, when you press the Tab key on your keyboard, the next in sequence becomes active. So if the Save As field is active, it becomes inactive when you press Tab, and the sidebar becomes active. Tab again, and the file list box becomes active. Press Tab again, and the Save As field becomes active again.

If you don't feel like pressing the Tab key, you can achieve the same effect by clicking the file list box, the sidebar, or the Save As field to make it active. Try it yourself and notice again how visual cues let you know which is active. When the file list is active, it displays a border; when the Save As field or the sidebar is active, the file list has no border, and the active field displays a border and is editable or navigable.

Putting your finger on the button

Most Save sheets contain the following three buttons (New Folder, Cancel, Save) and a Hide Extension check box. I describe them all briefly in the following list.

- ✔ **New Folder:** The New Folder button is a nice touch, but is present only in an expanded Save sheet. Click this button, and you create a new folder inside the active folder. You first get the opportunity to name the folder; then you can save your document there.

- ✔ **Cancel:** Clicking this button dismisses the Save sheet without saving anything anywhere. In other words, the Cancel button returns things to the way they were before you displayed the Save sheet.

The keyboard shortcut for Cancel is ⌘+. (⌘+ a period). Pressing the Esc key usually (but not always) does the same thing. This shortcut is a good command to memorize because it cancels almost all dialogs, and it also cancels lots of other things. If a program is dragging — your spreadsheet is calculating or your database is sorting or your graphics program is rotating, for example, and it's taking too long — try pressing either Esc or ⌘+. (period). (They work — usually.)

✔ **Save:** Click this button to save the file to the active folder.

But wait! What if the Save button is grayed out? This happens when the Save As field is blank; typing even one character will activate the Save button again.

Make sure that the folder you want to save your document in is showing in the (Where) popup menu. If you're not sure and you click the Save button, *you* could be the next one to say, "Well, I saved the file and now I don't know where it went."

✔ **Hide extension:** Marking this check box turns off the display of file name extensions, such as .rtf or .txt, in Save sheets.

It looks like Save and it acts like Save, so why is it called Save As?

The Save As command, which you can find in the File menu of almost every program ever made (at least those that create documents), lets you resave a file that has already been saved by giving it a different name.

Why would you want to do that? Here's a good (albeit kind of rude) example:

Suppose that you have two cousins, Kate and Zelda. You write Kate a long, chatty letter and save this document with the name Letter to Kate. At some point afterward, you decide that you want to send this same letter to Zelda, too, but you want to change a few things. So you change the part about your date last night (Zelda isn't as liberated as Kate) and replace all references to Kevin (Kate's husband) with Zeke (Zelda's husband). (Aren't computers grand?)

So you make all these changes to Letter to Kate, but you haven't saved this document yet. And although the document on your screen is actually a letter to Zelda, its file name is still Letter to Kate. Think of what would happen if you were to save it now without using the Save As feature: Letter to Kate reflects the changes that you just made (the stuff in the letter meant for Kate is blown away, replaced by the stuff that you write to Zelda). Thus, the file name Letter to Kate is inaccurate. Even worse, you would no longer have a copy of the letter that you sent to Kate!

The solution? Just use Save As to rename this file Letter to Zelda by choosing File⇨Save As. A Save sheet appears, in which you can type a different file name in the Save As field. You can also navigate to another folder, if you like, and save the newly named version of the file there.

Now you have two distinct files: Letter to Kate and Letter to Zelda. Both contain the stuff they should but both started life from the same file. *That's* what Save As is for.

An even better idea is to choose Save As just before you begin modifying the document and give it the new name. That way, when you're done with your changes you don't have to remember to choose Save As — you can just perform your habitual Save.

Open Sez Me

If you've read the earlier parts of this chapter, you probably already know how to use the Open dialog — you just don't yet know that you know. Open dialogs are so much like Save sheets that it's scary. To summon an Open dialog, launch your favorite program and choose File⇨Open (or use the keyboard shortcut ⌘+O, which works in 98 percent of all programs ever made).

Check out a typical Open dialog in Figure 8-7.

Figure 8-7:
The Open dialog in all its glory.

Knowing the differences between Open dialogs and Save sheets

After you master navigating the Save sheet, you should have smooth sailing when using an Open dialog. They work the same except for a few minor differences:

- **No Save As field:** A Save As field isn't needed in an Open dialog because it's the one you see when you want to open a file! Because you're not saving or naming a file here, you don't need the Save As field.

- **No Where pop-up menu:** In the Open dialog, you find the path pop-up menu instead. Why? Because you're opening a file *From* a certain folder, rather than telling your Mac *Where* to save it. The path menu has the same basic job as the path menu in an expanded Save sheet, and you see the same folders in it.

- **No Expand button:** You always have to be able to select a file, so the file list pane (and the sidebar) are omnipresent. I mean, if the Open dialog was not expanded, where would you select the file to open?

- **No New Folder button:** Why? Well, you can't open something that you haven't yet created, right? You don't need to create new folders when you're opening a file, basically.

You may notice a couple of other differences between the Save sheet and the Open dialog. At the bottom of the Open dialog (refer to Figure 8-7), note the Plain Text Encoding pop-up menu and the Ignore Rich Text Commands check box. These are specific to TextEdit and have to do with the format that TextEdit uses to save text files. Don't worry about these for now. Just remember that many applications add special items to their Open dialogs and Save sheets that help you to select formats and other options specific to those programs.

Navigate through the Open dialog just as you would a Save sheet. Don't forget the mantra, "The Open dialog and the Save sheet are just another view of the Finder."

Knowing what the Open dialog doesn't show you . . .

When you use a program's Open dialog, only files that the program knows how to open appear enabled (in a bold font) in the file list. In other words, the program filters out files that it can't open, so that you barely see them in the Open dialog. This method of selectively displaying certain items in

Open dialogs is a feature of most applications. Therefore, when you're using TextEdit, its Open dialog will dim all your spreadsheet files because TextEdit can only open text, rich text, and picture files. Pretty neat, eh?

Some programs such as AppleWorks, Microsoft Word, and Adobe Photoshop have a Show or Format menu in their Open dialogs. This menu lets you specify what type(s) of files that you want to see in the Open dialog. (Check it out in Figure 8-8.) You can often open a file that appears dimmed by choosing All Documents in the Show or Format menu.

Figure 8-8:
Photoshop's
Format
menu offers
to show you
many
different
types of
files.

Chapter 9

Haggling with Removable Media

· ·

· ·

*I*n this chapter, I show you disk basics: how to format them; how to format them so that our Windows-using brethren (and sisteren) can use them; how to eject them; how to copy or move files between disks; and much more. Onward!

Now, some of you may be thinking, "My Mac doesn't even have a floppy drive. Why should I read a whole chapter about disks?" Well, I'll tell ya. In this chapter, I tell you lots of info that applies to every Mac user, including folder management and moving or copying files to and from disks other than your internal hard drive. I also show you how to work with other types of removable magnetic media, such as Zip, Jaz, and optical media such as CD-R, CD-RW, DVD-R, DVD-RW, and DVD-RAM, types of media many Mac users deal with regularly. If you have a Power Mac G4, for example, you may have an internal Zip drive or an Apple SuperDrive (DVD-R). Or you may have added an external floppy disk drive, or iMation SuperDisk drive which can read both standard 1.4MB floppies and 120MB iMation SuperDisks (not to be confused with Apple's DVD-burning drive, which they call "SuperDrive").

The bottom line is that removable media drives allow you to easily copy files for friends, regardless of whether they use a Mac or a PC, and to move your files between home and work. And, as you'll see in Chapter 17, they allow you to protect your valuable data by backing up your hard disk to another type of media for safekeeping.

Comprehending Disks

You should think of the disk icons that appear on the Desktop (and/or in the sidebar of Finder windows) as if they were folders. That's because disks are nothing but giant folders. When you double-click them, their contents appear in the Finder window, just like a folder. You can drag stuff in and out of a disk's window, and you can manipulate the disk's window in all the usual ways, just like a folder. In fact, for all intents and purposes, disks are folders.

The only exception to the disks-are-folders rule that I can think of is that you can't use the Duplicate keyboard shortcut (⌘+D) on a disk, although you can use it on a folder.

Making Sure Your Disks are Mac Disks

Brand-new disks sometimes need to be *formatted* — prepared to receive Macintosh files — before they can be used. (This is especially true for floppy disks, if your Mac has a floppy drive.) I say *sometimes* because you can buy new disks that are preformatted. Formatting a disk takes only a few minutes to do, so don't pay a whole lot more for preformatted disks unless you really believe that time is money.

When you insert a floppy disk, your Mac may take a bit (or sometimes quite a while) before it recognizes that a disk is present and displays it on your Desktop or in the Computer window. Be patient with floppies; they're old and slow.

Is that a disk or a disc?

So how do you spell this critter, anyway? Sometimes you see it spelled d-i-s-k; other times you see it spelled d-i-s-c. If you're wondering what's up with that, here's the skinny. In the good old days, the only kind of disk was a disk with a *k*: floppy disk, hard disk, Bernoulli disk, and so on. Then one day, the compact disc (you know, a CD) was invented. And the people who invented it chose to spell it with a *c* instead of a *k*, probably because it's round like a *disc*us (think track and field). From that time on, both spellings have been used more or less interchangeably.

Now some people will tell you that magnetic media (floppy, hard, Zip, Jaz, Orb, and so on) are called *disks* (spelled with a *k*). And that optical media — that is, discs that are read with a laser (such as CD-ROMs, audio CDs, DVDs, and CD-RWs) — are called *discs* (spelled with a *c*). Maybe that's true, but the two terms have been used pretty much interchangeably for so long that you can't depend on the last letter to tell you whether a disk is magnetic or optical.

The bottom line is that I'm going to compromise and use the word *disk* in this chapter. If you're offended that I call CD-ROMs, audio CDs, DVDs, CD-RWs, and such *disks* instead of *discs*, I'm sorry.

My editors made me do it.

When you pop in any type of unformatted disk, your Mac pops up a dialog that asks whether you wish to format it, but your Mac usually calls this *initializing* rather than formatting. If you choose to format the disk, the Disk Utility program starts, and you can initialize the disk from the Erase tab.

The Erase command defaults to using Mac Extended as the format. If you're formatting a floppy disk, don't use Mac Extended — switch to Mac Standard. You should probably mark the check box to include OS 9 drivers as well if you or anyone who may need the floppies is still using OS 9 or earlier.

Moving and Copying Disks

Moving an icon from one disk to another works the same as moving an icon from one folder to another with one notable exception: When you move a file from one disk to another, you automatically make a copy of it, leaving the original untouched and unmoved. If you want to move a file from one disk to another, you need to delete the original by dragging it to the Trash.

Copying the entire contents of any removable disk (Zip, 120MB SuperDisk, or CD-ROM, among others) to your hard drive works a little differently. To do this task, click the disk's icon and while holding down the Option key, drag it onto the icon or window for the destination media (for example, your hard drive icon, your hard drive's open window, or onto any other folder icon or open folder window).

 If you don't hold down the Option key when you drag a disk icon to another icon, window, or disk volume, you get an alias of the disk instead of a copy of its contents. As you might expect, the alias will be worthless after you eject the disk.

When the copy is completed, a folder bearing the same name as the copied disk appears in the destination folder. The new folder now contains each and every file that was on the disk of the same name.

Surprise: Your PC Disks Work, Too!

One of the most excellent features of Mac OS X (if you have friends unfortunate enough not to own Macs and you want to share files with them) is that it reads both Mac- and DOS-formatted disks without any user intervention. *DOS disks* are formatted for use with personal computers (PCs) that run DOS or Windows. If a friend has a Windows computer, you can read his or her disks by just sticking them in your disk drive. Your unfortunate friend, on the other hand, can't do diddly squat with your Mac-formatted disks — yet another reason why Macs are better.

Although PC-formatted disks will work in your Mac, the files on them may or may not. If the files are documents, one of your Mac programs can probably open them. This applies also to other types of disks, including CD-ROMs, Zip, Jaz, Orb, and SyQuest.

But if the files are Windows programs (these often sport the *.exe* suffix, which stands for executable), your Mac won't be able to do anything with 'em without additional software.

That additional software is the almost magical *Virtual PC* from Microsoft (www.microsoft.com). This program emulates a Pentium-based PC on your Mac so that you can run genuine Microsoft Windows operating systems (Windows XP Professional or XP Home, Windows 2000, Windows Me, and Windows 98) on your Mac.

So with a copy of Virtual PC (around $200), your Mac *can* run those .exe files (and most Windows programs as well). Unfortunately, because emulating a Pentium processor and PC video card demands a lot from your Mac, it's slower than even a cheap PC. So although it's useful for most Windows applications (including Web browsers, which run remarkably well under Virtual PC), fast-moving games such as Doom, Quake, or Unreal Tournament, are mostly unplayable, which is a bummer. The Windows bundled solitaire game, on the other hand, works pretty well under Virtual PC.

Burning CDs and DVDs

Apple, or at least Steve Jobs, refers to the Macintosh as "your digital hub" and has been doing so since January 2001 at Macworld Expo (before Intel started touting the Pentium 4 as the "center of your digital world"). With Mac OS X (10.1 or later), this means that you can play, create, and publish audio and video. If your Mac is equipped with a CD-RW or SuperDrive, just insert a blank CD-R, CD-RW, DVD-R, or DVD-RW disc and you'll see the alert, as shown in Figure 9-1, that asks you what you want to do with the disk.

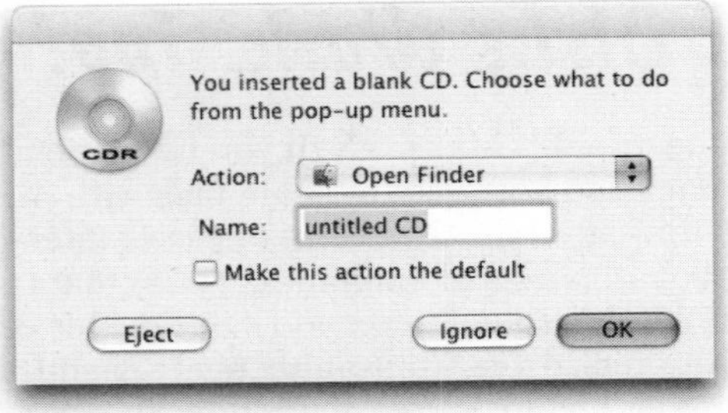

Figure 9-1:
Insert a
blank CD in
your CD-RW
drive and
get ready to
feel the
burn.

You inserted a blank CD. Choose what to do
from the pop-up menu.

Action: Open Finder

Name: untitled CD

Make this action the default

Eject   Ignore   OK

Name the disk and choose from the Action pop-up menu. The default choice is Open Finder, unless you've changed that default in the CDs & DVDs System Preference pane.

The other choices are Open iTunes and Open Other Application... If you choose the first, iTunes automatically opens when you insert a blank CD; if you choose the second, you are first presented with an Open File sheet where you can select the application you want to open; then the application itself opens. If you want to make this action the default so it occurs the next time you insert a blank disk (and every time thereafter), click the Make This Action the Default check box.

Let's go with Open Finder for now, though. So click the OK button, and your blank CD mounts on the Desktop just like any other removable disk but with a distinctive icon telling you that it's a recordable CD (or DVD), as shown in Figure 9-2. From that point on, just copy files onto it until you have it the way you want it. When you're ready to create your CD, start to drag the icon, and the Trash will turn into a Burn button (looks like the warning for radioactivity to me), as shown in Figure 9-3.

Figure 9-2:
Recordable optical discs get a distinctive, labeled icon.

Figure 9-3:
Just drag the disk icon to the Burn Disc button on the Dock when you're ready to burn your CD.

Alternatively, you could Control+click the disk's icon and choose Burn Disc (yes, Apple spells it with a *c*) from the contextual menu or select the icon and choose Burn Disc from the File menu (see Figure 9-4). If you choose Eject, either from the contextual menu or from the File menu, you'll be asked whether you want to burn the disk first.

Figure 9-4:
Two more
ways to
burn a disk.

MP3 players play files in the order that they're written, which will be alphabetically. So, if you want them to play in a particular order, be sure to name them with sequential numbers at the beginning. Fortunately, iTunes makes that easy with the Create File Names with Track Number option in your Importing preferences.

After you've chosen to burn a disk, you see the dialog box shown in Figure 9-5. Choose a speed from the Burn Speed pop-up menu; then click the Burn button, and you're done.

I always choose Maximum for the speed. If a burn fails for any reason, I will then try a slower burn speed. But that rarely happens.

Figure 9-5:
The last
step before
the burning
begins.

Getting Disks out of Your Mac

You now know almost everything there is to know about disks except one important thing: how to eject a disk. Piece of cake, actually. Here are several ways, all simple to remember:

- ✔ Click the disk's icon to select it, and then choose File➪Eject (or use the keyboard shortcut ⌘+E).

- ✔ Drag the disk's icon to the Trash. You'll notice that when you drag a disk's icon, the Trash icon in the Dock changes into an Eject icon, like that shown in the left margin here.

  The preceding method of ejecting a disk is something that used to drive me (and many others) crazy before Mac OS X. In the olden days, the Trash icon didn't change into an Eject icon. And this confused many new users, who then asked me the same question (over and over and over): "But doesn't dragging something to the Trash erase it from your disk?"

- ✔ Click the disk icon while holding down the Control key and then choose Eject from the contextual menu.

There's one more way if you like little menus on the right side of your menu bar, as shown in Figure 9-6.

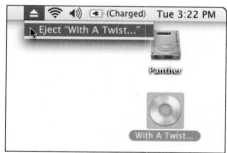

Figure 9-6:
The last
step before
the burning
begins.

To install your own Eject menu, navigate to System/Library/CoreServices/MenuExtras and then open (double-click) the Eject.menu icon. Your Eject menu will appear on the right side of your menu bar.

There are 17 other handy menus in the MenuExtras folder and they're all installed the same way — just double-click 'em. You can see a few of mine in Figure 9-6; from left to right are my AirPort, Battery, and Clock menus.

To move a menu extra after it's installed on your menu bar, hold down ⌘, click the menu, then drag left or right.

To remove a menu extra, hold down ⌘ and drag the menu off the menu bar and onto the desktop as shown in Figure 9-7. It disappears with a little poof.

Figure 9-7:
⌘+click and
drag, and
poof — the
Eject menu
is gone for
good.

Chapter 10

File Management without Tearing Your Hair Out

*I*n other parts of this book, you can discover the basics about windows and icons and menus. Here, you begin a never-ending quest to discover the fastest, easiest, and most trouble-free way to manage the files on your Mac. And, along the way, you'll discover what some of the special folders (most notably the multiple Library folders) in Mac OS X are all about.

I've been wrangling with Macintosh files and folders for more than 15 years now, and I've learned a lot about what works and what doesn't — for *me*.

And although Mac OS X is very different from earlier versions of Mac OS, the fundamentals of organizing files and folders haven't changed that much. So this chapter spares you at least part of my 15-year learning curve.

One thing I'll stress throughout this chapter is that what works for one user may not work for another. So I encourage you to develop your own personal style. I don't preach (much) about the right way to organize your files. After you've read this chapter, you'll have all the ammunition that you need to organize your files into a Mac environment designed by you, for you.

I won't pretend to be able to organize your Mac for you. Organizing your files is as personal as your taste in music. You develop your own style with the Mac. So in this section, I give you some food for thought: some ideas about how I do it as well as some suggestions that should make organization easier for you, regardless of how you choose to do it yourself.

Working with Files and Folders

Before I go any further, you first need to understand a bit about files and folders: the difference between a file and a folder, how you can arrange and move files and folders around, and how to nest folders. Then you can concentrate on becoming a savvier — and better organized — Mac OS X user.

Then, after I discuss *your* files and folders, I offer more about the folders that Mac OS X creates (and requires). In other words, by the end of this chapter, you'll not only know all about *your* files and folders, you'll also know about the files and folders that Mac OS X creates when you install it and what they do.

Files versus folders

When I speak of a *file*, I'm talking about any icon except a folder or disk icon. A file can be a document, an application, an alias of a file or application, a dictionary, a font, or any other icon that *isn't* a folder or disk. The main distinction is that you can't put something *into* a file icon.

When I talk about *folders*, I'm talking about, well, folders. They look like folders and they can contain files or other folders (*subfolders*). You can put any icon — any file or folder — into a folder.

Here's an exception: If you put a disk icon into a folder, you get an alias to the disk (as I explain in Chapter 9) unless you hold down the Option key. Remember that you can't put a disk icon into a folder on itself. In other words, you can only copy a disk icon to a different disk. Or, put another way, you can never copy a disk icon into a folder that resides on that disk.

Finally, *disks* are nothing more than big folders. A disk icon is, for all intents and purposes, the same as a folder icon. (Look in the margin to see a typical folder icon.)

File icons can look like practically anything. If the icon doesn't look like a folder or one of the numerous disk icons, you can be pretty sure that it's a file.

Creating new folders

So you think that Apple has already given you enough folders? Can't imagine why you'd need more? Think of creating new folders the same way that you'd think of labeling a new folder at work for a specific project. New folders help you keep your files organized, enabling you to reorganize them just the way you want. Creating folders is really quite simple.

To create a new folder, just follow these steps:

1. **Decide which window you want the new folder to appear in and then make sure that the window is active; or, if you want to create a new folder right on the Desktop, make sure that no windows are open or active.**

   You can make a window active by clicking it, and you can make the Desktop active if you have windows onscreen by clicking the Desktop itself.

2. **Choose File⇨New Folder (or press ⌘+Shift+N).**

   A new, untitled folder appears in the active window with its name box already highlighted, ready for you to type a new name for it.

3. **Type a name for your folder.**

   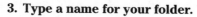

   If you accidentally click anywhere before you type a name for the folder, the name box will no longer be highlighted. To highlight it again, select the icon (single-click it) and then press Return once. Now you can type its new name.

   Name your folders with relevant names. Folders with nebulous titles like sfdghb or Stuff — or worst of all, Untitled — won't make it any easier to find something six months from now.

   For maximum compatibility with other users and other operating systems, avoid using punctuation marks in file and folder names. Periods, slashes, backslashes, and colons, in particular, can be reserved for use by other operating system.

   So while Panther will let you use almost any character except a period (as the first character) or a colon (anywhere in the name), it's a good idea to avoid using any punctuation marks in your folder or file names.

   While we're on the subject, it's not a good idea to use characters you have to hold down the Option key to type in file or folder names. I'm talking about ones like: ™ (Option+2), ® (Option+r) ¢ (Option+4) or even © (Option+g). So get in the habit of not using those, either.

   So, for files you might share with users of non-Macintosh computers, no punctuation and no Option key characters for maximum compatibility.

Navigating Nested Folders

Folders within other folders are often called *nested folders*. To get a feel for the way nested folders work in Mac OS X, check out Figure 10-1. You can see the following from the figure:

- Folder 1 is one level deep.
- Folder 2 is inside Folder 1, which is one level deeper than Folder 1, or two levels deep.
- Folder 3 is inside Folder 2 and is three levels deep.
- The files inside Folder 3 are four levels deep.

If the previous list makes sense to you, you're golden. What's important here is that you are able to visualize the path to Folder 3. That is, to get to files inside Folder 3, you open Folder 1 and then open Folder 2 to be able to open Folder 3. Understanding this concept is important to understanding the relationships between files and folders. Keep reviewing this section and eventually the concept will click — you'll slap yourself in the head and say, "Now I get it!"

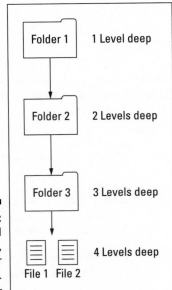

Folder 1   1 Level deep

Folder 2   2 Levels deep

Folder 3   3 Levels deep

File 1 File 2   4 Levels deep

Figure 10-1:
Nested
folders,
going four
levels deep.

Moving files and folders

You can move files and folders around within a window to your heart's content as long as that window is set to the Icon view. Just click and drag any icon to its new location in the window.

Some people spend hours arranging icons in a window so that they're just so. But because using Icon view wastes so much screen space, I avoid using icons in a window.

You can't move icons around in a window that's viewed as a list or as columns, which makes total sense when you think about it. Well, you can move them to put them in a different folder in List or Column view, but that's not moving them around, really.

As you may expect from Apple, the King of Having Lots of Ways to Do Anything, you have choices for how you move one file of folder into another folder. You can use these techniques to move any icon — folder, document, alias, or program icon — into folders or onto other disks.

✔ **Drag an icon onto a folder icon:** Drag the icon for one folder (or file) onto the icon for another folder (or disk) and then release when the second folder is highlighted (see Figure 10-2). The first folder is now inside the second folder. Put another way, the first folder is now a sub-folder of the second folder.

This technique works regardless of whether the second folder's window is open.

✔ **Drag an icon into an open folder's window:** Drag the icon for one folder (or file) into the open window for a second folder (or disk), as shown in Figure 10-3.

One Folder

One Folder

Another

Figure 10-2:
Placing one
folder into
another.

Figure 10-3:
You can also
move a file
or folder by
dragging
it into
the open
window of
another
folder.

If you try to move an item from one disk to another disk, it's only copied — not moved. If you want to *move* a file or folder from one disk to another, you have to trash the original manually after the copying is complete.

That is, unless you're using Mac OS X version 10.1 or later. If so, there's a great new trick: If you hold down the ⌘ key when you drag an icon from one disk to another, it's moved instead of copied, and the original is deleted automatically. The little Copying Files window even changes to read Moving Files. Nice touch, eh?

Copying files or folders

What if you want to *copy* an icon from one place to another, leaving the icon in its original location and creating an identical copy in the destination window? No problem — all it takes is the addition of the Option key.

If you're wondering why anyone would ever want to do that, trust me: Someday you will. Suppose that you have a file called *Long Letter to Mom* in a folder called Old Correspondence. You figure that Mom has forgotten that letter by now, and you want to send it again. But before you do, you want to change the date and delete the reference to Clarence, her pit bull, who passed away last year. So now you need to put a copy of Long Letter to Mom in your Current Correspondence folder.

Read about how to make a copy of a file by using Save As in Chapter 8. This technique yields the same result.

When you copy a file, it's wise to change the name of the copied file. Having more than one file on your hard drive with the same name is not a good idea, even if the files are in different folders. Trust me, having 10 files called Expense Report or 15 files named Randall's Invoice can be confusing, no matter how well-organized your folder structure is. Add distinguishing words or dates to file and folder names so that they're named something more explicit, such as Expense Report 10-03 or Randall's Invoice 10-30-03.

You have four ways to copy a file or folder, as follows:

✔ **Drag an icon from one folder icon onto another folder icon while holding down the Option key.**

Drag the icon for one folder onto the icon for another folder and then release when the second folder is highlighted (refer to Figure 10-2). This technique works regardless of whether the second folder's window is open.

When you copy something by dragging and dropping it with the Option key held down, the mouse pointer changes so that it includes a little plus sign (+) next to the arrow as shown in the margin. Neat!

✔ **Drag an icon into an open window for another folder while holding down the Option key.**

Drag the icon for the file or folder that you want to copy into the open window for a second folder (or removable media, such as a floppy disk), as shown in Figure 10-3.

✔ **Copy an icon and paste it in another folder's window.**

Introduced to the Mac with the OS X 10.1 release, you can now click an icon, choose Edit⇨Copy (or press ⌘+C), click where you want the icon to go, and then choose Edit⇨Paste (or press ⌘+V) — it's done.

✔ **Choose File⇨Duplicate or Control+click the file or folder that you want to duplicate and then select Duplicate from the contextual menu that appears.**

For more about the Duplicate command, check out Chapter 6.

You can have lots of files with the same name *on the same disk* (although, as I mentioned earlier, it's probably not a good idea). But your Mac won't let you have more than one file with the same name *in the same folder*.

Everything that I've discussed so far in this chapter works at least as well for windows using the List or Column views as it does for windows using the Icon view. (You gotta love those disclosure triangles in the List view! I sure do.) In other words, I only used the Icon view in the previous examples because it's the best view to show you what's going on. For what it's worth, I find moving and copying files easiest in windows when using the List view.

Opening files with drag-and-drop

Macintosh drag-and-drop is usually all about dragging text and graphics from one place to another. But there's another angle to drag-and-drop — one that has to do with files and icons. I tell you the real deal in this section.

You can open a document by dragging its icon onto the proper application. In other words, you can open a document that you created with Microsoft Word by dragging the document icon onto the Microsoft Word application's icon. The Word icon will highlight, and the document will launch. Of course, it's usually easier to just double-click a document's icon to open it. The proper application opens automatically when you do. Or at least it does most of the time. This brings me to why I'm explaining this drag-and-drop thing here.

If you try to open a file and Mac OS X can't find a program to open the file, Mac OS X prompts you with an error window, as shown in Figure 10-4. You can either click OK (and abort the attempt to open the file) or pick another application to open it.

Figure 10-4:
Oops! Mac helps you find the correct application.

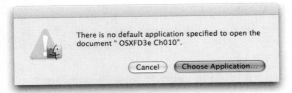

There is no default application specified to open the document " OSXFD3e Ch010".

Cancel   Choose Application...

Of course, you can click the Choose Application button and pick another program from a regular Open File dialog (see Chapter 8 for details). If you click the Choose Application button, a dialog appears (conveniently opened to your Applications folder, and shown in Figure 10-5). Applications that you can't use to open the file are dimmed. For a wider choice of applications, choose to view All Applications instead of Recommended Applications from the Show pop-up menu.

Here is a better way: Use drag-and-drop to open a file using a program other than the one that would ordinarily launch when you open the document. To do so, just drag the file onto the application's icon (or alias icon or Dock icon), and presto — the file opens in the application.

If the icon doesn't highlight and you release the mouse button anyway, the document will be dropped into the folder that contains the application (with the icon that didn't highlight.)

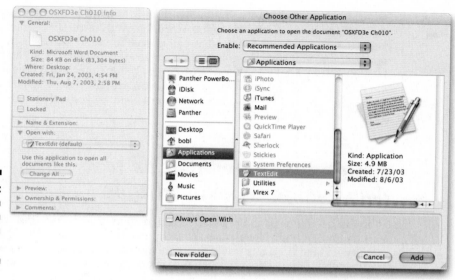

Figure 10-5:
Choose an
application
to open
a file.

If that happens, don't forget that the OS X Finder, unlike previous Finders, offers Undo. This is a case where it's a godsend. Just choose Edit⇨Undo (or press ⌘+Z), and the mislaid document magically returns to where it was before you dropped it. Just remember — you can't do anything else after dropping the file, or Undo may not work.

You can't open every file with every program. For example, if you try to open an MP3 (music) file with Microsoft Excel (a spreadsheet), it just won't work — you'll get an error message or a screen full of gibberish. Sometimes you just have to keep trying until you find the right program; other times, you won't have a program capable of opening the file.

Only applications that *might* be able to open the file will highlight when you drag the document on them. That doesn't mean the document will be usable, just that the application *can* open it.

Suffice it to say that Mac OS X is smart enough to figure out which applications on your hard drive can open what documents and to also offer you a choice.

You're usually best off clicking the Choose Application button and sticking to the Recommended Applications choice in the Choose Application dialog. But if that doesn't work for you, at least you now know another way — drag the file onto an application's icon and see what happens.

I don't know if you noticed, but in Figure 10-5, Mac OS X is recommending I use TextEdit to open this Microsoft Word file. And for the first time, Apple is giving users a word processor that can open Microsoft Word files, view them, modify them, and save them again. Why does this make me rant and rave? Because if they could do it now, why couldn't they have done it years ago? If you don't own a copy of Microsoft Word, you probably know what I mean — documents created by Word have for years been notoriously difficult to open without a copy of Microsoft Word.

Assigning an application to a document or document type

I don't know about you, but people send me files all the time that were created by applications I don't use . . . or at least that I don't use for that document type. Mac OS X lets you specify the application in which you want to open a document in the future when you double-click it. More than that, you can specify that you want all documents of that type to open with the specified application. "Where is this magic bullet hidden?" you ask. Right there in the file's Get Info window.

Suppose, for example, that you want all graphic files that default to opening in Preview JPEG to open with GraphicConverter (one of my favorite pieces of OS X-savvy shareware) instead. Just click one of these files in the Finder and then choose File➪Get Info (⌘+I). In the Info window, click the gray triangle next to disclose the Open With pane, as shown in Figure 10-6.

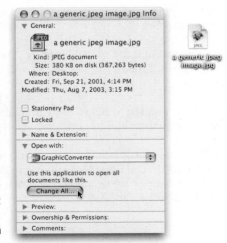

Figure 10-6:
Set a default application for this document or document type here.

Click and hold where it says GraphicConverter in Figure 10-6, and a pop-up menu appears offering the applications that Mac OS X believes will open this document type. Choose one (in Figure 10-6, I've already chosen GraphicConverter).

Now, GraphicConverter will open when you double-click this particular document; however, if you click the Change All button at the bottom of the window, as I've done in Figure 10-6, you'll make GraphicConverter the default application for all .jpg documents owned by Preview.

Organizing your stuff with subfolders

As I mention earlier in this chapter, you can put folders inside other folders to organize your icons. I call a folder that's inside another folder a *subfolder*.

Create subfolders based on a system that makes sense to you. Here are some organizational topic ideas and naming examples for subfolders:

- ✔ **By type of document:** Word-Processing Documents, Spreadsheet Documents, Graphics Documents
- ✔ **By date:** Documents May–June, Documents Spring '03
- ✔ **By content:** Memos, Outgoing Letters, Expense Reports
- ✔ **By project:** Project X, Project Y, Project Z

When you notice your folders swelling and starting to get messy (that is, becoming filled with tons of files), subdivide them again by using a combination of these methods that makes sense to you. For example, suppose that you start by subdividing your Documents folder into multiple subfolders, as shown in Figure 10-7. Later, when those folders begin to get full, you may subdivide them even further, as shown in Figure 10-8.

My point (yes, I do have one!): Allow your folder structure to be organic, growing as you need it to grow. Let it happen. Don't let any one folder get so full that it's a hassle to deal with. Create new subfolders when things start to get crowded.

If you want to monkey around with some subfolders yourself, a good place to start is the Documents folder — it's inside your home folder (that is, it's a *subfolder* of your home folder). I'll start your look at getting organized here.

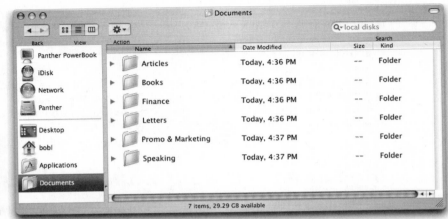

Figure 10-7:
Organize a folder with subfolders.

If you use a particular folder a great deal, make an alias of it and then move the alias from the Documents folder to the Dock, your home folder, or to your Desktop (for more info on aliases, see Chapter 4) to make the folder easier to access. For example, if you write a lot of letters, you could keep an alias to your Correspondence folder in your home folder, in the Dock, or on your Desktop for quick access. (By the way, there's no reason you can't have a folder appear in all three places if you like. That's what aliases are all about, aren't they?)

If you put the Documents folder in the Dock, you can click and hold on it (or Control-click) to reveal its subfolders, as shown in Figure 10-9.

Spring-loaded folders

Spring-loaded folders have been resurrected in Mac OS X version 10.2 Jaguar, and they work in all views and with all folder or disk icons in the sidebar. Because you just got the short course on folders and subfolders and various ways to organize your stuff, you're ready for your introduction to one of my favorite ways to get around my disks, folders, and subfolders.

Here's how they work: Select any icon except a disk icon and drag it onto any folder or disk icon but don't release the mouse button. The folder or disk icon will highlight to indicate that it's selected.

I call this *hovering* because you're doing just that — hovering the cursor over a folder or disk icon.

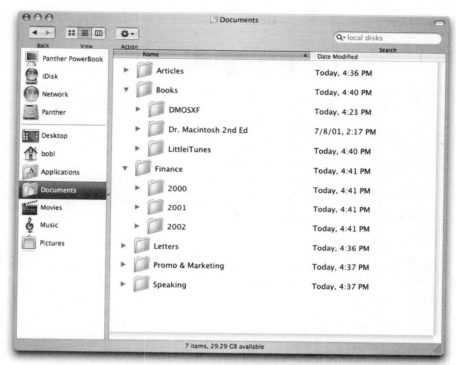

Figure 10-8:
Further
subdivide a
growing
folder.

In a second or two, the highlighted folder or disk will flash once or twice and then spring open right under the cursor.

You can continue to traverse your folder structure this way until you release the mouse button. When you do, the icon that you've been dragging will be dropped into the active folder at the time. That window will remain open but all the windows that you traversed will close.

Figure 10-9:
It's super
convenient
to have your
Documents
folder in
the Dock.

Creating subfolders . . . or not

How full is too full? When should you begin creating subfolders in a folder? That's impossible to say, but having too many items in a folder can be a nightmare, as can having too many subfolders with just one or two files in them. My guideline is this: If you find more than 15 or 20 files in a single folder, begin thinking about ways to subdivide it.

On the other hand, some of my bigger subfolders contain things that I don't often access. For example, my Bob's Correspondence 1992 folder contains more than 100 files. But because I want to keep this folder on my hard drive just in case I do need to find something there — even though I don't use it very often — it's overcrowded condition doesn't bother me. Your mileage may vary.

Here are some tips to help you decide whether to use subfolders or just leave well enough alone:

✔ **Don't create subfolders until you need them.** In other words, don't create a bunch of empty folders because you think that you may need them someday. Wait to create new folders until you need them to prevent opening an empty folder when you're looking for something else — a complete waste of time.

✔ **Let your work style decide the file structure.** When you first start working with your Mac, you may want to save everything in your Documents folder for a week or two (or a month or two, depending on how many new documents that you save each day). After a decent-sized group of documents accumulates in the Documents folder, at that point consider taking a look at them and creating logical subfolders for them.

You can toggle spring-loaded folders on or off in the Finder's Preference window. There's also a setting for how long the Finder waits before it springs open these spring-loaded folders. If you're impatient, you can spring a folder open instantly by pressing the Space bar as you hover your mouse over it.

Finally, to cancel a spring-loaded folder, drag the cursor away from the folder icon or outside the boundaries of the sprung window — the folder will pop shut.

After you get used to them, you'll wonder how you ever got along without them. They work in all three window views, and they work with icons in the sidebar. Give 'em a try and you'll be hooked.

Getting Up to Speed with the Mac OS X Folder Structure

In addition to your personal files and folders, your Mac OS X system has its own folder structure. These folders contain the system software that runs the

Mac, as well as folders that include system preferences, fonts, and other files that are used by everyone with access to this Mac. These shared files include applications, programs, utilities, and other software.

Also, each person who uses the Mac has his or her own set of folders that contain documents, preferences, and other information that's used by only that person. If you're the sole person who accesses your Mac, you have only one user. Regardless, the folder structure that Mac OS X uses is the same, whether you have one user or ten.

I realize that a lot of people don't share their Macs with others. And if you're one of these folks, you may wonder why I keep mentioning sharing and multiple users and the like. Well, Mac OS X is based on the UNIX operating system, which is a multi-user operating system that's used by high-end servers and workstations that are often shared by several people. Mac OS X has both the benefit of this arrangement and a bit of the confusion caused when a single user like you fires up a computer that could be set up for several people. That's why Mac OS X folders are organized the way that they are — with different hierarchies for each user and for the computer as a whole.

All these files are stored in a nested folder structure that's a bit tricky to understand at first. This structure makes more sense after you spend a little time with it and learn some basic concepts.

In this section, I walk you through these different folder structures one by one, starting with the place where you'll spend most of your time — your home folder.

The Mac OS X folder structure in depth

I start with the Computer folder, which is the top level of the folder hierarchy. The Computer folder shows all the storage devices (hard drives, CD- or DVD-ROM, Zip disk, and so forth) that are currently connected to your Mac. Figure 10-10 shows a hard disk and a Network icon, with which you can access servers or shared Macs on your network. (Don't quite know what file sharing is all about? Read Chapter 16 for the whole scoop on sharing files with other Macs and sharing your Mac with other users.

The computer name, Panther PowerBook in Figure 10-10, can be changed in the Sharing System Preference pane.

To find the Computer folder, use the keyboard shortcut ⌘+Shift+C or click its icon in the sidebar of any Finder window.

Figure 10-10:
Contents
of the
Computer
folder.

You may have more or fewer icons in your Computer folder than the two that you see in Figure 10-10 (depending upon how many disks that you have mounted), but I'm going to drill down on the one that holds your Mac OS X stuff. In Figure 10-10, that hard drive is called *Panther* — of course, I have no idea what yours is called; if you haven't changed it, it's probably called *Macintosh HD*. Double-click that icon to open it.

Inside your boot disk icon (the one with OS X installed on it; the one called *Panther* in Figure 10-10) is everything on that disk. You should see at least four folders (unless you've added some — if you installed the Developer Tools CD, for example, or an OS 9 System Folder, you'll have more). I'll go through each of them for you.

Applications

The Applications folder, located at the root level of your boot drive (the one with OS X installed on it), is accessible with a click of the Application button on the sidebar, from the Go menu, or by using the keyboard shortcut ⌘+Shift+A. In this folder, you find all the applications that Apple includes with Mac OS X. All users of a given Mac have access to the items in this Applications folder. Read more about the Applications folder in Chapter 13 and more about the sidebar in Chapter 6.

Library

The Library folder at the root level of your Mac OS X hard drive is like a public library because it stores items that everyone with access to this Mac can use. You'll find two different library folders on your hard drive — the one at the root level of your OS X disk and another in your home folder.

Okay, I wasn't entirely truthful but only for your own good: There's actually a third Library folder inside the System folder, which I discuss in a page or two. But for now, heed this warning: **Leave this folder alone** — don't move, remove, or rename it or anything within it. It's the nerve center of your Mac. In other words, you should never have to touch this third Library folder.

Think of the Library folder inside your home folder like a library in your own house (have you ever actually been in a house with its own library?) and the one at root level as a public library. I talk more about these Library folders in the upcoming sections.

You find a bunch of folders inside the Library folder at root level (the public Library folder). Most of them contain files that you never need to open, move, or delete. (For what it's worth, just about all of them are preferences of one kind or another.)

The Library folder that most users will work with is the Fonts folder, which houses all the fonts installed on the Mac. Fonts can either be available to everyone who uses the Mac (stored here) or only to a single user (stored in that user's Library folder, the one in their home folder). I discuss fonts more in Chapter 12. Some other subfolders that you may use or add to are the Internet Search Sites folder (where you put Sherlock plug-ins), the Printers folder (where you install new printer drivers), the Scripts folder (which houses AppleScripts accessible to all users), and Desktop Pictures (where you can place pictures to be used for Desktop pictures).

Leave the Library folder pretty much alone unless you're using the Fonts folder or know what you're adding to one of the other folders. Don't remove, rename, or move any files or folders. Mac OS X uses these items and is very picky about where they're kept and how they're named.

Note: Under most circumstances, you won't actually add or remove items from folders in this Library yourself. Software installers do the heavy lifting for you by placing all their little pieces into appropriate Library folders. You shouldn't need to touch this Library often, if ever. That said, knowing what these folders are and who can access their contents may come in handy down the road a-piece.

If you want to add something to a Library, it's usually best to add it to your Home/Library.

Mac OS 9

If you have Mac OS 9.2.2 installed on the same disk as OS X, this folder contains your Mac OS 9.2.2 System folder (which the Classic environment requires) as well as the System Disk program (which enables you to choose to boot your Mac from Mac OS 9.2.2 or OS X).

You can read more about Classic in Chapter 14.

System

The System folder includes the files that Mac OS X needs to start up and keep working. **Leave this folder alone** — don't move, remove, or rename it or anything within it. It's a part of the nerve center of your Mac.

If you've used any previous version of Mac OS, you should notice two things:

- ✔ The System folder doesn't include the same items or the same arrangement of files and folders.

✔ This folder is now simply called System rather than System Folder.

Also gone are the System file and Finder file that have been around since the first Mac. Located here instead are a large number of files that make up the Mac OS X system.

Users

When you open the Users folder, you see a folder for each person who uses the Mac as well as the Shared folder.

In the next section, I drill down from the home folder bob1 to see what's inside. If user bob1 logs onto this Mac using his username, his home folder (bob1) opens when he clicks the Home button.

The Shared folder that you see in the Users folder allows everyone who uses the Mac to use the files stored there. If you want other people who use your Mac to have access to a file or folder, this is the place to stash it.

Enough with the big picture folder structure! Read on as I dig into how to work with the folders and files in Mac OS X.

There's no place like home

Your home folder is the most important folder to you as a user — or at least the one where you'll probably spend most of your time — but it's only part of Mac's higher-level folder structure. I walk you through this configuration so that you understand where your home folder fits in and so that you'll be able to find applications and other items shared by everyone who uses your Mac. It's kind of complicated, especially if you're an old-time Mac user who's used to arranging things pretty much the way you want. Take heart, though: After you get the hang of the new way of arranging things, it makes sense.

I strongly recommend that you store all the files that you create or work with in one of the folders of your home folder, whether in the Documents folder or in another folder that you create. The advantage of using the Documents folder is that you can quickly locate the folder from the Go menu or with the keyboard shortcut ⌘+Shift+H — *H* for *home*, of course.

When you open your home folder, you see a Finder window with your username in the title bar. (I discuss this name in Chapter 15.) Seeing your username in the Finder window's title bar tells you that you're in your home folder. Every user has a home folder named after their short username in the Users folder. In Figure 10-11, you can see that my home folder is named bob1 — the short name I used when I first set up my Mac.

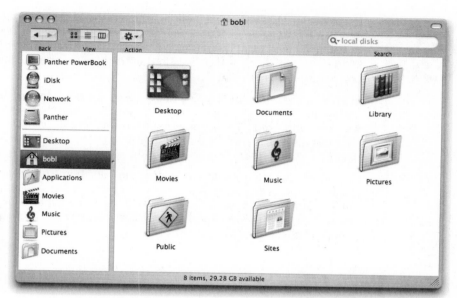

Figure 10-11:
My home
folder.

Your home folder has several folders inside it created by Mac OS X. You can create more if you like — in fact, every folder that you *ever* create (at least every one that you create on this particular disk or volume) should be within your home folder. I'll explain this as I describe the other main folders on your hard drive.

Your home folder contains eight folders by default. The following four are the most important ones:

- **Desktop:** If you put items (files, folders, applications, or aliases) on the Desktop, they appear on the Desktop. The files themselves, however, are actually stored in this folder.

- **Documents:** This is the place to put all the documents (letters, spreadsheets, recipes, and novels) that you create. For more on the Documents folder, check out Chapter 8.

- **Library:** Preferences (files containing the settings that you create in System Preferences and other places) are stored in the Library folder, along with fonts (ones that are only available to you, as described previously in this chapter), links to your favorite items, Internet search sites, and other stuff used by you and only you.

- **Public:** If you share your Mac, you can't work inside other users' folders. But you can share files with others by storing them in the Public folder of your home folder. (Read more about Public folders in Chapter 16.)

If you decide that you don't want an item on the Desktop anymore, delete it by dragging its icon from the Desktop folder to the Trash or by dragging its icon from the Desktop itself to the Trash. Both techniques yield the same effect — the file is in the Trash, where it remains until you empty the Trash.

In previous versions of Mac OS, there was no Desktop folder. Items stored on the Desktop appeared on the Desktop, and that same Desktop was seen and used by everyone that used this Mac. In Mac OS X, each user has his or her own Desktop, and the items there are stored in the user's Desktop folder.

✔ The other four folders that you may see in your home folder are Movies, Music, Pictures, and Sites. All these folders except Sites are empty until you put something in them; Sites contains a few files that your Mac needs if you enable Web Sharing (in the Sharing System Preferences pane, as I describe in Chapter 15).

Your Library card

The Library subfolder of your home folder is the repository of everything that Mac OS X needs to customize your Mac to your tastes. You won't spend much time (if any) adding things to the Library folder or moving them around within it, but it's a good idea for you to know what's in there. In the "Library" section earlier in this chapter, I discuss the Library folder that's used to specify preferences for the Mac as a whole. But *this* Library folder is all about you and your stuff.

Be cautious with the Library folder because OS X is very persnickety about how its folders and files are organized. As I discuss in the "Library" section earlier in the chapter, you can add and remove items safely from most Library folders, but **leave the folders themselves alone.** If you remove or rename the wrong folder, you could render OS X inoperable. It's like the old joke about the guy who said to the doctor, "It hurts when I do that," and the doctor replies, "Then don't do that."

To find the Library folder, click the Home icon in the sidebar of any Finder window and then open the Library folder. You should see several folders there. The exact number of folders in the Library folder depends on the software that you install on your Mac — for example, if you have an e-mail account, you should see a folder called Addresses (if not, it won't be there). Some of the more important standard folders in the Library folder include the following:

✔ **Documentation:** Where some applications store their Help files. Others store theirs in the main root level public Library folder.

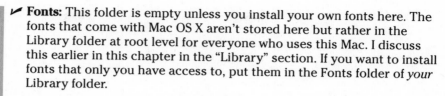

✔ **Fonts:** This folder is empty unless you install your own fonts here. The fonts that come with Mac OS X aren't stored here but rather in the Library folder at root level for everyone who uses this Mac. I discuss this earlier in this chapter in the "Library" section. If you want to install fonts that only you have access to, put them in the Fonts folder of *your* Library folder.

To install a font, drag its icon to this folder. It will only be available when you're logged in; other users won't be able to use a font stored here. To install a font that's available to anyone who uses this Mac, drag it into the Fonts folder in the public Library folder, the one at root level that you see when you open your hard disk's icon.

If your Mac is set up for multiple users, only users with Administrator (admin) privileges can put stuff into the public Library folder. (For more information on admin privileges, check out Chapter 16.)

✔ **Preferences:** The files here hold the information about things that you customize in Mac OS X. Whenever you change a system or application preference, that info is saved to a file in the Preferences folder.

Don't mess with the Preferences folder! You should never need to open or use this folder unless something bad happens — like you suspect that a particular preference file has become corrupted (that is, damaged). My advice is to just forget about this folder and let it do its job.

Part III
Doing Stuff with Your Mac

The 5th Wave   By Rich Tennant

"Brad! That's not your modem we're hearing! It's Buddy!! He's out of his cage and in the iMac!!"

In this part . . .

Moving right along, Part III comprises how to do stuff with your Mac. In this section, it's off to the Internet first — how to get it working and what to do with it after you do. Next, I help you decipher the myriad Print options to better help you become a modern-day Gutenberg. You'll also learn about the applications that come with OS X, the Classic Environment, and how to make your OS X look and feel the way you want it.

It's an excellent section if I do say so myself . . . one you definitely don't want to miss.

Chapter 11

Internet-Working

· ·

· ·

*S*imply put, use the Internet to connect your Mac to a wealth of information residing on computers around the world. Lucky for you, Mac OS X has the best and most comprehensive Internet tools ever shipped with a Mac operating system. In this chapter, I cover the top two: the *World Wide Web* (that's the *www* you see so often in Internet addresses) and *e-mail* (which stands for *electronic mail*). Okay, with Apple's release of iChat AV, I'm adding a third one: *live chatting*.

A Brief Internet Overview

The *Internet,* which is a giant conglomeration of connected computers, offers innumerable types of services. Sometimes referred to as the *Information Superhighway,* the Internet is a giant worldwide network of computers. With an Internet connection, you can view text and graphics on your computer, even if the text and graphics are sitting on a computer in Tokyo. Via the Internet, you can send and retrieve messages and computer files to and from almost anywhere in the world — in milliseconds.

Other Internet services include bulletin board discussions called *newsgroups,* File Transfer Protocol (FTP), and video conferencing. After you have your connection set up (I discuss this process in the "Setting Up for Surfing" section later in this chapter), I urge you to check out these nifty features. Unfortunately, although these other features are pretty cool, going into much detail about them is also beyond the purview of this book.

The most interesting part of the Internet, at least in my humble opinion, is the Web. This is the part of the Internet in which you traverse (that is, surf) to Web sites and view them on your computer with software called a *Web browser.*

Mac OS X offers built-in Internet connectivity right out of the box. For example, your machine comes with:

- ✔ Its own built-in **Point-to-Point Protocol** (PPP) client for making modem connections to the Internet

    If you don't even know what a modem is, don't worry. Skip ahead to the upcoming section "Setting Up for Surfing," and all will become clear.

- ✔ Apple **Safari** and Microsoft **Internet Explorer** (your choice of Web browsers with which you to navigate the Web, download remote files via FTP, and more)

- ✔ The **Mail** application (for e-mail)

- ✔ **iChat AV** (Apple's live online chatting client that works with other iChat users and people using AOL Instant Messaging [AIM] clients)

Because most Mac users like things to be easy, Mac OS X includes a cool feature in its Setup Assistant to help you find and configure an account with an Internet Service Provider (ISP). After your Internet connection is up and running, you can use Safari or Internet Explorer, which are both included with OS X Panther, to cruise the Internet.

But before I can talk about browsers, e-mail software, and chatting, I first have to help you configure your Internet connection. When you're finished, you can play with your browsers and the Mail application to your heart's content.

Setting Up for Surfing

Before you can surf the Internet, you need to do a few things first. In this section, I walk you through them all.

If you're a typical home user, you need three things to surf the Internet:

- ✔ A modem or other connection to the Internet, such as Digital Subscriber Line (DSL), cable modem, Integrated Services Digital Network (ISDN), or satellite Internet service

    If you use technology other than a regular (analog) modem, DSL, or cable modem to connect your computer to the Internet, your network administrator (the person who you run to at work when something goes wrong with your computer) or ISP will have to help you set up your Mac because setting up those other configurations is beyond the scope of this book.

> ✔ An account with an ISP (an Internet Service Provider such as EarthLink or RoadRunner) or America Online (AOL)
>
> ✔ Mac OS X default installation

It starts with the modem

A *modem* is a small, inexpensive device that turns data (that is, computer files) into sounds and then squirts those sounds across phone lines. At the other end, another modem receives these sounds and turns them back into data (that is, your files). All current Macs include an internal 56 Kbps modem.

Now plug a phone line into the modem. On Macs with internal modems, that simply means plugging one end of the phone cable into the phone plug-shaped port on the side or back of your Mac and the other end into a live phone outlet (or the phone jack on a surge suppressor that has a phone line running to your phone outlet). If you have an external modem, plug the phone cable into the modem and plug the modem cable into a USB port. Finally, plug the modem into an AC power source if it requires AC power (some don't because they obtain power from your Mac's USB port).

 The modem port on Macs with internal modems looks a lot like the Ethernet port, but it's smaller. You could plug a phone cable into the Ethernet port, but it wouldn't fit right and it wouldn't get you connected to the Internet. The modem port is the smaller of the two — look for the phone icon next to it. Conversely, the Ethernet port is the larger of the two. Look for an icon that looks something like this: <. . .>. Check out the differences: Both ports and their icons appear in the margin (the Ethernet port is on the left).

 Just in case you visit a store populated by computer geeks, a phone connector is called an RJ-11, and an Ethernet connector is called an RJ-45.

High-speed connections

If you have a cable modem, digital subscriber line (DSL), or other high-speed Internet connection — or are thinking about getting any of these — you can use them with your Mac. In most cases, you merely connect your Mac to the Internet via a cable plugged into the Ethernet port of your Mac and into an external box, which is either connected to a cable or phone outlet, depending on what kind of access you have to the Internet. Your cable or DSL installer-person should set everything up for you. If they don't, you'll have to call that service provider for help — troubleshooting a high-speed connection is, unfortunately, "beyond the purview of this book."

Your Internet service provider and you

After you make sure that you have a working modem, you need to select a company to provide you with access to the Internet. These companies are called *Internet Service Providers* (ISPs). Just like when choosing a long-distance company for your phone, the prices and services that ISPs offer vary, often from minute to minute. After you make your choice, you can launch and use Internet Explorer, Mail, iChat AV, or any other Internet application. Keep the following in mind when choosing an ISP:

- ✔ If you're using a cable modem, your ISP is your cable company. In most cases, the same applies to DSL — except that your provider is either your local phone company or an ISP that you've chosen to get your service connected. In that case, your ISP usually contacts the phone company and arranges for installation and setup for you.

- ✔ If you subscribe to AOL, then AOL is your ISP. You don't need to do anything more than install the AOL software and log on to AOL. You can ignore the rest of this chapter except for the parts about surfing the Web, iChat AV, and Apple's .Mac (dot-Mac) offerings, and preferences.

    You don't need Mail (the e-mail program included with OS X) if you get your mail exclusively through AOL, but if you've opted for a .Mac account, you can still use Mail to access it.

In addition to AOL, check out dedicated Internet service companies such as EarthLink and AT&T. Also investigate what your local cable or phone company offers. In other words, it pays to shop around for the deal that works best for you.

The going rate for unlimited access to the Internet, using a modem, is $10–$25 per month. If your service provider asks for considerably more than that, find out why. ***Note:*** If you have a cable modem, DSL, or other high-speed connection, you'll probably pay at least twice that much.

When you installed OS X (assuming that you did, and that it didn't come pre-installed on your Mac), the Installer program asked you a bunch of questions about your Internet connection and then set everything up for you. This process is detailed at the end of the book in the Appendix. If you didn't have an Internet connection (an ISP) at that time, you'll need to configure the Network System Preferences pane yourself. Although I cover the Network System Preferences pane in depth in Chapter 15, how to configure it so that your Mac will work with your ISP is something you'll have to work out with that ISP. If you have questions or problems not answered by this book, your ISP should be able to assist you.

And if your ISP can't help, it's probably time to try a different ISP.

Browsing the Web with Safari

In this chapter, I concentrate on Safari because it's my favorite of the two Web browsers installed with OS X Panther (Microsoft Internet Explorer is the other).

Why does Apple give you two browsers with OS X Panther? My best guess is that it's because there are still sites — including some major online banking and brokerage firms — that absolutely require Internet Explorer. You can't access these sites if you're using Safari.

Fortunately, there are fewer and fewer sites that discriminate against Safari, which is good, because Safari is noticeably faster than IE.

Getting up and running with Safari

Before you can browse the Web, the first step is to open your Web browser. No problem. As usual, there's more than one way. You can launch Safari by:

- Clicking the Safari icon on the Dock (look for the big blue stopwatch)
- Double-clicking the Safari icon in your Applications folder
- Double-clicking a link document representing a Web page

When you first launch Safari, it automatically connects you to the Internet and displays the default Apple home page (see Figure 11-1).

For those who don't care for Safari or Microsoft Internet Explorer

You can use any Internet browser you choose — such as Netscape, Mozilla, OmniWeb, iCab, Opera, or Chimera — but these browsers are not installed automatically with OS X like Safari and Internet Explorer. Instead, you'll have to download and install them first. You'll find the latest version of each by visiting www. versiontracker.com/macosx and searching for *browser*.

If you don't like Internet Explorer or Safari, I recommend OmniWeb. Unlike IE and Netscape, OmniWeb was designed exclusively for Mac OS X — and in my opinion, renders the best-looking pages. For more info, visit www. omnigroup.com.

The newest browsers on the OS X scene are Camino, iCab, and Opera.

Frankly, all the browsers are pretty darned good, and there's no penalty for installing a third or fourth one on your hard disk. So if you're not totally satisfied with the included browsers, try some of the others to decide which you like best.

Figure 11-1:
The Apple
home page,
powered by
Netscape.

Click the My Netscape button on this page (upper left, under the Apple Store
link) to customize the look and contents of your home page.

If a dialog box pops up asking whether you'd like to set Safari as your default
browser, click Yes. If you later change your mind and would prefer a different
browser to be your default, you can change it in the Internet System
Preference pane (covered extensively in Chapter 15).

I don't have room in this book to describe everything about Safari, but I'll hit
the highlights from the top of the Safari screen.

"What's this button do?"

The buttons along the top of the window from left to right — Back/Forward,
AutoFill, Reload/Stop, and Add Bookmark — do pretty much what their
names imply. Play with them a bit, and you'll see what I mean.

Other available buttons include Home, Text Size, and Bug (report a bug to
Apple); you add or delete them using Safari's View menu.

Below the Address field are some "bookmark" buttons that take you directly
to pages that may interest you, such as the Apple Web site, the Apple .Mac
Web site, Amazon.com, eBay, Yahoo, and others.

The News item at the far right of this row of buttons is a pop-up (actually a pop-down) menu, as shown in Figure 11-2.

Clicking any of these buttons or choosing one of the items in the News menu transports you to that page.

"Address me as Sir, rodent!"

To the right of the top row of buttons is the Address field. This is where you type Web addresses, or *URLs* (Uniform Resource Locators), that you want to visit. Just type one in and press Return to surf to that site.

Web addresses almost always begin with `http://www`. But Safari has a cool trick: If you just type a name, you usually get to the appropriate Web site that way without typing **http**, **//**, or **www**. For example, if you type **apple** in the Address field and then press Return, you go to `http://www.apple.com`. Or if you type **boblevitus**, you're taken to `www.boblevitus.com`. Try it — it's pretty slick.

Bookmarks

Choosing Bookmarks➪Show All Bookmarks, typing the keyboard shortcut ⌘+Option+B, or clicking the Show All Bookmarks button (shown in margin) brings up the Bookmarks window, as shown in Figure 11-3.

You can view the contents of any Collection (that is, a folder full of book-marks) by clicking its name in the Collections pane. In Figure 11-3, the contents of the Bookmarks Bar folder are displayed.

Open bookmarked pages by double-clicking them.

Use the Bookmark menu to add bookmarks or folders.

Figure 11-3:
The
Bookmarks
window in
all its glory.

Move bookmarks by dragging them. You can place bookmarks and folders of bookmarks on the Safari Bookmarks Bar or Menu by dragging them to the appropriate folder. If you drag a folder of bookmarks to the Bookmarks Bar folder (or directly onto the Bookmarks Bar itself), the result is a drop-down menu, as shown in Figure 11-2.

To delete a bookmark, select it and then press Delete or Backspace.

Bookmarks are favorites, and favorites are bookmarks. Both words describe the same exact thing — shortcuts to Web sites. In this chapter, I use Bookmark because that's what Safari calls them. Internet Explorer calls them Favorites.

Your copy of Safari comes pre-loaded with bookmarks that take you to other nifty Mac sites to check out. You'll find links to Apple sites, hardware and software vendors, Mac publications, and more. Take a look at the list of great Web pages that your pals at Apple have put together. Be sure and explore all the included bookmarks when you have some time; most, if not all, are worth knowing more about.

Searching with Sherlock

Looking for something on the Internet? Check out *Sherlock,* an application included with Mac OS X that can help you locate stuff on the Internet. You can scour general-purpose Internet search engines with the options under the Internet button or get more specific with one of the nine other Internet buttons.

In this section, you discover how to find Sherlock, how to use it to search the Internet, and how to get help with it when all else fails.

Starting Sherlock

You have two ways to invoke Sherlock:

- **Double-click the Sherlock icon in your Applications folder.**
- **Click the Sherlock icon on the Dock.** (Read more about the Dock in Chapter 3.)

Whichever way you choose, the Sherlock window appears, as shown in Figure 11-4.

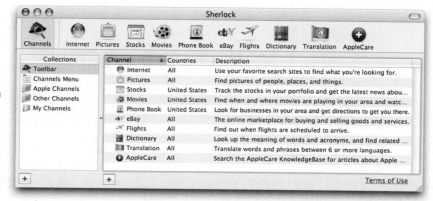

Figure 11-4: It's Sherlock's Channels screen.

A quick look at Sherlock's features

Before you use Sherlock, I'd like to point out a few of its more important features.

The top of the Sherlock window sports a series of buttons. From left to right they are Channels, Internet, Pictures, Stocks, Movies, Phone Book, eBay,

Flights, Dictionary, Translation, and AppleCare. You click the button that best represents what you're searching for. If you're looking for a Web site, click Internet. If you want to find where and when a movie is playing near you, click Movies. If you want to look up a word's meaning, click Dictionary. And so on.

The bottom part of the Sherlock window changes, depending on which button you've clicked (before a search). Then, it displays the results of your search (after you search, of course).

Searching with Sherlock

You use Sherlock to find things on the Internet. In this section, I first show you how to search with Sherlock.

Although I use an Internet search in the steps, you follow the same steps to search in any of the other channels. After you know how to search the Internet with Sherlock, you know how to search any Internet channel with Sherlock. To use Sherlock, follow these steps:

1. **Start Sherlock (I describe how in the previous section).**

2. **Click one of the ten Internet buttons to choose a channel.**

   Figure 11-5 shows the Internet channel.

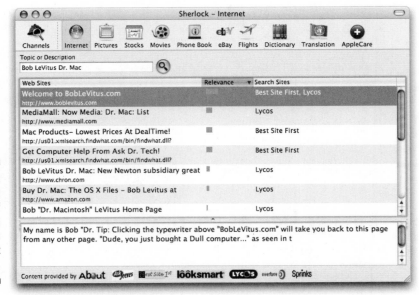

Figure 11-5: Searching for myself by using Sherlock's Internet search.

Yes, I know there are actually 11 icons, but the leftmost icon just describes what the 10 real search icons do, as you can see in Figure 11-4. The 10 to the right of the little dividing line are the actual buttons that you click for Internet searches.

3. **In the text entry field beneath the Sherlock search buttons, type a word or a phrase that you want to search for.**

4. **To begin your search, press Return or click the magnifying glass button to the right of the text entry field.**

   Sherlock passes your request along to the Web search engines and then displays a list of search results, similar to Figure 11-5.

5. **Click any search site listed along the bottom of Sherlock's window (About, Ask Jeeves, Best Site 1st, and so on) to launch your Web browser and access the search engine directly.**

   To start a new search, repeat Steps 2 through 5.

Some channels are slightly different in the way they look, such as the Movies channel shown in Figure 11-6, which doesn't let you search for movies by name but rather asks for your city and state or ZIP code and then displays the movies in a three-column browser.

Figure 11-6: The Movies channel works a bit differently than some of the others.

The Movies channel offers some nifty extras not found in other channels, including the movie poster and a QuickTime preview (lower-right pane of Figure 11-6) and the Map this Theater button (lower-left pane of Figure 11-6). Slick!

Checking out Help Center

I need to use another weasel-out here. I could write an entire chapter about using Sherlock, but one of the rules we *For Dummies* authors must follow is that our books can't run 1,000 pages long. So I'm going to give you the next best thing: Open the Help Center (by choosing Help⇨Sherlock Help from the Sherlock menu bar). A special Sherlock Help window appears; you can search for any topic here.

Getting Your E-Mail with Mail

Mail is a program that comes with Mac OS X that you use to send, receive, and organize your e-mail. You can also use Mail to access an address book that includes the addresses of your friends and family.

You can use other applications to read Internet mail. Netscape and AOL, for example, have their own mail readers, as does Microsoft Office (Entourage). But the easiest and best mail reader around (meaning, the best one on your hard drive by default) is probably Mail. And you can't beat the price; it's free!

Mail is fast and easy to use, too. Click the Mail icon on the Dock or double-click the Mail icon in the Applications folder to launch Mail. Mail icon looks like a cancelled postage stamp, as shown in the margin.

If this is your first time launching Mail, you'll see a Welcome message asking if you'd like to see what's new. If you click Yes, Help Viewer launches and shows you the What's New in Mail page.

Mail's main window looks like Figure 11-7.

Composing a new message

Here's how to create a new e-mail message:

1. **Choose File⇨New Message or press ⌘+N.**

   A new window appears; this is where you compose your e-mail message, as shown in Figure 11-8.

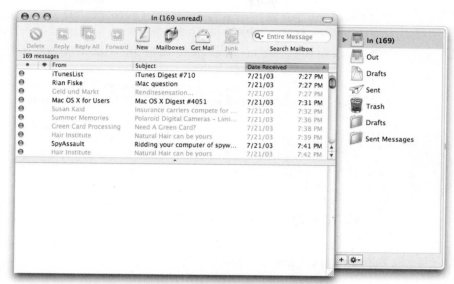

Figure 11-7:
Mail's main
window.

2. Place your cursor in the To field and type someone's e-mail address.

Use my address (`boblevitus@@boblevitus.com`) if you don't know anyone else to send mail to.

After you finish addressing a mail message, you can add the recipient to your address book. After you add an address to your address book, all you have to do is type the first few letters of the recipient's name, and Mail fills in the entire address for you. Neat, huh? (Choose Help⇨Mail Help to find out more about this feature.) You can even have Mail add the name and address of people who sent you mail by choosing Message ⇨Add Sender to Address Book (press ⌘+Y) when you're reading the mail from them.

Figure 11-8:
Composing
an e-mail
message.

3. **Press the Tab key twice to move your cursor to the Subject text field and then type a subject for this message.**

4. **Click in the main message portion of the window (refer to Figure 11-8) and type your message there.**

5. **When you're finished writing your message, click the Send button to send the e-mail immediately or choose File⇨Save as Draft to save it in the Drafts folder so that you can work on it later.**

If you do save your message to the Drafts folder (so you can write more later, perhaps), you can send it when you're ready by opening the Drafts folder, double-clicking the message, and then clicking the Send button.

Checking your mail

How do you check and open your mail? Easy. Just click the Get Mail button at the top of the main Mail window.

You can configure Mail to send and receive your mail every *x* minutes by choosing Mail⇨Preferences and then clicking the Accounts icon at the top of the window. Pull down the Check Accounts for New Mail pop-up menu and make a selection — every 1, 5, 15, 30, or 60 minutes — or choose Manually if you don't want Mail to check for mail automatically at all. The default setting is to check for mail every five minutes.

Dealing with spam

E-mail is a wonderful thing, but some people out there try to spoil it. If you think you get a lot of junk mail in your regular mailbox, just wait until some purveyor of electronic junk mail gets hold of your e-mail address. These lowlifes share their lists — and before you know it, your e-mail box is flooded with get-rich-quick schemes, advertisements for pornographic Web sites and chat rooms, and all the more traditional buy-me junk mail.

Mail comes with a Junk Mail filter that analyzes incoming message subjects, senders, and contents to determine which ones are likely to contain bulk or junk mail. Apple calls its initial configuration *training mode*. While training Mail to recognize which of its selections aren't junk, click the Not Junk button in the brown bar informing you that Mail thinks it found a piece of junk mail.

If a piece of junk mail slips past Mail's filters, select it in your Inbox and click the Junk button in the Mail window's toolbar.

After a few days (or weeks, depending upon your mail volume), Mail should be getting it right almost all the time. When you reach that point, choose

Automatic mode in the Junk Mail Preference pane and Mail will start moving junk mail automatically out of your Inbox and into a Junk folder where you can scan the items quickly and trash them when you're ready.

If, for some reason that escapes me, you prefer to receive and manually process your junk mail, you can turn Junk Mail processing off by disabling it in the Junk Mail Preference pane.

Changing your preferences

Actually, Mail's Preferences are more than you may expect from the name. This is the control center for Mail where you: create and delete e-mail accounts; determine which fonts and colors are used for your messages; decide whether attachments (such as pictures) are downloaded and saved; decide whether you send formatted mail or plain text; decide whether the spell checker is turned on; decide whether you have an automatic signature appended to your messages; and even establish rules to process mail that you receive.

As I've said before, space limitations make much of this beyond the scope of this book, but you should find everything perfectly straightforward, possibly with the assistance of Help⇨Mail Help. If you really want to tap the power of Mail, learn to set *Rules*. These little snippets let you automatically tag messages with a color, file them in a specific mailbox, reply to/forward/redirect the message (handy when you're going to be away for a while), or just delete the message *(kill-filing)* without even bothering to look at it.

Adding an item to your address book

If you have a fair number of contacts — relatives, friends, or the odd enemy that you keep in touch with for self-punishment purposes — you may want to check out the nifty Address Book application that comes with Mac OS X. You can enter new contacts in the Address Book application or while you're working in Mail or iChat AV (or any other program that interfaces with the Address Book).

Follow these steps to create a new entry in the Address Book:

1. **Launch the Address Book application by double-clicking its icon in the Applications folder or clicking its Dock icon.**

   The Address Book appears. The first time that you open Address Book, you see an empty address book.

2. **To create a new entry, click the Plus button at the bottom of the Address Book's Name column.**

   An untitled address card appears. The First name text field is initially selected. (You can tell by the border it now has, as shown in Figure 11-9.)

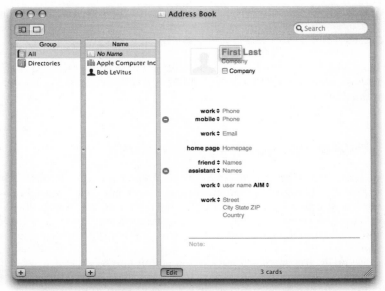

Figure 11-9:
A new
address
card in
Address
Book.

3. Type the person's first name in the First text field.

I type **Doctor**.

4. Press Tab.

Your cursor should now be in the Last text field.

You can always move from one field to the next by pressing Tab. And, in fact, this shortcut works in almost all Mac programs that have fields like these. Furthermore, you can move to the previous field by pressing Shift+Tab.

5. Type the last name for the person who you're adding to your Address Book.

Continue this process, filling in the rest of the fields shown in Figure 11-10.

6. When you're done entering information, click the Edit button to exit the editing mode.

The contact that I just created appears in Figure 11-9.

The little contact card is called a *vCard* (virtual business card).

To add more info about any Address Book entry, select the name in the Name column (<No Name> in Figure 11-9; you can tell when a name is selected because it has a gray field behind it), click the Edit button at the bottom of the Address Book window, and then make your changes.

Figure 11-10:
The address card displayed in the Address Book window.

You can do some pretty neat stuff with Address Book that I just don't have room to cover in this book. Just for starters, you can organize your contacts into groups so that you can e-mail everyone in a group (that you define) with one click. And you can create a blank e-mail message to a contact by clicking and holding the label next to the e-mail address and choosing Send Email from the pop-up menu that appears, as shown in Figure 11-11.

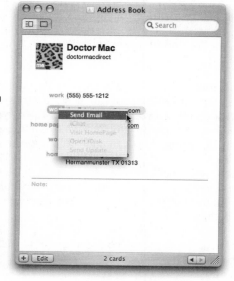

Figure 11-11:
Sending e-mail to someone in your Address Book is as easy as clicking here.

A Quick Overview of .Mac

.Mac is a set of Internet-based services provided by Apple. Although .Mac isn't specifically a Mac OS X feature (most of them are still available to Mac OS 9 users and have been since before Apple released Mac OS X), I'd be remiss if I didn't at least mention them and give you some background so you can check them out.

The seven .Mac services at the time of this writing are

- ✔ **Mac.com and Webmail:** An e-mail service run by Apple that lets you have an e-mail address in the form of `yourname@@mac.com`. For OS X users, Apple has added IMAP support and an SMTP server (is that enough geek-speak for you?). What this means is that you can now maintain your messages on the Apple server, and you don't have to use your ISP's server to send mail any longer. You can also access your Mac.com e-mail account from any computer with an Internet connection and a Web browser (that's called *Webmail*).

- ✔ **iDisk:** Your own personal 100MB Internet-based virtual disk.

- ✔ **HomePage:** The easiest way I know of to build your own home page.

- ✔ **Backup:** A utility to back up folders on your hard disk to either your iDisk or a CD-R or DVD-R disk.

- ✔ **iCards:** Electronic greeting cards that you can e-mail to your friends.

- ✔ **Anti-Virus:** A copy of the Virex virus-scanning and protection utility, including regular updates.

- ✔ **Support:** A consolidated link to a variety of support services, such as Network Status, online discussion boards concerning Apple hardware and software products, the AppleCare Knowledge Base, and Apple's customer Feedback page.

The first two services — Mac.com and iDisk — are beautifully integrated with OS X. For example, the aforementioned Mail program is set up to work perfectly with a Mac.com e-mail account. All you have to do is supply your username and password. And iDisk is a choice in the Finder's Go menu, although you can't use it until you visit the Apple Web site and create your own Mac.com account ($100/year).

You can even create a local copy of your iDisk on your hard drive and have it automatically synchronize with the remote iDisk via the Internet. See the .Mac System Preference pane for details.

If you want more than 100MB, Apple will lease you space — find out all about it on the Mac.com Web pages.

Even better, Apple keeps a folder on everybodys iDisk that's full of software for you to download and try out (and it doesn't count against your 100MB, either).

So what are you waiting for? To sign up, surf to `www.Mac.com`.

Communicating via iChat AV

Instant messaging and chat rooms provide for interactive communication between users all over the world. If you're into instant messaging, iChat AV gives you immediate access to all the other users of AOL Instant Messaging (AIM) and .Mac. All you need is their screen name and you're set to go. You can even join any AOL chat room just by choosing Go To Chat from the File menu.

OS X 10.2's built-in Rendezvous support makes it even better. With Rendezvous, which offers configuration-free connections, you don't have to do anything to be part of a Rendezvous network because your Mac configures itself and joins up automatically. For example, with Rendezvous enabled, I've sent and received messages from/to my AirPort-equipped PowerBook from/to my desktop computer without any network configuration. Just choose Rendezvous from the Window menu and select the person with whom you want to chat from the Rendezvous window.

Your chats can be one-to-one or they can be group bull sessions. Each participant's picture (or icon) appears next to anything he says, which is displayed in a cartoon-like thought bubble, as shown in Figure 11-12.

If you've attached a picture to a person in your Address Book, you'll even see that picture when you iChat with that person. Neat!

Figure 11-12: A chat with myself (I have two Macs on the same network).

If you find the thought bubbles a little too childish, you can turn them off from the View menu.

iChat AV even lets you transfer files, giving you a very convenient way to share photos or documents without resorting to file sharing or e-mail. Just drag the document's icon to the message box, as demonstrated in Figure 11-13, press Enter or Return, and the file will zip across the ether.

Figure 11-13:
Transferring
a file with
iChat AV.

iChat AV is integrated with the Address Book, so you don't have to enter your Buddies' information twice. It also communicates directly with the Mail application. Just select a Buddy in iChat AV's Buddy List, then choose Send Email from the Buddies menu (or use the keyboard shortcut ⌘+Option+E), and Mail will launch (if it's not already open), and address a new message to the selected buddy, ready for you to begin typing.

Gimme an A! Gimme a V!

The latest, greatest iChat development is audio/video chatting, which is what the *AV* in its name stands for. To conduct a video or audio chat, connect a FireWire camera and/or a supported microphone to your Mac. That's it — you're all set to chat using video and/or audio.

While many FireWire camcorders work fairly well for video chatting, Apple's $149 iSight camera/microphone combination is designed just for this purpose and works even better in most cases.

When you've got appropriate hardware connected to your Mac, your buddies' names in the Buddy lists will display little green telephone or camera icons if they've got the right hardware on their end. To start an audio or videoconference, click their green icons. Your buddies will receive an invitation to begin an audio or video chat. If they accept the invitation, a Video Chat window appears, as shown in Figure 11-14.

iChat's audio and video features are easy to set up and use.

If you've got a FireWire camcorder handy, give it a try. My chat handle is **levitus**; feel free to invite me to video chat if you see me online.

Figure 11-14:
I'm iChatting with my buddy Dave Hamilton.

Chapter 12

Publish or Perish: The Fail-Safe Guide to Printing

Printing is the process of getting what's on your screen onto paper. I know you probably know that, but my editor insisted I start this chapter by defining printing. And so I have.

Printing under OS X should be as simple as pressing the keyboard shortcut ⌘+P and then pressing the Return or Enter key. Happily, that's usually how easy printing something is. When it isn't, however, printing often turns into a raging nightmare. If you configure your printer and printing software properly, though, printing is as easy as can be. And that's pretty darn simple. In this chapter, I scare away the bogeymen to help you avoid any printing nightmares. I'll walk you through the entire process as if you just unpacked a new printer and plugged it in.

If you're upgrading from a 9.*x* version of Mac OS, you probably want to work through these steps because things have changed in OS X.

Before Diving In . . .

Before I even start talking about hooking up printers, you should know a few things. So here's a little list that tells you just what those things are:

✔ **Read the documentation that came with your specific printer.**
Hundreds of different printer makes and models are available for the Mac, so if I contradict something in your printer manual, follow your

manual's instructions first. If that effort doesn't work, try it my way — use the techniques that you'll be reading about in the rest of this chapter.

✔ **The Print and Page Setup sheets differ slightly (or even greatly) from program to program and from printer to printer.** Although the examples that I show you in this chapter are representative of what you will probably encounter, you may come across sheets that look a bit different. For example, the Print and Page Setup sheets for Microsoft Word include choices that I don't cover in this chapter, such as Even or Odd Pages Only, Print Hidden Text, and Print Selection Only. If you see commands in your Print or Page Setup sheet that I don't explain in this chapter, they're specific to that application; look within its documentation for explanation. Similarly, Adobe Illustrator CS has added numerous gadgets, list boxes, radio buttons, and so forth to the Print dialog box to the point where you might not even recognize it as a Print dialog box.

✔ **I use Apple's bare-bones word processor, TextEdit, for the examples in this chapter.** If you want to follow along, you'll find TextEdit in your Applications folder.

✔ **Don't forget about Mac OS Help.** Many programs support this excellent Apple technology, which can be the fastest way to figure out a feature that has you stumped. So don't forget to check the Help menu before you panic. (I cover the Help menu way back in Chapter 6.)

So, with those things in mind, get ready, set, print!

Ready: Connecting and Adding Your Printer

Before you can even think about printing something, you have to connect a printer to your Mac and then tell OS X that the printer exists. Here's how.

Connecting your printer

Once again, I must remind you that there are thousands of printer models that you could connect to your Mac. And each one is a little different from the next. In other words, if what you're about to read doesn't track with the printer that you're trying to connect, I again implore you to RTFM (that's *Read The Fine Manual*, in case you're wondering.) It should tell you how to load your ink or toner cartridges.

Remove all the packing material and little strips of tape, some of which you won't even see if you don't know where to look.

That said, here are some very general steps to connect a printer:

1. **Connect the printer to your Mac with the cable snugly attached at both ends (printer and Mac).**

   For your printer to work, you have to somehow connect it to a data source. (Think of your phone — you can't receive calls without some sort of connector between the caller and the callee.)

2. **Plug the AC power cord printer cord into a power outlet (yup, the regular kind in the wall or on a power strip).**

   Some printers require you to plug one end of the AC power cord into the printer; others have the AC power cord attached permanently. The point is that your printer won't work if it's not connected to a power source.

3. **Turn on your printer (check out your manual if you can't find the switch).**

4. **If your printer came with software, install it on your hard drive, following the instructions that came with the printer.**

5. **Restart your Mac.**

   That's it!

Any port on a Mac

You need to plug the printer cable into the appropriate port on the back of your Mac. Therein lies the rub. Mac technology has changed dramatically since the previous editions of this book, when I used to say, "Begin by connecting the printer to the Printer port on the back of your Mac (with both the Mac and the printer turned off, of course — but you knew that, didn't you?)." Now I tell you, "You need to plug the printer cable into the appropriate port. . . ." Why am I being so vague? Because I have to be. You see, these days, printers don't always connect to the same port. Some printers connect to the Ethernet port or to an Ethernet hub (which is, in turn, connected to the back of your Mac). Others connect through the Universal Serial Bus (USB) port. I've even seen a few that connect via the FireWire port. So read the instructions that came with your printer and plug your printer into the appropriate hole (port) for your Mac.

Typically, your printer connects to your machine with a USB, Ethernet, or FireWire cable. Don't confuse this with your printer's AC power cord (the kind you find on everyday appliances). If your printer didn't come with a cable that fits into one of the ports on your Mac, contact your printer manufacturer and ask for one; it's cheesy not to provide the proper cable with a printer. Unfortunately, some manufacturers make printers with different kinds of connectors on the back (to sell them to those poor souls stuck using Windows) and expect you to buy your own cable. Asking one of these manufacturers for a cable will be an exercise in futility.

Setting up a printer for the first time

After you connect your computer and printer with a compatible cable, provide a power source for your printer, and install the software for your printer, you need to configure your Mac so that it and your printer can talk to each other.

The Print Center application, which I am about to discuss, is the tool that you use to tell your Mac what printers are available. Note that many of the steps involving Print Center require that your printer is turned on and warmed up (that is, run through its diagnostics and start-up cycle).

Follow these steps to set up a printer for the first time:

1. **Launch Printer Setup Utility.**

   You'll find Printer Setup Utility in the Utilities folder, which is inside your Applications folder. Click the Applications button in the Sidebar of any Finder window to open the Applications folder. Now open the Utilities folder and double-click Printer Setup Utility.

2. **Choose Add Printer from the Printers menu.**

3. **From the Printer List window that appears (see the upcoming Figure 12-1), click the Add button in the window's toolbar.**

   If you have never set up a printer on this Mac, Steps 2 and 3 may be superfluous — the dialog box/sheet shown in Figure 12-1 should open automatically.

   If the dialog box/sheet appears, click the Add button, as shown in Figure 12-1.

4. **In the sheet that appears in front of the Printer List window, click the pop-up menu to select your printer's connection type.**

   Most printers are either connected directly to your Mac via a USB port — or over a network, using AppleTalk.

   Many USB printers (such as most of the compatible printers from Epson, Canon, Lexmark, and Hewlett-Packard) will be recognized immediately without you having to perform this step.

   For my example, I choose USB because the printer I'll be working with is an Epson Stylus Photo 900 USB printer, connected to the Mac via a USB cable.

   If your printer isn't recognized at this point, you may need to install its driver software first, either from the CD that came with the printer or by downloading the latest driver software from your printer manufacturer's Web site.

AppleTalk and USB are by far the most common kinds of printer connections for Macs. Another option available in the Add Printer window is IP Printing. If your printer is on a Transmission Control Protocol/Internet Protocol (TCP/IP) network, you need to configure the printer by using its network address. IP printers usually connect via Ethernet and are almost always found on large corporate networks. Fortunately, such large networks are almost always maintained by a network administrator, who should be able to help you set up an IP printer.

If you encounter trouble setting up a printer for Mac OS X, you may want to contact your printer's manufacturer about getting the latest, greatest driver. Many printer manufacturers are offering new drivers with enhanced functionality. You may find new drivers for your printer on the Web or a major Internet Service Provider, such as America Online. Apple often includes such new drivers in the Software folder on your iDisk. And Disk 2 of the Mac OS X 10.3 Installer disks has additional printer drivers as well. Check with your printer manufacturer for details.

After you choose your printer connection type, you see the names and kinds of available printers in the Printer List window. In Figure 12-1, my USB printer, named *Stylus Photo 900*, appears.

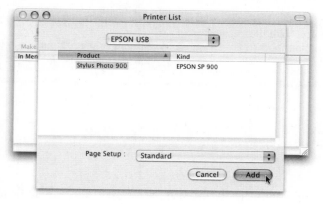

Figure 12-1:
Available printers with the specified connection type appear here.

5. **Click the name of the printer that you want from the list and then click the Add button.**

   This window closes and the Printer List window reappears, containing the printer that you just added. If you've added printers before, they appear here, too.

   Now you can print your first document! Make sure, though, that you have the document set to look how you want it to print. Read through the section "Set: Setting Up Your Document with Page Setup" later in this chapter for more info.

Checking for AppleTalk if you don't see your printer

If you have an AppleTalk printer but don't see it on the list when you click the AppleTalk option from the pop-up menu (look for the pop-up reading USB in Figure 12-1), check in System Preferences to see whether AppleTalk is active. (I cover System Preferences in Chapter 15, but here's how you check this.)

1. **Choose System Preferences from the Apple menu or by clicking its icon in the Dock.**

   The System Preferences window opens.

2. **Open the Network Preferences pane by clicking the Network icon in the System Preferences window.**

   The System Preferences window turns into the Network pane.

3. **Select Built-in Ethernet from the list and click the Configure button.**

4. **Click the AppleTalk button of the Network pane and check to see whether the Make AppleTalk Active check box is selected.**

5. **If the AppleTalk Active check box is not marked, check (select) it. You may have to click the padlock icon on the bottom left of the window and enter an Administrator password to do this.**

6. **After you make AppleTalk active, quit System Preferences and go back to the Print Center application (click its icon on the Dock; or, if you quit or restarted, launch it — it's in the Utilities folder inside your Applications folder) and add your AppleTalk printer. (See the section "Setting up a printer for the first time" where I detail adding your AppleTalk printer.)**

7. **When you've added and configured a printer, you can quit Print Center.**

Set: Setting Up Your Document with Page Setup

After you set up your printer, the hard part is over. You should be able to print a document quickly and easily — right? Not so fast, Buck-o. Read here how the features in the Page Setup sheet can help you to solve most basic printing problems.

Become familiar with Page Setup — you may not need to use it right this second, but it's a good friend to know.

Almost every program that can print a document has a Page Setup command on its File menu. Note that some programs use the name *Page Setup*, and others use *Print Setup*. (Print Setup is the quaint, old-fashioned term, more popular in the System 6 era and in Windows than on today's Macs.) Either way, in this sheet you can choose your printer, paper size, page orientation, and scaling percent (see Figure 12-2).

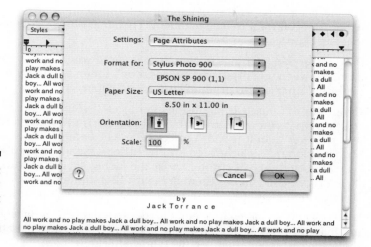

Figure 12-2:
The Page
Setup sheet
in TextEdit.

Users of network printers or PostScript printers may see slightly different versions of the Print and Page Setup sheet. The differences should be minor enough not to matter.

Click the little question mark in the lower-left corner at any time for additional help with the Page Setup sheet. Page Setup help will open immediately in the Help Viewer if you do.

The options within the Page Setup sheet are as follows:

✔ **Settings:** When the default Page Attributes displays in this pop-up menu, you see what configuration options are available. In that same pop-up menu, you can also choose

- **Custom Paper Size:** Define a paper size other than one supported directly by your printer driver as described under Paper Size in this list.

- **Summary:** Get a list of the options that apply to the current document, based on what you've set up in the Page Setup sheet.

- **Save As Default:** When you have everything configured the way you want it to be for most documents, choose this option to save the configuration as your Page Setup defaults.

✔ **Format for:** In this pop-up menu, you find the name of the active printer. If you have several printers configured, you can choose any of them from this list. As you see in Figure 12-2, the Epson Stylus Photo 900 printer that I set up earlier in this chapter (see the "Ready: Connecting and Adding Your Printer" section) is on the menu.

✔ **Paper Size:** Use options in this pop-up menu to choose the type of paper currently in the paper tray of your printer or to choose the size of the paper that you want to feed manually. The dimensions of the paper that you can choose appear below its name.

Page Setup sheet settings remain in effect until you change them. For example, when you print an envelope, don't forget to change back to Letter before trying to print on letter-sized paper.

✔ **Orientation:** Choose from options here to tell your printer whether the page that you want to print should be portrait oriented (like a letter, longer than it is wide) or landscape oriented (sideways, wider than it is long). Click the icons of the little person for the following (from left to right): Portrait, Landscape facing left, and Landscape facing right. You can see them in Figure 12-2 to the right of the Orientation heading.

✔ **Scale:** Use the Scale control percentages to enlarge or reduce your image for printing. Just type a new value into the Scale text entry box, replacing the default number 100 (shown in Figure 12-2).

Some programs also offer additional Page Setup choices. To see them (if your program offers them, of course), they'll usually appear in the Settings pop-up menu in the Page Setup sheet. Adobe Photoshop and Microsoft Word have them; TextEdit doesn't. The additional settings for Microsoft Word appear in Figure 12-3.

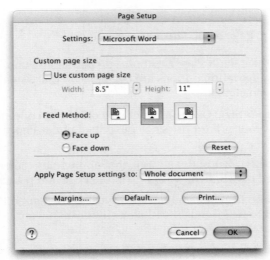

Figure 12-3:
The add-
itional Page
Setup
options in
Microsoft
Word.

Go: Printing with the Print Sheet

After you connect and configure your printer and then set up how you want your document to print, you come to the final steps before that joyous moment when your printed page pops out of the printer. Navigating the Print sheet is the last thing standing between you and your output.

Although most of the Print sheets that you see look like the figures that I show in this chapter, others may differ slightly. The features in the Print sheet are strictly a function of the program with which you're printing. Many programs choose to use the standard-issue Apple sheet as shown in this chapter, but not all do. If I don't explain a certain feature in this chapter, chances are good that it's a feature specific to the application or printer that you're using and is explained in that program's or printer's documentation.

Printing a document

If everything has gone well so far, the actual act of printing a document is pretty simple. Just follow the steps here and in a few minutes, pages should start popping out of your printer like magic. (In the sections that follow, I talk about some print options that you'll probably need someday.)

1. **Open a document that you want to print.**

2. **Choose File⇨Print (or use the keyboard shortcut ⌘+P).**

   You see the basic Print sheet, as shown in Figure 12-4.

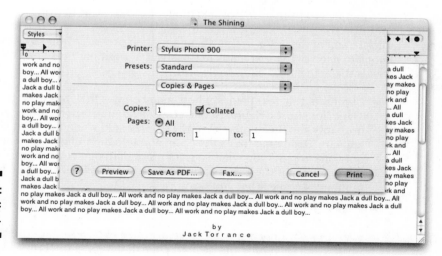

Figure 12-4:
Your basic
Print sheet.

3. **Change any settings that you like in the Print sheet and then click Print. Wait a few minutes and then walk over to your printer to get your document.**

Choosing from different printers

Just as you can in the Page Setup sheet, you can choose which printer you want to use from the Printer pop-up menu of the Print sheet. Remember that you can only choose from the printers that you have added via the Print Center, as you read in the section earlier in this chapter, the one I lovingly refer to as "Setting up a printer for the first time."

Choosing custom settings

If you've created a custom group of settings previously, you can choose from them in the Presets pop-up menu of the Print sheet. I touch more on this feature in the "Save Custom Settings" section later in this chapter.

The Print sheet also features another pop-up menu called `Copies & Pages` (refer to Figure 12-4) — that offers additional options.

I go through these options and their sub-options one at a time in the following sections.

Copies & Pages

When Copies & Pages is selected in the pop-up menu, you can choose how many copies to print and the page range that you want to print.

Click in any of the fields in this sheet and then press the Tab key. Your cursor jumps to each of the text fields in the sheet in rotation. Pressing Shift+Tab makes the active field jump backward.

- **Copies:** In this text field, set how many copies that you want to print. The Print sheet defaults to one copy (1) in most applications, so you'll probably see the numeral 1 in the Copies field when the Print sheet appears. Assuming that's the case, don't do anything if you want to print only one copy. If you want to print more than one copy of your document, highlight the 1 that appears in the Copies field and type the new number of copies that you want.

- **Pages:** Here you find two radio buttons to choose from: All or From. If you want to print your entire document, select the All option. If you want to print only a specific page or range of pages, mark the From radio button and then type the desired page numbers in the From and To text entry boxes.

Dictating perfection . . . sort of

The Print command appears in the File menu in the vast majority of the Mac programs that you'll use. Every so often, you may come across a program that doesn't follow these conventions, but I would say at least 98+ percent of commercial Mac programs put the Print command in the File menu and use ⌘+P for its keyboard shortcut.

One of the best things about the Mac is that Apple has published a set of guidelines that all Mac programs should use. Consistency among programs is one of the Mac's finest features. Notice how 98+ percent of all programs house the Open, Close, Save, Save As, Page Setup, and Print commands in their File menus and the Undo, Cut, Copy, and Paste commands in their Edit menus. That's the kind of convenience and consistency that the Macintosh Human Interface Guidelines recommend.

Macintosh Human Interface Guidelines also recommend that the keyboard shortcut ⌘+P should be reserved for the command "plain text" unless it is used for Print, in which case ⌘+T should be used for Plain Text (just like how

the keyboard shortcuts ⌘+B and ⌘+I are usually used to format bold and italic text, respectively). So ⌘+P is almost always the shortcut for the Print command in the File menu.

My point: Choosing File⇨Print (⌘+P) *won't* work for you if any one of the following is true with the software you're using:

- The Print command is on a different menu.

- There *is* no Print command.

- The Print keyboard shortcut is anything but ⌘+P.

If any of the above is true for a program that you're using, you just have to wing it. Look in all the menus and check out the product's documentation to try to get a handle on the Print command for that program. You can also write the software company a brief note mentioning that it could make things easier on everyone by putting the Print command in the proper place and using the generally agreed-upon keyboard shortcut.

For example, suppose that you have a 10-page document. You print the whole thing and then notice a typo on page 2. After you correct your error, you don't have to reprint the whole document — only the one with the correction. Reprint only page 2 by typing a **2** in both the From and To fields. You can type any valid range of pages (um, you can't print out page 20 if your document is only 15 pages long) in the From and To fields.

Layout

Choose Layout from the pop-up menu to set the number of pages per printed sheet, the layout direction, and whether or not you prefer a border. (See Figure 12-5.)

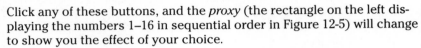

✔ **Pages per Sheet:** Choose from preset numbers here in this pop-up menu to set the number of pages that you want to print on each sheet. (*Note:* Pages appear smaller than full-size if you use this option.)

✔ **Layout Direction:** Choose from one of four buttons that govern the way the small pages are laid out on the printed page.

Click any of these buttons, and the *proxy* (the rectangle on the left displaying the numbers 1–16 in sequential order in Figure 12-5) will change to show you the effect of your choice.

✔ **Border:** Your choices from this pop-up menu are none, single hairline, single thin line, double hairline, and double thin line.

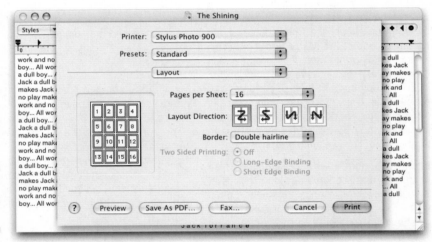

Figure 12-5:
The Layout
sheet.

Output Options

Choose Output Options from the pop-up menu to save your file as a PDF or PostScript. *PDF* stands for *Portable Document Format,* the file format made famous by Adobe and its Acrobat program. It's also a type of document that almost anyone with a computer can open and view (using Acrobat Reader or the OS X Preview application, which you'll find in the Applications folder).

Unless the program that you're using added something, Save as File is the only choice on this screen. If you mark that check box, you have a choice of PDF or (sometimes) PostScript. So why the heck is it called Output Options? I think it should be singular and say something more descriptive, such as *Save as File* and then just let you select the format for that file.

This is even more redundant with the presence of a Save As PDF button at the bottom of every Print sheet.

If you're preparing a file for someone else to use on another computer, PDF is often the best format to use because it preserves both text and graphics exactly as they appear onscreen.

Scheduler

The Scheduler lets you set a later time for printing (say, while you're asleep, at lunch, or in a meeting). The Scheduler is shown in Figure 12-6.

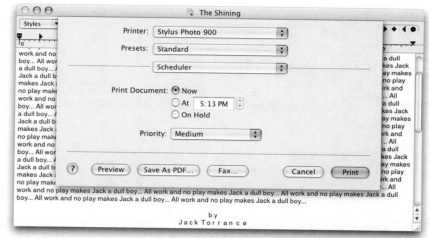

Figure 12-6:
The print scheduler sheet.

Printer Features

The options on this sheet vary from printer, but typically include such settings as print resolution, media type, and whether you're printing in color, grayscale, or black & white. Some printers may not even offer this sheet.

Summary

When you select Summary in the pop-up menu, you can see the printing details for your document, as shown in Figure 12-7. Look here for one final check to verify your print job settings: how many copies you want, whether you want them collated, the page range of your print job, your layout choice(s), and whether to save a file as a PDF, plus any settings specific to your particular printer or the application that you're printing from.

Paper Handling

Use this sheet to reverse the order your pages print or if you want to print only the odd or even numbered pages.

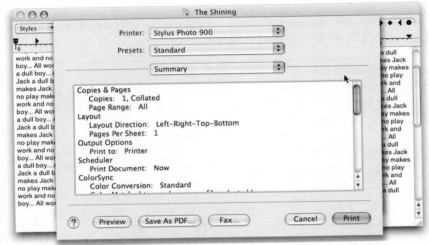

Figure 12-7:
Summary
for the
about-to-
be-printed
document.

ColorSync

Use this sheet to choose a color conversion method and/or to add a Quartz filter.

Quartz filters include Black & White, Blue Tone, Gray Tone, Lightness Decrease, Lightness Increase, Reduce File Size, and Sepia Tone. They do pretty much what they say they do when you apply them to a print job.

Print Settings

This sheet offers printer-specific choices such as type of paper, type of ink, and other settings specific to the selected printer.

Save custom settings

After you finalize the printer settings for Copies & Pages, Layout, Output Options, and any other options your printer driver provides, choose Save As from the Presets pop-up menu. Name the settings and from now on, that setting appears as an option in the Presets pop-up menu. Just choose your saved set before you print any document with which you want to use it.

Previewing Your Documents

When you click the Preview button, you see a version of the page or pages that you're about to print, displayed by the Preview utility at a size small enough to allow you to see the whole page at once, as shown in Figure 12-8.

Figure 12-8:
A Print
Preview of a
Safari
document.

If you have any doubt about the way that a document will look when you print it, check out Preview first. When you're happy with the document preview, just choose Print from the File menu (or press ⌘+P). Preview works with the Preview application that Apple includes with Mac OS X. With the Preview feature, you do cool things like

- ✔ **See all the pages in your document one by one.**

- ✔ **Zoom in or out to get a different perspective on what you're about to send to the printer (pretty cool!).**

- ✔ **Rotate the picture 90 degrees to the left or right.**

- ✔ **Spot errors before you commit to printing something.** A little upfront inspection can save you a lot of paper, ink (or toner), and frustration.

- ✔ **Add headers and footers.** Many applications include, or allow you to include, header or footer fields to fill in. *Headers* include information or page numbers that run at the top of each page, like this book uses. *Footers* — you guessed it — are the same thing, but they display at the bottom of a page. They aren't visible while you're working on a document, but they do appear in the printed version (if you set them to). Use Preview to get a look at the header or footer before you print a document. Just zoom in on that area of the page to take a closer look and make any changes that you want within the application that created the file.

Check out the Preview program's View menu and its toolbar. Here you can zoom in or out, rotate your document, move forward or backward (through multi-page documents), and other stuff. So I urge you to pull down the View menu and check it out. If you have a multi-page document (or multiple documents) open, a drawer will pop out of the side of the window to let you move through the pages.

To hide and show the drawer, click the Drawer button, choose View➪Drawer, or use the keyboard shortcut ⌘+T.

Just the Fax . . .

OS X Panther adds the ability to fax a document right from the Print sheet. Just click the Fax button at the bottom of every Print sheet and the sheet becomes the Fax sheet, as shown in Figure 12-9.

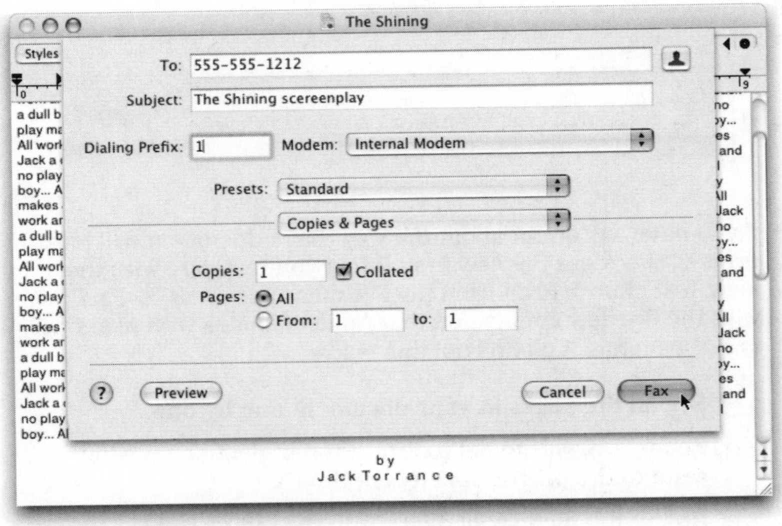

Figure 12-9:
In Panther, faxing is just as easy as printing.

To fax a document, click the Fax button on the Print sheet and then type the fax phone number of the recipient in the To field.

If you click the button with the silhouette on the right of the To field, you can select a recipient from the OS X Address Book.

Type a subject name in the Subject field if you so desire, add a dialing prefix if your phone requires one (such as 1, which most phones require to dial a ten-digit, long-distance phone number). Select your modem from the modem pop-up menu if it's not already selected (as mine is in Figure 12-9).

Everything else in the Fax sheet is just the same as it was in the Print sheet, which you read all about in the previous sections. Just click the Fax button, and your fax will be sent.

If you don't connect a phone line to your modem, the process will (of course) fail.

Font Mania

Jazz up your documents — or make them a little more serious — with different fonts. To a computer user, *font* means typeface — what the characters look like. Although professional typographers will scream at my generalization, I'll go with that definition for now.

Tens of thousands of different fonts are available for the Macintosh. You don't want to use the same font that you'd use for a garage sale flyer as you would for a résumé, right? Lucky for you, Mac OS X comes with a bunch of fonts, as shown in Figure 12-10. Some are pretty predictable, such as Times New Roman (it's the font of this paragraph), but OS X gives you some artsy ones, too, such as Brush Script. If you get really get into fonts, you can buy single fonts and font collections anywhere that you can buy software. Plenty of shareware and public domain fonts are also available from online services and user groups. Some people have thousands of fonts.

Figure 12-10:
Mac OS X includes these fonts and plenty more.

The pre-installed fonts live in two different folders, both called Fonts. One is in the Library folder at root level on your hard disk; the other is in the Library subfolder within the System folder, as shown in Figure 12-10.

OS X actually has four different Font folders. The third one, also called Fonts, is in the Library in your home directory. The subtle distinction between the three is explained below. The last one is in the Network/Library folder, and you see it only when you're connected to a network server.

Installing new fonts

To install any new font, drag its icon into one of the two Fonts folders that you have access to, as follows:

- ✔ **If you want other users to be able to access the new font,** drag the font's icon to the Fonts subfolder inside the Library folder, which is at the root level of your hard drive. This Fonts folder has universal access. (The two Library folders are covered in Chapter 10.)

- ✔ **If you want to limit access to the new font to solely yourself,** drag the font's icon to the Fonts subfolder located in the Library folder inside your home folder.

The Fonts folder on the right in Figure 12-10 — the one in the Library inside the System folder — is reserved for OS X and can't easily be modified. If you try to remove or add a font to it, you'll first have to "authenticate" yourself as an Administrator.

If you've designated a Classic System Folder, OS X will also load any fonts in its Fonts folder, for a total of five different folders named Fonts.

Some applications, in particular high-end design applications like Adobe Illustrator and Adobe InDesign, add yet another Fonts folder to the mix in the Application Support folder within the Library folder at the root level of your hard disk. These fonts are accessible only when running the program that installed them.

Types of fonts

There are many font formats with names like OpenType, Mac TrueType, Windows TrueType, PostScript Type 1, bitmap, and dfont. No problem — Mac OS X supports them all. In fact, the only font format I know of that OS X doesn't support is PostScript Type 3.

That said, the two most common formats for Macs are TrueType and PostScript Type 1, but OpenType is making big strides to join the elite.

- ✔ **TrueType fonts:** These Apple standard-issue fonts come with Mac OS X. In common use on Macs as well as on Windows machines, these fonts are scaleable. *Scaleable fonts* use only a single outline for the font, and your Mac makes these fonts bigger or smaller when you choose a bigger or smaller font size in a program.

- ✔ **Type 1 fonts:** These fonts are often referred to as PostScript Type 1 fonts, and they are the standard for desktop publishing on the Mac (as well as Windows and UNIX). Tens of thousands of Type 1 fonts are available. (Not nearly as many TrueType fonts exist.)

  Type 1 fonts come in two pieces: a bitmap font suitcase and a second piece (called a *printer font*). Some Type 1 fonts come with two, three, or four printer fonts, which usually have related names. Just toss all the parts in the appropriate library folder, and you'll have those fonts available in every program that you use.

- ✔ **OpenType fonts:** OpenType fonts are really TrueType fonts with PostScript information embedded. This gives you the greater typographic control that high-end typesetters require with the one-file convenience of TrueType.

And that's about it for printing and fonts. Onward!

Chapter 13

Applying Yourself to the Applications Folder

Mac OS X comes with a whole folder full of applications — software that you can use to do everything from surfing the Internet to capturing an image of your Mac's screen to playing QuickTime movies to checking the time. In this chapter, I give you a thumbnail view of each — at least the ones I don't cover in other chapters — and tell you a bit about working with applications in Mac OS X.

 Many software developers often get ideas for cool shareware and commercial applications from what they find in the Mac OS Applications or Utilities folders. They look at what Apple has provided for free and say, "Hey, I can add some cool features to that!" The next thing you know, you have new and improved versions of Mail, Terminal, Grab, TextEdit, and others. If you use an Apple-supplied application but find it lacking, check your favorite shareware archive (www.versiontracker.com, www.macupdate.com/, and www.tucows.com are a few good ones) for a better mousetrap.

Shareware, for those of you who haven't experienced the joy, is freely distributed try-before-you-buy software. There's a lot of it for Panther, much of which is as good as or better than commercial software.

Folder Full of Apps

The applications that you get with Mac OS X are all stored in (where else?) the Applications folder. Hang with me as I run 'em down!

First, though, you need to open the Applications folder, the contents of which you can see in Figure 13-1. You can get there in three ways:

- ✔ Click the Applications folder in the Places sidebar in any Finder window
- ✔ Choose Go➪Applications
- ✔ Use the keyboard shortcut ⌘+Shift+A

Address Book

 Just like it sounds, the *Address Book* is the place to store contact information for your family, friends, and anyone else whom you want to keep track of. It works with the Mail application, enabling you to quickly look up e-mail addresses when you're ready to send a message. Use it with iChat, too, to help you quickly chat with your online friends. It can also work with any other application whose programmers choose to make the connection.

 For example, my Sony Ericsson wireless phone can obtain my contact information (wirelessly!) from Address Book (through the magic of Bluetooth). I talk more about the Address Book in Chapter 11. For more on Bluetooth, see the sidebar entitled "Whither Bluetooth?" elsewhere in this chapter.

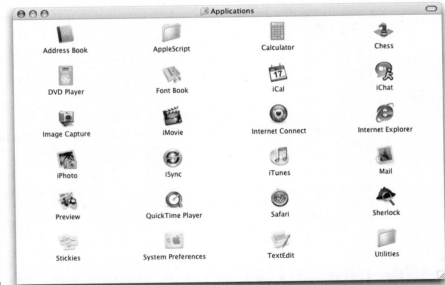

Figure 13-1: Checking out Mac OS X applications.

AppleScript

AppleScript is like a tape recorder for your Mac. It can record and play back things that you do, such as opening an application or clicking a button. You can use it to record a script for tasks that you often perform and then have your Mac perform those tasks for you later. You can write your own AppleScripts, use those that come with your Mac, or download still others from the Web. The following sections should give you some indication as to how much — or how little — you care about AppleScript.

Discovering whether you give a hoot about AppleScript

Describing AppleScript to a Mac beginner is a bit like three blind men describing an elephant. One man may describe it as the Macintosh's built-in automation tool. Another may describe it as an interesting but often-overlooked piece of enabling technology. The third may liken it to a cassette recorder, recording and playing back your actions at the keyboard. A fourth (if there were a fourth in the story) would assure you that it looked like computer code written in a high-level language.

They would all be correct. *AppleScript,* the Mac's built-in automation tool, is a little known (at least until recently) enabling technology that works like a cassette recorder for programs that support AppleScript recording. And scripts do look like computer programs (which could be because they *are* computer programs).

If you're the kind of person who likes to automate as many things as possible, you may just love AppleScript because it's a simple programming language that you can use to create programs that give instructions to your Mac and the applications running on your Mac. For example, you can create an AppleScript that launches Mail, checks for new messages, and then quits Mail. The script could even transfer your mail to a folder of your choice.

I call AppleScript a time-and-effort enhancer. If you just spend the time and effort it takes to understand it, using AppleScript will save you oodles of time and effort.

Therein lies the rub. This stuff is far from simple — entire books have been written on the subject. So it's far beyond the purview of a 408-page *For Dummies* book. Still, it's worth learning about if you'd like to script repetitive actions for future use.

You can put frequently used AppleScripts on the Dock or on your Desktop for easy access. Apple also provides a script menu extra, located in the Menu Extras folder (/System/Library/CoreServices/Menu Extras) folder; double-click it to install it in your menu bar. Apple also provides a number of free scripts to automate common tasks, many of which are in the Example Scripts folder in the AppleScript folder. Furthermore, additional scripts can always be downloaded from `www.apple.com/applescript`. Many AppleScripts are designed for use in the Toolbar of Finder windows, where you can drag and drop items onto them quickly and easily.

Checking out AppleScript

The Applications folder contains an AppleScript folder, which in turn contains the Script Editor program plus an alias to a folder full of sample AppleScripts.

Script Editor is the application that you use to view and edit AppleScripts. Although more information on Script Editor is beyond the scope of this book, it's a lot of fun. And the cool thing is that you can create many AppleScripts without knowing a thing about programming. Just record a series of actions that you want to repeat and use Script Editor to save them as a script. If you choose to save your script as an application by selecting Application from the Format menu in the Save sheet, you can then run it by double-clicking its icon.

If the concept of scripting intrigues you, I suggest that you open the Example Scripts folder and rummage through it to check out the scripts available at `www.apple.com/applescript`. When you find a script that looks interesting, double-click it to launch the Script Editor program where you can examine it more closely.

Calculator

 Need to do some quick math? The *Calculator* application gives you a simple calculator, with all the basic number-crunching functions that your pocket calculator has. To use it, you can either click the keys with the mouse or you can use your numeric keypad (on your keyboard) to type numbers and operators (math symbols such as +, −, and =). Check out the Calculator in Figure 13-2.

Calculator now has an Advanced mode (View⇨Advanced or ⌘+2), that turns the formerly anemic calculator into a powerful scientific calculator) and a paper tape (View⇨Show Paper Tape) to track your computations and if you want, provide a printed record. It can even speak numbers aloud (Speech⇨ Speak Button Pressed and Speech⇨Speak).

 I find it interesting that until the advent of MacOS X version 10.2 Jaguar, the only thing that had changed about the Calculator since the Mac was invented was the interface. In other words, no functionality had been added or removed in almost 20 years. How many computer programs can say that? (For the curious: Calculator was a Desk Accessory in early versions of the Mac OS and an Apple Menu Item in versions 8 and 9.)

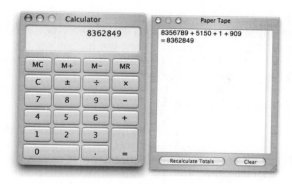

Figure 13-2:
The
Calculator,
basic
(top) and
advanced
(bottom).

Chess

This is a visual implementation of the GNU (stands for Gnu's Not Unix) chess-playing game. You can play against the computer at a variety of settings. Chess is a fairly strong player and should provide a good contest for any chess player who has less than a master ranking. You can see what it looks like in Figure 13-3.

Notice that in the figure, the Dock is hovering over the window. Don't forget that you can auto-hide the Dock by choosing ⌘⇨Dock⇨Turn Hiding On/Off (or by pressing ⌘+Option+D).

To play a game, launch Chess and then choose Game⇨New. If you're playing against the computer, you play as white, so click a white piece and move it. The computer responds by moving a black piece, making it your turn again. Because this is *Mac OS X Panther For Dummies* rather than *Chess For Dummies*, I won't even attempt to tell you how to improve your chess game here.

You can tinker with a couple of preferences in the Chess program. To make the computer a more formidable opponent, choose Chess⇨Preferences and drag the Level slider toward the word Hard. You can also choose to play human versus human or change the name that the computer uses from the rather unimaginative Computer to something more evocative (maybe Kasparov). The last option in the Preferences dialog lets you turn Voice Recognition on or off. (The default is On, which is why you see the circular Speech Recognition window on the right in Figure 13-3.) If you choose to use it, you press the Esc key, and then speak your moves ("Knight G1 to F3," and so on). It works pretty well but, of course, requires that you have an appropriate microphone connected to your Mac.

If you need a hint (as I often do) as to a good next move, choose Move⊅Hint or press ⌘+Shift+H. The program will show you the move that it calculates to be your best choice by blinking both the piece that it thinks you should move and the square to which you should move it. You don't have to take the program's suggestion — just make a different move if you decide to decline the suggestion.

DVD Player

 This application is present only on Macs that have a DVD player installed. Inserting a DVD in such a Mac automatically starts the DVD Player. You can then watch the movie on your Mac unless you've changed the default in the CDs & DVDs System Preferences, which is to Open DVD Player when you insert a video DVD.

Figure 13-3:
The super-
snazzy Mac
OS X 3-D
Chess
game.

The System Profiler application (in the Utilities folder) can tell you whether you've got a DVD drive in your Mac. Just launch it and then click the IDE (ATA) item in the contents column on the left; the details appear on the right.

If you choose ⌘⇨About this Mac in the Finder, there's a More Info button. Click it and System Profiler opens.

The DVD Player comes with a snazzy little on-screen remote control (redesigned in OS X 10.3 Panther), as shown in Figure 13-4.

To choose between the vertical (the two on top in Figure 13-4) and the horizontal (bottom two) controllers, choose Controls⇨Use Vertical/Horizontal Controller or use the keyboard shortcut ⌘+Option+C.

To open or close the little Controller drawer (as shown top right and bottom in Figure 13-4), choose Controls⇨Open/Close Control Drawer, use the keyboard shortcut ⌘+], or click on the little pull tab (where you see the arrow cursor in Figure 13-4) and drag.

The controls themselves should be self-explanatory to anyone who has ever used a set-top DVD player. If they're not familiar to you, hover the cursor over any control and a tool tip will pop up, as shown in Figure 13-5.

Figure 13-4:
DVD
Player's
onscreen
remote
control
gadget.

Font Book

Font Book is a new addition to the Applications folder in Panther. It lets you view your installed fonts, install new fonts, group your fonts into collections, and enable and disable installed fonts. If you ever used the commercial program Extensis Suitcase, Font Book does much the same job.

To install a new font, choose File⇨Add Fonts or use the shortcut ⌘+O. A standard Open dialog box allows you to select a font or fonts to be installed. You may choose to install the font for only you, all users of this Mac, or for use in Classic, as shown in Figure 13-6.

To view a font, click its name in the Font list. To change the size of the viewed font, choose a new size from the drop-down menu (it says "Fit" in Figure 13-7) or move the blue slider on the right side of the window up or down.

To disable a font so it no longer appears in applications' Font menus, choose Edit⇨Disable or click the Disable button at the bottom of the window.

To enable a previously disabled font, choose Edit⇨Enable or click the Enable button at the bottom of the window.

To create a new font collection, choose File⇨New Collection or use the keyboard shortcut ⌘+N. To add a font to a collection, first choose the All Fonts collection and then drag the font from the Font list onto the collection. To remove a font from a collection, select it in the Font list and choose File⇨ Remove Font.

If you remove a font from the All Fonts collection, it disappears permanently. This action cannot be undone, so be careful when you remove fonts.

iCal

 iCal is a wonderful utility that's a daily/weekly/monthly pocket and desktop calendar equivalent. You can publish your calendar(s) to a .Mac account or other compatible (WebDav) server as well as subscribe to calendars that others publish. Integrated with the Address Book, you can select people who you want to invite to a scheduled event. Figure 13-8 shows me inviting some friends to a small shindig.

Figure 13-6: Font Book's Open dialog box lets you install new fonts for you, for all users, or for Classic.

iChat

Text-based chatting on the Internet is an old and popular pastime. Numerous protocols abound with names such as IRC (Internet Relay Chat), ICQ (a mnemonic play on *I Seek You*), AIM (AOL Instant Messenger), and many others. *iChat* supports AIM and lets you communicate with other Mac.com members as well as others on your local network via Rendezvous. You can even hook up online with anyone connected to AOL's massive AIM network, including joining AOL chat rooms, even if you aren't an AOL subscriber. (***Note:*** You do have to know the chat room's name.) Figure 13-9 shows me having a brief conversation with someone we both know and love.

You can even drag and drop files (like photos from iPhoto) onto the message area when chatting with someone, and the file will be sent right to her iChat window! This is way easier than creating an e-mail to send the file while you're chatting.

Furthermore, if you have a FireWire DV camcorder or Apple's iSight camera connected, you can conduct video chats with iChat, and see and hear the person on the other end, as I discuss you in Chapter 11.

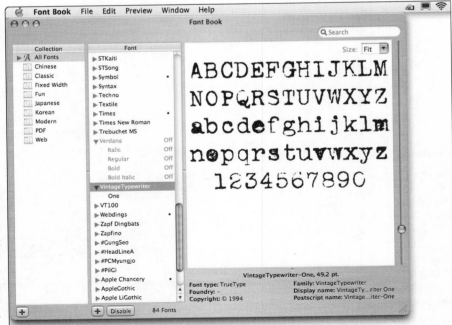

Figure 13-7:
Click a font in the Font list on the left to display it in the pane on the right.

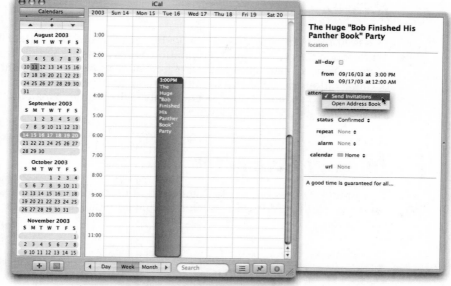

Figure 13-8:
iCal uses
Address
Book and
Mail to
invite
people to
scheduled
events.

Image Capture

Use this program to transfer images from your Universal Serial Bus (USB) digital camera, various SmartMedia readers, or from many supported scanners. If you don't have such a device, don't worry about it. If you do have one and the software that came with it doesn't work with OS X (or even if it does), try Image Capture.

I discuss Image Capture in a bit more detail in Chapter 22.

Figure 13-9:
I'm not
schizo-
phrenic,
and neither
is the
other Bob
"Dr. Mac"
LeVitus.

iMovie

 This is Apple's fantastic digital video editing program. You can use it to edit digital video files or to control compatible FireWire-equipped digital camcorders. You can also use it to create great slideshows for presentations, with both narration and background audio. Trying to cover this software could fill a book of its own, and it does — check out Todd Stauffer's *iMovie 2 For Dummies* (Wiley Publishing, Inc.).

Internet Connect

 This program replaces the old Point-to-Point Protocol (PPP) application in earlier versions of Mac OS. It is used to configure dial-up telephone modem connections.

Internet Explorer

 Internet Explorer (IE) is Microsoft's Web browser for the Mac, and (lucky you!) it ships with OS X. Read a discussion of IE in Chapter 11. Depending upon your version of OS X, there may be an Internet Explorer folder here in the Applications folder, and within that the Internet Explorer icon from which you can start IE. But the quickest way to open Internet Explorer is still to click its e-shaped icon on the Dock.

iPhoto

 If you have a digital camera — or even if you don't but have a large collection of photographs in digital form (maybe from Kodak PictureCDs or scans) — you'll love iPhoto. Use *iPhoto* to organize your pictures into albums (a single picture can be in as many albums as you want without having to create any duplicates); print them out; send them to Kodak for professional photo printing; or send them to Apple to be published in a coffee-table book, published as a Web page (or on your Mac.com Web page), exported as a slideshow, or for use as your Desktop picture.

iSync

 iSync is Apple's hot synchronizing software that lets you synchronize your Address Book entries and iCal calendars with over 20 cell phone models, your iPod, and/or your PDA (such as Palm, Visor, etc.). It also lets you synchronize your Address Book entries, iCal calendars, and Safari Bookmarks between multiple Macs in different locations.

iTunes

iTunes is another great piece of multimedia software from Apple. It lets you play CDs, create your own audio or MP3 CDs (assuming that you have a CD burner), play MP3, AIFF, WAV, and Audible.com files, integrate with your iPod or other MP3 player, listen to Internet radio stations, and view some rather pretty visual displays. (Whew!)

Mail

Mail is the free e-mail program that comes with OS X. I cover Mail in Chapter 11.

Preview

You use *Preview* to open, view, and print PDFs as well as most graphics files (TIFF, JPEG, PICT, and so on). *PDF files* are formatted documents that include text and images. User manuals, books, and the like are often distributed as PDF files. You can't edit a PDF file with Preview, but you can leaf through its pages or print it. It's also the application that pops open when you click the Preview button in the Print dialog, as you discover in Chapter 12.

Any OS X program that prints offers PDF as a file format from which you can print your own documents (via the Output Settings pop-up menu choice or the Save As PDF button found in all OS X 10.2 [and later] print dialogs).

QuickTime Player

Use the *QuickTime Player* to view QuickTime movies or streaming audio and video. The quickest way to launch it is by clicking its icon on the Dock. It also opens automatically when you open any QuickTime movie document file.

Safari

Safari is Apple's Web browser, discussed in some detail in Chapter 11.

Sherlock

I mention *Sherlock* — the cool search tool that you can use to find Web sites, people, software, stuff to buy, and lots more — in several chapters of this book. (The most comprehensive coverage is in Chapter 11.) To quickly open Sherlock, click its icon on the Dock (it looks like Sherlock Holmes' hat with a magnifying glass).

Stickies

Stickies are electronic Post-it Notes for your Mac. They're a convenient place to jot notes or phone numbers. Some Stickies are shown in Figure 13-10.

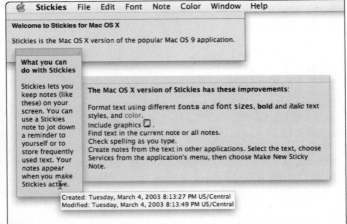

Figure 13-10:
Stickies —
Post-it
Notes for
your Mac.

Stickies are supremely flexible. Move them around onscreen (just drag 'em by their title bar) and change their text to any font and color that you desire by using the Note menu. Make your Stickies any color that you like by using the Color menu. You can collapse a Stickie by double-clicking its title bar. Also, you can print them and import and export text files from them.

If you hover the cursor over a Stickie note (but don't click), the creation and modification dates and times pop up in a little tool-tip style window, like the one just below the "What you can do with Stickies" note in Figure 13-10.

Anything that you type on a Stickie is automatically saved as long as you keep that note open. But when you close a note (by clicking its close box, choosing File⇨Close, or using the keyboard shortcut ⌘+W), you lose its contents forever. Fortunately, Stickies give you a warning and a second chance to save the note in a separate file on your hard drive. You can also export Stickies (choose File⇨Export Text) and save Stickies as plain text, rich text format (RTF) files, or as rich text format with attachments (RTFD) files. The last two formats support fonts and other formatting that plain text format does not.

Stickies have grown up in Mac OS X. They work pretty much as they always have, but now you have more options available, such as a spell checker. You can also import pre-Mac OS X Stickies, in addition to plain text files. The old Stickies application supported colors, but not fonts, as Mac OS X Stickies do.

System Preferences

 I mention System Preferences throughout this book. For complete details, though, check out Chapter 15.

You can open the System Preferences application in any of these three ways:

- ✔ Double-click its icon in the Applications folder.
- ✔ Click its icon on the Dock.
- ✔ Choose System Preferences from the menu.

TextEdit

 TextEdit is a word processor/text editor that you can use to write letters, scribble notes, or open Read Me files. Although it's not as sophisticated as AppleWorks or Microsoft Word, you can use it for some text formatting and to check your spelling. TextEdit supports images, too. (Just copy an image in another program and paste it into a TextEdit document. Or, you can use drag-and-drop to drop an image into a TextEdit document from many applications.)

 Here's a cool new Panther-only trick: TextEdit can open Microsoft Word documents. This is fabulous if you don't happen to have a copy of Microsoft Word on your hard disk. Neat!

Utilities

 Here's another folder full of stuff. Most of the items in the Utilities folder work with other applications to do some useful thing. You may never even open a lot of these applications. The Utilities folder appears in Figure 13-11; stick with me for a brief tour of each application that you find there.

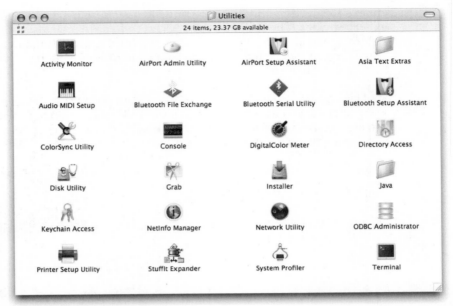

Figure 13-11:
The Utilities
folder.

Activity Monitor

 In *UNIX* (the operating system behind Mac OS X), applications and other things going on behind the scenes are called *processes*. Each application (and the operating system itself) can run a number of processes at once.

Activity Monitor is new in Panther, but its capabilities will be familiar to users of previous versions of OS X — it combines the functions of Process Viewer and CPU Monitor (both discontinued in Panther), and a little bit more, all in one convenient and easy to decipher application.

In Figure 13-12, you see 43 processes running. Interestingly, only three applications are open (the Finder, Snapz Pro X, and Activity Monitor itself).

To display the three CPU monitor windows on the right of the Activity Monitor window in Figure 13-12, choose Monitor➪ Show CPU Usage (keyboard shortcut ⌘+2), Floating CPU Window (no keyboard shortcut), and/or Show CPU History (keyboard shortcut ⌘+3).

You also select what appears in the Activity Monitor's Dock icon — CPU Usage, CPU History, Network Usage, Disk Activity, Memory Usage, or the Activity Monitor icon — from the Dock Icon submenu in the Monitors menu. All but the Activity Monitor icon appear "live," meaning they update every few seconds to reflect the current state of affairs.

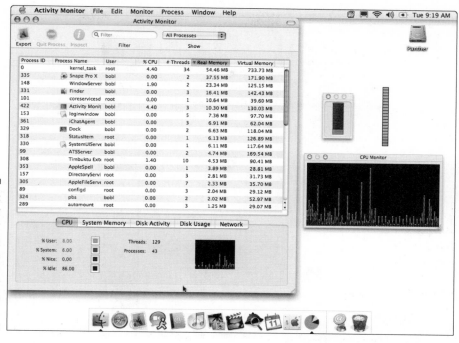

Figure 13-12:
The Activity
Monitor
(left) and
its three
little CPU
Monitor
windows
(right).

To choose how often these updates occur, use the Monitor⊠ Update Frequency submenu.

But be careful — shorter durations cause Activity Monitor to use more CPU cycles, which can decrease overall performance.

Finally, the bottom portion of the Activity Monitor window can display one of five different monitors. Just click the appropriate tab — CPU, System Memory, Disk Activity, Disk Usage, or Network — to see that particular monitor, as shown in Figure 13-13.

Geeks and troubleshooters can use Activity Monitor to identify what processes are running, which user owns the process, and how much of the CPU and memory that the process is using. You can even stop a process if you think that it may be causing problems for you.

Messing around in Activity Monitor is not a good idea for most users. If you're having problems with an application or with Mac OS X, try quitting open applications, force-quitting applications (press ⌘+Option+Esc), or logging out and then logging back in again before you start mucking around with processes.

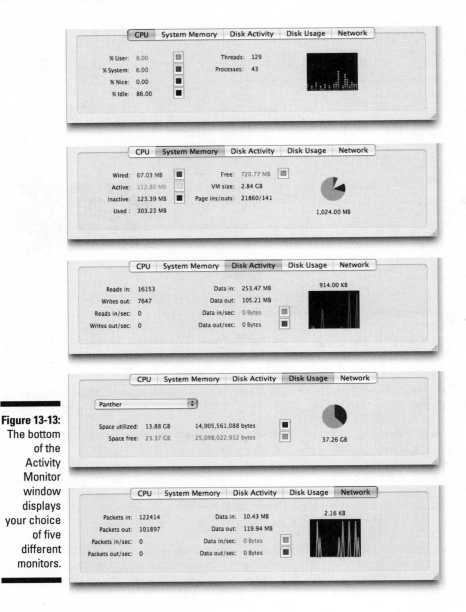

Figure 13-13: The bottom of the Activity Monitor window displays your choice of five different monitors.

AirPort Admin Utility

You use *AirPort Admin Utility* to change individual Internet settings of an AirPort Base Station, such as your Internet Service Provider's (ISP) phone number.

AirPort Setup Assistant

The name is pretty self-explanatory. You run this program to configure your AirPort card for wireless networking.

Asia Text Extras

This folder contains three items: Chinese Text Converter, IM Plugin Converter, and Plugin_Text_Sample. Because I speak no Asian languages, I have no idea what to do with them.

Audio MIDI Setup

This program is the control center for any MIDI devices built into or connected to your Mac.

Bluetooth File Exchange

If you have a Bluetooth device and your Mac has a Bluetooth adapter connected to a USB port (or has Bluetooth built in, although no Mac has it at the time of this writing), you can drag icons for Address Book items (vCard files), iCal items (vCal files), and pictures (.gif files) onto the Bluetooth File Exchange icon to copy the file from your Mac to the Bluetooth device wirelessly via Bluetooth.

If your Mac doesn't have Bluetooth built-in or a Bluetooth adapter connected to it and you try to launch any of the three Bluetooth utilities, they alert you that your Mac doesn't have the proper Bluetooth hardware connected to it and refuse to launch.

Bluetooth Serial Utility

This utility lets you add serial ports for specific Bluetooth devices. For example, one port may be dedicated to your Bluetooth PDA while another is dedicated to your Bluetooth Phone.

Bluetooth Setup Assistant

If you have a Bluetooth device (or devices), start by running this utility. It helps you set up each Bluetooth device to work with your Mac by asking a series of questions.

ColorSync Utility

This is a single-purpose program that verifies the contents of color-matching profiles installed on your Mac. If you don't use ColorSync (Apple's color-matching technology to ensure what you see onscreen is the same as what you print on any device), don't worry about it.

Console

Mac OS X is based on an operating system called *UNIX*, which is a powerful operating system with lots of incredibly geeky features and capabilities that most Mac users don't really want to know about (and that Apple hides from you unless you want to work with them). But for those who want to find out what's going on under the hood of Mac OS X (or even to tinker around with the engine), the Console application provides a window into the deep, dark world of UNIX. Console displays system messages that can help you to troubleshoot problems with Mac OS X — assuming that you know how to interpret them.

Don't let it scare you — most folks will never need Console.

DigitalColor Meter

 This is a little program that displays what's on your screen as RGB (red-green-blue) or CIE (the abbreviation for a chromaticity coordinate system developed by the Commission Internationale de l'Eclairage, the international commission on illumination) values. If you're not a graphic artist or otherwise involved in high-end color document production, you'll almost certainly never need it.

Directory Access

 This little program is meant for system administrators on large networks. If your computer is connected to a campus or corporate network, talk to your network administrator about these settings.

If you're a home user, just ignore it.

Disk Utility

 If you're having problems with your hard drive or need to make changes to it, Disk Utility is a good place to start. This application has five active components: First Aid, Erase, Partition, RAID, and Restore.

Whither Bluetooth?

Bluetooth is an upcoming standard for wireless communication between intelligent devices over short distances. At least that's my definition. The first devices have just come on the market, and one of them is the Sony Ericsson T68i wireless phone that I've been using.

Bluetooth is a smart protocol. When two Bluetooth devices have been prepared (actually, paired), they recognize each other when they are within range — 20–30 feet — and then automatically perform whatever task they've been instructed to perform when they pair.

My phone can receive calendar items, contacts, and little pictures from my Mac. And I can back up the phone's memory to my Mac's hard disk as well. If I attach the Bluetooth adapter to my PowerBook, I can use the phone as a wireless modem and surf the Internet or check my e-mail from the beach if I want to, just like on TV.

What AirPort is to wireless networking, Bluetooth is to intelligent wireless peripheral connections.

Bluetooth isn't very fast and has a limited range (around 20–30 feet from your Mac). But it's swell for sending small amounts of data back and forth between devices. Watch for digital cameras, printers, and other devices that you currently use via USB to offer Bluetooth connectivity soon.

First Aid

If you suspect that something's not quite right with your Mac, the First Aid portion of Disk Utility should be among your first stops. Use First Aid to verify and (if necessary) repair an ailing drive. To use it, click the First Aid button on the left side of the Disk Utility window. Click a volume's icon and then click Verify. You get information about any problems that the software finds. If First Aid doesn't find any problems, you can go on your merry way, secure in the knowledge that your Mac is A-OK. If verification turns up trouble, click Repair to have the problem fixed. You can also use First Aid to fix disk permission problems.

You won't be able to use the copy of Disk Utility in your Applications/Utilities folder to repair your OS X boot disk. To do that, you must reboot from the Mac OS X CD and run the copy of Disk Utility on that CD-ROM.

You can't use Disk Utility First Aid to fix a CD-ROM or DVD-ROM disk, nor can it fix most disk image files (see the discussion of Disk Copy just before this section). These disks are read-only and can't be altered.

You *can* fix Zip disks, SuperDisks, DVD-RAM discs, or any other writeable media that can be mounted by your Mac.

Erase

Use Erase to format (completely erase) a disk. You can't do this to the startup disc — the one with Mac OS X on it.

When you format a disk, you erase all information on it, permanently. Formatting can't be undone and shouldn't be attempted unless you are absolutely sure this is what you want to do. Unless you don't want or need whatever's currently on the disk, you need a complete backup of the disk before formatting. If the data is critical, you should have at least two (or even three) known-to-be-valid back-up copies of it before you reformat.

Partition

Use this tab to create disk partitions (multiple volumes on a single disk), each of which is treated as a separate disk by OS X.

RAID

By using Redundant Array of Individual Disks (RAID), you can treat multiple disks as a single volume, which is sort of the antithesis of partitioning.

Restore

Use the Restore tab to restore your Mac to factory-fresh condition from a CD-ROM or Disk Image file.

Of partitions and volumes

Partitioning a drive lets you create multiple volumes. A *volume* looks and acts just like a hard drive, but if it's a partition, it's not a drive at all. Rather, it's a section of the drive that's completely separate from all others. You can create any number of partitions, but it's a good idea to limit yourself to no more than a small handful. Lots of people, including me, use one partition for Mac OS X and another for Mac OS 9.

You can only create drive partitions on a newly formatted drive. So to partition a drive, first format it in Drive Setup and then create partitions. Before you do, give some thought as to how large of a partition that you want to create. You won't be able to change your mind later.

I think that partitions should be no smaller than 2GB. You can get away with 1GB if you have a 4GB or smaller drive, but you don't need to create a lot of little partitions just to store your stuff. Instead, use folders: They work just great for organizing things the way you like. The one exception to this rule is if you burn a lot of CDs with your CD-RW drive. In that case, a 650MB or 700MB (if you use that size CD) partition lets you "prototype" your CDs before you burn them to see just how much stuff will fit on a single 650MB or 700MB disk.

By the same token, I think you should limit the number of partitions that you create. A PowerMac G4 with a 20GB drive does just fine with two (or maybe three) partitions.

Speaking of disk images, the Panther version of Disk Utility contains the functionality formerly found in the (now discontinued) Disk Copy program.

In most cases, you install new software on your Mac from a CD-ROM or by downloading it from the Internet. Software vendors typically use an installer program that decompresses and copies files to their proper places on your hard drive. After you've installed the software, you're back in business.

Apple has a variation on this theme called the *disk image,* and more developers are adopting the disk image format for their downloadable installers and updaters. When mounted on your Desktop — more on what *mounting* means in a minute — a disk image looks and acts just like a real disk. You can open it and see its contents in a Finder window; you can copy files from its window to another disk; and you can drag it to the Trash to remove it from your Desktop. To make a disk image appear on your Desktop, you double-click the image file. At that point, the Disk Utility application takes over and puts an icon (which for all intents and purposes looks like a disk) on your Desktop.

Disk Utility not only mounts images when you double-click them, but it can also be used to create your own disk image files and to burn disk image files onto CD-ROM discs.

Because disk images can be transferred via the Internet and because they act just like disks, they're a great substitute for a CD-ROM or other disc-based software installer. A software maker can create both a CD version of an installer and a disk image that can be downloaded.

Grab

 Want to take a picture of your screen? I used to do this a lot so that I could bring you the screen shots (what you see in the figures) in this book. You can use Grab to take a picture of all or part of the screen and then save that file for printing or sending around (like to everyone that you think may want to see your Desktop pattern or how you've organized your windows). The first edition of this book used Grab, but I used the superb Snapz Pro X utility (Ambrosia Software; www.ambrosiasw.com) for the figures in subsequent editions. It's definitely worth the shareware fee.

 Grab's best feature is the ability to do a timed screen capture. Like those cameras that let you start the timer and then run to get into the shot, Grab gives you ten seconds to bring the window that you want to the front, pull down a menu, get the cursor out of the way, or whatever you need to do to get the screen just right.

 Grab's default behavior is to display no cursor. If you want to show a cursor in your screen shots, choose Grab⇨Preferences and then select a pointer from the ten choices in the Preference dialog box by clicking it. Or to have no cursor, click the topmost, leftmost item, which is an empty box (that indicates *no cursor*).

Installer

 Here's an application that you'll never need to open yourself. But don't get rid of it because software developers, including Apple, write installer scripts that automate the process of putting software on your Mac. These scripts know where everything should go and in what order — and in order to run, those installer scripts need to find this little program. So just leave it alone, and everything will be hunky-dory.

Java

 This folder contains five items:

- **Applet Launcher:** Used to run Java applets without launching your Web browser.

- **Java Plugin Settings (one for version 1.3.1; another for version 1.4.1):** A control panel for Java and plug-ins that you may run in your Web browser or Applet Launcher.

- **Input Method Hot Key:** Lets you designate a hot key that allows you to select from multiple input methods in a pop-up menu.

The hot key is available only while a Java application is the active application.

✔ **Java Web Start:** A nifty little tool that lets you launch full-featured applications written in the Java language with a single click from within your Web browser. One big advantage of an application written in Java is that you don't have to wait for the publisher to create a Mac OS X version. The same Java code that runs on Windows or Linux or Solaris (Sun's version of UNIX) will run on Mac OS X and inherit the Mac OS X interface.

Keychain Access

A *keychain* is a way to consolidate all your passwords — the one you use to log into your Mac, your e-mail password, and passwords required by any Web sites. Here's how it works: You use a single password to unlock your keychain (which holds your various passwords) and then you don't have to remember all your other passwords. Rest assured that your passwords are secure because only a user who has your keychain password can reach the other password-protected applications.

To create a new keychain, choose File⇨New Keychain.

To add passwords to the keychain, you must first create a keychain and a password. Then you can add passwords to the chain.

After you set up a keychain, just open Mail or another application that supports the keychain and change your password. Respond *Yes* when prompted whether you want to add the password to the keychain.

How do you know which programs support the Keychain utility? You don't until you're prompted to save your password in a keychain in that Open dialog, connect window, or so forth. If a program supports Keychain, it offers a check box for it in the user ID/password dialog or window.

The Keychain utility is particularly cool if you have multiple e-mail accounts that each has a different password. Just add them all to your keychain, and you can get all your mail at once with one password.

To add a Web site password to a keychain, open the Keychain Access application and click the Password button. In the New Password Item window that opens, type the URL of the site in the Name text field, type your username in the Account text field, and then type your password in the Passphrase text field, as shown in Figure 13-14.

To use the new URL password, double-click the URL in the Keychain Access window. A small Get Info window will pop up. Click the Go There button to launch your browser (if it isn't already running) — you're taken and logged in to the Web site that you choose. This will work even with Internet Explorer, but if you type a URL into IE's Address field, it won't check your keychain.

Figure 13-14:
Add a URL
to the
keychain in
Keychain
Access.

NetInfo Manager

Here's another little program for system administrators on large networks or power user administrators of shared Macs. If you're a home user, just ignore it.

Network Utility

And here is yet another little program for system administrators on large networks. But unlike the others — the ones I've told you to ignore if you're a home user — this one can come in handy if you're a veteran Internet user. It offers common Internet utility functions such as `ping`, `traceroute`, `whois`, `finger`, and such. If you don't know what any of this means, don't worry. Just ignore this program and you'll be fine.

ODBC Administrator

If you have need to access corporate databases using Open Database Connectivity (ODBC), your database administrator will give you the values that you need to plug into this tool. If you're not going to be doing that, don't worry about this tool.

Printer Setup Utility

Print Center is the program that you use to configure your Mac to use printers and to manage print jobs. I discuss Print Center in Chapter 12.

StuffIt Expander

Nowadays, you encounter compressed files and archives of compressed and encoded files and folders everywhere you turn, especially if you get any files from the Internet. *StuffIt Expander* can decompress or decode StuffIt (`.sit`), PC Zip (`.zip`), UNIX gzip (`.gz`), UNIX compress (`.z`), BinHex (`.hqx`), and a whole host of other compression and encoding formats.

I strongly recommend putting StuffIt Expander's icon on the Dock, which will allow you to just drag the compressed files onto the icon to decompress them.

System Profiler

System Profiler is a little program that gives you information about your Mac. What a concept! If you're curious about things such as what processor your Mac has or what devices are currently connected to it, give the Profiler a try. Poke around the Commands menu and check it out; this little puppy is benign and won't hurt anything.

If you ever have occasion to call for technical support for your Mac, software, or peripherals, you're probably going to be asked to provide information from System Profiler. So don't get rid of it just because you don't care about this kind of stuff.

Terminal

Mac OS X is based on UNIX. If you need proof, or if you actually want to operate your Mac as the UNIX machine that it is, Terminal is the place to start.

Because UNIX is a command-line based operating system, you need to use Terminal to type commands. You can issue commands that show a directory listing, copy and move files, search for filenames or contents, or establish or change passwords. In short, if you know what you're doing, you can do everything on the command line that you can in Mac OS X. For most folks, that's not a desirable alternative to the windows and icons of the Finder window. But take my word for it; true geeks who are also Mac lovers get all misty-eyed about the combination of a command line and a graphical user interface.

If you do decide to tinker with Terminal and the UNIX-y innards of Mac OS X, please take some time to bone up on UNIX itself. Everything that you learn about UNIX will work on your Mac OS X. A good book on the subject is *Learning the UNIX Operating System (Nutshell Handbook)* by Jerry Peek, Grace Todino, and John Strang. Or try *UNIX Visual QuickStart Guide* by Deborah S. Ray and Eric J. Ray, which is the UNIX book that I keep on my desk, just in case.

Chapter 14

The Classic Environment: Like Mac OS 9, Only Better

*M*ac OS X is capable of running two different operating systems. Mac OS X, of course, runs your machine, but Mac OS 9.2.2 — the Mac OS version just before Mac OS X — is available too, if you need it.

Why would Apple give you two operating systems, and what in the world do you do with more than one? I explain this in the following section, and later I explain how two operating systems on one computer work together, how you can use them, and why you would want to.

Mac OS X version 10.3 Panther requires version 9.2.2 of Mac OS to provide the Classic environment. But most (if not all) programs don't distinguish between Mac OS 9, 9.0.1, 9.0.2, 9.0.3, 9.0.4, 9.1, 9.2, 9.2.1, and 9.2.2. So when I call a program a *Mac OS 9 program,* what I mean is that it's not an OS X program and that it will (usually) run under any version of Mac OS 9.

In other words, when I talk about stuff that works with (or appears in) all versions of Mac OS 9, I say *Mac OS 9* or *Mac OS 9.x.* When I'm talking about Classic or another feature or program that requires OS 9 version 9.2.2, I say *Mac OS 9.2.2.*

If you're not sure whether to or how to install Classic on your system, see the Appendix of this book, where I discuss the different ways that you can install Classic.

You Can Call It Classic

Mac OS X is the software that controls your Mac (as I describe in Chapter 1) — it's the magic that starts your computer, displays the Desktop, and gives you access to all the tools that you use every day to work with your files and applications.

Mac OS 9.2.2, called *Classic* when running under Mac OS X, actually runs inside an operating system (OS) *emulator* — software that does most, but not all, of what an operating system does by pretending to be one. When you launch an older application, it's as if you've booted a computer within your computer; that is, Classic first emulates the OS 9 startup process, loading all the extensions and control panels that it needs to mimic Mac OS 9.2.2 and run the application.

Retail boxed copies of Mac OS X version 10.3 Panther don't include a Mac OS 9 install CD. Classic is supported fully, but you'll have to come up with your own copy of a Mac OS 9 install CD (or a copy of your Mac OS 9 System Folder) to use it. Also, Macs sold after January 1, 2003 won't be able to boot into Mac OS 9, although they will still be able to run Classic.

If you have an older Mac OS 9 install CD lying around, you might be able to install that version and then use the OS 9 Software Update control panel to update it to 9.2.2. It's worth trying if you don't have another way of getting an OS 9 System Folder on your Mac. And, of course, you must have an OS 9 (9.2.2) System Folder on a local disk or volume to use Classic.

Running under Mac OS X, Classic is an application, just like AppleWorks, Internet Explorer, or TextEdit. With the Classic application running, you can use Mac OS 9.2.2's Apple menu (if at least one Classic program is running) and you can run Mac OS 9 applications.

You also have access (by switching to any OS X window) to your Mac OS X Home, Desktop, and applications. Finally, you can switch to another program (when a Classic program is active) by choosing it from the Application menu, located on the far right of the Mac OS 9.2.2 (Classic) menu bar.

Most Macs sold after January 1, 2003 can't start up in Mac OS 9. Which means the only way to run older software on newer Macs is via Classic.

All currently open applications — including any Classic apps — appear in your Dock for easy access.

What's so great about Classic?

If you're a Mac newbie or don't have applications or other tools that work with Mac OS 9, you may wonder why Apple would go to the trouble of including Classic in Mac OS X and why you'd want to use it. Well, I think Classic makes OS X a lot better by making available a panoply of older programs that would otherwise be relegated to the slagheap. And long-time Mac users love Classic because it provides access to programs that haven't been updated for Mac OS X. (The following section discusses this in much greater detail.)

Doin' the Classic dance and liking it

If you're a former Mac OS 9 user, you probably have lots of applications and documents that ran under Mac OS 9. For example, suppose that you have Adobe's Photoshop 6.5. You don't have the Mac OS X-native version of Photoshop (version 7) yet, but you do have your copy of Photoshop 6.5, which worked perfectly with Mac OS 9. Classic lets you use version 6.5 until you decide to upgrade to the OS X version of Photoshop. Are you with me? Old software, old files, new operating system.

Although you certainly will want programs written for OS X (often called *OS X native* applications) rather than programs that run as Classic applications, sometimes you have no choice: The program that you want isn't available as a native OS X app — it either runs in Classic or not at all.

To make software work with Mac OS X, the folks who write it *(developers)* have to rewrite *(port)* OS 9 programs for Mac OS X. Or they have to create them from scratch by using special programming tools designed to create *native* Mac OS X applications. Not all developers have done this yet because lots of people still use older Macs with older versions of Mac OS and because rewriting programs costs money and takes time.

When emulation *isn't* the sincerest form of flattery

Emulators aren't just for Mac OS 9/Classic. Some, like Classic, do everything that an operating system does except boot up the computer. Some bridge the PC/Mac gap: With Pentium emulators (such as Virtual PC) for Mac OS, for example, you run Windows software on your Mac in a window that looks like, well, Windows. Other kinds of emulators, such as those used in companies in which a Mac or PC needs to connect to a mainframe or other big computer, run the mainframe's software in a window on your desktop computer. Most emulators, including Classic, enable you to use the keyboard shortcuts and commands that the emulated system (Mac OS 9, in the case of Classic) uses.

But Apple has encouraged them, and they have responded. These days, there are no new OS 9 (Classic) apps being released; 99.9 percent of software for the Mac today is OS X native.

Working with Classic

Frankly, there's not much to working with Classic. If you launch an old program, it launches itself and just works. But, in the inimitable *For Dummies* tradition, I'm going to tell you all about it anyway. First I talk about launching Classic. Then I talk about opening Classic applications. Last but not least, I show you how to boot up with OS 9.2.2 for those occasions where Classic just won't do.

Launching Classic (or letting it launch itself)

You don't really have to launch Classic, per se. It launches itself whenever you open any Mac OS 9 application (or a document that belongs to that application). When you do, your Mac figures out that the program or document is a *classic,* and the Classic environment launches automatically.

That's not exactly true. Although you can't launch it in the traditional sense (by opening its icon), you can make it launch from the Classic System Preferences pane. In the upcoming "Setting Classic Preferences" section, I'll show you how.

The first time that you launch Classic, a dialog appears asking you to allow Mac OS X to install some files in the Mac OS 9.2.2 System Folder — the folder that runs the Mac OS 9.2.2 environment that you'll be working with. These files are needed to bridge the gap between Mac OS X and Mac OS 9.2.2, so click OK when you see the dialog.

After you launch Classic, you first see a small status window (shown in Figure 14-1) with a progress bar and a Stop button . . . just in case you change your mind and don't want Classic to launch.

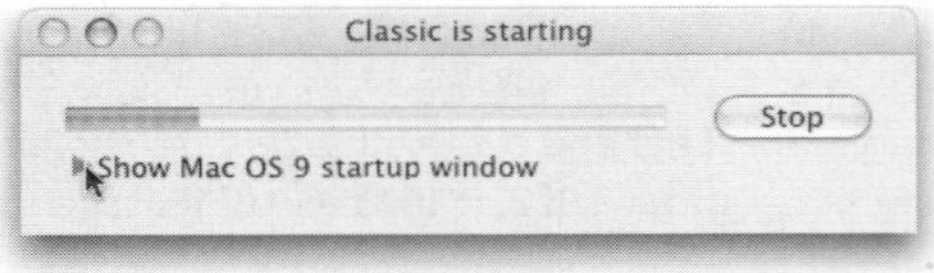

Figure 14-1:
Opening
Classic
launches
the Mac
OS 9.2
emulator.

○ ○ ○	Classic is starting
▭▭▭▭▭▭▭▭▭▭▭▭▭▭▭▭▭▭▭▭▭▭▭▭	(Stop)
▶Show Mac OS 9 startup window	

After you start Classic, you can watch the emulator load by clicking the right-pointing triangle below the progress bar (under the arrow cursor in Figure 14-1). Clicking this triangle expands the window to show you the progress of the startup process (as shown in Figure 14-2). If you're a Mac OS 9 user, you'll recognize the welcome screen.

If you don't choose to view the startup process by expanding the Classic window, just wait a bit and watch the progress bar inch its way along until Mac OS 9.2.2 launches and is ready to use. At that point, the Classic window disappears, your Classic application becomes active, and you see the Mac OS 9.2.2 menu bar. Check it all out in Figure 14-3.

Opening a Classic app

With Classic you can launch any pre-Mac OS X application by double-clicking its icon. If Classic isn't already running, double-clicking a Classic application automatically launches both Classic and the application. When you double-click a MacWrite (or other document) file associated with a Classic app, for example, the Classic application launches and so does MacWrite (or whatever Classic application created the file).

Figure 14-2: Expand the window and view the familiar OS 9 welcome screen.

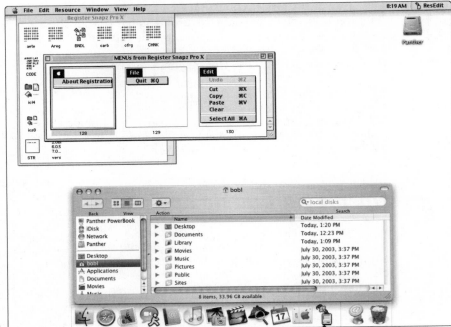

Figure 14-3:
The Classic program, ResEdit, is active; the OS X Desktop and Finder window (my Home) are inactive but can still be seen in the background.

You can tell when you're using a Classic program because when it's active (front-most on your screen), you see the old OS 9-style menu bar, complete with a multi-colored Apple menu in the upper-left corner of your screen. Figure 14-4 shows the old striped Apple menu and its blue OS X counterpart.

The OS X Apple icon will be gray instead of the default blue if you select the Graphite Appearance in the General System Preferences pane. In any event, it's always a solid color in the OS X menu bar and always rainbow-colored in Classic menu bar.

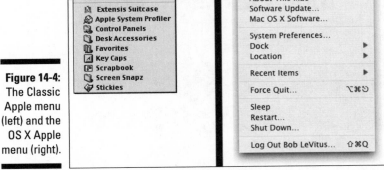

Figure 14-4:
The Classic Apple menu (left) and the OS X Apple menu (right).

Getting oriented ("Toto, we're not in OS X, anymore . . .")

Classic is a strange bird, combining things that are familiar from each of the two operating systems on your Mac. In the following sections, I walk you through what to expect when Classic is active.

Menu bar

The menu bar that you see when working in a Classic application is the Mac OS 9.2.2 version. You'll know it by the multi-hued Apple logo in the top-left corner. Compare that with the Mac OS X Apple, which is a solid color (either blue or gray depending on your choice in the General System Preference Pane).

The Mac OS 9.2.2 menu bar appears when you have a Mac OS 9 application open and active. If Classic has been launched but no Classic application is running, you'll see the Mac OS X menu bar.

Because space here won't allow me to go over all the features that you can access from the Classic menu bar, I'll point out a few and encourage you to explore them on your own. Although most of the menus on the menu bar belong to the Classic application that's open (ResEdit in Figure 14-3), a couple — sometimes more — are part of Mac OS 9.2.2.

The first feature of the Mac OS 9.2.2 menu bar is the Apple menu (topped by that rainbow Apple logo, as shown in Figure 14-5). The old customizable Apple menu is among the coolest of all Mac OS 9 features and one that lots of Mac OS X users miss. This menu contains all sorts of things: It houses tools for working with parts of Mac OS 9 (control panels, the calculator, and so forth), as well as aliases to folders (or files, if you've put them there). The beauty of the Apple menu is that it's available in all Classic Mac applications.

Figure 14-5:
Access the OS 9 Apple menu (l.) or Application menu (r.) when a Classic application is open.

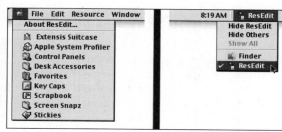

Another menu that I want to tell you about is the Application menu, located at the top far-right corner of the OS 9.2.2 menu bar. You'll know it by the application's name and icon — ResEdit in Figure 14-5. The Application menu displays a listing of all applications that are currently running, including both Classic and Mac OS X applications.

Dock and icons

Just like in Mac OS X, the Finder's Desktop and windows are visible when you're working in the Classic environment. That includes the Dock and any icons that you have on the Desktop. The Dock is pretty smart about Classic: When you open a Classic application, the application's icon appears on the Dock; the icon disappears when you quit the application. In Figure 14-6, you can see the Dock with one Classic application icon in the middle of some Mac OS X application icons. Telling them apart is tricky — the Classic application icons are, well, sometimes a little *uglier* than the Mac OS X ones. Where OS X icons have clean lines, OS 9 icons can look jaggy and . . . well . . . ugly. (That's because they're old, lower-resolution icons.) Check out Figure 14-6 to see for yourself.

Figure 14-6:
ResEdit's jack-in-the-box icon doesn't look so good when it's surrounded by beautiful photoreal-istic OS X icons on the Dock.

Finder windows

Whether a Classic application or the Mac OS X Finder is active, you might see Mac OS X Finder windows (assuming that any are open and that your Classic application isn't blocking your view of them). You can use them to open or move files as you normally would with Mac OS X alone. If you double-click a file that belongs to a Mac OS 9 application, that program opens when you launch the Classic application.

Getting back to OS X

To get out of Classic and back to OS X, just click the Desktop, any OS X icon in the Dock, any OS X application in the Application menu, or any Finder window, and you're back to good ol' Mac OS X as quick as a bunny.

To quit the Classic application, you'll need to use the Classic System Preference Pane as described in the next section.

Setting Classic preferences

In Chapter 15, I talk about System Preferences panes, but because the preferences for Classic are important to this discussion, I cover them here and now.

If you have multiple hard drives or partitions with Mac OS 9.2.2 installed on them, you can choose which one to use as the operating system for the Classic environment. You make that choice in the Classic pane of System Preferences. (See Chapter 15 for more on System Preferences in general.) Just select the drive or partition (mine is Macintosh HD in Figure 14-7), and the next time that you launch Classic, it uses that volume's copy of Mac OS 9.2.2. Volumes that don't include Mac OS 9.2.2 appear dimmed in the preferences window.

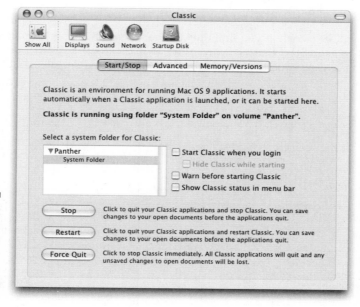

Figure 14-7:
Classic
System
Prefer-
ences.

By selecting the Start Classic When You Log In check box, you tell Mac OS X to do just that. The advantage is that you won't have to wait a minute or two for Classic to launch the first time that you launch a Classic application. The disadvantage is that Classic uses a hefty amount of RAM and other system resources.

If you select the Warn Before Starting Classic check box, when you open a Classic application or a document owned by a Classic application, OS X will present a dialog warning you that Classic is about to start up and offers the choice of starting or not starting it, as shown in Figure 14-8.

Figure 14-8:
OS X tells you that Classic is starting and asks what you'd like to do.

The third check box — Show Classic Status in Menu Bar — adds a useful Classic status indicator and menu to the right side of your menu bar, as shown in Figure 14-9.

Running Classic when you don't need it can slow OS X's performance, so I prefer to keep Start Classic When You Log In disabled and Warn Before Starting Classic enabled. Classic then only runs when I'm sure that I want and need it — and never when I don't.

Figure 14-9:
The Classic status menu adds a useful shortcut to your OS 9 Apple Menu Items.

Note the three buttons at the bottom of the System Preferences Classic pane's Start/Stop tab. (The last two are used mostly when the Classic environment crashes, freezes, or otherwise acts improperly.)

- ✔ **Stop/Start:** Launches Classic without first launching a Classic program. (If Classic is not running, this button toggles to Start.)

  In the earlier section "Launching Classic (or letting it launch itself)," I offer this tip: *Although you can't launch it (Classic) in the traditional sense (by opening its icon), you can make it launch using the Classic System Preferences pane.* The Start/Stop button is what I was talking about.

- ✔ **Restart:** Restarts Classic (big surprise), which is like rebooting OS 9.2.2 without having to reboot OS X.

  You can continue to work in OS X — listen to iTunes, edit movies in iMovie, surf the Web, get your mail, and so on — while Classic starts or restarts. Which is just another reason OS X is better.

- ✔ **Force Quit:** Forces the Classic environment to quit, even if it's crashed or frozen.

Getting more info on Classic

To get the most from Classic, take a look at the version of this book that was written especially for Mac OS 9: *Mac OS 9 For Dummies* (well, duh!). I'm very proud of it. Read the chapters on the Apple menu and those that cover the contents of the System Folder. You'll discover a lot more about the wonders available to you in the Classic environment.

Booting from Mac OS 9.2.2

Before I finish with Classic, here's one more thing you may want to know — how to boot your Mac so it runs OS 9.2.2 instead of OS X.

As I mention earlier in the chapter, if you bought a Mac after January 1, 2003, it may not be capable of booting OS 9 at all. If that's the case, Classic is the only way that you can run OS 9 software.

And as I mention earlier in the chapter, some programs — mostly games — just won't work when you try to run them in the Classic environment under OS X. When that happens, you'll have to start up your Mac with OS 9.2.2 if you want to use that program.

No problem; it's a snap. Here's how:

1. **Open System Preferences by clicking its icon in the Dock or choosing System Preferences from the menu.**

2. **Click the Startup Disk icon to open the Startup Disk pane.**

3. **Click a Mac OS 9.2.2 icon to select it, as shown in Figure 14-10.**

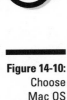

   If you've installed OS 9.2.2 on two or more volumes, you'll see two or more OS 9 System Folders; select the one that you want to boot from.

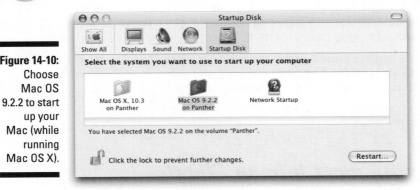

Figure 14-10:
Choose
Mac OS
9.2.2 to start
up your
Mac (while
running
Mac OS X).

4. **Restart your Mac by choosing Restart from the menu or by clicking the Restart button.**

   That's all there is to it. When your Mac comes back to life, you'll be running Mac OS 9.2.2.

If you have both OS 9.2.2 and OS X on the same volume or disk, be careful not to rename any of OS X's folders or throw any of OS X's folders in the Trash (while you're running OS 9.2.2). The results could be catastrophic — you could easily render OS X inoperable.

When your Mac runs OS 9.2.2 and you want to run OS X again, you can't open the Startup Disk System Preferences pane because it's part of Mac OS X and it isn't available while running OS 9.2.2. Now what?

Again, no problem. You do it the old-fashioned way — by using the Startup Disk control panel.

1. **Open the Startup Disk control panel by choosing Control Panels⇨ Startup Disk from the menu.**

2. **Click the folder representing Mac OS X, as shown in Figure 14-11.**

3. **Click the Restart button in the Startup Disk window.**

   That's it. In a few moments, you'll be back up and running with Mac OS X.

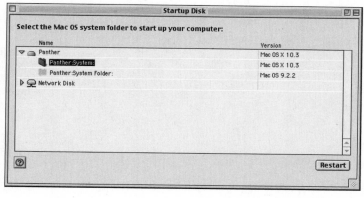

Figure 14-11: Choose Mac OS X to start up your Mac (while running Mac OS 9.2.2).

Chapter 15

What Your Mac Prefers

*E*veryone works a bit differently, and we all like to use our Macs in a certain way. System Preferences is the place in Mac OS X where you can set options that are just right for you. You can set everything from the appearance of your screen to the kind of network or Internet connection that you have — and a whole lot more. In this chapter, I take you on a tour of all the Mac OS X System Preferences panes. Hang on; it's gonna be a long, but informative, ride.

Introducing System Preferences

You find System Preferences on the Apple (🍎) menu and in the Dock. Choose System Preferences from the 🍎 menu or click it in the Dock to get a look at all the options that I discuss in this chapter. Check out all the features that you can change from the System Preferences window, as shown in Figure 15-1.

What you see in Figure 15-1 is the System Preferences window. But when you click any of the icons here, the bottom part of the window changes to reflect the options for the icon that you click. When this happens, I call the bottom part of the window a *pane*. So, for example, when you click the Date & Time icon in the System Preferences window, the bottom part of the window becomes the Date & Time System Preference pane.

System Preferences are similar to OS 9's Control Panels, but Control Panels (mostly) loaded at start up, displaying an icon on the screen when they loaded. System Preference panes don't load at start up; they're just there.

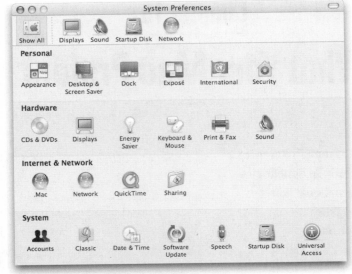

Figure 15-1:
The System
Preferences
window:
Change
your world.

Just where? The actual files for Preference Panes are stored in the Preference Panes folder, in the Library folder in the System folder. (*Note:* This is the OS X System folder, not the OS 9 System Folder-with-a-capital-F.) If you choose to install third-party preference panes, they can go either in that folder (if you want them to be available to all users) or in the Preference Panes folder in the Library in your Home folder (if you want to keep them to yourself).

Some System Preferences relate to topics that I cover in other chapters. The most notable of these are the Network and Internet preferences, which I discuss in Chapter 11. I let you know in this chapter any time that I skip a preference that you can read about in another chapter.

Look back at the System Preferences window in Figure 15-1. By default, four System Preference icons — Displays, Sound, Startup Disk, and Network — appear in the toolbar. Apple kindly put them up top so that you can find them more easily and because these are probably the ones that you'll use most frequently. Also on the toolbar (far left) is the Show All button. I tell you more about this in the upcoming section "Using System Preferences." Below that, Apple has divided System Preferences into four categories: Personal, Hardware, Internet & Network, and System.

Who is Apple to decide which System Preferences you'll be using most? If you want to change this configuration, add your own favorites to the toolbar by simply dragging any icon you like from the bottom of the window onto the toolbar. Your new custom design is waiting for you each time that you open System Preferences. To remove an item, just drag it off the toolbar — it'll disappear with a poof.

As a nice touch, you can change these frequently accessed items from name-and-icon to just icon or to just name (in two sizes each, no less) and back again by ⌘+clicking the Hide/Show Toolbar button (the gumdrop in the upper-right corner) as shown in Figure 15-2.

Using System Preferences

Before I examine the items in the System Preferences window, I need to explain a couple of things about using them. This info applies to all System Preferences, so listen up.

To use a System Preference, just click it once to open its pane. You can double-click if that habit is ingrained in your mouse finger, but there's no need.

Okay, so you've finished working with a System Preferences pane, but you want to open another one. You could simply close the one that you've been working on, or you could cut to the chase by clicking the Show All button, located at the far left of the top row of icons on the System Preferences window (as shown in Figure 15-1). Clicking the Show All button returns the icons for all available System Preferences to view on the screen.

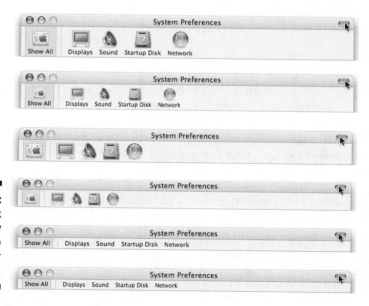

Figure 15-2:
⌘+click
the gray
gumdrop to
change your
toolbar.

Here's an even more convenient way: Choose the System Preferences that you want from the View menu. All the icons that you see in Figure 15-1 also have an entry on this menu; choose one, and its System Preference pane appears immediately.

Here's another nifty tip: You can get rid of the categories all together and display the icons in alphabetical order. As a bonus, it makes the System Preferences window roughly 25 percent smaller onscreen.

When you choose View⇨Organize Alphabetically, the categories disappear, the window shrinks, and the icons are alphabetized, as shown in Figure 15-3.

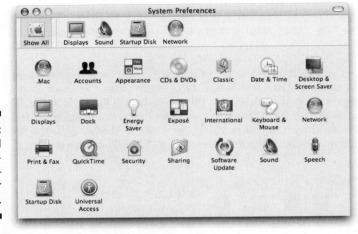

Figure 15-3:
Alphabetical or categorical — however you prefer.

To switch from alphabetical view back to category view, choose View⇨Show All In Categories or use the keyboard shortcut ⌘+L.

Unlocking a preference

Many System Preferences need to be unlocked before you can use them because some of these settings are applicable for all users and thus require an Administrator password. After all, you can't have just any user of your Mac change the Network configuration and break it for everyone. See Figure 15-4 to see what a locked preference looks like. Notice the locked lock icon in the lower-left corner and that everything is grayed out and unavailable. Now compare that with Figure 15-5, where the lock has been unlocked (by supplying an administrator user name and password) and all items are enabled.

You don't have to unlock all System Preferences to change them, just some of them. When I come to a System Preference that must be unlocked before you can use it, I'll let you know up front. Deal? Good.

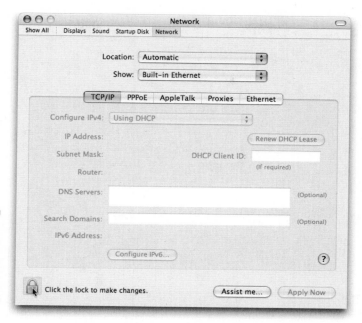

Only users with Administrator privileges can unlock some System Preferences. See Chapter 16 for more info on administrators and permissions.

To unlock a preference, do the following:

1. **Click the lock icon in the lower-left corner of the System Preferences pane (shown in the margin).**

   Mac OS X responds with an Authenticate dialog in which you enter your user name and password.

   The user name and password that you use here must be a user with administrator privileges on this Mac. If your user account isn't set up with administrator privileges, you can't unlock locked panes or change them. You'll need to supply an administrator's user name and password or learn to live with it the way it is.

   The first user that you create with OS X (when you first install it) is always an administrator.

2. **Enter this user information and then click OK.**

   Mac OS X unlocks the System Preference that you're working with.

In Figure 15-5, you see the Network System Preferences pane after being unlocked. Notice that you can now make changes to it; before you unlocked it, all the options were grayed out and impossible to change.

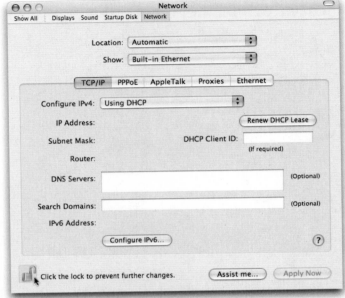

Figure 15-5:
An unlocked
System
Preference
displays its
options.

Locking a preference

To relock a System Preferences pane (after you unlock it), merely click the lock icon again. It will lock itself instantly.

Setting Preferences

Ready to dig into each of the System Preferences? Great. I start with the first category (Personal, as shown in Figure 15-1) and work from left to right.

Personal preferences

The following preference panes are displayed in the Personal category.

Appearance

In the Appearance pane, you can choose specific aspects of how your Mac looks and feels (see Figure 15-6).

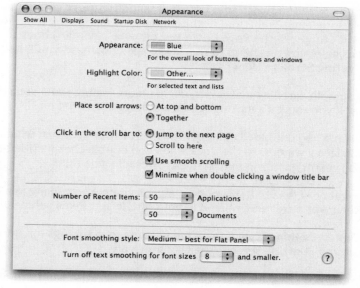

Figure 15-6:
The
Appearance
System
Preferences
pane.

Appearance options

✔ **Appearance pop-up menu:** Use choices from this menu to choose from different appearances, changing the overall look of buttons and window controls (the jellybeans in the scroll bars).

Apple, however, in its infinite wisdom, provides only two choices — Blue and Graphite.

✔ **Highlight Color pop-up menu:** From here, you can choose the color that text becomes surrounded by when you select it in a document or in an icon's name in the Finder window. This time Apple isn't so restrictive. You have seven highlight colors to choose from, plus Other, which brings up a color picker from which you can choose almost any color.

Scroll bar behavior

The Place Scroll Arrows radio buttons let you choose whether you have the traditional single arrow at either end or the default (introduced in OS 8) of both arrows together at the bottom or right of the scroll bars.

Select from two radio buttons next to the Click in the Scroll Bar To heading to move your view of a window either up or down by a page (the default behavior for OS 9) or to the point in the document roughly proportionate to where you clicked in the scroll bar.

Select the Scroll to Here radio button if you often work with long (multi-page) documents. You'll find it quite handy for navigating long documents. And don't forget — the Page Down key on your keyboard does the same thing as selecting the Jump to the Next Page choice, so you'll lose nothing by selecting Scroll to Here.

Using smooth scrolling makes documents more legible while you scroll. Give it a try; if you think it's making things feel sluggish, turn it off.

Minimize When Double-Clicking a Window Title Bar does just what it says — it minimizes a window to the Dock when you double-click its title bar. And yes, the yellow gumdrop button does the exact same thing.

The Number of Recent Items pop-up menus control how many applications and documents are remembered in your ⌘⇨Recent Items submenu.

The Font Smoothing Style pop-up menu offers four settings for anti-aliasing (smoothing) fonts on screen. The categories are

- **Standard - Best for CRT:** You know, your standard, clunky tube-type monitor. If your monitor isn't a flat panel LCD, this is probably your best bet.

- **Light:** Just a hint of the essence of smoothing for your text.

- **Medium - Best for Flat-Panel:** For those sleek, flat-panel monitors and notebooks, too.

- **Strong:** Mondo-smoothing. I happen to like it on my flat-panel display, but you might not.

Ignore Apple's editorial comments and try all four. Then choose the one that looks best to your eyes.

The Turn off Text Smoothing for Font Sizes x and Smaller pop-up menu (where x is the pop-up menu setting) does just what it says. Fonts that size and smaller are no longer *anti-aliased* (smoothed) when displayed.

Desktop & Screen Saver

The Desktop & Screen Saver pane lets you set your Desktop color or picture as well as choose a screen saver for your Mac.

Desktop

Click the Desktop tab to specify a desktop picture or pattern. Apple provides a number of collections from which you can choose via the Collection pop-up menu, or you can choose a different folder of images if you want. You can also drag an image file into the *well* (that indented box in the upper-left corner of the pane).

Screen Saver

Click the Screen Saver tab to choose a screen saver module.

Mac OS X comes with several screen saver modules; to see what the selected module looks like in action, click the Test button. Press any key to end the test.

To set up the screen saver, first choose a screen saver from the list on the left side of the pane. Next, drag the Start Screen Saver slider to the number of minutes that you want the Mac to wait before activating the screen saver.

Click the Use Random Screen Saver checkbox to have your Mac choose a new screen saver at random each time the screen saver kicks in.

You can require a password to wake your Mac from sleep or a screen saver. This option appears in the Security System Preference pane as a checkbox: Require a Password to Wake This Computer from Sleep or Screen Saver.

Finally, click the Hot Corners button to choose which corner(s) of your screen activates the screen saver and which deactivates it. Now when you move your mouse to a selected corner, you activate or deactivate the screen saver.

That's it. You're done!

If you like Screen Savers/Effects, find plenty more available at your favorite downloadable software repository (mine's www.versiontracker.com). Many are free, and some cost a few bucks. Some of those, like Marine Aquarium in Figure 15-7 (from www.order-n-dev.com), are even worth paying for.

Figure 15-7:
Search the
Web for
other cool
screen
savers.

I paid my $21.95, and it was worth every penny. It's so lifelike I sometimes believe those are real fish in my monitor. Plus, unlike other fish I've owned, these never float belly-up (or explode from overeating). I love this saver/effect; it's the only one I use anymore.

Dock

I cover the Dock and its preferences in great detail in Chapter 3. Rather than waste any more trees, I'll just move along to . . . .

Exposé

Exposé is a cool new Panther feature that lets you quickly see all open windows or all the windows open in the application you're currently using by rearranging the windows on screen and "graying out" everything else. It can also hide all windows so you can see your desktop.

By default, you use the function keys to choose the way Exposé displays your windows:

- To see all open windows, press F9.
- To see all open windows belonging to the current application, press F10.
- To hide all open windows and display the desktop, press F11.

A picture is worth a thousand words, so take a gander at Figure 15-8, where I've got several applications running with multiple windows open in each of them.

While using Exposé, if you point to a window but don't click, the window's title appears. If you click on any window — even one that's grayed out — at any time, Exposé deactivates and that window becomes active.

The four Active Screen Corners pop-up menus allow you to configure the corners of your screen to activate and deactivate Exposé features.

The three Keyboard pop-up menus let you change the keys Exposé uses from F9, 10, and 11, or disable the keyboard commands completely (by choosing the dash in any of the pop-up menus).

The three Mouse pop-up menus let you assign alternate mouse buttons to activate or deactivate Exposé features.

International

If you're in the U.S., you might assume that you don't need to set anything in the International System Preferences pane. After all, you chose to see your Mac's menus and commands in U.S. English when you first installed Mac OS X. But wait — the International System Preferences pane has more in it than just a choice of language. Here's where you can set date and time formats — probably the most useful feature for U.S. folks — and yes, you can choose a new language here, too.

The International System Preferences pane has three tabs: Language, Formats, and Input Menu. I describe each in the following sections.

Language

This is where you set your Mac's order of preference for languages used in applications. Choose the languages you want your Mac to use by clicking the Edit button and checking or unchecking checkboxes; to organize your choices, drag an entry up or down in the list on the left. If an application uses the first language that you indicate in this list, you see the application's commands and menus in that chosen language. If your first language choice isn't available, the next option is used, and so on.

The Customize Sorting button lets you select a script to attach to the languages that you chose in the top part of this pane. The script that you choose affects sort order, case conversion, and word definitions.

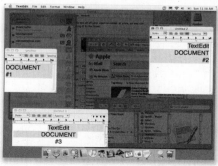
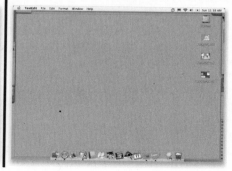

Figure 15-8: Clockwise from top left: Exposé off; F9 — All open windows; F11 — Desktop only; F10 — All applications windows (TextEdit here).

Formats

First choose your present location from the Region pop-up menu. Then, select a format for the way date, time, and numbers are displayed by clicking appropriate Customize button. A sheet appears with all the options available. Make your choices and click OK.

Note that when you change an option in any of these sheets, the way it will look if you click OK appears in a gray rectangle near the bottom of the sheet.

Input Menu

Use the Input Menu tab to select keyboard layouts, input methods, and palettes that appear in the input menu, which you can display in the menu bar by clicking the Show Input Menu in Menu Bar checkbox, as shown in Figure 15-9.

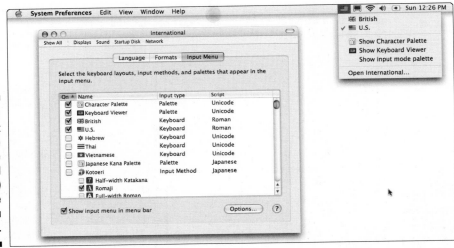

Figure 15-9: The Input Menu tab in the International pane (left) and the Input Menu menu (right).

While many users will never need an alternative keyboard layout, two of the palettes — the Character and Keyboard Viewer — can be quite handy, as shown in Figure 15-10.

Do not under any circumstances click the Options button on the Input Menu tab unless you have good reason to use foreign keyboard layouts on occasion. The ⌘+Option+spacebar keyboard shortcut, when turned on, can cause unpredictable behavior if you later forget that you turned it on. Use this thingy with caution, especially if you use Photoshop (which uses ⌘+Option+spacebar as the shortcut for Zoom Out).

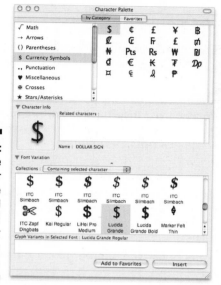

Figure 15-10: The Character Palette (left) and Keyboard Viewer palette (right).

Security

This pane offers four checkbox items that deal with your Mac's security:

✔ **Require password to wake this computer from sleep or screen saver.**

This item causes your Mac to require a password to wake it from sleep or to dismiss the screen saver.

Turning this preference on won't prevent another user from turning off the computer and restarting it, and then logging into their account. If you think this could happen, be sure to save your work before you leave your computer.

✔ **Disable automatic login.**

This item causes your Mac to require every user to provide a user name and password each time the Mac is started up or restarted.

If you want your Mac to start up to the Finder without first asking for a user name or password, select the Automatically Log In option in the Accounts preference pane. And, of course, this item must remain unchecked.

✔ **Require password to unlock each secure system preference.**

This item locks all the System Preference panes that affect all users so they cannot be changed without an administrator name and password.

✔ **Log out after __ minutes of inactivity.**

This item causes your Mac to log out automatically after a set number of minutes pass without any keyboard or mouse activity.

Hardware preferences

The following preference panes are displayed in the Hardware category.

CDs & DVDs

Introduced with Mac OS X version 10.2 Jaguar, this preference pane lets you decide what your Mac should do when you insert a blank or pre-recorded CD or DVD. Choose here from five pop-up menus; you can also set your Mac to launch certain applications, run AppleScripts, or nothing at all.

Displays

This pane has two tabs — Display and Color — to set various options for your monitor.

Display

The Colors pop-up menu lets you choose the number of colors your monitor displays.

The list of resolutions governs how much stuff you see on your monitor. The smaller the numbers, the less you'll see and the bigger you'll see it. Bigger numbers mean you see more, but it's smaller. Got it? Most monitors and video cards support multiple resolutions, and some also allow you to choose from multiple refresh rates.

Many monitors offer settings to adjust their brightness and some also enable you to adjust their gamma settings in this tab. If your monitor supports these features, you will see Brightness and/or Gamma Control slide bars in this tab. If you have these features, adjust them the way that looks best to your eyes.

The Show Displays in Menu Bar check box gives you the little menu that you see at the upper-right of most of the figures in this book, so you can change the resolution and color depth without opening the System Preferences application.

The Number of Recent Modes pop-up menu controls how many settings appear in the Displays menu (assuming you've enabled the Displays menu; if you haven't, it does nothing.)

If you have a laptop, you will see a Detect Displays button; if you have a desktop Mac, you won't have it. It does just what its name implies: When you connect an external display to your laptop Mac, if that display isn't recognized automatically (which it usually is), you can click this button (or choose Detect Displays from the Displays menu), and the monitor will be instantly recognized without restarting!

This OS X-only detail is good to remember if you use several different external displays or projection systems in different locations. It saves you from shutting down/restarting and makes the whole process a little sweeter. Just click and you're done.

Color

Choose a pre-configured profile for your monitor (for Apple branded monitors) and calibrate your display (any brand including Apple). To calibrate, click the Calibrate button; an assistant will walk you through the process.

Arrange

Finally, if you have two video cards or are using a PowerBook and external monitor together, you'll see a third tab called Arrange. Drag the little pictures representing your monitors around in the window to arrange your screens. Make it match the physical set up of your monitors as closely as possible. If you want to place the menu bar on the other screen, drag the little picture of the menu bar from one little screen to the other.

The Arrange tab only appears on PowerBooks with an external display connected to them, and on desktop Macs with more than one graphics card installed.

Energy Saver

All Macs are Energy Star compliant and have been for years, allowing you to preset your machine to turn itself off at a specific time or after a specified idle period. It offers three tabs: Sleep, Schedule, and Options.

If you have a battery-powered Mac, you'll also have a checkbox to enable or disable the battery status indicator in the menu bar.

Sleep

To enable Sleep mode, move the slider to the desired amount of time. You can choose any number between 1 minute and 3 hours, or turn Sleep off entirely by moving the slider all the way to the right to Never.

You can also set separate sleep times for your Mac's display and choose whether to let your hard disk go to sleep if it supports sleep mode. Setting the display to sleep might come in handy if you want your Mac to keep doing what it's doing and you don't need to use the monitor. The hard drive sleep option is less useful unless you've got a PowerBook or an iBook. Checking this option will force your hard drive to sleep after a few minutes of inactivity, which will save your battery.

To activate display sleep, select the Put the Display to Sleep when Computer is Inactive for check box and then drag the slider to the idle time that you want.

To wake up your Mac from its sleep, merely move your mouse or press any key on the keyboard.

Drag the slider to 30 or 45 minutes for sleep; then remember to turn off your Mac manually when you're not going to need it for a day or more.

Schedule

To start up, shut down, or put your Mac to sleep at a predetermined time, check the appropriate checkbox and choose the appropriate choices from the Schedule tab's popup menus.

Options

The Options tab is home to a small collection of useful settings. On this tab, you'll find check boxes telling the Mac to automatically wake up when the modem detects an incoming call (useful for fax software), to automatically wake for Ethernet network administrative access (handy in a corporate setting where an IT person maintains system configurations), and to restart automatically after a power failure.

PowerBook and iBook users get additional Energy Saver options including the ability to display a battery status indicator in the menu bar near the clock as well as a pop-up menu called Processor Performance that offers two options: Highest and Reduced.

Choose Highest when AC power is connected and Reduced when you need to conserve battery power.

Keyboard & Mouse

This pane lets you modify how your keyboard and mouse respond. It offers three tabs (plus a fourth tab — Trackpad — for iBooks and PowerBooks):

Keyboard

Drag the Key Repeat Rate slider to set how fast a key repeats when you hold it down. This feature comes into play, for example, when you hold down the dash (-) key to make a line or the asterisk (*) key to make a divider.

Drag the Delay Until Repeat slider to set how long you have to hold down a key before it starts repeating.

You can type in the box at the bottom of the window to test your settings before exiting this tab.

The Show Eject in Menu Bar checkbox lets you add an Eject menu to your menu bar, which can come in handy when you've got a recalcitrant disc that doesn't want to come out of your CD or DVD drive.

Mouse

The Mouse tab is where you set your mouse speed and double-click delays. Move the Tracking Speed slider to change the relationship between hand movement of the mouse and cursor movement on the screen. A faster tracking speed settings (moving the slider to the right) sends your cursor squirting across the screen with a mere flick of the wrist; slower mouse speed settings (moving the slider to the left) make the cursor crawl across in seemingly slow motion, even when your hand is flying. Set this setting as fast as you can stand it — I like the fastest speed. Try it: You might like it.

The Double-Click Speed setting determines how close together two clicks must be for the Mac to interpret them as a double-click and not as two separate clicks. Move the slider arrow to the leftmost setting (Very Slow) for the slowest. With this setting, you can double-click at an almost leisurely pace. The rightmost position (Fast) is the fastest setting, which I prefer. The middle area of the slider represents a double-click speed somewhere in the middle.

Changes in the Mouse System Preferences pane take place immediately, so you should definitely play around a little and see what settings feel best for you. You can test the effect of your changes to the Double-Click Speed setting in the Double-Click Here to Test text box at the bottom of the window before you close this preference pane.

Trackpad

If you have a portable Mac with a trackpad, such as a PowerBook or iBook, you'll see an additional tab — Trackpad — where you can set the tracking speed and double-clicking behavior of your trackpad.

Note: If you have a PowerBook or iBook, there will also be a tab for trackpad settings with the same two settings and options to specify just what tasks the trackpad can be used for, such as tapping it rather than pressing the button when you want to click something. You can even tell OS X to ignore the trackpad while you're typing. But all these goodies are only for notebook Macs — the only kind that include trackpads.

Keyboard Shortcuts

The Keyboard Shortcuts tab is a new feature in Panther and a welcome one at that. It lets you add, delete, or change keyboard shortcuts for many operating system functions such as taking a picture of the screen and using the keyboard to choose menu and dock items. It also allows you to add, delete, or change keyboard shortcuts for applications.

To change a shortcut, double click it and then hold down the new shortcut keys. To add a new shortcut, click the + button; to delete a shortcut, click the – button.

The Turn on Full Keyboard Access checkbox lets you use the keyboard to access all the controls in a window or dialog, which lets you tab to buttons and check boxes and avoid using the mouse (if that's your preference).

When it's enabled, you press a key combination specified above to use the tab or arrow keys to move among items in the menu bar, Dock, a window's toolbar, or palettes (floating windows). If you really hate to use your mouse or if your mouse is broken, these keyboard shortcuts can come in really handy. I like to use them on my PowerBook when I'm traveling and don't have room to hook up a mouse because I really don't like using the built-in mouse-thing (technically called a *trackpad*).

Print & Fax

 This pane lets you configure printers and the new built-in Fax capability. It offers two tabs: Printing and Faxing.

Printing

Click the Set Up Printers button to launch the Printer Setup Utility and configure a new printer.

The Selected Printer in Print Dialog pop-up menu lets you choose which printer is selected by default in Print dialog boxes and sheets.

The Default Paper Size in Page Setup pop-up menu lets you choose the default paper size your Mac will use in Page Setup dialog boxes and sheets.

The Share My Printers with Other Computers checkbox allows printers connected to this Mac to be available to other Macs on the local area network.

Faxing

Click the Receive Faxes on This Computer checkbox to enable faxing.

Type your fax line's phone number into the My Fax Number field.

Set the number of rings you want the software to wait before answering a fax call in the Answer after __ Rings field.

Click the Save To checkbox to enable a pop-up menu that lets you select which folder incoming faxes will be saved to.

Click the Email To checkbox to send an email to yourself (or anyone) when a fax arrives.

Click the Print on Printer checkbox to automatically print incoming faxes, which you choose from the pop-up menu next to the checkbox.

Finally, the Let Others Send Faxes through This Computer checkbox allows other Macs on the local area network to send faxes through this Mac.

Sound

 This pane controls the way your Mac plays and records sound and offers three tabs: Sound Effects, Output, and Input.

To make your Mac's volume louder or softer, use the Output Volume slider at the bottom of the window. Select the Mute check box to turn off all sound. Click the Show Volume in Menu Bar check box to add a volume control menu to your menu bar.

These three items appear at the bottom of the Sound pane no matter which of the three tabs is active.

Sound Effects

Choose an alert (beep) sound by clicking its name; set its volume using the Alert Volume slider control.

You can also specify through which output device they play, if you have more than one, by selecting from the Play Alerts and Sound Effects Through pop-up menu.

The Play User Interface Sound Effects check box turns on sound effects for actions such as dragging a file to the Trash.

The Play Feedback When Volume Keys Are Pressed check box tells your Mac to beep once for each press of the increase or decrease volume keys (usually F4 and F5).

 You can find new sounds on the Internet at your favorite shareware archive (www.versiontracker.com, www.macupdate.com/, and www.tucows.com are a few that I like and recommend).

To install new sounds, move them into the Sounds folder inside the Library folder at root level on your hard drive if you want them to be available to all users of this Mac. Or put them in the Sounds folder inside the Library folder in your home folder if you want to be the only one that can use them. (See Chapter 10 for more info on these two Library folders.)

Output

The Balance slider in the Output tab to make one stereo speaker louder than the other.

Two that won't show (unless . . .)

Two more preference panes might appear in the Hardware section, but only if your Mac has the appropriate hardware connected to it.

Bluetooth

Bluetooth is wireless networking for low-bandwidth peripherals introduced in Mac OS X version 10.2 Jaguar. If your Mac is equipped with a Bluetooth adapter, you can synchronize wirelessly with phones and Palm devices, print wirelessly to Bluetooth printers, and who knows what else (it's very new technology).

Bluetooth is designed to work with *iSync,* Apple's new synchronizing technology, to let you synchronize your address book, calendar, and bookmarks wirelessly with Bluetooth phones such as the Sony Ericsson T68i.

Ink

Ink is Mac OS X's built-in handwriting recognition engine, also introduced in Version 10.2 Jaguar. If you have a stylus and tablet connected to your Mac, just turn it on in this pane and you can write anywhere you can type with the keyboard.

The Ink pane is another one you'll only see if you have one of the handful of tablets that Ink supports connected to your Mac.

All currently supported tablets are from Wacom (www.wacom.com) with prices as low as $100 for a small wireless stylus and tablet.

Internet & Network preferences

The following preference panes are displayed in the Internet & Network category.

.Mac

The .Mac pane lets you configure your .Mac subscription and iDisk (if you have them). It offers two tabs:

.Mac (formerly iTools)

If you have a .Mac account, you can type your name and password here so that you don't have to type them every time that you use your iDisk or Mail. (See Chapter 11's section on .Mac if you want to know what this is all about.)

Click the Sign Up button, and your Web browser will open and take you to the Apple .Mac Sign Up page.

iDisk

This tab shows how much of your iDisk (your remote disk maintained on Apple's servers for .Mac members) is used and how much is available. It also allows you to keep a local copy of your iDisk on your hard disk and synchronize it automatically or manually, and make your Public Folder Read/Write or Read-Only with or without a password.

Network

This pane offers options for connecting your Mac to the Internet or to a network. Although I talk a little about this pane in Chapter 11, I promised you more detail here. So here's some detail.

If you're part of a large office network, check with your System Administrator before you change anything in this pane. If you ignore this advice, you run the risk of losing your network connection completely.

At the top of this pane is the Location pop-up menu. If you use your Mac in more than one place, you can set up a separate configuration for each location and then choose it from this menu. A *location*, in this context, consists of all the settings in all the tabs in the Network System Preferences pane. After you have this entire pane configured the way that you like, pull down this menu and choose New Location. Type in a name for the new location and then click OK. Then you can change all the settings in this pane at once by choosing that location from the pop-up menu.

If your Mac has a single network or Internet connection, like most home users have, just choose Automatic from the Location menu and be done with it.

Below the Location menu is the Show pop-up menu. Here you choose your Internet connection, network status, and port configuration. If you use a modem to connect to the Internet, choose Internal Modem. If you have another type of Internet access, such as ISDN, cable modem, or Digital Subscriber Line (DSL), choose either Ethernet or Built-in Ethernet.

Depending on which type of connection you choose in the Show menu, you'll see four or five tabs. Unfortunately, you'll need to talk to your ISP or network administrator to find out how to configure them; I can't tell you how in this book because there are just so many configurations that depend upon your particular ISP and service. I will, though, give you a brief rundown on the most important ones:

- ✔ **TCP/IP:** *TCP/IP* is the language of the Internet. On this tab, you specify things such as your IP Address, Domain Name Servers, and Search Domains.

- ✔ **PPP or PPPoE:** These acronyms stand for Point-To-Point Protocol and Point-To-Point Protocol over Ethernet. Which one you see depends on what you've selected from the Show menu. All modems use PPP; some cable and DSL modems use PPPoE. Your ISP will tell you whether you need to do anything with this tab.

- ✔ **AppleTalk:** *AppleTalk* is a homegrown network protocol invented by Apple. Some (but not all) networked printers require it to be turned on for them to function. For more information about AppleTalk in general, this tab in particular, and printers, see Chapter 12.

✔ **Proxies:** If you're on a large network or your Mac is behind a firewall, you might need to specify one or more proxy servers. If so, your network administrator can help you with this tab's settings. If you're a home user, you'll probably never need to touch this tab. Finally, some ISPs require you to specify proxy servers; if you need to do this, ask your ISP what to do.

QuickTime

QuickTime is Apple's multimedia technology for both Mac and Windows. When you watch a movie on your Mac (unless you're watching a DVD, of course), chances are good that it's a QuickTime file.

Chances are also good that QuickTime is already configured properly.

The QuickTime pane has five tabs: Plug-In, Connection, Music, Media Keys, and Update. Just check to make sure that QuickTime is set as follows and then leave this preference alone.

Plug-In

This tab deals with the way your Internet browser handles multimedia files; it contains three checkboxes:

✔ Select the **Play Movies Automatically** check box if it's not already checked if you want your browser to play movies when it encounters them.

✔ Select the **Save Movies in Disk Cache** check box to save QuickTime movies in the browser's cache folder (in your Home/Library/Preferences folder; if you use Internet Explorer, they're in Explorer/Temporary Items.)

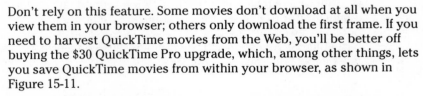

Don't rely on this feature. Some movies don't download at all when you view them in your browser; others only download the first frame. If you need to harvest QuickTime movies from the Web, you'll be better off buying the $30 QuickTime Pro upgrade, which, among other things, lets you save QuickTime movies from within your browser, as shown in Figure 15-11.

✔ Select the **Enable Kiosk Mode** check box to hide the QuickTime controller (Play/Pause/Volume/and so on) within your browser.

The Allow Multiple Simultaneous Streams check box lets you have more than one QuickTime movie or file streaming into your Mac over the Internet or network at a time.

If streaming movies or sounds are stuttering or not playing properly, try unchecking this option.

Figure 15-11:
Control-
click to save
a movie
(left) with
QuickTime
Pro; if you
don't pay for
the Pro
upgrade,
Save As is
disabled
(right).

The MIME settings button at the bottom of this pane offers advanced options for receiving files over the Internet. I suggest you leave this alone unless you're instructed to change it by someone knowledgeable, such as your ISP.

Connection

This tab is where you select the speed of your Internet connection by choosing the appropriate option from the Connection Speed pop-up menu. If you're not sure what your connection speed is, ask your ISP. (If you're not sure what an ISP is, I suggest that you read Chapter 11.)

The Instant On button lets you adjust how quickly streaming movies and sounds start playing. Alas, turning this feature on may degrade streaming media performance.

The Transport Setup button offers advanced options for receiving files over the Internet. I suggest you leave this alone unless you're instructed to change it by someone knowledgeable, such as your ISP.

Music and Media Keys

I strongly suggest you ignore the Music and Media Keys tabs. I have yet to need them even though they've been in QuickTime for years. If you want to use a music synthesizer other than the built-in QuickTime Music Synthesizer or if someone sends you a secured media file (or you download one), you'll have to play with their settings, but I have never had to touch either one.

Update

Change settings in the Update tab to update your QuickTime software automatically (if you have an Internet connection). Because each successive version of QuickTime has added cool and useful features, I suggest that you select the Check for Updates Automatically check box. After you do, your Mac will check for new versions of QuickTime whenever you connect to the Internet.

Sharing

This is another option that you'll use when networking your Mac. There are two facets of Sharing — sharing a single Mac with other users and sharing files via an office network or the Internet. Read all the gory details in Chapter 16.

System System preferences (kind of redundant)

The following preference panes are displayed in the System category.

Accounts (formerly Users)

This pane, which is only useful to users with Administrator access, is where you create and administer user accounts on your Mac. I cover this in greater detail in Chapter 16, but I promised earlier to show you how to get rid of logging in entirely if you don't like it. Here's what to do.

If you don't have any reason to worry about someone else logging on and making mischief (or if you don't share your Mac), you can disable the log-in screen by clicking the Login Options button beneath the list of accounts.

When you disable logging in, you also affect the preferences set by anyone else who shares your Mac. So, if your Desktop pattern, keyboard settings, and so forth are different from those of someone else who uses your machine, those preferences won't be properly reflected if each of you don't have your own log-in account. Even if you're not worried about security, consider keeping logging in enabled if any other users have accounts on your machine.

To disable the logging in requirement, you may first need to unlock the Accounts System Preference. (For more on unlocking a preference, see the "Using System Preferences" section earlier in this chapter.)

To disable log in, select yourself in the list of users, click the Login Options button below the list, then check the Log In Automatically as checkbox and choose your account from the pop-up menu.

Note that only one account is allowed to use auto-login. If another user wants to use this Mac, you need to choose Log Out from the menu or press ⌘+Shift+Q. And if you've disabled automatic login in the Security System Preference pane, you can't enable it here.

For non-automatic logins, the Login Options tab has additional choices. You can choose to have your login window display just two fields — user name and password — or the flashier list of users of this Mac, complete with those cute little pictures.

The Disable Restart and Shut Down buttons and Show Password Hint after 3 Attempts to Enter a Password check boxes do just what their names imply.

 One cool new feature you'll find in Login Options is the Enable Fast User Switching checkbox. It lets you switch from one user to another without first logging out by choosing their name from the Fast User Switching menu that appears when this option is enabled, as shown in Figure 15-12.

Figure 15-12:
Fast user switching is much faster than logging out and back in under another account.

Classic

 Open the Classic System Preferences pane to choose the drive or drive partition that contains a Mac OS 9.2.2 System Folder to use when working in the Classic environment. I dig deep into the Classic environment in Chapter 14. Suffice it to say that if you have Mac OS 9 applications or if you're nostalgic for the way things were in Mac OS 9, you need to use the Classic System Preferences pane.

 I'll repeat what I said in Chapter 14 about version numbers to avoid any confusion:

Mac OS X (10.3) requires version 9.2.2 of Mac OS, commonly referred to as Mac OS 9.2.2, to provide the Classic environment. But most (if not all) programs don't distinguish between different versions of Mac OS 9. So when I call a program a *Mac OS 9 program,* what I mean is that it's *not* an OS X program and that it will run under any version of Mac OS 9. In other words, when I talk about stuff that works with (or appears in) all versions of Mac OS 9, I say *Mac OS 9.* When I'm talking about Classic or another feature or program that *requires* OS 9.2.2, I say *Mac OS 9.2.2.*

Date & Time

Within the Date & Time System Preferences pane, you can configure your Mac's internal clock (which many programs use) and the clock that you see in the menu bar. Three tabs appear: Date & Time, Time Zone, and Clock.

Date & Time

To change the date, click a day in the current month's calendar or click the date field above the calendar and use the up- and down-arrows that appear to the right of this field.

To set the time, type in the correct values in the Current Time field that appears above the clock face, or click the number that you want to change and use the up- and down-arrows that appear to the right of this field.

You can also use the arrow keys on the keyboard to increase or decrease the number. Or you can type a new number right over the selected number.

When you have the time how you want it, click the Save button. Or, if you mess up, click the Revert button to return to the way it was before you began.

Use the Tab key to move from number to number. The settings for the hour, minute, and second are selected in sequence when you press the Tab key. If you want to move backward through the sequence, press Shift+Tab. As long as you hold the Shift key down, you cycle through the numbers in reverse order when you press Tab.

You won't be able to set the date or time if you've already checked the Set Date & Time Automatically check box.

Network time servers are very cool, enabling you to synchronize your Mac's clock to a super-accurate time server on the Internet. To use a time server, however, you must be connected to the Internet when your Mac checks the time.

To set up access to a time server, just click the Set Date & Time Automatically check box, then choose a network time server from the pop-up menu.

Apple's Network Time Server is `time.apple.com`. You're allowed to use it, of course.

If you have trouble with the network time server feature, Apple posts a technical note that lists dozens of alternative network time servers. You can find this tech note (and several other tech notes you may find useful) by going to the Apple Knowledge Base (`http://kbase.info.apple.com`) and searching for *network time server*.

Time Zone

This tab lets you set your machine according to what time zone you're in. Click your part of the world on the map that appears or choose a time zone from the pop-up menu. The map is updated to show your time zone when you do.

Clock

This tab controls the display of the clock in the right corner of your menu bar. The options in this tab are accompanied by a check box to turn each on or off. Those options are:

- The Show the Date and Time in the Menu Bar or in a Window radio buttons let you choose to see a clock on the right side of the menu bar or in a floating window.

- The View As pop-up menu lets you choose to see your clock (in the menu bar or window) as an analog or digital version. If you choose analog, the following options aren't available:

  - The Display the Time with Seconds check box determines whether the time with seconds (04:20:*45*).

  - The Show AM/PM check box determines whether you see AM or PM after the time (4:20 *PM*).

- The Show the Day of the Week checkbox determines whether the day is included before the time (*Monday* 4:20 PM). If this check box is not marked, all you see is the time (4:20 PM).

- The Flash the Time separators check box determines whether the separating colons (:) between the hours and minutes (and seconds if you select the Display the Time with Seconds check box) blink on and off. If you deselect this check box, you still see the colons but they don't blink.

- The Use a 24-hour Clock checkbox does what it says. If you're military or have lived abroad, you may prefer the 24-hour clock, where 1 p.m. is expressed as 1300 hours and so on. If so, mark this check box.

Software Update

 Occasionally, Apple releases a new version of some of the software that's part of a Mac system. Such releases may be a patch for the system software, a bug fix for a utility program, or even a new version of Internet Explorer. You can set Software Update to check for new software, as well as to notify you of changes and download the fresh, hot files to your Mac. ***Note:*** You must have an Internet connection to use this feature.

Software update has two tabs:

Update Software

Use this tab to choose to update your software automatically by marking the lone check box on the Update Software tab in this preference pane. If you do, you can choose how often your Mac checks for updates from the pop-up menu.

Click the Check Now button at the bottom of the window to manually check for updates any time you like, even if you've selected the Automatically radio button.

Installed Updates

This tab shows which updates, if any, you've already installed. Click the Open as Log File button, and the installed update log will open in the Console application for you to review or save.

Speech

This pane lets you configure your desired Speech settings. It offers three tabs:

Speech Recognition

This is where you set up *speech recognition* — the ability to talk to your Mac and have it understand you. Alas, I'm going to have to use another weasel-out here — I just don't have a chapter's worth of space left to explain all the other Speech goodies. Sigh. Well, okay, here are a few more tips, hints, and rants.

You'll need a decent microphone to use this feature. Unfortunately, Macs don't come with one, and the mike that's built into iMacs isn't quite good enough. Even worse, many new Mac models, including the Titanium PowerBooks, don't even have a microphone port, so you have to use a microphone that connects via your Universal Serial Bus (USB) port. Luckily, both USB microphones and converters for connecting standard microphone connectors to USB are fairly common these days.

Dr. Bott is a great little Mac-only company that specializes in little items like USB microphones and analog-to-USB converters. Its Web address is www.drbott.com, or you can call 877-611-2688. Eric Prentice is the CEO; tell him that Bob sent you.

You can't use this feature to dictate text to your Mac — you'll need IBM's ViaVoice or MacSpeech's iListen to do that. But you can use it to launch programs ("Computer, open Microsoft Word") and other stuff, like emptying the Trash, when you say to. Frankly, I haven't used it for more than a few minutes — it just doesn't work well enough yet. Still, it's kind of neat and worth playing with if you have the time and a decent Mac microphone.

Default Voice

Use this tab to set the voice your Mac uses to communicate with you. Choose from the list of voices on the left side of the pane to select the voice your Mac uses when it reads to you. After you make a selection, a sample of the voice that you selected will play aloud.

Each voice's characteristics (the language, gender, age, and description) appear on the right when that voice is selected. Use the Rate slider (bottom-right of the window) to speed up or slow down the voice. Then click the Play button to hear this voice at its new speed.

I like Fred, who says, "I sure like being inside this fancy computer."

Spoken User Interface

This tab is where you choose to have your Mac speak the text in alert boxes and dialogs, such as, "The application Microsoft Word has quit unexpectedly" or "The Finder requires your attention."

Two additional (and quite useful) settings on the Spoken User Interface tab are the Text under the Mouse and the Selected Text when the x Key is Pressed check boxes (where x is the name of the key that you've assigned).

Startup Disk

This pane lets you select which hard drive, server volume, or hard drive volume (if you've partitioned your hard drive or have more than one hard disk) should act as the startup disk when more than one drive with system software is connected to the Mac. To use it, first unlock the Startup Disk preference if you have to (for more on unlocking a preference, see the "Using System Preferences" section earlier in this chapter) and then click the icon for the drive that you want to start up the Mac the next time that you restart.

This feature is very useful if you have both a Mac OS X start-up disk and a start-up disk with another version of Mac OS on it, such as Mac OS 9 or Mac OS 8.6. If you want to start up with the older operating system, just click that disk's icon in the Startup Disk System Preferences pane and restart your Mac; it now starts up with OS 8.6.

If you have OS 9.2.2 installed on the same volume as OS X, you can set this preference to choose which OS you boot from. You see two System Folder icons at the top of the pane — one with OS 9.2.2 and the other with OS X. Click the one that you want to boot from and then restart.

When you've selected the OS with which you want to restart, click the Restart button in the window.

For more information on using the Startup Disk System Preference pane, skip to the end of my discussion of the Classic environment in Chapter 14.

As I mention elsewhere in this book, Macs sold after January 1, 2003 may not be able to boot into OS 9. They will still run Classic but won't be capable of booting into 9.

Universal Access

Many years ago, Apple pioneered Easy Access to assist computer users who had disabilities or difficulty in handling the keyboard and mouse. Universal Access is the OS X implementation of that assistance. This pane has three check boxes and four tabs.

Mark the Allow Universal Access Shortcuts check box if you want the keyboard shortcuts listed throughout this pane on the various tabs to be enabled.

Mark the Enable Access for Assistive Devices check box to use special equipment to control your computer.

Mark the Enable Text-to-Speech for Universal Access Preferences check box to have this pane's text read to you.

The Seeing tab lets you turn on a terrific feature: hardware zoom. Turn it on and off with the shortcut ⌘+Option+* (asterisk). Zoom in and out using the shortcuts ⌘+Option++ (plus key) and ⌘+Option+– (minus key), respectively. Try this feature even if you're not disabled or challenged in any way; it's a great feature for everyone.

You can also display the screen as white on black (like a photographic negative), as shown in Figure 15-13. The shortcut is ⌘+Option+Control+*; use the same keyboard shortcut to toggle back to normal.

Finally, the Zoom Options button lets you specify minimum and maximum zoom levels, display a preview rectangle when zoomed out, and toggle image smoothing on or off.

The Hearing tab lets you choose to flash the screen whenever an alert sound occurs.

This feature, created for those with impaired hearing, is quite useful if you have a PowerBook or iBook and want to use it where ambient noise levels are high.

The Keyboard tab offers two types of assistance: Sticky Keys and Slow Keys. *Sticky Keys* treat a sequence of modifier keys as a key combination. In other words, you don't have to simultaneously hold down ⌘ while pressing another key. For example, with Sticky Keys enabled, a standard keyboard shortcut is accomplished by pressing ⌘, releasing it, and then pressing the other key. There are check boxes to inform you with a beep and/or on-screen display what modifier keys have been pressed.

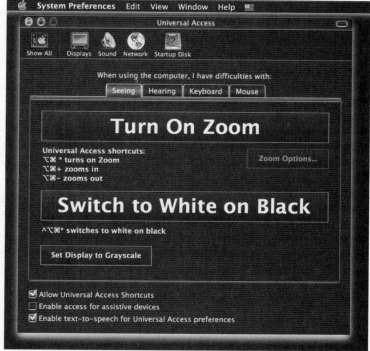

Figure 15-13:
The White
on Black
option
reverses
what you
see on
screen
like this.

Slow Keys lets you adjust the delay between when a key is pressed and when that key press is accepted.

Finally, the Mouse tab lets you specify that you want to use the keys on the numeric keypad in place of the mouse. In this situation, everything centers around the numeric keypad's 5 key (which means clicking the mouse): 8 is up; 2 is down; 4 is left; 6 is right; and 1, 3, 7, and 9 are diagonal movements. Pressing 0 (zero) means that the mouse is held down so that the other numeric keys now drag in the indicated directions.

Part IV
U 2 Can B a Guru

The 5th Wave   By Rich Tennant

"I just can't keep up with the cosmetics industry. That woman we just passed has a makeup case with a screen and keyboard."

In this part . . .

Here I get into the nitty-gritty underbelly of Mac OS X. In this part, I cover semi-advanced topics including sharing (files, that is) and automating your Mac by using AppleScript, complete with some easy-to-follow info that's guaranteed to get you scripting. Don't skip the chapter on backing up your files, followed by the all-important troubleshooting chapter, which takes you on a quick tour of Dr. Mac's (okay, Dr. Bob's) top troubleshooting tips for those times when good software goes bad.

Chapter 16

"Mine! Miiiiine!": Sharing Your Mac and Liking It

*H*ave you ever wanted to grab a file from your Mac while you were halfway around the world or even around the corner? If so, I've got good news for you — it's not difficult with OS X, believe it or not, even though computer networking in general has a well-deserved reputation for being complicated and nerve-wracking. The truth is, you won't encounter anything scary or complicated about sharing files, folders, and disks (and printers, for that matter) among computers as long as the computers are Macintoshes. And, if some of the computers are running Windows, Mac OS X version 10.3 Panther even makes that (almost) painless. Your Macintosh includes everything that you need to share files and printers. Everything, that is, except the printers and the cables (and maybe a hub). So here's the deal: You supply the printers and cables, and this chapter will supply the rest.

Mac OS X is a multi-user operating system. After you create a user account for someone to share your Mac, that user can log on to your Mac two different ways with the same username and password. They can log *on* while sitting at your Mac or they can log *into* your Mac from a remote location via the Internet or a local area network (LAN).

The first sections of this chapter provide an overview and tell you everything that you need to know to set up new user accounts and share files successfully. I won't show you how to actually share a file, folder, or disk until the "Consummating the Act of Sharing" section later in this chapter. Trust me, there's a method to my madness. If you try to share files without doing all the required prep work, the whole mess becomes confusing and complicated — kind of like networking a pair of PC clones.

One last thing: If you're the only one who uses your Mac and you don't intend to share it or its files with anyone else, you can safely skip this whole chapter if you like.

Introducing File Sharing

Macintosh file sharing enables you to use files, folders, and disks from other Macs on a network — any network, including the Internet — as easily as if they were on your own local hard drive. If you have more than one computer, file sharing is a must. It's fun, it's easy, and it's way better than SneakerNet. (*SneakerNet* is the moving of files from one computer to another via floppy disk or other media, such as CD-R, DVD-R, Zip, and so on, according to the unpublished epic, "The Dr. Macintosh Unabridged Dictionary.")

Before diving in and actually sharing, first check out a few necessary terms:

- **Network:** For our purposes, a network of two or more Macs connected by Ethernet cables or AirPort wireless networking.

- **Ethernet:** A network protocol and cabling scheme that lets you connect two or more computers so they can share files, disks, printers, or whatever.

- **Ethernet ports:** Where you plug an Ethernet cable into your Mac.

Be careful. On your Mac and printer, the Ethernet ports look a lot like phone jacks, and the connectors on each end of an Ethernet cable look a lot like phone cable connectors. But they aren't the same. Ethernet cables are typically thicker, and the connectors (RJ-45 connectors) are a bit larger than the RJ-11 connectors that you use with telephones. (See examples of both types of connector ends in the margin.) When you connect an Ethernet cable to your Mac, you won't be able to put it into your RJ-11-friendly modem port (and you shouldn't try). Standard phone cables fit into Ethernet ports, but you shouldn't try that either because they'll probably fall out with the slightest vibration. It's unlikely that either mistake will cause any permanent damage, but it won't work and will frustrate you to no end.

✔ **Local devices:** Devices that are connected directly to your computers, such as hard drives or CD-ROM drives. Your internal hard drive, for example, is a local device.

✔ **Remote devices:** Devices that you access (share) over the network. The hard disk of a computer in the next room, for example, is a remote device.

✔ **Protocols:** Kinds of languages that networks speak. When you read or hear about networks, you're likely to hear the words AppleTalk, EtherTalk (or Ethernet), SMB, and TCP/IP bandied about with great regularity. These are all protocols. Macs can speak several different protocols, but every device (Mac or printer) on a network needs to speak the same protocol at the same time in order to communicate.

Support for the AppleTalk protocol is built into every Mac. Your Mac includes all the software that you need to set up an AppleTalk network; the hardware that you need to provide comprises Ethernet cables and a hub (unless you use crossover cables) or an AirPort base station. I'm using *hub* here generically — its more powerful cousins, switches and routers, will also work. The AirPort base station, by the way, is a member of the router class.

Although you can use Transfer Control Protocol/Internet Protocol (TCP/IP) to do a lot of the same things that you can with AppleTalk, I concentrate on Apple's protocol, AppleTalk. By learning how to activate and use it, you'll master the basics that you need to dig into the language of the Internet.

AppleTalk is particularly useful when you have all Macs on your network. It's the easiest to configure and doesn't require additional information such as IP addresses. If you want to use the Internet to connect to another computer (or have it connect to yours), however, you need to use TCP/IP.

Mac OS X version 10.2 Jaguar added support for a protocol called Bluetooth, and this support has been enhanced in OS X 10.3 Panther. Bluetooth is wireless connectivity with devices such as cell phones in addition to other computers; however, it works over very short ranges and at lower speeds than Ethernet or AirPort. Further, it requires an adapter, called a *dongle*, on most Macs employing Bluetooth.

Portrait of home office networking

A typical Mac home office network consists of two Macintoshes, an Ethernet hub, and a network printer (usually a laser printer, although networked inkjet printers are becoming more common). Check out Figure 16-1 to see the configuration of a simple network. In the figure, the black lines between the devices are Ethernet cables; the rectangular device with those cables going into it is a hub. (I tell you more about cables and hubs in the section "Three ways to build a network" later in this chapter.) You need enough Ethernet cable to run among all your devices.

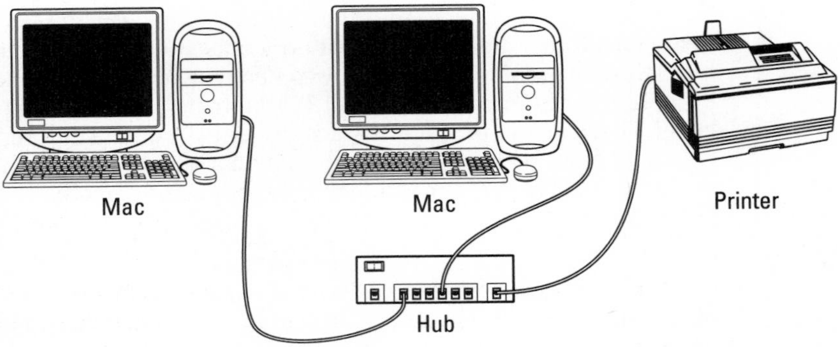

Figure 16-1:
Two Macs and a printer make up a simple Mac network.

Mac   Mac   Printer

Hub

With the setup that you see in Figure 16-1, either Mac can use the other Mac's files, and both Macs can print to the same printer.

A network can and often does have, however, dozens or hundreds of users. Regardless of whether your network has 2 nodes (machines) or 2,000, the principles and techniques in this chapter apply.

Three ways to build a network

Back when you could connect a whole bunch of Macs and printers by simply running cables among them, most small Mac networks were pretty much the same. You attached a small device (a LocalTalk connector) to the first Mac and then ran plain old telephone cable to the next Mac, which also had a LocalTalk connector. By stringing more phone cable and more LocalTalk connectors, you had yourself a little network.

Today, building a Mac network is a little more complicated. Most Macs that support Mac OS X don't include LocalTalk ports, and Ethernet and wireless networks require a little more setup.

In this chapter, I assume that you're working on a small network, the kind typically found in a home or small business. If you're part of a mega-monstrous corporate network and you have questions about your particular network, talk to the PIC (*person in charge,* also known as your *network administrator*). If you're trying to build one of these mega-networks, you'll need a book a lot thicker than this one.

The following list gives you three common ways to build a modern network:

- **AirPort:** If all your Macs are equipped with AirPort wireless cards and if you have the AirPort Base Station, you don't need cables at all. Just plug in the base station, and Macs with AirPort cards can communicate with each other. If you use an Ethernet printer (connected to your Mac by Ethernet cable), you need to connect it to the base station before you can print from your wireless Macs. Both the Base Station and printer have Ethernet ports, so you can use a crossover cable to make the connection.

  Although this setup is more expensive than Ethernet cables and a hub, it's also more flexible because you can move your devices anywhere. (Well, almost anywhere; you're limited to 150 feet per AirPort.)

  For more information about wireless networking, check out the Apple AirPort Web page at www.apple.com/airport/.

- **Small Ethernet:** If you have only two devices to network (two Macs, or a Mac and an Ethernet printer, in most cases), you can use an Ethernet crossover cable to connect them directly to one another via the Ethernet ports. You can purchase a crossover cable (which looks just like a standard Ethernet cable) at your local electronics store. *Note:* Be sure to ask for a crossover cable, or your network won't work. Plug one end of the crossover cable into one of your two devices and the other end into the other.

  An Ethernet crossover cable won't work with a hub; a regular Ethernet cable won't work without one (in many Macs, as explained in the sidebar "To cross over, or not?"). Therefore, it makes sense to label your crossover cable(s) as such because they look exactly like regular Ethernet cables, and it's easy to become confused if you have a bunch of similar-looking cables.

- **Traditional Ethernet:** All modern Macs have an Ethernet port. To connect your Mac to a network, you need Ethernet cables for each Mac and a little device called a *hub*. (A hub is like the middle of a wagon wheel, with spokes representing the wires coming out of it.) A typical Ethernet hub includes two to eight Ethernet ports. You plug the hub in to an electrical outlet and then connect Ethernet cables from each of your Macs and printers (from their Ethernet ports) to the hub. Voilà! — instant network. Hubs are pretty cheap, starting below $10; cables start at a few bucks, increasing in price as the length (and quality and shielding) of the cable increases.

  If you have a cable modem or Digital Subscriber Line (DSL) as your Internet connection, you may need a router or switch instead of a hub. They're similar but cost a bit more and have additional features that you may or may not need. Your ISP can tell you whether you're going to need one. For what it's worth, I have a cable modem, but it works fine with a cheap hub; I didn't need a more expensive router until I wanted to have more than one of the Macs talking to the Internet at the same time.

To cross over, or not?

The type of Ethernet cable required to connect two Macs without a hub or other middle-device has changed over time. In the old days, you absolutely had to have a crossover cable or the Macs wouldn't be able to see each other.

The basic rule had always been that to connect two Macs, you had to use a crossover cable. And if you had a hub or router or other intermediary device, you had to use regular Ethernet cables.

It's less true today because many Macs built in the past couple years — and every Mac sold today — has new and improved Ethernet that can determine what type of cable (regular or crossover) you're using and then automatically adjust itself so that cable works properly.

These days, you may encounter three possibilities: If you want to connect two older Macs, you need a crossover cable. If you want to connect an older Mac to a newer Mac, you may or may not need a crossover cable. And, if you want to connect two late-model Macs, you can use either a regular Ethernet cable or a crossover cable.

When in doubt, check Mac OS Help in the Help menu (press ⌘+Shift+?).

Setting Up File Sharing

Before I get into the nitty-gritty of sharing files, you must complete a few housekeeping tasks, such as turning on file sharing, turning on AppleTalk (if you want to share files with an AppleTalk-enabled file server or print to an AppleTalk printer), and enabling sharing over TCP/IP (that is, over the Internet) if you plan to share that way.

Turning on file sharing

Before you can share files, you have to turn on Mac OS X's built-in File Sharing feature. Follow these steps to do so:

1. **From the menu on the Finder menu bar, choose System Preferences (or click the System Preferences icon on the Dock) and then click the Sharing icon.**

   The System Preferences Sharing pane appears. Unless you've changed it, your long user name appears by default as the Computer Name.

2. **If you want to change the computer name at this time, do so in the Computer Name text field at the top of the Sharing pane.**

   In Figure 16-2, you can see that I named mine `Panther PowerBook`. You can name yours anything you like.

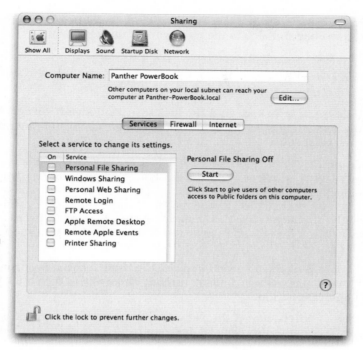

Figure 16-2:
Turning
personal file
sharing on
and off.

3. **On the Services pane, mark the sharing services that you want to use (such as Personal File Sharing) and then click the Start button (beneath the heading Personal File Sharing Off) or just click inside the check box in the On column to activate file sharing (see Figure 16-2).**

Why does it say `Personal File Sharing Off` above the button? Because it *is* off. After you click the Start button, the button name changes from *Start* to *Stop,* and the text above the button changes to `Personal File Sharing On,` indicating that file sharing is on.

Starting AppleTalk

If you want to share files with an Apple file server or print to a networked printer that requires AppleTalk, as many do, you have to enable AppleTalk. (See the "Introducing File Sharing" section earlier in this chapter for a definition of AppleTalk.) Here's how:

1. **From the menu on the Finder menu bar, choose System Preferences (or click the System Preferences icon on the Dock).**

   The System Preferences window appears.

2. **In the System Preferences window, click the Network icon (located in the toolbar and also in the main part of the window).**

   The Network System Preferences pane appears.

   You can get here in one step by choosing ⌘⇨Location⇨Network Preferences.

3. **If the pane is locked, click the lock icon (bottom-left corner) to unlock the Network System Preferences, type your name and password, and then click OK.**

   If your Mac is set up for multiple users, only users with administrative privileges (or, at least, knowledge of the Administrator password) can unlock these locks. Those with such privileges are the first user (created when you installed OS X) and any other user who you've given administrative privileges to in the Accounts System Preference pane, which I discuss in the "Access and Privileges: Who Can Do What" section later in this chapter.

4. **Choose Built-in Ethernet or AirPort (whichever you use) from the Show pop-up menu (if it isn't already chosen) and then click the AppleTalk button.**

   The AppleTalk view of the Network System Preferences pane appears in all its glory — onscreen and in Figure 16-3.

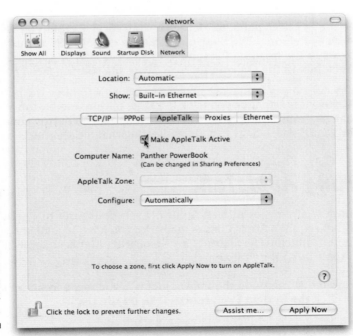

Figure 16-3:
The AppleTalk tab of the System Preferences Network pane.

5. **Mark the Make AppleTalk Active check box.**

6. **Click the Apply Now button in the lower-right corner of the AppleTalk tab to confirm your action.**

   That's it. You can quit the System Preferences application now.

Sharing with TCP/IP

TCP/IP is the network protocol used on the Internet. It's also the protocol used by OS X for sharing files. It enables Macs, PCs, and other computers to communicate with each other (sometimes, but not always, via the Internet), even if they're running different operating systems. TCP/IP is always on, so you don't have to do anything further about it.

If you want remote users to be able to use an File Transfer Protocol (FTP) client program (instead of using File Sharing on another Mac) to upload and download files to and from this computer, mark the FTP Access check box in the Sharing System Preferences pane's Services pane. If you want to enable Windows or Linux — or to allow other users of other operating systems to share files with you — this check box needs to be marked. (I talk more about FTP and FTP clients in Chapter 22.) Windows users can also share files if you turn on Windows File Sharing in the Sharing pane's Services pane. This feature, introduced in Mac OS X version 10.2 Jaguar, takes most of the pain out of working with people using Microsoft Windows systems.

Mac users could use an FTP client to access your Mac, but they'll probably want to use File Sharing instead because it's easier.

Security risks are involved in allowing FTP access. I strongly suggest that you go to Apple's Web site (www.apple.com) and read about them before you enable this feature.

Computers connect to one another by using a number-based addressing system *(an IP address)* that's standard all over the world. You can (and most big companies do) use this system to communicate in offices and over the Internet. If you need to know more about using TCP/IP to connect to computers on your network than I've told you here, talk to the system administrator or the network geek in charge of these things where you work.

I touch more on TCP/IP in the "Connecting to a shared disk or folder" section later in this chapter where you can read how to use it to connect to a Mac or other server that's running it.

Rendezvous, the relatively new, zero-configuration network protocol included in Mac OS X version 10.2 Jaguar (and later versions, of course) makes networking simple. If two devices (and this includes all Macs running version 10.2 Jaguar or later) speak Rendezvous, you don't have to do any configuration (besides turning the sharing on). Rendezvous queries the other available networked devices to see what services they offer and support and then configures the connections for you automatically.

Access and Privileges: Who Can Do What

Before you can share your Mac with other users or share files over a network, you need to tell your Mac who is allowed to do what. Lucky for you, this process just happens to be what I cover in this section.

Users and groups and guests

Macintosh file sharing (and indeed, Mac OS X as well) is based on the concept of users. Shared items — drives or folders — can be shared with no users, one user, or many users, depending on your needs.

- **Users:** People who share folders and drives (or your Mac) are *users*. A user's access to items on your local hard drive is entirely at your discretion. You can configure your Mac so that only you can access its folders and drives or so that only one other person (or everyone) can share its folders and drives.

  When you first set up your Mac, you created your first user. This user automatically has administrative powers, such as adding more users, changing preferences, and having the clearance to see all folders on the hard drive.

For the purposes of this book, I assume that some users for whom you create identities won't be folks who actually sit at your Mac but rather those who only connect to it from a remote location when they need to give or get files. But they *could* use the same name and password to log on while sitting at your desk.

For all intents and purposes, a remote user and a local user are the same. In other words, after you create an account for a user, that user can log on to this Mac while sitting in your chair in your office or log on to this Mac from a remote location via AppleTalk/Ethernet or the Internet.

✔ **Administrative users:** Although a complete discussion of the special privileges that a user with administrator privileges has on a Mac running OS X is far beyond the scope of this book, note two important things:

- The first user created (usually when you install OS X for the first time) is automatically granted administrator (admin) powers.

- Only an administrator can create new users, delete some (but not all) files from folders that aren't in his or her Home folder, lock and unlock System Preference panes, and a bunch of other stuff. If you try something and it doesn't work, make sure that you're logged in as a user with admin privileges.

You can give any user administrator privileges by selecting that user's account, clicking the Security button, and then selecting the Allow User to Administer This Computer check box in the Security pane. You can set this check box when creating the user account or subsequently.

✔ **Groups:** *Groups* are UNIX-level designations for privilege consolidation. For example, there are groups named staff and wheel (as well as a bunch of others). Your main account, for example, is in the wheel group.

If you're wondering whether you can create *your own* groups, as you could under OS 9 and earlier Mac operating systems, the answer is, well, yes and no. If you want to delve into the intricacies of the NetInfo Manager application to do it yourself, then "Yes;" but if you don't, then the answer is "No, please don't." UNIX-related tasks such as this are far beyond the scope of this book. Very far beyond. . . .

✔ **Guests:** Those who access public folders on your Mac via file sharing are *guests*. They don't need a username or password. If they're on your network, they can see and use your public folder(s), unless you or the public folder's owner has altered the permissions on one or more public folders. If they're on the Internet and know your IP address, they can see and use your Public folder(s). Public folders are all that guests can access, luckily.

Creating users

Before users can share folders and drives (or share your computer for that matter), you need to create user identities for them. You perform this little task in the Accounts System Preferences pane.

Guests can use your public folder(s) — but no other folders — without having a user account.

To create users for the purposes of file sharing, you need to add the user as a user of your computer, too. In other words, giving a user access to certain folders on your system means that that user also has folders of his or her own on the Mac. When you add (create) a user, you need to tell your Mac who this person is. This is also the time to set passwords and administrative powers of this new user. Here's the drill:

1. **From the 🍎 menu on the Finder menu bar, choose System Preferences (or click the System Preferences icon on the Dock), click the Accounts icon, and then make sure that the Password pane is selected.**

   The Accounts System Preferences pane appears. In this pane (shown in Figure 16-4), you can see the name of the first user (boblevitus) and the administrative control that this user has (look beneath the user's name).

   As I mention previously, the first user created (usually at the same time you installed OS X) always has administrator privileges.

2. **Click the + button beneath the list of users.**

   All the text fields in the Password pane empty out, waiting for you to fill in the new user's account information.

   If the + button is dimmed, you'll need to first click the lock (lower-left), supply your user name and password in the resulting dialog, and then click OK.

3. **In the Name text box, type the full name of a user you want to add.**

   In the Short Name text box, your Mac inserts a suggested abbreviated name (or *short name,* as it's called). Check out Figure 16-5 to see both.

Figure 16-4: The Accounts System Preferences pane shows who can use this Mac.

In Figure 16-5, I added **Steve Jobs** as a user, typing the full name in the Name field. You don't really need to type the user's full name, but I do so in this example to show you the difference between a name and a short name.

The name of each user's folder (in the Users folder) is taken from the short name that you enter when you create a user.

4. **Press the Tab key to move to the next field.**

Mac OS X suggests an abbreviated version of the name in the Short Name field (as shown in Figure 16-5). Because he's the only Steve that matters around here, I'll change the suggested *stevejob* to just plain *steve,* which is shorter than the short name recommended by OS X. (In other words, I type **steve** into the Short Name field, replacing the suggested *stevejob*.)

Users can connect to your Mac (or log on to their own Macs, for that matter) by using the short name, rather than having to type their full names. The short name is also used in environments in which usernames can't have spaces and are limited to eight or fewer characters. While OS X Panther allows longer user names (but no spaces), you may be better off keeping your short name shorter than eight characters, just in case.

Figure 16-5:
Name the new user; your Mac suggests a short name.

5. **Tab to the New Password field and enter an initial password for this user.**

6. **Press the Tab key on your keyboard to move your cursor to the Verify text field.**

7. **In the Verify text box, type the password again to verify it.**

8. **(Optional) To help remember a password, type something to jog the user's memory in the Password Hint text box.**

   If a user forgets his or her password and asks for a hint, the text that you type in the Password Hint field will pop up, hopefully causing the user to exclaim, "Oh yeah . . . *now* I remember!" A password hint should be something simple enough to jog the user's memory but not so simple that an unauthorized person may guess. The hint that I typed in Figure 16-5 for Steve is not a very good nor secure hint. Perhaps something like, "Your first teddy bear's name backwards" would be a better hint.

9. **(Optional) Click the Picture button to assign a picture to the user.**

   OS X will suggest one from its default collection, but you can select a different one from the scrolling row or drag one in from the Finder (or iPhoto).

10. **If you want this user to administer the Mac (that is, have access to preferences, be able to create users, and so forth), click the Security button and select the Allow user to administer this computer check box.**

   The new user now appears in the Accounts System Preferences pane's Users list.

Changing a user

Circumstances might dictate that you need to change a user's identity, password, or accessibility, or perhaps delete a user. Follow these steps to change a user's name, password, or administration privileges:

1. **From the menu on the Finder menu bar, choose System Preferences (or click the System Preferences icon on the Dock).**

   The System Preferences window appears.

2. **In the System Preferences window, click the Accounts icon.**

   The Accounts System Preferences pane appears.

3. **Click the user's name in the scrolling list to select it.**

   The information for that person appears in the Password view.

4. **Make your changes by selecting the existing username, short name, password, picture, and/or capabilities and then replacing the old with new text or a different setting.**

In order to change a user, you must be logged in using an account that has administrator powers.

5. **Quit the System Preferences application or choose a different System Preference pane.**

Your changes are saved when you leave the Accounts pane.

Removing a user

To delete a user — in effect, to deny that user access to your Mac — select the user who you want to delete and then click the – button. You will be asked to confirm that you really want to delete the user. Click OK to delete the user but save their Home folder files in the Deleted Users folder or click Delete Immediately to delete the user *and* their Home folder.

To remove a user from your Mac, you must be logged in using an account that has administrator privileges. When you delete the user, the files and folders that user owned will now be in the Deleted Users folder in a Disk Image file.

Limiting a user's capabilities

Sometimes, especially with younger children or computer-phobic family members, you want to limit what they can access. For example, you might want to make certain programs off-limits. With Mac OS X version 10.3 Panther, you do this via the Limitations button on the Accounts System Preferences pane.

1. **From the menu on the Finder menu bar, choose System Preferences (or click the System Preferences icon on the Dock).**

The System Preferences window appears.

2. **In the System Preferences window, click the Accounts icon.**

The Accounts System Preferences pane appears.

3. **Click the user's name once to select it and then click the Limitations button.**

The Limitations information for that person appears, as shown in Figure 16-6. Note that you can't limit an account with administrator privileges.

4. **Click a button to determine how much you wish to restrict this user.**

   • **Simple Finder:** Click this button to replace the normal Finder interface with one where many menu choices have disappeared as have a number of icons.

Figure 16-6:
You have
three levels
of limitation
available
to you.

- **No Limits:** This is the default setting for an account and means that you haven't applied any limitations (other than, possibly, not letting them Administer the Mac).

- **Some Limits:** Clicking this button displays some check boxes and a scrolling list, as shown in Figure 16-7. The four check boxes under This User Can: are pretty self-explanatory. Deselect the check box and the user loses that capability. Selecting the This User Can Only Use These Applications: check box makes the list active and you can click the check box next to a category to allow everything in that category or you can click the disclosure triangle and control the availability on an application-by-application basis.

If you disallow some, but not all, the applications in a category, the check box displays a minus sign rather than being empty or showing a check mark.

In order to change a user's capabilities, you must be logged in using an account that has Administrator powers.

5. **Quit the System Preferences application or choose a different System Preference pane.**

Your changes are saved when you leave the Accounts pane.

Figure 16-7:
Limiting
some user
capabili-
ties and
program
access is
easy.

Mac OS X knows best: Folders shared by default

When you add users in the Accounts System Preferences pane as I describe earlier in this chapter, Mac OS X automatically does two things behind the scenes to facilitate file sharing: It creates a set of folders, and it makes some of them available for sharing.

Each time you add a user, Mac OS X creates a folder hierarchy for that user on the Mac, as I describe in Chapter 10. The user can create more folders (if necessary) and also add, remove, or move anything inside of these folders. Even if you open a user account solely to allow him or her to exchange files with you, your Mac automatically creates a folder for that user. Unless you, as the owner of your Mac, give permission, the user can't see inside or use folders outside the Home folder (which has the user's name) except for the Shared folder in the Users folder and the Public folders in every other user's folder, as described below.

✔ **Public:** A Public folder is located inside each user's folder. That folder is set up to be accessible (shared) by any user who can log onto the Mac. Furthermore, any user can log on (as a guest) and copy things out of this folder as long as he knows your Mac's IP address, even if he doesn't have an account on this Mac at all. Files put into the Public folder can be opened or copied freely.

Inside each user's Public folder is a Drop Box folder. Just like the name implies, this folder is where others can drop a file or folder for you. Only the owner can open the Drop Box to see what's inside or to move or copy the files that are in it. Imagine a street corner mailbox — after you drop your letter in, it's gone, and you can't get it back out.

✔ **Shared:** In addition to a Public folder for each user, Mac OS X creates one Shared folder on every Mac for all users of this Mac. The Shared folder *isn't* available to guests, but it's available to every person who has an account on this machine, when they're logged in at the machine. You find the Shared folder within the Users folder (the same folder where you find folders for each user). The Shared folder is the right place to put stuff that everyone with an account might want to use. In Figure 16-8, you can see the Users folder for Bob's Mac, where Bob (bob1), Mr. Clean (clean), Simple Simon (simple), and Steve Jobs (steve) each have user folders. You can also see the Shared folder that all three use.

Here's an example of how all this works. If Bob has a user account called bob1 on his Mac, he can log in and work with any item in his user directory — the bob1 Home folder. He can also put files in his Shared folder that he wants to share with others users who sit at this particular Mac. Or he can put them in the Public folder if he wants them available to everyone with an account as well as guests logged on remotely via a LAN or the Internet. If bob1 wants to share a file with just clean, he can put it in the Public folder under the clean user account; or, if he wants to be sure that no one but clean sees it, he can put it into the Drop Box folder inside the Public folder for clean. The privileges to do all of this are set up when the user account is created — you don't have to lift a finger.

Sharing a folder or disk by setting privileges

As you might expect, access privileges control who can use a given folder or any disk (or partition) other than the startup disk.

Why can't you share the startup disk? Because OS X won't let you. Why not? Because it contains the operating system and other stuff that nobody else should have access to.

Throughout the rest of this chapter, whenever I talk about sharing a folder, I also mean disks and disk partitions other than your startup disk (which, when you think of it, are nothing more than big folders anyway). Why am I telling you this? Because it's awkward to keep typing "a folder or any disk (or partition) other than your startup disk." So anything that I say about sharing a folder also applies to sharing any disk (or partition) other than your startup disk. Got it?

Figure 16-8:
Each user has a folder and can open or copy items from the Shared folder.

You can set access privileges for the folder's owner, for a subset of all the people having accounts on the Mac (a group), or for everyone who has the Mac's address whether they have an account or not (guests). To help you better understand, I'll talk a little first about owners and groups.

Contemplating privileges

When you consider who can use which folders, there are three distinct kinds of users on the network. I describe each of them in this section. Then, in the "Useful settings for access privileges" section later in this chapter, I show you how to share folders with each of them.

✔ **Owner:** The owner of a folder or drive can change the access privileges to that folder or drive at any time. The name that you enter when you log onto your Mac — or the name of your Home folder — is the default owner of shared folders and drives on that machine. Ownership can be given away (more on that in the "Useful settings for access privileges" section later in this chapter). Even if you own the Mac, you can't change access privileges for a folder on it that belongs to another user (unless you get UNIX-y and do so as root). The owner must be logged in to change privileges on his or her folders.

OS X is the owner of many folders outside the Users folder. If OS X owns it, you'll see that system is its owner, as shown in Figure 16-9. Folders that aren't in the User directories generally belong to System.

You *can* change those access privileges without resorting to third-party utilities or using the Terminal (which I describe briefly in Chapter 13), as was necessary in OS X versions before Jaguar. Be careful. It's not a good idea to change them unless you know exactly what you're doing and why. Unfortunately, that discussion is far beyond the purview of this book.

✔ **Group member:** In UNIX systems, all users belong to one or more *groups*. The group that includes everyone who has an account with administrator privileges on your Mac is called admin. Everyone in the admin group has access to Shared and Public folders over the network as well as to any folder that the admin group has been granted access to by the folder's owner.

✔ **Others:** This category is an easy way to set access privileges for everyone with an account on your Mac at once. Unlike the admin group, which includes only users with administrative privileges, others includes, well, everyone (everyone with an account on this Mac, that is).

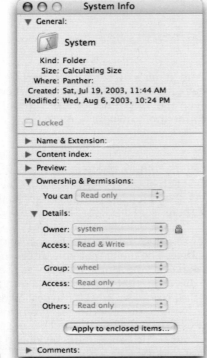

Figure 16-9:
Mac OS X (system) owns this folder, and you can't easily change its access privileges.

If you want people without an account on this Mac to have access to a file or folder, it needs to go in your Public folder, where they can log on as a guest.

Sharing a folder

Suppose that you have a folder that you want to share but with slightly different rules than those set up for the Public folder, the Drop Box folder within, or for your personal folders. These rules are *privileges,* and they tell you how much access someone has to your stuff.

Actually, the rules governing Shared and Public folders are privileges, too, but they're set up for you when Mac OS X is installed.

I suggest that you only share folders that are located within your Home folder or a folder within it. Because of the way UNIX works, the UNIX permissions of the enclosing folder can prevent access to a folder for which you *do* have permissions. Trust me, if you only share folders in your Home folder, you'll never go wrong. If you don't take this advice, you could wind up having folders that other users can't access, even though you gave them the appropriate permission.

You can set access privileges for folders within your Public folder (like the Drop Box folder) that are different from those for the rest of the folder.

Whatever happened to users and groups?

Mac OS X users who have used Mac OS 9 might wonder what's happened to the Users and Groups feature, which enabled you to create any number of user groups on a Mac. Because Mac OS X is based on the UNIX operating system, which deals very differently with permissions and access privileges than older versions of Mac OS did, it can't support old-style users and groups.

If you're brave or knowledgeable enough to dig into UNIX, you can make your own groups in Mac OS X. Creating a UNIX group confers identical access privileges and powers on its members. Although the process of creating a group is beyond the scope of this book, the process basically involves either gaining root access to the UNIX system and working from the Terminal command line or tinkering with the groups directory by using NetInfo Manager (requires Administrator access).

If you feel adventurous and know a little UNIX, try this: Open the Terminal program (in the Utilities folder inside the Applications folder) and type **man group**. Terminal will display the manual pages for the topic *group*. Press Space as many times as needed to scroll through the entire document. It probably won't help you create a group, but reading it won't hurt anything.

The admin group includes every user of a given Mac who has administrative privileges. Although it's not as good as the old Users and Groups feature (in OS 9 and earlier), it's a little better than no groups at all.

REMEMBER

I said this before, but it bears repeating: Whenever I talk about sharing a folder, I also mean disks and disk partitions other than your startup disk (which you just can't share, period). So don't forget that anything I say about sharing a folder also applies to sharing any disk (or partition) other than your startup disk. Though you can't explicitly share your startup disk, anyone with Administrator access can mount it for sharing from across the network (or Internet).

To share a folder with another user, follow these steps:

1. **Select (single-click) the folder or drive icon and then choose File⇨Get Info (or use the keyboard shortcut ⌘+I).**

   The Info window for the selected item opens.

2. **Click the triangle to the left of the Ownership & Permissions panel near the bottom of the window, then click the Details disclosure triangle.**

   The sharing options appear, as you see in Figure 16-10.

3. **Set access privileges for this folder by using the access privileges pop-up menus to control how much access each type of user has to the shared folder or drive.**

   When you click one of these pop-up menus, you see the privilege description.

   You can choose from three types of access for each user or group, as shown in Table 16-1.

   If you are the folder's owner (or have Administrator access), you can click the padlock icon and change the owner and/or group for the file or folder.

Table 16-1	Access Privileges
Access Privilege	*What It Allows*
Read & Write	A user with read and write access can see, add, delete, move, and edit files just as if they were stored on his or her own computer.
Read Only	A read-only user can see and use files that are stored in a shared folder but can't add, delete, move, or edit them.
Write Only (Drop Box)	Users can add files to this folder but can't see what's in it. The user must have read access to the folder containing a Write Only folder.
No Access	With no privileges, a user can neither see nor use your shared folders or drives.

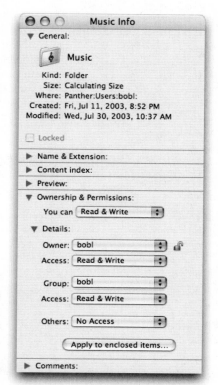

Figure 16-10:
Set file
sharing
here.

Useful settings for access privileges

The following sections show you just some of the more common ways that you can combine access privileges for a folder. You'll probably find one option that fits the way you work and the people you want to share with.

Allow everyone access

In Figure 16-11, I configure settings that allow access for everyone on a network. Everyone can open, read, and change the contents of this shared folder. Do this by choosing Read & Write for Others in the Access pop-up menu in the Ownership & Permissions section of the folder's Get Info window.

Allow nobody but yourself access

The settings shown in Figure 16-12 reflect appropriate settings that allow owner-only access. No one but me can see or use the contents of this shared folder. Choose No Access in both the Group Access and the Others pop-up menus to do it yourself.

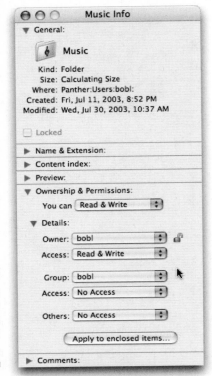

Figure 16-11:
Allow
everyone
access if
you want.

You need to change the Others pop-up menu to No Access first because Group member privileges must be at least as broad as Others privileges.

Allow all administrative users of this Mac access

Check out Figure 16-13 to see settings that allow the group wheel (in addition to the owner) access to see, use, or change the contents of the shared folder. Choose Read & Write in the Group Access pop-up menu.

Allow others to deposit files and folders without giving them access (a Drop Box)

The settings in Figure 16-14 enable users to drop their own files or folders without being able to see or use the contents of the shared folder. After a file or folder is deposited in a drop folder, the dropper can't retrieve it because he or she doesn't have access privileges to see the items in the drop folder. To let everyone use this folder as a Drop Box, choose Write only (Drop Box) from both the Group Access and the Others pop-up menus.

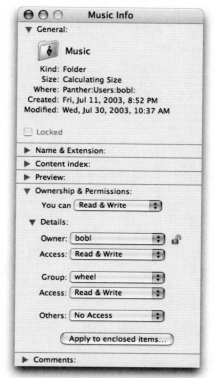

Figure 16-12:
Allow
access for
no one but
the folder's
owner.

Read-only bulletin boards

If you want everyone to be able to open and read the files and folders in this shared folder, choose Read Only from the Group Access and the Others pop-up menus. If you do this, however, only the owner can make changes to files in this folder.

One more privilege

The Apply to Enclosed Items button, at the bottom of the access privileges section, does exactly what its name implies. This feature is a fast way to assign the same privileges to many subfolders at once. After you set privileges for the enclosing folder the way you like them, click this button to give these same privileges to all the folders inside it.

Be careful — there is no Undo for this action.

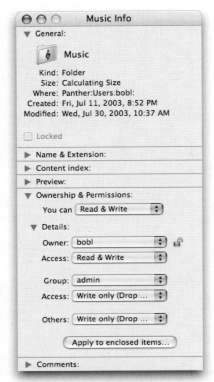

Figure 16-13:
Allow
access to
one group.

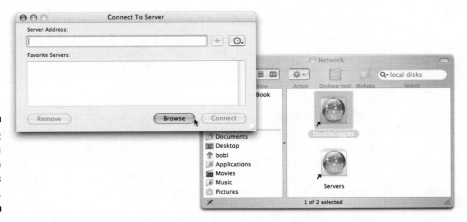

Figure 16-14:
Everyone
can drop
files in this
folder.

Consummating the Act of Sharing

After you set up sharing and assign access privileges, you can access folders remotely from another computer. (Just make sure first that you have access privileges to it.)

File sharing only has to be activated on the Mac where the shared files/folders reside, not on the Mac accessing them. When file sharing is turned off, you can still use it to access a remote shared folder on another machine as long as its owner has granted you enough access privileges and has file sharing enabled on his or her Mac.

If file sharing is turned off on *your* Mac, though, others won't be able to access your folders, even if you've assigned access privileges to them previously.

If you're going to share files and you leave your Mac on and unattended for a long time, logging out before you leave it is a very good idea. This prevents anyone just walking up to your Mac from seeing your files, e-mail, applications, or anything else that's yours unless you have given them a user account and granted them access privileges for your files.

Connecting to a shared disk or folder on a remote

On to how to access your Home folder from a remote Mac, which is a super-cool feature that's only bound to get more popular as the Internet continues to mature.

The following steps assume that you've got an account on the remote Mac, which means that you have your own Home folder on that Mac.

To connect to a shared folder on a Mac other than the one you're currently on, follow these steps:

1. **Make sure that you are already set up as a user on the computer that you want to log in to (DoubleGiggles in this example).**

   If you need to know how to create a new user, see the "Creating users" section earlier in the chapter.

2. **On the computer that you're logging in from (Panther PowerBook in this example), choose Go⇨Connect to Server.**

   The Connect to Server dialog appears.

3. **Click the Browse button.**

   A Finder window opens, set to show (aliases to) all the computers available on your local network, as shown in Figure 16-15.

4. **Double-click the remote Mac's name (DoubleGiggles) in the Finder window.**

   The Connect dialog box appears. The person logged in on Panther PowerBook name automatically appears in the Name field (Bob LeVitus in Figure 16-15). If that's not you, type your username in the Name field.

   TCP/IP must be active on Panther PowerBook (the Mac I'm using in the example). If it's not, you won't see any other machines on the network, nor will you be able to use any remote shared folders. In other words, file sharing doesn't have to be turned on (on the computer you're using), but TCP/IP does.

5. **Type your password into the Password field and then click the Connect button.**

   You would mark the Guest radio button if you didn't have an account on DoubleGiggles. Pressing ⌘+G is the same as marking the Guest radio button, and pressing ⌘+R is the same as marking the Registered User radio button. All you would get to see then are the Public folders of every user with an account on DoubleGiggles. A registered user (like me in this example) also gets to see his Home folder plus everyone else's Public folder.

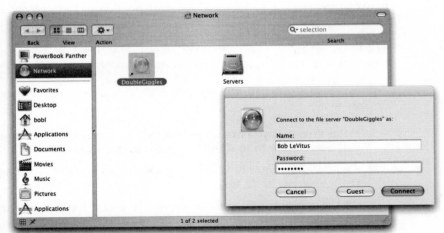

Figure 16-15:
The Connect to Server window (front window) and the Finder window that results when you click the Browse button (back window).

The available volumes appear in the Finder window, as seen in Figure 16-16.

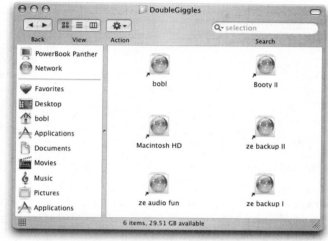

Figure 16-16:
The 5 disks connected to Double-Giggles and my home directory (bobl) on Double-Giggles. Mac.

Volume is the Mac OS X term for all the shared folders or disks. You can see what some volumes look like in Figure 16-17 — there are six of them available (plus my home directory, bobl).

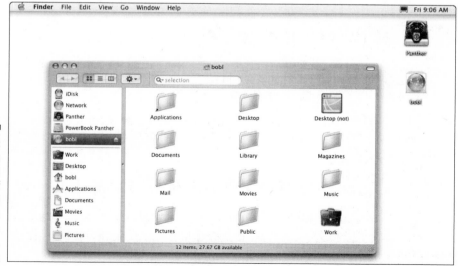

Figure 16-17:
The folders in the Home directory of the remote Mac (Double-Giggles).

When you log onto a Mac on which you have a user account, you will always see a volume with your name. You will also see other volumes with usernames of every other user who has an account on this computer. If those users have not given you access privileges for specific folders, the only thing you'll see when you open their volume is their Public folder (and the Drop Box folder within it). If they've given you privileges for other folders, you'll see those as well. If you have Administrator privileges on that Mac, you'll also see the various hard disks and other volumes.

If multiple items appear in the Finder window (as shown in Figure 16-17), you can select more than one. Click the first item, hold down the ⌘ key, and then click each item once that you want to add to the selection. After you select all the items that you want to use, choose File➪Open (or press ⌘+O) and they're all mounted on your Desktop.

6. **Select the volume that you want to use (bob1 in Figure 16-17) and then click OK.**

   An icon appears on your Desktop (the Desktop of BobsTiBook), as shown in Figure 16-18. This icon represents a volume named bob1, which resides on the computer GiggleHurts. Notice that the icon for bob1 doesn't look like a drive or folder icon. This icon is what you see whenever a remote volume is mounted on your Desktop. You'll also see it if you add a server to your Favorites folder (more on that later) or view a server in the Finder window.

   Open the volume icon, and its folder window appears (also called bob1), as shown in Figure 16-17.

Unsharing a folder

To unshare a folder that you own, change the Group Access and Others privileges to None. After you do, nobody but you will have access to that folder anymore.

If you're not sure how to do this, see the "Sharing a folder" and "Useful settings for access privileges" sections earlier in this chapter.

Disconnecting from a shared volume

When you finish using the shared volume, disconnect by using one of these methods:

✔ Drag the shared folder icon to the Eject icon in the dock.

   When a disk or volume is selected (highlighted), the Trash icon turns into a little arrow, which represents eject. Nice touch, eh?

✔ Hold down the Control key, click the volume, and then choose Eject from the contextual menu that appears.

✔ Select the icon and choose File➪Eject.

✔ Select the icon and press ⌘+E.

✔ In a Finder window Places pane, click the little Eject symbol to the right of the server's name or select the server and choose Eject from the Action popup.

✔ If you've finished working for the day, choose Shut Down or Log Out from the menu. Shutting down or logging out automatically disconnects you from shared disks or folders. (Shut Down also turns off your Mac.)

Changing your password

You can change your password at any time. Changing your password is a good idea if you're concerned about security — if there's a chance your password has been discovered by someone else, for example.

You can change the password for your Mac, or you can change the password that you use to connect to your account on a remote user's Mac. I show you how to do both in the following sections.

Changing your Mac's password

To change the password on your Mac, just follow these steps:

1. **Choose System Preferences from the menu on the Finder's menu bar (or click the System Preferences icon in the Dock) and then click the Accounts icon.**

   The Accounts System Preference pane appears.

2. **Select your account in the list on the left.**

   Your account information appears in the area on the right.

3. **Select the contents of the Password field and start typing. A sheet will drop down telling you that you need to verify who you are before you can change your password. Type your current password into Current Password field to demonstrate that you are who you're supposed to be and not someone who just walked up to your unattended Mac.**

   Assuming you entered your current password correctly, the sheet disappears.

4. **Type your new password into the Password field in the Password pane.**

5. **Retype your password in the Verify field.**

6. **Close the System Preferences window.**

Changing the password for your account on someone else's Mac

When you log into a remote Mac, you can change your own password if you like. Follow these steps to do so:

1. **Log into the remote computer on which you want to change your password (see the "Connecting to a shared disk or folder" section earlier in this chapter if you don't know how to log in to a remote computer).**

   The Connect dialog appears.

2. **Type your username into the Connect dialog if it's not already there.**

3. **Click the Options button in the Connect dialog.**

   The Options dialog appears, as shown in Figure 16-18.

   The Options dialog includes several options for encrypting your password as it is sent over the network. Mark the Add Password to Keychain check box to store your passwords in a single place on the Mac, meaning that you don't have to retype them each time you access a Mac or other remote resource. Read more about the keychain in Chapter 13.

4. **Click the Change Password button.**

   The Change Password dialog window appears, as shown in Figure 16-19.

5. **Type your current password in the Old Password field.**

6. **Type your new password in the New Password and Confirm Password fields.**

7. **Click OK.**

   Your password is changed, and you return to the Connect dialog.

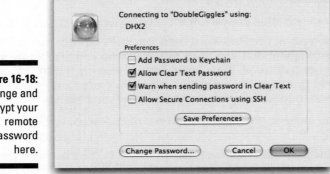

Figure 16-18:
Change and encrypt your remote password here.

Connecting to "DoubleGiggles" using:
DHX2

Preferences

☐ Add Password to Keychain
☑ Allow Clear Text Password
☑ Warn when sending password in Clear Text
☐ Allow Secure Connections using SSH

(Save Preferences)

(Change Password...)   (Cancel)   (OK)

Figure 16-19:
Enter your
old and new
passwords.

8. **(Optional) Type your new password and click then Connect to log onto the other Mac.**

    You can skip this step by clicking the Cancel button in the Connect dialog if you don't need to use anything on the remote Mac at this time. Your password is still changed, and you'll need to use the new password the next time that you log onto this Mac.

Setting up shortcuts to remote volumes (and folders)

Here are three ways that you can make using remote volumes and folders easier. The first is to use aliases, the second is to use OS X's Favorites, and the third uses aliases and the Dock. The following sections describe each of these methods.

Setting up a shortcut using aliases

After you've mounted a volume for the first time, you can make it easier to use in the future by creating an alias for it. The next time that you want to use that volume, just opens the alias, and the Connect dialog appears. You type your password, and the volume appears (is mounted) on the Desktop. No Connect to Server; no other dialogs; no muss and no fuss.

You can do this to any folder within the volume, too. It works just the same with one minor difference: The alias opens that folder, but it also mounts the volume that contains the folder and opens it, too. If you find this bothersome, just close the Home folder's window. The folder within — the one you made the alias of and want to work with — remains open, and you can continue working with it.

Setting up a shortcut using favorites

Here's another easy way to mount a volume: Just click the remote volume's icon (or any folder icon within that volume), and then while it's selected (highlighted), choose File⇨Add to Favorites (or press ⌘+T) from the Finder's menu bar. An alias to the remote volume or folder appears in the Favorites folder and on the Favorites submenu of the Go menu.

Setting up shortcuts in the Dock (and on the Desktop)

If you use remote folders often, follow these steps to create a folder that sits on your Dock, ready to call remote computers at your very whim:

1. **Log onto each remote volume (or folder) that you want to be included in the shortcut folder on your Desktop.**

2. **Create an alias for each remote volume or folder that you want easy access to.**

3. **Move the aliases that you created in Step 2 to a new folder on your Desktop (call it Remote Folders or something equally obvious).**

4. **Drag the Remote Folders folder onto the Dock.**

   Here are two easy ways to open any of the volumes or folders in the Remote Folders folder.

   • You can open the Remote Folders folder and double-click any of the aliases in it.

   • You can click and hold (or Control+click) the Remote Folders icon in the Dock, which causes a menu to pop up that shows all the aliases in the Remote Folders folder.

   Either way, that volume or folder will appear on your Desktop almost instantly.

Connecting to your own computer from a remote computer

In this section, I show you several file-sharing tricks that you can use on the road. The first explains how to log onto your home Mac easily from anywhere in the world by plugging into someone else's network. The second is a trick that I call *office-on-a-disk,* which is a way to take your shortcuts (see the previous section) with you, even when you use some-one else's Mac. Finally, I'll take a look at how to access your files remotely via modem connection.

These techniques are especially useful for iBook or PowerBook users or if you need to connect to your Mac from someplace other than your home or office network. The only thing you have to remember is that your Mac must be on and that you need File Sharing turned on as well.

Assume for the moment that you're on a network, perhaps at a client's office. In this section, I show how you would make the connection with a modem. For example, say you take a plane trip. You bring your PowerBook so that you can work on the plane. When you get to your destination, you want to copy the files that you've been working on to your home Mac to back them up. Well, you can do that with file sharing, which is easy if you've read about file sharing in the earlier sections of this chapter and understand how to connect to a remote Mac. (If you aren't sure how to do that, please reread the previous sections of this chapter now. If you don't, the following technique will only confuse you.)

Because you are the owner of your home Mac, you have full access privileges to both your Home folder and also to the rest of your Mac, just as you would if you were working from home. Also, because you own your Mac, you don't need to make any changes to file sharing privileges in order to log on and use your stuff.

You can connect to your home Mac via an Ethernet network or a modem. I'll talk about Ethernet first, then the nifty office-on-a-disk, and finally I'll talk about using a modem.

Logging on remotely via Ethernet

Okay, so you've arrived at your destination. The first thing to do is plug your PowerBook's Ethernet cable into the network and find out what TCP/IP address info that you need to use this network (by asking the PIC, or *person in charge;* also sometimes known as the network administrator, IT person, or resident geek). With those tasks completed, you're ready to do some sharing.

To connect to your home Mac from a remote computer, follow these steps:

1. **Choose Go⇨Connect to Server (on your PowerBook or other remote Mac, of course).**

2. **Type in the TCP/IP address of your Mac at home in the Address field and then click the Connect button.**

   The Connect to Server dialog appears.

3. **Type your username (it might be the same on the PowerBook as on your home Mac) and password and then click the Connect button.**

   The Volume Selection dialog appears. You see your Home folder, your startup hard drive, and any other disks or partitions that appear on the Desktop of your home machine.

4. **Choose a volume and then click OK.**

   The volume mounts on your PowerBook Desktop, and you're in business!

Logging on remotely via office-on-a-disk

Here's a great tip of an even easier way to use your hard drive while working at someone else's Mac. Before leaving your computer, make an alias of your hard drive and copy it to a Zip disk, an iPod, burn it onto a CD-R, or copy it to your PowerBook's hard drive. At a remote computer, open the alias of your hard drive. The Connect dialog appears, and as long as you type the correct password and your Mac can be found through the network connection, your hard drive mounts on that Mac's Desktop. Neat!

This technique is often called *office-on-a-disk*. If you work in a largish office and find yourself trying to connect to your hard drive from someone else's computer, carry one of these office-on-a-disk disks with you at all times. And if you're using a PowerBook, keep the aliases to your Mac (and any others you use on the road) on the Desktop for quick access. You could also put them in a folder and drag the folder to the Dock. Then all the aliases are available in a pop up menu when you click and hold (or Control+click) on the folder's Dock icon.

If you have no Zip or other removable media disk, don't despair. Just because your Mac has no removable-media drive doesn't mean that you can't use a disk alias. The first time that you mount your hard drive on a remote Mac (see "Logging on remotely via Ethernet"), make an alias of the mounted drive. Leave it on the Desktop or some other convenient location, and you can use it to quickly mount the drive.

Logging on remotely via a modem

Mac OS X includes Point-to-Point Protocol (PPP) software — Internet Connect — that enables you to connect to another computer or the Internet by modem.

With Internet Connect, you can access your home hard drive from a remote Mac when you're at another location. You do need a modem, and you also need to configure this modem for remote access, which luckily is a pretty simple process. Because remote access uses the same Accounts and File Sharing tools as network file sharing, you should probably bone up on file sharing in the sections earlier in this chapter if you haven't already.

To use a modem to log on remotely, follow these steps:

1. **Choose System Preferences from the menu or click the System Preferences icon in the Dock.**

2. **Click the Network icon.**

   The Network pane appears.

   You can consolidate Steps 1 and 2 by choosing ⌘⇨Location⇨Network Preferences.

3. **Choose Internal Modem from the Show pop-up menu, unless you have an external modem; in that case, choose that option.**

   If you've been using Ethernet rather than a modem, notice that two new tabs appear after you choose Internal Modem from the menu: the PPP tab and the Modem tab.

4. **Click the PPP tab.**

   PPP options appear, as shown in Figure 16-20.

5. **(Optional) Type a name for this connection in the Service Provider field.**

   This gives a name to the connection information that you're now creating so you can easily reuse it in the future. Doing this will make life easier if you need to use this modem connection again.

6. **Type your account name (Internet username) in the Account Name field.**

7. **Type your password in the Password field.**

8. **Type the phone number that you want to dial (including any dialing prefix and area code) into the Telephone Number field.**

9. **(Optional) Type an alternate phone number, if there is one, in the Alternate Number field.**

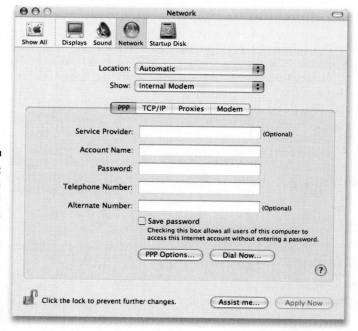

Figure 16-20:
The PPP tab of the Network pane is where you set up for remote access via a modem.

10. **(Optional) If you want to log on without having to enter your password each time, select the Save password check box.**

Selecting this check box means that someone with access to your Mac can log on to your account, so be careful, especially if you're working on an iBook or PowerBook.

11. **Click the PPP Options button to set preferences for how your connection is made and maintained.**

The PPP Options sheet appears, as shown in Figure 16-21. Of the many options you find here, I'll point out a few of the most useful in the following list:

- Select the Connect automatically when needed check box if you want your modem to connect to the Internet when you launch your browser, connect to a remote server, or retrieve e-mail. This check box must be marked, or your Mac won't connect to the Internet automatically when you choose Go⇨Connect to Server.

- Leave the Prompt every x minutes to maintain connection check box selected if you're paying long distance charges or Internet access charges. If you don't set this auto-disconnect timer, you could rack up a lot of toll charges if you forget that you're connected and online. If you choose this option, set the number of idle minutes by clicking within the number box and typing the number that you want.

- Select the Redial if busy check box to do just that. You can choose the number of attempts that your modem will make and how long it should wait between attempts if it gets a busy signal instead of connecting.

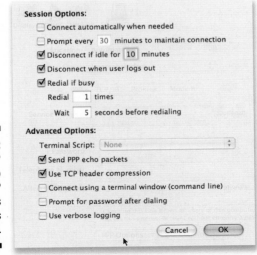

Figure 16-21:
Use PPP options to set how PPP connects and stays connected.

12. **When you're done setting PPP options, click OK to close the PPP Options sheet.**

13. **(Optional) Click the Modem tab in the Network pane.**

Your modem should be selected in the Modem pop-up menu. If you're having problems connecting, use the menu to find your particular modem and select it.

You won't need to do much with these settings unless you're having a problem connecting with the modem, but you can set little options here, too. Some options of note are

- Some modems, such as the Apple 56K modems included in most Macs, are capable of performing some error checking and data compression. It's not industrial-strength compression, but it can speed up data transfer.

- You can tell the modem to wait until it detects a dial tone before dialing. In less friendly environs, you have to know to insert commas into the phone number to pause.

- Choose whether to turn your speaker sound off (to rid yourself of that horrid screeching noise that modems make).

- Choose from tone or pulse dialing, if you need the latter for some strange reason.

And that retires the side. Just choose Go⇨Connect to Server and log onto the remote machine. (If you still don't know how, reread the "Connecting to a shared disk or folder" section earlier in the chapter.)

Chapter 17

Back Up Now or Regret It Later

*A*lthough Macs are generally reliable beasts (especially Macs running OS X), someday your hard drive will die. I promise. They *all* do. And if you don't back up your hard drive (or at least those files that you can't afford to lose) before that day comes, chances are good that you'll never see your files again. And if you do see them again, it will only be after paying Scott of DriveSavers Data Recovery Service a king's ransom, with no guarantee of success.

DriveSavers is the premier recoverer of lost data on hard drives. They understand Mac hard disks quite well, do excellent work, and can often recover stuff that nobody else could. (Ask the producers of *The Simpsons* about the almost-lost episodes.) Understandably, DriveSavers charges accordingly. Here's the phone number for DriveSavers: 415-883-4232. Now pray that you never need it — and if you back up often, you won't. But if, somehow, none of this sinks in, tell Scott that I said, "Hi."

In other words, you absolutely, positively, without question *must back up* your files if you don't want to risk losing them. Just as you adopt the Shut Down command and make it a habit before turning off your machine, you must remember to back up important files on your hard drive and back them up often.

How often is often? That depends on you. How much work can you afford to lose? If your answer is that losing everything you did yesterday would put you out of business, you need to back up daily or possibly twice a day. If you would only lose a few unimportant letters, you can back up less frequently.

Backing Up Is (Not) Hard to Do

You can back up your hard drive in basically two ways — the brute force method, or the easy way. Read on to discover both. . . .

Backing up by using the manual, brute-force method

The most rudimentary way to back up your files is to do it manually. Accomplish this by dragging your files a few at a time to removable disks, such as to a Zip, SuperDisk, or Jaz drive. Or, if you have a CD-R, CD-RW, DVD-R, or DVD-RW drive, burn a disc with the files that you want to back up. In effect, you're making a copy of each file that you want to protect. (See Chapter 9 for more info on removable storage.)

Yuck! If doing a manual backup sounds pretty awful, trust me — it is. This method takes forever; you can't really tell whether you copy every file; and you can't copy only the files that have been modified since your last backup. Almost nobody sticks with this method for long.

Of course, if you're careful to only save files in your Documents folder, as I suggest several times in this book, you can probably get away with backing up only that. Or, if you save files in other folders within your Home folder, back up the Home folder. As you'll read in a moment, it's even easier with back-up software.

Backing up by using commercial back-up software

If you ask me, a good back-up program is the best investment that you can make. Frankly, I like the security of knowing that every document that I modify today is being backed up automatically. And that's what back-up software is all about.

Back-up software automates the task of backing up, remembering what is on each back-up disk (if your backup uses more than one disk) and backing up only those files that have been modified since the last backup.

Furthermore, you can instruct your back-up software to only back up a certain folder (Home or Documents) and to ignore the hundreds of megabytes of stuff that make up OS X, all of which can be easily reinstalled from the Mac OS X CD-ROM.

Your first backup with commercial software should take anywhere from a few minutes to many hours and use one or more pieces of removable media — Zip, Jaz, CD-R, CD-RW, DVD-R, DVD-RW, magneto-optical disks, or any kind of tape backup. Subsequent backups, called *incremental backups* in back-up-software parlance, should take only a few minutes.

Be sure to label all the disks that you use for your backups during incremental backups because the back-up software may prompt you with a message like `Please insert backup disk 7`. If you haven't labeled your media clearly, you could have a problem figuring out which disk *is* disk 7.

For some unfathomable reason, Apple has almost never seen fit to provide back-up software with new Macs or include it with Mac OS. I know that some early-90s Macintosh Performas had a crummy back-up program, and if you pay the 99 bucks for .Mac, you get Apple's decent Backup program. But other than those two attempts, Apple has left millions of Mac owners clueless, for years, giving them nothing more than a brief passage regarding backing up in the Macintosh *User's Guide*.

Information on backing up should be in big red letters, in the first chapter of the guide, and include a warning from the Surgeon General or something. And it wouldn't kill Apple to provide a back-up utility, either. Sheesh, even Windows has a back-up command, albeit a lousy one. C'mon, Apple, give Mac owners a fair shake — include Backup with those $129 OS X upgrades.

Fortunately, plenty of very good back-up programs are available for well under $150, including the excellent Retrospect family of backup solutions from Dantz Development (www.dantz.com).

Retrospect Desktop protects up to three networked desktops and notebooks for $129; Retrospect Workgroup protects a single server and up to 20 networked desktops and notebooks for $499; Retrospect Server protects up to 100 networked clients, including Windows and Macintosh desktops and notebooks, as well as Mac OS X servers for $799.

Here's a nice touch: The included network client (all three versions of Retrospect use it) runs on Windows XP, Windows 2000 Professional, Windows NT 4.0 Workstation, Windows 95/98/Me, Red Hat Linux (versions 6.2, 7.1, 7.2, 7.3, and 8), and, of course, Mac OS 9 or X. So if you've got any non-Mac computers, chances are Retrospect can back them up over your local area network at no additional expense.

Other backup offerings include TriBackup 3 (around $50) from Tri-Edre (www.tri-edre.com); and more modest synchronizer programs such as ChronoSync ($20) from Econ Technologies (www.econtechnologies.com), or ExecutiveSync ($20) from Jason Weber Products (www.jasonweber.com).

If you want the most flexible, top-of-the-line back-up software, spend a little more and pop for Retrospect Desktop. It can do everything the others can do and more. It's the only backup software that you'll ever need.

Why You Need Two Sets of Back-Up Disks

You're a good soldier. You back up regularly. You think that you're immune to file loss or damage.

Now picture yourself in the following scenario:

1. One day you take a Zip disk, or your portable FireWire hard disk to QuicKopyLazerPrintz to print your resume on the high-resolution laser printer there. You make a few changes while at QuicKopyLazerPrintz and then take the disk home and stick it into your Mac (or connect it if it's the FireWire drive). Unbeknownst to you, the disk became infected with a computer virus at QuicKopyLazerPrintz. (I discuss viruses in the sidebar "Virus trivia," elsewhere in this chapter.)

2. When you insert or connect the disk, the infection spreads to your boot drive like wildfire.

3. Then you do a backup. Your back-up software, believing that all the infected files have been recently modified (well, they have been — they were infected with a virus!), proceeds to back them up. You notice that the backup takes a little longer than usual, but otherwise, things seem to be okay.

4. A few days later, your Mac starts acting strangely. You borrow a copy of an excellent virus-detection software, such as Virex or Norton AntiVirus (formerly Symantec Anti-Virus), and discover that your hard drive is infected. "A-ha!" you exclaim. "I've been a good little Mac user, backing up regularly. I'll just restore everything from my back-up disks."

   Not so fast, Buck-o. The files on your back-up disks are also infected!

This scenario demonstrates why you need multiple backups. If you have several sets of back-up disks, chances are pretty good that one of the sets is clean.

I always keep at least three current sets of back-up disks going at any one time. I use one set on even-numbered days, one on odd-numbered days, and update the third set once a week and store it somewhere other than my office (such as a neighbor's house or a safe deposit box). This scheme ensures that no matter what happens — even if my office burns, is flooded, is destroyed by a tornado or a hurricane, or is robbed — I won't lose more than a few days' worth of work. I can live with that.

Virus trivia

A computer *virus,* in case you missed it in *Time* or *Newsweek,* is a nasty little piece of computer code that replicates and spreads from disk to disk. Most viruses cause your Mac to misbehave; some viruses can destroy files or erase disks with no warning.

If you use disks that have been inserted in other computers, you need some form of virus-detection software. If you download and use files from Web and File Transfer Protocol (FTP) sites on the Internet, you need some form of virus detection as well.

You don't have too much to worry about if

- ✔ You download files only from commercial online services, such as America Online, which is very conscientious about viral infections.

- ✔ You use only commercial software and don't download files from Web sites with strange names.

You should definitely worry about virus infection if

- ✔ An unsavory friend told you about a Web site called Dan'sDenOfPiratedIllegal StolenBootlegSoftware.com.

- ✔ You swap disks with friends regularly.

- ✔ You shuttle disks back and forth to other Macs.

- ✔ You use your disks at service bureaus or copy shops.

- ✔ You download files from various and sundry places on the Internet, even ones that don't sound as slimy as Dan'sDenOfPiratedIllegalStolen BootlegSoftware.com.

- ✔ You receive e-mail with attachments (and open them).

If you're at risk, do yourself a favor and buy a commercial antivirus program. Although you can choose from many shareware and freeware antivirus solutions, none that I know of are as trustworthy as Virex or Norton. The big advantage of buying a commercial antivirus program is that the publisher contacts you each time that a virus is discovered and provides you with a software update to protect you against the new strain. Or, for a fee, the publisher can send you a new version of the software every time that a new virus is found.

On the commercial front, two leading virus-detection utilities are Virex and Norton AntiVirus (NAV; formerly Symantec Anti-Virus). Each has its advocates. I've used NAV for years and I have never been infected with a virus. My editor uses Virex and has also been virus-free. You'll find more info about Virex at: www. networkassociates.com/us/products/ mcafee/antivirus/desktop/virex.htm, and more info on Norton AntiVirus at www. symantec.com/nav/nav_mac/index. html.

Note: Most of the virus scares that you hear and read about won't affect you because they are specific to users of Windows systems. Most viruses are specific to an operating system — Mac viruses won't affect Windows users, Windows viruses won't affect Mac users, and so forth. The one real exception here is a "gift" from the wonderful world of Microsoft Office (Word, Excel, for example) users: the dreaded *macro viruses* that are spread with Word and Excel documents containing macros written in Microsoft's VBA (Visual BASIC for Applications) language. But you're even safe from those if you practice safe computing as I describe.

(continued)

(continued)

As it happens, so far almost all the viral activity affecting OS X involved various Windows macro virii. In fact, at the time of this writing, I know of no OS X-specific viruses nor of any that attack Mac OS X exclusively. And, at least so far, none that cause damage. Still, the advice in this chapter is sound — one never knows when the little boys out there will decide to attack the Mac. OS X viruses aren't impossible or non-existent; they just don't exist at this moment in time. But they could someday, so be safe rather than sorry.

Chapter 18

Troubleshooting Mac OS X

· ·

· ·

As a bleeding-edge Mac enthusiast with 18 years of Mac under my belt, I've had more than my share of Mac troubles. Over those years, I've developed an arsenal of surefire tips and tricks that I believe can resolve more than 90 percent of Mac OS X problems without a trip to the repair shop.

Alas, if your hardware is dead, then, sadly, neither you nor I can do anything about it because this is now a job for your friendly Mac repairman and your fat checkbook.

But if your hardware is okay, you have a fighting chance of using the suggestions in this chapter to get your machine up and running.

Dem Ol' Sad Mac Chimes of Doom Blues

Although you usually see a stylish Apple logo when you turn your computer on, once in a blue moon you might see the dreaded Sad Mac icon (shown in the left margin) and hear that melancholy arpeggio in G minor (better known as the *Chimes of Doom*), or the sound of breaking glass or a car wreck, or any of the other horrible sounds that Macs make when they're dying.

The Sad Mac usually indicates that something very bad has happened to your Mac; often some hardware component has bitten the dust. But Sad Macs are rather uncommon — many Mac users go their entire lifetime without seeing one. If you ever have a Sad Mac experience, don't despair immediately. Before you diagnose your Mac as terminally ill, disconnect any external FireWire and USB devices (everything except your keyboard and mouse), and try booting from CD-ROM to bring it back to life.

If you have your OS X installation CD-ROM ready, you can skip to the section "Booting from CD-ROM" later in this chapter. If you're not sure about your OS X installation CD-ROM, see the next section.

The ultimate startup discs: The OS X installation CD

I bet you have a copy of the ultimate startup disc right there on your computer table — the installation CD that came with your computer or, if you purchased a boxed retail copy of Panther, Install Disk 1.

You see, in addition to the system software that you need to make your Mac work, all OS X installation discs are bootable and include a working copy of Disk Utility, which I discuss in the section "Step 1: Run First Aid" section later in this chapter.

If you see a flashing question mark-on-a-folder, prohibitory sign, kernel panic alert, or a spinning disc cursor that doesn't go away (see Figure 18-1) when you start up your Mac, the first thing to do is attempt to repair hidden damage to your hard drive with the Apple Disk Utility program's First Aid feature.

Another of Disk Utility's features lets you verify and repair disk permissions, which is a handy thing to do if your Mac is telling you that you don't have enough permission to do things that you used to be able to do, such as move a file or folder, or move an icon to the Trash.

You'll learn more about using these utilities throughout the rest of this chapter.

Better safe than Mac-less

The bootable Mac OS X CD-ROM is soooo important — try to have more than one copy around. That way, if one gets misplaced, damaged, eaten by the dog, scuffed, scratched, or otherwise rendered useless, you won't be out of luck. I keep the Mac OS X CD in my middle desk drawer and several other bootable CDs on the bookshelf. An older version of Mac OS and the CD that came with your computer are examples of extra bootable CDs that you might have hanging around. The Mac OS X installation CD is bootable as well. All these will boot your Mac in an emergency, which is why they're so important to have handy.

One thing that I would do if I only had one of these valuable CDs is to use Apple's Disk Utility (in Applications/Utilities) to create a disk image of the CD and then burn a copy or two as spares. Don't forget to test the burned discs to ensure that they work and are bootable.

If you don't have a bootable CD-ROM, preferably a Mac OS X Install CD-ROM, you can't do most of the rest of the stuff in this chapter. So if you don't have it handy, go find it now. If you really can't find one, consider calling Apple or your Apple dealer to arrange for a replacement — you really shouldn't be without it.

Booting from CD-ROM

To boot your Mac from a CD-ROM installation disc, follow these steps:

1. **Insert a bootable CD-ROM (the Mac OS X installer CD is a good choice).**

   If your Mac uses a tray to hold the CD, make sure that it retracts and that the disk is in.

   If you have a tray-loading CD-ROM drive and it's closed, you can get it to open by restarting (or starting up) your Mac while pressing the mouse button. Continue pressing until the drive tray pops out, then release it.

2. **Shut down or restart your Mac.**

   If you shut it down, wait a few seconds and then start it up the usual way.

Figure 18-1:
If you see a flashing question mark (top left), prohibitory sign (top center), spinning disc cursor (top right), or kernel panic alert (bottom) at startup, it's troubleshooting time.

3. **Press and hold down the C key immediately and keep it pressed until your Mac either boots from the CD (you see a Welcome screen) or doesn't (you see a flashing question mark, prohibitory sign, spinning wheel-of-death, or anything but the first screen of the OS X Installer, the login window, or the Finder).**

If your Mac doesn't boot from the CD when you hold down the C key, and your Mac is new enough to support the built-in Startup Manager (most OS X-capable Macs are, but not all of them), hold down the Option key while booting to display the built-in Startup Manager (Figure 18-2). It displays icons for any bootable discs that it sees and allows you to select one (including the installation CD).

Figure 18-2:
Hold down the Option key during startup to bring up the built-in Startup Manager.

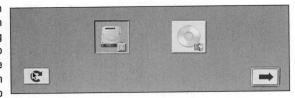

Click the CD-ROM icon to select it (on the right in Figure 18-2, unselected), then click the right-arrow button to boot from it.

This technique is quite useful if your usual boot disk is damaged or having issues during startup.

If you can boot from CD-ROM . . .

If you see the Mac OS startup (Welcome) screen when you boot (start up) from your CD-ROM, hope flickers for your Mac. The fact that you can boot from another disc (a CD-ROM in this case) indicates that the problem lies in one of two places: your hard drive and/or Mac OS X itself. Whatever the tangle, it will probably respond to one of the techniques that I discuss throughout the rest of this chapter.

So your Mac boots from the installation CD-ROM, but you still have this little problem: You prefer that your Mac boot from your (much faster) hard drive than the system software CD-ROM. Not to worry. All you need to do is reinstall Mac OS X (see the Appendix at the end of this book).

If you can't boot from CD-ROM . . .

If the techniques in this chapter don't correct your Mac problem or you still see the Sad Mac icon when you start up with the CD, your Mac is toast and needs to go in for repairs (usually to an Apple dealer).

Before you drag it down to the shop, however, try calling 1-800-SOS-APPL, the Apple Tech Support hotline. The service representatives there may be able to suggest something else that you can try. If your Mac is still under warranty, it's even free.

Another thing you might consider is contacting your local Macintosh user group. You can find a group of Mac users near you by visiting Apple's User Group Web pages at www.apple.com/usergroups.

If you get the Sad Mac immediately after installing random access memory (RAM) — and this is quite common — double-check that the RAM is properly seated in its sockets. Don't forget to power down your Mac first.

Follow the installation instructions that came with the RAM chips or the ones in the booklet that came with your Mac. But even if they don't say to, you should either use an anti-static strap (available from most RAM sellers) or discharge static electricity by touching an appropriate surface (such as the power supply case inside your Mac) before you handle RAM chips.

If problems occur immediately after installing RAM (or any new hardware, for that matter), remove and reinsert the RAM chips to make sure that they're seated properly. If you still have problems, remove the RAM temporarily and see whether the problem still exists.

Question Mark and the Mysterians

When you turn on your Mac, the first thing that it does (after the hardware tests) is to check for a start-up disc with Mac OS 9 or X on it. If your system doesn't find such a disc on your internal hard drive, it begins looking elsewhere — on a FireWire or Universal Serial Bus (USB) disk or on a CD or DVD.

If you have more than one start-up disc attached to your Mac, as many users do, you can choose which one your Mac boots from in the Startup Disk System Preference pane. (See Chapter 15 for details.)

At this point, your Mac usually finds your hard drive, which contains your operating system, and the start-up process continues on its merry way with the happy Mac and all the rest. If your Mac can't find your hard drive or doesn't find on it what it needs to boot OS X, you'll encounter a flashing question-mark icon or the prohibitory sign.

Don't go cryin' *96 Tears*. Those icons just mean that your Mac can't find a startup disc — a hard drive, or bootable CD-or-DVD-ROM disc with valid system software (either Mac OS X or a previous version supported by your particular Mac).

Think of the flashing question mark or prohibitory sign as your Mac's way of saying, "Please provide me with a startup disk."

If Apple can figure out a way to put a flashing question mark or prohibitory sign on the screen, why the heck can't the software engineers find a way to put the words `Please insert a startup disk` on the screen as well? The curtness of these icons is one of my pet peeves about the Macintosh. I know — you're clever and smart (you're reading *Mac OS X For Dummies*, aren't you?), so you know that a flashing question mark or prohibitory sign means that you should insert a startup disk. But what about everyone else?

If you encounter either of these warning icons, go through the steps that I outline in this section. I give you some different options to try, such as rebuilding your Desktop, using Disk Tools and First Aid, or zapping the parameter RAM (PRAM). If one doesn't work, move on to the next.

In the meantime, here are some less severe potential remedies for you.

Step 1: Run First Aid

In most cases, after you've booted successfully from the OS X CD, the first logical troubleshooting step is to use the First Aid option in the Disk Utility application.

Every drive has several strangely named components such as B-trees, extent files, catalog files, and other creatively named invisible files. They are all involved in managing the data on your drives. Disk Utility's First Aid feature checks all those files and repairs the damaged ones.

Here's how to make First Aid do its thing:

1. **Boot from your Mac OS X CD by inserting the CD and restarting your Mac while holding down the C key.**

   The OS X Installer appears on your screen.

2. **Choose Installer⇨Open Disk Utility to launch the Disk Utility application that's on the CD.**

3. **When the Disk Utility window appears, click the First Aid tab to select that function of Disk Utility.**

4. **Click the icon for your boot hard drive at the left of the Disk Utility window (*Panther* in Figure 18-3).**

   Your boot drive is the one with OS X and your Home folder on it. I call this one *Panther*.

5. **Click the Repair Disk button.**

   Your Mac whirs and hums for a few minutes, and the results window tells you what's going on. Ultimately, First Aid tells you (you hope) that the drive has been repaired and is now okay, as shown in Figure 18-4. If so, go back to work.

6. **Quit Disk Utility by choosing Disk Utility⇨Quit Disk Utility or by pressing ⌘+Q.**

7. **Reboot without holding the C key down.**

If First Aid finds damage that it can't fix, a commercial disk-recovery tool, such as Alsoft's DiskWarrior or Norton Utilities, may be able to repair the damage. And even if First Aid gave you a clean bill of health, you may want to run DiskWarrior anyway just to have a second opinion. Make sure that you're running a current version because older versions were not Mac OS X compatible.

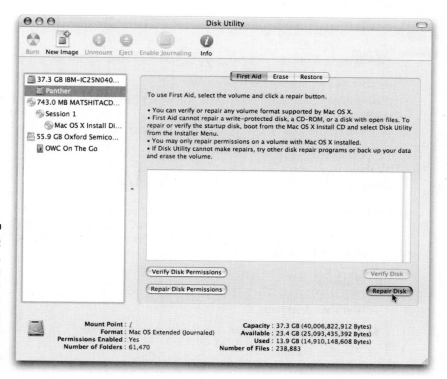

Figure 18-3:
First Aid, ready to perform its magic on the disk named Panther.

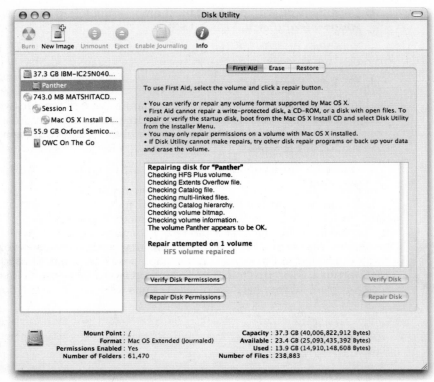

Figure 18-4:
First Aid
repaired the
disk and
gives it a
clean bill
of health.

If everything checks out with First Aid, eject the CD and try to boot from your hard drive again. If you still get the flashing question mark or prohibitory sign, proceed to the next section to try a little dance called zapping the PRAM.

Step 2: Zapping the PRAM

Sometimes your parameter RAM (PRAM) becomes scrambled and needs to be reset. *PRAM*, a small piece of memory that's not erased or forgotten when you shut down, keeps track of things such as printer selection, sound level, and monitor settings.

PRAM stores:

- Time zone setting
- Startup volume choice
- Speaker volume

✔ Recent kernel panic information, if any

✔ DVD region setting

To reset (often called "zapping") your PRAM, restart your Mac and press ⌘+Option+P+R (that's four keys — good luck; it's okay to use your nose) until your Mac restarts itself. It's kind of like a hiccup. You may see the flashing question mark or spinning disc cursor for a minute or two while your Mac thinks about it; then the icon disappears, and your Mac chimes again and restarts. Most power users believe that you should zap it more than once, letting it chime two, three, or even four times before releasing the keys and allowing the start-up process to proceed.

Now restart your Mac without holding down any keys.

If the PRAM zap didn't fix your Mac, move on to Step 3.

Remember that your chosen start-up disk, time zone, and sound volume are reset to their default values when you zap your PRAM. So after zapping, open the System Preferences application to reselect your usual boot disk and time zone, and set the sound volume the way you like it.

Unlike prior versions of the Mac OS, Mac OS X does not store display or network settings in PRAM. If you are having problems with video or networking, resetting PRAM will not help.

Step 3: Safe Boot into Safe Mode

Booting your Mac in Safe Mode by holding down the Shift key during startup, as shown in Figure 18-5, may help you resolve your startup issue.

Figure 18-5:
Your Mac lets you know you're booting into Safe Mode by adding the words *Safe Boot* to the bottom of the startup screen as shown.

Booting in Safe Mode does three things to help you with troubleshooting:

- ✔ It forces a directory check of the startup (boot) volume.
- ✔ It loads only required kernel extensions (some of the items in /System/Library/Extensions).
- ✔ It runs only Apple-installed startup items (some of the items in /Library/Startup Items and /System/Library/Startup items). Note that startup items are different from login items.

Taken together, these changes can work around issues caused by software or directory damage on the startup volume.

Some features do not work in Safe Mode. Among them are DVD Player, capturing video (in iMovie or other video-editing software), using an AirPort card, using some audio input or output devices, or using an internal or external USB modem. Use Safe Mode only if you need to troubleshoot a startup issue.

If your Mac boots in Safe Mode, you may be able to determine what is causing it — usually a damaged Preference file (in Home/Library/Preferences) or one of your Startup Items (in the Accounts System Preference pane).

If your Mac still has problems, try Step 4.

Step 4: Reinstalling OS X

I present the procedure to reinstall the system software last in this section because it takes the longest and is the biggest hassle. I detail this procedure at great length in the Appendix.

Read the Appendix and follow the instructions. If you're still unsuccessful after that point, you'll have no choice but to consider Step 5 . . .

Step 5: Take your Mac in for repair

If none of my suggestions work for you and you're still seeing anything you shouldn't when you start up your Mac, you have big trouble.

You could have any one of the following problems:

- ✔ Your hard drive is dead.
- ✔ You have some other type of hardware failure.
- ✔ All your startup discs and your system software CDs are defective (unlikely).

The bottom line: If you still can't start up normally after trying all the cures that I list in this chapter, you almost certainly need to have your Mac serviced by a qualified technician.

If You Crash at Startup

Startup crashes are another bad thing that can happen to your Mac. These crashes can be more of a hassle to resolve than flashing question mark problems but are rarely fatal.

You know that a *crash* has happened when you see a System Error dialog, a frozen cursor, a frozen screen, or any other disabling event. A *startup crash* happens when your system shows a crash symptom any time between flicking the power key or switch (or restarting) and having full use of the Desktop.

Try all the steps in the previous section before you panic. The easiest way to fix startup crashes (in most cases) is to just reinstall OS X from the CD. I detail this procedure at great length in the Appendix. Read the Appendix and follow the instructions. If you're still unsuccessful after that point, come back and reread the "Step 5: Take your Mac in for repair" section earlier in this chapter.

Part V
The Part of Tens

The 5th Wave   By Rich Tennant

"Because I can't find my regular cake stand."

In this part . . .

These last chapters are a little different — they're kind of like long top-ten lists. Although I'd like for you to believe that I included them because I'm a big fan of Dave Letterman, the truth is that Wiley always includes The Part of Tens section in its *For Dummies* books. This book continues the tradition. And because Wiley pays me, I do these chapters how I'm asked. (Actually, it's kind of fun.)

First, I tell you how to speed up your Mac experience. I then move on to a subject near and dear to my heart — awesome things for your Mac that are worth spending money on. Stay tuned for a collection of great Mac-related Web sites and finish out this section with a discussion of cool OS X applications that you may need someday.

Chapter 19

Ten (Or So) Ways to Speed Up Your Mac Experience

*T*his chapter is for speed demons only. At some time in their Mac life, most users have wished that their machine would work faster — even those with Power Macintosh G5s. I can't help you make your processor faster, but I do cover things in this chapter that can make your Mac at least seem faster, and most of these tips won't cost you a red cent.

Use Those Keyboard Shortcuts

Keyboard shortcuts (see Table 19-1 for a way-groovy list of the more useful ones) can make navigating your Mac a much faster experience compared to constantly using the mouse, offering these benefits:

✔ By using keyboard shortcuts, your hands stay focused on the keyboard, reducing the amount of time that you remove your hand from the keyboard to fiddle with the mouse.

✔ If you memorize keyboard shortcuts with your head, your fingers will memorize them, too.

✔ The more keyboard shortcuts that you use, the faster you can do what you're doing.

Trust me when I say that learning the keyboard shortcuts for commands that you use often will save you a ton of time and effort.

Make a list of keyboard shortcuts and tape it to your monitor or somewhere where you'll see it all the time when using your Mac. (Heck, make a photocopy of the upcoming table!)

Table 19-1	Great Keyboard Shortcuts	
Keyboard Shortcut	*What It's Called*	*What It Does*
⌘+O	Open	Opens the selected item.
⌘+. (period)	Cancel	Cancels the current operation in many programs, including the Finder. Also the keyboard shortcut for the Cancel button in most dialogs.
⌘+P	Print	Brings up a dialog that enables you to print the active window's contents. (See Chapter 12 for info on printing.)
⌘+X	Cut	Cuts whatever you select and places it on the Clipboard. (I cover the Edit menu and the Clipboard in Chapter 6.)
⌘+C	Copy	Copies whatever you select and places it on the Clipboard.
⌘+V	Paste	Pastes the contents of the Clipboard at the spot where your cursor is.
⌘+F	Find	Brings up Find window in the Finder; brings up a Find dialog in most programs.
⌘+A	Select All	Selects the entire contents of the active window in many programs, including the Finder.
⌘+Z	Undo	Undoes the last thing you did in many programs, including the Finder.
⌘+Shift+?	Help	Brings up the Mac Help window in the Finder; usually the shortcut to summon Help in other programs.

Keyboard Shortcut	What It's Called	What It Does
⌘+H	Hide	(Usually) Hides the current application. Use the Application menu (the one that reads *Finder* when you're in the Finder) to Show All applications again. Some applications, such as BBEdit and Illustrator have long used ⌘+H for something else and hiding the application would really confuse their longtime users, so they don't use this shortcut.
⌘+Q	Quit	Perhaps the most useful key board shortcut of all — quits the current application (but not the Finder because the Finder is always running).
⌘+Shift+Q	Log Out	Logs the current user out; the login window appears onscreen until a user logs in.
⌘+Delete	Move to Trash	Moves the selected item to Trash.
⌘+Shift+Delete	Empty Trash	Empties the Trash.

Learn to Type Better

One way to make your Mac seem faster is to make your fingers move faster. The quicker you finish a task, the quicker you're on to something else. Keyboard shortcuts are nifty tools, and improving your typing speed and accuracy *will* save you time. Plus, you'll get stuff done faster if you're not always looking down at the keyboard or up at the screen when you type.

You'll also find that as your typing skills improve, you spend less time correcting errors or editing your work.

The speed and accuracy that you gain has an added bonus: When you're a decent touch typist, you fingers will fly even faster when you use those nifty keyboard shortcuts (I list a gaggle of these earlier in the chapter in Table 19-1).

The Mac is not a typewriter

The Macintosh is more of a typesetting machine than a typewriter. So when you use a Macintosh, you should follow the rules of good typography, not the rules of good typewriting. If you want your documents to look truly professional, you need to understand the difference between inch and foot marks (" and ') and typographer's quotation marks (' and ' or " and "), in addition to putting single spaces after punctuation. You also need

to know where and how to use a hyphen (-), an en dash (–), and an em dash (—).

For more on making your documents look more elegant and professional, get a hold of an excellent book by Mac-goddess Robin Williams, *The Mac Is Not a Typewriter* (published by Peachpit Press).

Resolution: It's Not Just for New Year's Anymore

Another setting that you can change to potentially improve your Mac's performance is the resolution of your monitor. Most modern monitors and video cards (or onboard video circuitry, depending upon your Mac model) are capable of displaying multiple resolutions on your monitor. You change your monitor's display resolution in the same place where you choose the number of colors you want: the Display System Preference pane. Click your resolution choice from the Resolutions list, which is located on the left side of this tab.

In Displays System Preferences, check the Show displays in menu bar box to change resolutions and color depth without opening System Preferences. You can then select your resolution from the Displays menu that appears near the right end of your menu bar, as shown in Figure 19-1.

Figure 19-1:
Use the handy Displays menu to switch resolutions right from the menu bar.

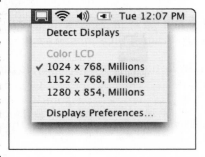

Here's the deal on display resolution: The smaller the numbers that you use for your monitor's resolution, the faster your screen refreshes. For a computer monitor, *resolution* is expressed as a dimension-type set of numbers (*number* x *number*). The first number is the number of pixels (color dots) that run horizontally, and the second number is the number of lines running vertically. Fewer pixels refresh faster. Therefore, a resolution of *640* x 480 updates itself faster than a resolution of *832* x 624; *832* x 624 updates faster than *1,024* x 768; and so forth.

This isn't always true if you have an LCD (flat-panel) monitor or a PowerBook. In that case, the native resolution is usually faster. Which is the native resolution? Depends upon the monitor. For the Apple Studio Display 15-inch and most PowerBooks, it's 1,024 x 768. For my Apple Cinema Display, it's 1600 x 1024. If you have a different flat screen, check out the documentation to see what the vendor recommends.

On the other hand, the speed difference between resolutions these days is relatively minimal. In fact, I can almost never tell the difference between one and the other. Furthermore, because you can see more onscreen at higher resolutions, a higher resolution reduces the amount of scrolling that you have to do and lets you have more open windows on the screen. Therefore, you could say that higher resolutions can speed up your Mac as well.

The bottom line is this: Choose a resolution based on your preference rather than which one you think might be faster. That said, if your Mac seems slow at a resolution setting of 1,600 x 1024, try a lower resolution and see whether it feels faster. Although you can use Mac OS X at resolutions of less than 1024 x 768, Apple has really designed the OS X windows and dialogs on the assumption that your resolution will be at least 1024 x 768.

A Mac with a View — and Preferences, Too

The type of icon display and the Desktop background that you choose affect how quickly your screen updates in the Finder. You can set and change these choices in the View Options windows. From the Finder, choose View⇨Show View Options (or use the keyboard shortcut ⌘+J).

The View Options window, like our old friend the contextual menu, is . . . well . . . contextual. Depending on what's active when you choose it from the View menu, you see one of three similar versions shown in Figure 19-2: folders in Icon view or the Desktop (left), folders in List view (middle), and folders in Column view (right).

Figure 19-2:
Your
choices in
the View
Options
windows for
Icon view,
List view,
Column
view, and
the Desktop.

The All Windows and This Window Only radio buttons in the View Options window display identical options. You choose the All Windows radio button to set the default appearance for all your Finder windows, and you choose the This Window Only radio button to set up just the current window. These buttons only appear for Icon and List view windows; Column windows are one-size-fits-all.

When bigger isn't better

The smaller the icon, the faster the screen updates. In the Icon view of the View Options windows, moving the Icon Size slider to the left makes icons smaller (faster) and moving it to the right makes them bigger (slower). In List view, select one of the two Icon Size radio buttons to choose smaller (faster) or larger (slower) icons. The difference is greater if you have an older Mac.

Calculated moves

I recommend that you deactivate Calculate All Sizes (that is, deselect, or clear, its check box). If you activate it, the Finder calculates the size of every folder of every open window in List view and displays that number in the Size column. At least to me, the screen feels as if it redraws faster with this feature turned off. This feature is offered only for windows using the List view.

The Finder is kind of smart about the Calculate All Sizes option. If you try to do anything in the Finder while folder sizes are calculating — when you make a menu selection, open an icon, or move a window, for example — the Finder interrupts the calculation so that you can complete your task before it resumes calculating. So, in theory, you should never notice a delay when Calculate All Sizes is selected.

Try the Calculate All Sizes option both on and off. I don't know about you, but I find any noticeable delay unacceptable, and I notice a delay when this option is turned on, even on very fast Macs. Maybe this feature is just annoying and not actually slowing things down, but I can't stand having it on. If you want to know how big a folder is, just click it and choose File⇨Get Info (or use the ⌘+I keyboard shortcut).

Getting ahead-er and other stuff

The Show Columns check boxes in the View Options window for List view — Date Modified, Date Created, Size, Kind, Version, and Comments — have a slight impact on screen update speed when you open a Finder window in List view. The Finder has to draw everything that you select here: With fewer items checked, the Finder updates windows faster.

The effect of these items on screen updating is pretty small, so your choice should be made based on what information you want to see in Finder windows, not on whether choosing them slows down your Mac. Play around with these options if you like, but unless your Mac is very slow, you probably won't notice much (or any) difference between on and off.

Get a New, Faster Model or Upgrade Yours

Apple keeps putting out faster and faster Macs at lower and lower prices. From time to time, Apple and other vendors offer reasonably priced upgrades that can transform your older, slower Mac into a speedy new one.

Check out the latest iMacs and eMacs — they're usually an excellent value. Or, if you crave portability, iBooks and PowerBooks are rocking good computers. Or consider a used Mac that's faster than yours. The big-time honcho of auction Web sites, eBay (www.ebay.com), has hundreds of used Macs up for auction at any given time. Shopping on eBay might just get you a better Mac at an outstanding price. Give it a try!

Get a G4 Accelerator

An *accelerator* is a card that replaces the processor (CPU) in your Mac with a faster one. Even if you have a G4 in your Mac already, you might be able to upgrade to a faster one.

But before you plunk down the cash for an upgrade, be sure that it's compatible with Mac OS X. Some upgrades only work with older versions of Mac OS, and those won't help you.

Visit www.macworld.com for information on the various upgrade options available and how they compare with each other. Upgrades start at a few hundred dollars and go up to more than a thousand clams. The older your Mac, the more bang you'll get for your G4 upgrade buck.

Get an Accelerated Graphics Card

An *accelerated graphics card* is designed to speed up one thing: the screen update rate. Accelerated graphics cards blast pixels onto your screen at amazing speeds. They're extremely popular with graphic arts professionals who would otherwise suffer slower screen redraws when working with 24-bit graphics. Most of them are also awesome for playing 3-D games. And because OS X's Quartz Extreme imaging architecture hands off part of its load to the processor on an accelerated graphics card, it might even make other tasks faster because it does some of the work that your Mac's main processor (CPU) used to do.

You can use a graphics accelerator only if your Mac has a slot for it; that's where you install one. Currently, you'll need a PowerMac G4 or G5 to use a graphics accelerator with OS X.

Visit www.macworld.com for information on the various graphics cards available and how they compare with each other. Cards start at around a hundred dollars and go up from there. And remember, the older your Mac, the more of a performance boost you'll see for your graphics card upgrade buck.

Get a New Hard Drive

Depending on how old your Mac is, a faster hard drive could provide a substantial speedup. If you have a relatively new Mac — any Mac with a G4 or G5 processor — the internal hard drive that came with it is pretty fast already. Unless you also need more storage space, a new hard drive may not be the best way to spend your bucks. On the other hand, if you have an older G3 model, a faster (and larger) hard drive could be just the ticket.

Fire Up Your Mac with FireWire

If you really crave speed, get a FireWire hard drive — all Macs released since February 2001 include at least one FireWire port.

FireWire is the name for the fastest *bus* (or data pathway) on your Mac.

FireWire, the state-of-the-art in connecting devices that need fast transfer speeds, is used to connect devices that require high-speed communication with your Mac, such as hard drives, CD burners, scanners, and camcorders.

In other words, FireWire is the fastest, easiest way to add storage to Macs that include it. Hard drives that connect via the Universal Serial Bus (USB) port work fine if you don't have FireWire, but they're as slow as molasses by comparison (USB runs at about 3 percent of the speed of FireWire). So if you have the need for speed, be sure you opt for a FireWire hard drive and not a USB model. You just plug it in and start using it. There's nothing to it!

Chapter 20

Ten (Or So) Ways to Make Your Mac Better by Throwing Money at It

This is one of my favorite chapters. As you've probably figured out by now, I love souping up my Macs. I live to find ways of working smarter, saving time, and saving hand motion, and reveling in tweaking my Mac OS X machines. So it gives me great pleasure to share in this chapter my personal top ten things that you can buy for your Mac to tweak it and make it faster, easier to use, and (I hope) more fun.

The items listed in this chapter are things I have, use every day, love dearly, and would (and probably will!) buy again.

RAM

RAM, or *random access memory,* is your computer's primary working memory. The more you have, the smoother your Mac runs — period. If you have anything less than 512MB in your Mac, you'll like your Mac *a lot* better if you upgrade to 512MB or more. If you like to do a few things at once, more megabytes of RAM will make you a happier camper. (For what it's worth, RAM has never been cheaper than it is today — it's worth every penny.)

Back-up Software

The only two kinds of Mac users are those who have lost data and those who are going to. If your work means anything to you, get something that helps automate the task of backing up your files. Retrospect Desktop, Workgroup, or Server, all from Dantz Development (www.dantz.com), are the names to trust. And please, please read Chapter 17, which is titled, appropriately, "Back Up Now or Regret It Later." It may well be the most important chapter in this book.

A Better Monitor (Or a Second One)

If you have a tiny monitor, get a bigger one. With a larger monitor, you spend less time scrolling and rearranging windows and more of your time getting actual work done — which is a good thing, right? For example, one of my setups includes two monitors: a 22-inch Apple Cinema flat-panel LCD display, and an old fashioned CRT display, a 24-inch NEC MultiSync. It's an awesome setup — one that I highly recommend. With two monitors, you can have the menu bar and Finder windows on the first monitor, and document(s) that you're working on displayed on the second monitor. Or, when using a program like Photoshop (which has lots of floating palettes), you can put the palettes on one monitor and a document that you're working on can be displayed on the big one. And so on.

Flat-panel LCD displays, such as the Apple Studio and Cinema Displays, have come down dramatically in price over the past year. In my humble opinion, LCD displays are brighter and easier on the eyes than traditional CRT (glass picture tube) monitors. Apple must agree, because they no longer sell CRTs other than the ones built into eMacs. If you can afford one, that's what you really want. Alas, owners of older iMacs, as well as most iBook owners, are out of luck on this tip — it's not possible to add a second monitor to these models. If you've got a more recent (snow globe flat screen) iMac that includes a video port, go ahead and get a bigger second monitor.

A Fast Internet Connection

High-bandwidth connections (that is, fast Internet access) just *rock*. By adding a high-speed Internet connection, such as digital subscriber line (DSL) or cable modem, your capacity to communicate electronically will increase tenfold. With this add-on, you can join an online service, surf the Internet, e-mail your friends, and much, much more, at speeds ten or more times faster than a 56 Kbps-speed modem. Web pages that once took minutes to load appear onscreen almost instantly. If you can afford cable/DSL (around $45-$50/month in most places) and are in an area where you can get cable modem or DSL (not all places can yet), it's worth every penny.

Additional Hard/Removable/ Optical Drive(s)

Apple stopped including floppy disk drives with new Macs a couple of years ago. So now the only ways that you can load new files (programs, documents, games, or whatever) onto your Mac are by copying files from some other kind of removable media (like a Zip disk or a CD or DVD, see Chapter 9), or by downloading from the Internet.

If you want to back up your Mac or hand your buddy a disk with files on it, you'll need some kind of removable media drive. Zip and SuperDisk are the most popular magnetic media, but they are quickly losing popularity for being too small to be useful (around 200MB maximum per disk). On the other hand, there are millions of both types of drive in use today, making it a good choice if you plan to swap data with anyone who has this type of device.

Perhaps the best choice these days is a CD-R (recordable CD-ROM) drive or CD-RW (with unlimited writing capabilities) drive so that you can make your own CDs that contain files, music, or both! Both kinds of drives let you *burn* CDs (CD-RWs just let you burn 'em again and again). The new Apple SuperDrives even let you burn DVDs and these hold 4.7GB each. If you don't already have a burner, it's worth considering.

If you have a relatively new Mac, you may have a built-in Zip, CD-RW, or SuperDrive drive. If you do (or if you get an external one), for goodness sake — use it to back up your stuff!

Games

Gaming on the Mac has never been better, and the game developers are getting better and better at coaxing even more performance out of OS X.

Some of the games I *love* include *The Sims* (and all the add-ons), *Links Championship Edition,* and every pinball game LittleWing has ever created. Try one — you'll be amazed at how far computer gaming has come.

Multimedia Titles

Many great games, references, and educational titles come on CD-ROM or DVD-ROM these days. You'll love 'em, and so will your kids. Your Mac is more than a computer — it's a full-blown multimedia player. Enjoy it.

Some Big Honking Speakers with a Subwoofer

Face it: Most Macs have crummy speakers (or worse, only one crummy speaker). With a decent set of speakers, games are more fun, music sounds like music instead of AM radio, and the voiceovers in your multimedia titles suddenly become intelligible. If you're into sound, you'll enjoy your Mac much more if you add a set of window-rattling speakers, preferably one with a massive subwoofer to provide that booming bass that sound lovers crave. So crank it up! I'm partial to EV SonicXJR Multimedia Speaker System, from Telex/ElectroVoice (www.telex.com) but any good speakers kick the stuffing out of the speakers in any Mac.

If you have a DVD-ROM drive, a killer set of speakers makes watching movies on your Mac a zillion times better.

A New Mouse and/or Keyboard

If you're still using that hockey-puck mouse that came with your iMac, G3, or G4, do yourself a favor and beat it to death with a hammer. Then buy a real mouse. You'll be so much happier if you upgrade to a mouse that's easier to move around and maybe even has two or more buttons or a scroll wheel. You'll be amazed at how much easier it is to work with a mouse that fits your hand. OS X knows about multi-button mice and scroll wheels. With a two-button mouse, you no longer have to hold down the Control key while clicking to display a contextual menu — just click with the right-hand button.

Also, consider ditching that silly Chiclet keyboard if you're stuck with one (you know, those curved, tiny-keyed annoyances that first came with iMacs and that Apple continued to foist on users for many years). Third-party Mac keyboards on the market today are also a huge improvement over what probably came with your Mac and the new Apple Pro keyboard is an excellent product.

I'm partial to so-called ergonomic keyboards, which I find more comfortable for prolonged writing sessions. I also think I type faster with this kind of keyboard. My current axe is a Microsoft Natural Keyboard Pro. Even though it's a Windows keyboard and the modifier keys are mislabeled (the Command key says Alt and the Option key has a Windows logo on it), Microsoft offers excellent Mac drivers for OS X. Although this particular model has been discontinued, sadly, Microsoft offers other ergonomic keyboards in the Natural line of products. Shop around to find one that works for you.

Look into the clear Apple Pro keyboard and Pro Mouse if they didn't come with your Mac. They're pretty cool and have a nice tactile response.

A PowerBook or an iBook

Because one Mac is never enough. With a portable Mac, you can go anywhere and continue to compute. And both iBooks and PowerBooks are capable of using Apple's AirPort wireless networking, so you can surf the Net, print, and share files from the couch or the pool.

A New Mac

If you have any money left, consider upgrading to a newer, faster Mac. They've never been faster, cheaper, or better equipped; if yours is getting a bit long at the tooth, consider a newer, faster model.

Timing can be everything when shopping for a new Mac. Historically, new models are announced at Macworld Expo in January (in San Francisco) and at the Apple Worldwide Developer Conference in the summer (in San Francisco). So it's usually a bad idea to buy a new Mac in December or June because chances are good that what you buy will be discontinued in a month or two. On the other hand, Apple occasionally lowers prices the month before Macworld Expos to clear out old inventory before introducing new models. Keeping that in mind, *my* advice is to wait until after a Macworld Expo to choose your new Mac. But, if a December or June deal is so good you can't pass it up, go for it. Bear in mind, however, that the model you're buying might be discontinued shortly and replaced with a faster, better model at around the same price.

One great truth of computer shopping is that no matter when you hop on the highway, a faster and less expensive ride will be along pretty soon. You just have to realize that if you wait for the ultimate machine at the ultimate price, you're never going to have a computer or get anything done with it.

Caveat emptor.

Chapter 21

Ten (Or So) Great Web Sites for Mac Freaks

In This Chapter

▶ Mac troubleshooting Web sites

▶ Mac freeware and shareware on the Web

▶ Mac news Web sites

▶ Mac shopping Web sites

*A*s much as I would love to think that this book tells you everything that you need to know about using your Mac, I know better. You have a lot more to discover about using your Mac, and new tools and products come out almost daily.

The best way to gather more information than you could ever possibly soak up about all things Macintosh is to hop onto the Web. There you'll find news, freeware and shareware software to download, troubleshooting sites, tons of news and information about your new favorite OS, and lots of places to shop. So make sure that you read Chapter 11 to get set up for the Internet because this chapter is all about finding cool stuff on the Web to help you use your Mac better while having lots of fun.

The sites in this chapter are the best, most chock-full-o'-stuff places on the Web for Mac users. By the time you finish checking out these ten Web sites, you'll know so much about your Mac and Mac OS X that you'll feel like your brain is in danger of exploding. On the other hand, you may just be a whole lot smarter. Happy surfing!

MacFixIt

www.macfixit.com

Frequent *Macworld* contributor and consultant Ted Landau put together an excellent troubleshooting site to help users solve common problems and keep current on compatibility issues with new system software and third-party products.

Alas, Ted has taken a less active role in the site of late, and there is now a surcharge to search the archives. This site isn't as useful as it once was if you don't purchase a Pro membership (currently $25 a year). But even without paying it's worth checking this site when you have any problem with your Mac. Chances are MacFixIt has a solution.

But I encourage you to go Pro if you can afford the $2 a month. It's worth more than that to have unlimited access to MacFixIt's extensive troubleshooting archives and special reports.

Don't tell the MacFixIt gang, but I'd consider it a bargain at twice the price.

VersionTracker.com

www.versiontracker.com

For free or shareware stuff, try VersionTracker. It's one of the best sites to search for software — for any version of Mac OS — by keyword. This treasure trove of software and updates is worth visiting even if you aren't looking for anything in particular. So check it out and download some useful utilities or games or something. I love this site and visit daily.

MacInTouch

www.macintouch.com

For the latest in Mac news, updated every single day, check out MacInTouch.com. Authored by longtime *MacWeek* columnist Ric Ford and his staff of news hounds, this site keeps you on the bleeding-edge of Mac news, including software updates, virus alerts, and Apple happenings. I consider this a site that's essential to keeping up with Mac OS X.

MacMinute

www.macminute.com

Here's another great source of up-to-the-minute Macintosh news. It's a great site, updated many times a day with lots of useful stories, links, and other Mac info.

Apple Knowledge Base

http://kbase.info.apple.com

Do you have a technical question about any version of Mac OS or any Apple product — including OS X? March your question right over to the Knowledge Base, Apple's searchable archives of tech notes, software update information, and documentation. The Knowledge Base is especially useful if you need info about your old Mac because Apple archives all its info here. Choose from a preset list of topics or products and type a keyword to research. You're rewarded with a list of helpful documents. Click any one of these (they're all links) to take you right to the info you seek. The site even has tools that can help narrow your search.

The Mac OS X Home Page

www.apple.com/macosx

Part of Apple's main Web site, this section is all about Mac OS X, its cool features, how to get the most from it, what applications are available for it, and so on. Check in here to see what Apple has cooking; think of it as one-stop-shopping for your Mac.

ramseeker

www.macseek.com

One of the best ways to make your Mac better is to buy more random access memory (RAM). *RAM* is the readily available memory that your computer uses; the more you have, the smoother programs run. Although Mac OS X can run on a Mac with only 64MB of RAM, officially it requires 128MB and works even better and faster with more than that. As cheap as RAM is, the price that you pay for it can vary quite a lot. The best way I know to get the lowdown on RAM prices is ramseeker, which organizes memory prices by Mac type.

Outpost.com

www.outpost.com

Recently taken over by the great electronics retailer, Fry's, Outpost.com is all about buying stuff — and what big kid doesn't love his toys? Here you can find lots and lots and lots of Mac products, including Apple CPUs, memory, drives, printers, scanners, and other miscellaneous accessories. You'll love the prices, as well as the massive selection of Mac and non-Mac electronics products.

EveryMac.com

www.everymac.com

The author of this site claims that it is "the complete guide of every Macintosh, Mac Compatible, and upgrade card in the world." You can't argue with that. Become a member and sign up for forums. Check out the Forums and Q & A sections, too, for your Mac-related questions.

Inside Mac Games

www.imgmagazine.com

This is the best of the Mac gaming sites on the Web (at least in my humble opinion). Order CDs of game demos, download shareware, check out game preview movies, or shop for editors and emulators. Find forum camaraderie and troubleshoot gaming problems, too.

dealmac

www.dealmac.com

Shopping for Mac stuff? Go to dealmac ("Because cheap Mac stuff rocks," this site boasts) first to find out about sale prices, rebates, and other bargain opportunities on upgrades, software, peripherals, and more.

Chapter 22

Ten (Or So) Mac OS X Apps That You Might Need Someday

Dig around the Mac OS X Applications folder or take a gander at the System Preferences application's main window, and you'll run across some programs and preferences that you won't use every day but are still kind of cool.

In this chapter, I tell you what some of these items do and whether you're likely to get much from them. Unfortunately, because of space limitations, I didn't talk much about any of them elsewhere in this book. And I can't really explain how to use each of these potentially useful goodies in much detail here. Instead, my objective is to briefly describe each one and then provide some insights on whether you need it or not.

 Almost everything that I mention in this chapter includes a Mac OS Help feature. Use it to discover more about how these goodies work. Just search Mac OS Help for the item that you're interested in, and you'll get an eyeful.

Web Sharing

Web Sharing enables others to share documents on your computer through the Web. You can set up a Web site just by adding HyperText Markup Language (HTML) pages and images to the Sites folder in your home folder, and then activating Web Sharing in the Sharing pane of System Preferences.

Web Sharing works only while your Mac is connected to the Internet or an internal network. In other words, if you use a modem and connect to the Internet by dialing up, this application won't be a lot of use to you because your server (your Mac) will only be on the Internet when you've dialed up and made a modem connection. When you're not connected, your server won't be available except to other computers on your local network. That's not to say that Web Sharing can't be used this way, but you'll have to tell remote users when they'll be able to find it @md and then make sure you dial up and make a connection at that time. Another downside to this method is that almost without exception, dial-up users will have a different IP address every time they connect, so you would have to tell folks your new address every time.

Furthermore, even if you keep your modem connected to the Internet 24 hours a day with a Digital Subscriber Line (DSL) or cable modem connection, using this feature could violate your agreement with your Internet Service Provider (ISP) because some ISPs prohibit you from running a Web site. And, most cable and DSL connections use dynamic IP address assignment through Dynamic Host Configuration Protocol (DHCP), which means that your IP address will change from time to time.

On the other hand, some ISPs don't care. Check with yours if you're concerned.

I do use this feature occasionally, but because I don't use it 24/7, I never bothered to check with my ISP. Do me a favor and don't rat me out.

FTP Access

File Transfer Protocol (FTP) is kind of like Web Sharing: It allows folks on the Internet to have access to files on your Mac. The difference is that FTP access is specifically designed to let you make files available for download, and Web Sharing is designed to let people view Web pages.

When you activate FTP by selecting the Allow FTP Access check box in the Sharing pane of System Preferences, users on the Internet have the same access to the contents of your Mac that they would if they were using file sharing. (See Chapter 16 for more on file sharing.) People who don't have accounts on your Mac can access Public folders and Drop Boxes — or any folder to which you grant everyone access, as I describe in Chapter 16.

Internet users can connect to your Mac with any FTP client application.

An *FTP client* is a program that offers FTP features — uploading files, downloading files, and so on. Better FTP clients can also do stuff like rename and delete remote files. On the Mac, Transmit (my personal fave), Interarchy, and Fetch are probably the best known FTP clients. Another Mac client that you may find easy to use is RBrowser or its freeware sibling, RBrowserLite. You can also find FTP clients for Windows, Linux, and most other operating systems (but because I use Macs, I don't know the names of the good ones).

Most Internet browsers can serve as FTP clients, as well as browsers (although they're mostly good only for downloading, and not much use for uploading, deleting, renaming, and other useful functions).

Applet Launcher

The *Applet Launcher* is an application that you can use to work with Apple's version of Java. *Java* is a programming language (or a platform, depending on who you ask) that's most frequently used in Web pages that you view on the Internet. Stand-alone Java programs, called *applets*, are available as well.

With Applet Launcher, you can run programs written in Java on your Mac, with no Web browser required. Mac OS X and Internet Explorer (the browser that comes with Mac OS X) also support Java within Web pages. So you have a choice — run stand-alone applets with Applet Launcher, or have your browser do the work of loading and launching Java programs that are part of a Web page. A nice variety of example applets are available via the Applets menu within Applet Launcher.

You'll find Applet Launcher in the Java folder within the Utilities folder (in your Applications folder).

ColorSync Utility

ColorSync helps ensure color accuracy when scanning, printing, and working with color images. This package includes ColorSync software as well as pre-made ColorSync profiles for a variety of monitors, scanners, and printers.

A *ColorSync profile* is a set of instructions for a monitor, scanner, or printer, which tells the device how to deal with colors (and white) so that the device's output is consistent with other devices output (as determined by the ColorSync profiles of other devices). In theory, if two devices have ColorSync profiles, their output (on screen, on a printed page, or in a scanned image) should match perfectly. Put another way, the red (or green or blue or white or any other color) that you see onscreen should be exactly the same shade as the red that you see on a printed page or in a scanned image.

You'll find the ColorSync Utility in /Applications/Utilities; use it to pick a profile or check to see that the profile ColorSync is using is the right one for your display, input, output, or proof device.

To calibrate or not to calibrate?

One thing you might want to try, even if you never plan to use ColorSync, is to calibrate your monitor. This process adjusts the red, green, blue, and white levels, and could make what you see on your screen look better than it does now.

To calibrate your monitor, follow these steps:

1. **Open the Displays System Preferences pane.**

2. **Click the Color tab and then write down the Display Profile that your Mac is currently using (it's highlighted in the Display Profile list).**

3. **Click the Calibrate button.**

The Display Calibrator Assistant appears.

4. **Follow the simple onscreen instructions to calibrate your monitor and create a custom display profile.**

5. **Give your profile a name then click the Continue button.**

If you decide that you don't like the results of your calibration, just click the Display Profile that you wrote down in Step 2 from the Display Profile list in the Displays System Preference pane, and your monitor will go back the way it was before you calibrated it.

If you're not a graphics artist working with color files and calibrating monitors and printers to achieve accurate color matching, you probably don't need ColorSync (unless you've gotten hooked on iPhoto and want your printed inkjet color pictures to match up correctly).

Image Capture

Image Capture is a nifty little application that you use to download images from a digital camera to your Mac or from a variety of scanners. You'll find it in your Applications folder. You can use it with many kinds of digital cameras and a number of different scanner models, so if you have more than one, you may be able to avoid having to install an application for each.

Unfortunately, Image Capture doesn't work with every digital camera. For example, Image Capture did not recognize my relatively new Olympus digital camera. To find out whether Image Capture works with your digital camera, plug the camera into one of your Mac's USB ports and open Image Capture. If the Camera menu at the top of the window reads No devices found, you're out of luck. The same steps apply to your scanner, except that you'll be checking the Scanner menu.

Image Capture can automate some parts of the image downloading process. For example, you can set it up to download all images from the camera into a pre-selected folder or to open automatically when you connect your camera to your Mac.

You may not want to use Image Capture if you prefer the program that came with your digital camera (the program that you use to import pictures from the camera) or iPhoto. On the other hand, you may have to use Image Capture if that program hasn't been upgraded to support Mac OS X and doesn't run under Classic (some programs just don't work with Classic). Because this is true of most scanner software at this time, Image Capture could be your best bet.

If Image Capture doesn't support your scanner, a shareware program for Mac OS X called VueScan from Hamrick Software (www.hamrick.com) supports scanning images with many different scanners, including ones that don't work with Image Capture. Its $40 price tag is a small price to pay if your scanner is going to otherwise just collect dust.

Finally, if the program that came with your camera doesn't run under Classic and Image Capture doesn't work with your camera, you'll have to reboot with OS 9 to run the program. (For more info on running Classic and OS X, and rebooting under OS 9.2.1, read through Chapter 14.)

Text-to-Speech

Use Text-to-Speech to convert onscreen text into spoken words from your Mac. This application is pretty much unchanged from earlier versions of Mac OS. With a whole slew of voices to choose from, you can have Text-to-Speech read dialog boxes, or even documents, aloud.

Sometimes hearing is better than reading. For example, I sometimes use Text-to-Speech to read a column or page to me before I submit it. If something doesn't sound right, I give it a final polish before sending it off to my editor.

You can activate this feature in the Speech System Preferences pane. Click the Spoken User Interface tab to check it out.

Text-to-Speech is kind of cool (the talking alerts are fun), but having dialog boxes actually produce spoken text becomes annoying real fast for most folks. But check it out! You might like it and find times when you want your Mac to read to you.

Speech Recognition

Speech Recognition enables your Mac to recognize and respond to human speech. With this feature, you can issue verbal commands such as, "Get my mail!" to your Mac and have it actually get your mail. You can also create AppleScripts and then trigger them by voice.

An *AppleScript* is a series of commands, using the AppleScript language, that tells the computer (and some applications) what to do.

You create AppleScripts with the Script Editor program, which you'll find in the AppleScript folder in the Applications folder.

You'll need a microphone (some Macs have them built-in) to use Speech Recognition. And you'll only be able to talk to your Mac when using applications that support Speech Recognition.

You'll find the Speech Recognition tab to the Default Voice tab's left in the Speech pane of System Preferences.

This application is clever and kind of fun, but it's also slow and requires a microphone. And I've never been able to get Speech Recognition to work well enough to continue using it beyond a few hours at best. Still, it's kind of neat (and it's a freebie), and I've heard many users profess their love for it. So you might want to check it out.

NetInfo Manager

NetInfo is a hierarchical database that contains much of the configuration information needed to manage what goes on behind the scenes of Mac OS X. NetInfo knows all your settings, who has an account on your Mac, what network addresses you're using, and lots, lots more. With NetInfo Manager, which you'll find in Applications/Utilities, you can view and edit some of this information. Although it has a Mac interface, the database info displayed there will be pretty much incomprehensible to most folks.

NetInfo is a central location for a lot of important information. With NetInfo Manager, a savvy Mac user can do cool things that can't be done with the Network or Sharing System Preferences panes. But most average users won't want to play here. One suggestion: If you're at all curious about the internals of the UNIX operating system on which Mac OS X is based, start by learning a bit about NetInfo before you dive into the hard-core UNIX stuff (see the next section).

UNIX Tools: Terminal, Console, and Activity Monitor

Mac OS X is based on the UNIX operating system, although its UNIX underpinnings are mostly hidden. While most Mac users are grateful to be able to ignore UNIX, if you know UNIX (or think you might like to), you'll find that you can do a lot of very geeky things with the UNIX tools included in Mac OS X.

You'll find all three programs in the Utilities folder within your Applications folder.

UNIX is not for the inexperienced or faint of heart. Before you even begin experimenting with it, you should get yourself a good UNIX primer and learn the ropes. And as usual, be very careful. Mucking around in the Mac OS X UNIX files gives you access to lots of stuff that isn't ordinarily available to you, which can very quickly lead to major problems if you're not absolutely sure what you're doing. If you want more info on UNIX, check out *Unix Bible,* 2nd Edition by Yves Lepage and Paul Iarrera (published Wiley Publishing).

Terminal

Basically, *UNIX* is a command-line operating system. Instead of clicking buttons and dragging icons around the Desktop, you type commands (not in English, by the way) at a command line. To do this in Mac OS X, you use a program called Terminal, which you'll find in the Utilities folder in the Applications folder.

Terminal is nothing more than a single window with a line (or many lines) of very geeky-looking text — there are no menus or buttons to make your life easier. So Terminal is mostly useless unless you speak a decent amount of UNIX.

Console

Console is another UNIX tool that's used to show you technical messages from Mac OS X — in UNIX-speak, of course. It shows what UNIX processes are running, what devices are in use, and so on. Think of it as a UNIX troubleshooting and status-checking tool. Unfortunately, like Terminal, Console's only window is a wall of super-geeky-looking text — still no menus or buttons to make your life easier. Like Terminal, Console is mostly useless unless you speak a decent amount of UNIX.

Activity Monitor

Activity Monitormight be more useful for seeing what's going on under the hood than Console because it has a Mac interface (or at least it has some menus), a Find text field, and columns that you can sort. Think of it as another UNIX troubleshooting and status-checking tool.

Part VI
Appendix

The 5th Wave   By Rich Tennant

AFTER INSTALLING OSX,
NED AND LORETTA SELECT THE
COMPUTER'S BACKGROUND

© RICHTENNANT

"Oh — I like this background _much_ better than
the basement."

In this part . . .

Last but certainly not least, I cover installing/reinstalling Mac OS X in this appendix. The whole process has become quite easy with this version of the System software, but if you have to install OS X yourself, it would behoove you to read this helpful appendix first.

Appendix

Installing Mac OS X Panther
(Only If You Have To)

. . . .

In This Chapter

▶ Installing (or reinstalling) Mac OS X Panther

▶ Setting up OS X Panther with Setup Assistant

▶ Running OS X Panther and OS 9 on the same Mac

. . . .

You'll probably never need this Appendix. Some of you will get Mac OS X pre-installed on a new Mac, and others will have installed it long before buying this book. And so, I expect that few of you will have to refer to this Appendix to install OS X on your Mac for the very first time.

But (and there's always a but, isn't there?), someday something unexpected might happen to your Mac. You could have a hard drive crash or a problem starting up from your hard drive, or maybe you'll see the flashing question-mark icon when booting — all meaning that you'll need to *reinstall* OS X. And so, I expect some of you (and I hope not many) will have to refer to this Appendix for instructions on reinstalling OS X.

A Mac OS X reinstallation is a drastic final step. Be sure that you've tried all the stuff in Chapter 18 before even thinking about reinstalling OS X. If nothing else fixes your Mac, reinstalling Mac OS X could well be your final option before invasive surgery (that is, trundling your Mac to a repair shop). I save this solution for here at the very end of the book because it's the biggest hassle, and you don't want to reinstall OS X if something easier can correct the problem. So if you have to do a reinstallation, realize that this is more or less your last hope.

In this Appendix, you'll discover all you need to know to install or reinstall OS X, if you should have to. I say reinstalling is a hassle because although you won't lose the contents of your Home folder or stuff in your Documents folder (unless something goes horribly wrong or you have to reformat your hard disk), you could lose some System Preferences, which means that you'll need to reconfigure those panes manually after you reinstall. It's not the end of the world, but it can be inconvenient. That said, reinstalling OS X usually corrects all but the most horrifying and malignant of problems. And the process is relatively painless, as you'll soon see.

I'll stay with you through it all; be brave.

How to Install (or Reinstall) Mac OS X

In theory, you should only have to install OS X once. And in a perfect world, that would be the case. But you may find occasions when you have to install/reinstall it, such as

 ✓ If you get a new Mac that didn't come with Mac OS X pre-installed

 ✓ If you have a catastrophic hard drive crash that requires you to initialize (format) your boot drive

 ✓ If any essential Mac OS X files become damaged, corrupted, or are deleted or renamed

The following instructions do double duty: They're what you do to install OS X for the first time on a Mac, and they're also what you do if something happens to the copy of OS X that you boot your Mac from. That is, the process for installing or reinstalling OS X is exactly the same.

If you've backed up your entire hard drive, you might prefer to reinstall from your backup disk or tape rather than reinstalling OS X from the Install Mac OS X CD. That way, you'll be certain that everything is just the way you left it, which is something you can't be sure of if you reinstall from the Install Mac OS X CD.

Here's how to install (or reinstall) OS X, step by step:

1. **Boot from your Install Mac OS X CD Disc 1 by inserting the CD into your machine's CD-ROM or DVD drive and then restarting your Mac while holding down the C key.**

   When Mac OS X has finished booting your Mac, the Install program launches automatically. Here is where you begin the process of installing or reinstalling Mac OS X.

2. **Unless you want to use a language other than English for the main language of Mac OS X, click the Continue button in the first screen you see; if you do want to use another language, select the language by clicking its name, and then click the Continue button.**

3. **Read the Welcome, Important Information, and Software License Agreement screens, clicking the Continue button after each.**

A sheet drops down querying whether you agree to the terms of the license agreement. If you don't, you can't go any further, so I advise you to go ahead and click the Agree button.

If you're currently using any version of Mac OS except version 9.2.2, you might next see a dialog with the warning that you can't run Classic applications unless you have Mac OS 9.2.2 or a later version installed. You can't install Mac OS 9.2.2 right now (you're installing OS X!), but you can click OK and install it later. (Mac OS X, version 10.3 Panther does not come with a Mac OS 9.2.2 Install CD, so you're on your own here.) If you have Mac OS 9.2.2 installed, you won't see this dialog.

4. **Choose the disk that you want to install or reinstall Mac OS X on by clicking its icon once in the Select a Destination screen.**

At the bottom of the Select a Destination screen is the Options button, which offers three mutually exclusive choices:

a. **Upgrade Mac OS X:** Choose this option to upgrade an earlier version of OS X installed on the disk that you choose in Step 4 above. Your Home and other files are left undisturbed; after the upgrade, things will be (more or less) as they were before, except that you'll be running a factory-fresh installation of OS X.

b. **Archive and Install:** Choose this option to move all the System components from your existing OS X installation into a folder named Previous System and then install a fresh new copy of OS X. The Previous System folder cannot be used to boot but it does contain any and all files that were in any of the OS X folders before you upgraded.

If you select this option, a check box for a second option — Preserve Users and Network Settings — becomes available. Mark it if you want to import all the existing users of this Mac, their Home folders, and their network settings — but still archive all the old System stuff into the Previous System folder.

If you choose this option, you skip the Setup Assistant discussed later in this Appendix.

c. **Erase and Install:** Choose this option if you want to completely erase the disk that you selected in Step 4, starting completely from scratch.

If you choose the Erase and Install option, the disk that you selected in Step 4 will be erased, and all your files will be deleted immediately! You should only choose this option if you've backed up all your documents and applications. In most cases, erasing the start-up disk is not necessary.

If you select this option, the Format Disk As pop-up menu becomes available. Your choices are Mac OS Extended (Journaled), which is the one you want, or Unix File System, which is the one you don't want.

Unix File System is not a good choice for most OS X users. Suffice it to say that 99.9 percent of you should absolutely and positively avoid Unix File System like the plague (and the other tenth of one percent know who they are and why they need a UFS disk). 'Nuff said.

After you make your selection in this window, click OK to return to the Select a Destination screen and then click Continue.

Now you have the choice to perform an easy install or a customized install. The Easy Install copies all of Mac OS X onto your chosen hard drive (as you choose in Step 4); the Custom Install (click the Customize button at the bottom of the screen) enables you choose to install only the items that you want to install.

In almost all cases, Easy Install is the right way to go, and that's what I assume that you'll choose for the rest of these steps because you're either doing a complete install or reinstall of your operating system.

5. **To begin the installation, click the Install button.**

   The install process takes 10 to 20 minutes, so now might be a good time to take a coffee break. When the install process finishes, your Mac will ask you to insert OS X Install Disk 2. When it's done installing, your Mac will restart itself, and you can begin using Mac OS X . . . hopefully, trouble-free.

   After your Mac reboots, the Setup Assistant appears, unless you've chosen Archive and Install and also selected the Preserve Users and Network Settings option, which obviates the need for the Setup Assistant (since you'll still have all your settings from before the installation).

6. **Work your way through all of the Setup Assistant screens (you have to before you can begin working in OS X), which I show you how to do in the next section.**

Getting Set Up with Setup Assistant

Assuming that your installation (or reinstallation) process goes well and your Mac restarts itself, the next thing you should see (and hear) is a short, colorful movie that ends by transforming into the first Setup Assistant screen, fetchingly named Welcome.

To tiptoe through the Setup Assistant, follow these steps:

1. **When the Welcome screen appears, choose your country from the list by clicking it once, and then click the Continue button.**

   If your country doesn't appear in the list, select the Show All check box, which will cause a bunch of additional countries to appear in this list. Choose yours by clicking it and then click the Continue button.

   The Personalize Settings screen appears.

2. **Choose a keyboard layout from the list by clicking it once; then click the Continue button.**

   If you're an American or want to use an American keyboard setup, click the U.S. listing. If you prefer a different country's keyboard layout, select the Show All check box, and a bunch of additional countries (as well as a pair of Dvorak keyboard layouts) appears in the list. Choose the one you prefer by clicking it and then click the Continue button.

   The Your Apple ID screen appears.

3. **Click the appropriate radio button — My Apple ID is, Create an Apple ID for me, or Don't create an Apple ID for me. If you have an Apple ID, type your user name and password in the appropriate fields. Now click the Continue button.**

   Click the Learn More button to learn more about an Apple ID and what it can do for you. In a nutshell, it lets you make one-click purchases at the iTunes Music Store, iPhoto, or the Apple Store. If you get one now, you'll also get a free, limited 60-day trial to .Mac.

   When you're finished reading, click OK, and then click the Continue button.

   The Registration Information screen appears.

4. **Fill out the fields (name, address, phone number, and so on) and then click the Continue button.**

   If you're interested in what Apple will and will not do with this information, click the Privacy button on this screen and read the Privacy Policy.

   The Thank You screen appears.

5. **Click the Continue button.**

   The Create Your Account screen appears.

6. **Fill in the Name, Short Name, Password, Verify, and Password Hint fields and then click the Continue button.**

   This first account that you create will automatically have administrator privileges for this Mac.

   Each of these fields has an explanation beneath it.

   You can't click the Continue button until you've filled in all five fields.

   The Get Internet Ready screen appears.

7. **Select from four radio buttons — I'd like a free trial account with EarthLink; I have a code for a special offer from EarthLink; I'll Use My Existing Internet Service; or I'm Not Ready to Connect to the Internet — and then click the Continue button.**

If you choose to use your existing Internet service, you'll see another series of screens in which you provide specific information about how you connect to the Internet, your IP address (if you have one), what kind of connection you have, and so on. If you don't know one (or more) of the items in this series of screens, don't worry. Just leave them blank and keep clicking the Continue button. Later, after the Setup Assistant finishes and you're up and running with OS X, you can ask your ISP (Internet Service Provider) about any empty fields, and then put in that information in the appropriate place (the Network and/or Internet System Preference panes).

The Set Up Mail screen appears.

8. **If you want to set up the Mail program now, click the appropriate radio button — Use my Mac.com account only or Add my existing email account, fill in the blanks, and then click the Continue button.**

The Select Time Zone screen appears.

9. **Click your part of the world on the map, then choose a city from the pop-up menu, and then click the Continue button.**

The Set the Date and Time screen appears.

10. **Set today's date and the current time, and then click the Continue button.**

11. **When the next screen appears, click the Done button.**

The assistant will quit and in a few moments, the Mac OS X Desktop will appear. That's it. You're done.

For the very last time, don't forget that Macs sold after January 1, 2003 will not be able to boot into Mac OS 9 at all. Classic will be the only option for running OS 9 software on Macs made in 2003 and beyond.

Two ways to run two systems

If you're planning on using Classic applications at all, I need to tell you a little about how Mac OS X and Classic (Mac OS 9.2.2) co-exist on the same computer. (If you'd rather just learn how to use Classic, you can skip this section and read Chapter 14 instead.)

Both Mac OS 9.2.2 and OS X can either be installed on the same volume — usually the single hard drive in your Mac — or on separate volumes. If they're installed on a single volume, as they would be if you got your Mac with Mac OS X pre-installed, the files that make up Mac OS 9.2.2 are buried within the complicated hierarchy of Mac OS X components. You probably won't have much to do with them, other than customizing some preferences. If you've used any version of Mac OS 9 (9.0.1, 9.0.4, or even 9.1), you won't find the familiar System Folder or be able to work with its files in the way that you're used to.

In some cases, Mac OS 9.2.2 and Mac OS X are installed on separate volumes on your Mac.

Volumes can be individual hard drives, or they can be partitions of a single hard drive. A *partition* looks and behaves like a hard drive, but it's actually just a section of the disk that is completely separate from the rest of the drive. In this arrangement, Mac OS X and Mac OS 9.2.2 each have their own partitions on the same hard drive. That means that you can install and customize a Mac OS 9.2.2 drive without affecting Mac OS X. They behave as if they were completely separate drives. When you launch Classic while running Mac OS X, Mac OS 9.2.2 launches from the other partition, and you have access to its System Folder, just as you would on a Mac with Mac OS 9.2 as the primary operating system.

If you're installing Mac OS X from scratch and you're comfortable with concepts such as drive partitioning and the like, I recommend that you install Mac OS 9.2.2 on two partitions or hard drives. In other words, install 9.2.2 on both partitions and then install OS X on one of them. Let the copy of OS 9.2.2 on the same disk (or partition) as OS X be the one that you use for Classic. Use the other copy of OS 9.2.2 to boot from when you need to run Classic apps or use Classic extensions/control panels that aren't supported by Classic (such as DVD Player, CD Audio Player, some CD burning software, full functionality for iTunes, and so on). You'll have more flexibility when using Mac OS 9.2.2 if you follow this advice, and you'll be able to troubleshoot both operating systems more easily if you keep them on separate drives. You'll also find that Classic starts up faster because it won't have all the extra control panels and extensions to load. You might also find it more convenient to store all your Classic applications on the partition or drive with OS 9.2.2 only rather on the OS X drive or partition. That's how I have the Mac I used for writing this book arranged (check the screen shots).

If you have multiple partitions or drives — each of which has a copy of Mac OS 9.2.2 — you can choose which copy to use when launching Classic. Make this choice in the Classic pane of System Preferences. (Read more about this in Chapter 14.)

Index

• *Q* •

Windows 95 Answers: Certified Tech Support

Martin S. Matthews
Carole Boggs Matthews

Osborne **McGraw-Hill**

Berkeley · New York · St. Louis
San Francisco · Auckland · Bogotá
Hamburg · London · Madrid · Mexico
City · Milan · Montreal · New Delhi
Panama City · Paris · São Paulo
Singapore · Sydney · Tokyo · Toronto

Osborne **McGraw-Hill**
2600 Tenth Street, Berkeley, California 94710, USA

For information on software, translations, or book distributors outside of the U.S.A., please write to Osborne McGraw-Hill at the above address.

Windows 95 Answers: Certified Tech Support

1234567890 DOC 99876

ISBN 0-07-882128-2

Acquisitions Editor Wendy Rinaldi	**Computer Designer** Peter Hancik
Project Editor Claire Splan	**Illustrator** Lance Ravella
Copy Editor Gary Morris	**Series Design and Illustrator** Marla Shelasky
Proofreader Stefany Otis	**Quality Control Specialist** Joe Scuderi
Indexer Valerie Robbins	**Cover Design** Ted Mader Associates

About the Authors

Marty Matthews and Carole Boggs Matthews are the best-selling authors of more than 40 computer books covering topics as diverse as Windows networking, Excel, PageMaker, CorelDRAW!, and Paradox. They have been working with software for over 25 years and are experts in Windows, spreadsheets, graphic design, and desktop publishing.

Contents

Foreword

Few things are as frustrating as having a computer problem that you can't solve. Computer users often spend hours trying to find the answer to a single software question! That's why the tech support experts at Stream International Inc. have teamed up with Osborne/McGraw-Hill to bring you the **Certified Tech Support Series**—books designed to give you all the solutions you need to fix even the most difficult software glitches.

At Stream, we have a dedicated support staff that handles over 675,000 software questions every month. These experts use the latest hardware and software technology to provide answers to every sort of software problem. Stream takes full advantage of the partnerships that we have forged with all major software publishers. Our staff frequently receives the same training that publishers offer their own support representatives and has access to vender technical resources that are not generally available to the public.

Thus, this series is based on actual *empirical* data. We've drawn on our support expertise and sorted through our vast database of software solutions to find the most important and frequently asked questions for Windows 95. These questions have also been checked and rechecked for technical accuracy and are organized in a way that will let you find the answer you need quickly—providing you with a one-stop tech support solution to your software problems.

No longer do you have to spend hours on the phone waiting for someone to answer your tech support question! You are holding the single, most authoritative collection of answers to your software questions available—the next best thing to having a tech support expert by your side.

We've helped millions of people solve their software problems. Let us help you.

Judy Salerno

Judy Salerno
Senior Vice President, Worldwide Service Operations
Stream International Inc.

Acknowledgments

We are appreciative of Stream International for the time and effort that they put into the collection of the questions and drafting of the answers. Special thanks to Steven F. and Lala M. Thanks also to Dianne S., Todd B., Andrea G., Bob B., Allen M., Tony F., Lori F., Gretchen J., Kevin P., Michael W., Margaret M., Peter S., Scott H., Scott T., Joseph Y., Joseph K., Joseph H., George W., Dan G., Phil J., Chris L., Daniel W., John T.

We also appreciate John Cronan, who technically reviewed the book and then read all of the typeset pages. John, who is an author in his own right, is every author's dream in that he thoroughly tests everything the book says and gives you lots of feedback on the results without trying to rewrite the book.

This book marks the debut of Wendy Rinaldi into the ranks of acquisition editors. Wendy, for many years, has been a project editor who was always a joy to work with. Now we get to work with her even closer and it's an even greater joy.

Daniela Dell'Orco, editorial assistant, is always there with a smile in her voice that makes every call a pleasure. She also has a great can-do spirit that gets tasks accomplished.

Introduction

Windows 95 represents a major change in the way you use your computer and includes many new facilities and features that were not there in the past. It is therefore natural that you'll have a great many questions about how to use what is there as well as how to handle the situations when things don't go quite right. With literally hours waiting on a toll phone line to get tech support from Microsoft, almost nonexistent documentation, and online help never quite answering the question you are asking, there is a great disparity between the questions being asked and the answers that are available. The purpose of the book is to fill that void.

The over 400 questions that are answered here came out of Stream International's contract with Microsoft to provide tech support to Windows 95 users during the five months of the Preview period. To these real-world questions, the authors added their 21 months of using Chicago (the original code name for Windows 95) and Windows 95 itself in many beta versions. The authors have literally delved into every nook and cranny of the product and experienced a great many of the problems first hand. As a result, they have located practically every source of answers and have referenced many of them here.

The book then brings together the "on the firing line" experience of a company providing tech support on Windows 95 with about as much depth of experience in researching and using the product as you can have and not be one of the programmers writing Windows 95 (and the Matthewses have spent a lot of time talking to the people behind Windows 95).

Windows 95 Answers is divided into 11 chapters, each of which is a major subject. Within each chapter the questions and answers are further divided into topics, grouping like questions. To find a particular answer, use the Table of Contents to identify the chapter and section in which it's located. Around your particular question, you'll find others that relate to it and will add to the original answer. You can also use the thorough Index to alphabetically locate a topic that doesn't pop out of the Table of Contents.

Besides the questions and answers, there are many **Tech Tips** throughout the book that give you insight into how best to do something that only considerable experience would otherwise bring. In addition to the Tech Tips, there are a number of **Tech Terrors** that that point out areas that can cause considerable problems if they are not avoided. Finally, all but the first chapter have a section labeled **Frustration Busters**. These sections give you an introduction to the chapter's subject and how to address or accomplish the issues related to it. Reading all of the Frustration Busters will give you a broad understanding of Windows 95 and answer many of your questions before you ask them.

Top Ten Tech Terrors

Whenever you install a new piece of software, questions arise simply because of its unfamiliarity. When the software is an operating system, those questions take on an even greater significance because the operating system is so basic to everything that is done on your computer. Among all the Windows 95 questions collected by Stream International during the Windows 95 Preview, the following ten questions repeatedly

caused the most consternation among callers. Here are the answers.

How do I find my files and programs?

To find any file, whether a program or a data file, Windows 95 has three independent paths that you can take using My Computer, the Explorer, or Find.

To use My Computer, follow these instructions:

1. Double-click on the My Computer icon on the desktop. The My Computer window will open, as you see in Figure 1-1.

2. Double-click on the drive that you want to search and then on the directories or folders that you believe contain the files. Each folder that you double-click on opens a new *folder window*, as shown in Figure 1-2.

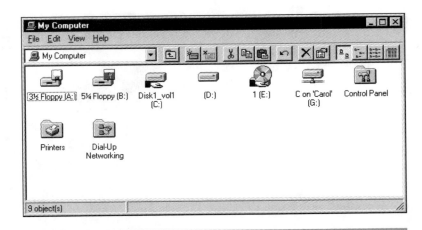

FIGURE 1-1   My Computer window

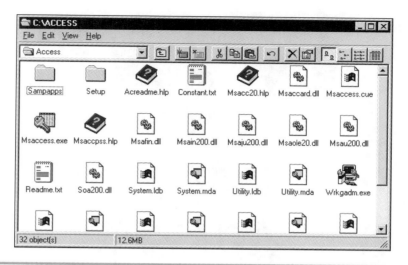

FIGURE 1-2   Folder window

3. When you find the file and the file is a program, you can load or start it by double-clicking on it.

Tech Tip: If the file is a data file that is *associated* with a program (you can tell a file is associated with a program if it uses the program's icon), you can start that program and open the data file by double-clicking on the data file.

To use the Explorer, use these steps:

1. Click on the Start button in the lower left of your screen. The Start menu will open.

2. Move the mouse pointer to Programs (you *don't* have to click), and then click on Windows Explorer, as you see in Figure 1-3. Figure 1-4 shows how the open Explorer window will look.

3. Click on the drive and folder you want to open in the left pane, and then double-click on the file you want to start or open in the right pane.

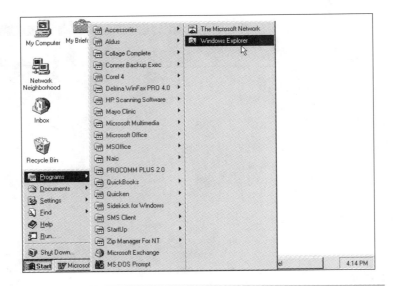

FIGURE 1-3   Start and Programs menus

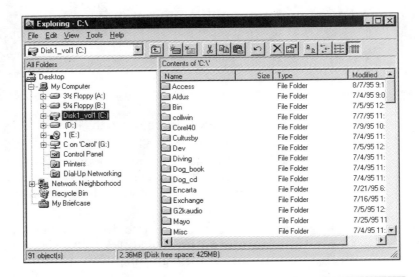

FIGURE 1-4   Explorer window

Tech Tip: Right-clicking on a file in the right pane of the Explorer or in a folder window opens a popup menu, shown next, that allows you to copy, move, delete, or send a file to a floppy disk or to a fax.

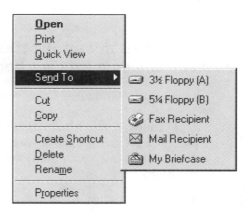

The next set of steps show you how to use Find:

1. Click on the Start button, point on Find, and then click on Files or Folders. The Find dialog box opens as shown in Figure 1-5.

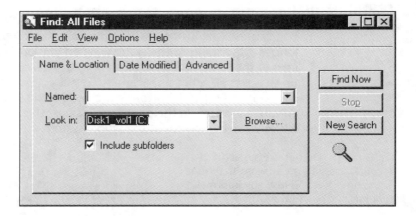

FIGURE 1-5   Find dialog box

2. Select the drives and possibly folders you want to search and click on Find. When the search is complete, the files will be listed below the Find dialog box. You can do anything with those listings (open, start, copy, move, and delete them) that you can do in either the Explorer or My Computer.

Do I have to reinstall my applications after installing Windows 95 on the system that had Windows before?

If you install Windows 95 over your existing Windows 3.*x* directory or folder, then you do not need to reinstall your applications. If you install Windows 95 into a new folder, then you will have to reinstall all your Windows applications. Copying files from your Windows 3.*x* folder to Windows 95 is not sufficient.

Tech Tip: There is almost no need to keep Windows 3.*x* on your computer (virtually all programs run as well or better under Windows 95), so Windows 95 should be installed over your existing Windows 3.*x*.

What do I do if an application I am running stops responding?

You can use CTRL-ALT-DELETE to end an application that is no longer responding to the system. When you press these three keys at the same time, the Close Program dialog box will come up that lists all active applications. Select your application and click on the End Task button. Windows 95 will allow you to continue working in the other applications that are running without having to reboot the whole system.

Tech Terror: Do not press CTRL-ALT-DELETE a second time unless you want to reboot your computer and lose any information that has not been saved.

4 How do I do a clean boot for Windows 95?

When troubleshooting Windows 95 or a specific application, you sometimes have to run the system in the simplest possible configuration to single out the source of the problem or a conflict. In the previous operating systems, you had to create a separate boot disk and boot off this floppy. Windows 95 gives you an easier way of creating a clean environment. Use these steps for that purpose:

1. Restart your computer.

2. When you see the message "Starting Windows 95," immediately press F8. You will see a menu of the following options:

■ **Normal**   Starts regular Windows 95 without changes.

■ **Logged**   Starts regular Windows 95 but creates a file called Bootlog.txt that lists all the steps during bootup. This is very useful in tracking down Windows 95 startup failure. You can read the Bootlog.txt file with Notepad.

■ **Safe Mode**   Windows 95 is started using the most generic default settings: VGA display driver, no network, Microsoft mouse driver, and the minimum device drivers necessary to start Windows. No CD-ROM drives, printers, or other peripheral devices. Config.sys and Autoexec.bat are ignored. You can also get this by pressing F5 at the "Starting Windows 95" message.

■ **Safe Mode with network support**   Starts Windows 95 in a minimum mode, as before, but adds networking for the situation where you must have access to network drives. You can also get this by pressing F6 at the "Starting Windows 95" message.

■ **Step-by-step confirmation**   Also called *interactive start.* Starts Windows 95 but asks if you want to execute each line in your Config.sys and Autoexec.bat files (or the Windows 95 default if you don't have these files). Type **Y** if you want to process the line; type **N** if you don't. You will receive an error message if one of the command lines fails (an indicator of where the system fails). It will process the Registry and load all Windows drivers.

- **Command prompt only**   Starts only the DOS part of Windows 95. All drivers are loaded and all command files processed, but the graphic user interface (GUI) is not started. You are left at the C:\ prompt. You can type **win** to load the GUI. You can also get the Windows 95 DOS command prompt by pressing ALT-F5 at the "Starting Windows 95" message.

- **Safe Mode command prompt only**   Same as Safe Mode but stops at the C:\ prompt without loading the GUI. Type **win** to load the GUI. You can also get this by pressing SHIFT-F5 at the "Starting Windows 95" message.

- **Previous version of MS-DOS**   (Only available if you have dual-boot MS-DOS/Windows 95 setup on your system.) Starts your computer in the previous version of MS-DOS that was on your computer when you installed Windows 95. (See the next question.) You can also get this by pressing F4 at the "Starting Windows 95" message.

How can I go to my previous version of MS-DOS? I tried pressing F4 while booting when it says "Starting Windows 95," but nothing happens and I don't get the option "Previous version of MS-DOS" when I press F8.

If F4 does not work, dual booting is not enabled on your computer. You can enable this feature with these steps:

1. Open Notepad (Start menu, Programs, Accessories, Notepad) and open a file called Msdos.sys in your root directory or folder.

2. Locate the section entitled "Options," and change the line **BootMulti=0** to **BootMulti=1**.

3. Save the changes and reboot. Pressing F4 during booting will load your previous version of MS-DOS, and pressing F8 will give you an option to start the previous MS-DOS version.

Tech Tip: If you boot into your previous version of MS-DOS, you must reboot your computer to return to Windows 95.

Tech Tip: If you have installed Windows 95 into a new directory without deleting Windows 3.*x* from your computer, you can start Windows 3.*x* by booting into the previous version of MS-DOS and then typing **win.**

6 I have installed Windows 95 into a separate folder or directory. Now, when I am trying to run most of my programs, I get an error message that the specified path is invalid. But the path is correct, and the file is right there on the hard drive; I can see it. How do I run my applications and not get this message displayed?

Windows 95 gives an error message because it cannot locate different program components like *.DLLs that you probably have in your Windows 3.*x* \Windows\System folder. Since you did not install Windows 95 over your previous setup of Windows, Windows 95 is not aware of the location of these components. Under most circumstances, the only sure way around this is to reinstall your programs.

7 How do I recover from a power failure or unintentional rebooting during the Windows 95 installation process?

The Windows 95 installation program includes a Safe Recovery option. Depending on where the installation was interrupted, you may be able to turn your computer off and then on (don't just press CTRL-ALT-DELETE), run Setup again, and choose the Safe Recovery option when you are prompted. If this doesn't work the first time, try running Setup a second time.

I have deleted a file by mistake. Can I get it back?

Yes, any files that you delete in My Computer, the Explorer, or any Windows 95 application are automatically moved to the Recycle Bin on your desktop. The deleted files can be recovered by opening the Recycle Bin, selecting the files, and choosing Restore from the File menu.

Tech Terror: You can permanently delete files in the Recycle Bin by right-clicking on the Recycle Bin and choosing Empty Recycle Bin. Once done, though, the files cannot be recovered.

I have accidentally deleted a file through File Manager and immediately tried to recover it through the Recycle Bin, but the file was not there! I thought it stored all deleted files. Why can't I see it, and how do I recover it?

The Recycle Bin stores files deleted through 32-bit native Windows 95 utilities only. You will recover files deleted in My Computer, Explorer, or any Windows 95 application. File Manager is a 16-bit Windows 3.*x* application, and it does not support file recovery through the Recycle Bin. You can try to recover your file using disk utilities for Windows 95, such as Norton Utilities for Windows 95.

Tech Tip: Use only native Windows 95 file management utilities to have use of the Recycle Bin and long filenames.

10 After I completed Setup, the system was trying to reboot but died. Now what do I do?

1. Turn the PC off and then back on (do not just press CTRL-ALT-DELETE).

2. Press F8 when you see "Starting Windows 95," to open the Startup menu and choose Safe Mode.

If Windows 95 starts, change the video driver to the standard VGA driver by following these steps:

1. Right-click on the desktop, choose Properties, click on the Settings tab, and then click on the Change Display Type button.

2. Click on the Change button in the Adapter Type section, and click on Show All Devices.

3. In the Manufacturers list, click on Standard display types, and then click on Standard Display Adapter (VGA). Click on OK.

4. Click on the Start button, choose Shut Down, and choose Restart the computer.

If Windows 95 still does not work, reboot from a floppy disk with your previous DOS, rename your Config.sys and Autoexec.bat (at a DOS prompt, type **ren autoexec.bat autoexec.tmp** and **ren config.sys config.tmp**), and restart off your hard disk again.

If the problem persists, use these steps:

1. Restart off your hard disk, press F8 at "Starting Windows 95," and choose Safe Mode.

2. Right-click on My Computer, choose Properties, click on the Performance tab, and click on the File System button.

3. Click on the Troubleshooting tab.

4. Check all of the available boxes, and then click on OK in all dialog boxes and reboot.

Installing Windows 95

Given that Windows 95 replaces both DOS and Windows 3.1, you might expect that it would have a fairly complex and lengthy installation. In fact, just the opposite is the case. If you use the Typical installation and have a reasonably standard system running Windows 3.1 or above, the Windows 95 installation is simplicity itself. You have to type **a:\setup** in the Run command and answer less than half a dozen questions—that's it! It takes only a few minutes of your time, although it will take between 30 and 60 minutes of your computer's time.

Of course there are always the unplanned hitches and that is what this book is for! The first tip is to do some preparation *before* the installation. The Frustration Busters tell you what you should do to get ready.

FRUSTRATION BUSTERS!

To prepare for the installation of Windows 95, take the added time to run through the following steps. This will ensure that you and your computer are in the best possible shape for the installation.

- **Compare your hardware** with the minimum and recommended hardware needed for Windows 95, as shown in Table 2-1, and consider upgrading your hardware before upgrading to Windows 95.

- **Clean up your hard disk** by removing all unused files. Windows 95 requires a lot of disk space (40 to 80MB for file space and 10 to 20MB for temporary space). Use the installation of Windows 95 as an excuse to do the disk cleaning you always intended to do. Uninstall or remove the programs you aren't using and delete the data and miscellaneous files that are no longer of value.

Tech Tip: While it is a drastic step and you should consider it carefully, the very best way to clean up your hard disk is to back up all important files, reformat it (which erases everything on your hard disk), and then after installing Windows 95, to reinstall just the application and data files you need. You'll be amazed at how much more space you have.

- **Back up important files** on your hard disk. While the installation of Windows 95 will probably go without a hitch, there is nothing like the comfort of having a backup of *all* your important files in case the worst should happen. You need to back up all the data files you don't want to lose (these include word processing, spreadsheet, database, and drawing files). Back up your Config.sys and Autoexec.bat

FRUSTRATION BUSTERS!

files in your root (\) directory or folder, and back up your .INI, .DAT, and .PWL files in your Windows folder. You may also have network and/or communications configuration and script files that need to be backed up. You don't need to back up your applications, since you already have them on their distribution disks.

- **Create a bootable floppy** from your current version of DOS using the **format a:/s** command and a new disk or one that can be written on in your A: floppy drive. This allows you to recover if something happens to your hard disk that prevents you from booting from it.

- **Optimize your hard disk** by running ScanDisk (Thorough option) and Defrag *before* you run Windows 95 Setup. ScanDisk checks your disk for both physical and software errors and in many instances corrects them for you. Defrag defragments your disk by putting related file segments together in the same area of the disk. Use the version of ScanDisk in the \Win95 folder on the Windows 95 CD or on the first Windows 95 floppy disk. You can't easily get to the Windows 95 version of Defrag before installation, so use the DOS 6.*x* version if you have it or use a recent version of Norton Speed Disk that is part of the Norton Utilities from Symantec.

- **Review the four primary decisions** that you will have to make during installation:

  - **Install from Windows or from DOS?** If you are currently running Windows 3.1, 3.11, or Windows for Workgroups, it is recom- mended that you start Windows 95 Setup from Windows. In all other circumstances you need to start Setup from DOS.

FRUSTRATION BUSTERS!

- **Install into the current Windows directory?** When you install Windows 95 into your current Windows directory or folder, you'll replace your current version of Windows and it will no longer be available. This is the recommended approach. If you want to keep your current version of Windows available to you, you need to install Windows into a new folder.

Tech Tip: If you install Windows 95 into a new folder, you'll have to reinstall any Windows applications you want to use with Windows 95.

- **Save your current DOS and Windows files?** If you choose to install Windows 95 in the same directory as your old Windows, you will then be given this choice. While it takes up to 10MB of your local hard disk (it can't be on a network drive or a floppy), it allows you to completely and cleanly uninstall Windows 95 and reinstall your previous DOS and Windows.

Tech Tip: If, after Windows 95 is running for a while, you want to remove your old Windows and DOS files, you can do so by clicking on Old Windows 3.*x*/MS-DOS System Files and then on Remove in the Install/Uninstall tab of the Add/Remove Programs control panel reached from the Start menu, Settings, Control Panel options.

- **Use Typical, Portable, Compact, or Custom installation?** If you have a portable (laptop or notebook) computer or if you have a computer with very limited disk space, you should use the

FRUSTRATION BUSTERS!

Portable or Compact installations. If you know you want to install components not installed in a Typical installation, then use the Custom installation. In most circumstances, a Typical installation is the easiest and preferred type. See the discussion later in this chapter on the differences between the types of installation. Also see Appendix A for a list of components that are installed in the various types.

Tech Tip: By using the Add/Remove Programs Windows Setup tab in the Windows 95 Control Panel (opened from Start menu Settings), you can easily add or remove Windows 95 components after installing it and without rerunning Setup.

Element	Minimum	Recommendation
Processor	386DX-20	486DX2-66
Memory	4MB	8MB
Free Disk Space	40MB	80MB
Display	VGA (640 x 480, 16 colors)	SVGA (800 x 600, 256 colors)
Mouse	None	Microsoft-compatible device
CD-ROM	None	Double-speed (2X)
Modem	None	14.4 Kbps fax/modem
Sound board	None	16-bit

TABLE 2-1   What you need to install Windows 95

Pre-Installation Considerations

I have just bought the Windows 95 upgrade. I have completely erased all information from my hard disk and formatted it, so that it is all empty, clean, and ready for Windows 95 Setup. Can I start installing Windows 95 now?

Not just yet. Since you have an operating system upgrade, you have to have an operating system already installed on the computer to start Windows 95 Setup. Install your previous version of DOS and then use it to start Windows 95 Setup. Also, since this is a Windows upgrade, you must have available an original installation disk (although the program does not need to be installed) for Windows 3.0 or above, Windows for Workgroups, or OS/2 version 2.0 or above. You'll be asked to insert the prior version's first installation disk if Setup can't find it on your hard disk.

My company is planning a migration to Windows 95. What are the resources that I can use to help me with this migration?

Microsoft Press has released the Windows 95 Resource Kit, which has a wealth of technical information on how to implement Windows 95. It contains the following:

- A guided tour.
- A planning guide.
- Technical information on installing, configuring, and networking.
- Software utilities.

Tech Tip: The complete Windows 95 Resource Kit is on every Windows 95 CD as a help file (Win95rk.hlp) in the \Admin\Reskit \Helpfile folder. As you can see in Figure 2-1, this folder also contains help files for Apple Macintosh users and system administrators.

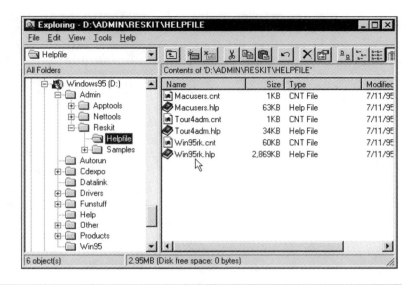

FIGURE 2-1   The Windows 95 Resource Kit, available on the Windows 95 CD

Microsoft also offers the Windows 95 Migration Planning Kit, which contains the Resource Kit text in a help file format; demo kit; deployment guide; Microsoft project deployment plan template; and business analysis tool. Contact Microsoft at (800) 426-9400.

You can order Microsoft Windows 95 TrainCast, which is a series of four videotapes that explain and demonstrate how to plan, support, and implement the migration to Windows 95. For information on ordering tapes and local broadcast availability, call MSTV at (800) 597-3200.

Third-party support is available through companies such as Stream International, which offers consulting services to help your company plan and implement enterprise-wide migration to Windows 95.

What is the difference between different types of setup?

There are four options presented to you during Setup, as shown in Figure 2-2: Typical, Portable, Compact, and Custom. The four choices allow you to choose the components that will be installed with Windows 95, depending on your disk space and whether you have a portable computer. The components that are installed by each option are listed in Appendix A. Briefly, the four choices are as follows:

- **Typical Setup** resembles the Express setup in Windows 3.*x*. This type of setup will run through most of the setup routine without requiring user input. The only choices that the user will have to make are the location of the Windows 95 folder and whether to create a startup disk.

- **Portable Setup** will install the files necessary to run Windows 95 on a laptop or notebook PC, including such components as power management; My Briefcase, a tool for file synchronization; and the system files necessary to establish cable link between two computers for file exchange.

- **Compact Setup** will install the bare minimum files necessary to run Windows 95.

- **Custom Setup** resembles the Custom setup in Windows 3.*x*. This option will allow users to make their own choices on what components to install.

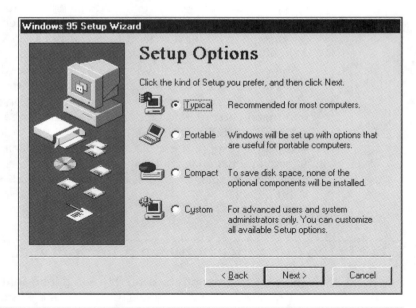

FIGURE 2-2   The four options presented to you during installation

Does the setup of Windows 95 require that I make a lot of decisions?

The installation procedure is more automated and user-friendly than in all previous operating systems. One of the advantages of the installation is that it can be done entirely from within Windows. If Windows has never been installed on the system, the setup procedure will install a small subset of Windows 3.*x* just to run the installation process. During the setup, the Setup Wizard walks you through making choices and selecting options, as you can see in Figure 2-3. At all times, extensive context-sensitive help is just a mouse click away, and you always have the option to return to the previous screen(s) if you decide that you made a wrong choice.

Windows 95 Setup autodetects the hardware components that are installed on your computer and automatically loads necessary drivers, configures them, and writes all the information into the Registry—the database that stores all configuration information for the system.

FIGURE 2-3   The Setup Wizard makes installation easy

During the setup, every operation is recorded in the setup log. If the setup fails at some point, Windows 95 will recover from just before the action that caused the setup to fail, and the user will be presented with an option to make necessary adjustments in the choices.

Can I install Windows 95 without user input?

Windows 95 allows system administrators to create batch setup scripts so that no input will be required from the users. The administrators can create an automated mandatory installation routine for the users on the network.

This new feature involves setting up Windows 95 on the file server using the file Netsetup.exe, which you can find on the Windows 95 CD in the \Admin\Nettools\Netsetup folder. You then create custom batch scripts with the Batch.exe program in the same directory and store scripts in the Msbatch.inf file. Finally, you run the workstation setups using the MS SMS (System Management Services) network login or any other network software management system to perform the mandatory setup. See the Batch.hlp file as well as the various text files in the \Admin\Nettools\Netsetup folder on the Windows 95 CD. Also, read the applicable parts of the Windows 95 Windows Resource Kit or its help file described earlier in this chapter.

Equipment Considerations

How much RAM do I need to run Windows 95?

The absolute minimum is 4MB, and despite what you may have heard, Windows 95 will run fine with only 4MB. It is just that most people want to also run one or more applications. While that's possible with 4MB, it is recommended you have at least 8MB, and you will notice a major boost in performance with 16MB of RAM. The primary consideration is what applications you will be running and how many of them at one time. If you are running Microsoft Word or Excel alone, 8MB is fine; you can even run them together in that space, although you can switch back and forth much faster with 16MB. If you are running CorelDRAW!, you will be happier with 16MB.

How much hard disk space do I need for Windows 95?

The installation requirement for hard disk space varies depending on the options you choose. For the basic components of the operating system in both a Typical and Compact installation, you will need the disk space as shown in Table 2-2. If you choose to install some of the features not in a Typical install, you can as much as double the amount of disk space required. For example, if you install the Microsoft Exchange and the Microsoft Network, it will add 20MB, and Networking will add 5 to 10MB. Additionally, when you are done with the installation, you should have at least 10 to 20MB left for temporary files.

Tech Tip: A good rule of thumb is that you need 50MB for minimum installation and 100MB for a full installation.

Can I install Windows 95 on my PowerPC?

No. Windows 95 is designed to run only on the Intel-based computers. This means that you cannot install it on computers using PowerPC or DEC Alpha chips.

Installation Option	Additional Disk Space Required	
	Compact	**Typical**
New Installation	30MB	40MB
Windows 3.x Upgrade	20MB	30MB
Windows for Workgroups 3.x upgrade	10MB	20MB

TABLE 2-2   Disk space required for basic Windows 95

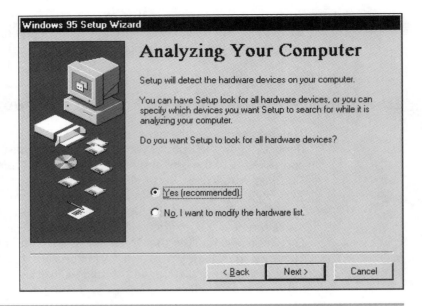

FIGURE 2-4   Setup Wizard asks if you want it to analyze your hardware

During the installation process, does Windows 95 detect hardware devices and configure them?

Yes. During the installation, Windows 95 analyzes your computer, if you choose (see Figure 2-4 above) to identify the hardware resources that are available. To the extent possible, it configures the appropriate drivers and stores the hardware information in the Registry.

Will Windows 95 run on my 286?

No. Windows 95 is a 32-bit operating system and requires a 32-bit processor. You will need a 386-based or higher computer to run Windows 95.

Can I install Windows 95 correctly on a hard disk partitioned with OnTrack Disk Manager?

Yes. Windows 95 is compatible with all versions of Disk Manager. It also provides a protected-mode driver for Disk Manager version 6.03, and if you use this version, Windows 95 automatically uses its protected-mode driver, which will give you faster 32-bit disk access.

Can I set up Windows 95 if I have compressed my hard disk with Stacker?

Yes. Windows 95 Setup is compatible with Stacker version 2.0 or above. Before you start Setup, verify that there is at least 1.5MB of free hard disk space on the host drive or 8MB if you use a permanent swap file. If there is not enough free space on the host drive, you must run the compression software to increase this amount.

Tech Note: Windows 95 Setup may not find your boot drive if you have compressed it with SuperStor. If you get a message to that effect, you will need to uncompress your hard drive, remove SuperStor, and then rerun Windows 95 Setup.

Operating Systems Considerations

What versions of MS-DOS and Windows do I need to upgrade to Windows 95?

Windows version 3.0 and higher, Windows for Workgroups version 3.1 and higher, or MS-DOS or PC-DOS version 3.2 or higher. You can also upgrade from OS/2 version 2.0 and higher.

Tech Tip: If you have Windows 3.0 or OS/2, you must run Setup from MS-DOS and then, in the case of Windows 3.0, choose to install Windows 95 in the same folder as Windows 3.0.

Can I have more than one operating system installed on my PC at one time?

Yes. You can install Windows 95 in its own folder and retain your old DOS and Windows. If you boot and do nothing, you will get Windows 95. If you boot and press F4, you'll get your old DOS, from which you can run your old Windows. Or you can partition your drive and use OS/2's Boot Manager to select the application operating system. Windows 95 must first be installed, and then you can partition your drive and make the new partition bootable. Then use OS/2 to install the Boot Manager menu system in the new partition. When you start, a menu will open asking which operating system you want to run this session. You have 30 seconds to choose, or by default it will go into the first partition that was made active—Windows 95.

Tech Terror: If you install Windows 95 into its own folder, you'll have to reinstall the applications you want to run under Windows 95.

Which is better to start Setup from, Windows or MS-DOS?

Starting Windows 95 Setup from Windows is the preferred option. However, you should start the setup from MS-DOS in the following cases:

- You don't have Windows installed.
- You have Windows 3.0 or an earlier version installed.
- You have OS/2 installed either by itself or as dual boot.
- You have Windows NT installed either by itself or as dual boot.

If Windows 95 is the operating system upgrade, what operating systems can I upgrade over?

You can install the Windows 95 upgrade over the following:

- MS-DOS version 3.2 or above, or an equivalent version of DR DOS or PC DOS that supports partitions greater than 32MB

- Windows 3.0 and above

- Windows for Workgroups 3.1 and above

- Dual-boot OS/2 with MS-DOS installed on the FAT partition

- Dual-boot Windows NT with MS-DOS installed on the FAT partition

Can I install Windows 95 on a computer that has OS/2 and Windows and still dual-boot?

Yes, you can do that. You have to be aware of the fact that Windows 95 cannot access the HPFS partitions used in OS/2, so you have to have a FAT partition with enough disk space to install Windows 95. Don't install Windows 95 on top of your existing Windows if you also want to keep it.

To install Windows 95, boot into DOS and start the Windows 95 Setup. Setup disables the OS/2 boot manager, because during the setup process Windows 95 Setup has to have full control over the system. You can re-enable OS/2 Boot Manager after the setup is complete.

To do this:

1. Start Windows 95.

2. Click on the Start button, choose Run, and type **fdisk**.

3. Choose Set Active Partition, as shown in Figure 2-5. Enter the number of the Boot Manager Partition. This partition is the 1MB Non-DOS partition.

4. Close Fdisk, and restart the computer. You can now use the Boot Manager.

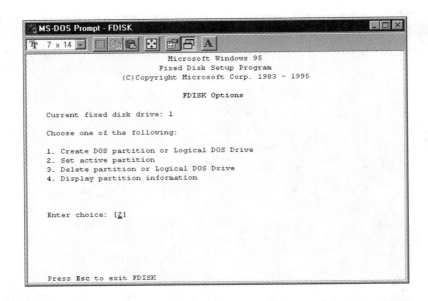

FIGURE 2-5   Fdisk allows you to set partitions for dual operating systems

How can I install Windows 95 on my PC that has Windows NT 3.5 installed?

You can install Windows 95 on a Windows NT machine only if you have a dual boot between Windows NT and MS-DOS. To install Windows 95:

1. Start the Windows NT computer in MS-DOS mode.

2. If Windows 3.1 or above is installed, start it, and then in the Program Manager's File Run command type **d:\setup.exe**, where d:\ is your Windows 95 CD-ROM or Setup disk.

3. If Windows 3.1 or above is not installed, type **d:\setup.exe** at the DOS prompt.

4. Follow the onscreen prompts of the Setup Wizard. Make sure to install Windows 95 into a separate folder rather than on top of existing Windows or Windows NT.

After you complete the setup, Windows 95 will become an option on your startup menu, along with Windows NT and MS-DOS.

How do Windows 95 and NT 3.5 operate on the same machine?

Windows 95 Setup will detect the presence of a Windows NT boot sector, and it will not overwrite it if you start Setup from MS-DOS or Windows 3.*x* and not NT. Setup will then load. However, Setup will make several changes to the folder structure and the files in the System folder that will affect the operation of Windows NT.

Setup rewrites the Windows 3.*x* default .DLL files (such as Shell.dll) in the System folder. This is by design so that Windows 95 can run both 16- and 32-bit Windows applications. However, Windows NT's Windows on Windows (WOW) subsystem relies on the original Win16 .DLL's to run Win16 applications. If Windows 95 is installed, certain Win16 applications, such as some of Microsoft's Setup programs and WinBUG, may not run under Windows NT.

Windows 95 moves all the screen fonts to a newly created Fonts folder. Since Windows NT uses the screen fonts normally present in the System folder, it will be forced to use a default Courier-type font rather than the normal system font. This default font is not proportioned correctly for Windows NT's dialog boxes, and some text may be unreadable.

If I am not ready to make the changeover, can I set up Windows 95 and Windows 3.1 as a dual boot and still have access to all of my files on the hard disk using either version?

You can do this. When you install Windows 95, the Setup prompts you for the folder to install to. The default is your existing Windows folder. Select a different folder to install Windows 95 into, and you'll be able to access your old Windows 3.*x* through dual boot.

Once installed, Windows 95 will not recognize your installed applications. To correct that, start Windows 95 and reinstall your applications into their existing folders. The result is that Windows 95 will register the applications, and you can still use them in your old Windows without having to make two copies of each program, one for each operating system. If you install new applications, make sure to do two installs—one under Windows 3.*x*, one under Windows 95.

Situations During Installation

 ### Setup fails to start. What do I do?

You can do any of the following:

1. Check for sufficient conventional memory. Windows 95 requires 420K. If this is not available, remove any unnecessary drivers from your Config.sys file or TSR programs that are started in your Autoexec.bat file. As a general rule, to install Windows you need drivers only for your hard disk and maybe your CD-ROM, and you normally do not need any TSR. Use either Windows Notepad or DOS Edit to clean out all unnecessary commands in your Config.sys and Autoexec.bat files.

2. Check the RAM configuration in Config.sys.

   ■ Using MS-DOS 4.*x*, the commands should include

      Device=Himem.sys

   ■ Using MS-DOS 5.*x* or later, the commands should include

      Device=Himem.sys
      Device=EMM386.exe NOEMS
      DOS=High,UMB

   ■ Check for adequate extended or XMS memory; the requirement is at least 3MB of XMS. If you are using MS-DOS 6.*x*, when you first see the MS-DOS message, press F8 and choose Step-by-step confirmation to verify that Himem.sys is loading. If it is not, verify that the file exists in your DOS or Windows directory and that your Config.sys file has the Device=Himem.sys statement.

■ At the DOS prompt or in a Run command, type **mem /c /p** to check for free conventional and XMS memory.

What switches can I use with Setup.exe?

The Setup switches allow you to alter the Setup in a specific way. You type the switches at the time you enter a Setup command, as shown here:

Following is a list of the command line switches you may use with Setup when you start it in either the Run command or at the DOS prompt:

■ **/?** Gives help on the possible switches of the Setup.exe.

■ **/c** Prevents Windows 95 Setup from loading the SMARTDrive disk cache.

■ **/d** Prevents Windows 95 Setup from using the existing version of Windows for the first stage of Setup. Instead, it will load a brand new small subset of Windows. This option is useful if the existing version of Windows is experiencing some problems.

■ **/id** Prevents Windows 95 Setup from checking for the necessary disk space. This option can be used if the Setup reports less space than you know you have.

■ **/il** Tells Windows 95 to load the Logitech Series C mouse driver. This option is needed if you have a Logitech Series C mouse.

■ **/im** Prevents Windows 95 Setup from checking for the necessary memory space.

■ **/in** Prevents Windows 95 Setup from running the Network Setup module.

■ **/iq** Prevents Windows 95 Setup from running ScanDisk at the beginning of setup from MS-DOS. This option is useful if you are using non-Microsoft disk compression software.

- **/is** Prevents Windows 95 Setup from running ScanDisk at the beginning of setup from Windows. This option is useful if you are using non-Microsoft disk compression software.

- /T:*tmpdir* Tells Windows 95 Setup to use the path and folder named *tmpdir* to store all its temporary files.

- /nostart Copies the minimal required Windows 3.*x* DLLs required by Windows 95 setup and then exits without installing Windows 95.

- *batchfile* Tells Windows 95 Setup to use the file and path *batchfile* to get the script containing the Setup options.

How do I restart Setup after an earlier attempt has failed?

Use the following steps to restart:

1. Turn off your computer (do not press CTRL-ALT-DEL), and wait 10 seconds. Then turn it back on.

2. Start Setup again. Setup will prompt you to use Safe Recovery to recover the failed installation.

3. Choose the Safe Recovery option, and click on Continue. Hardware detection will skip the part that caused the initial failure.

4. If the computer stops again during the detection process, restart Setup, and repeat the process until the hardware detection process is finished.

5. After Setup is complete and Windows is running, you can use the information in Setuplog.txt and Detlog.txt to check for the devices that caused the problems.

When I am installing Windows 95, I get an error message indicating that I don't have enough disk space available. I know that I do have enough space. Is there anything I can do to get around this error message?

You can have Setup ignore the checking for available disk space by using the /id switch with the Setup.exe command (at the DOS prompt or in a Run command, type **setup /id**).

What does it mean when I get the error message "Standard Mode: Fault in MS-DOS Extender" when running Setup from DOS?

There may be a conflict in the upper memory area. Upper memory blocks (UMBs) are the unused part of upper memory from 640K to 1MB. If an EMM386 statement appears in your Config.sys file (use Windows Notepad or DOS Edit to view it), it is enabling upper memory blocks. Disable this statement by typing **REM** in front of it, save your altered Config.sys, reboot, and then rerun Setup.

When I start Setup, I am advised by Setup to exit Windows and run ScanDisk in MS-DOS. I do that, but ScanDisk does not find any errors. I restart Setup and get the same error again. What do I do?

You can force Setup to run without running ScanDisk by adding the /is switch to the Setup.exe command line. (At a DOS prompt or in a Run command, type **d:\setup /is** where d:\ is the drive with Setup on it.)

I received the error message "Cannot open file" while running Setup. What does this mean?

You may need to free up memory by disabling (typing **REM** in front of it) or removing the Smartdrv.exe statement in your Autoexec.bat or by closing any applications that may be running in Windows. Windows 95 does not use SMARTDrive, so it is not necessary to have it in your Autoexec.bat.

During setup I get the error message "B1." What does that mean?

A "B1" error message indicates that Setup has detected an older 80386 processor that is not supported and instructs you to upgrade your processor. If your 80386 chip was made before April 1987 or has a label that reads "16-bit operations only," contact your hardware manufacturer for an upgrade.

When running Setup, why do I get an error message that my path is invalid?

The drive you are trying to install Windows 95 on has zero bytes available (such as a CD-ROM would have), or the drive is not ready or not mounted with a removable hard drive. Install Windows 95 to a different drive or make the removable hard disk drive ready.

   If more than zero bytes of hard disk space are available, but not enough for Windows to be installed, you will receive an error message: "Insufficient disk space" or "Not enough disk space."

I terminated the installation of Windows 95 after it requested the folder name to contain the Windows 95 files. On my second install, I was waiting for the prompt for the folder name but never got it. Windows 95 remembered my first try and automatically created the folder name originally entered. How do I remove Windows 95 and start the installation over?

Windows 95 installation created a file called Setuplog.txt to keep track of each step of Setup. If the setup fails at some point, Windows 95 Setup refers to this file to determine the last successful step. To restart Setup from scratch, delete this file (it is in the root folder). You might also want to delete the Detlog.txt and Detcrash.log files if you have them.

How can I set up Windows 95 into a folder separate from my current Windows?

During setup you are prompted to enter a directory or folder in which to install Windows 95, and your current Windows folder is suggested as a default, as shown in Figure 2-6.

To install Windows 95 into a new folder:

1. Click on the Other directory button.

2. Click on Next, and enter the new folder name. If the folder does not exist, the setup routine will create it for you.

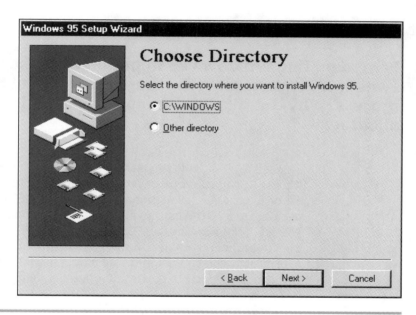

FIGURE 2-6 Setup Wizard asking where to install Windows 95

I was running Setup and it stopped during hardware detection. What do I do now?

Use the following steps:

1. Turn the computer off, wait ten seconds, and turn it back on. (Do not press CTRL-ALT-DEL if Setup hangs!)

2. When the PC is back online, restart Setup using Safe Recovery (you'll be prompted to do this). This will bypass the portion of hardware testing detection that caused the problem. If your system stops again, it will be in a different detection module. Perform these steps as many times as necessary to allow your system to complete detection.

I am installing Windows 95 from the CD-ROM. The system went dead after the first reboot late in the process. Why did this happen and what can I do about it?

You might have both real-mode and protected-mode drivers installed for the CD-ROM, and they are in conflict. Remove the CD-ROM real-mode drivers from your Config.sys and Autoexec.bat files (all mention of your CD-ROM). If the problem persists, boot into Windows in Safe mode by pressing F8 when you see "Starting Windows 95" and choosing Safe mode from the Startup menu. If Windows will not start even in Safe mode, reinstall it. If you can get into Safe mode, reboot, press F8 again, and choose Logged to create a Bootlog.txt file to see where the system fails.

Look for the Detcrash.log file. If it is present, the problem is with hardware detection. Check Ios.ini in your Windows folder and remark out the drivers that are loading in Config.sys (by putting **rem** and a space at the left of lines that load any drivers found on the unsafe list in the Ios.ini file) in case there is a problem with these protected-mode drivers. From the Start menu, select Settings, Control Panel, and then double-click on System. Then check the Device Manager for any conflicts. Change the display driver to standard VGA.

Try the Step-by-step confirmation boot after pressing F8 when you see "Starting Windows 95" and observe what is being loaded. Rename Autoexec.bat and Config.sys so they don't load on the next boot.

I am using a Logitech mouse on my computer. When I run Windows 95 Setup, the mouse does not work until I restart the computer to boot into Windows 95.

If you have a Logitech mouse, you have to start the Setup program with the following command: **setup /il**. This will make your mouse available during the initial stages of Setup.

Post-Installation Questions

How do I know that Windows 95 Setup installed the components that I wanted?

Windows 95 Setup creates the following log files during the setup: Setuplog.txt, Detlog.txt, and Bootlog.txt. If the setup fails, another file is created called Detcrash.log. All of these files are in the root (\) directory or folder. You can view these files (but do not change them) by using Notepad, as shown in Figure 2-7.

- Setuplog.txt is the file that keeps track of each step of setup. If the setup fails at the stage before the hardware detection, Windows 95 Setup refers to this file to determine the last successful step. Setuplog.txt ensures that the setup does not fail twice due to the same cause. It will make the correction in the failed step and continue the setup.

- Detcrash.log is created if the setup fails during hardware detection. This file stores information on what hardware component caused the failure and what resources the setup routine was accessing just before the crash. After such a crash, if you rerun Setup, it will automatically go

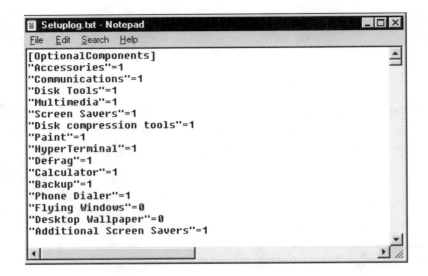

FIGURE 2-7   You can view the Setup log files using Notepad

into the Safe recovery mode and will continue the process, skipping the module that failed. If Setup is successful, Detcrash.log is deleted upon completion of Setup.

- Detlog.txt contains a list of detected hardware components and the parameters for each detected device.

- Bootlog.txt is the file that describes what takes place during the system startup processes.

What do I do if I want to install a feature of Windows 95 that I did not originally install?

To add or remove a Windows 95 component outside of Setup, use the following steps:

1. Click on the Start button, choose Settings, and click on Control Panel.

2. Double-click on the Add/Remove Programs icon.

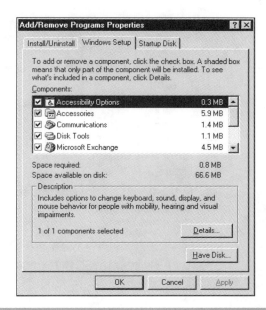

FIGURE 2-8   Add/Remove Programs dialog box allows you to install programs you did not install during Setup

> **3.** Click on the Windows Setup tab, as shown in Figure 2-8, and select/deselect the items you want to add or remove. Click on OK when you are done.

I installed Windows 95 on a system with two CD-ROM drives. One of the CD-ROM drives was not detected. Why?

> This happens if Windows 95 loads protected-mode drivers for the primary CD-ROM drive, but the secondary CD-ROM drive is running with real-mode drivers loaded by the Config.sys and Autoexec.bat files. Windows 95 assumes that both drivers reference the same device, so it assigns the same drive letter for both, making them appear as one drive.

Assign the CD-ROM drive that is running to a different drive letter with these steps:

1. Click on the Start button, choose Settings, and click on Control Panel.

2. Double-click on the System icon, and then click on the Device Manager tab.

3. Select the CD-ROM you want to change, click on the Properties button, and click on the Settings tab, shown in Figure 2-9.

4. In the Reserved drive letters section, set Start drive letter and End drive letter to the drive letter you want the CD-ROM to use. Click on OK.

5. Click on the Start button and click on Shut Down.

6. Then click on the Restart the computer option.

FIGURE 2-9   You can change a CD-ROM's drive letter in the drive's Properties dialog box

How do I remove Windows 95 from my computer?

If during Setup you chose the option of saving your system files so that you could uninstall Windows 95, as described at the beginning of this chapter, then, after completing installation and finding you want to remove Windows 95, you can use the following steps to completely restore your previous DOS and Windows:

1. Open the Start menu and choose Settings and then Control Panel.

2. Double-click on Add/Remove Programs and, if necessary, on the Install/Uninstall tab.

3. Select Windows 95 and click on Remove.

Tech Note: If you are having problems starting Windows 95 and want to remove it, boot into DOS by pressing F8 when you first see "Starting Windows 95," choose Command prompt only, and type **uninstal** at the DOS prompt.

If you did not choose the option of saving your system files so you could uninstall Windows 95, use the following steps to remove Windows 95 and reinstall your previous system:

1. Reboot your computer using a DOS disk that contains the SYS.COM command.

2. At the DOS prompt, type **sys c:**. Remove the disk and reboot your computer.

3. Reinstall your previous version of DOS.

4. Delete the folders that contain Windows 95 files and reinstall your previous version of Windows and all your Windows applications.

When I look at the Windows 95 Installation diskettes in the Explorer, it only shows one *.CAB file on each disk. How can I get a list of all the files that are there?

Follow these steps to list all files on the installation disks:

1. Insert the Windows 95 diskette into a:\ drive.

2. From the Start menu, choose Programs and MS-DOS Prompt. Then at the c:\ prompt, type the following command: **extract /d a:\win95_xx.cab > win95_xx.txt** where *xx* stands for the disk number. This action will generate a text file named after the .CAB file, and it will have the listing of the disk contents.

Alternatively, open an MS-DOS window, and for the Windows 95 CD, type the following to create a master list: **extract /a /d d:\win95\win95_02.cab > win95.txt** where d:\Win95_02.cab is the filename of the first .CAB file. This will process all the .CAB files in sequence and generate a list of all files in the file Win95.txt.

What's New in Windows 95

One of the first impressions you'll have of Windows 95 is that it contains so many new features—and it does. Not only is the appearance of the product different, but the content is as well. Windows 95 represents a major step forward in functionality on desktop and portable PC platforms by providing a system that is even easier, faster, and more powerful to use. In addition, it is designed to maintain compatibility with the existing Windows and MS-DOS applications and hardware in which you have invested. The Frustration Busters will give you an overview of some of the more important enhancements in Windows 95.

FRUSTRATION BUSTERS!

Here are some of the most important new features of Windows 95.

- **32-Bit Architecture** takes advantage of the 32-bit data paths that have been available since the 386 processor. With this come faster response times and more sophisticated software.

- **Backward Compatibility** ensures that most of the programs and hardware with which you ran Windows 3.*x* and MS-DOS will run with Windows 95. There may be some glitches, but they are few.

- **Taskbar and Start Menu** are the focal points of a new graphic interface that provides an intuitive way to find the functions and programs you want. You simply click on Start and a menu of your computer's contents makes it very easy for you to navigate the new operating system. This interface is called "discoverable" because a user can discover how to use it with little or no training. Instead of searching for ways to perform a task, the user will easily discover the way to do it.

- **Explorer, My Computer,** and **Network Neighborhood** provide the file management tools. With them, you can find out where files and devices are located—on your own disk or computer or within your network—and open, copy, delete, rename, move, or perform other file and disk tasks.

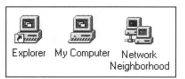

Explorer   My Computer   Network Neighborhood

- **Microsoft Exchange** acts as a centralized communications facility for sending and receiving e-mail, files, and faxes to and from LAN and remote computers. It also provides a way of connecting with information services such as CompuServe or the

FRUSTRATION BUSTERS!

Internet. It can be accessed by the Inbox icon, allowing you to quickly get your messages.

- **Microsoft Network** is Microsoft's information service, which provides bulletin boards and chat rooms, as well as access to forums on a wide variety of subjects.

- **Plug-and-play** allows you to "plug in your new hardware and play it." Windows 95 figures out what hardware you have or are installing and handles the configuration setup and management for you (for the most part!).

- **Recycle Bin** is where your deleted files are automatically placed. From there, you can throw them away or restore them, as you wish. It is protection against inadvertently deleting a file you want to keep.

- **My Briefcase** allows you to keep the original and copies of a file synchronized. After you have edited a file (perhaps on another computer, or just in another directory or

FRUSTRATION BUSTERS!

folder), you synchronize the original with the edited copy to keep all copies current with the latest changes.

■ **Multimedia** accessories, including CD Player, Media Player, and Sound Recorder, are available to play and display your audio, video, and animated files. Also, Volume Control lets you control the volume for your special input and output devices, such as the CD player or microphone.

■ **Multitasking and Multithreading** allow you to easily and effectively run several programs at the same time. Multitasking was available in Windows 3.*x*, but multithreading is new to Windows 95.

■ **Drag and Drop** allows you to use the mouse to drag a file or folder from one location to another. You can use this to open, copy, or move files, or even to print a document.

■ **Object Linking and Embedding** (OLE2) enables you to insert another application's files into a document by linking or embedding it. It facilitates how you update or modify the inserted file by calling in the creating application's toolbars and menus and then allowing you to continue with the current application. Although this is a facility that has been previously available, its handling of the interfaces with various applications has been enhanced.

■ **Accessories**, such as Calculator, Paint, Character Map, Notepad, and WordPad as well as games (Solitaire, Hearts, Minesweeper, and FreeCell) enhance Windows 95's usability and enjoyment.

FRUSTRATION BUSTERS!

- **Security** of access can be controlled on several levels. For instance, you can restrict access according to an accepted password or to a list of persons allowed to log onto your computer.

- **Sharing** of Windows 95 files and devices over a network is handled at several levels as well. You can share with others on your network everything on your computer, or just certain files or devices.

What About the Name?

What is Windows 95? And what was Chicago?

Windows 95 is the official product name of this new major version of Microsoft Windows. It replaces Windows 3.*x* and Windows for Workgroups 3.*x*. Chicago was the code name for the development project that produced the successor to these earlier products. Chicago was used as the name until the official product name, Windows 95, was announced.

What does the name Windows 95 really mean? Does the numbering system mean that Microsoft will release a new version of Windows every year?

No. The version numbers will help give users a sense for the "model year" of their software, in the same way that customers have a sense of the model year of their cars today.

New Features and Enhancements

 ## What is Plug-and-play?

Plug-and-play makes it easier for you to add new hardware to your computer. It is a term for the PC architecture standard developed jointly by leading hardware and software vendors. Hardware labeled Plug-and-play has been built according to these standards. When you add or remove Plug-and-play hardware components and peripheral devices, such as modems, printers, video cards, and so on, the computer automatically recognizes the device (or its absence) and adapts to the new configuration. This eliminates some of the tedious procedures required to install hardware under previous versions of operating systems. Often you were required to manually change jumpers on the device to configure, for example, the IRQ, and then spend hours troubleshooting hardware conflicts.

Full Plug-and-play depends on having the following components:

- A Plug-and-play operating system, such as Windows 95
- A Plug-and-play BIOS on the computer's motherboard
- Plug-and-play hardware devices (when you buy hardware, ask if it is Plug-and-play-compliant)

With Windows 95 you can still get some of the benefits of Plug-and-play without the computer and other hardware being Plug-and-play-compliant, but as you buy new equipment, consider Plug-and-play.

Windows 95 is the first PC operating system that supports Plug-and-play. Information about the installed hardware devices is stored and maintained in the Registry database. When a new device is being added to the system, Windows 95 will check the Registry for available resources, such as IRQs, I/O addresses, and DMA channels and dynamically assign it to the new device, avoiding the possibility of hardware conflicts.

Where are configuration data maintained? (What is the Registry?)

The Registry is the database Windows 95 uses to store and retrieve information about user settings, hardware configurations, installed applications, application file types, and other system information. While there is no single file entitled Registry, there are two files, System.dat and User.dat, that contain the Registry information. You access much of the information in the Registry by opening the Start menu and selecting Settings and then Control Panel. The Control Panel window, shown in Figure 3-1, is displayed. Each category of information contains its own access, such as Keyboard, Mouse, Passwords, Add New Hardware, Multimedia, or Network. Double-click on the icon representing the data you want to change or add to.

FIGURE 3-1   Control Panel, which provides access to the Registry

Windows 95 and Windows 95 applications use the Registry to store configuration and file association information. Whenever a new 32-bit application is installed, its information is stored in the Registry. Whenever a new hardware component is added or removed, or a user makes changes to the desktop, the information goes into the Registry.

Tech Tip: In Windows 3.*x*, this information was stored in multiple .INI files (System.ini, Win.ini, and Progman.ini) plus the application-specific files (Winword.ini, Excel.ini, 123r4.ini, and so on), while the information for OLE was stored in the Reg.dat file. For compatibility purposes, Windows 95 will still maintain the .INI file settings for use by older applications.

The two Registry files, Systems.dat and User.dat, can be directly edited using the Regedit.exe program in the Windows folder. It is strongly recommended that this NOT be done because there is nothing to tell you what you are doing, and you can cause major changes in the behavior of Windows 95.

Tech Tip: If you inadvertently make a change in the Registry files, System.dat and User.dat, you can recover with a backup set of files that Windows 95 maintains, System.da0 and User.da0. Revert to the backup files by renaming the .DAT files to .BAD and then the .DA0 files to .DAT.

What are multitasking and multithreading, which I hear so much about?

Multitasking enables you to run several programs at one time. Multithreading is a technique used to ensure that tasks run in the most efficient way possible without one program degrading the system by taking all the resources.

Windows 95 handles the scheduling of processes to allow multiple applications to run at the same time: multitasking. There are two types of multitasking: cooperative and preemptive. Under cooperative multitasking (implemented in Windows 3.*x*), the system required applications to check the system message queue and to give up control of the system to other running applications. Windows 95 supports cooperative multitasking for 16-bit Windows applications. For 32-bit applications, however, Windows 95 implements preemptive multitasking. In this environment, Windows 95 assigns system time to running applications, preventing a single resource-intensive application from monopolizing the system resources. In Windows 95, the applications do not have to yield to other applications to share resources due to the feature called multithreading. Each 32-bit application can have multiple threads, or distinct units of code that can receive a time slice from the system. A complex application can have several threads processed by the system at the same time through preemptive multitasking. This gives the application more stability and robustness.

What is the Recycle Bin?

The Recycle Bin holds deleted files. Files are placed there automatically when you delete a file in My Computer or Explorer. Figure 3-2 shows the Recycle Bin window. You can also delete files in 32-bit applications like Microsoft Word 7 and

Name	Original Location	Date Deleted	Type
CD06TIF.ZIP	C:\CD6bk	8/10/95 2:59 AM	Zipped
CD11F01.TIF	C:\CD6bk	8/22/95 2:39 AM	Corel F
CD11F02.TIF	C:\CD6bk	8/22/95 2:39 AM	Corel F
Cd11f03.tif	C:\CD6bk	8/22/95 2:39 AM	Corel F
CD11F04.TIF	C:\CD6bk	8/22/95 2:39 AM	Corel F
CD11F05.TIF	C:\CD6bk	8/22/95 2:39 AM	Corel F
CD11F06.TIF	C:\CD6bk	8/22/95 2:39 AM	Corel F
CD11F07.TIF	C:\CD6bk	8/22/95 2:39 AM	Corel F
CD11F08.TIF	C:\CD6bk	8/22/95 2:39 AM	Corel F
CD11F09.TIF	C:\CD6bk	8/22/95 2:39 AM	Corel F
CD11F10.TIF	C:\CD6bk	8/22/95 2:39 AM	Corel F
CD11I01.TIF	C:\CD6bk	8/22/95 2:39 AM	Corel F
CD11I02.TIF	C:\CD6bk	8/22/95 2:39 AM	Corel F
CD11I03.TIF	C:\CD6bk	8/22/95 2:39 AM	Corel F

21 object(s)   3.13MB

FIGURE 3-2   Recycle Bin window allows you to recover deleted files and folders

CorelDRAW! 6, where you can delete files by right-clicking on a file in many dialog boxes, such as Open and Save As, and choosing Delete. Items in the Recycle Bin can be cut, copied, pasted, or dragged to another location; or they can be restored to their original location by double-clicking on the Recycle Bin icon, opening the Edit menu, selecting files to restore, and choosing Undo Delete. The Recycle Bin can easily be emptied when you are sure you want to get rid of its contents by right-clicking on it and choosing Empty Recycle Bin.

Tech Tip: To delete a file without placing it in the Recycle Bin (to save disk space), press SHIFT-DELETE. But be aware that files deleted in this way cannot be restored.

Are there special keyboard shortcuts for the Microsoft Natural keyboard?

Yes. Here is a list containing the shortcut keys for the Microsoft Natural keyboard:

WINDOWS R	Display the Run dialog box
WINDOWS M	Minimize All
WINDOWS SHIFT-M	Undo Minimize All
WINDOWS F1	Open Help
WINDOWS E	Open Windows Explorer
WINDOWS F	Find Files or Folders
WINDOWS CTRL-F	Find Computer
WINDOWS TAB	Cycle through Taskbar buttons
WINDOWS BREAK	Display the System Properties dialog box

Accessibility Features

Where do you access the features for disabled persons?

Windows 95 contains a number of accessibility options to alter the way information is presented visually and aurally and to alter the way the mouse and keyboard are used. You get to it by following these steps:

1. Open the Start menu and select Settings, Control Panel, and then double-click on the Accessibility Options. The Accessibility Properties dialog box is displayed, as shown in Figure 3-3.

2. Select the tab you want:

   ■ **Keyboard** for changing the way the keyboard is used

   ■ **Sound** for having sounds displayed on the screen

   ■ **Display** for making the screen easier to see

   ■ **Mouse** for implementing the mouse on the keyboard

   ■ **General** for overall settings for when the Accessibility Options are used

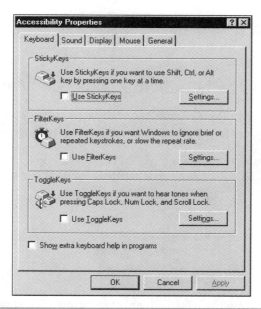

FIGURE 3-3   Accessibility Properties dialog box for persons with disabilities

What are the new features for people with vision problems?

Using the Accessibilities options (Display and Mouse tabs) or the Mouse or Display Control Panels, users who have limited vision or eyestrain when working in windows can

- adjust the size of window titles, scroll bars, menu text, borders, and other standard screen elements.

- pick between two sizes for displaying the standard system font.

- choose one of three sizes for the mouse pointer: normal, large, or extra large. Also, the color can be adjusted or animation added to increase the pointer's visibility.

- select a high-contrast color scheme to optimize the visibility of screen objects, making it easier for users to see them. High-contrast mode has been added for users with low vision who require a high contrast between foreground and background objects so they can distinguish them.

What are the new features for the hearing-impaired?

The Accessibilities Properties dialog box, Sound, and General tabs present features for the hearing impaired that allow you to

- set a global flag to let applications know they want visible feedback instead of or in addition to sound.

- request a blinking title bar or screen flash instead of the system beep.

- support alternative input devices such as headpointers or eyegaze systems.

What is available for tremors or limited hand motion?

The Accessibilities Properties dialog box, Keyboard, and Mouse tabs have options for assisting those with limited hand motion or tremors that allow you to

- press a function key such as SHIFT, CTRL, or ALT with another key, one at a time so that you don't have to press two keys simultaneously. This is called StickyKeys.

- desensitize the keyboard so that tremors do not produce unwanted keystrokes by slowing the rate that a key may be pressed and ignoring repeated keystrokes. This is called FilterKeys.

- toggle the CAPS LOCK, SCROLL LOCK, and NUM LOCK keys to produce a sound when one of those keys is pressed so that you'll know it. This is called ToggleKeys.

- use the numeric keypad on the right of your keyboard to move the mouse pointer on the screen and press the mouse button without using the mouse itself. This is called MouseKeys.

What tools and utilities for my system are included with Windows 95?

Win 95 has the following utilities for system maintenance:

- **System Monitor** Monitors system resources, threads, processor usage, and other system uses.

- **Drive Space** Compresses hard and floppy disks and configures disk drives that you have already compressed using DoubleSpace or DriveSpace.

- **Backup/Restore** Backs up or restores files to tape, floppy disk, and network drives.

- **Disk Defragmenter** Optimizes and speeds up your hard disk.

- **Net Watcher** Monitors network resource usage on your computer.

- **ScanDisk** Checks and repairs your hard drives for logical and physical errors.

Tech Tip: Not all utilities might be installed during Setup. You may have to add them through Add/Remove programs. To do this, click on the Start button, choose Settings, Control Panel, and double-click on Add/Remove Programs.

Enhancements to Previous Versions

Is there a macro recorder, like Windows 3.*x* used to have?

Not anymore. You are expected to use the scripting capabilities of the applications or a third-party batch programming language like WinBatch from Wilson WindowWare in Seattle at (206) 938-1740.

What happened to Paintbrush?

Paintbrush was replaced by Paint, a new 32-bit application. Paint is an OLE server, which allows the creation of OLE object information that can be embedded or linked into other documents. It is also MAPI-enabled, so it is easily integrated with Microsoft Exchange for sending images as e-mail or fax messages.

I keep hearing rumors that Microsoft is working on a portable version of Windows 95 (one that works on multiple processors). Is this true?

No. Microsoft is not working on a portable version of Windows 95. Windows NT is a portable operating system, and it's already available for high-end Intel, MIPS, Alpha, and Clipper machines; it will be available on the PowerPC and other high-end platforms over time.

Windows 95 is optimized for Intel processors and much of its internal code is Intel Assembler, which puts Windows 95 at the heart of today's mainstream line (but dedicates it to the Intel line).

My favorite games require exclusive access to the system. Will Windows 95 be able to handle that?

Most MS-DOS applications can run concurrently with other MS-DOS, Windows 16-bit, and Win32-based applications. There are some MS-DOS applications (mostly games) that require exclusive access to the system. Such applications can be run in MS-DOS mode, which is still Windows 95. It is created by the Virtual Memory Manager as an exclusive operating environment. This mode does not allow multitasking and directs all resources to the MS-DOS application. To run in MS-DOS mode, choose Shut Down from the Start menu and select Restart the computer in MS-DOS mode.

 In Windows 3.x, I could only keep one piece of data on the Clipboard. This is a serious limitation when I need to manipulate multiple portions of documents. Do I still have the same limitation in Windows 95?

Yes and no. You still can retain only one item when you do Copy or Cut. However, Windows 95 provides a new mechanism for temporarily storing "document scraps" on the desktop. These are selected segments of a document that become a separate file when you drag it to the desktop.

To create a document scrap, open the original document and select the text or graphic that you want to copy, and then drag it to the desktop. This will create a "document scrap" on the desktop—a file with the copied piece of data. The item will have a title that includes the words "Document scrap ..." and then the first several words of the copied piece, as seen here:

WordPad
Document
Scrap 'This
section of ...'

You can now drag this scrap to other documents or programs. You can create as many scraps as you want, and you can have not only text scraps, but pictures as well. You can only use this feature if the program used to create the document supports OLE2 drag-and-drop functions. For example, it will work with WordPad and Paint, but not Notepad.

In previous versions of Windows, I was constantly running out of system resources. What improvements have been made to this limitation of the system resources?

While the system resources are still there, much of what was using them up is now handled in other ways. Specifically, much of the code has been moved from 16-bit into 32-bit code, which does not suffer from the 64K limitation. It is very unlikely that you will run out of system resources in Windows 95.

I understand Windows 95 allows drag and drop between applications. Does this mean a new version of OLE is being used, and will "normal" Windows 3.1 applications lose their OLE functionality?

The 16-bit applications will not lose their existing OLE functionality because Windows 95 still runs the 16-bit applications in the same manner that Windows 3.1 did; 32-bit applications will have additional OLE2 functionality that 16-bit applications don't have, such as the ability to create scraps on the desktop.

How does Windows 95 handle memory?

Memory allocation is provided through the Memory Pager and is based on the *demand-paged virtual memory system.* Windows 95 is treating the memory as a flat linear address space that can be accessed through 32-bit addressing. Each process is allocated a virtual address space of 4GB. This virtual memory space is divided into pages. A certain amount of information is stored in memory, and the rest is written back to the temporary storage space on the hard drive, called a *page file* (*swap file* in Windows 3.*x*). When the application needs the information that is stored in this space, the information is paged back to memory. This process is called *demand paging.* Each process is only aware of its own memory, so it cannot accidentally overwrite information paged out by another process. This makes the whole system much more stable. Obviously, the more memory you have, the less disk activity you have for this purpose. Windows 95, therefore, can make good use of lots of memory.

How are the system resources handled by Windows 95?

In Windows 95, system resources are handled by Virtual Machine Manager, which replaced Win386.exe in Windows 3.1.
  Virtual Machine Manager creates an environment in memory called the virtual machine. Each application sees this virtual machine as a separate computer that is running only this one application and dedicating all its resources to it. This allows each application to access all the resources it needs. Each Windows-based application, both 16-bit and 32-bit, run in a single virtual machine called System VM. Each MS-DOS based application runs in its own DOS VM.

What network security features are implemented in Windows 95?

Windows 95 has several security features implemented directly in the system. These features are listed here:

- Logon security can prevent a user from getting access to Windows 95 in two different ways. In a stand-alone system or peer-to-peer network, you can set the Primary Network Logon by opening the Control Panel, double-clicking on Network, and choosing the Configuration tab. In addition, in a client-server network, you can get server validation of the user logging on by opening the System Policy Editor (found on the Windows 95 CD under \Admin\Apptools\Poledit) and choosing Require

Validation By Network For Windows Access. This is an improvement over Windows 3.*x*, where a user could still access Windows even if the server validation failed; he or she was only prevented from accessing the network resources.

- In Windows 95, a user or administrator can enable user-level security. This security level can allow or prevent individual users or groups access to drives on that computer. A list of valid users and passwords is stored on a Windows NT or Novell NetWare server, and the access level for local resources is specified on the actual Windows 95 computer. This feature is accessed through Control Panel, Network, Access Control tab.

- Share-level security allows or restricts access to specific resources, such as printers, disks, folders, and CD-ROM on a computer. The password is assigned when sharing a resource through the Control Panel or Start menu (for Printers), and My Computer or Explorer for disks and folders. This feature is available only in the peer-to-peer environment under Windows 95 or other Microsoft networks, but not under Novell NetWare. This feature is accessed through Control Panel, Network, Access Control tab.

- In Windows 95, a system administrator can define user profiles through the System Policy Editor. In doing so, individual users can be prevented from accessing specific resources on the network or the workstation, and they can be restricted from modifying the system configuration or installing new hardware and software.

Help

How can I learn the basics of Windows 95?

Use Windows 95 Help to learn the basics by clicking on the Start button and choosing Help. You will find an online user's guide, as shown in Figure 3-4. Here you can take a ten-minute tour of Windows 95, get a quick introduction, or find many tips and tricks on its use.

FIGURE 3-4   Windows 95 Help window

How do I use the online help in Windows 95?

In Windows 95, online help is not just context-sensitive, but interactive. You can still hit F1 and get the help that is appropriate for the situation you are in, but the Help in Windows 95 goes a step further. In many Help windows, you will find a "Click here . . ." button that will walk you through the necessary steps to complete the task and take you to the necessary location.

You can resolve a lot of your problems and issues by going into Help, selecting the Index tab, and typing the word "troubleshooting." This will take you to a menu with different troubleshooting scenarios. For example, if you are having problems printing, you can select "Troubleshooting, Printing . . ." and it will present you with an interactive printing troubleshooting guide (as you can see in Figure 3-5), which will step you through different troubleshooting steps. You will be able to quickly resolve the majority of common problems without having to call technical support or your friendly computer guru.

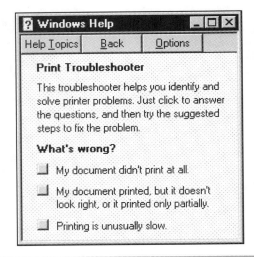

FIGURE 3-5 Troubleshooting using Help can solve many of your problems

Is there a way I can view the online help in the old Windows 3.1 way?

When first launching Help, seeing the books and chapters of the contents tab view but no search engine may be disconcerting, but click on the Index tab and the search feature is there, looking very much like the default Help view of the Windows 3.1 online help.

How can I get more information about Windows 95?

For more information about Microsoft Windows 95, take a look on most major online services and networks.
    The following list tells how to access this information.

- On the Internet, use the World Wide Web (http://www.microsoft.com).

- On the Microsoft Network, open Computers and choose Software, Software Companies, Microsoft, Windows 95.

- On CompuServe, type **go winnews**.

- On Prodigy, type **jump winnews**.

- On America Online, use the keyword **winnews**.
- On GEnie, download files from the WinNews area under the Windows RTC.

What keyboard shortcuts are used in Windows 95?

Appendix B contains the shortcut keys used in Windows 95.

Hardware Considerations

Will Windows 95 and Windows NT share the same device drivers?

Generally not, since Windows 95 and Windows NT have different device driver models. However, since both products support a modular, layered device driver architecture, there are areas of substantial synergy. For example, SCSI miniport adapters for Windows NT will be binary-compatible with Windows 95, as will printer drivers and NDIS drivers for Windows NT.

Can I use Windows 95 with an IDE hard drive larger than 540MB?

Windows 95 will work on a hard drive over 540MB capacity in any of the following conditions:

- Your PC's ROM BIOS supports Logical Block Addressing (LBA).
- Your hard disk controller supports LBA or geometry translation.
- You only use the first 1024 cylinders of the drive.
- You have a vendor-provided real-mode driver for geometry translation.

If you are using any of the first three options listed previously, you can take advantage of the Windows 95 protected-mode IDE disk driver, ESDI_506.PDR, which allows the use of 32-bit disk access. With the last option, 32-bit disk access is available through ESDI_506.PDR only if you have OnTrack Disk Manager's XBIOS drivers version 7.0 and above.

I have a lot of serial devices that I used to run with my DOS sessions. Are there any limits on the number of ports supported by Windows 95?

In Windows 95 there are actually more ports supported than in the previous versions of Windows. The actual number of ports with which Windows 95 can communicate is 128 serial and 128 parallel.

Can I have a RAM Disk in Windows 95? How do I use it?

Sure you can. Do the following:

- Edit your Config.sys file to create a RAM drive by adding the line: Device=c:\Windows\Ramdrive.sys. This will create a 64K RAM drive and assign the next available drive letter to it. If you have enough memory available, you can specify a bigger size, for example: Device=c:\Windows\Ramdrive.sys 256. This is still a very small area to serve as a temporary disk—2MB are needed in many instances to be effective.

Tech Tip: The purpose of a RAM drive is to give you a very fast disk by using RAM as temporary disk storage. However, this takes away from the memory you have available and can slow your programs, depending on the memory you have. So use with caution.

- To create a RAM drive in expanded memory, use the /E switch, as in: Device=c:\Windows\Ramdrive.sys /E

- After rebooting your computer, you will see the new drive in the My Computer or Windows Explorer.

After all the great things I've heard about Windows 95, I heard that these improvements will be available only if I am running 32-bit applications. Is this true?

It is true that 32-bit protected-mode applications will utilize the robustness of Windows 95 to the full extent. However, Windows 95 has made important changes in the way that 16-bit applications are handled. Although 16-bit applications are still run very similarly to the way Windows 3.1 ran them (in the same memory space so they can see each other, or their OLE functionality would no longer exist), Windows 95 has improved cleaning up after the 16-bit applications. That is, while any 16-bit application is running, Windows 95 cannot track what resources are being used; once all 16-bit applications are closed, Windows 95 will go in, clean up the memory, and release any system resources the 16-bit applications may not have released. But during the execution of any 16-bit application, Windows 95 cannot clean up these resources, and the 16-bit applications will continue to use and not release the resources.

What is the cluster size on a disk under Windows 95?

The cluster size for storing data on a disk is the same as for MS-DOS 6.*x* and Windows 3.*x*, which can be up to 32KB, depending on the size of the logical partition. The sectors are 512 bytes in size.

Setting Up, Customizing, and Optimizing Windows 95

A basic human trait is that different people like different things. That is as true with computers as with anything else. Windows 95 provides more accommodation for this facet of our nature than any previous operating system. Almost everything that you find in the Control Panel represents a way that you can set up, customize, or optimize Windows 95. These control panels allow you to set up your mail system, modem, network, and printer; customize how your keyboard, mouse, and display behave; as well as optimize how you use your file system and memory. In the Display control panel alone, you can change not only the color of the screen and the type of wallpaper displayed but also the size, color, and font used in windows and their components like title bars, scroll bars, and message boxes.

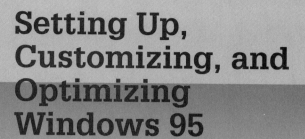

FRUSTRATION BUSTERS!

The principal way that you can change your system is through the Control Panel, which you can open by selecting Settings Control Panel from the Start menu. The options you have in your Control Panel will depend on what Windows 95 components you installed during setup. Some of the more common options and their function are described in Table 4-1.

Icon	Name	Function
Accessibility Options	Accessibility Options	Allows you to customize the keyboard, mouse, display, and use of sound to compensate for various disabilities
Add New Hardware	Add New Hardware	Leads you through the configuration of your system to accommodate the adding and removing of hardware
Add/Remove Programs	Add/Remove Programs	Provides the means to install or uninstall application programs, to add or remove Windows 95 components, and to create a Windows 95 Startup disk
Date/Time	Date/Time	Allows you to set the current date and time that are being maintained in your computer and to identify your time zone
Display	Display	Enables the selection of patterns and wallpaper to be used on your desktop; the screen saver you want to use; the appearance of your screen, including colors, sizes, and fonts; and the resolution and number of colors that are used in your display
Fonts	Fonts	Displays the fonts currently installed on your computer and provides the means to add and remove fonts
Keyboard	Keyboard	Allows the changing of the sensitivity, the language that is implemented, and the type of keyboard that Windows 95 thinks you are using

TABLE 4-1   Control Panel Options

Icon	Name	Function
Mail and Fax	Mail and Fax	Provides the means to configure the Microsoft Exchange and its Internet Mail, Microsoft Mail, Microsoft Fax, and Microsoft Network services
Microsoft Mail Postoffice	Microsoft Mail Postoffice	Enables the establishment and maintenance of a Microsoft Mail Postoffice for the immediate workgroup
Modems	Modems	Leads you through the configuration of your modem(s)
Mouse	Mouse	Provides the means to determine the use of the mouse buttons, the speed of double-clicking, the type of mouse pointers, the motion of the mouse pointer on the screen, and type of mouse you are using
Multimedia	Multimedia	Allows the selection and configuration of audio, video, MIDI, CD, and other multimedia devices
Network	Network	Allows for the configuration of your network components, the identification of your workstation, and the type of access you want to allow to your files
Passwords	Passwords	Allows you to change your logon password and the passwords used in other services, to enable the remote administration of your computer, and to determine if everyone using your computer will use the same preferences
Printers	Printers	Leads you through the setting up and sharing of a new printer, as well as providing for the management of the work waiting to be printed
Regional Settings	Regional Settings	Provides for the setting of your preferences for number, currency, date, and time formatting
Sounds	Sounds	Enables the association of sounds with events such as the receipt of mail and exiting Windows
System	System	Allows you to manage and optimize your hardware resources

TABLE 4-1   Control Panel Options (*continued*)

Changing Your Display

How can I change the fonts used on my desktop?

Use the following steps to change the fonts used in Windows:

1. Right-click on the desktop and choose Properties to open the Display Properties dialog box. Then click on the Appearance tab, which is shown in Figure 4-1.

2. In the Item list, choose the desktop element that you want to change the font for (Icon, Title Bar, and so on); and in the Font list, choose the font you want.

Tech Tip: You can also change the size, color, and style (whether it's bold or italic) of each font used on the desktop.

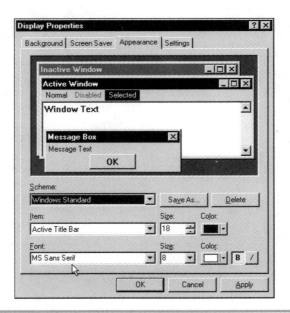

FIGURE 4-1   Change your desktop fonts in the Display Properties dialog box

What is an easy way for me to customize my desktop—change colors, wallpaper, screen savers?

All are easily changed! Right-click on an empty spot on the desktop and choose Properties. This will open the Display Properties dialog box. In the Background tab you can set the pattern or wallpaper that you want to use. In the Appearance tab that you saw in Figure 4-1, you can change the color of your desktop, and in the Screen Saver tab you can choose which you want to use.

How do I change the wait time before my screen saver kicks in?

To change the characteristics of your screen saver, do the following:

1. Right-click on the desktop, select Properties, and click on the Screen Saver tab.

2. In the Screen Saver list, choose the screen saver you want.

3. If the screen saver offers it, click on the Settings button and complete the options for configuring that type of screen saver.

4. In the Wait spinner, pick the time you want the system to wait before the screen saver appears.

5. If you want to protect access to the computer by using a password to turn off the screen saver, make sure the Password protected box is checked and click on the Change button to specify the password.

6. Click on the Preview button to test the screen saver and click on OK when done.

I am trying to use the Pipes screen saver from Windows NT. It says that I need the Opengl32.dll file. Where do I find this?

Support for OpenGL is not shipped with Microsoft Windows 95. OpenGL for Windows 95 will be available separately as a set of redistributable .DLL files. You can download them from Microsoft online forums (Internet: http://www.microsoft.com; ftp://ftp.microsoft.com; and CompuServe: Go MSWIN95, among others).

How can I create my own background (wallpaper)?

You can create your own Windows wallpaper with your company's logo or any graphics that you want using the Paint program with the following instructions:

1. Click on the Start button, choose Programs, and click on Accessories.

2. Click on Paint and create an image or Open an existing bitmap image (files ending with .BMP, .PCX, and .TIF, among others) for the background that you want.

3. Open the File menu, choose Save As, and give a name to your new background.

4. Choose File, select either Set as Wallpaper (Centered) or Set as Wallpaper (Tiled), and it will replace your current background with your new one.

I have seen animated cursors in NT. How can I get this for Windows 95?

Animated cursors are available in Microsoft Plus! However, you need protected-mode disk drivers and a Windows 95-compatible version display driver running at 256 or more colors that uses the device-independent bitmap (DIB) engine. Animated cursors are not supported with the following display types: ATI Ultra (mach8), Diamond Viper, Standard display adapter (VGA), and Super VGA.

How can I make sure I am using protected-mode disk drivers?

You can determine if you are using protected-mode disk drivers with these steps:

1. From the Start menu choose Settings, Control Panel, and then double-click on System.

2. Open the Performance tab, click on File System, and choose the Troubleshooting tab.

3. If you have NOT checked Disable all 32 bit protect-mode disk drivers, as you can see in Figure 4-2, you are using protected-mode drivers.

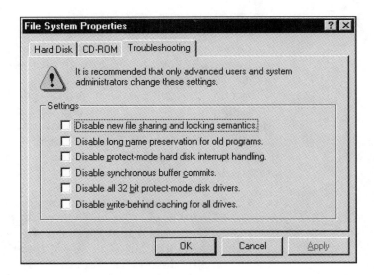

FIGURE 4-2   You are using protected-mode disk drivers if Disable all 32 bit protect-mode disk drivers is not checked

How can I get files and folders on my desktop?

Very simply—drag them there from either My Computer or Explorer. Use these two steps:

1. Open My Computer or the Explorer and locate the file or folder you want to move.

2. Drag the file or folder to an empty spot on the desktop.

Tech Tip: When you drag a file or folder to the desktop, unless the file is a program, you will physically move the file or folder from its original folder to the desktop ("folder"). If what you really want is a copy on the desktop, then press and hold CTRL while dragging the object. You should also consider a third alternative, placing a shortcut on the desktop that points to a file or folder.

What is a shortcut, and how do I use it to start programs from the desktop?

A *shortcut* is a very small file that represents or points to a usually much larger file or a folder in another location. A shortcut is useful because you can use it to remotely start a program, open a data file, or open a folder. For example, if you have an application that you use often, you can place a shortcut to that application on the desktop and start the application by double-clicking on the shortcut, all the while leaving the application program file in its original folder.

To create a shortcut on the desktop, use one of the following techniques:

■ If you want a shortcut of a program file (one with an .EXE or .COM extension), all you have to do is drag the program file to the desktop or wherever else you want the shortcut and one will automatically be created for you. The original program file will remain where it was originally.

■ Press and hold *both* CTRL and SHIFT while dragging any file or folder to the desktop, and a shortcut will be created for you. Make sure you release CTRL-SHIFT before you release the mouse button.

- Right-drag the file or folder to the desktop and select Create Shortcut(s) Here from the popup menu that appears.

- Right-click on the file or folder, select Create Shortcut from the popup menu, and drag the shortcut to the desktop.

How can I change the icons for the folders I have placed on my desktop?

If you drag the original folder or file to the desktop, you cannot change its icon. To work around this, create a shortcut for the folder or file, pick the icon you want for it, and place the shortcut on the desktop, rather than the original folder itself. To change an icon for a shortcut:

1. Right-click on the icon, and choose Properties.

2. Click on the Shortcut tab, and then click on the Change Icon button, as you can see in Figure 4-3.

3. Enter or browse for the file in which you want to search for an icon, and then select an icon, as you see here:

Tech Tip: You can find Windows 95 default icons in the \Windows\System\Shell32.dll, in \Windows\System\Iconlib.dll, and in \Windows\Moricons.dll.

 ## I want to change the name of the My Computer icon. How can I rename the icons on my desktop?

To rename desktop items, do the following:

1. Click on the item you want to rename (for example, My Computer).

2. Press F2, and just type the new name that you like (for example, Bob's Computer).

 **Tech Tip:** Using the above steps, you can rename My Computer, Network Neighborhood, Inbox, My Briefcase, and The Microsoft Network desktop icons. You cannot rename the Recycle Bin.

How do I get rid of the Network Neighborhood icon on a PC that is not networked?

It is not simple to get rid of the Network Neighborhood. You cannot just delete the icon from the desktop or drag it to your Recycle Bin. You can turn it off using the System Policy Editor, which you can find on the Windows 95 CD in the \Admin\Apptools\Poledit\ folder as Poledit.exe. Use the following steps:

1. Double-click on \Admin\Apptools\Poledit\Poledit.exe on the Windows 95 CD and open the default template, Admin.adm, when you are asked which template you want to use.

2. From the File menu, choose Open Registry, and then double-click on Local User.

3. Click on the plus sign opposite Shell to open it and then the plus sign opposite Restrictions.

4. Click on Hide Network Neighborhood to enable it, as shown in Figure 4-4. Click on OK and then close the System Policy Editor. You'll need to reboot for the icon to go away.

I want my printer shortcut to be on the right side of the screen. I drag the icon there, but it snaps back to its position on the left. What can I do?

The icons are being automatically rearranged by Windows 95. Right-click on the desktop, choose Arrange Icons from the popup menu, and then click on AutoArrange to turn the check mark off. Without AutoArrange, the icons will remain wherever you drag them.

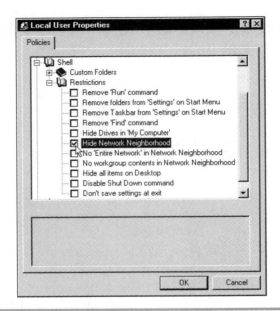

FIGURE 4-4   The System Policy Editor can be used to customize some elements of your desktop

I have chosen 800 x 600 small fonts, yet my fonts and icons are not as small as I expect them. What could be causing this and how can I change it?

Most probably, one of the Accessibility options, High Contrast, has been enabled. To turn off this feature:

1. Click on the Start button, choose Settings and Control Panel, and double-click on Accessibility Options.

2. Select Display tab, as shown in the following illustration, and clear the Use High Contrast check box.

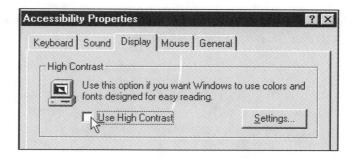

 ## Can I modify the Windows 95 Logoff screens?

There are two bitmap files in the \Windows folder that are used during logoff. Logow.sys is the "Wait while shutting down..." screen, and Logos.sys is the "You may now safely turn..." screen. Both are normal bitmaps. Back them up (right-click on them, choose Copy, right-click on white space in the Windows folder, and choose Paste), and modify them with Paint, opened from the Start menu under Programs Accessories. Figure 4-5 shows Logos.sys being modified. Be sure to save the modified files under the original names. Windows will then use them when shutting down.

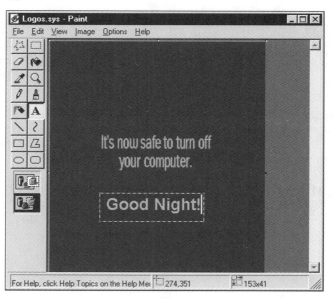

FIGURE 4-5   Paint can modify the Windows 95 logoff screens

How can I easily change screen resolution in Windows 95?

Screen resolution is the result of the number of pixels used to cover your screen and the number of colors that can be displayed. Standard VGA, the minimum for Windows 95, is 640 x 480 pixels and 16 or 256 colors (8-bit). A higher resolution, sometimes called Super VGA, is 800 x 600 pixels and 16- or 24-bit color. You can change screen resolution in the Display properties dialog box with these steps:

1. Right-click on the desktop for the popup menu, and choose Properties to open the Display Properties dialog box.

2. Click on the Settings tab. Then change the pixel density (Desktop area) and the number of colors (Color palette) to get the resolution you want, as shown in Figure 4-6.

> **Tech Tip:** The display and display adapter that you are using will determine the resolutions that you can use.

Taskbar

What customization can I do to the Taskbar?

You can customize the Taskbar by right-clicking on an empty area of the Taskbar and choosing Properties. The Taskbar

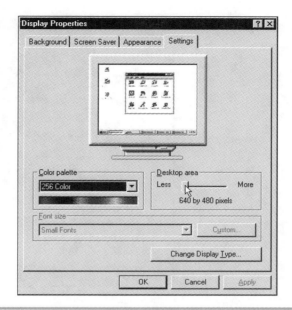

FIGURE 4-6 You can change your display's resolution in the Display Properties dialog box

Properties dialog box will open as shown in Figure 4-7. Here you can control four attributes of the Taskbar, as follows:

- **Always on top** prevents the Taskbar from being covered by other windows. If this is turned off, then maximizing a window would cover the Taskbar.

- **Auto hide** will hide the Taskbar until you move the mouse pointer to the edge of the screen containing the Taskbar, and then the Taskbar will appear.

Tech Tip: Always on top must be enabled for Auto hide to work with maximized windows.

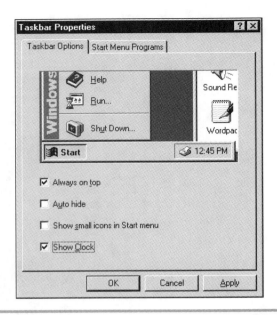

FIGURE 4-7   The Taskbar can be customized in the Taskbar Properties dialog box

- ■ **Show small icons in Start menu** allows you to contain more options in the Start menu.
- ■ **Show Clock** turns the display of the clock in the Taskbar on and off.

In addition to the Taskbar Properties dialog box, you can customize the position and size of the Taskbar, as you will see from the next question.

How do I change the location and size of the Taskbar?

You can drag the Taskbar to any of the four sides of the screen, and you can drag an edge of the Taskbar to size it. Use these steps:

1. Point on a blank area of the Taskbar, hold down the left mouse button, and drag the Taskbar to another edge of the screen. For example, Figure 4-8 shows the Taskbar on the right edge of the screen.

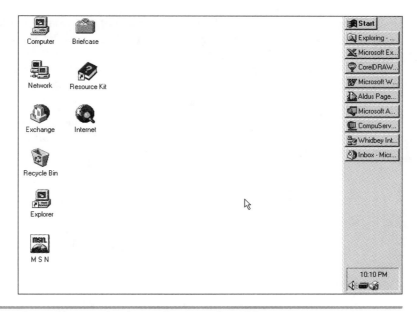

FIGURE 4-8   The Taskbar can be dragged to any edge of the screen

2. Resize the Taskbar by moving the mouse pointer to the inside edge of the Taskbar. When the pointer becomes a double arrow, drag the mouse pointer in or out to size the Taskbar as you desire. You can see a three-task-high Taskbar in Figure 4-9.

How can I add options to my Start menu?

The top part of the Start menu can contain options that you place there to start applications and/or open folders, as shown in Figure 4-10. You can place options on the Start menu in three ways:

■ Drag files and/or folders from My Computer or Explorer to the Start button on the Taskbar. This will automatically create a shortcut, place the shortcut in the \Windows\Start Menu folder, and an option named after the shortcut will appear on the Start menu.

■ Right-click on a vacant area of the Taskbar, choose Properties, and open the Start Menu Programs tab. Click on Add, browse for the program file of the program you want on the Start menu, click on Next, click on Start Menu and on Next again, type the name you want to use on the Start menu, and click on Finish.

■ Open the Explorer and locate the file or folder in the right window that you want to add to the Start menu. In the left window of the Explorer, click on the plus sign opposite the Windows folder and then scroll the list of folders until you can see the Start Menu folder. If the option you want to add is a program, simply drag it to the Start Menu folder. A shortcut will be created in the Start Menu folder. For other types of files, press and hold both CTRL and SHIFT while dragging the file to the Start menu.

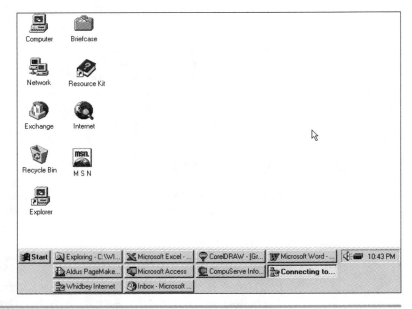

FIGURE 4-9   You can size the Taskbar by dragging its inside edge

| Access |
| Collage |
| CorelDRAW |
| Excel |
| Explorer |
| PageMaker |
| Wincim |
| WinWord |
| WinZip |

FIGURE 4-10   The Start menu can contain options to start your applications

 ## How can I turn off the clock on my Taskbar?

The clock is controlled in the Taskbar Properties dialog box. Use these steps to turn it off:

1. Right-click on an empty spot on the Taskbar and choose Properties.
2. Click the Taskbar Options tab, and clear the Show Clock check box to disable it. Choose OK.

Tech Tip: You can set the clock (set the system time, date, and time zone) by double-clicking on the clock in the Taskbar.

Tech Tip: If you hold the mouse pointer over the Taskbar clock, you can see the date displayed, as shown here:

Wednesday, September 06, 1995

11:45 PM

Customizing the way you use Windows 95

Can I bypass the Windows 95 startup logo?

Yes. You can turn off the logo by adding an entry to a file named Msdos.sys in your root folder. Msdos.sys, though is a hidden, read-only file, so you must go through some extra steps. Do so with these instructions:

1. In the Explorer, open the View menu and choose Options. In the View menu, choose Show all files, as you see in Figure 4-11.

2. Also in the Explorer, locate and right-click on the file Msdos.sys (NOT Msdos.dos) in the root folder of your boot drive, and choose Properties to open the Msdos.sys Properties dialog box.

3. Click on the Read-only and Hidden check boxes to turn them off, and then click on OK.

4. Make a copy of Msdos.sys to serve as a backup by right-clicking on Msdos.sys, choosing Copy, right-clicking on an open area of the right pane of the Explorer in the root folder, and choosing Paste. You can either leave the name Copy of Msdos.sys or change it to some other name like Msdos0.sys.

5. Right-click on Msdos.sys, choose Open With, scroll the list of programs, and double-click on Notepad, with which you will edit the file.

6. Locate the section entitled Options and add the line **Logo=0** like the one shown in Figure 4-12.

7. Choose Save As from Notepad's File menu, change the name to Msdos.sys (remove the "0"), and click on Save. Close Notepad and reboot your computer. You will no longer see the Windows 95 logo.

Tech Tip: If you change your mind, changing the line to read Logo=1 or removing it altogether will enable the logo again.

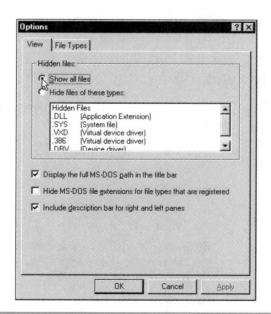

FIGURE 4-11   To display all your files, use the Explorer's View menu Options dialog box

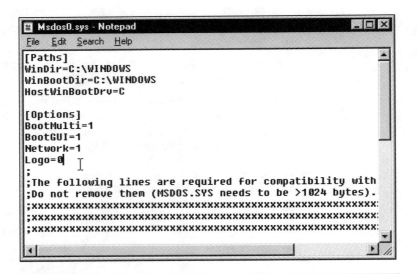

FIGURE 4-12   The file Msdos.sys provides some startup parameters to Windows 95

How can I get my old Windows 3.1 Program Manager to be easily available?

To get easy access to the Windows 3.1 Program Manager, do the following:

1. Click on the Start button, choose Settings, and click on Taskbar.

2. Click on the Start Menu Programs tab and click on Add.

3. Click on the Browse button and double-click on the \Windows folder.

4. In the \Windows folder, scroll down past the folders to the program files, select Progman.exe, click on the Open button, and click on Next.

5. Click on Start Menu to select it as the folder where you want to place the Progman shortcut, and then click on Next.

6. Type the full name **program manager**, click on Finish, and then click on OK. Now when you click on the Start button, the Program Manager option will be available.

Tech Terror: The Program Manager is a 16-bit application; by using it, you give up many of the features of Windows 95—most importantly, long filenames. You'll notice that the Rename option is gone from the File menu for this reason and you can't click twice on a name in a Program Manager to change it. You also can't drag a file from the Program Manager to the desktop, My Computer, or the Explorer.

I need to exclude a certain area in upper memory. How do I do this in Windows 95?

Upper memory is the area between 640KB and 1MB. It is used for many purposes, including your ROM BIOS and video memory. Some of it can and should be used for the storage of Windows 95 itself, but you may want to prevent Windows 95 from loading into a certain area so you can use it for some other purpose. To do that, use the following steps:

1. Right-click on My Computer and choose Properties. The System Properties dialog box will open. (This is the same dialog box you get when you open the System control panel.)

2. Click on the Device Manager tab, and then double-click on Computer. The Computer Properties dialog box will open, as shown in Figure 4-13.

3. Click on the Reserve Resources tab and select Memory.

4. Click on the Add button and type your Exclude range. Click on OK three times to close the various dialog boxes you opened.

How do I get rid of the list of files under the Documents menu under Start?

To clear the files in the Documents menu, do the following:

1. Right-click on a blank area of the Taskbar and choose Properties.

2. Click on the Start Menu Programs tab.

3. Click on the Clear button in the Documents Menu section of the dialog box.

How can I get my file extensions back? Just seeing the files and icons confuses me.

Use the following steps to show file extensions:

1. Open the Explorer's or My Computer's View menu and choose Options.

2. In the View tab, uncheck the box Hide MS-DOS file extensions for the file types that are registered.

3. Click on OK.

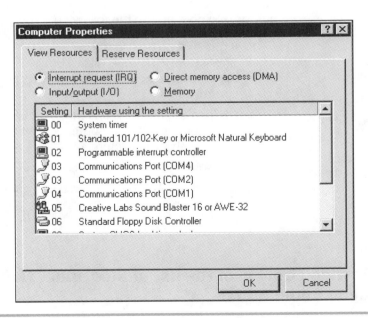

FIGURE 4-13   The Computer Properties dialog box allows you to view and reserve computer resources

How can I drag a screen and still see the contents of the screen? I don't want just the outside of the window.

This is a feature called Full Screen Drag and Drop. It is available in Microsoft Plus! as part of its visual enhancements. Many vendors are shipping Microsoft Plus! along with Windows 95. You can also buy it as an add-on.

Working with Programs

What are the techniques I can use to start my programs?

You can use several techniques to start your programs, depending on how frequently you use them. Some of the most common options are to place shortcuts to your programs in the following locations (see the discussion earlier in this chapter on creating shortcuts):

Tech Tip:
Objects on the desktop get covered by open windows and you cannot use ALT-TAB to reach them. You can right-click on the Taskbar and select Minimize All Windows to see your desktop and then right-click again on the Taskbar and select Undo Minimize All.

- **Directly on the desktop** by dragging the shortcut there. The shortcuts will remain where you drag them until you move or delete them.

- **On the Start menu** by dragging the program files there. Up to 12 programs can be placed on the Start menu itself. (See the discussion on this earlier in this chapter.)

- **In a folder on the desktop** by creating a new folder there and dragging shortcuts to it. If you leave the folder open, the shortcuts will be available at all times and you can ALT-TAB to the folder from any other program.

- **In the Programs menu** by dragging shortcuts in the Explorer to the \Windows\Start Menu\Programs folder, either directly or to a new or an existing subfolder to group the programs. When you group them, you get to them by opening the Start menu, selecting Programs, and then the group.

- **In the StartUp folder** by dragging shortcuts in the Explorer to the \Windows\Start Menu\Programs\StartUp folder. Programs in the StartUp folder are automatically started when Windows 95 is started.

How do I remove an item from the Start menu on a local computer?

To edit the Start menu, do the following:

1. Click on Start, choose Settings, and click on Taskbar.

2. Click on the Start Menu Programs tab, and click on the Remove button. A list of Shortcuts and Folders in the Start menu will be displayed, as you can see in Figure 4-14.

3. Select the shortcut or folder you want to remove and then click on Remove.

FIGURE 4-14   Removing items from the Start menu

The program folders are listed alphabetically under Start, Programs. Is there any way I can change the order?

Yes. To reorder them, you can rename the folders with a number on the left of the name. With such a number, the folders will be sorted by number rather than alphabetically.

Use the following steps to rearrange the order of the folders:

1. Right-click on the Start button and choose Open.

2. Double-click on Programs. Every folder in this group appears under Start, Programs.

3. Click once on the folder you want to appear on the top of the list.

4. Press F2 to rename and type **1.** in front of the name.

5. Repeat this for the rest of the folders. For example, if you want the Microsoft Office folder to appear first, click on it once, press F2, and type **1.** in front of the "Microsoft Office" label.

How can I have a program load automatically when I start Windows 95?

Use the following steps to load a program when Windows 95 starts:

1. Click on the Start button, choose Settings, and click on Taskbar.

2. Click on the Start Menu Programs tab, and then click on the Add button.

3. If you don't know the exact filename of the application, click on Browse, select the item you need, and click on Open.

4. In the Create Shortcut window, click on Next.

5. In the Select Program Folder window, select the \Start Menu\Programs\StartUp folder. Then click on Next.

6. In the Select a Title for the Program window, type a name for the shortcut, and click on Finish.

7. Click on OK to complete the task. The program will automatically start the next time you start Windows.

Can I uninstall a program?

If you installed an application with the "Developed for Windows 95" logo on it, you can uninstall it using the Add/Remove Programs control panel. This will remove the application and all its files. Try that next with these steps:

1. Open the Start menu and select Settings, Control Panel; then double-click on the Add/Remove Programs icon.

2. Select the Install/Uninstall tab.

3. Select the program to be uninstalled, as shown in Figure 4-15, and click on Remove.

4. Click on OK.

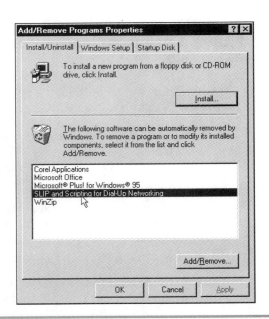

FIGURE 4-15   Windows 95-compliant applications can be uninstalled in the Add/Remove programs control panel

I installed Windows 95 in a folder other than Windows 3.1. Can I convert my Windows 3.1 program groups to the Windows 95 folders?

Yes. Do the following:

1. Click on the Start button and choose Run.
2. Type **grpconv /m.**
3. Select the group you want to convert.
4. Click on Open and then click on Yes in the Program Manager Group Converter dialog box. Close the Select a Group to Convert dialog box when you are done.

You can also convert the group by double-clicking on the group name.

How do I add command line switches to shortcuts for applications that are on my desktop?

Use the following steps to add command line switches to a shortcut:

1. Open the shortcut's Properties dialog box by right-clicking on the shortcut and choosing Properties.
2. Click on the Shortcut tab.
3. In the Target box, you should see the command line that is run when the icon is double-clicked. Add the switches to this line.

For example, to run Word for Windows with the /n switch so that it doesn't automatically open up a new document, you would put the following entry in the "Target:" line: **C:\Msoffice\Winword\Winword.exe /n**.

How do I create a program group in Windows 95?

In Windows 95, a program group is nothing more than a folder in the \Windows\Start Menu\Programs folder. To create a new group, use the following steps:

1. Right-click on the Start button, and choose Open.

2. Double-click on Programs folder. Here are all your program groups.

3. Right-click inside the folder, choose New, and click on Folder. This creates a new group, as shown in Figure 4-16. You can rename it to the name you want and drag to it the shortcuts you want there.

FIGURE 4-16   A folder in the \Windows\Start Menu\Programs folder is a program group

How do I assign a hot key to quickly launch an application?

You can assign a hot key to any shortcut. Use the next set of steps to do this:

1. Right-click on the Shortcut icon and choose Properties.

2. Click on the Shortcut tab, click in the Shortcut key box, and press a key combination you want to use for the shortcut key.

3. Click on OK to complete the operation.

How do I create a file association in Windows 95?

A file association relates a data file to a program that can open it, so that you can double-click on the file in the My Computer or Explorer and it will launch the application, which in turn will load the file. To create file association, use these steps:

1. Open My Computer, open the View menu, and choose Options.

2. Click on the File Types tab and on New Type. The Add New File Type dialog box will open.

3. Enter the description and extension, and click on New under Actions.

4. Type **open** for the Action and then click on Browse to find the application to associate with the file type. Click on OK and then Close to complete the process.

How can I specify a working folder for a program?

You cannot change the working folder for the original file in Windows 95—it must be done from within the program itself. However, you can create a shortcut to the original file and specify the working folder in the Properties. See the discussion earlier in this chapter on how to create a shortcut. Use the following steps to specify the working folder for a shortcut:

1. Right-click on the shortcut and choose Properties from the popup menu.
2. Click on the Shortcut tab.
3. Enter the working folder in the Start in text box.

Tech Tip: Many applications, such as Microsoft Word for Windows, that have the capability within them to specify a working folder will override the specification in the shortcut.

 I want to run a program minimized in the background at all times, but I don't want to have to manually minimize it every time it starts. How can I have a program load automatically and run minimized when I start Windows 95?

First you must place a program in the StartUp folder, as described earlier, so that the program will be automatically started when Windows 95 boots. Then follow these instructions to have it minimized:

1. After placing a program in the StartUp folder, click on the Start button, choose Settings, and click on Taskbar.
2. Click on the Start Menu Programs tab and click on the Advanced button.
3. Double-click on the Programs folder and open the StartUp folder.
4. Right-click on the program you need and choose Properties.
5. Click on the Shortcut tab and select Minimize in the Run drop-down list.
6. Click on OK and exit. the program will now start up minimized.

Video Drivers

How can I change my video driver?

To change your video driver, use the following steps:

1. Click on the Start button, choose Settings, and click on the Control Panel.
2. Double-click on the Display icon and then click on the Settings tab.
3. Click on the Change Display Type button.
4. Click on the Change button in the Adapter Type box, and then click on the Have Disk button in the Select Device window.
5. Specify the path to the disk or folder containing the driver that you would like to use.
6. Select the driver to use from the list and click on OK to install.

I thought that when I change my display driver in Windows 95 I would no longer have to restart my computer to have the change take effect. Aren't these changes dynamic?

They will only be dynamic if you don't change the color palette. If the color palette is changed, then a new driver file will have to be loaded, and hence the system needs to configure the color scheme based on what is available now with the newly installed driver.

Disk Drives

My hard drive space is compressed with a third-party compression package. I wanted to partition using Fdisk to create an extra logical drive, but Fdisk shows only half of the disk space I can see using the DIR command. How can I modify partitions?

If you installed a disk compression program from Microsoft or another vendor, Fdisk displays only the uncompressed, not the compressed, size of the drives. In some instances Fdisk cannot delete partitions created by third-party applications. You will have to use that application to delete or modify that partition.

I want to have my swap file on drive D. How do I change the location of the swap file?

To change the location, do the following:

1. Right-click on My Computer and choose Properties.
2. Click on the Performance tab and click on the Virtual Memory button.
3. Select Let me specify my own virtual memory settings. Then, opposite Hard disk, select the drive you want to use, as shown in Figure 4-17. Make sure to indicate that the Maximum size is the total amount of free space on the drive. Windows will then dynamically manage the swap file, and it will grow and shrink as needed.

Tech Terror: Under most circumstances, Windows 95 can do a better job of real-time management of your swap file than you can. So you should not need to take over that function.

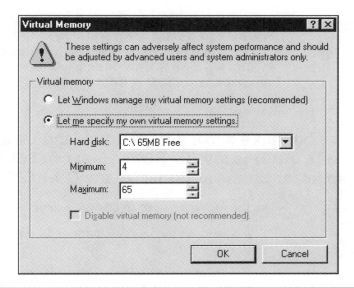

FIGURE 4-17   The Virtual Memory dialog box lets you specify the drive and amount of space to be dedicated to a swap file or virtual memory

How do I change the partitions on the hard drive?

The functionality for this did not change from DOS and Windows 3.*x*. Unlike Windows NT, you cannot adjust the partitions or create volume sets in Windows 95. You still have to use Fdisk to create partitions. See discussions in Chapter 2 on the use of Fdisk.

How do I use Windows 95 with SyQuest Drives?

In order to enable the support, one has to put **RemovableIDE=True** in the 386Enh section of the System.ini file. If this line is not there, then Windows 95's protected-mode IDE driver will not load. When the line mentioned here is added to the 386Enh section of System.ini, the Ios.log file will disappear, and the Windows 95 file system will provide 32-bit support for your SyQuest.

The other requirements for this support are that the SyQuest drive must have a formatted cartridge inserted when Windows

95 starts, and there must not be another 32-bit module loaded in System.ini such as the one provided by DTC for their IDE boards.

There is another setting called "Virtual Memory" in Windows 95. This will be in "MS-DOS compatibility mode" if C: drive is a removable drive, SCSI or IDE.

I have bought a second hard drive, and I want it to be drive D, but D is my CD-ROM. How can I change the drive letter that is assigned to my CD-ROM?

Use the following steps to change a drive letter:

1. Click on Start, choose Settings, and then click on Control Panel.

2. Double-click on the System icon.

3. Click on the Device Manager tab.

4. Click on the plus sign next to CDROM and select your CD-ROM, click on Properties, and click on the Settings tab.

5. In the Reserved drive letters section, you can set Start drive letter and End drive letter to be the drive letter you want the CD-ROM to use, as you can see in Figure 4-18. Set it the way you want, then click on the OK button.

6. Reboot the computer. The CD-ROM will have the new letter. Remember, however, if you had some applications already installed from the CD-ROM using the old drive letter, you might have to reinstall them.

Mouse

In my previous version of Windows I needed to have two mouse drivers—one for DOS and one for Windows. Do I still need two separate drivers?

A single mouse driver is used in Windows 95, eliminating the need for two separate mouse drivers. This will even save you some system resources!

FIGURE 4-18   Change a CD-ROM's drive letter in its Properties dialog box

How do I change my mouse driver?

Use the following steps to change the mouse driver using the System Device Manager:

1. Click on the Start button, choose Settings, and click on Control Panel.

2. Double-click on the System icon and click on the Device Manager tab.

3. Open the Mouse device, select your current pointing device, and click on the Properties button.

4. Click on the Driver tab and then click on the Change Driver button. The Select Device dialog box will open.

5. Select the new driver to be used, or click on Have Disk to use a non-Microsoft driver, and click on OK.

Alternatively, you can change the mouse driver using the Mouse control panel in the next set of instructions:

1. Click on the Start button, choose Settings, and click on Control Panel.

2. Double-click on the Mouse icon.

3. In the Mouse Properties sheet, click on the General tab.

4. Click on the Change button. The Select Device dialog box will open.

5. Select the new driver to be used, or click on Have Disk to use a non-Microsoft driver, and click on OK.

How do I change my mouse behavior?

You can adjust your mouse behavior with the following steps:

1. Click on the Start button, choose Settings, and click on Control Panel.

2. Double-click on the Mouse icon to open the Mouse Properties dialog box that you see in Figure 4-19.

3. Click on the tab for the behavior you want to change.

   - **Buttons** allows you to switch the left and right buttons and to change the speed of a double click.

   - **Pointers** allows you to customize the pointers that appear in specific circumstances.

   - **Motion** allows you to specify whether you want to use pointer trails and the speed at which the pointer moves across the screen.

   - **General** allows you to specify the type of mouse you have and to change its driver.

4. After changing the settings, click on OK.

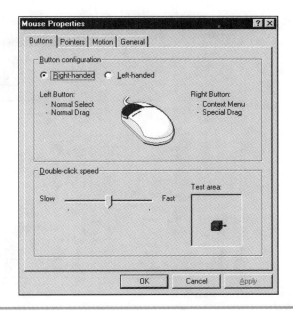

FIGURE 4-19   Mouse behavior is controlled in the Mouse Properties dialog box

Explorer

How can I get the Explorer to open up at the My Computer level instead of at my C:\ level, so I can get to all my drives without using the scroll bar or Up one level button?

To get the Explorer to open up at the My Computer level, as shown in Figure 4-20, you will need to add command-line

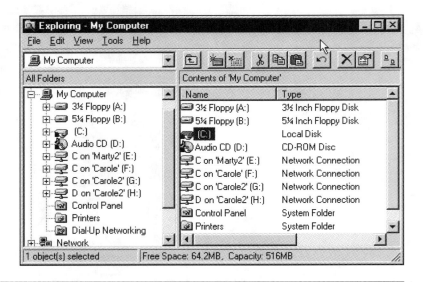

FIGURE 4-20   You can open the Explorer at different levels using command line switches in the shortcut

switches in the Target command line of the shortcut used to open the Explorer. Use the following set of instructions to do that:

1. Create a shortcut for the Explorer on your desktop or in your Start menu that you will use to open the Explorer.

2. Right-click on the new shortcut and choose Properties to open the Explorer Properties dialog box.

3. In the Shortcut tab, edit the Target command line so that it reads **C:\Windows\Explorer.exe /e,/select,C:**. (The C:\Windows\Explorer.exe may be different on your computer if you installed Windows 95 on a different drive and folder. Leave that part unchanged in your command line.) The command-line switches /e,/select, are explained in answer to the next question. The ending C:\ should be the first hard drive within My Computer.

4. Click on OK and double-click on your shortcut (or select it in the Start menu) to try it out. Your results should look like Figure 4-20.

What are the command-line switches that can be used with the Explorer in shortcuts and batch files?

The Explorer has several command-line switches that you can use in shortcuts and batch files to set it up in various ways as you saw in the answer to the previous question. The switches are entered following Explorer.exe and a space on a command line like the Start menu Run command, a DOS command line, or the Target command line in a shortcut.

- **/e**   Specifies that the Explorer view will be used. Otherwise the folder view is used.

- **/n**   Specifies that a new window will be opened. Otherwise the new view will use the existing Explorer window if one is open.

- **,/root,*object***   Specifies that the root of the folders displayed will be *object*, where object is a drive (network or local) or a folder. Otherwise the Desktop is the root. For example, the command line **Explorer.exe /e,/root,*netdrive***   opens an Explorer window with the network drive *Netdrive* as the root drive. This would allow browsing Netdrive, but only that drive.

- **/select,*subobject***   Specifies that *subobject's* parent folder is opened and *subobject* is selected. In the answer to the previous question, **Explorer.exe /e,/select,c:** opened an Explorer window with My Computer (the parent of C:\\) opened and C:\\ selected, as you saw in Figure 4-20.

- **,subobject**   Specifies that *subobject* is the initial selected object unless it follows /select. Otherwise nothing is initially selected.

Is there any way I can get a separate window for each drive in the Explorer, like I could in File Manager?

No. The only way to get two windows with different drives is to open two instances of the Explorer. In the Explorer though, you can select one drive and have it displayed in the right pane, then scroll the left pane so you can see and open the second drive.

You can then drag objects from a folder in the first drive to a folder in the second drive.

Accessibility Options

Tech Tip: If you did not install the Accessibility Options during Setup, you can still add them to your system. Open the Start menu, select Settings, Control Panel, and double-click on Add/Remove Programs. In the Windows Setup tab, place a check mark next to Accessibility Options. Insert your Windows 95 Install disk, click on Have Disk, and follow the prompts.

What are MouseKeys, and how do I implement them?

MouseKeys are part of the Accessibility Options that let users control the mouse pointer using the numeric keypad as follows:

- Use the arrow keys on the numeric keypad to move the pointer horizontally or vertically.

- Use HOME, END, PGUP, and PGDN to move the pointer diagonally.

- Use 5 in the middle of the keypad as a single click and the + as a double-click.

Tech Tip: You don't need to have a mouse to use the MouseKeys.

- Use / at the top of the keypad to specify that the left mouse button will be clicked when 5 is pressed; also at the top of the keypad, use - to specify the right button, and use * to specify both buttons.

- Use 0 or INS at the bottom of the keypad to lock down the mouse button for dragging and/or DEL to release the mouse button.

- Hold down SHIFT while you are using the mouse keys to move the pointer a single pixel at a time.

To implement MouseKeys, use the following steps:

1. Open the Start menu, select Settings, Control Panel, and double-click on Accessibility Options.

2. Click on the Mouse tab, shown next, and select Use MouseKeys.

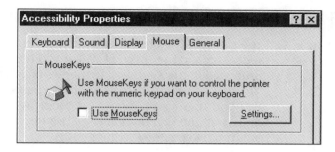

3. Click on Settings to open the Settings for MouseKeys, shown in Figure 4-21, to vary the pointer speed and acceleration, to use CTRL or SHIFT to speed up or slow down the speed, or to use NUM LOCK as a toggle to switch MouseKeys on or off.

4. To turn MouseKeys on and off with a shortcut key, select Use shortcut to turn it on. This enables you to turn MouseKeys on or off by pressing the LEFT ALT-LEFT SHIFT-NUM LOCK keys.

5. Click on OK twice to finalize the settings.

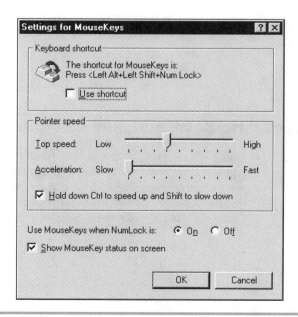

FIGURE 4-21   Settings for MouseKeys lets you determine how fast the mouse pointer will move

How can I adjust the keyboard repeat rate?

You can vary the time a key is held down before it begins repeating and the speed at which additional characters are produced in the Keyboard Properties dialog box. While these "RepeatKey" settings are not officially part of the Accessibility Options, they are important for people who can't lift their fingers off the keyboard quickly. Use the following steps to adjust the RepeatKey settings:

1. Click on the Start button, choose Settings, Control Panel, and double-click on Keyboard.

2. Click on the Speed tab, shown in Figure 4-22, if it is not already displayed.

   ■ To adjust how long a key must be held down before it begins repeating, drag the Repeat delay slider to the setting you want.

   ■ To adjust how quickly characters repeat when you hold down a key, drag the Repeat rate slider to the appropriate setting.

3. Click in the test box and press a key to see if your settings are correct for you. If not, make the necessary adjustments and test them again.

4. When you are satisfied with the settings, click on OK to finalize them.

What are FilterKeys, and how do I implement them?

FilterKeys desensitize the keyboard so that it is less likely that you will get unwanted keystrokes. Keystrokes that are not held down for a minimum period of time are ignored. This is useful for people who have tremors. FilterKeys are part of the Accessibility Options. Use the following steps to enable FilterKeys:

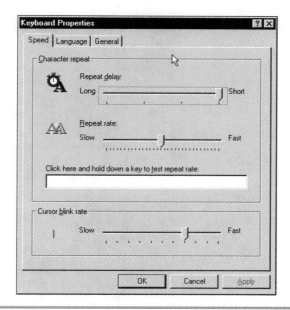

FIGURE 4-22 Keyboard Properties dialog box allows you to adjust the repeat rate

1. Open the Start menu and select Settings, Control Panel, and then double-click on Accessibility Options.

2. From the Keyboard tab, click on Use FilterKeys to enable the feature.

3. Click on Settings to open the Settings for FilterKeys dialog box, shown in Figure 4-23; to enable the shortcut (holding down Right SHIFT for eight seconds); to ignore repeated keystrokes or quick keystrokes and slow down the repeat rate; to test the FilterKeys settings; and to determine the type of notification you want that FilterKeys is working: by a beep or showing the status on the screen.

4. When you are finished, click on OK twice to finalize the settings.

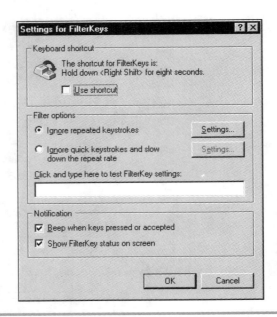

FIGURE 4-23   FilterKeys remove unwanted keystrokes

What are StickyKeys and how do I implement them?

StickyKeys, part of Accessibility Options, allows users to press the keys of a key combination one at a time and Windows responds as if the keys were pressed together. It is used with the CTRL, SHIFT, or ALT keys. Use the following steps to implement StickyKeys:

1. Open the Start menu and select Settings, Control Panel, and then double-click on Accessibility Options.

2. From the Keyboard tab, click on Use StickyKeys.

3. Click on Settings to enable the shortcut (pressing SHIFT five times); to press ALT, SHIFT, or CTRL twice to lock them in for repeated use; to turn off StickyKeys when two keys are pressed at the same time; and to determine notification by sounds when CTRL, SHIFT, or ALT are pressed, or to show the status on the screen.

4. When you are finished, click on OK twice to finalize the settings.

What are ToggleKeys, and how do I implement them?

ToggleKeys, which are part of Accessibility Options, provide audio cues—high and low beeps—to tell users when CAPS LOCK, NUM LOCK, and SCROLL LOCK keys are pressed. A high tone will be sounded when one of the toggle keys is turned on, and a low tone when they are toggled off. Implement ToggleKeys with these steps:

1. Open the Start menu and select Settings, Control Panel, and then double-click on Accessibility Options.
2. From the Keyboard tab, click on Use ToggleKeys.
3. Click on Settings to enable the shortcut (holding down NUM LOCK for five seconds).
4. When you are finished, click on OK twice to finalize the settings.

Optimizing Windows

In Windows 3.1, a permanent swap file works better than a temporary one. Is it still true for Windows 95?

No. Windows 95 dynamically manages the swap file, which can grow and shrink as necessary. In this sense, its behavior is closer to a Windows 3.*x* temporary swap file. However, it is free of many limitations of Windows 3.*x* swap files as listed below.

- Windows 95 swap file does not have to occupy contiguous disk space.
- Windows 95 swap file can be located on a compressed drive.
- Windows 95 swap file can be located anywhere the user wants, not just in the root of the boot drive.
- It is recommended that you let Windows 95 manage the swap file for you.

I've got Windows 95 installed, but it's not performing as well as I had hoped. Is there anything I can do to increase performance?

Windows 95 is self-optimizing, so there isn't much you can do short of buying more memory. However, here are some things to try:

- Click on the Start button, choose Settings, and click on Control Panel. Then double-click on the System icon. Once the System control panel is opened, click on the Performance tab and Windows 95 may give you some suggestions on what you can do to increase performance or tell you that your system is configured for optimal performance, as shown in Figure 4-24.

- Defragment your hard drive(s) using the Windows 95 Disk Defragmenter utility (from the Start menu, select Programs, Accessories, System Tools). This can greatly increase disk performance.

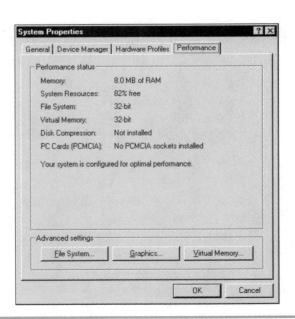

FIGURE 4-24   The System Properties Performance tab will tell you if your system is optimally configured

I increased my virtual memory swap file size to 30MB, and now my system seems to run at a much slower pace. Why is this?

By default, Windows 95 will optimize your virtual memory settings for peak performance. When you force a given swap file size, it may adversely affect performance by causing Windows to manage (use) more of a swap file than it would otherwise be using in optimal circumstances.

Tech Tip: For your best performance, let Windows maintain your virtual memory settings.

How can I speed up the Start menu?

You can use Regedit to make changes to the Registry that speed up the menu display.

Tech Terror: Regedit is a very crude editing tool and gives you no help about what you are doing. It's like doing surgery with a scalpel blindfolded. Incorrect changes to the Registry can cause Windows not to boot. You therefore need to make very sure that you only change what you intend to change and that you understand exactly what to change. **Always back up System.dat and User.dat before using Regedit!**

The Registry uses two files, System.dat and User.dat and maintains a backup System.da0 and User.da0. All four of these files are in the \Windows folder. The .DA0 backups are frequently modified by Windows, so it is worthwhile creating your own known good backup before modifying the files with Regedit. Use the following instructions to make an additional backup and then use Regedit:

1. In the Explorer, open the \Windows folder, right-click on System.dat and choose Copy from the popup menu that appears.

2. Right-click on a blank area of the right Explorer pane within \Windows and choose Paste to paste a copy of System.dat. It will be named "Copy of System.dat."

3. Repeat Steps 1 and 2 for User.dat.

4. Click on the Start button and choose Run.

5. Type **regedit** and click on OK to open Regedit.

6. In the left pane, click on the plus signs opposite HKEY_CURRENT_USER and Control Panel to open them. (My Computer should already be open.)

7. Right-click on desktop and select New and String Value, as shown in Figure 4-25.

8. In the new entry that appears in the right pane, type **MenuShowDelay**, all one word, for the name, and press ENTER.

9. Double-click on the new entry to open the Edit String dialog box. In the Value data text box, type a value from 10 to 1, 1 being the fastest. Try 4 and click on OK.

10. Exit Regedit (the file is automatically saved) and restart Windows. Take a look at how fast you can access your Start menu items!

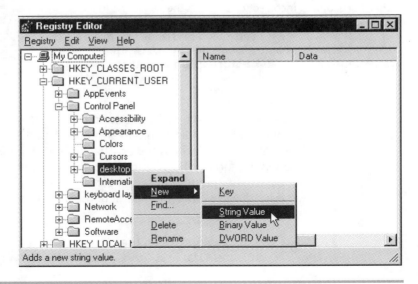

FIGURE 4-25   Creating a new Registry entry

If you make a mistake and your system won't boot, boot into DOS, change to the \Windows folder, copy Copy of System.dat to System.dat and Copy of User.dat to User.dat, and then boot again.

 ## It takes forever for my screen to refresh. Why is my video performance not what I expected?

The controls that are available to change video performance vary, depending on your display adapter card. The controls you do have are reached by opening the Control Panel, double-clicking on the System icon, selecting the Performance tab, and clicking on Graphics. Depending on your controls, try dragging the Hardware acceleration slider to Full. Try fast ROM emulation. Choosing this option will allow the system to emulate video ROM drivers in protected mode, letting the system write to the screen faster. Or try Dynamic Memory Allocation. If set, this switch will allow memory used by the application for video display. This is very useful if you switch from text and graphics modes frequently.

 ## I tried to use DriveSpace, the disk compression program that comes with Windows 95, to increase the capacity of my new 850MB hard drive, but it is only compressing 512MB. Why?

The version of DriveSpace (version 2) in Windows 95 is only capable of creating a compressed drive of up to 512MB. Try Microsoft Plus! for Windows 95, which includes DriveSpace 3. This will give you a compressed drive up to 2GB and a better compression algorithm than DriveSpace 2.

Using Windows 95

Using Windows 95 begins with finding your way around the computer. You'll learn that it's easy and intuitive. First, you have a Start menu that calls to you, "Start here!" When you do, you'll find a series of options that display programs neatly listed in a menu, documents and files that you frequently use, important settings that control your display and many other elements of your computer, a Find command for searching your files, system Help, and a Run option where you can enter DOS commands. In addition to these basic Start menu options, you can place up to 12 other options on the Start menu that let you quickly access the programs and folders you use most frequently.

On the Start menu and in Windows 95, there are a number of tools and convenient ways of getting around that make it easy and fun to use. The Frustration Busters lists some of the first you'll encounter.

FRUSTRATION BUSTERS!

For the first-time user of Windows 95, understanding four facilities of the system is of primary importance in effectively using it. These are the Start menu, the Taskbar, the right-mouse button, and file management with the Explorer, My Computer, and the Network Neighborhood. If you are just beginning, take a minute and look at what you can do with each of these.

The **Start menu** contains all the information, programs, and tools to get you started using your computer. You open the Start menu by clicking on it, and you can select one of the menu *options* by clicking on it. The top four options, though, open a submenu with additional options, and you need only to point to—you don't have to click on—an option if its function is to open a submenu. The purpose of the seven initial Start menu options (before adding any of your own) is as follows:

- **Programs** displays two or more *program groups* at the top of the submenu that, when you point on them, display another submenu listing programs and folders making up that group, as you can see in Figure 5-1. You'll find Windows 95 groups, such as Accessories, with many valuable small applications or "applets," and your own groups, perhaps with word processing, spreadsheet, or database programs. At the bottom of the Programs submenu you will have two to four programs (depending on what Windows 95 options you installed) that you simply click on to activate.

- **Documents** lists the last 15 documents that you worked on and were directly activated by double-clicking on them or a shortcut. When you click on a document or file that is *associated* with an application, that application will load and the selected file will be opened ready to use. You will find that this list rapidly fills up with documents, graphics, clip art, and other files that are handy to have at your fingertips.

- **Settings** gives you fast access to the Control Panel, where you can change most of the hardware and user settings (Chapter 4's Frustration Busters describes the most common control panels). Settings also gives you access to a Printers folder, where you can control all the printers, local and networked, including fax machines, that you have available. Finally, Settings gives you direct access to the Taskbar properties, which allows you to vary

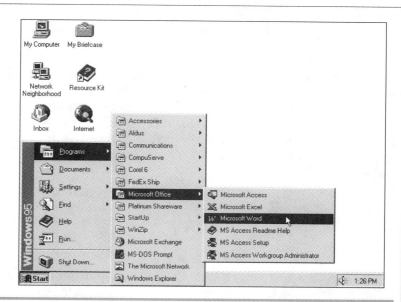

FIGURE 5-1   From the Start menu you can open a program group and select a program

the Taskbar display, even hiding it if you want, and enables you to add programs to the Start menu, either on the top of it or contained within the Programs submenu.

- **Find** allows you to search for files and folders on any disk drive to which you have access; to search for a computer on your network; or to search for an item on the Microsoft Network. Find is a powerful tool that allows you to search using criteria other than name, such as date, text content, or file type.

- **Help** brings up the Windows 95 Help system, which is comprehensive in its coverage of the features and how to use them. You can look at an overview of the Help system, learn some Tips and Tricks, or be lead through a troubleshooting procedure. You can search for an item by subject, indexed alphabetically. Finally, you can search for all references to a subject in a database consisting of all words and phrases in the Help system.

- **Run** provides a command line on which you can type a DOS command or directly initiate a program or open a folder by typing in its path and name. This is the same as the Run Command line in Windows 3.*x*.

■ **Shut Down** allows you to gracefully shut down Windows 95 by first saving any open files or reminding you to do so and then deleting any temporary files that have been in use and are no longer needed. The Shut Down option gives you the option to restart your computer, the equivalent of rebooting, either back into Windows or to DOS.

Tech Tip: Protect yourself from losing unsaved information by always using Shut Down when leaving Windows 95 and, only when you are told it's safe, turning off your computer.

■ The **Taskbar**, which is normally at the bottom of the screen, enables you to switch among multiple programs that are running on your computer. It displays the programs as *tasks* on the Taskbar—a rectangle with the name and icon of the program (Figure 5-2). After a program is started (see the discussion in Chapter 4 on starting programs), its task appears on the Taskbar. When you want to switch from one program to another, you simply click on the task for the program you want to use. The program you are switching to opens on the screen. The program you left is still active in memory; it just may not be visible. With the Taskbar, you will always know what programs are active, and you'll be able to get to them immediately. In addition to the active program tasks, the Taskbar contains a *notification area* with special status icons that, for example, tell you that you have mail waiting or that your printer or modem are active, or allow you to control the volume of your sound system.

Tasks

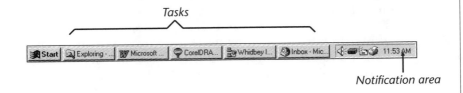

Notification area

FIGURE 5-2 The Taskbar lets you switch among programs that are running

■ The **Right-mouse button**, which was largely ignored in previous versions of Windows, has taken on a significant role in Windows 95. Most importantly, when you *right-click* on an object (a folder, a file, the desktop, or Taskbar), a *popup* menu appears that provides options related to the object you clicked on. These popup menus, some of which are shown in Figure 5-3, contain many different options, but most of them contain a Properties option that will open a Properties dialog box that gives you information about the object and lets you change its settings. Additionally, you can drag files and folders using the right-mouse button and, when you are done dragging, get a popup menu that allows you to copy, move, or create a shortcut for the object you dragged.

A. Taskbar popup

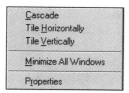

B. Desktop popup

C. Folder popup

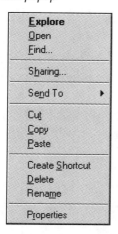

D. File popup

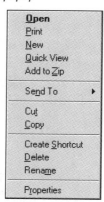

FIGURE 5-3   The Right-mouse button opens popup menus such as these

> ■ **Explorer, My Computer, Network Neighborhood** are the navigating and file management tools within Windows 95. You use them to find a file, a folder, or a networked computer. Chapter 6 discusses these tools more. Explorer is found on the Start, Programs menu. You'll want to place a shortcut to it on the Start menu, or even on the desktop. My Computer and Network Neighborhood are already on the desktop for your quick use.

Booting Situations

 ## How do I create a Windows 95 startup disk if I didn't do it during Setup?

 **Tech Tip:** A startup floppy disk can be a lifeline if you can't boot from your hard disk. You should create, try out, and keep handy a startup disk now before you need it.

You can easily create a startup or "boot" disk from within Windows 95. Follow these steps:

1. Click on Start, choose Settings, and then Control Panel, and double-click on Add/Remove Programs.

2. Click on the Startup Disk tab and click on the Create Disk button, as shown in Figure 5-4. Follow the prompts.

FIGURE 5-4   Creating a new startup disk after installation

Make sure you are using a blank high-density diskette because all of the files on the diskette will be deleted and replaced with the boot programs.

Tech Tip: If you originally installed from a CD-ROM, you'll be asked to insert your Windows 95 CD-ROM in order to create the startup disk.

When I reboot the system, I receive the following error message: "Bad or missing Command Interpreter, enter name of Command Interpreter (c:\windows\command.com)". What does this mean and what do I do about it?

This message can occur when the Windows 95 or the MS-DOS command interpreter (Command.com) is missing or has become corrupted.

To restore the operating system and make the disk bootable, do the following:

1. Boot the system using your Windows 95 startup disk.

2. To move the Windows 95 basic programs to the hard disk from the floppy, type **sys c:** at the MS-DOS command prompt.

3. After the programs have transferred from the floppy disk to the hard disk, remove the diskette and reboot the computer. You may need to reinstall Windows 95, but you will now be able to from your hard drive.

The Control Panel folder insists on loading every time I start my PC in Windows 95. How do I get it to stop loading on startup?

There are three possible ways a folder will be automatically opened at startup. These are as follows:

- The folder was open when Windows 95 was shut down. If so, close the Control Panel, and then restart Windows 95. That should normally take care of it.

- A shortcut to the Control Panel was placed in the \Windows\Start Menu\Programs\StartUp folder. If so, drag the Control Panel icon out of the folder.

- The Win.ini file has a Run=Control Panel statement. Use Notepad to edit the Win.ini file and change the statement to just Run=.

What switches are available to start Windows from the command prompt when I need to isolate an error?

Using switches during booting enables you to diagnose problems. When you are having problems bringing up Windows 95, you can use the /d (for diagnostics) switch. This allows you to create an environment to troubleshoot your problem.
Follow these steps:

1. Boot to the MS-DOS environment either by selecting Restart the computer in MS-DOS mode from the Shut Down menu or by pressing F8 and selecting MS-DOS mode during startup.

2. At the command prompt, type the following command:

   win /d:*switch*

   where *switch* is one of the following switches:

   - **f** Disables 32-bit disk access. Use this if the computer seems to have disk problems or if Windows stalls. (This is the same as the statement "32bitdiskaccess=false" in the System.ini file.)

   - **m** Starts Windows in Safe Mode. Use this if you are having trouble booting. You can accomplish the same thing by pressing F5 when you first see "Starting Windows 95" while booting.

- **n** Starts Windows in Safe Mode with networking. Use this if you need network access for your Windows 95 files. You can accomplish the same thing by pressing F6 when you first see "Starting Windows 95" while booting.

- **s** Prevents Windows from using the upper-memory ROM address space between F000 and FFFF for a break point. Use this if Windows stalls during startup. (This is the same as the "SystemRombreakpoint=false" statement in the System.ini file.)

- **v** Causes the system ROM to handle interrupts from the hard disk controller instead of Windows 95. Use this if you are having disk problems. (This is the same as the statement "VirtualHDIRQ=false" in the System.ini file.)

- **x** Prevents Windows from using any of the upper-memory area A000-FFFF. Use this if you suspect an upper-memory conflict. (This is the same as the statement "EMMexclude=A000-FFFF" in the System.ini file.)

On one of my PC's I used to have the NT 3.5 Server with a dual-boot configuration. Since then I installed Windows 95 and deleted NT from my hard disk. When I boot, I still must choose between Win 95 or NT. How do I safely get rid of that dual boot?

To eliminate the NT dual boot, do the following:

1. Make sure you have recently backed up your critical files in case this gets messed up.

2. Use your Windows 95 startup floppy disk (see earlier) to boot into MS-DOS.

3. Type **sys c:**, which overwrites the NT boot sector on the C drive with a DOS boot sector.

4. Reboot off your hard disk into Windows 95.

I installed Windows 95 to a clean folder instead of updating my current version of Windows 3.*x*. When I boot to my previous version of DOS and then launch Windows 3.*x*, I get a message that states my swap file is corrupt and that I can delete it and create a new one. What should I do so I can boot both versions of Windows at different points?

You can do one of three things to rectify this problem:

- Delete the swap file as prompted and when Win3.*x* starts, go to the Control Panel and then to 386 Enhanced. Click on the Virtual Memory button and then click on the Change button. Then you want to create a temporary swap file instead of a permanent one.

- You could install Windows 95 on a different drive than the previous version of Windows 3.*x*.

- You could set up a permanent swap file in Win3.*x* and then add the following lines to the 386Enh section of the Windows 95 System.ini:

  - PagingFile=<Win31xPagingFile>
  - MinPagingFileSize=<SizeInk>

<Win31PagingFile> is the swap file (usually C:\386part.par) and <SizeInk> is the size of <Win31PagingFile> divided by 1024.

Can I warm-boot Windows 95 without rebooting the PC?

Yes. Do the following:

1. Click on the Start button and choose Shut Down.
2. Click on Restart the computer.
3. Hold down SHIFT and click on Yes. This will only restart Windows 95, not the computer (warm boot). This is a lot faster than a normal (cold) reboot.

While Windows 95 is loading, an error occurs during video adapter initialization. My computer stalls and I have to press CTRL-ALT-DELETE to restart it. How do I change my video driver back to VGA?

To change your video driver, do the following:

1. Restart your computer, and as soon as you see "Starting Windows 95...", press F8 and choose Safe Mode.

2. When in Windows 95, click on the Start button, choose Settings, and click on Control Panel.

3. Double-click on the Display icon, and click on the Settings tab.

4. Click on the Change Display Type button, and then click on the Change button in the Adapter Type section.

5. Click on Show all devices, click on Standard display types, Standard Display Adapter (VGA) (Figure 5-5), and then click on OK.

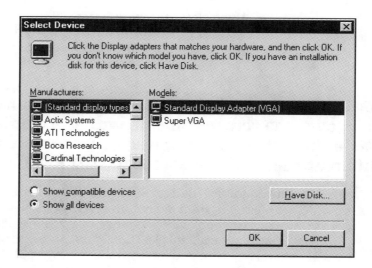

FIGURE 5-5   Returning your display driver to standard VGA

6. When asked to use current driver or a new driver, select Current.

When I start Windows 95, it comes up with an error message asking me to change my video display settings. How can I find the problem?

To troubleshoot the problem:

1. Reboot your computer.

2. As soon as you see the "Starting Windows 95..." message, press F8. Select Safe Mode. This starts with the most basic VGA display driver.

3. If step 2 works, then open the Display control panel Settings tab and use Change Display Type to install and test (see steps in the previous question) successively more sophisticated display drivers. If you use a third-party display driver, you may have to get a new driver from the card manufacturer.

4. Using Notepad, check System.ini to see what driver is installed by looking at the line display.drv=*some.drv*, where *some.drv* is the driver name you are looking for.

My system crashed, and the next time I started Windows, the screen came up with the words "Safe Mode" in each corner of the screen, the colors are different, and I cannot access my CD-ROM. Why?

If Windows 95 detects a problem during startup or detects that a previous startup did not successfully complete, it then starts in a special troubleshooting mode called Safe Mode. This means that all your system files (Config.sys, Autoexec.bat, and all .INI files) are by-passed; no network, printer, or CD-ROM drivers are loaded; and only the standard VGA driver is loaded. This is done so that you can identify the reason for the system crash and make necessary changes.

To figure out what caused the problem, question yourself about what's been happening on your computer. For example: What was the last thing you did before the crash? Added a new driver? Retrace your steps and remove the driver. Did you install a printer? Remove it. If you were just working with an application, run ScanDisk (Start, Programs, Accessories, System Tools, ScanDisk). It will report any problems with your hard drive. Then click on the Start button, Shut Down, and choose Restart the computer. If everything is OK, you will get your regular Windows screen. If you are still getting Safe Mode screen, you might have to continue troubleshooting.

Shortcuts

How are shortcuts used?

A shortcut is a small (under 1KB) file that references another file. A shortcut allows you to remotely load a program, open a folder, or access an object (like a printer or a dial-up network connection) by double-clicking on the shortcut. You can place a shortcut in a convenient location, for example, on the Start menu (where you only have to single-click on it) or on the desktop. That way, you don't have to search the computer or open a number of folders to find the original object, program, or folder.

You can create a shortcut in several ways, as explained in Chapter 4. Probably the easiest is to right-drag the original file, folder, or object to where you want the shortcut and then select Create Shortcut(s) here from the popup menu. If the file is a program file (a file with an .EXE, .COM, .BAT, or .PIF extension), you can drag it normally (using the left-mouse button) to where you want the shortcut, and a shortcut will be created. You can tell that an icon represents a shortcut if the icon contains an arrow, like this:

Word

Sometimes I create a shortcut and then it seems to disappear. Where does it go?

As a rule of thumb, the shortcut is created in the same folder with the original. If the original is on the desktop, the shortcut will be added to the desktop. In My Computer or Explorer, the shortcut will be created in the same folder as the original. On the other hand, if you are in the Find window and create a shortcut, you may not see it unless you rerun the search. The shortcut to an object, such as a printer or a modem, will by default be placed on the desktop.

Registry

How do I access the Registry settings?

You can access the Registry settings in four ways. These, in the order of their ease and safety (with the first being the easiest and the safest) are as follows:

- Using the **Control Panel** items allows you to change many of the settings in the Registry. The dialog boxes associated with the Control Panel give you a lot of information about what you are doing and are generally easy to use. To use the Control Panel, click on Start, Settings, Control Panel, and then choose the area you want to access.

- **File type** associations (the associations between document types and the programs that can open them) are a major component in the Registry. To create an association for a file type (generally indicated by the three-letter file extension) that does not have one, simply double-click on the file, and the Open With dialog box will appear. Here you can enter a description and identify the program you want used to open the file. If you want to change, delete, or add new file associations, open the View menu in either the Explorer or My Computer, choose Options, and then click on the File Types tab, which is shown in Figure 5-6.

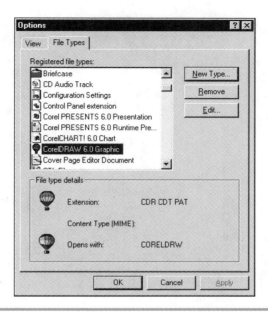

FIGURE 5-6   Change the Registry's file type associations from the Explorer's View menu Options dialog box

- The **System Policy Editor**, which is hidden in the \Admin\Apptools\Poledit folder on your Windows 95 CD-ROM, provides access to many areas of the Registry to allow the implementation of policies on the use of computers within an organization. The Policy Editor's settings, of course, can also be used to make desired Registry changes on a single machine. See example in Chapter 4. To use the Policy Editor with your local Registry, insert your Windows 95 CD and use the Explorer to open the \Admin\Apptools\Poledit folder. Then double-click on Poledit.exe, open the File menu, and choose Open Registry.

- The **Regedit.exe** program in your \Windows folder gives direct access to all of the Registry's settings. The problem is that there is no information about what your options are or what the effect of a change will be. You simply select a setting and make a change, as shown in Figure 5-7, hoping the change will give you the desired

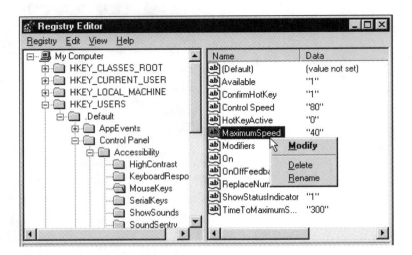

FIGURE 5-7   Regedit provides direct access to the Registry but little help in changing it

results. You can access and use Regedit with the following steps:

1. Click on the Start button, choose Run, and type **regedit**. (If you will be using it a lot, create a shortcut to it on your desktop or under Programs). This will bring up the Registry Editor.

2. To display settings, double-click on the folder and its subfolders for the key you want to access until you see the value you want to change on the right.

3. Right-click on the value you want to change to bring up the popup menu shown in Figure 5-7. Alternatively, double-click on the value if you just want to modify it. This will bring up the Edit String dialog box shown here:

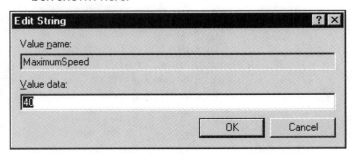

Tech Terror: Make sure you back up the Registry's User.dat and the System.dat files in your \Windows folder BEFORE making modifications to the Registry.

How can I find a specific setting in the Registry?

You can use Regedit to locate a setting:

1. Click on the Start button, choose Run, type **regedit,** and click on OK.
2. Open the Edit menu and choose Find.
3. Type a string to look for. For example, if you want to find the settings associated with a modem, open the Edit menu, choose Find, and type **modem**, like this:

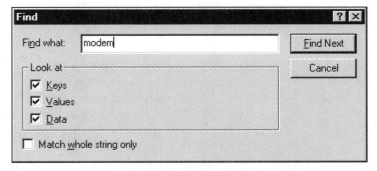

4. Click on Find Next. To find another instance of the same string, press F3.

What are the files System.dat, System.da0, System.1st, User.dat, and User.da0?

The System.dat file is your system registry. This file stores all information about your computer and software. The System.da0 file is a backup copy of System.dat, which is created whenever you start Windows. If Windows finds that your registry is damaged, it attempts to use System.da0 from the previous session of Windows instead of System.dat.

The System.1st file is a copy of System.dat from the first time your computer booted successfully after the last installation of Windows 95.

The User.dat contains specific user information. A copy of the User.dat always exists locally. When the User.dat is placed in the user's logon folder on a server, a copy of that file is made on the user's local computer when the user logs on. User.da0 is a backup copy of User.dat. Like System.da0, it is created every time you start Windows and is automatically used if Windows thinks User.dat is corrupted.

Tech Terror: User.dat and System.dat are very important to your system. Even though the system maintains a backup, it is only as old as the last time Windows 95 was started. You should make your own backups of these files periodically.

What do the different keys in the Registry contain?

The Registry keys are

- **HKEY_CLASSES_ROOT** Contains information similar to that in Reg.dat in Windows 3.*x*—information about file associations and OLE parameters. All the file association information is here, as are drag and drop rules. Windows 95 has added information on shortcuts and some information on the user interface.

- **HKEY_CURRENT_USER** Contains user-specific information that is generated when the user logs on and is based on information for that user in HKEY_USERS.

- **HKEY_LOCAL_MACHINE** Contains information about the computer being referenced. It includes the drivers loaded on the system, what kind of devices are installed, and the current configuration of installed applications. This is machine-specific, not user-specific, information.

- **HKEY_USERS** Contains information about all users of the PC, plus a description of a default (generic) user. The information stored here is applications configuration, desktop settings, and sound schemes, among other things.

- **HKEY_CURRENT_CONFIG**   Contains information about the current configuration of the workstation. This is used when you create different configurations for the same workstation—for example, Laptop vs. Docked configuration.

- **HKEY_DYN_DATA**   Contains dynamic status information for system devices used in Plug-and-play. The device information includes its current status and any detected problems.

Windows 95 stores the recent history of RUN commands somewhere. Where can I find it?

They are in the registry under HKEY_CURRENT_USER\Software\ Microsoft\Windows\CurrentVersion\Explorer\RunMRU.

How do I recover if I ever corrupt or have a problem with the Windows 95 Registry?

The short answer is to copy System.da0 and User.da0 to System.dat and User.dat, respectively. The problem is that these are hidden, read-only files. Also, you probably cannot start Windows, so you must use DOS. If you are in Windows, shut down and restart in MS-DOS mode. Here are the DOS commands to type:

```
cd c:\windows                           ┐── Where c:\windows is your Windows folder.
attrib -h -r -s system.da?              │
attrib -h -r -s user.da?   ┘
copy system.da0 system dat ┐── The "0" in ".da0" is the numeral zero.
copy user.da0 user.dat     ┘
```

When you have completed the previous steps, reboot your computer and start Windows 95 normally. If you still have problems and you have another different backup, replace the .DA0 files in the previous instructions with your backup files.

The instructions for recovering the Windows 95 Registry files are also contained in the Registry Help file. To see and possibly print them, start the Registry as described in the questions earlier, click on Help, Help Topics, select Restoring the registry, and click on Display. To print the topic, click on Options and Print Topic, as you can see in Figure 5-8.

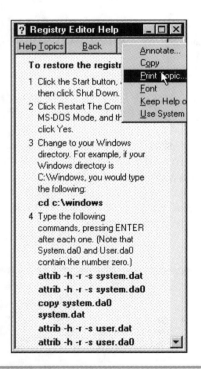

FIGURE 5-8   Print the Help Topic for restoring the registry

Drag and Drop

 How can I use drag and drop with the left mouse button and also with the right mouse button? Is there a difference?

Using the left mouse button and dragging a folder or file, you will have different results depending on the keys you hold down as you are dragging, as follows:

Keys held	Effect
none	Moves folders and non-program files, makes a shortcut of program files (one with an extension of .EXE or .COM)
CTRL	Copies all folders and files
SHIFT	Moves all folders and files
CTRL-SHIFT	Makes a shortcut for all folders and files

Right drag and drop gives you a popup menu when you drop the object, asking if you want to copy, move, or create a shortcut, like this:

 If I am dragging an .EXE file from the Explorer to the desktop, I get a shortcut. If I drag a document file, it is copied to the desktop! How do I know what the outcome is of the drag and drop?

By design, Windows 95 treats program files differently from data files. If you drag an .EXE or .COM file to the desktop, you receive a shortcut. If you drag holding down the CTRL key, the file is copied to the desktop. If you drag holding down the SHIFT key, the file is moved to the desktop.

If you drag a data file to the desktop, a .DOC, .BMP, .XLS, or any type other than .EXE or .COM, the file is moved to the desktop. You get the same result of moving the file if you drag holding down the SHIFT key. If you drag holding down the CTRL key, the file is copied to the desktop, and if you hold down both CTRL and SHIFT, you will create a shortcut to the data file.

How do I drag an item from a Program Manager group to the Windows 95 desktop?

Program Manager, designed to ease the transition between Windows 95 and earlier versions, does not provide drag and drop from its groups to the Windows 95 desktop. Even though Program Manager ships with Windows 95, it is still a 16-bit application and only has drag and drop within its windows.

Windows Environment

I see the terms *real mode* and *protected mode* used a lot in conjunction with Windows 95, but what's the difference between them, and is it really important?

Yes, it is important. *Real mode* was the original way that the 8086 and 8088 processors operated and the foundation on which DOS was built. It was a single-tasking, 16-bit environment limited to slightly over 1MB of address space. The 80286 processor added *protected-mode* instructions, and the 386 and 486 significantly improved on them. These protected-mode instructions, which are 32-bit, provided for multitasking, where two or more programs could be in memory at the same time, and allowed addressing up to 4GB in the later processors. (The term "protected" comes from the memory protection routines that are necessary when two programs run in memory at the same time, whereas "real" addressing is what takes place if only one program is running at a time.) DOS never made use of protected mode, and all Intel processors (including the Pentium) have kept the real-mode instructions for that reason. Since all processors have real-mode instructions and it is the initial startup mode, most disk drivers used real-mode instructions. This meant that every time you went from Windows, which runs in protected mode, to the disk driver in real mode, you had to switch the processor from protected to real mode, taking time and going from a more efficient to a less efficient environment. For these reasons, Windows 95 has made a considerable effort to replace real-mode drivers with protected-mode drivers.

Tech Tip: Wherever possible, use protected-mode drivers. The easiest way to do that is to only use the drivers that come with Windows 95 by removing any statements in your Config.sys and Autoexec.bat files that load drivers (under many circumstances you should be able to completely get rid of your entire Config.sys and possibly your Autoexec.bat files).

How do I find how much system resources I currently have?

In My Computer, Explorer, or a number of other windows, open the Help menu and select About Windows 95. The About dialog box opens with both the free system resources and the free physical memory, as shown in Figure 5-9.

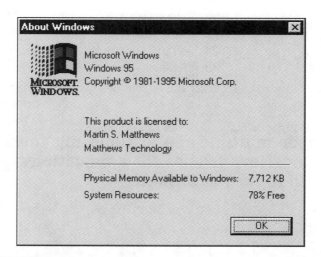

FIGURE 5-9   The About dialog box from most Help menus will give you the free system resources

How can I access the desktop if it is hidden behind open applications?

Right-click on an empty area of the Taskbar, and choose Minimize All Windows from the popup menu shown next; or press ALT-M when the Taskbar is selected.

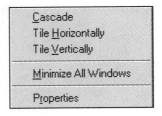

Tech Tip: After using Minimize All Windows, you can again right-click on the Taskbar and select Undo Minimize All and restore the windows you closed to their original position.

When I am running an application, why does my Taskbar sometimes disappear?

The Auto hide feature is enabled. Here are the steps to clear this:

1. Move your cursor to the edge of the screen where the Taskbar is located and the Taskbar will reappear.

2. Click on the Start button, choose Settings, and click on Taskbar.

3. Clear the Auto hide box, as you can see in Figure 5-10, and click on OK when you are done.

As I open multiple applications, my Taskbar gets very crowded. How do I see the applications that I am running in the list format?

The easiest way is to drag the inside edge of your Taskbar in so you can easily see all of your tasks, like this:

FIGURE 5-10   If Auto hide is checked, the Taskbar will only be visible when you move the mouse pointer to the edge of the screen where it's located

You can also switch to each task individually using ALT-TAB. Or you can press CTRL-ALT-DELETE (this is equivalent to pressing CTRL-ESC in Windows 3.*x*), and you will get a list of all running applications with the option to end tasks. Click on Cancel to continue without ending a task.

How do I use the question mark icon on the right side of the title bars?

This is a Help aid found in dialog boxes. The question mark is known as the "What's this?" button. Click on it and the pointer changes to a question mark, as shown here. Click on any object in the dialog box and a short description of the object is shown.

How do I get rid of the Inbox icon on my desktop? Why is it there at all when I told it not to install MSN?

The Inbox icon is there because you have chosen to install Microsoft Exchange and/or Microsoft Fax. You must remove them to get rid of the icon. You can do so with the following steps:

1. Click on the Start button, choose Settings, and click on the Control Panel.

2. Double-click on Add/Remove Programs and then click on the Windows Setup tab.

3. Scroll the list of components until you can see Microsoft Exchange and Microsoft Fax, as shown in Figure 5-11.

4. Uncheck the Microsoft Exchange and the Microsoft Fax check boxes, click on OK, and click on Yes to restart your system. When Windows comes back up, the Inbox icon will be gone.

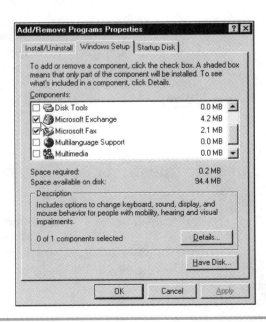

FIGURE 5-11   Uninstalling MS Exchange and MS Fax will remove the Inbox

Why does Windows 95 change the look of certain parts of my applications and not other parts?

The programming code is often inconsistent throughout an application, probably since it was written by multiple programmers. In some instances an application may use Windows 95 tools to create some parts. For example, in Access 2.0, which uses Windows 95 to create its dialog boxes, the check boxes now come equipped with check marks and there is a single-click "X" for closing the application in the upper-right corner. Some applications just show a slight appearance change such as fonts and colors.

How can I rebuild Windows 95 default folders?

You can run the Grpconv.exe program that rebuilds the Windows 95 folders (for example, all the folders within the \Windows folder). Follow these steps:

1. Click on the Start button and choose Run.

2. On the Run dialog box, type **grpconv /s**. While the program is running, you will see the Start Menu Shortcuts message box appear, like this:

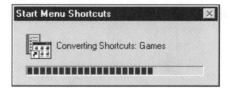

The program Grpconv.exe is principally used to convert Windows 3.1 program groups to Windows 95 shortcuts in the \Windows\Start Menu\Programs folder. When Grpconv.exe is used with the /S switch, it rebuilds the default Windows 95 folders.

How do I tile or cascade windows in Windows 95?

Right-click on an empty spot on the Taskbar. You will see the options to Cascade, Tile Horizontally, or Tile Vertically, as shown next:

```
Cascade
Tile Horizontally
Tile Vertically

Minimize All Windows
Undo Minimize All

Properties
```

How can I capture my screen in Windows 95?

The PRINT SCREEN key on your keyboard will copy the image on your screen to the Clipboard. You can then paste that image into a document. You can use PRINT SCREEN in the following ways:

■ To copy an image of the entire screen, press PRINT SCREEN.

■ To copy an image of the window that is currently active, press ALT-PRINT SCREEN.

■ To paste the image into a document, open the Edit menu in the document window, and then click on Paste.

How can I stop opening multiple windows each time I open a new folder in My Computer?

In your current window, select the View menu, choose Options, and on the Folder tab, choose Browse folders by using a single window that changes as you open each folder, as shown in Figure 5-12.

When using the Explorer, I get an Edit option when I right-click on the Autoexec.bat file, but not when I right-click on Config.sys. How can I edit Config.sys from the Windows Explorer window?

Windows 95 has attached a special property to .BAT files that brings up the Edit option. You can edit your Config.sys file in Explorer in several ways:

■ Double-click on it and then select Notepad as the application to open the file.

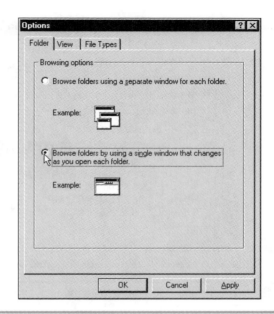

FIGURE 5-12   The View menu, Options option contains a control for displaying a single window rather than cascading ones

- Right-click on it, choose Open With, and select Notepad to open the file.

- Run Sysedit by clicking on the Start button, choosing Run, and typing **sysedit** on the command line. This opens the System Configuration Editor (Figure 5-13), which opens many of the system files for editing.

Tech Tip: If you don't see the system files in the Explorer, open the View menu, choose Options, and select Show All Files. By default Windows 95 will hide files with system and hidden attributes.

There is no File, Run option. How can I install a program in Windows 95?

You may install a program in two ways: by directly loading the program's Install or Setup programs (see the following steps), or by using Windows 95's Add/Remove Programs utility. If you use the Add/Remove Programs, you will be guided through placing

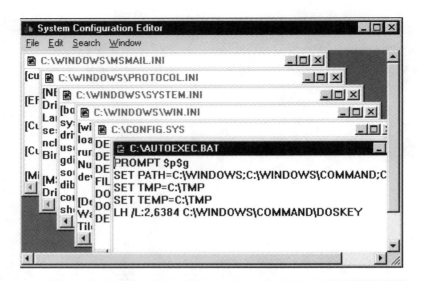

FIGURE 5-13   The System Configuration Editor allows you to edit your system files

the program on a menu, perhaps within a program group, and can assign an icon to it.

Follow these steps to directly run the program's own installation procedure:

1. Click on the Start button and choose Run.

2. Type in the command (for example, **a:\setup**) or choose it from the drop-down list if you have recently run Setup from your a: drive.

Follow these instructions to use Add/Remove Programs:

1. Click on the Start button, choose Settings, and click on Control Panel.

2. Double-click on Add/Remove Programs and the Add/Remove Programs Properties dialog box will open, as shown in Figure 5-14.

3. Click on Install and follow along as the Installation Wizard leads you through the process.

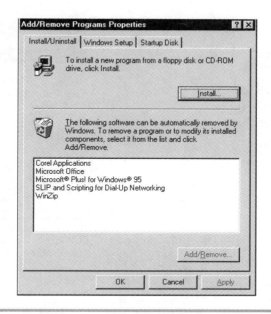

FIGURE 5-14   Add/Remove Programs leads you through the installation of your programs

Tech Tip: Only applications written specifically for Windows 95 can be completely removed using Add/Remove Programs.

How do I open a file with a different application than the one with which it is already associated?

An option of the right-click popup menu contains the Open With option in which you can select the application you want to open the file. Follow these steps to get the Open With question on the right-mouse popup menu:

1. In My Computer or the Explorer, *left*-click on the file to select it.

2. Hold down the SHIFT key and right-click on it. The Open With command will appear in the popup menu, as you can see in the following illustration:

Open
Print
Open With...
Quick View
Add to Zip
Send To ▶
Cut
Copy
Create Shortcut
Delete
Rename
Properties

Tech Tip: You must first select the file before SHIFT right-click will cause Open With to appear.

 Are there any alternative ways that I can run an application other than using the Programs menu system?

Yes, there are a number of alternatives. Here are some of them:

- Double-click on a shortcut icon created on the desktop by dragging the program's .EXE file there.

- Click on an option in the Start menu itself (not the Programs submenu), created by dragging the program's .EXE file to the Start button.

- Double-click on a shortcut icon created in a special folder left open on the desktop by dragging the program's .EXE file there.

Tech Tip: A special folder left open on the desktop containing shortcuts to your frequently used applications is superior to placing the shortcuts directly on the desktop, because you can use ALT-TAB to get to the folder but not to the desktop—you must minimize any open applications.

- Click on Start, choose the Run command, type the application's path and filename, and press ENTER.

In the Add/Remove Programs (Windows Setup tab), the size in bytes in the Components list is different from the size specified for the Space Required displayed below it. Why?

The two sizes are calculated differently and give you different information. The size you see beside each component listed is the total of the files in that Component. The size for the Space Required is calculated using the cluster size of the hard disk drive you are installing them on, which varies depending on the size of the hard disk and how it is formatted.

WordPad

How do I use WordPad?

WordPad is a 32-bit editor that replaces the Write application that was in Windows 3.1. WordPad uses the same file format as Microsoft Word 6, but it also supports the reading and writing of text files (.TXT) and rich text files (.RTF) and the reading of Write files (.WRI).

To start WordPad, open the Start menu, and select Programs, Accessories, and then WordPad. Alternatively, you can open the Start menu, select Run, type **wordpad**, and press ENTER.

If you create a new document in WordPad, you are given a choice of the type of document you want to create, as shown next. You need to determine what you will do with the document and how much formatting it will have. Word 6 and rich text can handle a lot of formatting, but those formats cannot be used with system files like the Autoexec.bat, Config.sys, and Win.ini.

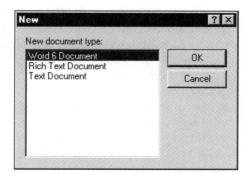

How do I set a manual page break in WordPad?

There is no provision for page breaks. They are handled automatically.

I am in WordPad, and I am trying to save a file with a name c:\Test.txt, but I am getting an error message "This filename is not valid." What is going on?

If all characters in the name are valid, the problem might be that all 512 root folder entries are used up. In MS-DOS and Win 3.*x*, you could have 512 files and folders defined in the root (C:\) directory or folder. MS-DOS used one root folder entry for each file and folder. In Windows 95, the 512 entry maximum still applies, but you might get to use a lesser number of actual items because Windows 95 uses additional root folder entries to store long filenames and their associated 8.3 aliases, plus the normal files and folders. This means that you can run out of available root folder entries even if you have less than 512 files or folders in the root folder. To avoid this problem, save your files to a folder other than in the root. Folders other than the root do not have the root entries limitation—the only limitation is actual free disk space.

Equipment Related Problems

Do I absolutely have to have a mouse?

It is strongly recommended that you use a mouse in Windows 95 because the whole environment is object-oriented and is strongly tied to pointing and clicking, now with both the left and right mouse buttons.

You can substitute the keyboard for many mouse actions by, among other things, using the shortcut keys listed in Appendix B. Also, the underlined letters in the menus and dialog boxes represent a shortcut—you can hold down the ALT key and press the underlined letter on the keyboard to activate the menu option or dialog box feature.

However, there are a few tasks, such as the following examples, that cannot be performed without a mouse:

■ In the Explorer, you cannot move the vertical bar that divides the folder tree on the left and list of files on the right without a mouse.

■ In the Explorer, when you are viewing files in Details view, there is no way without a mouse to change the size of the fields for the filename, type, total size, and free space listings.

■ Very long filenames may be truncated on dialog box properties tabs, and you can only see the whole name by holding a mouse pointer over it.

Tech Tip: Even if you don't have a mouse, you can use the MouseKeys option to simulate the mouse pointer on the keyboard. You can access this option through Start, Settings, Control Panel, and selecting the Accessibility Options icon. On the Mouse tab, enable the Use MouseKeys option. (You might have to install the Accessibility Options because it is not installed in every type of install.)

Where can I get an accurate view of my memory size?

There are two places where you can see the physical memory you have on your computer:

■ As Windows 95 is booting, it displays the memory size.

■ In Explorer or My Computer, select Help, and then About Windows 95. The Physical Memory Available to Windows will be displayed as well as the percentage of System Resources currently available, as shown previously in Figure 5-9.

Do I need Himem.sys or Emm386.exe in Windows 95?

Yes, Windows 95 does need Himem.sys, but you do not need to include it in a Config.sys file. It is automatically loaded through the Io.sys file. If the Himem.sys file is missing or damaged, you will not be able to run Windows 95.

Emm386.exe is not required by Windows 95.

Can I use an upper-memory manager such as QEMM with Windows 95?

There is no need for such utilities. Windows 95 utilizes its internal memory management system, which is superior to QEMM.

My SCSI controller isn't working under Windows 95. What can I do?

This is probably due to a conflict between a real-mode driver in your Config.sys file and Windows 95 trying to use a protected-mode driver. (See discussion earlier in this chapter on real and protected modes.) Use either of the following two methods to correct this problem.

- First, try removing the SCSI driver (it probably has ASPI in its name) from your Config.sys file so that only the Windows 95 protected-mode driver is loaded.

- Alternatively, edit the Iso.ini file in your \Windows folder and remove the reference to the real-mode driver.

I have been changing my video display back and forth to different resolutions, and now suddenly I cannot change it back to what I want. The option is no longer available. How do I restore the original defaults?

Somehow you changed your display type and thereby your video device driver to one that does not have the resolution options of your original driver. You need to reselect your original display type and the list will be set back to its original defaults. To do that, follow these steps:

1. Open the Start menu and select Settings, click on Control Panel, and double-click on Display.

2. Click on the Settings tab, and click on the Change Device Type button. Click on Change for the Adapter Type.

3. If you see your display adapter listed, select it and click on OK three times to return to the Control Panel.

4. If you do not see your display adapter in the Models list, click on Show all devices, select your display adapter, as you can see being done in Figure 5-15, and click on OK three times to return to the Control Panel.

5. If asked, restart your computer. When you are done, you should be able to select from among your original resolution settings ("Desktop Area").

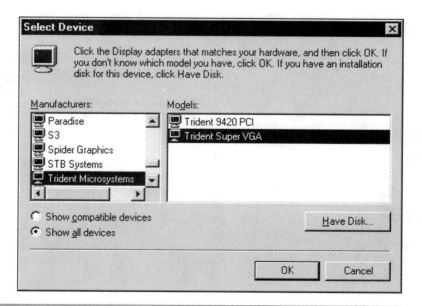

FIGURE 5-15 Getting back to your original video driver will return your resolution options

My display blinks (flickers). How do I avoid this?

You probably selected the wrong display type, and your monitor is running at a different frequency than your video card. Use the steps in the previous question to select the correct video device driver. If you don't know the display type, choose Standard Display Adapter (VGA).

I'm having a problem with my Conner external tape drive. The Conner program is attempting to back up 800MB of data, when there is only 500MB of data. What is going on?

The Conner backup program is having problems with long filenames in Windows 95. To back up your data, use the Backup program that comes with Windows 95. You can access Backup by opening the Start menu and selecting Programs, Accessories, System Tools, and clicking on Backup. Backup is a 32-bit application that is very easy to use and displays the standard tree and file list view you see in Explorer.

Tech Tip: If you can't find Backup, you may not have installed it, in which case you must rerun Setup—you cannot use the Add/Remove Programs Windows Setup tab to install Backup.

Tech Tip: Only some types of backup tape drives are supported by Windows 95 Backup. QIC 40, 80, and 3010 drives connected to the primary floppy controller and made by Colorado, Conner, Iomega, and Wangtek are supported. All drives on a secondary floppy controller and QIC Wide tapes, QIC 3020, and SCSI tape drives as well as all drives made by Archive, Irwin, Mountain, Summit, and Travan are NOT supported. If your tape drive is not supported, contact your tape drive manufacturer for software that works with Windows 95.

Other Problems

 ALT-TAB switches me to any open applications, but it does not switch me to an open Properties dialog box. How do I get back to the Properties dialog box?

You can use ALT-ESC to switch to a Properties dialog box or a Wizard. ALT-TAB only works with applications.

 One of my 16-bit applications has crashed and has not returned the resources it uses. How can I refresh the resources without restarting?

Windows 95 will return all 16-bit resources once *all* 16-bit applications have been closed. This includes screen savers such as MS Scenes, MS Office Manager (MOM), and other 16-bit Windows applications.

 I have deleted a large number of files over the last couple of days. When I wanted to recover some of them, I could not find them in the Recycle Bin! How can I avoid this?

You probably have exceeded the limit of the size of the Recycle Bin.

Tech Terror: By default, the system allocates 10 percent of disk space to hold the deleted files in the Recycle Bin. When you exceed this limit, the system purges the oldest files to make space for the newly deleted files. You are NOT notified when this happens! You can avoid this in the future by increasing the disk space allocation.

Use the following steps to increase the disk space allocated to the Recycle Bin:

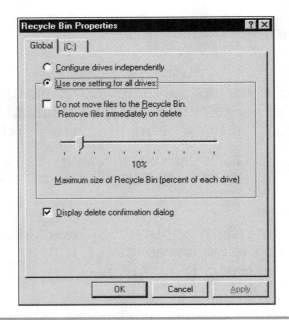

FIGURE 5-16   You can change the size of memory allocated to the Recycle Bin in its Properties dialog box

1. Right-click on the Recycle Bin and choose Properties.

2. Click on the Global tab, as shown in Figure 5-16, and adjust the Maximum size of Recycle Bin setting. Click on OK when you are done.

Tech Tip: Remember also that you can have a separate Recycle Bin for every hard drive (or partition) that you have. To do this, click on the individual drive tabs and adjust the disk space accordingly.

 ## How do I close a failed application?

If you cannot use any facilities within the application and you cannot close the DOS window it is running in (or if it isn't a DOS program), use the following steps to close it:

1. Press CTRL-ALT-DELETE. Windows will display a list of all running applications so you can specify which one you want to end.

2. If Windows detects that any application is not responding to messages from the system, the text "not responding" appears after the related application in the list. In the Close Program dialog box, select the application you want to close and click on End Task.

Tech Tip: After you use the Cancel or the End Task button to close the Close Program dialog box, the next time you press CTRL-ALT-DELETE, the Close Program dialog box appears again and the computer is not restarted. If you want to press CTRL-ALT-DELETE to restart the computer, you must press the keys again while the Close Program dialog box is displayed.

Tech Terror: If possible, you should use the Shut Down button in the Close Program dialog box or the Shut Down command on the Start menu to quit Windows. This ensures that all current information is saved in the Registry, and that each application is closed correctly before quitting Windows.

I ran a virus utility on WIN 95 and it seemed to see the virus, but it will not remove it from my system. Is there a problem with my antivirus program or my system?

Under Windows 95, most virus detection software will detect a virus, but it will not remove it from your system. This is because the virus utility uses low-level write commands to repair the damage to the disk. DOS-based virus utilities can only be run using the LOCK command. You need to get a Windows 95 antivirus program such as Norton AntiVirus for Windows 95.

Why did Windows 95 put "rem" in front of the SMARTdrive statement in my Autoexec.bat file?

Windows 95 made the SMARTdrive statement a remark so SMARTdrive will not be loaded during startup. Windows 95 replaces SMARTdrive with a protected-mode caching system that shrinks and grows as needed. The SMARTdrive was not totally deleted because you may need it if you boot into your previous DOS.

I think that a couple of the Windows 95 files are damaged. How do I find where these files are located on the distribution disks so that I can manually expand them?

Unlike Windows 3.*x*, Windows 95 will spare you this effort. If you have Windows 95 installed on the system, you can run Setup to verify the integrity of files. When you run Setup, it will offer you a choice of reinstalling Windows 95 or just verifying the files. If you choose to verify the files, Setup will consult Setuplog.txt, the file that was placed into the root folder by the Windows 95 installation process, and verify the integrity of each of the installed components. If one or more files are missing or corrupt, Setup will reinstall them.

Can I use Norton Utilities 8.0 or PC Tools for Windows with Windows 95?

You should never use Norton Utilities, PC Tools, or any other type of disk or file utility that was not specifically designed for Windows 95. The Windows 3.*x* versions of these utilities cannot handle long filenames in Windows 95 and might report the files as corrupt. An attempt to repair the "corruption" will lead to data loss and can seriously damage your whole system. Norton Utilities for Windows 95 is currently available.

File Management

File management, the handling of information written onto and read off of disks, was the primary focus of the first operating systems. Operating systems today do many other things, but file management remains critically important. It is a major area of enhancement in Windows 95 over the previous combination of Windows 3.*x* and DOS 6.*x*. Windows 95 provides a full 32-bit file system, many protected-mode drivers (see Chapter 5), long filenames, and the Explorer, in addition to many smaller enhancements. The net of all these changes is a file system that is easier to use, more intuitive, and faster. Windows 95 almost transparently provides these most basic of services, without which computing would be useless.

FRUSTRATION BUSTERS!

Here is a brief summary of some of the more important file management tools in Windows 95.

- **Backup**, accessed through the Start menu, Programs, Accessories, System Tools, will compress selected files and store them on multiple floppy disks or magnetic tape.

- **Cut and Paste** can be used to move or copy a file, as well as text or graphics within a file. Use CTRL-X to delete or cut, CTRL-C to copy, and CTRL-V to paste. You can also click on the Cut, Copy, and Paste icons in the folder window's toolbar, as shown here:

- **Drag and Drop** allows you to move or copy files or folders (directories in DOS and Windows 3.*x*) by pointing on them with the mouse, pressing and holding a mouse button, and dragging them from one location to another. Using the right-mouse button gives you a menu, shown on the left, when you release the mouse button ("drop" the object), whereas the left mouse button does different things depending on the type of file and the keyboard keys held down (see discussion in Chapter 5).

Move Here
Copy Here
Create Shortcut(s) Here
Cancel

FRUSTRATION BUSTERS!

- **Explorer, My Computer,** and **Network Neighborhood** are your primary access to files and folders within Windows 95. They allow you to locate files, folders, disks, and computers on a network; look at files and folders in different views; open, copy, move, delete, and rename files and folders, create folders and shortcuts to files and folders; format and copy disks; and share disks and folders and map disks on a network.

- **Folder Window** is the standard window used by the Explorer, My Computer, the Network Neighborhood, and all folders that are opened. Figure 6-1 shows you its standard features.

- **Long Names** are now allowed—up to 255 characters—and you can include spaces and all other characters *except* \ / : * " ? < > and |. You can give files descriptive names that are easily remembered, rather than the eight-character names with three-character extensions required in previous versions of Windows and DOS.

- **My Briefcase** is used to synchronize files that are being modified or edited on another computer. This is a way to keep multiple copies of a file up-to-date.

- **Recycle Bin** holds deleted files until it's emptied. You can cut, copy, paste, and restore files from this folder.

- **Renaming Files** can be done by clicking on the filename to select the file, clicking again to open the name editing (or pressing F2), and then typing the new name. It is fast and efficient.

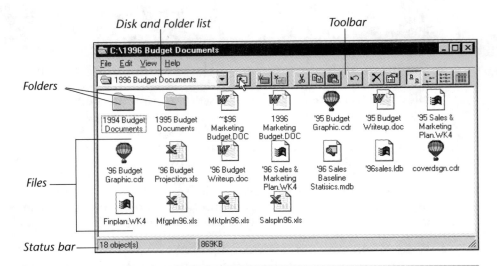

FIGURE 6-1   The Folder Window is used for all file management functions in Windows 95

Disk Backup and Copy

How do I make backup copies of my original Windows 95 disk set?

Windows 95 disks are shipped in Distribution Media Format (DMF), and the floppy disks are not compatible with the DOS Copy or the DiskCopy commands. You cannot create backup copies of the Windows 95 disks. You must call Microsoft's customer service center at 1-800-426-9400 if you need replacement disks.

Can I restore backups made from previous versions of Microsoft backup?

No. The Windows 95 Backup program only restores backup files that it has created.

How do I copy a diskette?

You can copy a diskette in either My Computer or the Explorer. Follow these steps:

1. Open My Computer by double-clicking on the icon on the desktop. Alternatively, open the Explorer by opening the Start menu, selecting Programs, and clicking on Windows Explorer.

2. Right-click on the floppy disk drive to be copied. This will open the popup menu shown on the left.

3. Click on the Copy Disk command. The Copy Disk dialog box will be displayed, as shown here:

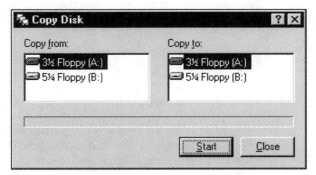

4. From the Copy from list, select the disk drive to be used as the source of the copy.

5. From the Copy to list, select the disk drive to be used as the destination of the copy.

6. Click on Start and follow any prompts.

Other Disk Utilities and Tasks

How do I format a diskette in Windows 95?

You can format a diskette from either My Computer or the Explorer using these steps:

1. Insert a diskette into the floppy drive.

2. Double-click on the My Computer icon or open the Explorer by selecting Start, Programs, Windows Explorer.

3. Right-click on the disk drive that contains the diskette and choose Format.

4. Choose the Capacity and Format type, or just accept the defaults that Windows 95 is offering if you are not sure (if the capacity is incorrect, you will have another chance to change it). Type in a Label if you want one on the diskette. You can also select No Label, Display summary when finished, and Copy system files (which will produce a bootable disk).

5. Click on the Start button.

Tech Terror: Formatting a used disk erases all data on it, and the lost data cannot be restored.

How can I label a diskette?

You can label a diskette while formatting it, as described in the previous question. You can also label a diskette after it has been formatted by following these steps:

1. If you want to label a diskette, place it in the disk drive.

2. Double-click on the My Computer icon or open the Explorer by selecting Start, Programs, Windows Explorer.

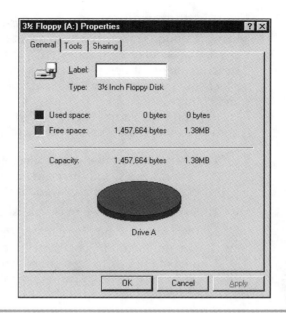

FIGURE 6-2   The Disk Properties dialog box allows you to label a disk

3. Right-click on the disk drive that contains the diskette and choose Properties. Select the General tab if it is not already selected, as shown in Figure 6-2.

Tech Tip: If you click on the Tools tab, you can find out the last time the disk was error-checked, backed-up, or defragmented. If it has not been recently, you can run the disk tools ScanDisk, Disk Defragmenter, and Backup from this dialog box.

4. Type the text for the label in the Label text box and then OK.

Windows 95 seems to have two versions of ScanDisk. What is the difference in the two versions?

One version of ScanDisk on the Windows 95 startup disk is a DOS program that checks your hard drive for errors before allowing setup. The other is a Windows-based version that can be run through Explorer or from the Start menu. Both versions check the File Allocation Table (FAT), long filenames, system structure, folder structure, surface damage (bad sectors and lost allocation units), and any DriveSpace or DoubleSpace volume and compression.

After Windows 95 has been installed, you can use ScanDisk from your Accessories menu with these instructions:

1. Open the Start menu and select Programs, Accessories, Systems Tools, and then click on ScanDisk. The ScanDisk dialog box will be displayed, as shown in Figure 6-3.

2. Select the disk drive to be checked.

3. Click on the Type of test, Standard or Thorough. If you choose Thorough, you can click on Options to select the area of the disk to be scanned, and to choose whether to perform write testing and to repair bad sectors in hidden or system files.

4. If you want the errors automatically fixed without alerting you, click on Automatically fix errors.

5. Click on Start to begin the error checking.

After I ran a disk utility (an older version of Norton Utilities, for example), all my long filenames disappeared. Why?

You have to run a disk utility that supports long filenames or the utility will look at the information in the Virtual File Allocation Table (VFAT) that stores the long filename information and consider it corruption or garbage and clean it up. Be sure to use Windows 95 utilities, such as the Norton Utilities for Windows 95 or the new version of ScanDisk that is long filename-aware.

What is Defrag and how do I use it?

The Defragmenter (which has a filename Defrag.exe) is a system utility that optimizes disk performance by reorganizing the files on a drive. When your disk begins to get full and you continue

FIGURE 6-3   ScanDisk searches your disk drives for errors

to save files, the files are broken up into segments and the segments are spread out over the disk in any unused space. Defrag's reorganization gathers up the segments and places them in one contiguous location. This considerably speeds up disk access. Unlike previous versions of Defrag, it can run from within Windows and even while you are performing other tasks, although this is NOT recommended since Defrag restarts every time you write something on the disk. You can defragment your local hard drives, compressed drives, and floppy drives. You cannot defrag network drives or CD-ROM drives.

We recommend that you run Defrag on a regular basis, at least monthly if you use your PC fairly often.

Follow these steps to start the Defragmenter:

1. Open the Start button and choose Programs, Accessories, System Tools, Disk Defragmenter.

2. Click on the down arrow to open the drive drop-down list and select the disk drive to be defragmented. It will default to your hard drive. Click on OK.

3. The Disk Defragmenter dialog box will examine your disk and display a percentage of fragmentation in your disk and recommend whether you should defragment the drive or not. Click on Select Drive to select a different drive. Click on Advanced to set some options for how the defragmenting will be done. If you decide to proceed, click on Start and a message box will open, giving you the status as shown here:

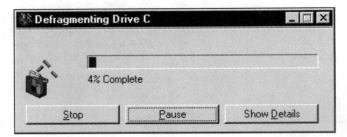

Is there an easier way than going through the maze of menus, if I want to run the drive utilities such as ScanDisk and Defrag?

There are two other ways to start the disk utilities: from the Start menu Run option and from the disk Properties dialog box. Follow these steps to use the Run option:

1. Open the Start menu and choose Run.

2. Type **scandskw** to start ScanDisk or type **defrag** to start the Disk Defragmenter, and in either case, press ENTER or click on OK.

Follow these steps to use the Properties dialog box:

1. Open My Computer or the Explorer.

2. Right-click on the drive you want to work on and choose Properties. The Properties dialog box will appear. Click on the Tools tab as shown in Figure 6-4.

3. Click on Check Now to run ScanDisk, Backup Now to run Backup, and Defragment Now to run the Disk Defragmenter.

FIGURE 6-4   Disk Properties dialog box provides access to some of the important
disk utilities

Folder and Filenames

I renamed a folder in Explorer. Can I get back to my original name?

Yes. After you perform a move, copy, or rename operation on a file or folder in Windows 95, you can undo it. Just press CTRL-Z. In the Explorer or My Computer, open the Edit menu and choose Undo. If you are undoing a rename, the option will actually be Undo Rename, or if you are undoing a move, it will say Undo Move. In this way you will have some idea what you are undoing.

Tech Tip: You can undo the last *ten* copy, move, or rename operations that you performed.

Filenames

What are the valid filenames I can use in Windows 95?

Filenames in Windows 95 can be up to and including 255 characters in length and can use all of the valid DOS filename characters, plus additional characters now valid in Windows 95. Windows 95 filenames are not case-sensitive, but the case is preserved. Also in Windows 95 you can have any number of characters after a period and multiple periods so long as the total number of characters does not exceed 255. In addition to the normal letters and numbers on your keyboard, the special characters shown in Tables 6-1 and 6-2 can be used.

Symbol	Valid in DOS and Windows 95
$	Dollar sign
%	Percent sign
'	Apostrophe or closing single quotation mark
'	Opening single quotation mark
-	Hyphen
@	At sign
{	Left brace
}	Right brace
~	Tilde
!	Exclamation point
#	Number sign
(	Opening parenthesis
)	Closing parenthesis
&	Ampersand
_	Underscore
^	Caret

TABLE 6-1   Valid special characters in DOS and Windows 95

Symbol	Valid only in Windows 95
	Space
+	Plus sign
,	Comma
.	Period
;	Semicolon
=	Equal sign
[	Opening bracket
]	Closing bracket

TABLE 6-2   Valid special characters in Windows 95 only

To see the DOS 8.3 name corresponding to a long filename, right-click the file and then click on Properties. You will see the long filename at the top of the dialog box and the MS-DOS name in the middle, as you can see in Figure 6-5.

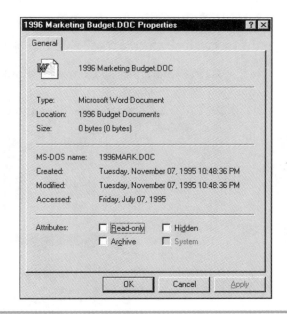

FIGURE 6-5   A file or folder's Properties dialog box shows both the long and short filename

After I restored a tape backup, I lost my long filenames. Why?

Not all tape backup programs support long filenames. Windows 95 includes a backup utility that supports long filenames. You access it by opening the Start menu and selecting Programs, Accessories, System Tools, and then Backup.

File and Folder Operations

How do I copy files and folders in Explorer or My Computer to a different name in the same folder? For example, I want to make a copy of Win.ini to Win.old. How do I do this?

You can make such a copy with the following instructions:

1. In Explorer or My Computer, right-click on the file you want to copy.

2. Choose Copy from the popup menu, as shown here:

3. Then right-click on an empty area inside the same folder you copied from, and choose Paste. This will create a copy of your file at the end of the folder. If the original was called Win.ini, the copy will be called "Copy of Win.ini".

4. Type the name you want in place of the default name.

Can I create a copy of a file on my A:\ drive without using a second disk or copying the file to my hard drive?

Yes, so long as there is enough room on your floppy to hold the copy. You can use the technique discussed in answer to the previous question, or you can do the following:

1. Open My Computer, double-click on A:\ disk drive, and select the file or files you want to copy.

2. Open the Edit menu and choose Copy.

3. Open the Edit menu again and choose Paste. A copy of the selected file or files will be created with the words "Copy of" in front of the filename.

4. Select the name and type the name you want over the default name.

I am getting a message: "This folder already contains a file . . ." What does that mean?

The message you speak of is shown in Figure 6-6. It's telling you that you are trying to place two copies of the same file in the same folder and asking if you want to replace the original file with the one you are trying to copy or move there. You cannot have more than one file with exactly the same name in the same folder. You can replace the existing file with the new one by clicking on Yes. Alternatively, you can click on No and copy or move the file to a different location or modify its filename.

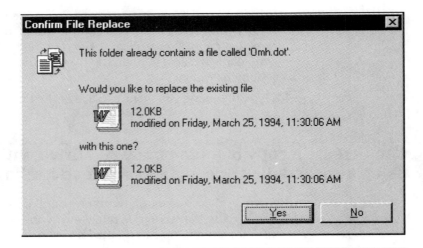

FIGURE 6-6   You get this message when you try to place two files with the same name in the same folder

How do I drag one file to another folder using just the Explorer?

To drag a file from one folder to another using only one instance of the Explorer, use the following steps:

1. Locate the file or folder you want to move in the right pane of the Explorer.

2. Drag the file or folder into the left pane near but not on top of the top or bottom border of the pane. This will cause the pane to scroll, either up or down, depending on whether you moved to the top or bottom (this is called "nudging"). When you see the destination folder, drag the file or folder you are moving to it.

What are some tips and tricks for quickly moving and copying files?

If you drag an object varying the use of SHIFT and CTRL while you drag, you'll get these results:

- If you drag a file or folder *without* using SHIFT or CTRL you will have these effects:
  - Dragging within the same drive will move the object.
  - Dragging to a different drive will copy the object.
- The exceptions to this are if you drag a file without using SHIFT or CTRL, and it is a program file (one with an .EXE or .COM extension), then:
  - Dragging within the same drive will create a shortcut.
  - Dragging to a different drive that is not removable will create a shortcut.
  - Dragging to a different removable drive will create a copy.
- Using SHIFT only always moves the object.
- Using CTRL only always copies the object.
- Using SHIFT and CTRL together while dragging always creates a shortcut.

Tech Tip: Certain folders do not allow objects to be dragged to them, such as the Control Panel and Printers folders. Dragging to other folders always creates a move regardless of SHIFT and/or CTRL status, such as to the Recycle Bin.

How can I select multiple folders or files?

The method used depends on whether the files are contiguous or not.

For contiguous files use one of these methods:

- Click just above or to the right of the first item (not on an item), hold down the left mouse button, and drag the resulting outline box to include all items you want included.
- Click on the first file in a group, press SHIFT, and then click on the last file in the group. All files in the group will be selected.

For noncontiguous files, click on each file while holding CTRL.

What is My Briefcase?

My Briefcase is a tool that you can use to synchronize files on different computers. You can change a file and then make sure that a copy on another computer is also changed. To install the Briefcase on your desktop, choose the Portable option when you set up Windows 95. If you do not do this, you can install it later using the Windows Setup tab on the Add/Remove Programs control panel.

To use My Briefcase, follow these procedures:

1. Using the Explorer or My Computer, drag the files you want to maintain or keep synchronized from folders on your computer to the My Briefcase icon in the Explorer on your desktop. That places a copy of the files in the folder named My Briefcase.

2. Drag the My Briefcase icon to a floppy that you will use to transport the files to another computer.

3. Update your files in My Briefcase on the other computer, making sure that updates are saved to the My Briefcase folder.

4. When finished working on the files on the other computer, insert the updated floppy onto your main computer.

5. Double-click on the My Briefcase icon and the My Briefcase window will be displayed, as shown in Figure 6-7.

6. From the Briefcase menu, select Update All to update your files on the main computer. Select Update Selection if you only want to update some of the files. The files on the main computer are automatically revised.

Why is a shortcut not created when I drag a file from File Manager to the desktop?

File Manager is a Windows 3.1 application. It does not support the functionality of creating shortcuts. Nor does it support dragging and dropping in any form outside of its windows. Use My Computer or the Explorer to create shortcuts.

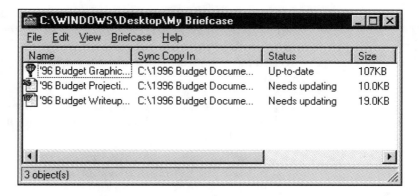

FIGURE 6-7   My Briefcase tells you when two copies of a file are not in synch

Can I add new options to the Send To menu that I get when I right-click on a file?

Initially, the Send To menu shows the floppy drives and other destinations that you have installed, as shown in Figure 6-8. However, you can specify any other disk and/or folder as a destination by adding shortcuts to the \Windows\SendTo folder. For example, adding a shortcut to the Recycle Bin saves

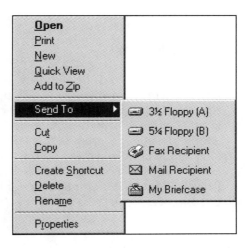

FIGURE 6-8   The Send To menu initially shows the destinations you have installed

time and avoids the prompt, "Are you sure you want to send *filename* to the Recycle Bin?" Alternatively, any other folder such as a temporary folder can also be used.

To add a disk and/or folder to the Send To folder, follow these steps:

1. In the right pane of the Explorer, locate the drive and folder or device (such as a printer) to place in the Send To folder.

2. In the left pane, locate \Windows\SendTo, but do not select it. Simply display it on the left of the Explorer window.

3. Drag the drive and/or folder from the right pane to the \Windows\SendTo folder in the left pane.

Now when you right-click on a file and select Send To, the new destination will appear.

Tech Tip: Here is a bonus. If you have different but related places to send a file, you can create another level of submenu. You place an additional folder (not a shortcut) in the SendTo folder, for example, a Customers folder. Then, within that folder, place shortcuts to all your customer's individual folders, naming each shortcut appropriately. As a result, when you right-click a file icon, your Send To quick menu will show the new Customers option. When you can move to it, you will see a submenu listing all your customer's shortcuts. (You may want to remove the "shortcut to" text from the icons in the SendTo folder.)

 ## What is the Recycle Bin?

The Recycle Bin holds deleted files. These are automatically placed there when you delete a file by pressing DEL or by selecting Delete from the Edit menu or a popup menu. Items in the Recycle Bin can be cut, copied, pasted, or dragged to another location; or they can be restored to their original location by double-clicking on the Recycle Bin icon, opening the Edit menu, and choosing Undo Delete. Items remain in the Recycle Bin until it is emptied by right-clicking on it and choosing Empty Recycle Bin.

Tech Tip: In Windows 95-compliant applications, such as Microsoft Word 7 for Windows 95, if you right-click on a file in the Open dialog box and choose Delete, the file will be placed in the Recycle Bin.

Where do I find the Recycle Bin files?

There is a hidden system folder, \Recycled, in the root folder of every drive. This folder stores the deleted files.

The following are procedures that you can use when working with the Recycle Bin.

- If you delete or rename this folder in Explorer, Windows 95 will recreate a new one when you restart Windows 95. Of course, the new Recycled folder will not contain your previously deleted files.

- If you rename the old Recycle Bin back to its original name, all the previously deleted files will be displayed in the Recycle Bin again.

When I delete a shortcut from my desktop, it is placed in the Recycle Bin. How can I just delete a file and not have it go into the Recycle Bin?

First select the file and then hold down the SHIFT key and press the DELETE key. You can also right-click on the file and then hold down the SHIFT key before selecting Delete from the menu.

Tech Terror: Of course, if you delete a file without sending it to the Recycle Bin, it cannot be restored.

Viewing Files and Folders

What is a folder?

A folder is just a directory as that term was used in earlier versions of Windows and DOS. It is a subdivision of a disk in which you can store files or other folders.

How do I make a new folder?

Making a new folder is easy. Use the following steps:

1. Open the Explorer or My Computer and open the folder to contain the new folder (the contents of the folder should either appear in its own window or in the right pane of the Explorer).

2. Right-click on an empty area in either the folder window or the right pane of the Explorer.

3. Choose New and click on Folder, as shown next. The new folder is created and placed in the parent folder.

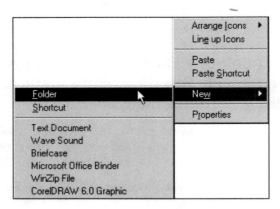

4. Type the name over the New Folder default name, and you're done.

I thought I moved some files around in My Computer, but they still show up in the old place. Why does this happen?

You probably haven't done anything to cause the screen to be refreshed. Press F5 and the display will be refreshed.

How do I view only one type of file (for example only .DLL files) in the Explorer?

You can look at all your .DLL files in two ways using either the Explorer directly or the Find option in either the Explorer Tools menu or the Start menu.

Follow these steps to sort the Explorer so all the .DLL files in a given folder are together:

1. Open the Explorer and select the folder in which you want to see the .DLL files.

2. Open the View menu and select Details to see the file types.

3. In the right-hand pane, click on the Type button in the heading above the files. This will sort the files in ascending order on the file type or file extension as shown in Figure 6-9.

> **Tech Tip:** If you click once on a filename, you will sort the files in ascending order; if you click twice, you will sort in descending order.

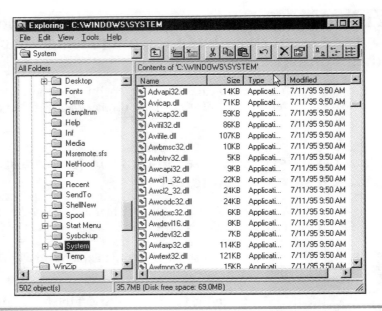

FIGURE 6-9 Clicking on the field names in the heading of the Details view sorts the files on that field

Follow these steps to use Find to gather together the .DLL files in all folders:

1. In the Explorer, open the Tools menu, choose Find, and click on Files or Folders.

2. In the Name & Location tab, type ***.dll** in the Named box. Choose the disk or folder to be searched in Look in. Use Browse if you are not sure.

3. Then click on the Find Now button. Your results will look like those shown in Figure 6-10.

How do I know which .DLL files are being called by a given program?

Right-click on the program file (a file with an .EXE or .COM extension) in the right pane of the Explorer and choose Quick View. The Import Table will show you the list of DLLs being called by the program, as shown in Figure 6-11.

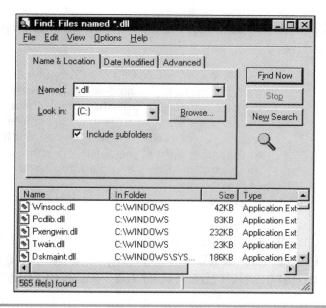

FIGURE 6-10   The Find option can gather similar files across many folders

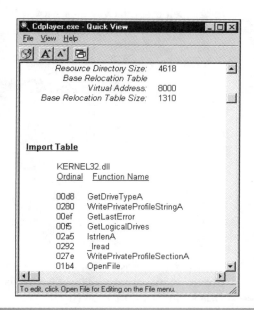

FIGURE 6-11   The Quick View Import Table of a program file will tell you the .DLL files loaded by the program

In My Computer, how do I select the details that appear in a folder?

To select a file or folder in My Computer or the Explorer, you must click on the filename or the icon itself. You cannot click on the details that appear to the right of the icon and filename in Details view. My Computer and the Explorer are designed this way so you can select multiple files and/or folders by pointing to the upper right of the objects, pressing and holding the mouse button down, and dragging a rectangle to the lower left of the objects.

The Quick View feature is supposed to allow users to preview a file without having to open the application that created the file. How do I access this feature?

To use Quick View to see a file, follow these instructions:

1. Right-click on the file in the Explorer or My Computer.

2. Select Quick View, as shown here:

If the file extension cannot be opened by Quick View, this popup menu option will not be available. If you don't get the Quick View option at all (try it on a .DOC or .TXT file), Quick View may not be installed. To do this, use these steps:

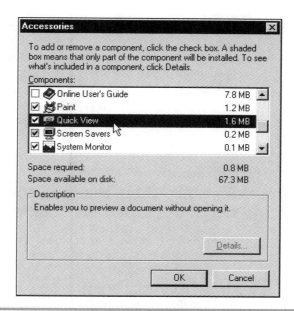

FIGURE 6-12   Select Quick View by placing a check mark next to the name

1. Click on the Start button, choose Settings, and click on Control Panel.

2. Double-click on Add/Remove Programs, and click on the Windows Setup tab.

3. Select Accessories and then click on the Details button. If Quick View doesn't have a check mark next to it, as shown in Figure 6-12, it means that it was not installed during the initial setup. In this case, just click on this item to select it, choose OK, and follow the prompts for the disks.

What file formats can I see in the Quick View?

The following are among the file formats Quick View can open: .ASC ASCII text; .BMP Windows bitmap; .CDR CorelDRAW!; .DOC Microsoft Word for DOS 5-6, Microsoft Word for Windows

2-7, WordPerfect 4.2-6.1; .DRW Micrografx Designer; .INF Setup information; .INI Windows initialization; .MOD MultiPlan 3-4.1; .RTF rich text format; .SAM and .AMI AmiPro; .TXT text; .WB1 QuattroPro; .WKS, .WK1-.WK4 Lotus 1-2-3 1-4; .WPD WordPerfect demo; .WPS Works word processing; .WQ1 QuattroPro 5 for DOS; .WRI Write; .XLC and .XLS Excel 4-7.

Other viewers might be available from the vendor that manufactures a specific application.

 In Windows 95, since there really is not a File Manager, is there any way I can still view files by type?

Yes, there are two ways you can see all files of a certain type together: by sorting the files by Type and by excluding the files you don't want to see.

To sort the files by file type in My Computer or the Explorer, use these instructions:

1. Open the View menu and choose Arrange Icons.

2. Click on by Type, as shown in Figure 6-13.

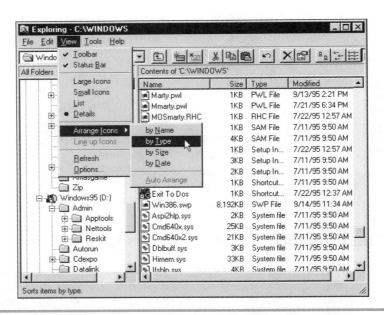

FIGURE 6-13   Any Explorer or My Computer view can be sorted with Arrange Icons

Tech Tip: In Details view you can sort by clicking
on the heading buttons in the upper part
of the window.

You can exclude certain system file types from being viewed
and therefore see only the files that were not excluded. The
following steps allow you to restrict the files view in that way:

1. In either the Explorer or My Computer, open the View
   menu and select Options, and the Options dialog box
   View tab will open.

2. Click on Hide files of these types. This will hide all of the
   system and hidden files, leaving only the files that you
   might normally use.

3. Click on OK. You'll only see the file types that were
   excluded from the list.

How do I search for a document that contains a specific word?

Using Find, you can conduct a search using specific text for the
criteria. Use these instructions:

1. Click on the Start button, choose Find, and select Files or
   Folders. (Alternatively, you can start by selecting Find
   from the Tools menu in the Explorer.)

2. In the Name & Location tab in Look in, type the disk
   drive or the path to be searched. Click on Include
   subfolders if you want the search to be extended to
   these. If you do not know the name of a folder or disk
   drive you want to search, click on Browse and find it
   that way.

3. Click on the Advanced tab, type the keyword or phrase
   for which you want to search in the Containing text entry
   box, as shown in Figure 6-14.

4. Click on Find Now to activate the search.

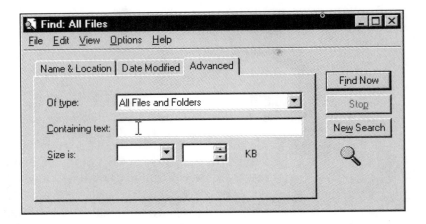

FIGURE 6-14 Find allows you to search for a document containing specific text

Tech Tip: You can quickly open Find by pressing F3. The currently active drive and folder will be the basis for the search, so if you select the drive and folder first and then press F3, you will get exactly the Find dialog box you want.

I often use Find to search for the same files. How can I save and reuse my criteria?

You can save your search criteria with these steps:

1. Open the Start menu, select Find, and choose Files or Folders.

2. Fill in the details of the search such as the filename to search for and the disk and/or folders to search in.

3. After all of the search parameters have been entered, click on Find Now to perform the search and confirm that the criteria produced the desired results.

4. When the search is complete, open the File menu and select Save Search. Your search will be saved on the desktop with a filename that contains the search criteria and the file extension of .FND.

Tech Tip: You can also save the *results* of a search, not just the criteria, by selecting Options and then Save Results.

To use a saved search, simply double-click on the Find file (one with an extension .FND) on the desktop.

When I save a search that contained a wildcard, the filename of the search contains different characters in place of the wildcard. Why does this happen?

This is because wildcards (asterisks and question marks) are not valid characters to use in filenames. Windows 95 replaces asterisks with the @ symbol and question marks with !, the exclamation point, but only in the filename. When you use the saved search, the original criteria with the wildcards reappears as you can see in Figure 6-15.

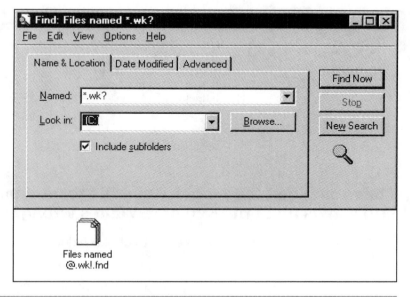

FIGURE 6-15   Although wildcards are replaced in the filename of a saved search, the actual search criteria remains unchanged

I really prefer File Manager from Windows 3.x to Explorer. Is there any way to get it back?

Sure there is. Do the following to restore the File Manager:

1. Right-click on the desktop.

2. Choose New and click on Shortcut.

3. Type in the filename **winfile.exe** and choose Next.

4. Type in the name of the shortcut **file manager**, and then click on Finish. A shortcut to the old Windows File Manager will appear on your desktop, like this:

Tech Terror: The File Manager is a 16-bit application without the ability to display or change long filenames; use drag and drop outside of its window; directly change filenames; or have access to the right-mouse button popup menu. If you move, copy, or try to rename files with long filenames, you will lose the long filename.

I have changed the property of a file to hidden, but it still shows up in the Explorer. What's wrong?

You have the Explorer set to display hidden files. To change that, do the following:

1. Open the Explorer's View menu and choose Options.

2. Choose Hide files of these types.

3. Click on OK.

When I save a file in Word 6.0, it does not appear under Documents in the Start menu. If I save the same file in WordPad, the file shows up on the list! Why?

The documents will only show under Documents in the Start menu if they were saved by a Windows 95 application. Word 6 is a 16-bit Win 3.*x* application and does not support the Windows 95 environment in this way. If you use Word 7 for Windows 95 you will see your documents on the list.

How do I clear out the files from the Documents menu?

To remove files from the Documents menu, do the following:

1. Click on the Start button, choose Settings, and click on the Taskbar.

2. Click on the Start Menu Programs tab, and click on the Clear button in the Documents Menu section, as shown in Figure 6-16.

FIGURE 6-16   Clear the Documents Menu by clicking on the Clear button

File Allocation Table (FAT)

Does Windows 95 utilize a File Allocation Table (FAT) File system?

It does; however, it is a protected-mode implementation of the FAT system known as VFAT (Virtual File Allocation Table). FAT limits a file or folder's name to the 8+3 design; for example, Filename.ext, which provides eight characters for the name and a three-character extension. VFAT allows for both short and long conventions. The 32-bit VFAT driver provides a protected-mode code path for managing the file system stored on a disk that provides smoother multitasking performance.

I have both FAT and HPFS (OS/2) partitions on my computer. Windows 95 Explorer does not seem to recognize the HPFS partition. Why?

Windows 95 can only read an HPFS formatted file from a remote server or with the use of a third-party application that will convert it to VFAT. Windows 95 does not have the capacity to recognize the HPFS partition directly.

I am getting errors trying to save from a Windows 95 application to another folder on my PC. I have a configuration that allows dual booting between Windows 95 and Windows NT. I know it is not a matter of insufficient disk space because the FAT partition that I created under NT is 4GB. Why am I getting these errors?

Windows 95 only supports a 2GB primary partition. Windows NT can create FAT partition of up to 4GB. The reason is that for Windows 95 (like MS-DOS), the maximum cluster size is 32KB, while for Windows NT it is 64KB. (The maximum number of clusters in both cases is 64KB.) This means that Windows 95 can create a maximum drive of 32KB x 64KB = 2048MB (or 2GB). For Windows NT, the numbers are 64KB x 64KB = 4096MB (4GB).

Tech Tip: Fdisk in MS-DOS or Windows 95 can create extended partitions of more than 2GB and then create several logical partitions of under 2GB. But it cannot create primary partitions over 2GB.

Printing

After getting information into your computer and saving it, the next most important job is printing it out. Sometimes this is the most troublesome and often the most time consuming of the tasks. You have the problems associated with the mechanical device, with connecting it to your computer, with using the correct software drivers, and with scheduling and handling the print queue. And if you are printing over a network, all of these problems go up exponentially. If that wasn't enough, with today's printers you also have to worry about fonts—loading, using, managing, and removing them.

FRUSTRATION BUSTERS!

Windows 95 addresses all of the major printing concerns and goes a long way toward making printing truly easy. Among the many enhancements in Windows 95 are the following:

- **Easier printer** installation and setup using Plug-and-play, the Add Printer Wizard, and Point and Print. With a Plug-and-play-compliant printer, all you need to do is plug it in and start Windows 95; the rest is done for you. With the Add Printer Wizard, you are quickly led through the setup process step-by-step. Using Point and Print, you use the Network Neighborhood to locate a shared printer on the network and then double-click on it. This starts the Add Printer Wizard to complete the process.

- **Faster printing** is a reality as a result of a 32-bit printing system, bidirectional communications, enhanced metafile (EMF) spooling, and support for the extended capabilities parallel port (ECP). Windows 95 replaces the Windows 3.*x* Print Manager with a faster 32-bit protected-mode print spooler using 32-bit virtual device drivers for the popular printers. With the printers that can support it, these device drivers will more closely interact with the printers through bidirectional communications and the extended capabilities parallel port. Using the enhanced metafile encoding scheme, Windows 95 can quickly spool a print job to the disk and then, with very little overhead, feed the job to the printer. This gets the user back to his or her work sooner and provides true background printing.

More printing support with image color matching (ICM), deferred printing, improved font handling and flexibility, and the sharing of printers through a NetWare server. Using image color matching, you can better match the colors on the screen with those produced with a color printer. If you are using a portable computer or are for some other reason disconnected from your printer, you can use deferred printing to hold the print job until you are next connected to a printer, at which time the job will automatically be printed. Windows 95 provides for font substitutions, enhanced and more accurate font generation, and

FRUSTRATION BUSTERS!

the ability to store and print many more fonts. Windows 95 also allows its printers to be shared through a NetWare server.

Installing a Printer

How do I install a new printer on my computer in Windows 95?

You can install a new printer using the Add Printer Wizard from your Printer's dialog box. The Wizard will prompt you in the installation of your printer. Use these steps:

1. Click on the Start button, choose Settings, and click on Printers.

2. Double-click on Add Printer. The Add Printer Wizard window will be displayed.

3. Click on Next. Choose Local printer.

4. Click on Next. The lists of Manufacturers and Printers will appear, as you can see in Figure 7-1.

5. In the Manufacturers list, select the manufacturer's name and double-click on the model you want to install, or select the model and click on Next.

6. If you are installing a local printer, select the port it will use. The LPT1 parallel port is the most common choice.

7. Click on Next. The wizard will prompt you for a friendly name (type a name that easily identifies the particular printer).

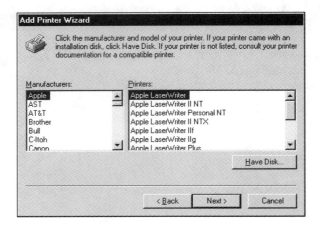

FIGURE 7-1   Windows 95 gives you a very wide choice of printer manufacturers and models to choose from

8. Decide if this printer will be your default printer and click on Next.

9. Decide if you want to print a test page, and then click on Finish. Windows begins to copy the necessary files. If the files are already installed, you can use them or choose to install new files. You can install new files from Windows source files or from a disk from the manufacturer.

I keep hearing about Point and Print. How does it work?

Point and Print allows you to easily install a printer driver on your computer so you can use a shared network printer. Here's how:

1. Double-click on the Network Neighborhood to open it.

2. Browse through your network by opening (double-clicking on) various computers until you find the printer you want to use.

3. Double-click on the printer and click on Yes to install it on your computer.

4. Answer the various questions from the Add Printer Wizard, clicking on Next and finally on Finish. The print queue for the network printer will open. Click on Close.

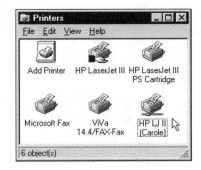

FIGURE 7-2   A network printer appears in your Printers folder with a cable beneath it

The network printer is now set up on your computer and can be used by any of your Windows (and DOS, if you selected that option) programs. You can see the new printer on your computer by double-clicking on Printers in My Computer or by opening the Start menu and selecting Settings, Printers. In both cases, the Printers folder will open and display a new networked printer, one with a cable beneath it, as shown in the lower right of Figure 7-2 above.

Using a Printer

What is drag-and-drop printing?

If you create a shortcut to your printer on your desktop, you can drag a file from My Computer or the Explorer and drop it on the printer shortcut. This will send the document to the printer without you having to open the application that created the file. To create a shortcut to a printer, follow these instructions:

1. From My Computer, the Explorer, or the Control Panel, double-click on Printers. The Printers folder will open.

2. Drag the printer for which you want a shortcut to the desktop.

3. Answer Yes, indicating that you want to create a shortcut.

4. Rename the shortcut if you wish.

Tech Tip: Drag-and-drop printing only works for documents that have a registered association with an application and have a printing option defined.

To see if drag-and-drop printing has been defined for a type of file, use these steps:

1. From the Explorer or My Computer, open the View menu and choose Options.

2. Click on the File Types tab and select the file type you want to check in the Registered file types list box.

3. Click on Edit. The Edit File Type dialog box will open, as you can see in Figure 7-3.

4. Check to see if the list of actions includes Print. If so, drag-and-drop printing will work with that file type.

5. If Print is not a defined action, you can define it by clicking on New, typing **Print** in the Action box, and using Browse to select the application you want to use to print the job.

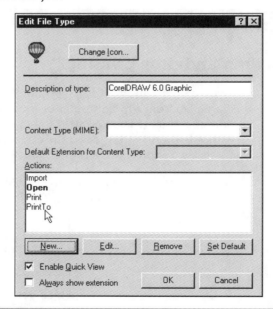

FIGURE 7-3   The drag-and-drop actions available for a file type are listed in the File Type dialog box

How can I print a file from the Explorer?

If printing has been defined as an option in a file type's registration, then there are three ways to print that file type from the Explorer:

- Drag the file from the Explorer and drop it on a shortcut to a printer that you have created on your desktop. (See the previous question.)
- Right-click on a file and select Print from the popup menu that opens.
- Right-click on a file and select Send To, Printer, if you add a shortcut to your printer in your \Windows\SendTo folder.

To add an item to the Send To list, use the following steps:

1. Create a shortcut to a printer on your printer as described in the previous question.
2. Open the Explorer and then the \Windows\SendTo folder.
3. Right-click on the right pane of the Explorer, which should be the \Windows\SendTo folder.
4. Choose New Shortcut from the popup menu that appears.
5. Click on Browse in the Create Shortcut Wizard that appears.
6. Select Desktop in the Look in drop-down list and All Files in the Files of type list. Your printer shortcut should appear in the list of objects on the desktop.
7. Double-click on the printer shortcut, and click on Next.
8. Type the name you want to use, and click on Finish. Your printer will now appear in your Send To list.

How can I print to a file, and can I do it from the Explorer?

You can send your output to a file and print later from a different PC. You must either create a new printer or change the configuration of one of your existing printers so that you have a printer defined that prints to a file. Then you can use one of the techniques in the previous question to do the printing. Here's how you change the configuration of an existing printer to have it print to a file (if you want a new printer to serve that purpose, use the Add Printer Wizard, as described in an earlier question):

1. Right-click on the printer you want to reconfigure, and select Properties. The printer's dialog box will open.

2. Click on the Details tab and open the Print to the following port drop-down list box.

3. Select FILE, as shown in Figure 7-4. Click on OK.

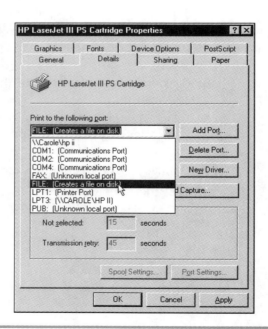

FIGURE 7-4   You can direct a printer to a file or a fax as well as an actual printer by changing the port you are printing to

When you issue the Print command, the print will be sent to a file and you will be prompted for a filename as you can see here:

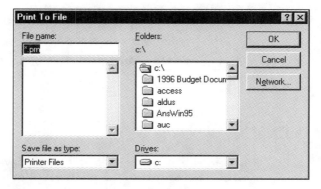

To print the file later, use these steps:

1. From the Start menu, choose Programs, MS-DOS Prompt to open a DOS window.

2. At the DOS prompt, type **copy c:\\<path>\\filename lpt1**, where <path>\\filename is the full path and name of your file, and LPT1 is your printer port. Make sure you are printing using the same type of printer you selected when you printed to a file.

I was trying to print something to a file (for example, Device Manager information). Why isn't it readable?

When Windows 95 prints information to a file, it uses printer language output rather than straight text format. To print to a file and have it in a readable format, you have to print to the Generic Text Only printer. To install the Generic Text Only printer, do the following:

1. Click on the Start button, choose Settings, and then click on Printers.

2. Double-click on the Add Printer icon and click on the Next button.

3. When you are prompted, click on the Local printer button, and then click the Next button.

4. In the Manufacturers box, select Generic; in the Printers box, select Generic/Text Only.

5. Click on Next and in the Available ports box, select FILE, and click on Next.

6. Enter the name you want for the printer and answer No to "Do you want your Windows-based programs to use this printer as the default printer?"

7. Click on Next. Answer No to testing the printer, and click on Finish.

What is EMF?

EMF is an enhanced metafile. It is a non-device-specific picture of what is being sent to the printer. A print job can be quickly captured as an EMF on disk and then sent to the printer in the background. Spooling with an EMF allows you to get back to work faster after printing a file and to do more while the EMF is being sent to the printer.

As I understand, Windows 95 does not use a "Print Manager" but sends the pages to be printed in a queue as metafiles. Being in a metafile format, will my printer be required to have enough memory to print a full page of my graphics?

This will not put additional strain on the printer. The Windows 95 EMF format (see previous question) increases the actual printing speed but does not require the printer to hold or process more information.

I have printed a document, but nothing is coming out. How do I avoid this problem?

If you are trying to use a network printer or one that is sometimes not connected to your computer, check to make sure the printer has not been set to work offline. Use these steps to do that:

1. Click on the Start button, choose Settings, and click on Printers, or open My Computer and double-click on the Printer icon.

2. Right-click on the printer you are trying to use. The printer's popup menu, shown here, will open.

3. If Work Offline is selected and you can in fact connect to the printer, deselect the Work Offline option.

If you are using a local printer and having the problem, check all the obvious things like the cable being connected to the port you think you are using, the printer being turned on and online, and the driver you are using being the correct one for your printer. Windows 95 has an excellent printer troubleshooting section in online Help. The next set of steps will open it for you:

1. Click on the Help menu in the Explorer, My Computer, or Printers windows and select Help Topics. The Windows Help dialog box will open.

2. In the Contents tab, double-click on Troubleshooting and then double-click again on it if you have trouble printing. The Print Troubleshooter will open, as shown in Figure 7-5.

3. Click on the button that best describes your problem and follow along as additional questions are asked until your problem is fixed.

 If I am printing offline, will I lose my print job if I turn off my laptop?

No, the whole idea behind deferred printing is that you can process the print job while not being actually connected to the printer. The job is spooled to the disk, and an EMF (enhanced

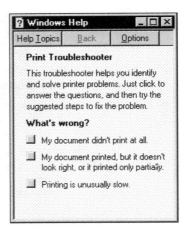

FIGURE 7-5   The Print Troubleshooter will help you solve your printing problems

metafile) print output is created. It will stay on your hard disk until you connect to a printer. Then when you connect to the printer and turn Work Offline off, your print job will be completed and the temporary spool file deleted.

I used to be able to print offline on my laptop computer, but then I changed something in my settings and this option is gone. What did I do?

If you have turned off spooling in your printer properties, you cannot print offline. Follow the next set of steps to turn this back on:

1. Use the Start menu, Settings, Printers to open the Printers folder.

2. Right-click on the printer and select Properties from the popup menu.

3. Click on the Details tab and on the Spool Settings button. The Spool Settings dialog box will open, as shown in Figure 7-6.

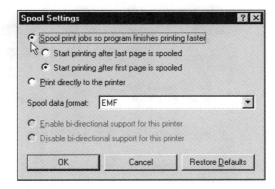

FIGURE 7-6   The Spool Settings dialog box allows you to turn print spooling
on and off

Tech Tip: The Spool Settings dialog box allows
you to begin printing after one page has spooled
(which increases printing speed) or after all
pages have spooled (which gets you back to
your application faster).

Tech Tip : If you have shared your printer on a
ntwork, you will not be able to turn spooling off.

4. Click on the Spool print jobs. . . option and click on
OK twice.

I have sent a number of files to the printer. One of them is urgent. How can I change the order in which the files will be printed?

To change the print order, do the following:

1. Double-click on the printer icon in the notification area
on the right of the Taskbar. Your printer's print queue
window will open, as you can see in Figure 7-7.

HP LaserJet III				_ □ ×

Printer Document View Help

Document Name	Status	Owner	Progress	Started At
Microsoft Word - W95ans04.doc	Printing	marty	2 of 34 pages	10:18:46 AM 9/16/95
Benz.cdr:CorelDRAW		marty	1 page(s)	10:21:55 AM 9/16/95
C:\MPUB\KENRTNEV.PM5		marty	2 page(s)	10:25:57 AM 9/16/95
Microsoft Word - W95ans03.doc		marty	18 page(s)	10:28:34 AM 9/16/95

4 jobs in queue

FIGURE 7-7   The print queue window shows you what is waiting to be printed and in what order

2. Select the file you want to print sooner, hold down the left mouse button, drag it up to the top of the queue, and then let go of the mouse button.

In Windows 3.*x*, printing was closely connected to the video driver and I could resolve a lot of strange printing problems by replacing the video driver. Is this troubleshooting option still available?

In Windows 95, printing and video display are completely independent. The Windows 95 video driver and the Windows 95 printer drivers get graphical display information from separate sources and not from a common graphical device interface (GDI), as was the case in previous versions of Windows.

This is true only for the native 32-bit Windows 95 printer drivers. If you are using Windows 3.*x* printer drivers, it would still access GDI for printing information. In this case, changing the video driver might directly affect printing.

In Windows 3.1, the colors on the printout did not match the colors on the screen. Does Windows 95 improve color printing?

This has been addressed by a new Windows 95 feature called Image Color Matching (ICM), which provides the user with real color WYSIWYG (what you see is what you get). Applications that directly support ICM will match the formatting of the printed output to colors onscreen based on the specifications of the printer and display. Even older applications that are not ICM-aware (Windows 3.*x* applications) would benefit from this because the ICM can be enabled directly through the printer driver. The printer driver has to be a native 32-bit Windows 95 driver that supports color printing.

I thought I should be able print to a printer connected to a UNIX machine because I am running TCP/IP and can see the UNIX box. Why am I not able to do this?

In Windows 95, you cannot print directly to a printer on a machine running UNIX only. You can print to a printer on a Windows NT 3.5 server or a NetWare server that are also running UNIX. For example, you can connect to a UNIX printer through a Windows NT machine and then share it to Windows 95 clients.

When I print from my DOS application, I get an error message and I can't print. Why does this happen?

This will happen because you only configured the printer to print from Windows applications. You will need to reconfigure the printer to print from DOS applications by deleting the current driver and using the Add Printer Wizard to install a new one with support for DOS. Use these steps to do that:

1. Open the Start menu, and choose Settings, Printers.
2. Select the printer you want to reconfigure, press DEL, and answer Yes you are sure you want to delete the printer.
3. Double-click on Add Printer and click on Next.
4. Select Network printer and click on Next.
5. Type in or browse for the path to the printer; select Yes you want to print from MS-DOS-based programs, as you can see in Figure 7-8; and click on Next.

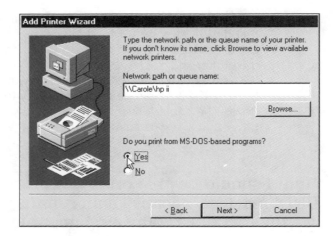

FIGURE 7-8   You must establish the capability to print from DOS applications while you are setting up the printer

6. Click on Capture Printer Port; select the device, such as LPT3; click on OK; and click on Next.

7. Type in a name for the printer, decide if you want to make it your default printer, and click on Next.

8. Print a test page if you wish and click on Finish.

Tech Tip: DOS programs cannot print directly to a network printer. You must map the network printer to a port address on your computer (such as LPT3, as was done in step 6) that DOS can print to.

How do I print from Lotus Notes under Windows 95?

When you install a network printer on your computer, the default port is the path to the printer in the form *server\printername*. This works fine with many products. Notes, like DOS applications, is looking for a port address such as LPT3, as opposed to just \\server\printername. You can fix this problem by capturing the network printer to a port address on your computer. Use these instructions to do that:

1. Click on the Start button, choose Settings, and choose Printers.

2. Right-click on the icon for the printer you want to use, and choose Properties.

3. Click on the Details tab, and then select Capture Printer Port.

4. In the Device list, select the port address that you want to use.

5. Select or type the network path for the printer, select Reconnect at logon, as shown next, and then click on OK.

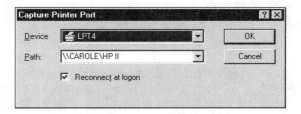

6. In the Print to the following port box, select the port you mapped, and click on OK.

How do I print out information about my computer configuration?

To print your computer configuration information, use the following steps:

1. Right-click on My Computer.

2. Choose Properties, and click on the Device Manager tab.

3. Select Computer, and then click on Print.

4. Make sure the System Summary option is selected in the Print dialog box, and click on OK.

Fonts

How do I preview my fonts without actually having to format text in an application?

You can see the fonts without using them in text by doing the following:

1. Open My Computer, and double-click on Control Panel.

2. Double-click on the Fonts folder.

3. Double-click on the font you want to see. The font's dialog box will open as shown in Figure 7-9.

4. Click on Print to print out the sample fonts and click on Done when you are.

Tech Tip: To print samples of several fonts, in the Fonts folder, select all the fonts at once while holding down CTRL, open the File menu, and choose Print. (You'll have to click on OK in the Print dialog box and Done in the font's dialog box for each of the fonts to complete the printing.)

FIGURE 7-9   You can see what a font looks like by double-clicking on it

When I remove a font, Windows 95 deletes the file and places it in the Recycle Bin. In previous versions of Windows, if font trouble occurred, I could "remove" the font without removing the file from the hard disk. Does this functionality still exist in Windows 95?

Windows 95 accomplishes the same end by moving the fonts to the Recycle Bin. You can then return the font to its folder by opening the Recycle Bin and choosing Restore from the File menu.

What is the maximum number of True Type fonts that I can install on my PC?

Because Windows 95 uses the registry to store fonts, there is no limit to the number of True Type fonts that can be installed. You can select and use nearly a 1000 different fonts and styles on any document without any problems.

Networking

Computer networking has become more the rule than the exception, and Windows 95 has responded to that by making networking an integral part of the operating system and not an add-on. And what Windows 95 has provided is significant. It is both a full and very competent *client* for Novell NetWare and Windows NT servers, and a complete peer-to-peer networking system among Windows 95 or Windows for Workgroups computers, with all the features needed for many organizations. In addition, Windows 95 supports networking with several other vendors' software including Artisoft LANtastic, Banyan VINES, and DEC Pathworks. Not only can Windows 95 be a client in a client-server network and a full peer in a peer-to-peer network, it can do both at the same time. In all senses, Windows 95 is a networking operating system.

FRUSTRATION BUSTERS!

To utilize Windows 95 networking, you'll need the hardware required to set up the applicable Windows 95 components. Windows 95 makes the software setup easy by leading you through dialog boxes with lists of alternatives, and if your network adapter is Plug-and-play-compliant, setting it up is a snap. Here are some tips on setting up Windows 95 networking:

- You will need a network adapter card in your computer and in each computer in your network. The most common adapter cards are combination Ethernet cards that handle several types of cabling. Depending on your network adapter card and several physical considerations like the distances to be covered and the number of stations to be connected, you will need one of the following types of cabling:

  - **10Base-T** twisted-pair cabling is the most common today and is the most flexible form of network cabling.

  - **10Base-2** thin coaxial cable is common in small networks and for them, it is very cost-effective.

  - **10Base-5** thick or standard coaxial cable was the original networking standard. But it is both expensive and difficult to use, and so it has been eclipsed by the other forms of cabling.

  - **Fiber optic** cabling is appearing for long-distance and high-speed networking, but is expensive and probably will not replace 10Base-T in the near term.

  - **Wireless** networking is beginning to be used where running a cable is very difficult. It too is expensive and may encounter problems with interference.

- If your networking hardware is running prior to installing Windows 95, Setup will often detect and properly set up Windows 95 to operate with your hardware.

- If you install a Plug-and-play adapter after setting up Windows 95, it will automatically set up your network the first time you start up Windows 95.

FRUSTRATION BUSTERS!

- If you add networking after Windows 95 has been set up and without a Plug-and-play adapter, you will need to set up the network manually. You can do this by opening the Start menu, selecting Settings, Control Panel, and then double-clicking on Add New Hardware. You will be guided through the network installation.

- How you set up Windows 95 networking depends on whether you want your computer to be a peer in a peer-to-peer network or a client in a client-server network. In peer-to-peer networking, generally used in smaller networks, all computers in the network share their resources equally. In this mode, all computers typically run either Windows 95 or Windows for Workgroups, although other possibilities exist. Client-server, on the other hand, supports many computers, known as clients, accessing the resources of one or more designated server computers. The clients can be running Windows 95 or other client software, but for Windows 95 clients, the server must be running either Novell NetWare or Windows NT.

- To set up or change the Windows 95 networking software configuration, open the Start menu, select Settings, Control Panel, and double-click on Network. The Network dialog box will open, as shown in Figure 8-1. It allows you to install or change four types of networking software components:

  - **Clients,** which allow you to access other computers in order to use their resources, are used for both peer-to-peer and client-server networking. The Client for Microsoft Networks and the Client for NetWare Networks are the two most common choices.

  - **Adapters,** which are the interfaces or drivers between your network adapter cards and Windows 95, are unique to your particular adapter card and, like a printer, you must select a manufacturer and a model.

    Tech Tip: Generic NE1000-, NE2000-, and NE3200-compatible adapters are found under Novell/Anthem, and the Dial-Up Adapter is under Microsoft.

FRUSTRATION BUSTERS!

- **Protocol**, which is the communication language that will be used between computers, is determined by the type of networking you will be doing. In a Windows 95 peer-to-peer network or with a Windows NT client-server network, you should use Microsoft NetBEUI. With a NetWare client-server network, you should use Microsoft IPX/SPX or Novell IPX. With dial-up networking to the Internet, you should use Microsoft TCP/IP.

- **Service**, which allows you to share your resources with other computers or to provide other services such as network backup, is primarily needed to provide the server functions in a peer-to-peer network.

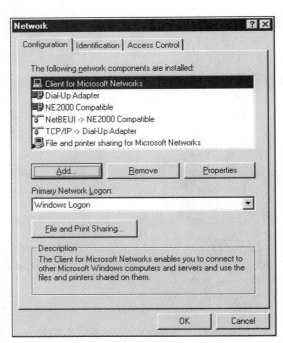

FIGURE 8-1   The Network dialog box allows you to select the software components you'll use in networking

Network Compatibility

What types of networking are supported in Windows 95?

Windows 95 can be a client or a peer in the following networks, but it may need additional software from the particular manufacturer:

- **Artisoft LANtastic** version 5.0 and above
- **Banyan VINES** version 5.52 and above
- **DEC PATHWORKS** version 4.1 and above
- **IBM OS/2 LAN Server**
- **Microsoft LAN Manager** and **Windows NT**
- **Novell NetWare** version 3.11 and above
- **SunSoft PC-NFS** version 5.0 and above

I understand Windows 95 ships with NetWare client software from both Microsoft and Novell. What's the difference and how do I install my choice?

Windows 95 does include both the Microsoft Client for Novell Networks and the comparable software from Novell (Novell NetWare Workstation Shell for either 3.*x* or 4.*x* networks). The Microsoft version is 32-bit protected-mode software versus 16-bit real-mode software from Novell. The Windows 95 file system operates in 32-bit protected mode, so to use the Novell software, the processor is going to have to switch between real and protected mode, which will slow performance. The Microsoft software also supports long filenames and peer resource sharing, neither of which is supported by Novell.

Tech Tip: Novell is expected to release 32-bit protected-mode software in the fall of 1995, so you may want to check into that as a third alternative.

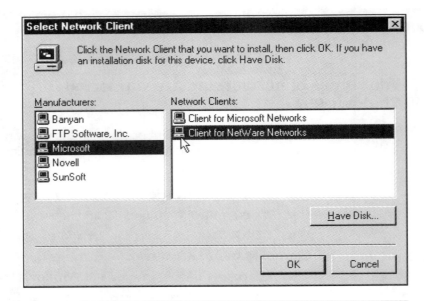

FIGURE 8-2   You can choose between Microsoft and Novell NetWare networking clients

You can choose and install a NetWare client using the following steps:

1. Open the Start menu, choose Settings, Control Panel, and double-click on Network.

2. In the Configuration tab, click on Add, select Client, and click on Add again.

3. Select from the Manufacturer's list, Microsoft or Novell, choose the network client you want, as shown in Figure 8-2 (above), and then click on OK.

Can I use Windows 95 with a Banyan VINES network?

You can, provided you have VINES version 5.52(5) or later. The best way would be to have the Banyan VINES client installed and configured before upgrading to Windows 95. To make your Windows 95 PC work as a client on Banyan VINES network, you have to have the following components installed in the Network control panel:

- Your network adapter should be set for a real-mode 16-bit NDIS driver (choose this by clicking on your adapter in the Network dialog box, Configuration tab, and then clicking on Properties).

- Your client software should be Banyan DOS/Windows 3.1 (choose this by clicking on Add in the Network dialog box, Configuration tab, choosing Client, and then clicking on Add again).

- Your network protocol should be Banyan VINES Ethernet Protocol (choose this by clicking on Add in the Network dialog box, Configuration tab, choosing Protocol, and then clicking on Add again).

Make sure your system files contain the following lines (assume that Banyan VINES is your primary network, that your Banyan files are in the \Vines folder, and that Exp16.dos is your NDIS2 driver):

```
Autoexec.bat:
cd \Vines
ban
ndisban                  ; ndtokban if you are using token ring
redirall
arswait
z:login
c:
cd\
Config.sys:
device=c:\vines\proman.dos /i:c:\vines
device=c:\vines\exp16.dos
Protocol.ini:
[PROTOCOL MANAGER]
drivername=protman$
[VINES_XIF]
drivername=ndisban$   ; ndtokban$ if you are using token ring
bindings=MS$EE16
[MS$EE16]
drivername=EXP16$
interrupt=5
ioaddress=0x300
iochrdy=late
```

Banyan VINES servers will not appear in the Network Neighborhood, because Banyan VINES servers do not support browsing. You can use Windows 95's Map Network Drive to locate and connect to the Banyan servers.

Tech Tip: Banyan is planning on having 32-bit protected-mode client software in the fall of 1995.

Can a Windows 95 computer act as a Novell NetWare server?

If you install file and printer sharing for NetWare networks service, the Windows 95 machine can act as a NetWare file and print server. To install this service, do the following:

1. Right-click on Network Neighborhood, and click on Properties.
2. On the Configuration tab, click on Add, select Service, and click on Add again.
3. Select Microsoft and select File and printer sharing for NetWare Networks, as shown in Figure 8-3. This will load a virtual device driver (called Nwserver.vxd) that enables Windows 95 computers to process NCP-based requests for file and printer input/output.

Does Windows 95 come with support for DEC PATHWORKS?

Yes, Windows 95 provides 32-bit protected-mode drivers for DEC PATHWORKS version 4.1 and above. You should use

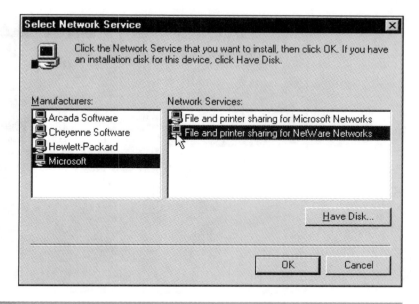

Select Network Service

Click the Network Service that you want to install, then click OK. If you have an installation disk for this device, click Have Disk.

Manufacturers:
- Arcada Software
- Cheyenne Software
- Hewlett-Packard
- Microsoft

Network Services:
- File and printer sharing for Microsoft Networks
- File and printer sharing for NetWare Networks

Have Disk...

OK   Cancel

FIGURE 8-3   A Windows 95 workstation can share its files and printers over a NetWare network

Microsoft's Client for Microsoft Networks and a DEC PATHWORKS protocol. Follow these steps:

Tech Tip: DEC is supposed to have a 32-bit protected-mode client available in the fall of 1995.

1. Right-click on the Network Neighborhood icon and choose Properties.
2. On the Configuration tab, click on Add.
3. Choose Client and click on Add.
4. Choose Microsoft Client for Microsoft Networks, and click on OK.
5. Choose Protocol and click on Add.
6. Click on Digital Equipment (DEC) and a list of DEC network protocols will be listed, as shown in Figure 8-4.
7. Select the one you want to use and click on OK.

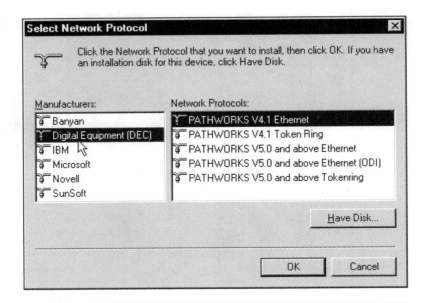

FIGURE 8-4   DEC offers several network protocols that can be installed

Can I use Windows 95 with Artisoft LANtastic 6.0?

Yes, you can use LANtastic 5.0 and above with Windows 95. Be sure and have LANtastic installed and running *before you run* Windows 95 Setup. Windows 95 does not supply the LANtastic software—you must get the Windows 95 LANtastic *.INF files from Artisoft. When you do, you must then install them as client software following these steps:

Tech Terror: You cannot install LANtastic after you have installed Windows 95. Also, you must start LANtastic before starting Windows 95 Setup.

1. Open the Start menu, select Settings, Control Panel, and double-click on Network.

2. From the Configuration tab, click on Add.

3. Click on Client and click on Add again.

4. Insert the disk with your LANtastic *.INF files into a floppy drive and click on Have Disk.

5. Follow the prompts to install the client software.

The LANtastic resources will only be accessible for you through the LANtastic utilities, which you can find by opening the Start menu and selecting Programs and then the LANtastic program group. You will not be able to access LANtastic through Network Neighborhood.

How do I install Windows 95 on a computer that has networking support from a network vendor other than Microsoft or Novell?

First, before you install Windows 95, you should be sure that your network client software is correctly installed under MS-DOS, Windows version 3.1, or Windows for Workgroups, and that the network is running when you start Setup.

During Setup, Windows 95 should detect a network adapter and install the Microsoft Client for Microsoft Networks by default. Notice that the Configuration tab in the Network control panel provides the same controls for adding and removing networking components after Windows 95 Setup is complete.

Tech Tip: Install any non-Microsoft network *before* you install Windows 95 and then install networking support during Windows 95 Setup, not after the fact.

Setting Up

Will I need new networking software to connect Windows 95 to my network server?

No. Windows 95 will continue to run existing real-mode networking components while enhancing the 32-bit protected-mode networking components first delivered with Windows for Workgroups.

After installing Windows 95, I no longer can connect to my network. Why?

If your network is supported in Windows 95 with Windows 95 protected-mode drivers (primarily Microsoft and Novell networks when this is written), you may have a conflict between real and protected-mode drivers. Make sure the appropriate client software is installed by opening the Network control panel. Then use Notepad to open your Autoexec.bat and Config.sys files and remark out (put **rem** and a space on the left of the line) all real-mode network drivers (for a Microsoft or a Novell network with the Microsoft client, you do not need any statements in your system files that load network drivers).

If the network you have is not supported in Windows 95 with Windows 95 protected-mode drivers, you have to load real-mode client drivers in your Autoexec.bat or Config.sys files. If it is an unsupported network, make sure to have the network fully installed and operating *before* starting Windows 95 Setup.

If you think that all of your networking software is correct, make sure that the resources are correctly assigned to your network adapter. Use the following steps to do that:

1. Right-click on the Network Neighborhood and choose Properties.

2. In the Configuration tab of the Network dialog box, click on your network adapter and click on Properties.

3. In the adapter's Properties dialog box, click on Resources, and check on the Interrupt (IRQ) and I/O address range, as you can see in Figure 8-5. The settings you see should match what was set on your adapter card.

4. Make the necessary changes to the IRQ and I/O address and click on OK twice.

How do I install a NetWare client on my Windows 95 machine?

First, you must determine whether to use Microsoft's 32-bit NetWare client, or one of Novell's 16-bit clients. If your network

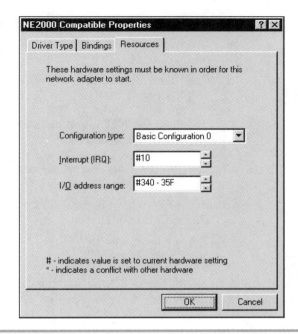

FIGURE 8-5   The resource settings in your network adapter's Properties dialog box must match those physically made on the card itself

is running either NetWare 3.*x* or 4.*x*, you can use the 32-bit Windows 95 Microsoft Client for NetWare. To do this:

1. Click on the Start button, choose Settings, open the Control Panel, and double-click on Network.

2. In the Configuration tab, click on Add, select Client, and click on Add again.

3. Select Microsoft and Client for NetWare Networks. This will give you full protected-mode support for NetWare, and you will not be using any conventional memory to load real-mode network drivers. Click on OK.

However, if you need to use any of the following NetWare services or functions, then you will need to use one of the Novell NetWare 16-bit real-mode Clients (NetWare Workstation Shell 3.*x* or NETX and NetWare Workstation Shell 4.*x* or VLM):

■ Load real-mode TSRs from your login script—use either NETX or VLM

■ Enable NetWare Directory Services (NDS)—use VLM

- Use NCP Packet Signature for security—use VLM
- Use NetWare Internet Protocol (IP)—use either NETX or VLM
- Use Novell utilities such as NETADMIN or NWADMIN—use VLM

If you want to use NETX, you have to load the Novell NetWare Workstation Shell 3.*x*. To do that:

1. Click on the Start button, choose Settings, Control Panel, and double-click on Network.
2. In the Configuration tab, click on Add, select Client, and click on Add again.
3. Select Novell and then Novell NetWare (Workstation Shell 3.*x*). Click on OK.

If you want to use VLM, install the Novell NetWare (Workstation Shell 4.*x*) client in step 3.

Can I connect to a Novell server through Dial-Up Networking?

You need to install the Microsoft Client for NetWare Networks and the IPX/SPX-compatible protocol, which you need to bind to the Dial-Up Adapter driver. To install the client software, see the previous question. The protocol is very likely to already be installed on your computer. Check this by opening your Network control panel and seeing if you see the following lines in the list of network components:

```
IPX/SPX-compatible Protocol -> Dial-Up Adapter
IPX/SPX-compatible Protocol -> NE2000 Compatible
```

If the protocol software is not already installed on your computer, follow these steps to install it:

1. From the Network dialog box Configuration tab, click on Add, select Protocol, and click on Add again.

2. Select Microsoft from the list of manufacturers and click on IPX/SPX-compatible Protocol, as shown in Figure 8-6.

3. Click on OK.

Next, make sure the protocol is bound to your Dial-Up Adapter. You can check this with the next set of steps:

1. Double-click on your Dial-Up Adapter in the list of Network components on the Configuration tab of the Network dialog box.

2. Click on the Bindings tab. Verify that the IPX/SPX-compatible Protocol is checked as shown in Figure 8-7. Click on OK.

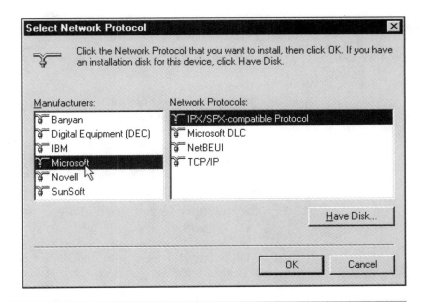

FIGURE 8-6   Selecting a Protocol from the list of those available

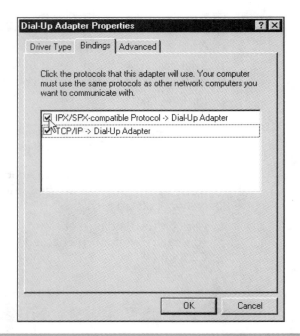

FIGURE 8-7   Protocols must be attached or "bound" to network adapters

Finally, set up the dial-up connection for use with a NetWare server using this last set of steps:

1. Open My Computer and the Dial-Up Networking folder, and then right-click on the dial-up connection you want to use (if you don't have one, double-click on Make New Connection and follow the instructions on the screen).

2. Click on Properties in the popup menu, and then click on Server Type. In the Type of Dial-Up Server list, click on NRN: NetWare Connect, as you see in Figure 8-8. Click on OK twice, and close both the Dial-Up Networking and My Computer folders.

 I am using both Microsoft's Client for NetWare networks and their Client for Windows networks. How do I write logon scripts?

Logon Scripts run when you log on to either a NetWare or Windows NT Server. If you have Supervisor's or Administrator's

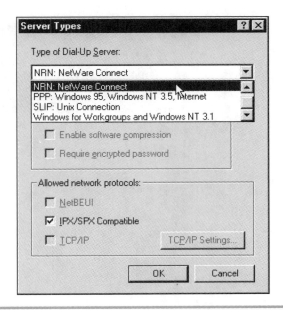

FIGURE 8-8 Selecting the correct server type allows you to dial into a
NetWare server

privileges on the servers, you can, in NetWare, type **syscon** and
either create or edit logon scripts or use User Management on
the NT Server.

Where do I find Interlink in Windows 95?

The Interlink that shipped with MS-DOS 6.*x* is now called
Direct Cable Connection. You can use it to connect between
PCs via a parallel or serial cable and share files between the two
computers. The Direct Cable Connection is found on the Start
menu by selecting Programs, Accessories, and then Direct
Cable Connection. If you don't have this option on your
Accessories menu, you will have to install it first. You can do
that with these steps:

1. Click on the Start button, choose Settings, Control Panel,
and double-click on Add/Remove Programs.

FIGURE 8-9   Install Direct Cable Connection

   2. Click on the Windows Setup tab, select Communications, and then click on the Details button for a list of the Communications components.

   3. If there is no check mark next to it, click on Direct Cable Connection to install it, as shown in Figure 8-9 (above). Click on OK twice. (If there is a check mark, it is already installed.)

I would like to specify settings normally stored in Net.cfg like the FILE HANDLES variable and such. How can I see and change settings in Net.cfg using Windows 95 and the Microsoft Client for NetWare?

In Windows 95, using Microsoft's 32-bit client software, file handles are set dynamically, and so you do not have to have a specific setting as you would make in Net.cfg. Windows 95 is doing this in the protected-mode redirector (NWREDIR).

Can I connect two Windows 95 computers together, or do I need to buy a special peer-to-peer network program?

Windows 95 has built-in networking capabilities. Provided you have the necessary network adapter cards and cables, linking two machines together is no problem. Just make sure both are using the same protocol, for example, NetBEUI.

To verify that both computers are using the same protocol, follow these steps on both computers:

1. Click on the Start button, choose Settings, Control Panel, and double-click on Network.

2. On the Configuration tab, click on the protocol and click on Properties. Check that the settings in the Bindings tab on both computers are as shown in Figure 8-10.

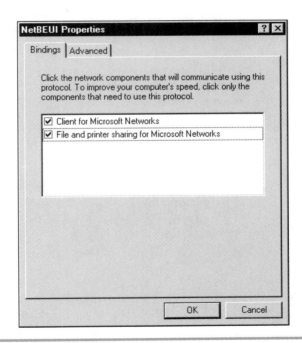

FIGURE 8-10   For peer-to-peer networking, all computers need to be using the same protocol and have both a client and file and printer sharing for Microsoft Networks

Why can't I connect to Novell servers?

One of the first steps is to verify that you have installed the IPX/SPX-compatible protocol and set the frame type to AUTO or to the specific frame type your server is using. (NetWare 3.11 servers use frame type of Ethernet 802.3, and NetWare 3.12 and 4.0 servers use frame type of Ethernet 802.2.) With the following steps you can check the protocol and frame type you are using.

1. Open the Start menu and select Settings, Control Panel, and double-click on Network.

2. On the Configuration tab, check that IPX/SPX-compatible Protocol is listed as one of the installed network components. (If not, install it by clicking on Add, selecting Protocol, clicking on Add again, and selecting Microsoft, and then IPX/SPX-compatible Protocol. Click on OK.)

3. To verify that the frame settings are accurate, click on the IPX/SPX-compatible Protocol and click on Properties.

4. Click on the Advanced tab and then on Frame Type. Select the type that is appropriate for you, as you can see in Figure 8-11.

If this does not solve your problem, use the Network Troubleshooter in Windows 95 Help to step through possible network problems. To do this:

1. Open the Start menu, and choose Help.

2. From the Contents tab, double-click on Troubleshooting.

3. Double-click on "If you have trouble using the network". The Network Troubleshooter will be displayed, as shown in Figure 8-12.

4. Step through the help screen as you are prompted.

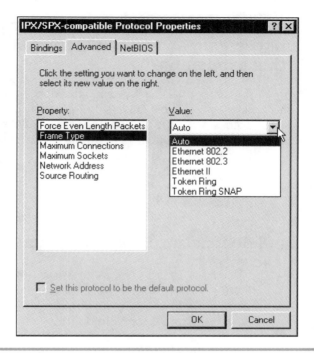

FIGURE 8-11 The default Auto Frame Type is typically the best choice

FIGURE 8-12 Windows Help provides a Network Troubleshooter to help you identify problems

I am trying to run an application from my Novell server, and I am receiving an error "Incorrect MS-DOS version." Why is this happening?

If you are using NetWare login scripts, you can have a script refer to a variable OSVersion to map a specific NetWare server according to the version of operating system the workstation is running. You will have to update the procedure to have MS-DOS version 7.0 recognized.

You might also have to modify the SETVER table to have the correct version reported to the program.

What can I do if Setup does not recognize my network adapter?

If your network adapter was not identified and/or installed during Windows 95 Setup, you can, as a first step, run the Add New Hardware Wizard. To do this:

1. Open the Start menu, choose Settings, Control Panel, and double-click on Add New Hardware. To begin, click on Next.

2. Allow Windows to detect the hardware and click on Next. Click Next again to initiate the search. Chances are that the search will find the adapter card.

   However, if the search again ignores the card, you can manually install it by continuing with these steps:

3. Click on Next, click on Network adapters, and click on Next again.

4. Select the manufacturer and model of your card from the lists, and click on OK.

5. If the card is not listed, click on Have Disk, insert the disk that came with your card, make sure the drive letter is correct, and click on OK.

6. If you don't have a disk with an Oemsetup.inf file, you will have to quit Add New Hardware and load the drivers through your Autoexec.bat file by following the instructions that came with the card. Having done that, open the Network control panel Configuration tab, click

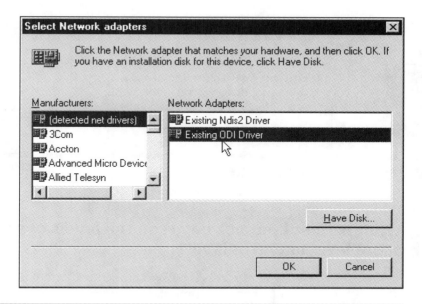

FIGURE 8-13   Use the Existing ODI Driver as the network adapter when you load the driver for the adapter in your Autoexec.bat file

Add, select Adapter, and click Add again. This time, select the Existing ODI Driver from the Network Adapters list, as shown in Figure 8-13 (shown above), and click on OK.

Can I set up my PC to act as a server to answer calls through Dial-Up Networking?

To enable Dial-Up Networking to act as a server, you need Microsoft Plus! If you have it, follow these steps:

1. Double-click on My Computer, and then double-click on Dial-Up Networking.

2. Open the Connections menu and click on Dial-Up Server. The Dial-Up Server dialog box will open.

3. Click on Allow caller access and click on OK. Your computer can now serve as a dial-up server.

If you don't have Microsoft Plus!, you only use Dial-Up Networking as a client to call out to external servers.

Tech Tip: You can see if someone is using your dial-up server in the Status box of the Dial-Up Server dialog box.

Security Considerations

What is the difference between the levels of security: share level and user level?

Share level access is password oriented. With it, a password can be attached to a computer, a printer, or a folder, and anybody on the network who knows the password can have access to the shared resource.

User level access is user oriented. With it, a security provider is specified, such as an NT domain or a NetWare server. This security provider supplies a list of users from which certain users can be specified for access to the shared resource as well as levels of access (read only, full access, or custom).

Tech Tip: User-level security is available only when you are attached to a NetWare or Windows NT server. In peer-to-peer networking you can only use share-level access.

How do I share a folder with another user?

Open the Explorer and find the folder to be shared. Then do the following:

1. Right-click on the folder and click on Sharing.

2. Choose Shared As and other options will become available, as shown in Figure 8-14.

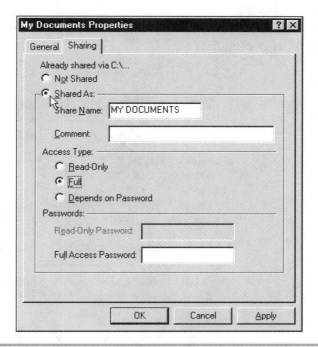

FIGURE 8-14 Changing a file or folder to be shared is done from the Properties dialog box

3. Fill in the Share Name, Comment, and specify the Access Type: Read Only, Full (read and write), or Depends on Password. Select whether you want a password, Read-Only Password, or Full Access Password. Then fill in the Password if appropriate.

4. Click on OK.

My NetWatcher shows that there is a user connected to my machine, but it shows no information about which file is opened from the remote machine. Why?

Some Windows applications do not keep files open. They are designed that way to save file handles. For example, applications like Notepad and WordPad open a file, load it into memory, and then close it. When there is a need to write back to the file, the application will open it again.

How do I grant access to others to use my computer's resources?

To allow others to use your computer resources, do the following:

1. Open the Explorer, and select the resource you want to share (disk, printer, folder, or CD-ROM drive).

2. Right-click on it, and choose Sharing.

3. Select the type of access you want to grant, and type the password if necessary.

If you want others on remote computers to be able to administer your resources, follow these steps:

1. Click on the Start button, choose Settings, Control Panel, and double-click on Passwords.

2. On the Remote Administration tab, click on Enable Remote Administration of this server, as shown in Figure 8-15.

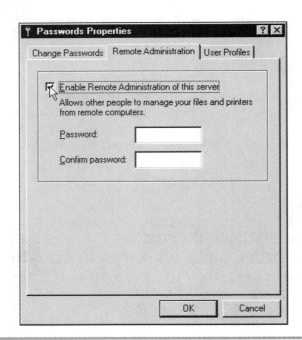

FIGURE 8-15 You can enable a remote site to manage your computer's resources

3. If you are using password-level security, fill in the password, and then confirm it. If you are using user-level security, click on Add, and select a person or groups from the list on the left.

4. Click on Add.

 I had a RESTRICTIONS section in the Progman.ini file to impose certain restrictions for the users on my network. Do I have to recreate the restrictions and how do I do that?

When you install Windows 95 on top of the existing Windows files, a program Grpconv.exe is automatically run. It converts the Windows 3.*x* program groups into Windows 95 folders. All data in the RESTRICTIONS section of the Progman.ini is migrated into the Policies section of the Registry.

If you installed Windows 95 into a different folder, you can convert the groups into folders by using the grpconv /m command (see Chapter 4 for further details). This will also migrate the restrictions.

 I am logging into several network servers, and my passwords are different for each of them. In Windows 95, do I have to type all the different passwords as I log in?

No. When you log into Windows 95 and its various facilities for the first time after setup, you will be prompted for passwords. You will have an option to save the passwords for future use. If you choose to do this, Windows 95 will store the passwords in the password cache. Next time you start Windows 95, you will be prompted only for your primary password. The correct password will unlock the password cache, and you will be connected to all your servers without having to type additional passwords.

I am not connected to a network on my computer at home. Why does it always come up with the "Enter network password" screen when I start Windows?

You probably have a network logon selected as your primary logon. To eliminate this, follow these steps:

1. Click on the Start button, choose Settings, Control Panel, and double-click on Network.

2. Under Primary Network Logon, choose Windows Logon, as shown here:

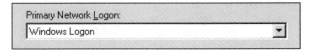

3. Restart Windows. You will no longer be prompted for a network password.

Using a Network

Do I have to have a disk or folder on my server mapped to a drive letter if I want to access this folder?

No. Windows 95 supports UNC (Universal Naming Conventions), so you don't have to have a drive letter explicitly assigned to a network resource to use it. (You have to have appropriate rights to that resource, of course.) You can, for example, create a shortcut to a network folder right on your desktop. Let's say you want to have a shortcut to a folder WinApps on the volume Drive C on the server Rock. Then use the following steps:

1. Open the Network Neighborhood, double-click on the Rock server, double-click on the Drive C volume, and then right-click on the WinApps folder.

2. Choose Create Shortcut. This will create a shortcut to the WinApps folder. You can drag it to your desktop or into another folder in My Computer.

Tech Tip: If you want to access a network drive or folder from within 16-bit or especially DOS applications, you will need to map the network resource to a drive letter on your machine.

 I cannot load both File and printer sharing for NetWare Networks and File and printer sharing for Microsoft Networks at the same time. I need to work with both Novell and Microsoft networks. What can I do about this?

Your Windows 95 machine can only act as one type of server—either the Novell or Microsoft Network server—at one time. You cannot do both simultaneously. You can have multiple clients loaded on the same machine, though. If you have File and printer sharing for Microsoft networks loaded, you can also load the Client for NetWare Networks and access your Novell servers.

 I often access a network drive. Can't I define that network drive as a drive on my computer?

Yes. This is called "mapping" a network drive. Follow these steps to map a network drive:

1. From the Explorer, click on the Map Network Drive icon (shown here), or select it from the Tools menu.

2. In the Map Network Drive dialog box, click on the Drive down arrow to find the Drive to be mapped. Click on it.

3. Enter the path to be mapped to it, using the format, \\computer\drivename.

4. Click on OK.

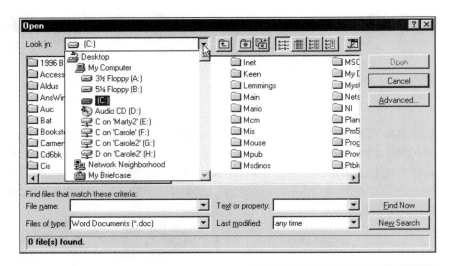

FIGURE 8-16   Once you have mapped a network drive to your computer, you can access that drive from within your applications

Now the network drive will appear not only in the Explorer and My Computer windows, but also in the File Open dialog boxes of all your applications, where you can open it and have immediate access to all the shared files. In Figure 8-16, drives E through H are mapped network drives.

How can I run an application from a network drive?

You can map a network drive to a drive letter on your computer, open that drive in My Computer, locate the application, and run it. You can also create a shortcut to the application and put it on your desktop, on your Start menu, or in a program group in the Programs menu.

Can I search for files on a network drive?

Yes. Use the following steps to search for files on network drives:

1. Click on the Start button, choose Find, and click on Files or Folders.

2. Type the filename you are searching for in the Named box.

3. Type the mapped drive letter and optionally a folder (**\drive\folder**) or the UNC path (**\\computername\drive\folder**) in the Look in box.

4. Click on Find Now.

Tech Tip: You can also look for network files in Network Neighborhood, Explorer, or My Computer.

 At work I have an icon right on my desktop called Network Neighborhood and at home I don't have this icon. Why?

The Network Neighborhood icon will only appear when you have a network installed. If you are on a stand-alone PC, you will not see the icon on your desktop.

 I am running Windows 95 and Novell NetWare. On my Windows 95 workstation, how can I run NetWare system utilities Syscon, Pconsole, and Fconsole?

To run these utilities, you can go to the DOS prompt, change to the appropriate drive, and type the command. If you will be using these utilities a lot, you can create shortcuts to them. To do this:

1. Right-click on the desktop.

2. Choose New, and click on Shortcut.

3. In the Create Shortcut dialog box, type the full path and the filename of the command, and click on Next. If you cannot remember what the path and filename are, you can click on Browse to find them.

I am only connected to a network occasionally. How can I prevent Windows 95 from attempting to reestablish the connection if I am not on the net?

When you are restarting Windows 95, select Cancel at the Network Password box. This will prevent Windows from reestablishing connections. If you are using a Microsoft Network, you have a more elegant way of doing this with these steps:

1. Right-click on Network Neighborhood, and choose Properties.

2. Select Client for Microsoft Networks, click on Properties, and select Quick logon, as shown in Figure 8-17.

This will allow you to get into Windows without reestablishing connections. The connections will be established only when you

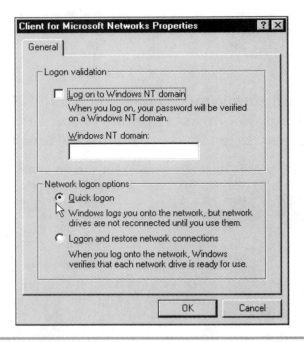

FIGURE 8-17   You can bypass the network logon until you want to use a network

need to utilize the network resource, for example, to start a program that resides on the network.

 How can I locate a computer without going through the Network Neighborhood or searching through My Computer or Explorer when I know right where I want to go?

Rather than use one of the file management programs, use the Find command.

1. Open the Start button, choose Find, and then click on Computer.

2. Type in the computer name. You can use wildcards.

3. Click on Find Now.

Another trick is to use the Run option. Use the following steps to locate a folder when you know where it is located:

1. Open the Start button and choose Run.

2. Type in the complete path in the form **\\computername\drive\folder**. For example, the run command (shown next) will open the folder window shown in Figure 8-18.

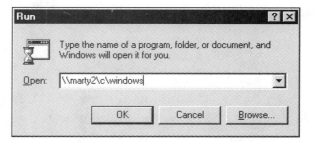

You can also just use the computer name by itself. If you're looking for a computer, this is a lot faster.

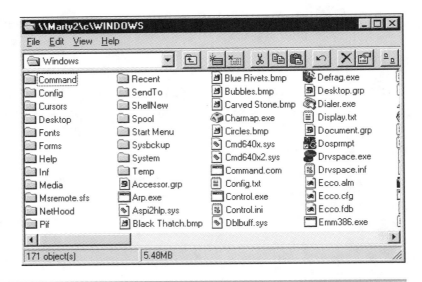

FIGURE 8-18   Using Run to find a remote drive and folder can give you fast access

I used the Direct Cable Connection option to get my two computers to talk to each other. The Network Neighborhood icon is now a permanent part of my desktop. How can I get the icon off of my desktop without disconnecting the Direct Connect capabilities?

You can hide the Network Neighborhood icon using System Policy Editor on the Windows 95 installation CD-ROM. Use the following steps to hide the Network Neighborhood:

1. Load your Windows 95 CD, and close the Autorun screen.

2. Using the Explorer, locate the System Policy Editor in \admin\apptools\poledit\ on the CD.

3. Run the Policy Editor by double-clicking on Poledit.exe, open the File menu, and choose Open Registry.

4. Double-click on Local User.

5. Open the folders as follows: Local User, Shell, Restrictions.

6. Under Shell Restrictions, click on Hide Network Neighborhood so that it has a check mark.

7. Click on OK and close the System Policy Editor.

Network Printing

 My network printer won't work. How can I troubleshoot the problem?

There are several factors that have an impact on correctly networking printers. Check the following items:

■ In the Network control panel, click on File and Print Sharing. Are both of the check boxes checked? If not, check them, click OK, and try your printer.

■ Check to see that the shared printer is identified as being shared on its local computer (does its icon have a hand beneath it?). From the Printers folder, right click on the printer and choose Sharing from the popup menu. Is the printer Share Name the same as the one on the other computer as found in the next step?

■ In the Printers folder on the client machine, right-click on the printer and select Properties from the popup menu. In the Details tab, check to see that the printer's name in the Print to the following port text box is the same as that found in the previous step.

■ In the Printers folder, Properties dialog box, Details tab on the client machine, click on Capture Printer Port and select a port other than the LPT1 that the local printer is probably using.

■ When you access the printer, be sure to use the port address and not the shared name.

Administering and Monitoring Networks

I am a network administrator, and I am planning to install Windows 95 on my network. How do I do Administrative Setup? Is it setup /a, like in Windows 3.x?

Tech Terror: You cannot run Server Based Setup (Netsetup.exe) from a machine that has only Windows NT installed. You can only run Netsetup from Windows 95.

In Windows 95, there are many tools for assisting an administrator in setting up Windows 95 throughout his or her network. First, Administrative Setup has been replaced with Server Based Setup, which is a separate program called Netsetup.exe. It is located on the Windows 95 CD-ROM in the \Admin\Nettools\Netsetup\ folder. (Before running Netsetup, you *must have installed Windows 95;* you can start Netsetup only from that operating system.) You use Netsetup to create and manage configuration information for each computer in the network. While still using Netsetup, this configuration information is used to create batch files or scripts that will automatically set up Windows 95 on each client workstation. Figure 8-19 shows Netsetup's primary dialog box and the tasks that program performs. Once the batch files are created, you can then set up each workstation by running Setup with the batch file as an argument (**setup msbatch.inf**). See the text files in \Admin\Nettools\Netsetup\ as well as Chapter 4 of the Windows 95 Resource Kit, or the Resource Kit's Help file on the Windows 95 CD-ROM under \Admin\Reskit\Helpfile\. Also, the CD has sample scripts in \Admin\Reskit\Samples\Scripts\.

How can I monitor access to my resources on the peer-to-peer network?

You can monitor the use of your computer by others with Net Watcher. You have to have the Client for Microsoft Networks installed, and the file and print sharing options for the network must be enabled. You also have to have the Net Watcher installed. If you don't, use the following steps to do that:

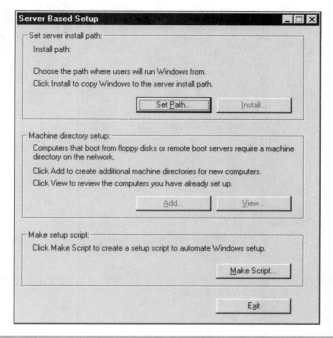

FIGURE 8-19   Server Based Setup is used to set up diskless and floppy-based workstations

1. Click on the Start button, choose Settings, and click on Control Panel. Double-click on Add/Remove Programs and click on the Windows Setup tab.
2. Select Accessories, click on Details, and select Net Watcher from the list.
3. Click on OK and Finish.

To start Net Watcher:

1. Click on the Start button, choose Programs, Accessories, System Tools, and click on Net Watcher.
2. Open the View menu and click on Connections. In the Net Watcher window, you'll see two panes. On the left are the names of all users currently connected to your PC.
3. Click on any user and you will see the full list of resources they are using on the right, as seen in Figure 8-20.

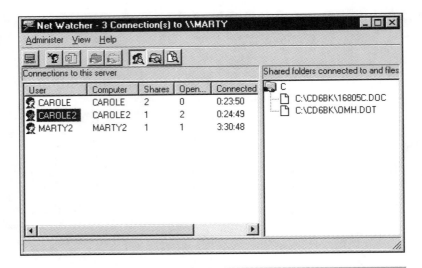

FIGURE 8-20   Using Net Watcher, you can monitor the users accessing your computer's resources

You can view the network by user, by shared folders, or by shared files using either the View menu or the right three tools in the toolbar.

How can I monitor network activity through my Windows 95 PC?

Windows 95 gives you several useful network monitoring tools. One of them is Net Watcher, discussed in the previous question. Another is the System Monitor. This application will allow you to monitor the amount of CPU resources used by local applications and by servicing remote requests of other users. If you don't have the System Monitor installed, do it now with these steps:

1. Click on Start, choose Settings, Control Panel, and double-click on Add/Remove Programs.

2. Click on the Windows Setup tab, select Accessories, click on Details, and select System Monitor from the list.

3. Click on OK twice.

To start and use the System Monitor:

1. Click on Start, and choose Programs, Accessories, System Tools, and System Monitor. The System Monitor window will be displayed as shown in Figure 8-21.

2. Select the resources to be monitored by clicking on the Edit or Add icons or selecting that option from the Edit menu.

3. Select from choices of viewing the data by a Line Chart, Bar Chart, or Numeric displays. You can either click on one of the icons in the toolbar or select the display option from the View menu.

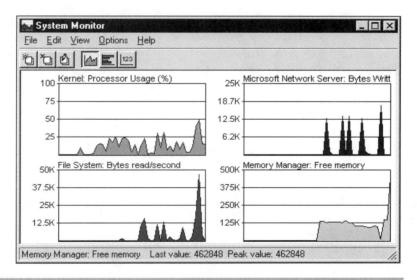

FIGURE 8-21 System Monitor allows you to monitor the system resources used on your computer

How can I have different users log on to the same PC?

Not only can you have different users log onto the same computer, but each user can retain a unique configuration. Each user can have different access to the computer's resources, determined by the password used to log on to the computer. To enable this option:

1. Click on Start, choose Settings, Control Panel, double-click on Passwords, and click on the User Profiles tab.

2. Select the option "Users can customize their preferences and desktop settings" as shown in Figure 8-22.

Now when the computer is booted, Windows 95 will ask for the configuration to be loaded and a password to validate it. Each computer configuration will have its own desktop settings, hardware configurations, Start menu contents, and shortcuts.

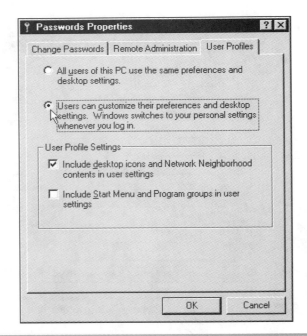

FIGURE 8-22   The Passwords Properties dialog box allows you to enable customized configurations for multiple users of one computer

How do I set up individual accounts and restrict portions of the system to my users?

After installation, you can use the System Policy Editor to restrict a user's access to some or all of the features of Windows 95. To utilize the System Policy Editor, follow these steps:

1. On the Administrator's PC, install the System Policy Editor from the \Admin\Apptools\Poledit\ folder on the Windows 95 CD.

2. Open the File menu, and choose New File. A Default User and a Default Computer icon will appear.

3. Double-click on first the Default User and then the Default Computer icons, and edit the policy lists. This will establish a standard or default set of system policies, so that when you go to each machine, all you need to do is enter the exceptions.

4. Once you have created the default policies, open the Edit menu and choose Add User for each user, Add Computer for each computer, and Add Group for each group. For each one you create, make the policy changes for the exceptions.

5. When you are done with the policies, make sure the specific user, computer, and group policies are stored in the NetLogon directory of a Windows NT server, or in the Public directory of a NetWare server. With the policies in these directories, Windows 95 in the remote clients will automatically download the policies during network logon and update the local registry with the policies.

6. In lieu of or in addition to establishing policies on the server, you can use the System Policy Editor's File menu Connect command to connect to a remote computer and edit that computer's registry files (User.dat and System.dat). This will establish a set of policies for that one computer.

Tech Tip: To set policies on remote computers, you must have administrative privileges for the remote computer, and in that case and when policies are downloaded at logon, the computer must be on a network with both user-level access and Remote Registry enabled.

Protocols

Which network protocol should I use with my network?

A network protocol is equivalent to a human language; it is the coding scheme used to communicate over a network. Different networks require different protocols. Here are the general rules of thumb:

- Use NetBEUI with Microsoft and IBM networks including Windows 95, Windows NT, Windows for Workgroups, and LAN Manager networks.
- Use IPX/SPX with all Novell networks.
- Use TCP/IP with dial-up networking to the Internet.

I'm using both TCP/IP and IPX/SPX-compatible protocols on my networked computer in my office, as well as through dial-up networking at home. In the office I get the IPX/SPX-compatible login dialog box immediately after booting. At home this box does not appear because I don't connect at boot time. How can I get this login dialog box? I would like to have one single action that produces the same NetWare access in both my office and my home. Can I invoke the login procedure by running a program?

There is a way to process the login script while in Windows. What you have to do is make sure that you attach to the server first. Use these steps to do this:

1. Go to Network Neighborhood and double-click on the NetWare drive on the server you want to connect to. This will prompt you to login. However, the system login script will not process.

2. After you attach to the network drive, open a DOS window and type the following: **NWLSPROC/SERVER**.

SERVER is your server name. For example, if my server is NWSERVER1, the command will be NWLSPROC/ NWSERVER1. Make sure to enter the server name in uppercase. If you enter it in lowercase, it will not work. This will force the script to run. You can make a shortcut to this on your desktop for use whenever you want.

Can I use the IPX/SPX-compatible protocol to access a Windows NT server?

Yes, do the following:

1. Right-click on Network Neighborhood, and choose Properties.
2. Select the IPX/SPX-compatible protocol, click on Properties, and click on the NetBIOS tab.
3. Select I want to enable NetBIOS over IPX/SPX, as seen here:

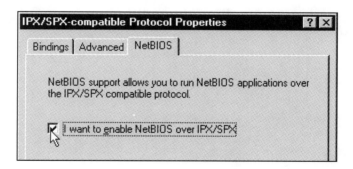

This will allow you to access Windows NT servers with IPS/SPX.

4. Click on OK.

Communications

While networking is connecting computers within a single facility or several closely located facilities, communications is connecting computers at remote facilities—anywhere in the world. Communications is primarily conducted over telephone lines connected to modems in the computers at either end. It consists of e-mail, faxes, bulletin boards, the Internet, information services such as CompuServe or Microsoft Network, and the simple transferring of files or information from one remote computer to another. Communications and networking do overlap. You can send e-mail via a network and use communications facilities (modems and phone lines) to do dial-up networking. Windows 95 provides a full complement of communications support including handling your modem and providing the software for e-mail, fax, transferring files, connecting to information services and the Internet, and doing dial-up networking.

FRUSTRATION BUSTERS!

Like networking, to utilize Windows 95 communications, you'll need the necessary hardware and you'll need to set up the Windows 95 communications components you want to use. The Add New Hardware Wizard or Windows 95 Setup leads you through the installation of your modem, and Windows Setup or its subset in Add/Remove Programs provides for the installation of the software components; in any case, communications setup in Windows 95 is considerably easier than it has been in the past. Here are some tips on setting up Windows 95 communications:

■ The modem hardware that you need for communications can be an adapter card in your computer or an external box that connects to your computer through a serial port. In either case a phone cable will plug into the modem and into a normal RJ-11 jack in the wall connecting you to your phone company and the worldwide telecommunications network beyond it. You can have a dedicated phone line for modem communications, or you may share a phone line between voice and data, or even among voice, data, and fax. With the majority of modems, you can use a phone line for only one type of communication at a time, and if, for example, you try to place a voice call while the modem is transmitting data, the data transmission will be interrupted and you'll have to restart it.

■ Many modems today can handle fax as well as data. This means that you can send information from your computer to a remote fax machine. For example, if you have a letter that you prepared on your word processor, you can send it to a fax machine across the world with Windows 95 Microsoft Fax.

■ If your modem or fax/modem is connected to or installed in your computer when you install Windows 95, in many cases Setup will detect your modem and properly set up Windows 95 to use it.

■ If you install a Plug-and-play modem after installing Windows 95, your system will automatically be set up to use the modem. In other circumstances you will need to

FRUSTRATION BUSTERS!

manually set up your modem. You can do this by opening the Start menu, selecting Settings, Control Panel, and then double-clicking on Add New Hardware. You'll be guided through the modem installation.

- With a modem installed, you can use the following Windows 95 communications tools without having to respecify your modem's characteristics.

  - **Dial-Up Networking** connects you as a client to a remote network server and allows the use of all the normal networking resources including file access and transfer, printing, and e-mail. Dial-Up Networking, also called Remote Access or "razz," is the principal way that you connect to the Internet with Windows 95.

  - **HyperTerminal**, which is a full-featured communications package, connects you to a remote computer so that you may send or receive files, or access an information service or a bulletin board.

  - **Microsoft Exchange,** Windows 95's messaging center, allows you to send and receive e-mail and fax messages in one location. You also may access the mail facilities of information services such as CompuServe or Microsoft Network or Internet mail.

  - **Microsoft Network** is Microsoft's new information service. It provides a multitude of services, such as bulletin boards, chat sessions, forums, opportunities to buy products, and information on a wide variety of subjects, including computing, science, business, education, and many others. You can connect to and use the Internet from within Microsoft Network.

  - **Phone Dialer** is used to dial the phone for you so you can talk to someone. You can either enter the number to be dialed or select it from a phone book that Windows 95 will maintain.

Setting Up a Modem

My system freezes when I try to set up my modem. What can I do about this?

Your problem may be one of conflicting port assignments or interrupt request lines (IRQs). Specifically, you may have either more than one serial device (for instance, your mouse and your modem) assigned to the same port or an interrupt request line used by two devices. Your serial ports are COM1 through COM4; your mouse is usually assigned to COM1 or COM3 and your modem to COM2 or COM4. Interrupt requests are usually assigned so that COM1 and COM3 use interrupt request line 4 (IRQ 4) and COM2 and COM4 use interrupt request line 3 (IRQ 3).

Plug-and-play devices help you avoid this problem, but if you have older equipment that is "hard-wired," you will have to search out the problem. To check the use of your ports and IRQs, use the following steps:

1. Click on Start, choose Settings, Control Panel, and double-click on System.

2. Click on the Device Manager tab. Here you can look at the IRQs assigned to your communications ports and see if there are any conflicts. You can do this in two ways: by looking at each port's properties and by looking at all the ports in the Computer's properties. Do both of these to see the different information presented.

3. Double-click on Ports to expand the list, select the Communications Port used for the modem (usually COM2), and click on the Properties button.

4. In the Communications Port Properties dialog box, click on the Resources tab, as seen in Figure 9-1. You will see Interrupt Request followed by a setting, usually 03. Also, at the bottom of the dialog box, look to see that it says "No conflicts." Close the Port Properties dialog box.

5. From the Device Manager tab, click on Computer in the list of devices. Then click on Properties. In the View Resources tab, click on Interrupt request (IRQ). You'll see

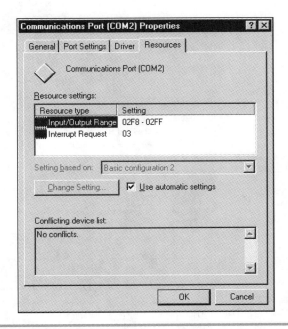

FIGURE 9-1   Verify your modem's IRQ in the Communications Port Properties
dialog box

a list of ports and the interrupt requests assigned to them,
like that shown in Figure 9-2. Here you can see that IRQ 3
is assigned to both COM2 and COM4 and IRQ 4 is
assigned to COM1, all as expected. Close Computer
Properties and the System Properties dialog boxes. Next,
check to see what is using the COM ports.

6. In the Control Panel, double-click on Modems and click
on the Diagnostics tab to open the Modems Properties
dialog box that you see in Figure 9-3. Here you can see
the assigned usage of each COM port and make sure that
your modem, mouse, and other serial devices are all
assigned to nonconflicting ports.

7. Click on your modem port (COM2 in Figure 9-3), and
then click on More Info. You will see a message telling
you that the system is communicating with the modem.
Your modem is being tested. The results are then
displayed, as you can see in Figure 9-4. If you see that the
first several of the AT (attention) commands return OK,

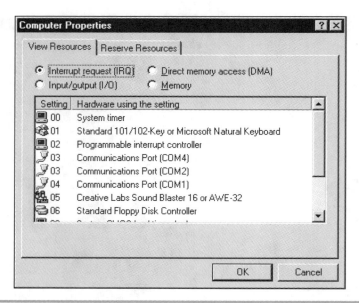

FIGURE 9-2   The Computer Properties dialog box will show you all your IRQ assignments in one list

FIGURE 9-3   The Modems Properties dialog box will show you what is assigned to each port

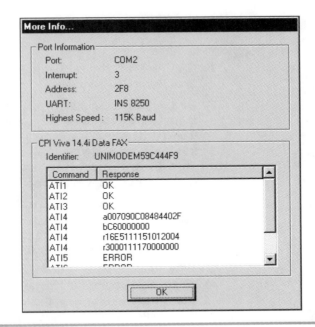

Port Information
- Port: COM2
- Interrupt: 3
- Address: 2F8
- UART: INS 8250
- Highest Speed: 115K Baud

CPI Viva 14.4i Data FAX
Identifier: UNIMODEM59C444F9

Command	Response
ATI1	OK
ATI2	OK
ATI3	OK
ATI4	a007090C08484402F
ATI4	bC60000000
ATI4	r16E5111151012004
ATI4	r3000111170000000
ATI5	ERROR

FIGURE 9-4   Clicking on More Info tests your modem and then displays the results

your modem is probably working. If some of the AT commands toward the end return ERROR, that simply means that your modem has not implemented that command.

8. If you do not see any response to the AT commands, then it is likely that your board is installed incorrectly and that some setting on the board needs to change. You or a technician needs to open your computer and look at the board.

9. Click on OK twice to return to the Control Panel.

I cannot dial or connect with my modem. Why?

There could be several reasons for this. Here are some tips for troubleshooting your modem problems:

■ Make sure the modem is set up properly. You should be using Windows 95 drivers, not Win 3.*x*, which might be incompatible. Open the Control Panel and run the Add New Hardware Wizard to automatically detect the existing modem and load the correct Windows 95 drivers.

■ After the modem is installed, verify that your modem is correctly configured with these steps:

1. Click on Start, choose Settings, Control Panel, and double-click on Modems.

2. On the General tab, verify that the manufacturer and model for your modem are correct, as shown in Figure 9-5. If it is not, click on Add and use the Install New Modem Wizard. If your modem is not on the list, try the Generic Modem Hayes-compatible modem. Make sure to remove any other modem listed as installed.

3. Verify that the modem is enabled. Open the System control panel. In the Device Manager tab, open Modem, select your modem, and click on Properties. Make sure that the Device status is "This device is working properly."

4. Verify the port while still in the Modems Properties dialog box by clicking on the Modem tab; also verify that the Port listed is correct (for example, COM2). If not, select the correct port by clicking on the Port down arrow and selecting the port you want. Then click OK.

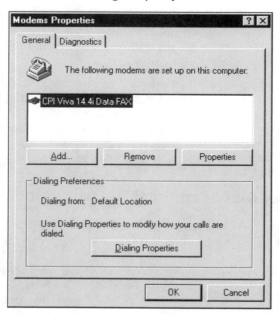

FIGURE 9-5 The Modems Properties General tab shows the modems that are installed

5. Verify the serial port I/O address and IRQ from the System Properties Device Manager, by opening Ports; choose the specific port for your modem; choose Properties; and then click on the Resources tab. Check the Conflicting device list on the bottom of the dialog box to see if the modem is using resources in conflict with other devices. If it is, select Change Settings (you may need to remove the check mark from Use automatic settings first), and then select a configuration that does not have resource conflicts. For example, if you have a serial mouse or other device on COM1, you cannot use a modem on COM3, because COM1 and COM3 ports use the same IRQ. The same IRQ addressing applies to COM2 and COM4. Click OK twice to return to the Control Panel.

6. Verify the port settings:

a) From the Control Panel, double-click on Modems.

b) Select your modem, click on Properties, and click on the Connection tab to check the current port settings, such as data bits, stop bits, and parity.

c) Click on Advanced to check Error Control and Flow Control. If you are using a Windows 3.*x* communications program, turn off these advanced features. Click on OK.

d) Now click on the Port Settings button to verify the UART type. Data transmission problems may occur on a slower 8036-based computer not equipped with a 16550 UART with a baud rate greater than 9600, or when multitasking during a file download. Try lowering the Transmit and Receiver Buffers and click on OK three times to return to the Control Panel, and then close it.

If you are still unable to connect, use the Troubleshooter for modem problems in Windows Help. Use the following instructions to open the Troubleshooter:

1. Click on Start, choose Help, select the Contents tab, and double-click on Troubleshooting.

2. Choose "If you have trouble using your modem." The window shown in Figure 9-6 will open. Click on the appropriate buttons to follow the problem-solving guide.

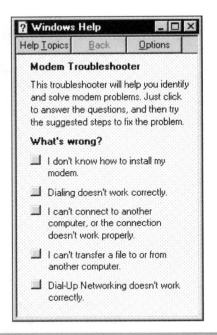

FIGURE 9-6   Windows Help can troubleshoot your modem problems

During setup, I let Windows pick my modem, and it didn't select the correct one. What can I do about this?

The modem automatically detected by Windows depends on the chip set and the type of modem. If you are having problems with the type of modem Windows has picked for you, you can manually choose your modem if it is on the list in Windows 95 (there are hundreds) or select a generic modem driver that will allow you to go online. To manually install a modem, follow these steps:

1. Open the Start menu, choose Settings, Control Panel, and double-click on Modems.

2. Click on Remove to clear the current installed modem from the system.

3. Click on Add to start the Install New Modem Wizard.

4. Click on Don't detect my modem; I will select it from a list, and click on Next.

5. From the list of manufacturers, select first the manufacturer and then the model of your modem. If you don't see your modem, try the same manufacturer and speed if not the exact model. If you don't see your manufacturer, select Standard Modem Types, and from the Models list, select one with the bps modem speed equal to yours, as shown in Figure 9-7. Click on Next.

6. Select the port to use with the modem. It is typically COM2 or COM4. Click on Next and Windows will install the modem. You will be able to see it in the Modems Properties dialog box.

Tech Tip: If you have a 14.4 Kbps modem, you often can run it at 19.2 Kbps. If you are using one on the Standard Modem Types, try the 19.2 model and see if it doesn't work.

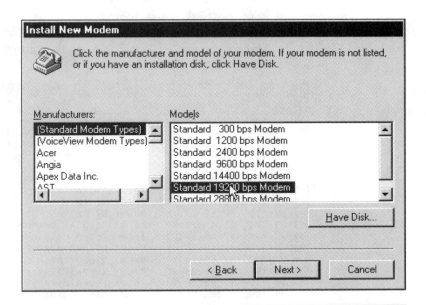

FIGURE 9-7   You can choose a modem that is different than the one Windows selects for you

My modem connection fails! How can I find out what is going wrong?

One possibility is to look at the log file. Do the following to have a log generated:

1. Open the Start menu and select Settings, Control Panel, and then double-click on Modems.

2. From the Modems Properties dialog box, click on Properties.

3. In the Modems Properties dialog box, click on the Connection tab, and click on Advanced.

4. In the Advanced Connection Settings dialog box, click on Record a log file. This will create a file called Modemlog.txt when you initiate the modem connection.

Now to view the log, follow these steps:

1. From the Explorer, locate the file, \Windows\Modemlog.txt.

2. Double-click on Modemlog.txt. The Notepad will open and display the log as you can see in Figure 9-8.

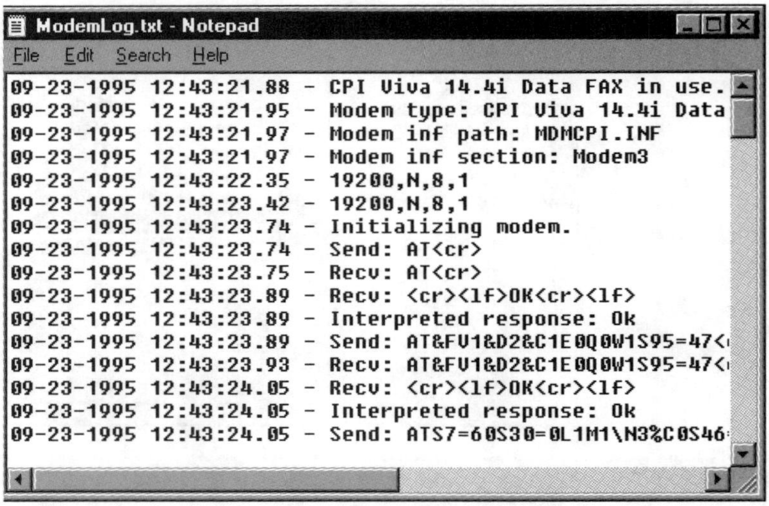

```
ModemLog.txt - Notepad                                    _ □ ×
File  Edit  Search  Help
09-23-1995 12:43:21.88 - CPI Viva 14.4i Data FAX in use.
09-23-1995 12:43:21.95 - Modem type: CPI Viva 14.4i Data
09-23-1995 12:43:21.97 - Modem inf path: MDMCPI.INF
09-23-1995 12:43:21.97 - Modem inf section: Modem3
09-23-1995 12:43:22.35 - 19200,N,8,1
09-23-1995 12:43:23.42 - 19200,N,8,1
09-23-1995 12:43:23.74 - Initializing modem.
09-23-1995 12:43:23.74 - Send: AT<cr>
09-23-1995 12:43:23.75 - Recv: AT<cr>
09-23-1995 12:43:23.89 - Recv: <cr><lf>OK<cr><lf>
09-23-1995 12:43:23.89 - Interpreted response: Ok
09-23-1995 12:43:23.89 - Send: AT&FU1&D2&C1E0Q0W1S95=47<
09-23-1995 12:43:23.93 - Recv: AT&FU1&D2&C1E0Q0W1S95=47<
09-23-1995 12:43:24.05 - Recv: <cr><lf>OK<cr><lf>
09-23-1995 12:43:24.05 - Interpreted response: Ok
09-23-1995 12:43:24.05 - Send: ATS7=60S30=0L1M1\N3%C0S46
```

FIGURE 9-8   Modemlog.txt displays what happened during a communications session

The Internet

How do I get on the Internet using Windows 95?

There are several ways you can connect to the Internet using Windows 95, depending on what you are planning to do and what applications and services you are using. The three most common ways of connecting to the Internet with Windows 95 facilities are with the Microsoft Network (MSN), with Microsoft Plus! Internet Tools, and with Dial-Up Networking. Besides Windows 95 and a modem, you need two other things to use the Internet: an Internet provider, a company or organization through whom you can connect to the Internet; and a program that allows you to search and retrieve information on the Internet. MSN is both a provider and has several facilities to allow you to search and retrieve Internet information. Microsoft Plus! provides the facilities and will help you get set up with a provider. Look at each of the three methods next.

The Microsoft Network (MSN) online service gives you some Internet access including browsing the World Wide Web, reading and posting to Internet newsgroups, and exchanging e-mail. To access the Internet from MSN, follow these steps:

1. Double-click on the Microsoft Network icon on the desktop.

2. If you have not already signed on, follow the prompts to sign up with Microsoft Network. After you are signed up, click on Connect.

3. You may be able to click on Getting on the Internet in the MSN Today window. Do that if you wish or click on Close to close the MSN Today window and open the main Microsoft Network screen.

4. If you went to Getting on the Internet, you can learn about Browsing the Web, Internet Newsgroups, and Internet E-mail by clicking on those areas at the top of the screen or you can download the web browser by clicking on Upgrade Instructions. When you are done reading the

Internet instructions and/or upgrading MSN for the web browser, click on Close to return to MSN Today and then click on Close again to return to MSN Central.

5. In MSN Central, click on Categories. Then click on Internet Center. The Internet folders will be displayed as shown in Figure 9-9. You will see folders such as Getting on the Internet, About the Internet Center, Netiquette, BBS offerings, File Libraries, Newsgroups, World Wide Web access, and much more. If you click on Newsgroups and follow on down the chain, you'll move through a series of windows that gives you a more detailed definition of what you want to see until you get to a list of postings on a particular topic. If you double-click on one of these postings, it will open and you can read it.

6. When you are ready to return to MSN Central, click on the house icon on the toolbar from wherever you are, or if you are ready to leave MSN, click on the broken wire icon to sign out and then click on Yes to disconnect.

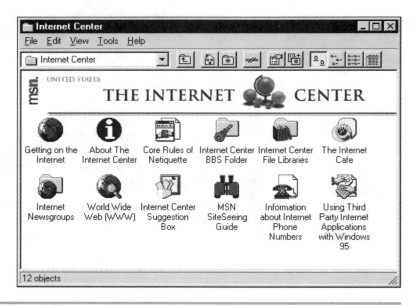

FIGURE 9-9   MSN provides access to many Internet services

Microsoft Plus! provides an easy way to sign up for the Internet, gives you the Internet Explorer to browse the World Wide Web, puts shortcuts to your Internet destinations on your desktop, and lets you use Internet mail. If Microsoft Plus! did not come on your computer, you must separately purchase it (it has a street price of under $50). To use Microsoft Plus!, insert the CD in your drive, click on Install Plus! from the Autorun window, and follow the instructions for installing Internet access.

Dial-Up Networking allows you to create a connection to an Internet access provider. See how to do this in the next question.

How do I set up a PPP dial-up Internet connection?

Setting up a PPP connection for using the Internet involves two steps. First, you must install and configure a modem, as described earlier. Then you have to install Dial-Up Networking. To install Dial-Up Networking, follow these steps:

Tech Tip: Once connected to the Internet with a dial-up connection, you will need software from other sources such as Microsoft Plus! or Internet in a Box to actually search and retrieve information or send and receive Internet mail.

1. Open My Computer and double-click on Dial-Up Networking. If you do not have a dial-up connection, the Make New Connection wizard Welcome message will be displayed. Click on Next.

2. If you already have a dial-up connection, the Dial-Up Networking folder will be displayed. In that case, double-click on Make New Connection. The Make New Connection wizard will be displayed.

3. Type a name for the computer you will be dialing, and verify that the modem is properly configured by clicking on Configure. It will display the Modems Properties dialog box as described in earlier questions in this chapter.

4. Click on the Options tab. If you need to enter your user name and password when you sign on to the Internet, then click on Bring up terminal window after dialing.

When you are satisfied with the modem properties, click on OK and then click on Next.

5. Enter the Area code, Telephone number, and Country code as needed. Click Next.

6. Click on Finish to complete the installation.

7. In the Dial-Up Networking dialog box, right-click on your new connection and click on Properties. The connection's Properties dialog box will open.

8. Click on Server Type. The Server Types dialog box will open as shown in Figure 9-10.

9. Make sure that PPP: Windows 95... is selected as the Type of Dial-Up Server. If NetBEUI and IPX/SPX protocols are enabled, click on them to disable those protocols. TCP/IP should be enabled (checked).

10. Click on TCP/IP Settings. The dialog box that opens has very important settings that only your Internet provider can tell you how to set. Discuss these settings with your Internet provider and set them accordingly.

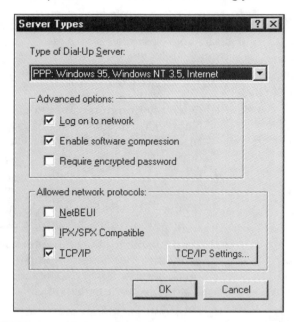

FIGURE 9-10   You can set up dial-up networking to connect to NetWare, Unix, and Windows for Workgroups servers in addition to Windows 95 and Windows NT

11. When you have made the TCP/IP settings the way you want, click on OK three times to return to the Dial-Up Networking folder.

Tech Tip: Remember the TCP/IP Settings dialog box reached from your dial-up connection's Properties and then Server Types dialog boxes. The TCP/IP Settings dialog box contains a number of settings that can cause you grief. In particular, if your Internet provider does not have a strong opinion on whether to use IP header compression (second from the bottom check box), disable it by removing the check mark.

The PPP protocol is installed by default because it is the most flexible, being able to work over NetBEUI, IPX/SPX, and TCP/IP. Now use the connection with these steps:

1. From the Dial-Up Networking window, double-click on the Internet connection you just created. The Connect To dialog box will open.

2. Enter your User name and Password, check on the correctness of the phone number, and click on Connect. You should hear your modem dial and will see a message that the system is trying to connect to your Internet provider. If the Terminal window opens, you will need to enter your user name and password again, possibly type **ppp,** and then press F7 to close the terminal window. Finally, you should see a connected message like this:

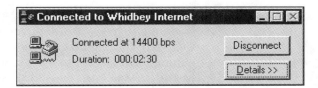

Once you have gotten the connection message, you can start your Internet mail, FTP (file transfer), or web browsing packages. With Microsoft Plus!, you can use the Microsoft Exchange for Internet Mail.

If you did not get connected, look at the Windows 95 Help Troubleshooter for your modem and for Dial-Up Networking. If that does not help, go over all of your settings with your Internet provider.

Microsoft Network

If I sign up on the Microsoft Network, how do I know my e-mail address?

Your Internet e-mail address on MSN is your *memberid@msn.com*, or within MSN, just *memberid*. Your memberid is the one you use to sign on to MSN.

Microsoft Exchange

How do I install Microsoft Exchange while running Windows 95 Setup?

The Custom option in Windows 95 Setup will allow you to install Microsoft Exchange. To accomplish that, follow these steps:

1. Place your Windows 95 first disk or CD in its drive and start Setup in one of the ways described in Chapter 2. Follow the instructions on the screen. When you are asked in the Setup Options dialog box what type of Setup you prefer, choose Custom and click on Next.

2. Continue to follow the onscreen instructions until the Get Connected dialog box appears where you can select communications components. At a minimum, click on Microsoft Mail as shown in Figure 9-11 and select Microsoft Fax and The Microsoft Network if you wish. Click on Next.

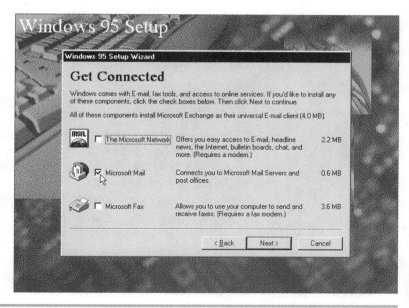

FIGURE 9-11   Installing Microsoft Exchange occurs automatically if you install one of its services such as Mail or Fax

3. In the Select Components dialog box that appears next, Microsoft Exchange should already be checked. Click on it and then on the Details button where Microsoft Exchange and Microsoft Mail services should both be checked. Click on OK and then continue with the setup by following the instructions on the screen.

4. At the end of setup, the wizards for configuring and adding Microsoft Mail and the other services you choose will guide you in configuring Microsoft Exchange on your computer.

How do I install Microsoft Exchange after Windows Setup has been run?

To install Microsoft Exchange after setting up Windows 95, use the following instructions:

1. Click on Start; choose Settings, Control Panel; and double-click on Add/Remove Programs.

2. Click on the Windows Setup tab. A list of components appears.

3. Click the box next to the Microsoft Exchange icon and then click on the Details button.

4. In the Microsoft Exchange components list, both Microsoft Exchange and Microsoft Mail Services should be checked. Click on OK to begin the setup (you'll need your Windows 95 Setup disk(s)). The Exchange Setup Wizard will prompt you through the configuration steps.

5. After the wizard is finished, shut down and restart Windows for the changes to take effect.

How do I specify the address book I want to use in Microsoft Exchange?

Microsoft Exchange creates two address books when you install it: a Personal Address Book for all your personal messages and a Post Office Address list for your network, maintained by the post office administrator. You can select an address book from either the Tools menu in Microsoft Exchange or from the toolbar of a new electronic mail message. To select an address book:

1. Open the Start menu, select Programs, and click on Microsoft Exchange. (You can also click on the Inbox icon on your desktop.)

2. Open the Tools menu and choose Address Book. The Address Book window is displayed as shown in Figure 9-12.

3. In the upper right of the Address Book dialog box, click on the name of the address book you want to use in the Show Names from the list box. All the names from the address book you selected are listed.

Tech Tip: You can choose which address book appears first on the list (and is therefore your default) by opening the Tools menu in the Exchange, choosing Options, and clicking on the Addressing tab. Then open the Show this address list first drop-down list and choose which you want. When you're done, click on OK.

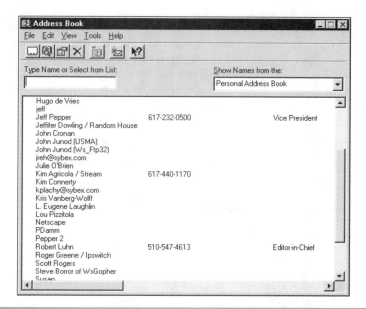

FIGURE 9-12 The Address Book in Microsoft Exchange provides phone numbers and street addresses as well as e-mail addresses

How do I use the Exchange's address book?

Once you open an address book as described in the previous question, here are some tips on how you can use it:

- To find a particular name in your address book, type the name or a sequence of letters beginning the name in the blank box on the left above the list. The name will be highlighted as you type. Press ENTER to open the entry.

- To add a name to your address book, choose New Entry from the File menu or click on the New Entry button on the left of the toolbar. Select the type of address you want to enter, and then fill in the information.

■ To create a message to be sent to selected address(es), select the addressees by holding down CTRL while clicking on them, then choose New Message from the File menu, or click the New Message button on the toolbar to create a new electronic mail message that is preaddressed to the selected people.

Faxing

How do I configure the Microsoft Fax?

Use the following steps to configure the Microsoft Fax:

1. Click on Start; choose Settings, Control Panel; and double-click on Mail and Fax.

2. Click on Show Profiles and choose a profile to which you want to add fax capabilities, and then click on the Properties button or click on Add to create a new profile with fax in it.

3. In the Services tab, click on the Add button to open the Add Service to Profile dialog box shown here.

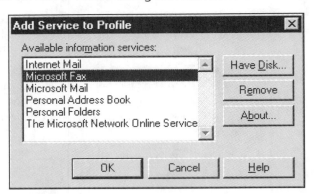

4. Click on Microsoft Fax and then click on OK. A message asks if you want to type your name, fax number, and fax modem now. Click on Yes.

5. In the Microsoft Fax Properties dialog box, click on the Message, Dialing, Modem, and User tabs to verify and enter appropriate information.

   ■ On the User tab, enter your fax number. Verify that the other information is valid. The information typed in the User tab automatically appears on the cover page.

   ■ On the Modem tab, the modem information will already be entered if your modem has already been installed. If you have not installed a modem or want to choose a different modem, click on the Add button in the modem folder and launch the Modem Wizard.

   ■ Check the information on the Dialing and Message tabs to see if it meets your requirements.

6. Click on OK and restart the Microsoft Exchange for the changes to take effect.

Tech Tip: Once you have set up Microsoft Fax, you can also change fax properties from Microsoft Exchange. Open the Tools menu and from Microsoft Fax Tools, choose Options.

How do I create a shortcut to the Fax printer?

You can place a shortcut to the fax printer on your desktop, drag a document to the shortcut icon and have it automatically start the Compose New Fax Wizard without going through any menus. Follow the steps listed below to create a shortcut to a fax printer:

1. Click on Start and choose Settings, Printers to display the currently installed printers.

2. Drag the Microsoft Fax printer icon to the desktop, and click on Yes, you want to make a shortcut.

3. If you want to change the name, click on the Fax Printer shortcut name and then click on it again after a pause.

A selection box will surround the name, allowing you to change it. Press ENTER to finalize the name.

When you have a document you want to fax, simply drag it to the fax icon on the desktop. The Compose New Fax Wizard will be loaded for you to address the document and send it.

How do I create a custom cover page for my faxes?

Use these steps to create a custom cover page:

1. Click on Start; choose Programs, Accessories, Fax; and then select Cover Page Editor.

2. Click on OK to bypass the Cover Page Editor Tips.

3. Follow these tips to create your fax cover page:

- From the Insert menu, click first on Recipient, then Sender, and finally Message. A submenu with options will be displayed. As you click on each field, an edit box with the place keeper will be displayed, as shown in Figure 9-13. Drag each box where you want it on the cover page.

- If you want an object, such as a graphic for a logo to be included, select Object from the Insert menu and then drag it where you want it.

- To include your own unique text, click on the Text icon. Your pointer will become a cross. Drag it to form a rectangle that will contain the text. You can then type, highlight, and format your text with the font, size, and style you want.

- To align objects, select them by dragging a marquee around them, and then select Align Objects from the Layout menu.

- When you are finished, save the cover page by selecting File, Save As, and putting it in your \Windows folder with the cover pages that come with Windows 95.

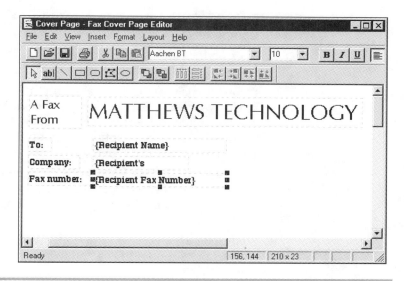

FIGURE 9-13 Fax Cover Page Editor allows you to create your own cover page

How do I attach to a predefined cover page to fax a message?

There are two ways to get predefined cover pages for your faxes. Windows 95 has some predefined cover pages (Confidential, For your information, Generic, and Urgent). These are presented to you at the time you compose a fax from Microsoft Exchange. You can select the one you want.

Another predefined cover page can be one that you have created in the Cover Page Editor and then saved. In this case, you can specify that filename or browse for it when you are asked if you want a cover page.

How do I send a fax from the Microsoft Exchange?

Assuming that you have set up the Exchange to send and receive faxes, use the following instructions to send a fax:

1. Open Microsoft Exchange by double-clicking on the Inbox icon.

2. From the Compose menu, choose New Fax to launch the Compose New Fax Wizard.

3. Click on the Address Book to select a fax recipient from that, or type the name and fax number. Click on Next.

4. If you want a cover page, make sure the "Yes. Send this one" is selected. Click on the type of cover page you want: Confidential, For your information, Generic, or Urgent. For additional options, click on the Options button. Click on Next when you are through.

5. In the Compose New Fax dialog box, type the subject, press TAB, and then type a message. If you want the fax note to be on the cover page, select that option. Click on Next.

6. To include a file with your message, type the path to the file, or click on Add File and follow the prompts. Click on Next.

7. To finish the fax and send it, click on Finish.

Tech Tip: You can also send a fax from many applications by, in a sense, "printing" to the fax—you select Microsoft Fax as the printer you want to use and the Compose New Fax Wizard will open and lead you through the process as described here.

How do I send a fax using Windows Explorer?

To use the Explorer to send a fax, do the following:

1. Right-click on My Computer and click on Explore.

2. Locate and right-click on the document you wish to fax.

3. Select Send To from the popup menu. A submenu will be displayed. Select Fax Recipient. This will launch the Compose New Fax Wizard, which will prompt you for information.

You can also drag the document to a shortcut to the Fax Printer on your desktop, if you have one.

HyperTerminal

What is HyperTerminal and how do I dial up a remote computer using HyperTerminal?

HyperTerminal is a full-featured communications program that can be used with a modem to connect two computers for the purpose of sending and receiving files or connecting to computer bulletin boards or other information services, including the Internet. To create a HyperTerminal connection, use these steps:

1. Click on Start; choose Programs, Accessories; and then click on HyperTerminal.

2. Double-click on Hypertrm.exe, which will load the HyperTerminal program.

3. In the Connection Description dialog box, type the name of the connection you want to create, select an icon to associate with it, and click on OK.

4. In the Phone Number dialog box, specify the Country code, Area code, Phone number, and Modem type for this connection, and click on OK. If you haven't already installed a modem, you will be prompted for it now.

5. In the Connect dialog box, click on Dialing Properties and look at the How I dial from this location section, as shown in Figure 9-14. If you need to dial a prefix to get an outside line, use a calling card, or if you want to turn off call waiting, this is the place to do it. Click on OK when you have completed the entries you wish to make.

   If you clicked on Dialing Properties and then checked to dial using a calling card, the Change Calling Card dialog box asks for the name and number of your card. If you click the Advanced button, you will see the Dialing Rules dialog box, which allows you to distinguish among calls made within the same area code, long-distance calls, and international calls.

6. When the Connect dialog box reappears, click on Dial to do that or click on Cancel to avoid dialing the connection

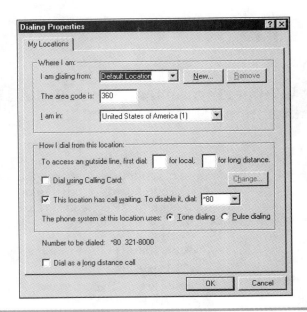

FIGURE 9-14   If you have call waiting, turn it off in the Dialing Properties dialog box

(you will still have a chance to save the session). When the connection is made, the computer you are dialing will display its own terminal window as you can see in Figure 9-15.

7. When you are finished with the connection, click on the Disconnect (hang up) button on the toolbar or open the Call menu and select Disconnect.

8. When you close the new HyperTerminal window after either dialing or canceling, it will prompt you to save your session definition. Click on Yes and you will see an icon for the new connection in the Program Files Accessories HyperTerminal folder.

FIGURE 9-15   The HyperTerminal window for a particular service, a local Internet provider

HyperTerminal adds a number 1 to a number that I am trying to dial. The number is in an area code that is different from mine, but it is not a long-distance call for me. How can I bypass this 1 that is added?

By default, Windows 95 will add a leading 1 if the area code is different from the area code entered by the user as local. This is standard for the USA phone system, but in other countries (for example, Canada) you may not have to dial 1 in some cases. Use the following steps to bypass a number 1 when dialing. Let us say you want to dial (333) 333-3333 from the (555) area code.

1. If you have already created a HyperTerminal connection for this number, double-click on its icon in the folder displayed when you open HyperTerminal from the Accessories menu, and click on Modify to change the Phone number.

2. If no connection exists for it, start one by double-clicking on Hypertrm.exe. Enter your name and choose an icon. Click on OK.

3. In the Phone number tab, enter your area code in the Area code field, and the whole number to be called, including the area code, in the Phone number field. For example, type **555** in the Area code box, and then **(333) 333-3333** (including the actual area code) in the Phone number box and click on OK.

4. Select Dial. HyperTerminal will not add a 1 because it thinks that the call is local, and it will not dial 555 for the same reason. The number dialed will be (333) 333-3333!

I am trying to type Attention (AT) commands in HyperTerminal, but I keep getting the New Connection dialog box. How can I bypass that box?

In addition to bypassing the New Connection dialog box, you must also set a switch that instructs HyperTerminal to bring up a terminal window before dialing the number. You can then enter your commands before dialing. To do this, follow these steps:

1. Open the Start menu; select Programs, Accessories; and then click on HyperTerminal. In the folder window, double-click on Hypertrm.exe.

2. In HyperTerminal, click on Cancel in the New Connection dialog box, leaving you in the New Connection window.

3. Open the File menu and choose Properties.

4. Click on the Configure button and then click on the Options tab.

5. Select the option Bring up terminal window before dialing, as shown in Figure 9-16. This will allow you to type modem commands directly in a terminal window.

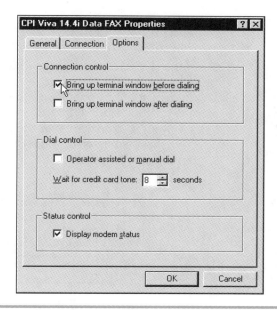

FIGURE 9-16   If you open a terminal window before dialing, you can set up your modem by typing commands to it

How do I get HyperTerminal to answer an incoming call?

This is a major oversight in the design of HyperTerminal, but there is a workaround, as described in the next set of steps:

1. Open the Start menu; select Programs, Accessories; and click on HyperTerminal.

2. Double-click on Hypertrm.exe, type a name like "AutoAnswer," select an icon, and click on OK.

3. Leave the Phone number blank. Open the Connect using drop-down list and choose Direct to Com x, where x is the Com port where your modem is installed, as you can see here:

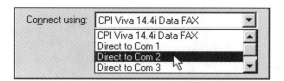

4. Click on OK. Correct your port setting, most importantly your speed, and click on OK again.

5. In the HyperTerminal window, type **ATS0=2** (that's a zero after the S, NOT the letter "o"), and press ENTER. Your modem should respond with an "OK" as shown next. This sets up your modem to answer after the second ring. If you want it to answer after the first ring, type **ATS0=1**. If you have an external modem, you will see the AA (autoanswer) light come on.

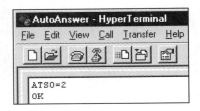

6. When a call comes in, it will be answered and you will see a message "Connected at x," where x is the speed you set your modem to. You can then type messages between your computer and the one you are connected to, and you can transfer files using the Transfer menu or the Send and Receive buttons on the toolbar.

7. To discontinue autoanswer, type **ATS0=0**, close the connection and the dialog box, and answer Yes to save the session.

When I use HyperTerminal I often get disconnected by an incoming call from "call waiting." How do I disable that?

You can disable call waiting by placing a code (the code can be *70, 70#, 1170, or *80, depending on the area) that is sent before an outgoing call (on your phone you would dial the code and then the area code and phone number). The best way to have the call waiting code sent is to do it for all calls made from a given location through your modem. You do this through the Modems control panel, Dialing Properties dialog box with the following steps:

1. Open the Start menu; select Settings, Control Panel; and double-click on Modems.

2. Click on Dialing Properties to open the dialog box of that name as shown earlier in Figure 9-14.

3. Click on the check box in the line next to the bottom with the label "This location has call waiting."

4. Open the drop-down list on the right of the call waiting line, and select the code that is correct for your area. (This code is often listed in your phone book. If not, call your phone company.)

5. Click on OK.

 I tried to connect to a bulletin board service, and it said to have my parity set to "odd." Where do I do that?

Parity allows the receiving computer to check on the integrity of the data being sent. There are several parity conventions: odd, even, mark, space, and none. To work, both computers must be set to the same convention. The most common is none. To check and possibly change your parity setting, follow these steps:

1. Open the Start menu; choose Programs, Accessories; and click on HyperTerminal.

2. Right-click on the connection that you want to change, and choose Properties.

3. Click on the Phone Number tab, and then click on Configure under the Modem list box.

4. In the Modems Properties dialog box, click on the Connection tab, as shown in Figure 9-17.

5. You will see the Parity under Connection preferences. Click on the down arrow to be able to choose between Even, Odd, None, Mark, or Space. Click on the one you want, and click on OK twice.

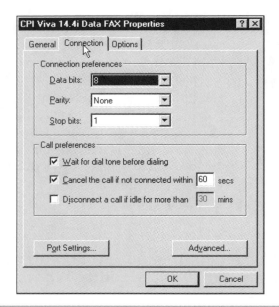

FIGURE 9-17   You can set the type of parity in the Modems Properties Connection tab

What file transfer protocols are supported by HyperTerminal?

HyperTerminal supports these file transfer protocols: Kermit, X-Modem, X-Modem-1K, Y-Modem, Y-Modem-G, and Z-Modem.

Phone Dialer

How do I start the Phone Dialer?

Use the following steps to start the Phone Dialer:

1. Click on Start; choose Programs, Accessories; and click on Phone Dialer. A dialog box appears with a telephone pad and speed dial buttons, as shown in Figure 9-18.

FIGURE 9-18   Phone Dialer dials your voice line telephone calls for you

2. Type a phone number from your keyboard or use the Phone Dialer numeric keyboard.

3. Click on Dial.

How do I create a speed dial button to use in Phone Dialer?

To create a speed dial button:

1. Click on Start; choose Programs, Accessories; and then click on Phone Dialer.

2. In the Phone Dialer dialog box, click on the Speed dial button (1 through 8) you want to set.

3. Type the Name that will appear on the button and the phone number to dial.

4. Click on Save or Save and Dial to call the number right now. The name you typed now appears on the button.

5. When you want to speed-dial the number, click on the button and the number will be dialed.

How do I change my speed dial settings in Phone Dialer?

To quickly change one or more speed dial numbers or names, follow these steps:

1. Click on Start; choose Programs, Accessories; and click on Phone Dialer.

2. When the Phone Dialer dialog box appears, open the Edit menu and choose Speed Dial.

3. Click on the speed dial button you wish to change.

4. Change or delete the information in the Name and the Number to dial boxes.

5. When you are done editing, click on the Save button.

Multimedia

Multimedia is to computing as spice is to food—
it may not fill you up, but it sure improves the taste.
Multimedia is the addition of sound and video plus the
use of CD-ROMs in a computer environment. Windows
95 provides a substantial enhancement to the support
for multimedia that has been available at the operating
system level. Windows 95 includes built-in programs to
record, edit, and playback digital audio, and to playback
digital video. Windows 95 also includes a substantial
enhancement in the playback of full-motion video, has
built-in support for many audio and video compression
schemes, allows sharing a CD-ROM over a network, and
includes a new media control interface for controlling
different types of media devices. Windows 95 is the first
multimedia operating system.

FRUSTRATION BUSTERS!

To make full use of multimedia and really of Windows 95, you need a CD-ROM drive (2x, or double speed, and above), an audio or sound board (preferably 16-bit), and a pair of speakers. You also need to install the multimedia components that come with Windows 95. You may install them during Setup or by using the Add New Hardware control panel. When installed, the programs are available from the Start, Programs, Accessories, Multimedia menus. Here are the most common multimedia applications that come with Windows 95:

- **CD-Player** plays your CD audio disks. It allows you to play CD music or other files. You can start, stop, fast forward and rewind, and skip to the beginning or end. You can play a CD continuously, or in random order, and select which tracks you want to play. You can also build and maintain a database of the selections on your CDs.

- **Media Player** is a general-purpose multimedia player that plays all types of multimedia files: audio, video, and animation. It allows you to control the play of a clip, create a new clip by inserting one file into another, and edit an existing clip.

- **Sound Recorder** allows you to digitally capture sound from either a microphone or the CD. With it you can record; stop; go to the beginning or end of the recording; insert other files into it; and perform special tasks, such as increasing the volume for specific parts of the recording, adding an echo, or mixing two recordings so both are heard.

- **Volume Control** controls the volume and balance of your audio files by providing a slider for each function. Depending on your equipment, you will have a dialog box for volume and balance of all multimedia, line in, synthesizer, CD, wave, and microphone devices.

Sound

 ## How can I assign sound to program events?

Events, such as opening files, completing a job, or encountering an error, can have sounds assigned to them if you have a sound card. Use the following steps to do this:

1. Click on Start; choose Settings, Control Panel; and double-click on Sounds. The Sounds Properties dialog box will open.

2. In the Events list, select the event you want to assign a sound to. (You can scan the list and see what events currently have sounds assigned to them, such as starting Windows. Events with sounds assigned are identified by a speaker icon, as shown in Figure 10-1.)

3. In the Name list, select the sound you want to hear when the event occurs. If you don't see the sound in the list, click on Browse, and locate the sound. Windows 95 has several sound schemes that come with it. More are

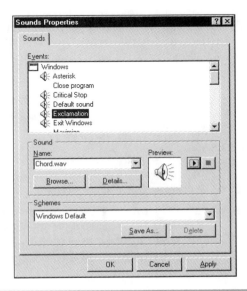

FIGURE 10-1   Assign a sound to an event by clicking on the event and then selecting a sound

available on the CD-ROM, although you might have to install them because they are not installed by default.

4. You can create a scheme that is used with your own chosen sounds and save it by clicking on Save As and naming the sound scheme.

5. Click on OK when you are finished.

Can I get sound from my PC speaker if I don't have a sound card?

Yes, if you have the PC speaker driver file Speaker.drv. You can obtain this file from Microsoft's bulletin board Download Service at (206) 936-6735 (you can use HyperTerminal to access this BBS). The filename on the BBS is Speak.exe because it is a self-extracting file that contains Speaker.drv as well as several other files. It is in the Windows 3.1 Audio drivers section. After you download the file (you should do it into an empty directory), double-click on it to extract Speaker.drv and the other files. Read the text files by double-clicking on them. When you are ready, use the following steps to install Speaker.drv.

Tech Tip: You won't get very high quality sound out of your PC speaker and, depending on your equipment, you may not get sound that you want to listen to. That's why Microsoft did not include it in Windows 3.1.

1. Click on Start; choose Settings, Control Panel; and double-click on Add New Hardware.

2. Click on Next to Start the Add Hardware Wizard.

3. Choose No to avoid having Windows 95 search for new hardware. Click on Next.

4. Select Sound, video, game controllers from the Hardware types list. Click on Next.

5. Click on Have Disk and then Browse to where you have your PC Speaker driver file. (The system looks for an .INF file. It will find the Oemsetup.inf file, which Windows 95 will use to set up the speaker driver.)

6. Choose OK to install. When it is done, you'll be asked if you want to restart your computer to complete the installation. Click on Yes.

To modify the settings for PC Speaker:

1. Click on Start; choose Settings, Control Panel; and double-click on Multimedia.

2. Click on the Advanced tab. Double-click on Audio Devices and you will see Audio for Sound Driver for PC Speaker.

3. Click on it to select it and then click on Properties to verify or change the settings. (If the Settings button is not available, the settings cannot be changed.)

4. Click on OK three times to finalize it and close all the dialog boxes. If you now go to the Sounds control panel, you should be able to click on a sound and hear something.

 I have added a sound card to my PC. What is the easiest way that I can set it up for use with Windows 95? The diskette that came with the card is for Windows 3.*x*. Should I use it?

Don't use the disk with the card, because the driver provided was written for Win 3.*x*. You should let Windows 95 do the setup for you. If your card is Plug-and-play-compliant (you will find that information in the card's label or User's guide), all you have to do is plug the card in and start Windows 95. If the card is not Plug-and-play, do the following:

1. Click on Start; choose Settings, Control Panel; and double-click on Add New Hardware.

2. Click on Next, and then click on Yes for the question Do you want Windows to search for your new hardware?

3. Click Next, and after several seconds, Windows 95 will automatically detect the card and load the appropriate 32-bit driver. Follow the prompts on the screen.

4. If Windows 95 did not automatically detect the card, manually select the manufacturer and model by first selecting Sound, video and game controllers.

5. You will be shown a group of possible resource settings that you can print out. Windows has considered the needs of the board and the available resources and determined these are the best. If these settings do not match what is set on the board, you can either open the Device Manager in the System control panel, or you can change the settings on the board. In either case, click on Next and follow the instructions to complete the installation.

CD-ROM

 ## How can I optimize the performance and change the configuration of my CD-ROM drive?

You can optimize the performance of the CD-ROM drive by setting up a cache large enough to contain an entire multimedia stream. To do that, follow these steps:

1. Click on Start; choose Settings, Control Panel; and double-click on the System icon.

2. In the System Properties dialog box, click on the Performance tab, and click on the File System button in the lower left.

3. Click on the CD-ROM tab in the File System Properties dialog box, as shown in Figure 10-2.

4. Open the Optimize access pattern for drop-down list and select the speed of the CD drive that you have.

5. Drag the Supplemental Cache Size slider to a setting according to these guidelines. (These settings are all based on 8MB of RAM or more.)

- **Single speed**, set to Small
- **Double speed**, set to one-third across from the left
- **Triple speed**, set to two-thirds across from the left
- **Quad speed**, set to Large

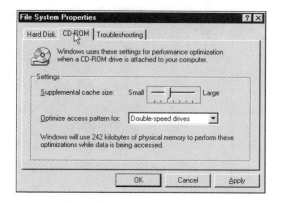

FIGURE 10-2   Optimize your CD-ROM from the File System Properties dialog box

> **6.** Click on Apply, then OK, and finally Close when you are finished.
>
> **7.** Answer Yes to Do you want to restart your computer now for changes to take effect?

Can I play a music CD on my PC?

You sure can. In fact, Windows 95 has an AutoPlay feature that begins playing the audio CD disk as soon as you insert the disk into the CD-ROM drive. (To prevent automatically playing the CD, hold down the SHIFT key when you insert it.) To permanently disable the AutoPlay feature so that it does not begin playing the CD automatically, follow these steps:

> **1.** Double-click on My Computer, open the View menu, and choose Options.
>
> **2.** Click on the File Types tab.
>
> **3.** Select AudioCD, and then click on Edit. The Edit File Type dialog box will be displayed, as shown in Figure 10-3.
>
> **4.** Click on Set Default to toggle AutoPlay off. If the Play command is bold, the CD will play when it is inserted; if Play is not bold, it will not.
>
> **5.** Click on OK when you're satisfied.

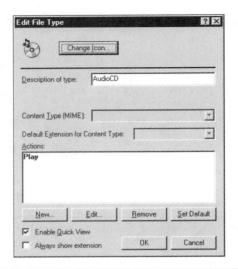

FIGURE 10-3   You can vary the default to automatically play a CD

I have installed Windows 95 and now my CD-ROM no longer works. How can I get it to work?

The problem could be because Windows is using the real-mode drivers from your Config.sys file. See the discussion on this subject in Chapter 2.

If your CD-ROM is a Sony, Mitsumi, Panasonic, Toshiba, or a number of others, Windows 95 will install the appropriate drivers. After removing the Config.sys statements, try running the Install New Hardware Wizard in the Control Panel and let the system autodetect the hardware.

If the system fails to detect the CD-ROM, you'll have to manually select the manufacturer and model.

I connected everything, but Windows 95 does not seem to recognize my CD-ROM drive. How do I install it?

Make sure that your controller is recognized. Use the following steps to do this:

1. Right-click on My Computer, choose Properties, and then choose Device Manager.

2. Locate the SCSI or IDE controller in the device tree.

3. Open the branch for your SCSI or IDE controller by clicking on the plus (+) sign at the left. Click on the controller, and then click on the Properties button.

4. On the General tab, verify that the Device Status message states "This device is working properly" as shown in Figure 10-4 and that the Device usage check box is enabled for the "Original Configuration." Click on OK to return to the Device Manager.

If you have several devices connected to the controller, and any of the SCSI or IDE devices does not have a Windows 95 driver, you can only use the devices connected to the controller with real-mode drivers.

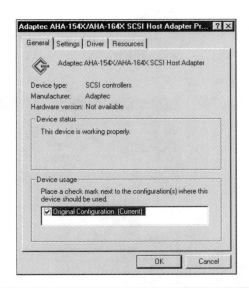

FIGURE 10-4   From the Device Manager, you can verify that Windows 95 thinks the device is operating correctly

With the Plug-and-play features of Windows 95, are the drivers that came with my CD-ROM necessary? Will Windows 95 already have drivers built in?

Yes. Windows 95 provides the drivers for the majority of CD-ROMs, so you don't need any drivers that come with your CD-ROM. You may need the drivers for use with the previous versions of MS-DOS if you are using a dual-boot system with an option of booting into a previous version of MS-DOS or Windows 95.

Are there any shortcuts or tricks that I can use with the Windows 95 CD player?

Yes. You can play or change songs using a variety of techniques. Try some of the following:

- Open the Explorer and click on your CD-ROM drive with an audio CD in it. In the right panel you will see Track01.cda, Track02.cda, and so on, listed as shown in Figure 10-5. If you right-click on a track, you can play it automatically by choosing Play from the popup menu. If you already are playing a track, it will be changed.

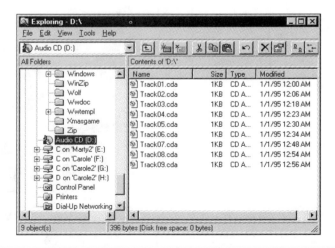

FIGURE 10-5 Viewing the tracks on a CD with the Explorer allows you to pick which one you want to play

■ If you double-click on a track displayed in Explorer, it will play automatically.

■ Try right-dragging a track onto your desktop and creating a shortcut. Rename the track's shortcut to the song's real name, as shown here. Whenever you have the CD in the drive, you can now double-click on its icon on the desktop to play it.

■ You can also drag tracks to your hard drive and put them in your Start Menu, or create a folder with CD tracks in it.

Tech Tip: When you drag a "copy" instead of a shortcut to your hard drive, you are not really copying the music file, only a pointer or link to it similar to a shortcut. To get the music on your hard disk, you must record it, although you should note that the .WAV file sizes are quite large (a 48-second piece in 16-bit stereo is over 8MB).

Media Player

What is Media Player?

Media Player is a multimedia application that allows you to play MIDI, video, and CD-Audio files. Unlike the Sound Recorder, this is a playback-only device. To access Media Player, you must have a sound card installed. If you have it installed, do the following:

1. Click on Start; choose Programs, Accessories, Multimedia; and click on Media Player. You will see the Media Player window open, as shown here:

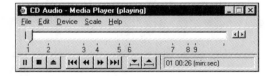

To play a file, first select the device, as follows:

1. Click on Device and choose the type you will be using: Video for Windows, Sound, MIDI, or CD Audio. The options you see will depend on the hardware you have installed.
2. Select the file for playback, and click on Open.
3. Click on the Play button.

Tech Tip: Sound files usually have the extension .WAV; video files, .AVI; MIDI files, .MID; and CD audio files, .CDA.

Volume Control

 Why can't I get the Volume Control utility included with Windows 95 to work with my sound card?

The Volume Control will only work if you install one of the sound drivers included with Windows 95 or a Windows 95-specific driver for your sound card. The Sound Blaster driver included with Windows 95 should work fine with Sound Blaster-compatible cards. To install that driver:

1. Click on Start; choose Settings, Control Panel; and double-click on Add New Hardware.
2. The Add New Hardware Wizard will be displayed. Click on Next to get it started. Choose No when it asks you if you want Windows to search for your new hardware. Then click on Next.
3. From the list of Hardware types, select Sound, video and game controllers, as shown in Figure 10-6. Click on Next.
4. Choose Creative Labs for the manufacturer and Creative Labs Sound Blaster as the model. Click on Next.
5. You will be shown the default settings that will be used for the new device. You have the opportunity to print the settings, and it is a good idea to do so. Click on Next.

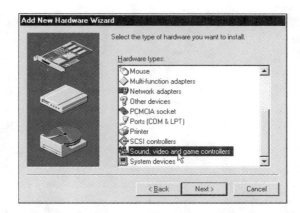

FIGURE 10-6   Select the sound device from the list of hardware types

> **6.** Files will be copied at this point, so you must insert the
> Windows 95 installation CD-ROM or floppy disks. Follow
> the onscreen instructions.

Can I put the volume control on the Taskbar?

A Volume Control icon on the Taskbar is very handy for
controlling the volume and turning the sound on and off
(for example, during phone calls!). You can do this using the
following steps.

> **1.** Click on Start; choose Settings, Control Panel; and
> double-click on Multimedia.
>
> **2.** Click on the Audio tab, and select the option Show
> volume control on the Taskbar. Click on OK.
>
> **3.** To use the Volume Control, double-click on the icon on
> the Taskbar to open the Volume Control dialog box,
> shown in Figure 10-7, or click on this icon to open the
> volume control slider, shown here.

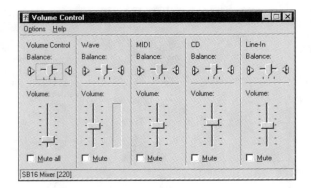

FIGURE 10-7   The Volume Control provides full audio level and balance control

Sound Recorder

How do I use the Sound Recorder?

If you have a microphone or a CD connected to your computer, you can record sound. Use the following steps to do this.

1. Click on Start; choose Programs, Accessories, Multimedia; and click on Sound Recorder. The Sound Recorder window will be displayed, as shown here:

2. Click on the red Record button on the right.

3. Click on the Stop button to end recording.

4. Open the File menu, choose Save As, and type a filename for this .WAV file.

I tried to start Sound Recorder and there is no Wave driver installed. What do I do?

The prerequisite is to have a sound card (or at least the Speaker.drv file described earlier). Then you can do one of the following:

- Install or reinstall the sound card using Add New Hardware as described in several instances before.

- If the sound card is Sound Blaster-compatible, use the Sound Blaster driver that ships with Windows. (See the question under CD-ROM for how to install that driver.)

- If the correct driver for the type of sound card being used is not listed, try using Windows 3.1 drivers for the specific card.

Windows 95 DOS

Why does a Windows 95 book talk about DOS? There are two good reasons. First, because there are literally thousands of DOS programs out there, especially games, that people are not willing to quit using; and second, because DOS and its command language *is* a very real and important part of Windows 95. Why in this point-and-click world would someone want to type DOS commands? Because certain tasks are easier for long-time DOS users to perform with commands and because some debugging tasks can only be performed at a DOS prompt. You therefore can look at DOS from two different, although related, standpoints: using DOS to run DOS programs, and using its command language.

FRUSTRATION BUSTERS!

In most cases, Windows 95 will run DOS programs better and easier than any prior version of DOS. This is true because Windows 95 takes less conventional memory (that below 640KB) than prior versions of DOS, and because Windows 95 does a better job of providing memory and disk resources than was the case in the past. Windows 95 also gives you a number of ways to start DOS programs. Among these are

- Locating the program in the Explorer or My Computer and double-clicking on it.

- Placing a shortcut to the program on the desktop where you can double-click on it or putting a shortcut on the Start menu where you can click on it.

- Typing the path and filename for the program in the Run option dialog box.

- Opening a DOS window or booting into DOS and typing the path and filename for the program.

While the last two methods of starting DOS programs are classical DOS, the first two are classical Windows, and the second, using shortcuts, is all Windows 95. As a matter of fact, shortcuts do more for DOS programs than for Windows programs. A shortcut for a DOS program allows you to specify a number of settings about how you want the program to run, including whether you want the program to run

- in DOS mode

- in a window

- full-screen

- without detecting Windows

- by shutting down Windows and starting DOS by itself

A shortcut for a DOS program can be created in the same ways as with other

FRUSTRATION BUSTERS!

programs: by dragging a program's .EXE file to the desktop or Start menu, or choosing Create Shortcut from either the File menu or popup menu. You can also create a shortcut to a DOS program by opening the Properties dialog box for the program. Since the program didn't come with properties, a shortcut is created for the program, and it is the shortcut's properties that you will be looking at.

The DOS commands in Windows 95 are a mixture of some new commands and some old (and familiar) DOS commands. The "old" commands remaining in Windows 95, while they have the same name and the same structure, have been rewritten to work in the 32-bit world and with long filenames. Windows 95 has also deleted some previous DOS commands. You can look up the commands not included in Windows 95 (see Figure 11-1) as well as all those that are in the Windows 95 Resource Kit help file located in the \Admin\Reskit\ Helpfile\ folder on the Windows 95 CD-ROM.

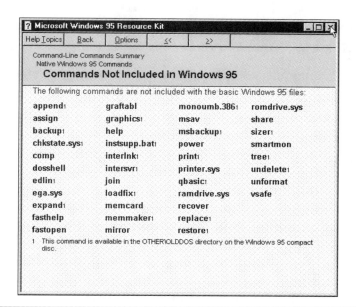

FIGURE 11-1   The Windows 95 Resource Kit lists the old DOS commands not in Windows 95

How Do I Do This in DOS?

I have created a new folder called My Letters. In the MS-DOS mode, I cannot access that folder! When I type CD \My Letters, **I get a message, "Too many parameters - Letters". Is MS-DOS mode not compatible with long filenames?**

> You just have to vary your command format. In order to switch to your new folder, type **cd \"my letters"**. Enclosing the name of the folder in quotes makes MS-DOS read the name of the folder as one block of text.

I have MS-DOS 3.3 on my system and I cannot boot into the previous MS-DOS version. I edited the Msdos.sys file as suggested and added BOOTMULTI=1, but it still does not work. How can I solve this problem?

> Unfortunately, you've just encountered a "no-solution" problem. To boot into the previous DOS version, you need DOS version 5.0 or greater.

How can I specify a working folder for a DOS application?

> A working folder is what the application uses as a default folder to store its output. You can specify a working folder in the properties for the program stored with its shortcut. Use the following steps to access the properties for a DOS application and specify a working folder:

Tech Tip: The Windows 95 shortcut replaces the .PIF files used in previous versions of Windows.

1. Open the Start menu, select Programs, and click on Windows Explorer.

2. Open the folder with your application, and then right-click on the application.

3. Choose Properties, and then click on the Program tab. You can specify the working folder in the Working box, as shown in Figure 11-2. Click on OK.

Tech Tip: From the Properties dialog box you can establish a batch file that will run before starting a DOS program. Type in the name of the batch file just below the working folder name. For example, if you want to use DOSKEY without loading it with Autoexec.bat, you can enter DOSKEY as the startup batch file. You'll save some conventional memory that way.

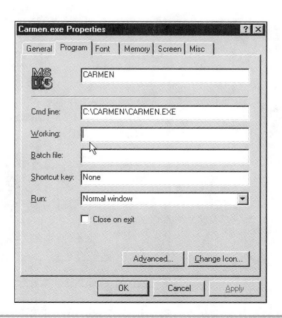

FIGURE 11-2 The Properties dialog box allows you to set a number of parameters for a DOS program

Can I change the way my MS-DOS window looks?

To change the DOS window, do the following:

1. Right-click on the Start button, and choose Open.

2. Double-click on Programs, find the MS-DOS Prompt, and right-click on it.

3. Choose Properties from the popup menu.

- On the Font tab, you can select between font types of Bitmap only, TrueType only, or Both font types. You can also change the point size for the font for your DOS window. As you choose a Font size, you can see how it will look by its effects on the Window preview and the Font preview, as you can see in Figure 11-3.

- On the Screen tab, you can choose to run the program full-screen or in a window, set an initial size or number

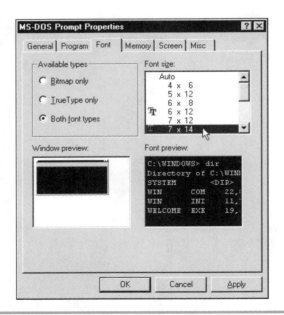

FIGURE 11-3   You can see how font changes will affect the DOS window

of lines in the screen, and set whether to display the toolbar.

 I want to start Windows 95 in the DOS mode at all times. Can I do this?

Yes. You can boot in DOS, and then start Windows 95 from DOS when you're ready for it. To do it, follow these steps:

1. Using the Explorer, open your root folder, right-click on the file Msdos.sys, and choose Properties. (If you don't see the file, open the Explorer's View menu, click on Options, in the View tab click on Show all files, and click on OK. Now try to right-click on Msdos.sys.)

2. In the Msdos.sys Properties dialog box, if Read-only and Hidden in the bottom of the dialog box are checked, click on them to remove the check marks, and then click on OK. This allows you to edit Msdos.sys and save your changes.

3. Right-click on Msdos.sys and choose Copy. Right-click on an empty area of the right pane of the Explorer and choose Paste. This creates a copy of Msdos.sys that you can use if you make a mistake while editing it.

4. Right-click on Msdos.sys again, choose Open With, and double-click on Notepad.

5. Locate the section entitled [Options], as seen in Figure 11-4.

6. Change the line: BootGUI=1 to BootGUI=0.

7. Save the changes and reboot.

8. The PC will now always start in DOS mode.

9. To go into Windows 95, type **win.**

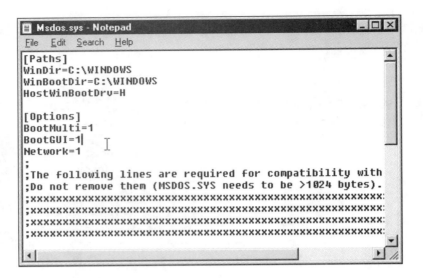

FIGURE 11-4 Msdos.sys is where you can change Windows 95 to boot into DOS mode

Can I run a Windows program from the DOS prompt, or do I have to start them from the Windows 95 desktop?

You can start both Windows and DOS programs from the DOS command line using the new START command. For example, to start Microsoft Excel from the DOS command line, type this:

```
***START [drive letter]:\[full path] excel.exe
```

An example of this syntax is **START C:\Excel\Excel.exe**.
   You can add the following switches to the START command, for example, START/m.

- **/m** Will run application minimized in the background.

- **/max** Will run application maximized in the foreground.

- **/r** Will run application restored in the foreground (default).

- **/w** Stands for wait. Will not return until the other program exits.

Is the DOS REPLACE command removed from Windows 95?

Yes, it has been removed from the DOS in Windows 95. However, you can use the new version of XCOPY that comes with Windows 95 with the /y switch to overwrite existing files without prompting or with the /-y switch to prompt before overwriting. This duplicates the functionality of Replace.

Tech Terror: You may find that REPLACE is on your CD-ROM in the \Other\Oldmsdos. These DOS commands are from version 6.2, even though they are dated with Windows 95. They are NOT designed to accept long filenames and can cause damage if they are used with long filenames.

Improving Performance

 My MS-DOS application slows down to a crawl when it runs in the background. How can I avoid this?

You can adjust the speed of the application by doing the following:

1. Right-click on the Start button, choose Open, and double-click on Programs.

2. Right-click on the MS-DOS Prompt icon.

3. Choose Properties, and then click on the Misc tab, as shown in Figure 11-5.

4. Move the Idle sensitivity slider to Low.

5. In the Background area, make sure that Always suspend is not selected.

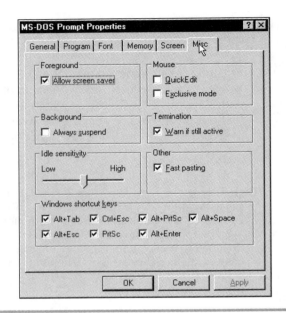

FIGURE 11-5 MS-DOS Prompt Properties can be modified for improved performance

Will Windows 95 allow me to customize/optimize my "DOS sessions" for individual DOS applications, as OS/2 does?

Yes, you can do that with the Properties dialog box for the DOS program. Here are the steps:

1. Using Explorer, find the program file (.EXE file) of the DOS program, and drag it to the desktop. That creates a shortcut to the DOS application.

2. Right-click on the shortcut and choose Properties from the popup menu. The program's Properties dialog box that you just saw will be displayed. Here you can change and modify the settings for the application. The functions of each of the tabs are as follows:

   ■ **General tab** displays the statistics and attributes about the program and allows you to set the Attributes for Read-only, Archive, Hidden, and System.

- **Program tab** displays the program name, path to find it, working folder, batch file, shortcut key, and with which type of window (normal, minimized, or maximized) it will begin. The Advanced button allows you to set whether or not the program can detect Windows and if you want the program to run in DOS only mode, as shown in Figure 11-6.

- **Font tab** is used to set the type and size of fonts used in the DOS window.

- **Memory tab** controls the settings for Conventional memory, Expanded memory, Extended memory, and MS-DOS protected-mode memory.

- **Screen tab** controls whether the DOS program will run full-size or in a window, what size it will be, whether a DOS toolbar is displayed, and whether to use Fast ROM emulation or Dynamic memory allocation.

- **Misc tab** controls miscellaneous settings for foreground and background operations, using the mouse, terminating the program, shortcut keys, and more.

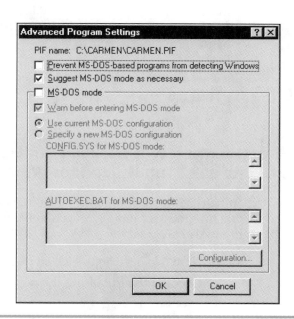

FIGURE 11-6   The Advanced Program Settings dialog box allows you to prevent a DOS program from seeing Windows

I am running Windows 95 as my operating system now. I would love to delete my old DOS to save some disk space. Do I still need it?

You only need your old DOS folder if you plan to use the F4 option to boot into the previous DOS version. If you don't think you will ever be doing that, you can safely delete the DOS folder. The new versions of DOS files that some applications might need are now in the \Windows\Command folder.

When typing the MEM /C command in an MS-DOS window to find out what free memory I have, I am told that I have zero kilobytes free memory in the upper memory area (UMA). I thought Windows 95 was better at allocating memory. How can that be?

Windows 95 is indeed managing the memory very effectively. MEM /C reports zero kilobytes because after loading all the real-mode drivers during startup, Windows 95 reserves all global upper memory blocks (UMBs) for Windows 95's own use or for expanded memory support.

Running DOS Programs

My DOS application will not load because Windows is running. How can I run this under Windows 95?

Some DOS-based programs are written not to load if they detect that Windows is running. So you must trick them a bit. Try this to run this program:

1. From Explorer, right-click on the program.

2. Choose Properties from the popup menu.

3. Click on the Program tab and then click on the Advanced button.

4. Click on Prevent MS-DOS-based programs from detecting Windows, as you saw in Figure 11-6, and click on OK.

5. Click on OK again. This will return a code to these applications that says Windows is not running.

 I realize that Windows 95 can do a lot for DOS applications in shortcuts, but what if my DOS application needs specific drivers?

You may find that you have certain DOS applications which still need to see specific drivers being loaded. Windows 95 can and will use a Config.sys file if the file is created. Also, in the Advanced settings of the program's Properties dialog box, an MS-DOS mode can be specified, in which case, you can load specific drivers only when launching that program. To set MS-DOS mode to be loaded, follow these steps:

1. Open Explorer and find your DOS program.

2. Right-click on the DOS application's icon, and choose Properties from the popup menu.

3. Click on the Program tab, and click on the Advanced button.

4. Then select MS-DOS mode. Other options will then become available, as shown in Figure 11-7.

5. You can type in the desired configuration changes, but a much easier way is to use a configuration checklist displayed when you click on the Configuration button. Do that now and the Configuration Options dialog box in Figure 11-8 will open.

6. Click on the options necessary for your program, and then click on OK.

7. Make any changes to the configuration that you need, and then click on OK twice more.

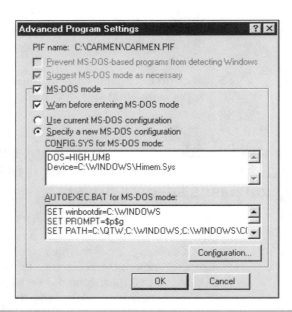

FIGURE 11-7   You can specify a specific Config.sys and Autoexec.bat to run only when you run a specific DOS program

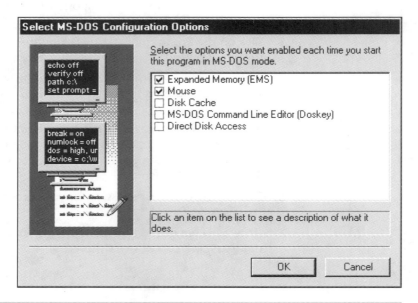

FIGURE 11-8   A Configuration Options dialog box gives you a checklist of possible options

What can I do with programs that won't run even in MS-DOS mode?

Many legacy DOS programs, especially those that needed a boot disk, will only run in MS-DOS mode under Windows 95. Sometimes, even when you specify that the program run in MS-DOS mode (see previous question for how to do this), the program will not run or will not run correctly. If you are using the current MS-DOS configuration for Config.sys and Autoexec.bat, beware that by default, Windows 95 gives you a "clean boot" configuration, and your DOS program may need specific device drivers and other settings not loaded by default in order to work. Finding and loading these drivers and settings manually can be quite a hassle. An easy way to do this is to copy the old Autoexec.bat and Config.sys files into the new ones that Windows 95 will use. Follow these steps to do this:

1. Find the appropriate boot disk the program used to work with.

2. Copy the Autoexec.bat and Config.sys files to your hard drive with identifying names (Darkfrce.aut and Darkfrce.cfg, for example).

3. From Windows 95, right-click on the program shortcut icon and choose Properties. Click on the Program tab and then on the Advanced button. Select the MS-DOS mode, and then click on Specify a new MS-DOS configuration.

4. While the Advanced Program Settings dialog box is open, open the Start menu and select Programs, Accessories, and then Notepad.

5. Open the configuration files (Darkfrce.aut and Darkfrce.cfg in this case) one at a time.

6. Select all the contents of the file, copy it to the Clipboard using CTRL-C, click on the Advanced Program Settings dialog box, and paste the Clipboard contents, using CTRL-V, into the Autoexec.bat and Config.sys text boxes, respectively.

7. Clean out any duplicate lines from the text boxes. Notice that some of the drivers from the old DOS folder should now be accessed from the Windows folder. Delete any of the default lines if necessary.

8. When you are finished, click on OK twice.

Tech Tip: If a DOS program tells you it can't run under Windows 95, don't assume that is a final answer. Try telling it to not detect Windows in its shortcut before giving up.

Why does the DOS window remain open with the text "Finished - *application name*" appearing on the title bar when it is finished?

The DOS window remains open so you can see any error messages that the DOS application may have displayed. You can change the program properties for the MS-DOS-based application so that it does close by following these steps:

1. From the Explorer, right-click the icon for the DOS application.

2. Choose Properties from the popup menu and click on the Program tab.

3. Select the Close on exit option, and click on OK.

When I am running a program in MS-DOS mode, why can't I press ALT-TAB to go back to Windows?

When you are running a program in MS-DOS mode, the application has exclusive access to the system, and all other applications are terminated, including the Windows 95 Explorer, which is the Windows 95 shell. You are effectively shutting down Windows to run this application. Windows will restart when you exit.

Managing Autoexec.bat and Config.sys Files

Do I need Autoexec.bat and/or Config.sys in Windows 95?

Windows 95 doesn't need Autoexec.bat or Config.sys. In fact, it speeds up your computer if you don't have them and may even make your DOS programs run better because Windows 95 does a better job of managing memory than if you try to do it in those files. The reason they are there is twofold: First, for compatibility—some programs look at these files and their contents. Second, you may need a driver that has no Windows

95 equivalent, in which case you can load them in real mode with Config.sys and Autoexec.bat.

If Windows 95 doesn't need Autoexec.bat or Config.sys, how does it load my necessary real-mode drivers, such as Himem.sys and Dblspace.bin?

In Windows 95, the functionality of Autoexec.bat and Config.sys is replaced by a new file, Io.sys. The drivers that are loaded by default through Io.sys are the following:

- Himem.sys
- Ifshlp.sys
- Setver.exe
- Dblspace.bin or Drvspace.bin (if found on the hard disk)

In addition to the above drivers, the following values are set by default with Io.sys:

Tech Tip: Contrary to what is said in the Windows 95 Resource Kit, Windows 95 DOES provide exPanded memory WITHOUT you having to load Emm386. See for yourself by removing the Emm386 statement and then looking at MEM /c in a DOS window.

- DOS=high
- Files=60
- Lastdrive=z
- Buffers=30
- Stacks=9,256
- Shell=command.com /p
- Fcbs=4

Io.sys is not an editable file, but an entry in Config.sys will take precedence over the Io.sys settings. For example, Io.sys does not load Emm386, so if you have an application that loads data into the high memory area, you can load Emm386.exe in Config.sys.

I have several lines in my Autoexec.bat file that I need to run specific DOS applications. Windows 95 Setup removes these lines! Does it mean that the commands are illegal? Why is that?

Setup remarks out lines starting with Rem to prevent files from changing that may be required for Setup to finish successfully. After the setup is complete, however, you can use any text editor, such as Notepad, to edit Autoexec.bat and enable the lines back. However, if you don't run these applications often, you might consider running them in MS-DOS mode with their own Autoexec.bat and Config.sys files and allow Windows to run the way it set itself up.

How do I add a "path" in Windows 95 similar to what existed in Autoexec.bat with PATH=?

Run Sysedit.exe and add a path statement to the Autoexec.bat file. It is still there, and it is still used by non-Windows applications.

Between DOS and Windows

Will Windows 95 run all my MS-DOS programs?

Windows 95 is designed to run MS-DOS programs. If you have problems with a specific MS-DOS program, try these steps in order (all of the settings are made in the program's Properties dialog box):

- Turn off the screen saver (Misc tab) and run Full-screen (Screen tab).

- Prevent the program from detecting Windows (Program tab, Advanced Program Settings).

- Force the program to run in an MS-DOS mode using the current configuration, which gives a program exclusive access to system resources but the standard setup (Program tab, Advanced Program Settings).

■ Force the program to run in an MS-DOS mode using a custom configuration, which gives a program exclusive access to system resources and its own setup (Program tab, Advanced Program Settings, Configuration Options).

Tech Tip: When you run a program in MS-DOS mode, it will shut down Windows 95 and will load the program exclusively in an MS-DOS environment. When the program completes, it will automatically reload Windows.

How can I pass parameters to my DOS application?

You can do this in three ways. First, you can start the program by typing its name and the parameters in the Start menu Run option. Second, if want to have a permanent set of parameters passed to the application every time you start it, you can enter those parameters in the Cmd line (command line) in the program's Properties dialog box Program tab. Finally, if you want to manually enter parameters when you run the program, you can add the **?** prompt to the end of the command line in the program's Properties dialog box Program tab, so that you will be asked to enter the parameters when the program starts. To add the prompt, follow these steps:

Tech Tip: You can check on a command's existence and see what parameters and switches are used with it by typing the command, followed by **/?** either in the Run command or at the command prompt in a DOS window.

1. Using the Explorer, find your DOS program shortcut and right-click on the icon. From the popup menu, choose Properties, and then click on the Program tab.

2. Add a **?** (question mark) to the end of the Cmd line (command line), as shown in Figure 11-9.

When you run the DOS program, you will be prompted to enter parameters in a little dialog box.

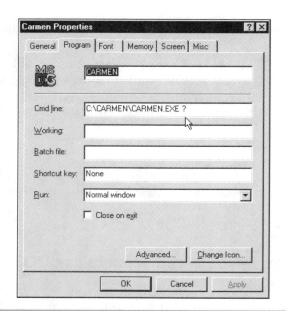

FIGURE 11-9   The system will prompt you to enter parameters if you add a ? to the command line

When I open a DOS window from Windows 95 I get a message "Parameter value not in allowed range." What did I do wrong?

Check to see if your MS-DOS Prompt settings are correct. Take a look at the properties for your MS-DOS Prompt. Make sure there are no additional settings that might confuse the system. To do this, follow these steps:

1. Click on Start, choose Program, and click on MS-DOS Prompt.

2. Then click on the Properties button in the Toolbar. (Or if you have a shortcut to MS-DOS Prompt on your desktop, right-click on it and choose Properties.)

3. Check on the settings and verify that they are OK.

What does Windows 95 Setup do to the DOS commands?

Windows 95 deletes and upgrades a number of DOS files during Setup. You can get a list of these files in the Windows 95 Resource Kit help file on the Windows 95 CD in the \Admin\Reskit\Helpfile\ folder. See Figure 11-1 at the beginning of the chapter.

Can I cut and paste between MS-DOS applications and Windows applications or between two MS-DOS applications?

Yes, if the applications are running in separate windows. To paste from a DOS window to a Windows application, do the following:

1. If the DOS program is running full screen, press ALT-ENTER to switch to window mode, open the File menu, choose Properties, and select Toolbar (if not selected).

2. Click on the Mark button on the toolbar, select the lines to be copied, and click on the Copy button.

3. Press ALT-TAB to switch to the Windows application, open the Edit menu and choose Paste.

To paste from a Windows application to a DOS window:

1. Select and copy the lines from the Windows application.

2. Switch to the DOS application.

3. Click on the Paste button.

I was looking through the \Windows\system folder and have come across a program called Mkcompat.exe. Is this how you make old DOS programs compatible with Windows 95? How do I use it?

Mkcompat.exe is used to make older Windows applications work with Windows 95. You use it by double-clicking on it, opening the File menu and specifying a program you want to work on.

You then select the functions you want set, save your settings, and exit MkCompat. It is a very unusual program that requires the use of this program. As a general rule the vast majority of both DOS and Windows programs work with Windows 95.

Effects of Long Filenames

Why, when I am in a DOS window within Windows 95 or when I boot Windows 95 to a command line, is the number of characters in a filename limited to 127?

The default command-line character limitation is 127 characters. In this default configuration, the DOS environment does not allow more than 127 characters to exist in a given command line. The command line character can be increased to its maximum by placing the following line in the Config.sys file: **shell=c:\windows\command.com /u:255**

When at a DOS prompt, I see many of my files have been renamed using a ~ character. Why is this?

While Windows 95 DOS does handle long filenames so that they are not lost or corrupted, it displays the 8.3 filename alias using a ~. It takes the first six characters, adds the ~, and starts numbering consecutively, starting with 1. So, for example, if you have Saturday's paper.doc, Saturday afternoon.doc; these will display as Saturd~1.doc and Saturd~2.doc.

Installation Components

The following table shows you which components are installed in the various types of installations. The files are available on both floppy disk and CD-ROM unless there is a "yes" in the CD-ROM Only column.

	Available on			
Component	**Typical**	**Portable**	**Compact**	**CD-ROM Only**
Accessories				
Accessibility Options	yes	no	no	no
Briefcase	no	yes	no	yes
Calculator	yes	yes	no	no
Character Map	no	no	no	yes
Clipboard Viewer	no	no	no	no
Desktop Wallpaper	no	no	no	no
Document Templates	yes	no	no	no
Games	no	no	no	no
Mouse Pointers	no	no	no	yes
NetWatcher	no	no	no	yes
Object Packager	yes	no	no	no
Online User's Guide	no	no	no	yes
Paint	yes	no	no	no
Quick View	no	no	no	yes
Resource Meter	no	no	no	no
Screen Savers	yes[1]	no	no	no
System Monitor	no	no	no	yes
Windows 95 Tour	yes	no	no	yes
WinPopup[2]	no	no	no	no
WordPad	yes	yes	no	no
Communications				
Dial-Up Networking	no	yes	no	no
Direct Cable Connection	no	yes	no	no
Hyper Terminal	yes	yes	no	no
Phone Dialer	yes	yes	no	no
Disk Tools				
Backup	no	no	no	no
Disk Compression Tools[3]	no	no	no	no
Disk Defragmenter	yes	yes	yes	no
Scan Disk	yes	yes	yes	no

Component	Available on			
	Typical	**Portable**	**Compact**	**CD-ROM Only**
Microsoft Exchange				
Microsoft Fax	no	no	no	no
Microsoft Mail	no	no	no	no
Microsoft Network	no	no	no	no
Multi-Lingual Support	no	no	no	yes
MultiMedia				
Audio Compression[4]	no	no	no	no
CD Player[5]	no	no	no	no
Media Player	yes	yes	no	no
Sound Schemes	no	no	no	yes
Sound and Video Clips	no	no	no	yes
Sound Recorder[4]	no	no	no	no
Video Compression	yes	yes	no	no
Volume Control[4]	no	no	no	no

[1] Flying Windows is the only screen saver installed. Others are available on both CD-ROM and on floppy disk.
[2] WinPopup is only installed if networking is detected.
[3] Disk compression is only installed if DoubleSpace or DriveSpace is detected.
[4] Audio Compression, Sound Recorder, and Volume Control are only installed if a sound card is detected.
[5] CD Player is only installed if a CD-ROM is detected.

Windows 95 Shortcut Keys

The following table lists many of the shortcut or hot keys that you can use in Windows 95.

ALT or F10	Activates the menu bar
ALT-Double-click	Displays properties of the selected object
ALT-ENTER	Displays properties of the selected object or switches between full screen and a window while a DOS program is active
ALT-ESC	Switches among the tasks on the Taskbar
ALT-F4	Closes the active window
ALT-M	Minimizes all windows when the Taskbar is selected
ALT-PRINT SCREEN	Copies the image of the active window to the Clipboard
ALT-S	Activates the Start menu if no applications are running
ALT-TAB	Displays the task switcher where you can switch to another running application
Arrow Keys	Moves the selection in the direction of the arrow
BACKSPACE	Opens the parent folder for the active window
CTRL	Copies a file while you drag it
CTRL-A	Selects all the objects in the current window
CTRL-C	Copies the selected objects to the Clipboard
CTRL-ESC	Opens the Start menu and selects the Taskbar
CTRL-G	Opens the Go To command in the Explorer
CTRL-Right-click	Displays a popup menu, usually different from the popup menu that appears with a right-click alone, when a file is selected in the Explorer or a Windows 95 application
CTRL-SHIFT	Creates a shortcut while you drag a file
CTRL-TAB/CTRL-SHIFT-TAB	Switches tabs in a dialog box
CTRL-V	Pastes the Clipboard contents into the selected window
CTRL-X	Cuts the selected object and places it on the Clipboard
CTRL-Z	Undoes the last copy, move, delete, paste, rename
DELETE	Moves the selected objects in the Recycle Bin
ENTER	Activates the selected object
END	Moves the selected object to the last object
ESC	Closes the active dialog box or menu without making a selection
F1	Opens Windows 95 Help
F2	Allows renaming of the selected object
F3	Opens the Find: All Files dialog box
F4	Opens the Go To Folder list in the Explorer
F5	Refreshes the current window
F6 or TAB	Moves among the panes in the Explorer or among the areas in a dialog box or the desktop

HOME	Moves the selection to the first object
LEFT ALT-LEFT SHIFT-NUM LOCK	Toggles MouseKeys on and off
LEFT ALT-LEFT SHIFT-PRINT SCREEN	Toggles High Contrast mode on and off
LEFT ARROW	Collapses the current selection if it is expanded, otherwise goes to the parent in the Explorer
Letter Keys	Moves the selection to the first object beginning with that letter
NUM LOCK held down for five seconds	Toggles ToggleKeys on and off
Numeric Keypad *	Expands everything under the current selection in the Explorer
Numeric Keypad +	Expands the current selection in the Explorer
Numeric Keypad –	Collapses the current selection in the Explorer
RIGHT ARROW	Expands the current selection if it is not expanded or goes down one level in the Explorer
RIGHT-SHIFT, held down for eight seconds	Toggles FilterKeys on and off
SHIFT five times	Toggles StickyKeys on and off
SHIFT-Click on the Close Button	For folders, closes the current folder plus all parent folders
SHIFT-DELETE	Deletes the selected object without placing it in the Recycle Bin
SHIFT-Double-click	Selects the second item on the popup menu, usually Explore or Open
SHIFT-F10	Opens a popup menu for the selected item
SHIFT while inserting a CD	Bypasses AutoPlay or AutoRun
WINDOWS-E	Opens the Explorer (Microsoft Keyboard)
WINDOWS-F	Opens the Find File or Folder dialog box (Microsoft Keyboard)
WINDOWS-CTRL-F	Opens the Find Computer dialog box (Microsoft Keyboard)
WINDOWS-F1	Opens Windows Help (Microsoft Keyboard)
WINDOWS-M	Minimizes all windows (Microsoft Keyboard)
WINDOWS-R	Opens the Run dialog box (Microsoft Keyboard)
WINDOWS-SHIFT-M	Restores all windows (Microsoft Keyboard)
WINDOWS-TAB	Cycles through tasks on the Taskbar (Microsoft Keyboard)
WINDOWS-BREAK	Opens the System Properties dialog box (Microsoft Keyboard)

Index

If you would like to **speak to the experts** who wrote this book, **call** Stream's Microsoft® Windows® 95 answer line! Trained specialists will answer your Microsoft Windows 95 questions including setup, built-in networking, printing, multi-media, Microsoft Exchange Mail client and Wizards.

Have we answered all your questions?

1-800-298-8215

$35 per problem. (Major credit cards accepted)

1-900-555-2009

$2.50 per minute. (First two minutes free)

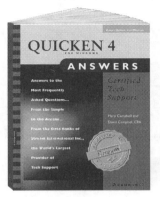
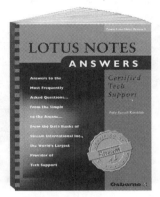
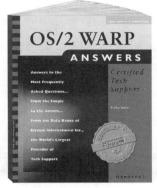

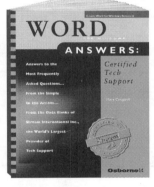
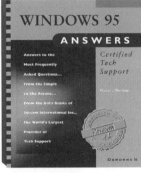

ORDER BOOKS DIRECTLY FROM OSBORNE/McGRAW-HILL

For a complete catalog of Osborne's books, call 510-549-6600 or write to us at 2600 Tenth Street, Berkeley, CA 94710

Call Toll-Free: *1-800-822-8158*
24 hours a day, 7 days a week in U.S. and Canada

Mail this order form to:
McGraw-Hill, Inc.
Customer Service Dept.
P.O. Box 547
Blacklick, OH 43004

Fax this order form to:
1-614-759-3644

EMAIL
7007.1531@COMPUSERVE.COM
COMPUSERVE GO MH

Ship to:

Name _____

Company _____

Address _____

City / State / Zip _____

Daytime Telephone: _____
(We'll contact you if there's a question about your order.)

ISBN #	BOOK TITLE	Quantity	Price	Total
0-07-88				
0-07-88				
0-07-88				
0-07-88				
0-07-88				
0-07088				
0-07-88				
0-07-88				
0-07-88				
0-07-88				
0-07-88				
0-07-88				
0-07-88				
0-07-88				

Shipping & Handling Charge from Chart Below		
Subtotal		
Please Add Applicable State & Local Sales Tax		
TOTAL		

Shipping & Handling Charges

Order Amount	U.S.	Outside U.S.
Less than $15	$3.50	$5.50
$15.00 - $24.99	$4.00	$6.00
$25.00 - $49.99	$5.00	$7.00
$50.00 - $74.99	$6.00	$8.00
$75.00 - and up	$7.00	$9.00

Occasionally we allow other selected companies to use our mailing list. If you would prefer that we not include you in these extra mailings, please check here: ☐

METHOD OF PAYMENT

☐ Check or money order enclosed (payable to Osborne/McGraw-Hill)

☐ AMERICAN EXPRESS   ☐ DISCOVER   ☐ MasterCard   ☐ VISA

Account No. ☐☐☐☐☐☐☐☐☐☐☐☐☐☐☐☐

Expiration Date _____

Signature _____

In a hurry? Call 1-800-822-8158 anytime, day or night, or visit your local bookstore.

Thank you for your order   Code BC640SL